Student Teacher to Master Teacher
A Practical Guide for Educating Students with Special Needs

FOURTH EDITION

Michael S. Rosenberg
Johns Hopkins University

Lawrence J. O'Shea
Director of Special Education
Intermediate Unit One
Coal Center, Pennsylvania

Dorothy J. O'Shea
Slippery Rock University of Pennsylvania

EARSON

Merrill
entice Hall

le River, New Jersey
mbus, Ohio

Library of Congress Cataloging in Publication Data
Rosenberg, Michael S.
  Student teacher to master teacher : a practical guide for educating students with special needs / Michael S. Rosenberg, Lawrence O'Shea, Dorothy J. O'Shea.—4th ed.
    p. cm
  Includes bibliographical references and index.
  ISBN 0-13-117311-1
  1. Children with disabilities—Education—United States—Handbooks, manuals, etc.
2. Special education—United States—Handbooks, manuals, etc. 3. Teachers of children with disabilities—Training of—United States—Handbooks, manuals, etc. I. O'Shea, Lawrence J. II. O'Shea, Dorothy J. III. Title.

LC4031.R68 2006
371.9—dc22   2005043114

Vice President and Executive Publisher: Jeffery W. Johnston
Acquisitions Editor: Allyson P. Sharp
Editorial Assistant: Kathleen S. Burk
Production Editor: Sheryl Glicker Langner
Production Coordination: GGS Book Services, Atlantic Highlands
Design Coordinator: Diane C. Lorenzo
Cover Designer: Thomas Borah
Cover image: Getty One
Production Manager: Laura Messerly
Director of Marketing: Ann Castel Davis
Marketing Manager: Autumn Purdy
Marketing Coordinator: Brian Mounts

This book was set in Palatino by GGS Book Services, Atlantic Highlands. It was printed and bound by King Printing Co., Inc. The cover was printed by King Printing Co., Inc.

Pearson Education Ltd.   Pearson Education Australia Pty. Limited
Pearson Education Singapore Pte. Ltd.   Pearson Education North Asia Ltd.
Pearson Education Canada, Ltd.   Pearson Educación de Mexico, S.A. de C.V.
Pearson Education—Japan   Pearson Education Malaysia Pte. Ltd.

7 8 9 10   V0CR   13 12 11 10
ISBN: 0-13-117311-1

Educator Learning Center:
An Invaluable Online Resource

Merrill Education and the Association for Supervision and Curriculum Development (ASCD) invite you to take advantage of a new online resource, one that provides access to the top research and proven strategies associated with ASCD and Merrill—the Educator Learning Center. At **www. educatorlearningcenter.com**, you will find resources that will enhance your students' understanding of course topics and of current educational issues, in addition to being invaluable for further research.

HOW THE EDUCATOR LEARNING CENTER WILL HELP YOUR STUDENTS BECOME BETTER TEACHERS

With the combined resources of Merrill Education and ASCD, you and your students will find a wealth of tools and materials to better prepare them for the classroom.

Research

- More than 600 articles from the ASCD journal *Educational Leadership* discuss everyday issues faced by practicing teachers.
- A direct link on the site to Research Navigator™ gives students access to many of the leading education journals, as well as extensive content detailing the research process.
- Excerpts from Merrill Education texts give your students insights on important topics of instructional methods, diverse populations, assessment, classroom management, technology, and refining classroom practice.

Classroom Practice

- Hundreds of lesson plans and teaching strategies are categorized by content area and age range.
- Case studies and classroom video footage provide virtual field experience for student reflection.
- Computer simulations and other electronic tools keep your students abreast of today's classrooms and current technologies.

LOOK INTO THE VALUE OF EDUCATOR LEARNING CENTER YOURSELF

A four-month subscription to Educator Learning Center is $25 but is **FREE** when packaged with any Merrill Education text. In order for your students to have access to this site, you must use this special value-pack ISBN number **WHEN** placing your textbook order with the bookstore: 0-13-154899-9. Your students will then receive a copy of the text packaged with a free ASCD pincode. To preview the value of this website to you and your students, please go to "**www.educatorlearningcenter.com**" and click on "Demo."

Preface

*A*s with previous editions, our basic purpose in preparing *Student Teacher to Master Teacher* is to provide a reflective guide for use during supervised special education student-teaching experiences or graduate field experiences. We believe that field experiences are often the single most important component of a preservice-level teacher development program.

The approach used in our guide is based on two interrelated assumptions. First, we believe that student teaching and initial field experiences should be rigorous and as realistic as possible. They should be developed to ensure that the preservice-level teacher enters the professional job market with the skills needed for both immediate survival and continued success. Few teacher educators would question this view, and many may regard it as an obvious, somewhat pious statement of fact. Interpretation and actual implementation of this view appear to vary considerably, however, affecting the validity of the basic assumption in reference to specific teacher-training programs. In the absence of structured and purposeful activities or requirements, there may be no valid criteria for assessing easily delineated teaching skills across varied settings. In fact, the apparent discrepancy between theory and successful application may significantly reduce program credibility.

Second, special education field experiences should incorporate a variety of structured requirements and activities that collectively "bridge the gap" between methods and/or laboratory courses and actual independent, professional teaching. We recognize the need for more structured, reality-based, and relevant preservice experiences. When observing, supervising, managing, and evaluating preservice and beginning teachers, we found a critical need to link preservice training and field experience requirements to real teaching skills and actual on-the-job requirements. Topics and activities in this guide were chosen because we believe they represent many of the most pertinent issues that new teachers will face when they begin their field experiences and when they manage their first classrooms on their own.

Through our own experiences as classroom teachers and supervisors of developing teachers, we also realized the needs of college supervisors. We believe that individuals involved with the supervision of student teachers and field-experience students often are the forgotten souls, desperately trying to promote best practices in the face of problems of logistics, timing, and the realities of modern schools. Often, these individuals must face experienced teachers' claims to novice teachers that "it can't be done like that" or "theory is only relevant in textbooks and it will never work here." We have heard the university instructors' calls for "increased best practices" in the classrooms, and we believe that college supervisors will welcome a commercially prepared resource to aid them in their roles. This guide was developed to reduce the amount of time needed by supervisory faculty and staff to review and possibly remediate key concepts associated with successful teaching. We hope the use of this guide will allow more time for the important tasks of observing and providing feedback to preservice teachers and of serving as liaisons to classroom teachers and administrators, university faculty, and preservice teachers.

We are also aware that there are large numbers of special educators who are entering the profession through alternative routes. For a number of reasons, most notably the ever-present and growing shortage of special education teachers, field-based preparation alternatives are proliferating, and large numbers of career changers are serving students with disabilities. Many of these individuals are teaching students who have not yet received their credentials; consequently, they have not fully acquired the multitude of skills necessary for a successful and satisfying career. We believe that portions of this text can serve to assist these individuals as they complete the myriad of challenges associated with on-the-job training.

In summary, throughout this guide we offer tips and insights to preservice and beginning teachers to help them grow professionally within their chosen career over time, starting during their initial field experiences and continuing through their beginning years in teaching. We recognize the enormous amount of information that teachers new to special education must obtain and be able to demonstrate during their initial work with students with mild to moderate disabilities. This guide is meant to help new teachers make the transition from the role of student at the preservice level to the role of professional at the in-service level. Each topic in the guide has been judged pertinent for new teachers and, we believe, will remain relevant to them as their experience grows. We have also added an appendix that links our contents to the Council for Exceptional Children's Knowledge and Skill Standards Common Core.

ORGANIZATION OF THE TEXT

Chapter 1 provides an introduction to the student-teaching experience and an overview of the field of working with students with mild to moderate disabilities. The chapter discusses the typical fears and concerns of student teachers and beginning special education teachers and reviews the characteristics of students with mild to moderate disabilities and the ways educational services are delivered to them (e.g., inclusion, continuum of service, and so on). The chapter also introduces ethical and professional standards of practice for teachers that will be highlighted throughout the subsequent chapters. Tips on using diplomacy in the workplace and an emphasis on maximizing people skills underscore our contention that both effective interpersonal communication skills and teaching skills are necessary to become master teachers.

Chapter 2 gives the novice teacher an understanding of the legal bases for assessment and programming for students with disabilities. Pertinent legislation and litigation of the past three decades, most notably the Individuals with Disabilities Education Improvement Act of 2004 and No Child Left Behind, are presented as the foundation of legal challenges that teachers today will face. Major components of federal mandates for school-age students and infants and toddlers are summarized, as are tips for working within the system to solve potential legal problems faced by teachers. Assumptions underlying successful mediation attempts with students, family members, and professionals are discussed as means to avoid unnecessary litigation.

Chapter 3 deals with the "nuts and bolts" of the actual instructional themes of the classroom. Tips on organizing and managing instructional time, with an emphasis on effectiveness and consistency, are presented. Ways of setting up and maintaining effective scheduling procedures are discussed, and a system for the development of classroom rules and procedures, as well as other management strategies (e.g., planning for group size, arranging the physical environment) is provided. Available resources at the new teacher's disposal and tips for beginning the school year are included.

The major focus of Chapter 4 is on how preservice and beginning teachers can link classroom-based assessment procedures to instruction. Initially, several basic assessment concepts are reviewed. These are followed by step-by-step procedures for implementing curriculum-based assessments in special education and inclusive education environments.

Chapter 5 discusses the need for effective planning as a catalyst to appropriate instruction. Successfully planned lessons are included to illustrate the relationship of instructional objectives to students' individualized education programs (IEPs), the teacher's preparation for the demonstration of understanding of prerequisite skills for students, task analyses and learning sequences, the need for concise descriptions of instructional activities and materials linked to predetermined objectives, systematic methods to evaluate lessons, and the need to anticipate problems that might occur anywhere along the implementation phase of instructional delivery to students. A section on lesson plan follow-up with tips on preventing and remediating actual problems observed during lessons, a review of instructional techniques used in varied lesson formats, and tips for lesson appraisal so that new teachers can practice self-evaluation are embedded within the chapter.

Chapter 6 stresses the importance of delivery of instruction. The concept of effective teacher behaviors is discussed in terms of the dimensions of a structured academic focus, the specific teaching of academic concepts, and a planned instructional sequence based on environmental variables and needs of students. Dimensions of direct instruction, the guided discovery approach, and strategic instruction are identified, with numerous examples of these teaching approaches provided throughout the chapter.

Chapter 7 provides developing and beginning teachers with a summary of the paperwork involved in special education and the documentation necessary in the referral process for special education. The chapter begins with the prereferral steps of helping students with problem behaviors or learning difficulties remain in the least restrictive environment (LRE) before calling for changes in these students' educational placements. New teachers are provided with the steps needed to work with other professionals and parents to document precisely the need for all changes in educational programs. Tips for working with parents, administrators, general educators, and others involved in educational planning teams are highlighted. In addition, IEPs and IEP meetings are discussed, stressing the IEP as a legal plan that parents and professionals develop together. The chapter concludes with suggestions to help developing and beginning teachers write reports of students' progress and to promote continuous communication with parents and other significant professionals.

Chapter 8 encourages positive behavior management and support by the new teacher from the beginning of his or her involvement with students. The chapter has been updated to underscore the importance of having a comprehensive school and classroom management program, as well as a series of specific strategies for the development of functional behavioral assessments of troubling behavior. A brief review of behavioral principles and rules governing classroom behavior is provided to highlight teachers' use of strategies to increase or maintain appropriate student behaviors and to decrease or eliminate inappropriate student behaviors. Tips for identifying, observing, recording, and illustrating problem behaviors are included. Logistical concerns in developing large-group management and means of designing individual behavior change programs and reports are discussed. Finally, the chapter provides some practical strategies teachers can use to facilitate and promote self-control strategies of their students.

Chapter 9 provides an overview of transition issues related to very young children with disabilities and their families. Highlighted are the evaluation and assessment needs of young children and the various medical and physical issues encountered by families. Step-by-step procedures are provided for the construction of individualized family service plans (IFSPs). Also provided is a discussion of the transition services offered to school-age children and youth with disabilities. A common theme throughout the chapter is the need for interagency coordination and planning.

Chapter 10 provides insights into the methods of collaborative consultation that new teachers will use when working with professionals and parents in school-based activities and educational meetings. Throughout this guide, teaming is stressed as an important strategy to encourage effective educational decision making for all students. Chapter 10 also builds a case for the necessity of strong interpersonal communication skills for teachers, as they form strong colleague relationships by stressing positive regard, empathy, and warmth toward peers.

Chapter 11 provides tips for the important search for employment. Typical job interview procedures are reviewed, and strategies for preparing attractive and relevant portfolios and résumés are described. Information regarding teacher tests such as Praxis has been added. Teacher burnout issues, which may impede the master teacher process, and means of recognizing and managing stress are also highlighted. Finally, the chapter concludes with suggestions for planning continued employment and advancement within the field. Specifically, readers are challenged to analyze their personal philosophy of special education as they maintain involvement in professional organizations, recertification and in-service programs, and advocacy groups.

By designing this guide as an easy-to-use, interactive resource, we hope its use will not end once the field experience, student teaching, or first year of teaching ends. We believe that the chapters of the book reflect concerns typically faced by many teachers as they continue to grow as special educators. This guide was written with the hope of assisting beginning special education teachers to become master teachers and to maintain their status as such throughout their teaching careers.

FEATURES OF THE TEXT

A new feature in this edition is the **Professional Glimpse** (case study) at the start of each chapter. These cases set the stage for the content of the chapter by providing readers with a real-life situation.

As with previous editions, brief **Pause and Reflect About the Profession** boxes are positioned frequently throughout each chapter to encourage the reader to think about what he or she has just read and relate the information to his or her own experiences and teaching situation.

Numbered boxes also frequently appear in each chapter to highlight issues and legislation, clarify definitions, and provide resources.

Following the Chapter Summaries are **Activities to Extend Your Knowledge**, exercises provided to challenge the reader to learn more about special education by completing the activities.

Finally, we have continued our practice of providing a **Point and Click About the Profession** section in most chapters. These sections contain web sites that provide useful materials and resources for both developing and beginning teachers.

ACKNOWLEDGMENTS

We wish to express our gratitude to the following individuals who devoted a great deal of personal and professional time to the task of helping us complete this book. The faculty and staff in the Department of Special Education at Johns Hopkins University, colleagues and staff at Intermediate Unit I in western Pennsylvania, and the faculty at Slippery Rock University provided much support and encouragement throughout all phases of this project. In particular, we acknowledge the artistic contributions of Sharon Lampkin and the overall assistance of Lori Jackman, Juliane Blyth, and Danielle Rollison. We owe special thanks to Sunil Misra, who devoted considerable time and effort in linking our text's content to the CEC standards and the Praxis requirements. We are especially appreciative of the efforts of our colleagues Janeen Taylor, Stephanie Carpenter, Peggy King-Sears, Sunil Misra, Kimberly Bright, David Batemen, and Vickie McGinley, who took the time to contribute important new content to our text. We also gratefully acknowledge the many contributions of the experienced teachers we have worked with who continually remind us that there is a vast number of master special education teachers. In addition, we appreciate the efforts of the numerous developing teachers we have supervised over the past 20 years. They have inspired us to focus on their needs for survival and success. We appreciate the efforts of significant individuals who served as role models to us, including Bob Algozzine, Bill Reid, Paul Sindelar, and James Van Tassel. We also wish to express our appreciation to Allyson Sharp and Kathy Burk at Merrill/Prentice Hall, as well as the reviewers of this edition: Susan Gately, Rivier College; Deborah Metcalf, East Carolina University; Eun-Ja Kim Park, California State University, Bakersfield; Stephanie M. Peterson, The Ohio University; and Lech Wisniewski, The Metropolitan State College of Denver.

Finally, we wish to express our love and appreciation to our families in providing us with the support, encouragement, and patience to finish our task.

Discover the Merrill Resources for Special Education

*T*echnology is a constantly growing and changing aspect of our field that is creating a need for new content and resources. To address this emerging need, Merrill Education has developed an online learning environment for students, teachers, and professors alike to complement our products—the *Merrill Resources for Special Education* website. This content-rich website provides additional resources specific to this book's topic and will help you—professors, classroom teachers, and students—augment your teaching, learning, and professional development.

Our goal is to build on and enhance what our products already offer. For this reason, the content for our user-friendly website is organized by topic and provides teachers, professors, and students with a variety of meaningful resources all in one location. With this website, we bring together the best of what Merrill has to offer: text resources, video clips, web links, tutorials, and a wide variety of information on topics of interest to general and special educators alike. Rich content, applications, and competencies further enhance the learning process.

The *Merrill Resources for Special Education* website includes:

Resources for the Professor—

- **The Syllabus Manager**™, an online syllabus creation and management tool, enables instructors to create and revise their syllabus with an easy, step-by-step process. Students can access your syllabus and any changes you make during the course of your class from any computer with Internet access. To access this tailored syllabus, students will just need the URL of the website and the password assigned to the syllabus. By clicking on the date, the student can see a list of activities, assignments, and readings due for that particular class.
- In addition to the **Syllabus Manager**™ and its benefits listed above, professors also have access to all of the wonderful resources that students have access to on the site.

Resources for the Student—

- Video clips specific to each topic, with questions to help you evaluate the content and make crucial theory-to-practice connections.
- Thought-provoking critical analysis questions that students can answer and turn in for evaluation or that can serve as basis for class discussions and lectures.
- Access to a wide variety of resources related to classroom strategies and methods, including lesson planning and classroom management.
- Information on all the most current relevant topics related to special and general education, including CEC and Praxis standards, IEPs, portfolios, and professional development.
- Extensive web resources and overviews on each topic addressed on the website.
- A message board with discussion starters where students can respond to class discussion topics, post questions and responses, or ask questions about assignments.
- A search feature to help access specific information quickly.

To take advantage of these and other resources, please visit the *Merrill Resources for Special Education* website at

http://www.prenhall.com/rosenberg

Brief Contents

Contents

Field Experiences with Students with Mild to Moderate Disabilities

Chapter Outline

Students with Mild to Moderate Disabilities: Definitions and Characteristics
> *Categories of Mild to Moderate Disabilities*
> *Category-Free Descriptions*

How Special Education Services Are Delivered
> *Continuum of Services*
> *Inclusive Education*

Roles and Responsibilities
> *University Supervisor*
> *Cooperating or Mentor Teacher*
> *Practicum Student*

Preparing for a Successful Practicum Experience

In this chapter, we will

- review the categories of mild to moderate disabilities, with an emphasis on current definitions and typical characteristics

- discuss how special education services are typically delivered to students with disabilities

- define the attributes of inclusive educational programming and describe how such programs are designed and implemented

- describe the roles and responsibilities of key individuals involved in field experiences

- enumerate some commonsense tips that enable practicum students to realize the greatest benefits from their field experiences

A PROFESSIONAL GLIMPSE

Naomi Crawford was ready for the final semester of her special education/general education teacher preparation program. Her major activity was a 10-week student teaching internship at Center City Middle School, a school not far from where she had grown up. Naomi picked out the clothing that she felt most comfortable in and allowed herself a little extra time to reflect on the range of emotions she was experiencing. On one hand, she was proud that she had made it through the rigorous training program provided by the university and earned solid grades in all of her courses. Yes, she could be a good role model for the students at Center City, a neighborhood kid who had made it through college. Naomi was also a bit nervous: What if she and her cooperating teacher did not hit it off? Would the cooperating teacher provide support in an instructive fashion? What about the students with special needs? Would they be in inclusive classrooms or would they be in segregated special classes? Would they listen to her even if she was just a student teacher?

Naomi had little to worry about. Over the years, the faculty and administration at Center City had provided successful field experiences for scores of potential educators. Upon her arrival at the school, the Assistant Principal (AP), Claude Gortner, oriented Naomi to the school and reviewed district and school policies and procedures. Naomi knew most of this, but the review was an opportunity for her to get to know the AP as well as to ask questions regarding her responsibilities in the enforcement of school rules and procedures. Following this meeting, Naomi observed her cooperating teacher, Sheila Parker, for two periods. During the first period, Ms. Parker cotaught with Ben Claxton in an inclusive seventh grade English class. Ms. Parker met with a subset of the class during the controlled practice activities. The second period was much different; Ms. Parker had a self-contained reading class of sixth graders with behavioral issues who were quite difficult to keep on task.

During lunch, Naomi and Ms. Parker reviewed the competencies related to the internship and mapped out a schedule of activities for Naomi. Ms. Parker also presented the school policies and procedures and then highlighted the responsibilities of all involved in the student teaching process. Naomi shared the mechanisms through which the university supervisor would monitor the success of the experience. A structured visitation schedule was provided along with specific targets for observation. To avoid problems in communication, Ms. Parker suggested that the two of them briefly discuss concerns at the end of each school day. The discussion concluded with Naomi answering a series of questions Ms. Parker had about her coursework.

A bit tired, but much relieved, Naomi left Center City Middle School with a clear understanding of what she would be required to experience and accomplish during the student teaching internship. Although still a bit apprehensive about how she would perform, Naomi was comforted by the structure and support provided by the university supervisor and the faculty and staff of Center City Middle School.

*F*ield experiences are among the most important components in the professional development of quality teachers. As is the case with a variety of other human service professions (e.g., medicine, social work, counseling), supervised field experiences provide appropriately trained candidates with opportunities to apply freshly acquired skills within nurturing and supportive environments. In most teacher-training programs, field experiences are viewed as critical transition activities. Experiences are designed to link the knowledge base presented in the college classroom to the independent activities expected of beginning teachers. In sharp contrast to the unidirectional and vicarious nature of textbooks, journal articles, university lectures, and classroom simulations, field experiences bring emotion and immediacy to the teacher-education process. With a built-in network of support, developing teachers are (1) placed in real-world situations that allow for the constructive discovery of strengths and weaknesses,

(2) given ample opportunities to improve on their assessed deficiencies, and (3) encouraged to enhance creatively their areas of strength. Working with students, parents, and colleagues, developing teachers experience the daily rewards and, at times, many of the challenges and frustrations inherent in their chosen profession.

In comparison with those of the past, today's teacher-training programs are allocating increased resources to and requiring increased amounts of time for field experiences as well as exploring ways to deliver such experiences to nontraditional preservice populations (Rosenberg, Jackson, & Yeh, 1996; Rosenberg & Sindelar, 2001). Through both traditional teacher-preparation programs and alternative routes to teacher development, developing teachers and their university supervisors are spending more of their time in direct contact with students and school personnel. Local education agencies (LEAs) and institutions of higher education are forming partnerships to ensure that developing and beginning teachers are provided with opportunities to become effective in today's schools.

Recognizing the importance of field experiences, state lawmakers and varied professional organizations involved in the education of teachers (e.g., American Association of Colleges for Teacher Education) are advocating that field experiences be expanded and improved even more (Wise & Leibbrand, 2001). For example, it has been recommended that clinical experiences include greater opportunities for analytic problem-solving activities and fewer tasks that merely require imitation (Case, Lanier, & Miskel, 1986; Feiman-Nemser, 2001). Such activities would produce reflective professionals who could apply their knowledge and skills to a range of challenges and, more important, use the results of their experiences to develop new approaches to the education of the children in their charge.

In this introductory chapter, we address a wide range of issues faced by developing teachers who are placed in field-based practicum experiences with students identified as having mild to moderate disabilities. First, we describe the characteristics of students with mild to moderate disabilities. We give special attention to issues surrounding the

Pause and Reflect About the Profession 1.1

For even the most prepared preservice special educator, the start of a new field experience can be a time of heightened anticipation. Clearly, this is a time of excitement, energy, enthusiasm, and, yes, even some stress. Finally, all the things learned in university classes will be put into practice. At times like these, it is often useful to write down some of the expectations and feelings you are experiencing. It is also useful to view how your teacher-development program has prepared you to meet your expectations and to deal with your emotions. In the space below, note some expectations you have for your field experience and some feelings you have regarding the start of this applied experience. Next, think back to your courses and previous experiences in your teacher-preparation program. How have they prepared you to succeed with this important step in your career? Use another sheet of paper if necessary.

Expectations/Feelings	Courses/ Experiences	How Prepared?

categorical and noncategorical descriptions of this heterogeneous population of students. Second, we explore the variety of systems for delivering special education services and discuss how these systems have changed in recent years. Specifically, we provide an overview of inclusive education and describe what developing and beginning teachers can expect in education settings that have adopted inclusionary service delivery procedures. In a similar fashion, we provide specific suggestions for planning for academic diversity. Third, we explore the roles of the key people involved in field-based practicum activities, including the university supervisor, the cooperating teacher, and the practicum student. We conclude this chapter with a series of strategies that can help practicum students understand the social reality of schools and become aware of their legal rights, responsibilities, and liabilities. We believe that these sensible tips can assist developing teachers in becoming effective participants in their field experiences and, ultimately, highly qualified teachers.

STUDENTS WITH MILD TO MODERATE DISABILITIES: DEFINITIONS AND CHARACTERISTICS

When developing teachers first enter the setting for students with mild to moderate disabilities, they realize that the children look like most other children. The children's outward appearance has no strange or alien quality; the layperson's conceptualization of what it means to have a disability doesn't seem to apply. From initial contacts, it seems nearly impossible to distinguish students with disabilities from students considered "normal." As the developing teacher spends more and more time in the classroom, however, learning and behavioral problems do become apparent, and students identified as having mild to moderate disabilities function with lower levels of success on academic tasks and have more difficulty in social situations than their nondisabled peers.

In most cases, children with mild to moderate disabilities are not identified until they enter school. There are two major reasons for the lack of success in the early detection of mild to moderate disabilities. First, many children display slight developmental difficulties that are virtually unnoticeable to the untrained eye. Even in cases where these difficulties are noted during the preschool years, there is no guarantee that these problems will persist into later developmental periods. Second, for many behaviors, there are no clear delineations as to what constitutes normal and abnormal functioning. In regard to hyperactivity or attention problems, for example, objective behavioral criteria that could assist in differentiating normal and problem preschoolers are virtually nonexistent. Thus, it is extremely difficult to differentiate a vigorous, unrestrained, and capricious three-year-old child whose behavior is considered age-appropriate from another three-year-old child whose behavior is overactive, inattentive, and impulsive to a clinically significant degree (Campbell, 1985). The beginning of school, however, is a time when professional educators first evaluate children's abilities in meeting age- and grade-appropriate expectations. Children who violate the norms of their school or grade level in terms of behavior, academic performance, acquisition of spoken and written language, motivation, or aspirations for achievement are those most often identified as having mild or moderate disabilities.

The definitions and descriptions of students' educational problems tend to vary according to the specific philosophies and policies of individual state education agencies (SEAs) and LEAs. As a result of these interstate and intrastate variations, developing and beginning teachers will encounter a variety of nomenclatural and administrative arrangements used to describe students with mild to moderate disabilities. Nonetheless, the variety of arrangements can be reduced to two broad approaches: the use of categorical referents and category-free clusters of characteristics. In the sections that follow, we (1) define the categories associated with mild to moderate disabilities and (2) describe the category-free cluster approach to problem identification.

Categories of Mild to Moderate Disabilities

The categories of exceptionality used most frequently to define students experiencing mild to moderate learning and behavioral problems are learning disabilities, emotional disturbance or behavioral disorders, mild/moderate mental retardation, and other health impairments (e.g., attention deficit disorders). Students identified as belonging to any one of these categories are presumed to share a specific behavior or pattern of behaviors. In recent years, the validity of this presumption has been a topic of considerable controversy.

Learning Disabilities. The vast majority of children having mild to moderate disabilities are considered to have learning disabilities. Central to the diagnosis of learning disabilities, the newest major category in the field of special education, are problems in academic achievement. Specific learning disability is defined in the 1997 iteration of the Individuals with Disabilities Education Act (IDEA) as:

> a disorder in one or more of the basic psychological processes involved in understanding or in using language, spoken or written, that may manifest itself in an imperfect ability to listen, think, speak, read, write, spell, or do mathematical calculations, including conditions such as perceptual disabilities, brain injury, minimal brain dysfunction, dyslexia, and developmental aphasia. The term does not include children who have learning problems that are primarily the result of visual, hearing, or motor disabilities, mental retardation, or emotional disturbance, or of environmental, cultural, or economic disadvantage. (U.S. Department of Education, 2004)

The National Joint Committee on Learning Disabilities (NJCLD), a national group of representatives of 10 major organizations (e.g., Council for Learning Disabilities [CLD], American Speech-Language-Hearing Association [ASHA], Learning Disabilities Association of America [LDAA]) committed to the education and welfare of individuals with learning disabilities, has defined learning disabilities as

> a general term that refers to a heterogeneous group of disorders manifested by significant difficulties in the acquisition and use of listening, speaking, reading, writing, reasoning, or mathematical abilities. These disorders are intrinsic to the individual, presumed to be due to central nervous system dysfunction, and may occur across the life span. Problems in self-regulatory behaviors, social perception, and social interaction may exist with learning disabilities but do not by themselves constitute a learning disability. Although learning disabilities may occur concomitantly with other handicapping conditions (for example, sensory impairment, mental retardation, emotional disturbance) or with extrinsic influences (such as cultural differences, insufficient or inappropriate instruction), they are not the result of those conditions or influences. (NJCLD, 1988, p. 4)

The major difference between the two definitions lies in the presumed causes of the disability (Smith, 1998). The federal definition, originally part of Public Law (PL) 94–142, the Education for All Handicapped Children Act (EHA), is older and reflects a biophysical or medical orientation. The more recent NJCLD definition states that an individual's learning disability may have a biophysical cause (e.g., central nervous system dysfunction), but it allows for the inclusion of individuals who may not have such a dysfunction.

Not surprisingly, the federal definition of learning disability has been criticized widely and continues to spark emotional debates among professionals in the field. Some critics (e.g., Hallahan & Kauffman, 1982) have argued that the definition of learning disability needs to be broadened so that any child not achieving up to potential can receive special education services. Such a definition would not rely on causal explanations or exclude children who may have other disability conditions along with their learning disability.

Other critics (e.g., Council for Learning Disabilities, 1986; Kirk & Gallagher, 1986) have tried to narrow the definition of learning disability and have remained steadfast in their view that not all underachieving students have a learning disability. In fact, these professionals view the excessive incidence of students with learning disabilities as a direct result of the inclusion of students whose low achievement or underachievement is a reflection of factors other than specific learning disabilities (e.g., depressed intellectual functioning, motivational problems, inadequate instruction). These professionals see learning disabilities as just one possible cause of underachievement and believe that interventions geared to specific learning disabilities can enhance remedial efforts. Underachievement stemming from extrinsic sources, such as poor environmental conditions, would be better served if society could change the living and learning environments.

Regardless of definitional controversies, most students identified as having a learning disability (LD) have average to above-average intellectual ability as measured by intelligence tests. On measures of achievement, however, these students do not perform at levels commensurate with their assessed intellectual abilities. These differences between a student's intelligence test scores and achievement test scores are typically referred to as discrepancies between intellectual ability and educational performance. If a severe discrepancy is found between the intellectual ability and actual achievement of a student, he or she may be considered to have a learning disability. Unfortunately, there is no clear consensus as to what level of discrepancy between ability and achievement constitutes a severe discrepancy. In fact, a number of researchers (e.g., Fletcher, Morris, & Lyon, 2003) have questioned the validity of using discrepancies for identification because they do not contribute to intervention planning. Rather, they have urged the field to examine a Responsiveness to Intervention (RTI) model to identify learning disabilities. RTI identification works as follows: All students are provided with effective instruction, and progress is monitored. Those who fail to respond get something more or something else from a teacher or resource person, and progress continues to be monitored. Those who still do not respond qualify for special education services (Fuchs, Mock, Morgan, & Young, 2003).

As the sentiment grows in favor of abandoning the discrepancy method of LD identification, it is clear that we will be witnessing a number of experiments evaluating the validity and utility of the RTI conceptualization of LD.

Emotional Disturbance or Behavioral Disorders. As with learning disabilities, it is difficult to identify and define formally the emotional and behavioral problems of school-age children. A major source of this difficulty is that a variety of terms is used to refer to problem behaviors. For example, professionals involved in the education and treatment of students with problem behaviors do not even agree on what generic name most appropriately captures the category. Under the provisions of the IDEA, children who are disabled by their behavior have been referred to as having an emotional disturbance. Although this term is commonly used, many professionals (e.g., Council for

Pause and Reflect about the Profession 1.2

What type of procedure or formula does your state and/or school district use to identify learning disabilities? Do such procedures account for all children who require services for their learning disabilities? Do the procedures overidentify or underidentify students for special education services? Can you think of better ways to define and identify learning disabilities? What is your view of Responsiveness to Intervention as a means for identifying learning disabilities?

Children with Behavior Disorders [CCBD]) believe that it is neither accurate nor beneficial to the educational process. The official position statement of the CCBD (Huntze, 1985) lists seven reasons for supporting the use of the term *behavioral disorder* over the traditional referent, *emotional disturbance*. These seven reasons are highlighted in Box 1.1

The IDEA continues to use the Bower (1969) definition of emotional disturbance to identify students who may need special education services. Briefly, a student with emotional disturbance exhibits one or more of the following characteristics to a marked extent and over a long period of time:

- An inability to learn that cannot be explained by intellectual, sensory, or health factors
- An inability to build or maintain satisfactory relationships with peers and teachers
- Inappropriate types of behavior or feelings under normal circumstances
- A general pervasive mood of unhappiness or depression
- A tendency to develop physical symptoms or fears associated with personal or school problems

The federal categorical definition of emotional disturbance does embrace children who may be schizophrenic but does not include those who are socially maladjusted unless it is determined that they possess a serious emotional disturbance. One advantage to this definition is that it is descriptive. It does not attempt to explain the causes of emotional disturbance, but rather describes likely manifestations of whatever the problem might be.

Nonetheless, as with the definition of learning disability, the IDEA definition of emotional disturbance has been the subject of widespread criticism, and it is quite possible that a new definition will be included in a future reauthorization of special education law. The major problem with the definition is that it contains many vague terms and the key terms and phrases are not defined, quantified, or operationalized. For

---

Box 1.1   **Seriously Emotionally Disturbed or Behaviorally Disordered? Is the Label Important?**

In a controversial position paper, the Council for Children with Behavior Disorders (CCBD) advocated replacing the term *seriously emotionally disturbed* with the term *behaviorally disordered* as a descriptor for children and youth who are disabled by their behavior. Listed below are seven reasons for its support of this change. Detailed explanations for each component of the rationale are available in Huntze (1985). Do you agree or disagree with each of the stated reasons? Why or why not?

1. The term *behaviorally disordered* has far greater utility for education than the term *seriously emotionally disturbed*.
2. The term *behaviorally disordered* is not associated exclusively with any particular theory of causation and therefore with any particular set of intervention techniques.
3. The term *behaviorally disordered* affords a more comprehensive assessment of the population.
4. The term *behaviorally disordered* is less stigmatizing than the term *seriously emotionally disturbed*.
5. The term *behaviorally disordered* is more representative of students who are disabled by their behavior and currently served under the IDEA.
6. The professional judgment of the field, generally, appears to be moving in the direction of the term *behaviorally disordered*.
7. The change in terminology is representative of a focus on the educational responsibility delineated in the IDEA and is descriptive of the population currently served.

example, the initial qualifying phrases "to a marked extent" and "over a long period of time" are not quantified easily and are open to subjective interpretation. Similarly, the phrase "satisfactory relationships with peers and teachers" is much too general for precise decision making. Other problems with the definition include (1) its failure to consider problem behaviors as existing within a social context (Rosenberg, Wilson, Maheady, & Sindelar, 2004) and (2) the seemingly incongruous inclusionary and exclusionary caveats regarding schizophrenia and social maladjustment. Clearly, five criteria within the definition indicate that children with schizophrenia must be included and that children with social maladjustment cannot be excluded from any conceptualization of emotional disturbance or behavioral disorder.

Unfortunately, there are no clear answers to the problems related to the identification of students with emotional disturbance. Many of us as educators believe that we know problem behaviors or indicators of emotional disturbance when we see them. The quantification of emotional disturbance under the present definition, however, is severely limited by a lack of measures for determining eligibility for services. This state of affairs has not limited the number of students referred as emotionally disturbed. In most school districts, emotional disturbance is defined socially by the relatively imprecise tolerance levels of teachers, administrators, and parents. Consequently, students identified as having emotional disturbance are a heterogeneous population that varies in behavioral characteristics both within and between individual classrooms, school buildings, and LEAs. At one extreme, these students may frequently act out or behave aggressively; at the other extreme, these students may be extremely withdrawn, with low rates of social interaction. In characterizing the range of behaviors associated with emotional disturbance, Rosenberg et al. (2004) have used the terms *high-incidence behavioral disorders* and *low-incidence behavioral disorders* to differentiate the types of behaviors that general and special educators tend to deal with on a regular basis. High-incidence behavioral disorders can include hyperactive behavior (overactivity, distractibility, impulsivity), aggression, rule-breaking/delinquency, and social withdrawal. Low-incidence behavioral disorders tend not to be observed by most educators and include a variety of psychotic behaviors exhibited by a relatively few children and youth in the general population. These behaviors can include self-stimulatory behavior, self-injurious behavior, extreme social withdrawal, and delusional thinking.

Mild/Moderate Mental Retardation. The IDEA formally defines mental retardation (MR) as significantly subaverage general intellectual functioning existing concurrently with deficits in adaptive behavior and manifested during the developmental period that adversely affects a child's educational performance.

In the past, for a student to be identified as having MR, he or she had to have two specific deficits: (1) below-average intellectual functioning as measured by standardized tests of intelligence and (2) deficits in adaptive behavior—those everyday behaviors believed to be necessary for survival in our society (Grossman, 1977). Those students meeting the definitional criteria were diagnosed as having a level or degree of MR based on the level of intelligence (as measured by intelligence test scores). Typically, students with scores between 55 and 69 on standardized intelligence tests were considered to have mild retardation, students with scores between 40 and 54 were considered to have moderate retardation, scores between 25 and 39 indicated severe retardation, and scores below 24 indicated profound retardation.

Under this classification system, the large majority of individuals with MR (approximately 85 percent) fell into the mild retardation range and were believed able to master academic skills up to about the sixth grade level and to learn job skills well enough to support themselves independently or semi-independently (Heward, 2003). Students with moderate retardation constituted approximately 7 to 10 percent of those identified as having MR and were believed to benefit from highly individualized instruction in those skills necessary for successful community integration (e.g., daily living skills, self-care skills, basic work skills, a functional vocabulary). Students with severe and profound mental retardation made up approximately 3 to 6 percent of those identified as having MR and were believed typically to require intensive instruction in self-care and basic communication skills.

However, in 1992, the American Association on Mental Retardation developed a new system for classifying mental retardation. Rather than using the level of measured intelligence, this new system is based on an individual's unique strengths, weaknesses, and needs for special supports. The intent of this new classification system is to describe more accurately the variability in the ways people with similar intelligence test scores can function (Kozma & Stock, 1993). The new system classifies individuals with MR by the amount of support or help that is needed across four dimensions—intellectual and adaptive skills, psychological and emotional considerations, physical/ health/ etiology considerations, and environmental considerations—related to success in their environment. For each of these dimensions, the four intensities of support are as follows:

1. **Intermittent:** Requiring short-term (yet not consistent) support (e.g., coaching during an acute medical crisis, assistance in preparing for a job interview).
2. **Limited:** Requiring time-limited (yet not intermittent) support consistently over time (e.g., time-limited job training, transitional supports for school-to-work period).
3. **Extensive:** Requiring support in some environments that is regular (e.g., daily) and not time-limited (e.g., long-term job support, long-term home living support).
4. **Pervasive:** Requiring support across environments that is characterized by constancy and high intensity. Supports typically involve more staff members and intrusiveness than do extensive or time-limited supports and may be of a life-sustaining nature.

Students with mild mental retardation typically require supports at the intermittent or limited intensity and most often have problems in communicating (e.g., delayed speech), attending to tasks, maintaining motivation, and generalizing from one task or setting to another as well as with incidental learning.

It bears mentioning that the use of mild mental retardation as a categorical referent is not without criticism. It has been argued that mild retardation is related more closely to such variables as socioeconomic status, family education level, and literacy than to intelligence test scores. In fact, some data support the view that children from poor families and minority groups tend to be overrepresented among the students identified with mild mental retardation. Although critics have noted that such students are questionable candidates for inclusion in the category of mild mental retardation, these children are undoubtedly in need of some type of special intervention if they are to succeed in school. The question posed by Edgar and Hayden (1985) remains: How can these students best be served?

Other Health Impairment (OHI). According to the IDEA, OHI refers to students who have limited strength, vitality, or alertness, including a heightened alertness to environmental stimuli, that results in limited alertness to the educational environment. This may be due to chronic or acute health problems such as asthma, attention deficit hyperactivity disorder (ADHD), diabetes, epilepsy, a heart condition, hemophilia, lead poisoning, leukemia, nephritis, rheumatic fever, and sickle cell anemia. For the health impairment to be considered a disability, it must adversely affect a child's educational performance.

A significant change in the current IDEA is the addition of ADHD to the conditions listed under OHI. Under previous iterations of the IDEA, it was specified that children with attention disabilities could receive special services only if (1) their characteristics met one of the disability categories listed in the statute and (2) special education was needed because of that disability. Unfortunately, it was determined that many students with attention difficulties were not receiving services and it was necessary to formally codify ADHD as a condition that could lead to special education eligibility under the law.

According to the fourth edition of the *Diagnostic and Statistical Manual of Mental Disorders—Test Revision* (American Psychiatric Association, 2000), the essential feature of ADHD is a persistent pattern of inattention and/or hyperactivity-impulsivity that occurs more frequently and is more severe than such behaviors found in individuals at comparable levels of development. Symptoms must be present in at least two settings (e.g., school, home), and there must be clear evidence of interference with developmentally appropriate social, academic, or occupational functioning. The primary characteristics are overactivity and fidgetiness, distractibility or inattention, impulsivity or judgment deficits, and excitability or negative affect. Among the secondary characteristics are learning problems or deficiencies in academic achievement, aggressive and antisocial behaviors, and poor self-concept or lack of self-esteem.

Category-Free Descriptions

Although the use of categorical referents is the traditional approach to the description of students with mild to moderate disabilities, many educators have found that it is more beneficial to adopt an alternative conceptualization—a category-free classification system. This category-free approach, often referred to as a noncategorical or cross-categorical perspective, puts greater emphasis on variables related to students' behavioral functioning than on the specific factors used to either include or exclude a student from a particular category. Operationally defined, behavioral functioning refers to the overt behaviors of students and their relationship to the environment. These are learned, often situation-specific behaviors that occur in response to the demands of different environmental settings (Gloecker & Simpson, 1988). Most important, students' levels of behavioral functioning are viewed as being, in part, modifiable through classroom intervention.

In general, the problem behaviors most typical of students with mild to moderate disabilities fall into several generic domains: academic underachievement, sensory and perceptual processing problems, perceptual-motor difficulties, attention deficit problems, long- and short-term memory deficits, receptive and expressive language disorders, hyperactivity, impulsivity, poor peer relationships, and deficient social-emotional skills. It should be remembered, however, that although students with mild to moderate disabilities as a group exhibit problem behaviors across all of these domains, rarely does any one student actually experience difficulties in all domains.

Proponents of the noncategorical perspective cite three major reasons for advocating their position. First, the categorical approach to the description of students with mild to moderate disabilities implies a homogeneity within each of the categories. This is not the case. In fact, there is such heterogeneity of characteristics among students within each of the categories that the result is a blurring of categorical boundaries. The overlap between the traditional categories is most often noted in a sharing of common behavioral features including (but not limited to) deficient academic functioning, poor social skills, memory problems, impulsivity, and problems in the generalization and maintenance of newly acquired skills.

The second argument supporting the noncategorical orientation involves the instructional procedures typical of most special education settings. In short, traditional methods of labeling students with learning and behavioral problems are basically administrative procedures that have little impact on how to best teach students. Many of the criteria used to determine categorical eligibility include generic references to traits and etiological considerations that have little instructional relevance. As a result, instruction based on strict categorical consideration has not been very successful (Hallahan, Kauffman, & Lloyd, 1985; Smith, Price, & Marsh, 1986). Rather, the precise definition of assessed problems constitutes the first step in providing appropriate instructional interventions.

The third reason offered by advocates for noncategorical programming is that the use of traditional categories promotes the faulty assumption that learning and behavioral difficulties can be attributed exclusively to the labeled student. Clearly, learning and behavioral problems are not solely student-based but are often the result of a myriad of interacting ecological factors, including classroom setting, teacher behavior, community characteristics, and the entry-level behavior of the student (Blankenship & Lilly, 1981).

HOW SPECIAL EDUCATION SERVICES ARE DELIVERED

By far, one of the most contentious issues in special education is how to best deliver special education services while ensuring access to the general education curriculum. Most of the controversy has centered on how to best meet the educational needs of individuals with disabilities while in the least restrictive environment (LRE). For many years, the cascade or continuum of services was the primary framework used to determine educational placement; recently, however, the principle of inclusion has been operationalized as an alternative means of delivery.

Continuum of Services

One of the first concepts presented to college students interested in pursuing a career in special education is the cascade of educational services. This cascade system, originally outlined by Reynolds (1962) and expanded by Deno (1970), suggests that the delivery of educational services to all students is best viewed as a continuum, as illustrated in Figure 1.1 and Box 1.2.

Several assumptions are inherent in the cascade conceptualization of available educational services. First, the model assumes that a variety of service delivery options should be available to meet the specific educational needs of individual students. Rather than focusing on classifications or labels, the ultimate goal is to tailor instructional programs and settings to meet the needs of students. Second, the triangular shape of the model indicates that the majority of students, those with disabilities and without disabilities, are appropriately placed in settings closest to the general education classroom. Third, the cascade assumes that placement within a particular setting is not permanent. Students should be able to move between levels of services on the basis of their educational performance. The greatest emphasis should be on returning students to less restrictive environments; movement to more restrictive settings should occur only when necessary.

Regardless of their categorical designation, most students with mild to moderate disabilities typically receive educational services within the general school environment. Therefore, many developing and beginning teachers find that they will be teaching in the traditional special education settings: full-time special classrooms, part-time special settings, and resource rooms. With the movement toward the increased integration of students with mild to moderate disabilities into general classroom settings, however, it is also possible that developing and beginning teachers will find themselves working in nontraditional service delivery roles—as consulting teachers, itinerant learning specialists, or cooperative partners in integrated classroom settings.

Some special education practicum students may sense an unusual estrangement from their general education colleagues. This feeling of separation is typically the result of a host of factors but is caused to a great degree by the lack of coordination between the special education and general education systems of educating students with problems. The significant growth and progress of special education have resulted in a dual system of education—with one set of instructional resources for nondisabled youngsters and another for those with learning and behavioral difficulties.

One major deleterious by-product of this development is misunderstandings between general and special educators as to who is responsible for the education of

FIGURE 1.1 Cascade of Educational Services

Source: Adapted from "Special Education as Developmental Capital," by E. Dene, 1970, *Exceptional Children, 37*, p. 235; and "A Framework for Considering Some Issues in Special Education," by M. C. Reynolds, 1962, *Exceptional Children, 28*, p. 368.

students identified as having disabilities. In settings where a dual system of education is institutionalized, many administrators and general classroom teachers believe they are no longer involved in the education of students with disabilities. Many general classroom teachers also believe they lack the specialized training that could enable them to teach the other 25 to 30 students in their classrooms along with students with disabilities. By virtue of their identification as students with disabilities, these challenging students have come to be viewed as the exclusive educational responsibility of a specialist—the special educator. Unfortunately, this attitude does little to promote the reintegration and mainstreaming of students with disabilities and often puts barriers between special and general educators. See Figure 1.1.

By the time they enter the school environment, developing and beginning teachers are keenly aware that the success of students with mild to moderate disabilities depends on the collaborative efforts of general and special educators. This need to bring together general and special educators has been approached in a number of ways and with varying degrees of intensity. Several special educators have advocated a complete merging of special and general education efforts into a single, unified, inclusive system. Such restructuring would radically change how students with disabilities would be identified and served in their local communities. As observed by Stainback and Stainback (1984), the adoption of a unified system of education for all students would affect many facets of special education. Possible affected areas are summarized in Table 1.1.

Box 1.2	**Levels of the Cascade: Examples of Students Receiving Services**

1. *Regular class:* The LRE for the education of students is the regular class.

   Example: Sara requires speech therapy for a diagnosed articulation problem although she displays no educational difficulties other than an articulation problem. Sara is five years old, and her LRE is the regular class at Public School #16.

2. *Regular class with consultation*: Resource room teachers and itinerant teachers consult with regular classroom teachers about modifications in the general curriculum. Prereferral strategies may be implemented for students who can profit by instruction with regular class peers.

   Example: Ellen demonstrates adequate comprehension skills but has trouble reading the text. Teachers at Taylor School have consulted about the use of a tape-recorded text for her regular class reading program. When she is allowed to hear stories read on tape, Ellen demonstrates no difficulty following the written discourse. The LRE for Ellen may be the regular class with consulting services. Use of the tape recorder may be monitored by her teachers through prereferral conferences.

3. *Regular class with supportive services*: The majority of the student's classwork is provided during regular class scheduling, but for a portion of the time, education is provided in a resource room setting.

   Example: Yusuf displays excellent reading and spelling skills but requires assistance by the teacher in the resource room for mathematics. Yusuf functions effectively in all aspects of the school curriculum. The LRE for Yusuf may be the resource room model at Tandy Elementary. His special education teacher may work on a consulting basis with the regular classroom teacher to monitor Yusuf's progress in the regular class.

4. *Part-time regular class and part-time special class or resource room*: Students with disabilities spend some part of the instructional week with regular peers.

   Example: Tommy displays problem behaviors—specifically, inattention to tasks during academic instruction. He displays excellent motor skills, however, and is especially proficient in rhythm activities during music class. The LRE for Tommy may be a placement in which he divides his time between instruction with regular students and instruction with students with disabilities at Santa Rosa High School.

5. *Full-time special class*: Students with disabilities are educated in a special class located on the grounds of a regular school.

   Example: Tara functions at a profound level of developmental delay although she displays no major problems with self-help skills or motor skills. She displays no medical difficulties. The LRE for Tara may be a full-time special class at Flanigan Middle School.

6. *Special day school*: Students with disabilities are educated in a special school with similar students.

   Example: Mary has been found to be functioning at a profound level of cognitive functioning. She requires the assistance of a wheelchair and feeding tubes during lunch. The LRE for Mary may be the Fanley Special Day Care Center.

7. *Full-time residential school*: Educational services are provided directly to the student at the hospital or institution where he or she resides.

   Example: John has been diagnosed as having severe developmental disability, is deaf-blind, and requires full-time medical assistance. The LRE for John may be the Maryhurst Residential School and Treatment Center.

TABLE 1.1 Comparative Effects of Dual Versus Unified Systems of Education on Selected Areas of Concern

Concern	Dual System	Unified System
1. Student characteristics	Dichotomizes students into special and regular	Recognizes continuum among all students of intellectual, physical, and psychological characteristics
2. Individualization	Stresses individualization for student labeled special	Stresses individualization for all students
3. Instructional strategies	Seeks to use special strategies for special students	Selects from range of available strategies according to each student's learning needs
4. Type educational services	Eligibility generally based on category affiliation	Eligibility based on each student's individual learning needs
5. Diagnostics	Large expenditures on identification of categorical affiliation	Emphasis on identifying the specific instructional needs of all students
6. Professional relationships	Establishes artificial barriers among educators that promote competition and alienation	Promotes cooperation through sharing resources, expertise, and advocacy responsibilities
7. Curriculum	Options available to each student are limited by categorical affiliation	All options are available to every student as needed
8. Focus	Students must fit regular education program or be referred to special education	Regular education program is adjusted to meet all students' needs

Source: From "A Rationale for the Merger of Regular and Special Education, by W. Stainback and S. Stainback, 1984, *Exceptional children*, *51*, p. 107. Copyright 1984 by The Council for Exceptional Children. Reprinted by permission.

Inclusive Education

Inclusive education is an effort to reconstruct general education classes so that all children, representing the range of diversity present in a local community, are welcome and provided with an appropriate, meaningful education (Giangreco, Baumgart, & Doyle, 1995). Therefore, inclusion means that students attend their home school with their age- and grade-appropriate peers, participate in extracurricular activities, and receive special education and support services, to the maximum extent possible, in the general education classroom. Inclusion does not mean that students must spend every moment of the school day in general education classes or that students never receive small-group or individualized instruction (see Box 1.3) (York, Doyle, & Kronberg, 1992). However, the focus for inclusion is on where things are happening and the types of practices that are being used (King-Sears, 1997).

Proponents of inclusion are quick to point out that inclusion is not synonymous with the term *mainstreaming*; mainstreaming occurs when a student with an identified disability leaves a special education class to participate in a general education class for part of the day to complete the same instructional goals set for other students. Within an inclusionary delivery system, special education and support services are delivered so that the student with a disability can benefit from being in the general education setting.

The rationale for inclusive education is quite compelling, particularly on philosophical and social grounds. Clearly, it is difficult to argue against the position that all children should reap the potential benefits of inclusive programming (e.g., attending their neighborhood school in classrooms where there is a climate of acceptance, ending the segregation of large numbers of students, having all students participate in shared educational experiences with individualized outcomes). Most discussions of inclusion, however, have (1) ignored the barriers and conditions within the schools that preclude successful inclusive efforts and (2) minimized the real-life, day-to-day demands on teachers who are expected to teach an increasingly diverse group of students with and without disabilities (Joint Committee on Teacher Planning for Students with Disabilities, 1995).

B ox 1.3	Inclusion: What It Is and What It Is Not

Inclusion IS	Inclusion is NOT
• teaching students with disabilities in their home schools in general education settings regardless of the degree or severity of their disabilities	• serving students with disabilities only in separate schools or classes based on their disability label
• having a school and district mission that sets high expectations for all students, including those with disabilities	• setting low expectations for students with disabilities
• making sure that all students are placed in schools and classrooms appropriate to their age	• teaching students with disabilities in schools and classrooms that are not age-appropriate
• providing the planning, support, and services necessary for successful participation of students with disabilities in general education programs	• placing students with disabilities in general education classes without the planning, support, and services needed for successful participation
• adapting teaching styles to meet the many different learning needs of all students	• failing to adapt instruction to meet the different learning needs of students
• providing professional development, training, and support for all staff regarding effective methods for the successful inclusion of students with disabilities	• providing separate staff development for regular teachers and special education teachers, thus reinforcing notions of separate systems
• encouraging activities that promote the development of friendships and relationships between students with and without disabilities	• maintaining separate daily activities for students with and without disabilities
• scheduling classes for all school activities in a way that maximizes opportunities for participation by students with disabilities	• scheduling students with disabilities for lunch and other activities at different times than other students are scheduled
• using "person first" language ("students with disabilities" instead of "disabled students") and teaching all students to understand and value human differences	• referring to students in stigmatizing terms such as "handicapped class" or the "retarded kids"

Source: Adapted from by Maryland Coalition for Inclusive Education, 1993, *Inclusion: What It Is and What It Is Not*. Laurel, MD: Author.

From the results of four large-scale studies, the Joint Committee on Teacher Planning for Students with Disabilities found that, for students with disabilities to be successfully included in the general education classroom, educators need to think in terms of "supported inclusion," not simply inclusion (see Box 1.4). Supported inclusion is defined as a set of instructional conditions in which classroom teachers

- are philosophically committed to meeting the needs of all students, including those with mild disabilities, in the general education classroom
- have sufficient time to think about and plan for the diverse needs of students in their class(es)
- incorporate teaching practices that enable them to better meet the needs of all students in their class(es)
- work collaboratively with special education teachers to assess, teach, and monitor student progress
- have the option for their students to receive short-term, intensive instructional support from a special education teacher
- have the option for their students to receive sustained instruction in basic skills or learning strategies that cannot be provided in the general education classroom (Joint Committee on Teacher Planning for Students with Disabilities, 1995, pp. 3–4).

Box 1.4　　　　**Inclusion Checklist for Your Placement**

Rodgers (1993) prepared a checklist designed to assist school personnel in evaluating whether their current practices are consistent with the best intention of the inclusive programming movement. Use this modified checklist to assess how your field placement measures up to some of the ideals proposed by inclusion advocates. Rate your placement with a + for each item in which the main statement best describes your placement and a 0 for each item in which the parenthetical statement best describes you school. As you consider the items, keep in mind that each 0 rating can serve as the basis for school improvement efforts.

_____ 1. Do the teachers, administrators, and staff at your school believe that each child belongs in the classroom that he or she would otherwise attend if not disabled (or do they believe that children with disabilities should be clustered into special groups, classrooms, or schools)?

_____ 2. Do the educators in your schools individualize the instructional programs for all children whether or not they are disabled and provide the resources that each child needs to explore individual interests in the school environment (or do they tend to provide the same sorts of services for most children who share the same label or classification)?

_____ 3. Are the educators in your school fully committed to maintenance of a caring community that fosters mutual respect and support among staff, parents, and students and in which the educators honestly believe that children with disabilities can benefit from friendships with non-disabled children (or do the educators' practices tacitly tolerate children teasing or isolating some as outcasts)?

_____ 4. Have the general educators and special educators in your school integrated their efforts and their resources so that they work together as integral parts of a unified team (or are they isolated in separate rooms or departments with separate supervisors and budgets)?

_____ 5. Do the administrators at your school create a work climate in which staff are supported as they provide assistance to each other (or are teachers afraid of being presumed to be incompetent if they seek peer collaboration in working with students)?

_____ 6. Do the educators in your school actively encourage the full participation of children with disabilities in the life of the school, including extracurricular activities (or do they participate only in the academic portion of the school day)?

_____ 7. Are the educators in your school prepared to alter support systems for students as their needs change through the school year so that they can achieve, experience successes, and feel that they genuinely belong in their school and classes (or do they sometimes provide students with such limited services that they are set up to fail)?

_____ 8. Do the educators in your school make parents of children with disabilities fully a part of your school community so they also can experience a sense of belonging (or do they give the parents a separate PTA and different newsletters)?

_____ 9. Do the educators in your school give children with disabilities just as much of the full school curriculum as they can master and modify it as necessary so that they can share elements of these experiences with their classmates (or do they have a separate curriculum for children with disabilities)?

_____ 10. Have the educators in your school included children with disabilities supportively in as many as possible of the same testing and evaluation experiences as their nondisabled classmates (or have they excluded them from these opportunities while assuming that they cannot benefit from the experiences)?

Source: Rodgers (1993)

These service delivery issues remain controversial within all levels of the teaching profession. Whether referred to as the regular education initiative, the general education initiative, inclusion, or simply a merger between regular and special education systems, it is heartening to see that educators are continuing to seek more effective ways of delivering special education services to those who need them. In this era of high-stakes testing and the No Child Left Behind legislative requirement that all students make annual yearly progress (AYP), such collaboration is essential. There is little doubt that these efforts will provide better strategies for coordinating the efforts of all educators in delivering specialized educational services to those students in need.

However individual LEAs decide to restructure their systems for identifying and educating students with disabilities, cooperation between general and special educators still comes down to individuals and their interactions. Cooperation and collaboration involve people skills and mutual respect. Developing and beginning teachers of students with mild to moderate disabilities should avoid the "us versus them" mind-set when working with their general education colleagues and should instead actively seek to develop collaborative relationships. Diplomacy is the key to achieving good working relationships and positive outcomes.

ROLES AND RESPONSIBILITIES

Thus far, we have limited our discussion to definitions and characteristics of students with mild to moderate disabilities and to descriptions of the various educational settings in which they are served. In this section, we focus on the developing teacher and describe the roles and responsibilities of the individuals who are influential in determining the success of field-based practicum experiences. For developing teachers of students with mild to moderate disabilities to derive the maximum benefit from field-based practicum experiences, a well-planned team effort must be initiated and maintained. The primary members of this team are the university supervisor, the cooperating classroom teacher, and, most important, the practicum student.

University Supervisor

The university supervisor assumes primary responsibility for the success of practicum students' field experiences. The supervisor is the direct representative of the university and serves to align the best interests of the practicum students and the requirements of the school or LEA. The university supervisor fosters professional development, provides honest performance feedback, and constructively smooths over possible rough spots during the teaching experience.

In addition to these generic responsibilities, the university supervisor typically assumes three responsibilities in the development of preservice special educators. First, the university supervisor arranges for the most appropriate placement for the practicum student. This entails the careful analysis of the practicum student's entry-level skills and the type of setting in which the student anticipates teaching (e.g., level of service, age or grade level, severity of disability). Factors also considered include the availability of both quality instructional settings and cooperating teachers within reasonable commuting distance of the practicum student and university supervisor.

Second, the university supervisor monitors the progress of the practicum student throughout the field experience. This typically involves periodic direct observations of lessons, meetings with the cooperating teacher and principal, and the critiquing of lesson plans, unit projects, and behavioral change efforts. A critical component of this monitoring process is the delivery of feedback. The university supervisor accentuates the strengths of the developing teacher and identifies weaknesses for the purpose of improving performance. Feedback, in many cases, will be specific to the lessons observed, and suggestions for improving student achievement should be offered.

Third, the university supervisor helps to reconcile the practicum student's university-inspired idealism with the real-world pressures of the school. The supervisor can serve as the buffer between the way-things-ought-to-be approach typical of college classrooms and the complex, less-than-ideal realities of school settings. Some practicum students observe that their cooperating teachers' behaviors are not consistent with many of the principles of effective teaching covered in methods classes. The supervisor should clarify such inconsistencies and diplomatically mediate any disagreements between the practicum student and the cooperating teacher.

Cooperating or Mentor Teacher

The cooperating teacher will have the greatest amount of direct contact with the practicum student. In the best of situations, a mentor relationship is forged between the cooperating teacher and the practicum student. Cooperating teachers (1) are models of effective instructional procedures and paragons of tempered professional practice, (2) are well schooled in the ability to share their instincts of teaching, (3) prepare their environment to maximize opportunities for novice teachers to succeed and learn from their errors, (4) observe and evaluate practicum student performance while ensuring that little damage is done to the often fragile self-concept of the novice teacher, and (5) set the pace for the integration of the practicum student into classroom activities, allowing gradually increased levels of responsibility. Box 1.5 lists the more commonly cited competencies desired of cooperating teachers. Although much is expected of cooperating teachers, it must be remembered that their first responsibility is to their students, ensuring that instruction of an appropriate quantity and quality is delivered consistently.

Box 1.5   **Commonly Cited Competencies Desired of Cooperating Teachers**

Competencies Related Primarily to the Working Relationship Between the Cooperating Teacher and the Practicum Student

The cooperating teacher

- remains available for consultation and moral support when needed
- analyzes with the practicum student the value of experiences and helps him or her discover which ones are most worthwhile
- helps the practicum student set his or her goals and formulate a personal educational philosophy
- shares in planning
- plans and teaches with another adult; originates and suggests new ideas without dominating the practicum student's thoughts and actions
- establishes a feeling of security for the practicum student by clarifying his or her responsibilities throughout the field experience
- offers criticism—continual, specific, and constructive—in an empathic manner
- invites the practicum student to participate in the professional and social activities of the staff
- helps the practicum student develop an understanding of his or her own strengths and weaknesses and build a healthy self-concept
- shows willingness to consider new and different techniques in an open-minded manner

Competencies Related to the Transition of the Practicum Student from Observer Status to Active Teaching Status Later in the Field Experience

The cooperating teacher

- gradually allows the practicum student to accept increasing responsibility until full teaching responsibility is assumed

- helps the practicum student understand his or her job in relation to the entire school program
- helps the practicum student build teaching skills through observation of his or her own teaching
- helps the practicum student link theories to practice

Competencies Related Primarily to Instruction, Classroom Procedures, and Techniques

The cooperating teacher

- gives suggestions in matters of discipline
- acquaints the practicum student with routine matters
- keeps accurate records
- creates a democratic setting for learning—one in which students share in some decision-making experiences
- assists the practicum student in setting reasonable standards of performance for his or her instructional group
- encourages creative thinking and planning by the practicum student
- models effective instructional procedures during his or her own teaching

Competencies Related Primarily to Personal Characteristics or Traits of the Cooperating Teacher That Might Be Emulated by the Practicum Student

The cooperating teacher

- sets a good example for the practicum student in personal appearance, grooming, speech, and appropriate mannerisms
- makes rational judgments, takes appropriate actions, and accepts responsibility for the consequences
- reflects a positive professional attitude and real liking of and respect for teaching
- exhibits interest in continual self-improvement and educational advancement
- reflects a mature personality with enthusiasm and broad interests

Competencies Related Primarily to Developing Broad Professional and School Responsibilities

The cooperating teacher

- is an active participant in local and state teachers' organizations
- perceives the opportunity to work with future teachers as a professional responsibility
- actively participates with his or her colleagues in developing and enforcing standards fundamental to continual improvement of the profession and abides by those standards in practice
- exhibits willingness to accept out-of-class responsibilities
- participates effectively in faculty meetings and the work of professional committees
- is acquainted with sources of current thinking—journals, conferences, yearbooks, workshops
- exhibits a cooperative attitude in relationships with other members of the staff

Source: Adapted from *Competencies of the Supervising Teacher*, by Ball State University, 1981, Muncie, IN: Author.

Practicum Student

For most practicum students, the transition from the role of university student to the role of professional teacher is challenging, yet completed with little difficulty. Nonetheless, the rigors and responsibilities of practicum experiences are considerable and should never be underestimated. How these responsibilities are met by the practicum student will dramatically affect the success of the experience itself as well as the individual's future career in teaching. It is best to conceptualize the many responsibilities of the practicum student as falling into six specific domains:

1. Students and their families
2. The cooperating teacher
3. The university
4. Awareness of legal rights, responsibilities, and liabilities
5. Personal professional growth
6. The profession

Responsibilities to Students and Their Families. Practicum students must realize that the instruction they deliver is of vital importance to the students in their classes. Every moment of available instructional time is of extreme value, particularly for students with mild to moderate disabilities. With this in mind, it is important that practicum students come prepared to teach effectively. This preparation should include thorough lesson planning and the necessary consultations with the cooperating teacher and university supervisor. Students' Individualized Education Programs (IEPs) and diagnostic test information should also be reviewed (see Chapters 3 and 4 for greater detail).

In general, students enjoy working with developing teachers. The teachers' youth, vitality, and creativity are often seen as welcome changes of pace. Practicum students should be aware, however, that the students in their classes will depend on them to follow through with planned activities. Therefore, practicum students should avoid unnecessary absences, be prompt in following through on promised events, and refrain from promising things that will not be delivered. Practicum students should be models of decorum, especially in their responses to negative or frustrating events. Initial student enthusiasm for working with developing teachers can be returned by becoming acquainted with students and by interacting with them in a lively, interested fashion. Practicum students should be careful not to become overly friendly, however, and should always conduct themselves in a firm, controlled, and impartial manner.

Practicum students may have the opportunity to interact with members of their students' families. This may be at a regularly scheduled IEP conference or at a meeting that results when some critical incident requires parental input. The practicum student must recognize family members as partners in the education process and, in concert with the cooperating teacher, must discuss constructively the behaviors of the student as they relate to the solution of any presenting problem.

Responsibilities to the Cooperating Teacher. Perhaps the most critical responsibility toward the cooperating teacher is to maintain clear communication. It is best to discuss situations in a direct, positive, and diplomatic manner without letting minor obstacles grow into major stumbling blocks. With the assistance of the university supervisor, the cooperating teacher should be made aware of the personal goals and aspirations of the practicum student, and a plan to achieve those goals within the context of the overall practicum experience should be developed and monitored. If questions about the methods used to pursue these goals arise, it is the responsibility of the practicum student to initiate requests for assistance. Finally, because the education of students in the class is ultimately the responsibility of the cooperating teacher, the practicum student should share activity or lesson plans well in advance of their implementation. This allows the cooperating teacher to provide constructive feedback prior to the delivery of the activity or lesson.

Responsibilities to the University. As a practicum student in the local schools, the developing teacher is a representative of the sponsoring university. By placing a practicum student within a particular setting, the university is stating that the developing teacher is ready to assume the multifaceted responsibilities associated with teaching students with mild to moderate disabilities. Consequently, the behavior of each practicum student reflects on the institution that trained that person.

To best represent their institutions, practicum students should (1) put forth the maximum effort possible in all facets of the field experience, (2) be open to suggestions from various school-based personnel, (3) become involved in team-based solutions to problems, (4) take on a fair share of the noninstructional and extracurricular duties required of teachers, (5) be enthusiastic and positive during instructional and noninstructional tasks, (6) facilitate the cooperative relationship between the visiting university supervisor and the school-based teachers and administrators, and (7) maintain a professional and ethical demeanor when dealing with students' problem behaviors and confidential records. Practicum students should avoid falling into the trap of lounge gossip and must be careful not to refer to students by name during social situations away from the classroom.

Awareness of Legal Rights, Responsibilities, and Liabilities. For better or for worse, we are living in an increasingly litigious society. In all of the human service professions, especially those that involve children, it is critical that the service provider be aware of his or her legal status. Because laws and procedural safeguards concerning those preparing to enter teaching vary from state to state, it is essential that each practicum student become aware of the specific requirements of his or her locality.

Roe and Ross (1994) have recommended that practicum students be particularly aware of their district's policies on (1) reporting possible child abuse, (2) reporting student accidents or injuries, (3) using specific techniques (e.g., time-out) for discipline and behavioral management, (4) searching students' personnel belongings, (5) dealing with physically and verbally abusive advances of students, (6) administering first aid, (7) making copies of instructional materials for students (so as to not violate copyright laws), (8) presenting seemingly controversial topics, and (9) needing liability insurance. Also, in this age of electronic information gathering and transmission, practicum students should be aware of policies regarding the acceptable use of technologies such as cell phones, computer networks, video, and the Internet. Such information can be obtained from the office that administers field-based placements in the school or district.

Although it is extremely rare for developing teachers to face problems that require massive legal involvement, it is important that sticky situations be fully documented and shared with appropriate personnel (e.g., cooperating teacher, university supervisor).

Personal Professional Growth. Although many practicum situations are the culmination of a set of experiences within a special education training program, they are actually the cornerstone for future professional development activities. Instructing and managing challenging students in busy classrooms tend to illuminate specific content or skill areas that require additional growth or refinement. This feeling will recur throughout a teacher's professional career. As a rule, professionals seldom let their acquired skills stagnate. In special education, research and instructional technology are advancing much too quickly for any teacher to neglect personal professional development.

Mechanisms exist for developing teachers to fulfill their need for professional growth. The most convenient method is to consult recent publications in the field and to scan the many web sites dedicated to special education and individuals with disabilities. A variety of professional textbooks, curriculum resource guides, and journals are available in regional resource centers, teacher development centers, and university libraries. Box 1.6 lists the professional journals that are of greatest interest to developing teachers of students with mild to moderate disabilities. Also, at the end of each chapter, we include a short list of web sites that provide both informative content and links to other sites of interest (see the Point and Click About the Profession sections).

B ox 1.6   Professional Journals of Interest to Developing and Beginning Teachers of Students with Mild to Moderate Disabilities

Listed below are the more prominent journals that are of interest to those involved in the education of students with mild to moderate disabilities. Most of these publications are available at major university libraries. To contact the journals directly, use the business addresses provided, or type in the title of the journal in your Internet browser.

American Journal of Mental Deficiency
American Association on Mental Deficiency
5101 Wisconsin Avenue, N.W.
Washington, DC 20016

Assessment for Effective Intervention
(formerly Diagnostique)
Council for Education Diagnostic Services
Council for Exceptional Children
1110 North Glebe Road
Suite 300
Arlington, VA 22201-5704

Behavioral Disorders
Division for Children with Behavior Disorders
Council for Exceptional Children
1110 North Glebe Road
Suite 300
Arlington, VA 22201-5704

Beyond Behavior
Division for Children with Behavior Disorders
Council for Exceptional Children
1110 North Glebe Road
Suite 300
Arlington, VA 22201-5704

Career Development of Exceptional Individuals
Division of Career Development
Council for Exceptional Children
1110 North Glebe Road
Suite 300
Arlington, VA 22201-5704

Communication Disorders Quarterly
Division for Communicative Disabilities and Deafness
PRO-ED
8700 Shoal Creek Boulevard
Austin, TX 78757-6897

Education and Training in Developmental Disabilities
Division on Developmental Disabilities
Council for Exceptional Children
1110 North Glebe Road
Suite 300
Arlington, VA 22201–5704

Education and Treatment of Children
Clinical Psychology Publishing Company
4 Conant Square
Brandon, VT 05733

Exceptional Children
Council for Exceptional Children
1110 North Glebe Road
Suite 300
Arlington, VA 22201–5704

Exceptional Parent
20 Providence Street
Boston, MA 03116

Focus on Exceptional Children
Love Publishing Company
1777 South Bellaire Street
Denver, CO 80222

Intervention in School and Clinic
PRO-ED
8700 Shoal Creek Boulevard
Austin, TX 78757–6897

Journal of Applied Behavior Analysis
Department of Human Development
University of Kansas
Lawrence, KS 66045

Journal of Emotional and Behavioral Disorders
PRO-ED
8700 Shoal Creek Boulevard
Austin, TX 78757–6897

Journal of Learning Disabilities
PRO-ED
8700 Shoal Creek Boulevard
Austin, TX 78757–6897

Journal of Special Education
PRO-ED
8700 Shoal Creek Boulevard
Austin, TX 78757–6897

Journal of Special Education Technology
Technology and Media Division
Council for Exceptional Children
1110 North Glebe Road
Suite 300
Arlington, VA 22201–5704

Learning Disabilities Quarterly
Council for Learning Disabilities
P.O. Box 4014
Leesburg, VA 20177

Learning Disabilities Research and Practice
Division for Children with Learning Disabilities
Council for Exceptional Children
1110 North Glebe Road
Suite 300
Arlington, VA 22201–5704

Mental Retardation
American Association on Mental Deficiency
5101 Wisconsin Avenue, N.W.
Washington, DC 20016

Physical Disabilities: Education and Related Services
Division for Physical and Health Disabilities
Boyd Printing Company, Inc.
49 Sheridan Avenue
Albany, NY 12210

Remedial and Special Education
PRO-ED
8700 Shoal Creek Boulevard
Austin, TX 78757–6897

Teaching Exceptional Children
Council for Exceptional Children
1110 North Glebe Road
Suite 300
Arlington, VA 22201–5704

Topics in Early Childhood Special Education
PRO-ED
8700 Shoal Creek Boulevard
Austin, TX 78757–6897

Young Exceptional Children
Division of Early Childhood
Council for Exceptional Children
1110 North Glebe Road
Suite 300
Arlington, VA 22201–5704

A second method for developing teachers to augment their skills is to attend local, regional, or state conferences sponsored by professional organizations and advocacy groups involved in the education and treatment of students with disabilities. Schedules of such events can be obtained directly from the sponsoring organizations or from listings in professional journals and newsletters.

A third means of professional development is in-service and staff development workshops provided by local school districts. These activities are usually open to all personnel within the district, and practicum students are typically urged to attend. Some workshops are even offered online with 24/7 convenience.

Finally, professional development can include taking additional courses in university settings. To identify the type of coursework or graduate program that most appropriately matches their professional development needs, practicum students can consult college catalogs. While university libraries contain these catalogs in either hard copy or microfiche format, it is probably most convenient to download information from university web sites on the Internet.

Responsibilities to the Profession. The most critical responsibility to the profession of special education is to behave in both an ethical and a professional manner throughout field experiences. The trademark of a profession is its willingness to establish and abide by (1) a code of ethics and (2) corresponding standards that provide a basis for evaluating professional practice related directly to the code of ethics (Connelly & Rosenberg, 2003; Heller, 1983). Whether or not special educators have reached the stage of true professionalism in the eyes of most members of society is arguable. What cannot be denied, however, is that all involved in the education and treatment of students with disabilities must continue to operate in a professional fashion if they are to expect those outside the profession to treat them as such.

In a major move toward the professionalization of special education, the Delegate Assembly of the Council for Exceptional Children (CEC) in 1983 adopted a Code of Ethics for educators of persons with exceptionalities. Responsibilities that form the basis of professional conduct in relation to three major areas—the exceptional student, the employer, and the profession—were formulated into a code of eight ethical principles. This Code of Ethics was translated into a corresponding set of minimum standards of conduct called the Standards for Professional Practice. Together, the Code of Ethics and the Standards for Professional Practice are viewed as providing guidelines for (1) professional etiquette, (2) effective interpersonal behavior, (3) resolution of ethical issues, and (4) professional judgments concerning what constitutes competent practice. This CEC Code of Ethics is presented in Box 1.7, and the complete set of standards is contained in Appendix A.

Box 1.7   **Council for Exceptional Children's Code of Ethics**

We declare the following principles to be the Code of Ethics for educators of persons with exceptionalities. Members of the special education profession are responsible for upholding and advancing these principles. Members of the Council for Exceptional Children agree to judge and be judged by them in accordance with the spirit and provisions of this Code.

I. Special education professionals are committed to developing the highest educational and quality-of-life potential of individuals with exceptionalities.

II. Special education professionals promote and maintain a high level of competence and integrity in practicing their profession.

III. Special education professionals engage in professional activities that benefit individuals with exceptionalities, their families, other colleagues, students, or research subjects.

IV. Special education professionals exercise objective professional judgment in the practice of their profession.

V. Special education professionals strive to advance their knowledge and skills regarding the education of individuals with exceptionalities.

VI. Special education professionals work within the standards and policies of their profession.

VII. Special education professionals seek to uphold and improve where necessary the laws, regulations, and policies governing the delivery of special education and related services and the practice of their profession.

VIII. Special education professionals do not condone or participate in unethical or illegal acts, nor violate professional standards adopted by the Delegate Assembly of CEC.

Source: From *What Every Educator Must Know: The International Standards for the Preparation and Certification of Special Education Teachers*, by Council for Exceptional Children, 2003, Reston, VA: Author.

Pause and Reflect About the Profession 1.3

You have just read what the expected roles and responsibilities typically are for university supervisors and cooperating teachers. On the basis of your unique needs and expectations, what types of supports would you like to receive from your university supervisor and cooperating teacher? What would be the most effective method for you to convey your expectations to these people? If problems with your placement arise, how would you like these individuals to approach you?

PREPARING FOR A SUCCESSFUL PRACTICUM EXPERIENCE

In the previous sections, we discussed the behavioral characteristics of students with mild to moderate disabilities as well as the many responsibilities of practicum students during their field-based experiences. In this final section, we offer tips that will enable practicum students to cope with their increased responsibilities and maximize the benefits of their field experiences.

1. Maximize the opportunity to succeed. The demands placed on practicum students during their field experiences are considerable. The time and effort required by most practicum experiences equal or even exceed those typical of full-time teaching positions. Wherever possible, limit the amount of time devoted to extracurricular activities, additional courses, and part-time jobs, and allow for the maximum opportunity for success. Plan to get some well-deserved rest; teaching students, particularly those with mild to moderate disabilities, is a challenging and demanding job.

2. Visit the assigned field-based setting prior to beginning the practicum. Much of the anxiety related to a practicum student's impending experiences is the result of nonspecific fears of the unknown. It is wise, therefore, to find out what will be experienced when the practicum officially begins. In addition to relieving some of the jitters, a visit to the school, for example, will (1) convey to the cooperating teacher a genuine interest in the practicum process, (2) allow for a brief introduction to students, (3) provide important first impressions regarding the standards of protocol and comportment within the school, and (4) allow for the learning of school and classroom-specific policies.

3. Prepare to make a favorable impression. Whether it is correct or not, people sometimes judge others rather superficially—on the basis of their appearance, comportment, and surface behaviors. To heighten the chances of making a favorable first impression, practicum students should be dressed and groomed appropriately. Moreover, the general tenor of how you express opinions and share personal lifestyles needs to be checked. Although many facets of a person's individuality are important components in the motivation of students, some forms of personal expression conflict with local community standards (however they tend to be defined) and are best saved for environments other than the school (Behling, 1978).

4. Monitor all written work. Practicum students are judged on the quality of the written documents (e.g., applications, personal statements) that are required for the field experience. Unfortunately, some developing teachers are identified as sloppy and careless because they do not make the extra effort needed for good written expression or do not proofread their written products prior to submission. Written products reflect directly on the author. Developing teachers should ensure that their written work contains correct punctuation and spelling, is grammatically correct, and presents ideas in a logical sequence.

5. Remain patient. The assumption of instructional responsibilities by the practicum student is a gradual process. Although you may feel "all fired up and ready to take charge," a gradual integration into the flow of activities allows for observations of the cooperating teacher in action and for a general orientation to the school's operating procedures. These observation periods also allow students in the class to become accustomed to the new teacher in the environment. Also, keep in mind that a practicum student must get the approval of the cooperating teacher prior to making any changes in instructional procedures or behavioral management programs. No matter how enthusiastic you may feel about implementing a change for a student, you must remember that the cooperating teacher is responsible for all programming within the classroom.

6. Remain diplomatic. Being the new person in the school means that many veteran teachers will give you advice on any number of topics related to education (and life in general). Although some of this real-world advice may be in sharp contrast with what you believe or have learned about education, it is best to treat these interactions with colleagues as valuable learning experiences, as opportunities to get others' perceptions of certain issues. During these interactions, avoid arrogantly flaunting your knowledge of the innovative instructional procedures you have discussed in methods classes. Keep interaction on a professional level, with efforts to engender mutual respect being initiated by the developing teacher.

7. Maintain enthusiasm in the face of others' disillusionment. As observed by Behling (1978), it is not unusual for practicum students to meet teachers and administrators who appear worn out, disillusioned, and apathetic. Although we anticipate that contacts with these people will be kept to a minimum, it is critical that developing teachers avoid catching these highly contagious feelings of hopelessness and frustration. Even with the most challenging of students with disabilities, there is enough potential job satisfaction to merit enthusiasm.

8. Think "team," rather than individual. Practicum students face an overwhelming number of challenges related to the education and treatment of their students. The problems faced by students in special education settings require collaboration and assistance from a variety of sectors within the school system. An effort should be made to avoid trying to save the world singlehandedly. As is fully described in Chapters 8 and 9, successfully meeting the challenges found in comprehensive special education programs typically requires the enthusiasm and cooperation of a multidisciplinary team of professionals.

9. Get to know the professionals and paraprofessionals. Each school has people who contribute to the effective schooling of children and youth. Developing teachers would be wise to use the practicum experience to learn the various roles and responsibilities of the individuals who populate the school. Certainly, visits with the school psychologist and social worker would allow for alternative perspectives on the student with mild to moderate disabilities. Also, getting to know the administrators of the school building and system could help when seeking a first teaching position.

 SUMMARY

In this chapter, we addressed issues associated with the initial field experiences of developing special education teachers. We opened with a brief description of the characteristics of students with mild to moderate disabilities. Specific emphasis was given to both categorical and noncategorical conceptualizations of these disabilities. This was followed by a discussion of the range of service delivery options that are typical of most LEA placements. Issues related to (1) the LRE and (2) possible changes in how educators deliver educational services to students with disabilities were highlighted. The bulk of the chapter was devoted to the many roles and responsibilities of the key individuals involved in field-based teaching experiences. Concerns related to communication maintenance, professionalism, and preparation were emphasized. We concluded with a list of nine sensible tips related directly to the practical aspects of field-based experiences.

ACTIVITIES TO EXTEND YOUR KNOWLEDGE

1. Learning disabilities, emotional disturbance, and mild mental retardation are typically regarded as separate diagnostic categories by many special educators. Recently, however, a vocal and prolific group of researchers, theorists, and practitioners has asserted that it is inappropriate and deleterious to continue using these nebulous and often overlapping categorical labels. Many of these dissenting special educators have advocated that services to students with mild to moderate disabilities be delivered through noncategorical (or multi- or cross-categorical) mechanisms. Can you clarify this categorical/noncategorical issue? Specifically,

   • Can you demonstrate via their definitions that you understand why learning disabilities, behavioral disorders, and mild mental retardation are traditionally treated as separate diagnostic entities?
   • Can you outline the major issues in the categorical/noncategorical controversy, including both data-based assertions and theoretical positions?
   • Can you explore the implications of adopting each of the service delivery alternatives in your LEA? How would the adoption of a noncategorical service delivery alternative affect instructional activities in your placement?
   • Can you provide your own view of this most complex issue? Given the choice, would you advocate a categorical or noncategorical approach to the identification and education of students with mild to moderate disabilities?

2. Characterize the recent research on service delivery alternatives (inclusion, full continuum of services). What types of student outcomes have the researchers been considering? Is there any best way to deliver special education services to students with mild to moderate disabilities? Be sure you can defend your response.

3. How do the CEC Code of Ethics and Standards for Professional Practice compare with the codes and standards found in other professions (e.g., law, medicine, psychology)? In making such comparisons, critically evaluate the inclusiveness and comprehensiveness of the CEC code and standards. On the basis of your review, do you believe that the CEC code and standards are too rigorous or too loose? What feedback would you provide to the CEC regarding the Code of Ethics and the Standards for Professional Practice?

POINT AND CLICK ABOUT THE PROFESSION

These web sites have information and links to additional information related to field experiences and students with mild to moderate disabilities.

Federal Resources for Educational Excellence (FREE)
www.ed.gov/free

IDEA Practices
www.ideapractices.org

K–12 Practitioners Home Page
nces.ed.gov/practitioners

Selected Abstracts on Current Educational Issues
www.ascd.org/services/eric/facts.html

National Information Center for Children and Youth with Disabilities
www.nichcy.org

What to Expect Your First Year of Teaching
www.ed.gov/pubs/FirstYear

McREL: Mid-continent Research for Education and Learning
www.mcrel.org

Council for Exceptional Children (CEC)
www.cec.sped.org

REFERENCES

American Psychiatric Association (APA). (2000). *Diagnostic and statistical manual of mental disorders* (4th ed.—text revision). Washington, DC: Author.

Ball State University. (1981). *Competencies of the supervising teacher.* Muncie, IN: Author.

Behling, H. (1978). *Some coping suggestions for student teachers* (Monograph No. 6). Annapolis: Maryland Association of Teacher Educators.

Blankenship, C., & Lilly, M. S. (1981). *Mainstreaming students with learning and behavior problems.* New York: Holt, Rinehart & Winston.

Bower, E. M. (1969). *Early identification of emotionally handicapped children in school.* Springfield, IL: Charles C. Thomas.

Campbell, S. B. (1985). Hyperactivity in preschoolers: Correlates and prognostic implications. *Clinical Psychology Review, 51,* 401–408.

Case, C. W., Lanier, J. E., & Miskel, C. G. (1986). The Holmes Group report: Impetus for gaining professional status for teachers. *Journal of Teacher Education, 37*(4), 36–43.

Connelly, V., & Rosenberg, M. S. (2003). *The development of teaching as a profession: Comparisons with careers that have achieved full professional standing* (COPSSE Document no. RS-9). Gainesville: University of Florida, Center on Personnel Studies in Special Education.

Council for Exceptional Children. (2003). *What every educator must know: The international standards for the preparation and certification of special education teachers.* Reston, VA: Author.

Council for Learning Disabilities. (1986). Inclusion of non-handicapped low achievers and underachievers in learning disabilities programs: A position statement by the Board of Trustees of the Council for Learning Disabilities. *Learning Disability Quarterly, 9*(3), 246.

Deno, E. N. (1970). Special education as developmental capital. *Exceptional Children, 37,* 229–237.

Edgar, E., & Hayden, A. H. (1985). Who are the children special education should serve, and how many children are there? *Journal of Special Education, 18,* 523–539.

Feiman-Nemser, S. (2001). Helping novices learn to teach: Lessons from an exemplary support teacher. *Journal of Teacher Education, 52,* 17–30.

Fletcher, J. M., Morris, R. D., & Lyon, G. R. (2003). Classification and definition of learning disabilities. In H. L. Swanson, K. R. Harris, & S. Graham (Eds.), *Handbook of learning disabilities* (pp. 30–56). New York: Guilford.

Fuchs, D., Mock, D., Morgan, P. L., & Young, C. L. (2003). Responsiveness to intervention: Definitions, evidence, and implications for the learning disabilities construct. *Learning Disabilities Research and Practice, 18,* 157–171.

Giangreco, M. F., Baumgart, D. M. J., & Doyle, M. B. (1995). How inclusion can facilitate teaching and learning. *Intervention in School and Clinic, 30,* 273–278.

Gloecker, T., & Simpson, C. (1988). *Exceptional students in regular classrooms: Challenges, services, and methods.* Mountain View, CA: Mayfield.

Grossman, H. J. (1977). *Manual on terminology and classification in mental retardation* (7th ed.). Washington, DC: American Association on Mental Deficiency.

Hallahan, D. P., & Kauffman, J. M. (1982). *Exceptional children: Introduction to special education* (2nd ed.). Upper Saddle River, NJ: Prentice Hall.

Hallahan, D. P., Kauffman, J. M., & Lloyd, J. W. (1985). *Introduction to learning disabilities* (2nd ed.). Upper Saddle River, NJ: Prentice Hall.

Heller, H. W. (1983). Special education professional standards: Need, value, and use. *Exceptional Children, 50*(3), 199–204.

Heward, W. L. (2003). *Exceptional children* (7th ed.). Upper Saddle River, NJ: Merrill/Prentice Hall.

Huntze, S. L. (1985). A position paper of the Council for Children with Behavior Disorders. *Behavioral Disorders, 10,* 167–174.

Joint Committee on Teacher Planning for Students with Disabilities. (1995). *Planning for academic diversity in America's classrooms: Windows on reality, research, change, and practice.* Lawrence: University of Kansas.

King-Sears, M. E. (1997). Best academic practices for inclusive classrooms. *Focus on Exceptional Children, 29*(7), 1–22.

Kirk, S. A., & Gallagher, J. J. (1986). *Educating exceptional children* (5th ed.). Boston: Houghton Mifflin.

Kozma, C., & Stock, J. S. (1993). What is mental retardation? In R. Smith (Ed.), *Children with mental retardation: A parent's guide* (pp. 3–16). Rockville, MD: Woodbine House.

Maryland Coalition for Inclusive Education. (1993). *Inclusion: What it is and what it is not.* Laurel, MD: Author.

National Joint Committee on Learning Disabilities (NJCLD). (1988). *Learning disabilities: Issues on definition.* Austin, TX: Author.

Reynolds, M. C. (1962). A framework for considering issues in special education. *Exceptional Children, 28,* 367–370.

Rodgers, J. (1993). The inclusion revolution. *Research Bulletin of Phi Delta Kappa, 11,* 1–6.

Roe, B. D., & Ross, E. P. (1994). *Student teaching and field experiences handbook.* Upper Saddle River, NJ: Merrill/Prentice Hall.

Rosenberg, M. S., Jackson, L., & Yeh, C. (1996). Designing effective field experiences for nontraditional preservice special educators. *Teacher Education and Special Education, 19*(4), 331–341.

Rosenberg, M. S., & Sindelar, P. T. (2001). *The proliferation of alternative routes to certification in special education: A critical review of the literature.* Arlington, VA: National Clearinghouse for Professions in Special Education, CEC.

Rosenberg, M. S., Wilson, R., Maheady, L., & Sindelar, P. T. (2004). *Educating students with behavior disorders* (3rd ed.). Needham Heights, MA: Allyn & Bacon.

Smith, D. D. (1998). *Introduction to special education: Teaching in an age of challenge* (3rd ed.). Needham Heights, MA: Allyn & Bacon.

Smith, T. E. C., Price, B. J., & Marsh, G. E. (1986). *Mildly handicapped children and adults.* New York: West.

Stainback, W., & Stainback, S. (1984). A rationale for the merger of special and regular education. *Exceptional Children, 51,* 102–111.

U.S. Department of Education. (2004). *IDEA: An act to amend the Individuals with Disabilities Education Act, to reauthorize and make improvements to that act, and for other purposes.* Retrieved from http://www.ed.gov/offices/OSERS/IDEA

Wise, A. E., & Leibbrand, J. A. (2001). Standards in the new millennium: Where we are, where we're headed. *Journal of Teacher Education, 52,* 244–255.

York, J., Doyle, M. B., & Kronberg, R. (1992). A curriculum development process for inclusive classrooms. *Focus on Exceptional Children, 25,* 1–16.

## CHAPTER 2

Legal Aspects of Special Education: A Brief Review

With Kimberly Bright

Chapter Outline

In this chapter, we will

- discuss the legal basis of educational rights for students with disabilities

- identify specific laws, rules, regulations, and procedural safeguards regarding students' planning and programming

- review recent court cases affecting special education and related services

- discuss legal principles, including rights and responsibilities of parents, students, teachers, and schools

A PROFESSIONAL GLIMPSE

Natalie C. is a student teacher assigned to an elementary learning support classroom (grades K–2) in a large suburban school district for the first 16 weeks of the new school year. She works under the supervision of a veteran teacher, Mrs. R. This elementary school houses kindergarten through fourth grade with approximately six hundred students. Currently, three special education classrooms operate in the building, including two learning support resource rooms (one for grades K–2; one for grades 3–4) and a part-time learning support classroom (grades K–4). A full-time speech and language clinician is assigned to this elementary school, and itinerant services are available for occupational therapy, physical therapy, and emotional support. The learning support classroom where Natalie will complete her student teaching is considered a resource room where students receive special education instruction in reading, writing, spelling, and/or mathematics. Mrs. R. does not teach social studies or science; all students on her caseload are integrated into the general education setting for those subject areas. Currently, Mrs. R.'s caseload consists of six first grade students and six second grade students. Eleven are identified as students with specific learning disabilities; one second grade student is identified as a student with mild mental retardation. The classroom is assigned a paraprofessional, Mrs. L., for three hours each morning. The principal of each elementary school is the local education agency representative (LEA), and the director of elementary special education supervises all elementary schools.

One of Natalie's early assignments is to attend and participate in a multidisciplinary team meeting for a first grade student who was referred for a multidisciplinary evaluation at the end of kindergarten as a result of a deficient score on the Metropolitan Readiness Test and poor performance in kindergarten. Natalie has been informed by Mrs. R. that she will be responsible for authoring an Individualized Education Program (IEP), if needed, and will conduct the IEP team meeting. After three weeks of school, the first grade general education teacher has reported to the team that the student is "struggling" with all areas of language arts, including reading, writing, and penmanship; math readiness skills; and social studies and science concepts. In addition to academic concerns, the general education teacher reports that the student is exhibiting behavioral problems described as noncompliance, a poor attitude toward learning, and being "antsy." The school psychologist has conducted a psychological evaluation, including an intelligence test and achievement testing, and the results indicate that the student is of average intelligence with achievement scores "significantly discrepant." The team agrees that the student has a specific learning disability and is in need of special education. An IEP team meeting is scheduled for one week after the multidisciplinary team meeting.

Natalie sets out to author a strong draft IEP by scheduling a classroom observation and curriculum-based assessment in reading, writing, math, and behavior to enhance the IEP goals. However, she is told by her cooperating teacher that she should take the IEP of another student in the learning support classroom and copy the goals. Mrs. R. says she always teaches the same language arts and math curriculum to students in first grade; therefore, the goals are the same. When Natalie appears confused, Mrs. R. tells her she does not have the time to "reinvent the wheel" and that the common goals will serve this student well. When Natalie inquires about writing goals for social studies, science, and behavior, Mrs. R. tells her that she does not teach social studies or science. In terms of behavior, Mrs. R. tells Natalie that she rarely has behavior problems in her classroom and does not think that behavioral goals will be necessary. Rightfully concerned about writing an IEP that is far from individualized, Natalie is worried about offending her cooperating teacher but also wants to learn to develop an appropriate program. This is the dilemma that Natalie confronts early in her student-teaching experience.

*L*egislation (laws and their accompanying regulations) and litigation (court cases) have resulted in many changes in special education and the interpretation of the rights and responsibilities of participants in the educational process. Recent changes in public policy have posed intense challenges for all professionals working with twenty-first-century students.

Preservice and beginning teachers who understand the important laws may deal more effectively with the complex issues involved in providing a free and appropriate public education (FAPE) to students with mild to moderate disabilities. Awareness of legal issues may help developing teachers to (1) provide a sound rationale for current administrative procedures and practices affecting their classrooms, (2) avoid past policy mistakes, and (3) ensure quality educational programming for the special-needs students they serve.

LEGAL BASIS OF EDUCATIONAL RIGHTS FOR STUDENTS WITH DISABILITIES

Germane to all students with disabilities is federal legislation that encourages comprehensive services, including multidisciplinary evaluations and intervention services. The Individuals with Disabilities Education Improvement Act, passed into law on November 19, 2004, amended the original federal legislation (the Education for All Handicapped Children Act of 1975 or EHA; the 1983 and 1986 EHA amendments; and the Individuals with Disabilities Education Act of 1990, 1992, and 1997 amendments) in order to

- strengthen the role of parents
- ensure access to general education curricula and reforms
- focus on teaching and learning, while decreasing unnecessary paperwork

Pause and Reflect About the Profession 2.1

Effective teachers require knowledge of and skills in meeting the legal requirements that protect students with disabilities and their families. These requirements can be very perplexing to new teachers, however. It may be useful to self-rate (5 highest, 1 lowest) your knowledge of and skills in the following areas.

Legal Issue	Self-Rating Scale
• Definition of individuals with exceptional learning needs	
• Screening and pre-referral procedures	
• Evaluation process for individuals with exceptional learning needs	
• Placement decision procedure after evaluation	
• Applicable laws, rules, and regulations regarding the students' educational placement and program	
• Procedural safeguards regarding the students' educational placement and program	
• Provision of FAPE; specifically, writing a legally defensible IEP.	
• Connections between the IEP, specially designed instruction, and educational placement	

- respond to the growing needs of an increasingly diverse society
- assist educational agencies in addressing the costs of improving special education
- ensure schools are safe and conducive to learning
- encourage parents and educators to work out differences using nonadversarial means.
- address the provisions under No Child Left Behind (NCLB). (IDEIA '04)

These elements extend the fundamental underpinnings of previous versions of the federal legislation that ensured students with disabilities a FAPE in the least restrictive environment (LRE). Additionally, the new IDEIA continues to attempt to balance schools' needs to maintain safe and orderly environments with the rights of students with disabilities to receive a FAPE (CEC, 2004).

Many educational practices have not always been in students' best interests. For example, in the past, students not meeting teacher or school expectations either were excluded from school altogether or were provided inappropriate services that did not match their needs. Such practices were to be eliminated through the enactment of federal and state laws, rules, regulations, and procedural safeguards upholding student and family rights in educational assessments and placements.

Unless teachers are informed users of legal knowledge, however, educational placement and programming decisions may be made inappropriately. Therefore, it is the responsibility of those who teach to have current knowledge of the legal issues affecting their students. Much progress and most educational innovations have resulted from the efforts of dedicated and informed individuals who sought to change public policy, reform educational services, and uphold educational rights through legal means.

Every teacher in a public school setting will come into contact with the principles of the new IDEIA(04). The original legislation and the subsequent amendments have changed the course of education for infants, children, and youth with special needs. During the mid–twentieth century, a social and political coalition of parents, concerned professionals, and advocates brought about passage of the landmark legislation at a time when children were being excluded from schools, misclassified through biased testing procedures, and/or served inadequately across the country. Without a strong commitment from a variety of people who challenged existing school policies and legal procedures, educational services and programs would have remained inadequate and inconsistent from locality to locality.

Specific Legislation

Legislation results from the political processes elected members of the local, state, or federal government use to effect policy changes—proposing, debating, and passing laws. New laws and regulations evolve continually as special education policies are challenged and redefined. For the new teacher, this means that educational responsibilities are not static; rather, they change continuously as parents, professionals, and advocates effect changes in legal mandates and educational practices. This phenomenon is euphemistically referred to as the "shifting sands of special education."

Prior to the passage of the EHA, some local and state statutes had guaranteed some degree of service to students in need of special help. Although these statutes were minimal and provided limited monies for the education of students with disabilities, they provided some direction (e.g., procedural safeguards, assurances in state plans, education for school-age students residing in institutions, expansion or initiation of local programs). These laws, passed between 1950 and 1975, eventually provided the initial basis for the federal mandate to provide services to all students in need of special education and related services. Box 2.1 presents pertinent laws directly bearing on special education. Today's professionals, familiar with these legal actions, may prevent educational injustices similar to those that occurred before these laws were passed.

Box 2.1

Laws Influencing Special Education

- **PL 83–531, Cooperative Research Act (1954)**, was implemented to assist cooperative research in education. Of the $1 million in appropriations, $675,000 was earmarked for research with students having mental retardation.

- **PL 85–926, Training of Professional Personnel Act (1958)**, expanded training for teachers of students with mental retardation and facilitated grants to state agencies and to tertiary institutions, establishing a model for support to teacher trainees in special education.

- **PL 88–164, Mental Retardation Facilities and Community Mental Health Centers Construction Act (1963)**, was a cornerstone legislative act for students with special needs. It brought together into one unit the "captioned film" program of PL 84–905 (1958), an expanded teacher-training program from PL 85–926, and a new research program for the education of students with disabilities.

- **PL 88–164, § 302, Research and Demonstration Projects in Education of Handicapped Students Act (1963)**, authorized the commissioner of education to make grants to various state and local agencies in order to educate students with disabilities. PL 89–105, discussed below, later supplemented PL 88–164, § 302, by allowing funds to be used for construction, equipment, and the operation of facilities for research and for the training of research personnel.

- **PL 89–10, Assistance to Students in Disadvantaged Areas (Title VI of the Elementary and Secondary Education Act) (1965)**, provided federal monies to initiate programs for the schooling of students who were educationally deprived, especially students with handicaps in low-income families.

- **PL 89–313, Elementary and Secondary Education Act Amendments (1965)**, encouraged programs to educate students with disabilities who were residing in state institutions and other similar state-operated or state-supported residential facilities.

- **PL 89–105, Community Mental Health Centers Act Amendments (1965)**, added traineeships and fellowships to the original legislation developed by Congress and provided additional funds for research and demonstration projects in the education of students with special needs. It authorized construction of at least one research facility.

- **PL 89–750, (Title VI of the Elementary and Secondary Education Act Amendments) Education for Handicapped Students (1966)**, allowed grants to states through the Elementary and Secondary Education Act (ESEA) for special needs students. Disbanded in 1965, PL89–750 reestablished block grants for districts serving students with special needs.

- **PL 90–538, Handicapped Students Early Education Assistance Act (1968)**, was developed exclusively for students with disabilities and authorized the commissioner of education, acting through the Bureau of Education for the Handicapped, to negotiate grants and contracts with both private and public agencies to establish experimental preschool and early education programs for special-needs students.

- **PL 91–61, National Center of Educational Media and Materials for the Handicapped Act (1969)**, provided the authority to the secretary of health, education, and welfare to contract with a university to develop, construct, and operate a national center of educational media and materials for persons with disabilities.

- **PL 91–230, Elementary and Secondary, Education Act Amendments (1970)**, consolidated a number of previous provisions on serving students with disabilities and divided into seven basic sections—Parts A through G—all of the programs and services for educating students with special needs that receive federal assistance. Part B was intended to authorize grants for the initiation, expansion, and improvement of state and local educational programs for students requiring specialized help and was meant to specify the kind and amount of federal dollars to be provided to public agencies for special education.

Box 2.1   **(continued)**

- **PL 92–424, Economic Opportunity Amendments (1972)**, mandated that a minimum of 10 percent of the enrollment slots in Head Start programs be made available to students with disabilities.

- **PL 93–112, § 504, Rehabilitation Act (1973)**, specified that no individual with a disability in the United States shall, solely by reason of his or her disability, be excluded from participation in, be denied the benefits of, or be subjected to discrimination under any program or activity receiving federal financial assistance.

- **PL 93–280, Education Amendments (1974)**, modified Part B to increase monies available to public agencies for the education of students with special needs and to expand the assurances in state plans for students' and parents' rights. Emanating from this law was the **Family Education Rights and Privacy Act of 1974, also referred to as the Buckley Amendment**, which protected the confidentiality of school records and provided procedures to challenge questionable information contained in the records. Title VI extended and revised the Adult Education Act, the Education of the Handicapped Act, the Indian Education Act, and the Emergency School Aid Act. It required states to locate and serve all students with disabilities and to protect the rights of students with disabilities and their parents when making educational changes, it assured an education with one's peers as much as possible, and it asked that evaluation materials be racially and culturally fair.

- **PL 94–142, Education for All Handicapped Children Act (1975)**, often referred to as the bill of rights for students with disabilities, guaranteed the availability of a "free appropriate education," including special education and related services programming, to all students with disabilities. It assured "due process" rights for students with disabilities and their parents or guardians and monitored effectiveness of special education at all government levels. It mandated that an individualized education program (IEP) or an individualized family services plan (IFSP) be drawn up for every student or youth found eligible for special education or early intervention, pinpointing the kinds of special education and related services or the types of early intervention services each preschooler, student, or youth would receive. It called for annual planning and the assessment of students' strengths, needs, and interests.

- **PL 98–199, Parent Training and Information Centers (1983)**, established centers to train and provide information to parents and volunteers.

- **PL 99–457, Education of the Handicapped Act Amendments (1986)**, extended the mandate from PL 94–142 to include special education and related services beginning at age three and created a discretionary early intervention program to serve students from birth through age two. It provided monies to train early intervention teachers in clinical settings and preschools.

- **PL 101–476, Individuals with Disabilities Education Act (1990)**, further amended the provisions of PL 94–142 and PL 99–457 and renamed the act. The IDEA promoted the linkage of school and community experiences, the development of postschool adult living objectives, and the development of daily living skills and functional vocational evaluations. It mandated that the IEP contain a statement of transition services, including, if appropriate, a statement of each public agency's and each participating agency's responsibilities or linkages, or both, before the student leaves the school setting.

- **PL 101–336, Americans with Disabilities Act (1990)**, prohibited discrimination based on disabilities in the areas of employment, public services, transportation, public accommodations, and telecommunications. It provided that all affected entities must ensure "reasonable accommodation" to persons with disabilities. The law highlighted fair employment practices pertaining to private employers, state and local governments, employment agencies, and labor unions. It prohibited the use of employment tests that screen out individuals with disabilities unless they are shown to be job-related, are required of all applicants, and are consistent with business necessity. It banned the use of preemployment medical examinations or inquiries to determine whether an applicant has a disability. It prohibited discrimination based on a relationship or association with a person with a disability (e.g., it protects people with spouses who are disabled from being denied employment because of an unfounded assumption that they would use excessive leave).

- **PL 101–392, Carl D. Perkins Vocational and Technology Education Act (1990)**, encouraged the competitiveness of the United States in the world economy by more fully developing the academic and occupational skills of all students. It provided resources to improve the educational programs providing the skills needed to work in a technologically advanced society. It guaranteed full vocational educational opportunities for all special populations.

- **PL 103–239, School to Work Opportunities Act (1994)**, promoted collaboration and problem solving by the U.S. Departments of Education and Labor. It encouraged partnerships between school-based and employment-based sites at the local level by encouraging schools and employers to plan, implement, and evaluate integrated school-based and work-based learning. This law matched students and employers stating a need for career education, career development programs, and work-based linkages. It encouraged interagency agreements, technical assistance, and services to employers, educators, case managers, and others. It promoted postschool planning and assistance. The law linked youth development activities, academic and vocation learning, and employer strategies for upgrading worker skills.

- **PL 105–17, Individuals with Disabilities Education Act (1997)**, added a number of provisions designed to improve outcomes for students with disabilities. Provisions in the reauthorized IDEA require that students with disabilities be included in state- and districtwide assessments, that students' IEPS address the issue of access to general education curricula, and that the states establish performance goals and indicators for students with disabilities.

- **PL _____ (Improving Educational Results for Children with Disabilities Act—The New IDEA)**, passed in 2004, amended PL 105–17. Supports many of the charges of IDEA '97, but emphasizes the defining of "highly qualified" for special education teachers with NCLB, reduces paperwork, solidifies personnel and paraprofessional qualification and addresses over identification and disproportionality, adds new language and provides alternative methods for identifying students with learning disabilities, eliminates short-term objectives and benchmarks for all students except those taking alternative assessments, adds additional discipline language and adjusts attorneys' fees in favor of districts when frivolous or unreasonable litigation is without foundation.

Specific Litigation

Litigation comprises court cases in which a judge and/or members of a jury examine evidence regarding the facts of an event or series of events. A decision is rendered about a particular case based on an application of the constructs of pertinent laws to the evidence (i.e., findings of fact). Through the litigation process, laws have been challenged and reinterpreted (Katsiyannis & Conderman, 1994; Turnbull, 1993; Weintraub, Abeson, Ballard, & LaVor, 1977). This process has resulted in significant changes not only for children and teachers but also for parents and guardians. For example, family members and professionals spearheaded litigation on issues that emerged from their combined collaborative struggles. In addition to the right of all students to an education, litigation centered on family involvement in educational decision making, the suspension and expulsion of students with disabilities, payment of attorneys' fees, extended school year programs, programs for children and youth with severe disabilities, and programs for children and youth with serious emotional disturbance.

Most special education *legislation* was enacted because parents, educators, and advocates questioned, through *litigation*, practices occurring within the educational system that, from their viewpoint, violated the rights of their children or others unable to defend themselves within the school setting. New special education teachers familiar with the legal principles affecting their students and their students' classrooms and homes can help ensure quality services.

Legal Principles

The Fourteenth Amendment to the U.S. Constitution (see Figure 2.1) forbids states from depriving anyone of life, liberty, or property without due process and equal protection of law. The developing teacher must keep the equal protection and due process clauses of the Fourteenth Amendment in mind because these components formed the basis for special education litigation and the resulting federal ligislation.

The Fourteenth Amendment applies to the states (not the federal government, which is bound by the first ten amendments to the constitution). Turnbull (1993) described the constitutional tenets under which today's professionals are held accountable for the educational treatment of students. Teachers are responsible for recognizing and respecting the legal principles that protect the students they serve. Box 2.2 presents legal principles and mandates having a direct bearing on special services.

Many litigants have relied on the Fourteenth Amendment when attacking legal injustices occurring in public school settings (Turnbull, 1993). As a result, they have argued, and courts have come to accept, that the benefits of an education are a property interest and the reputation of an individual is a liberty interest. When students with disabilities are denied access to a FAPE, they are deprived of property. And when exclusion and labeling negatively affect their reputations, they are deprived of liberty. Furthermore, litigants alleged they were treated differently by agencies of the state when they were denied "equal protection" against infringement of their property and liberty interests. Individuals or groups of individuals must have access to a set of procedures (i.e., due process) under which to contest their treatment by agencies of the state. Now, under the IDEA, parents or school districts can redress their differences through mediation services, prehearing

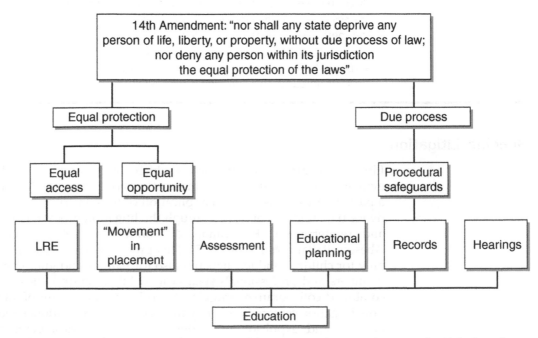

FIGURE 2.1 The Conceptual Structure of the Fourteenth Amendment to the U.S. Constitution as It Relates to Provisions for the Education of Students with Disabilities

Box 2.2   **Legal Principles Influencing Special Education Laws**

Procedural Due Process

Fair procedures must be followed before citizens can be denied certain interests. Due process entails procedural due process, under which a person has the right to receive notice and be heard and to protest if a government agency is about to take action affecting that person. Due process also entails substantive due process, under which certain rights are inviolate and cannot be taken away by any state agency.

An example of a violation of procedural due process by a first-year teacher or other school official is a change in the educational placement of a student without giving prior notice to and without consulting with the parents. The arbitrary institutionalization of a student by school officials is an illustration of a substantive due process claim. In other words, teachers must notify parents and students of their intent to change existing special education placements or services before such changes can be made in the students' education plans.

Equal Protection

The states must provide the same rights and benefits to individuals with disabilities as to persons without disabilities. They are guaranteed equal opportunity or access to participate in programs. Any variance must be justified.

For example, equal protection guarantees the opportunity for students with disabilities to participate in sports programs if such programs are available for students without disabilities. Also, band uniforms must be provided for special needs students if all other students are provided with band uniforms. School officials would be asked to justify a situation where students without disabilities warrant band uniforms, whereas students with disabilities do not.

Zero Reject

Individuals with disabilities must have the opportunity to be educated. No student can be denied educational services because of unalterable characteristics (including gender, cultural background, race, and disability). Zero reject means that any student or youth between the ages of 3 and 21 with disabilities must receive a free and appropriate education.

Assessment and Labeling

Traditionally, assessment and labeling procedures have been (and remain) powerful political tools capable of helping and harming diverse individuals. Assessment and labeling assist in identifying educational strengths and needs to serve the student better. Students are harmed by assessment that misplaces or wrongfully categorizes them in order to deprive them of educational opportunities and advancements. Some traditional assessment procedures are racially and culturally biased, and students are often labeled on the basis of a single criterion rather than multiple factors. Many assessments are administered inappropriately by untrained personnel. Federal law now requires a multidisciplinary assessment that is conducted by many professionals and that includes parent or guardian input. Multidisciplinary assessment uses multiple data sources to indicate what the individual student requires. All assessment and labeling must follow fair and appropriate procedures.

FAPE

Educational services must be free and appropriate to the individual student. This means that education and related services must be provided at no cost to students, parents, or guardians. In addition, each student must have available a full range of educational services based on what

Box 2.2   **(continued)**

he or she requires. Federal law also gives preference to placement in the school the student would have attended if nondisabled unless participants in the educational process agree to some other arrangement. If a school district does not have staff qualified to provide needed services, it may contract for these.

LRE

A continuum of special education service options must be available to meet the needs of each special student in the setting closest to the "normal" general classroom setting. Special education is characterized by the services, not the setting per se. However, whereas the LRE for most students will be the education they receive with their peers without disabilities in the general education classroom, for some students the LRE may be a special class or a special school.

Parent Participation and Shared Decision Making

Federal and state laws reaffirm parents' and guardians' legal right to participate in every decision related to the identification, evaluation, and placement of their student. Accordingly, school district professionals must attempt to notify and obtain the participation of the student's family when any changes are proposed, being considered, or made on behalf of the student. In addition, to initiate or change educational or related services, written parental or guardian consent is necessary.

conferences, due process hearings, and civil courts at the state or federal level. Consequently, new teachers should be aware of constitutional guarantees, and especially due process rights, which protect all students with disabilities from unilateral decisions by school personnel that deny students access to a FAPE in the LRE.

Central Issues

Special education litigation has affected the practices of school personnel during past years. Individuals have challenged unilateral decision making by school professionals by initiating due process proceedings and taking school districts to state or federal civil courts. Among the central issues of past litigation are separate but not equal standards; the disproportionate number of minority children assigned to special education; the fairness of referral, assessment, or placement practices; and the exclusion of students from programs (Ballard, Ramirez, & Weintraub, 1982).

After passage of the EHA, litigation followed a slightly different course. Litigation in the 1980s focused on the interpretation of federal laws and regulations at the state and local levels, including the delivery of special education programs and services, the definition of related services, the denial and/or unavailability of special education programming and services, the financial aspects of providing FAPE, and the expulsion/suspension of students with disabilities (*Education of the Handicapped Law Report*, 1977–1988; Turnbull, 1993).

During the 1990s, litigation addressed instruction for diverse students and where best to provide services. Funding issues, including attorneys' fees and mediation prior to due process, became central, and parents won the right to raise discipline strategies at students' IEP meetings (Zirkel, 1995).

In the twenty-first century, students' preschool needs, discipline practices, suspensions and expulsions, and the transition from school to adult years are central in many due process proceedings (Yell et al., 2000). Additionally, many citizen groups are calling for more efficient and effective instruction that will prepare all students for life in the twenty-first century. Many question the appropriateness of services addressing students' needs in technology (Hanley, 1995), of transitions across programs and services (Hodapp, 1993; McDonnell, 1993), and of opportunities affecting students' quality of life, such as the services that facilitate students' acceptance into their schools and communities (Yell et al., 2000).

Teachers are currently addressing the question of how to prepare all students to exercise the rights and responsibilities of citizenship. Foremost is the need to prepare them for productive employment in a modern economy. Recent reform agenda will have legal implications for and an impact on developing teachers as they focus their specially designed instruction (i.e., transition services) on preparing students with disabilities for life in the twenty-first century. Relevant are activities that will do the following:

- Define through the general education curriculum the academic knowledge and skills that students are expected to have by the time they graduate from public schools
- Encourage local school districts to design curricula allowing students to achieve learning outcomes leading to completion of high school graduation requirements
- Include students with disabilities in state- and districtwide assessment systems that measure student progress toward learning outcomes
- Encourage local school districts to implement educational reform according to a strategic plan developed at the local level
- Encourage active involvement of parents, businesses and other community representatives, teachers, students, and school personnel in the educational process (Pennsylvania Department of Education, 1995).

Major philosophical and logistical changes have resulted from IDEA (1997), which included new provisions designed to improve outcomes for students with disabilities. These include requirements that students with disabilities be included in state- and districtwide assessments, that students' IEPs address issues of access to the general education curriculum, and that states establish performance goals and indicators for students with disabilities (Hehir, 1999; McLaughlin, 1999; Ysseldyke & Olsen, 1999).

As many legal interpretations affecting school reform emerge, along with new perspectives on accepting and supporting students with disabilities, teachers continue to play a vital role: Teachers make appropriate services happen. Educational challenges in the form of technological advances, increasing community diversity, economic realities, and calls for school reform continue to set parameters for students with disabilities.

In addition, standards-based teaching, in which teachers provide high-quality instruction in order that students attain high-level goals, is influencing the quality of teaching and learning in the twenty-first century. The standards movement applies to students with disabilities in that differentiated instruction geared toward their needs must reflect the knowledge, skills, and dispositions valued by society (Tomlinson, 2000). These and other challenges require concerted efforts by new teachers to work with other professionals and students' families, using sharing processes and joint problem-solving skills to avoid legal injustices.

Box 2.3 presents a timeline of pertinent issues raised in litigation over the last half century. New teachers should be familiar with judicial decisions that ensure students with disabilities are subject to fair, appropriate educational practices.

MAJOR COMPONENTS OF THE FEDERAL LAW

The IDEIA as authorized in 2004 is the most important legislation supporting the education of children and youth with disabilities. It establishes the framework within which students with special needs are educated today. Preservice and beginning teachers will be involved actively in implementing its mandates no matter what type of class placement they work in or where they provide services. Mandated components of the

---

Box 2.3   **Pertinent Litigation Issues in Special Education**

Early 1950s–Mid-1970s	Mid-1970s–Early 1990s	Early 1990s–Present
• Separate but not equal standards • Disproportionate number of minority students in special education • Lack of fairness in referral, assessment, and placement • Exclusion of students from schools and programs	• Delivery of special education programs and services • Definitions of related services • Denial/unavailability of special education programs and related services • Transportation services and tuition • Expulsion/suspension of students with disabilities	• Serving diverse students • Instructional effectiveness • Technological advances • Transitions across programs • Graduation/learning outcomes • Attorneys' fees • Mediation processes • Funding appropriations

---

law form the basis of what teachers should know and be able to do and when or how they operate in the classroom. Teachers at the preservice level will be exposed to various aspects of the IDEIA as they progress in the student-teaching process.

Beginning teachers may be expected to demonstrate knowledge of the federal law from the first day of school. For example, the following activities require new teachers to be familiar with the requirements of the IDEIA:

1. Teachers in training may be involved in implementing and monitoring the measurable annual goals in a student's IEP under the guidance of the directing classroom teacher. They may be asked to observe a student who is being considered for special education. Their observational data may be used to monitor the student's progress in the general education curriculum and to make decisions about eligibility for special education.

2. Beginning teachers may be asked to attend IEP conferences prior to the beginning of the school year and to begin implementing the special education program during the initial week of classes. First-year teachers may be involved in screening and referral steps, formal or informal assessment processes, curriculum planning, or decisions to exit students from special education services.

A number of IDEIA mandates affect the educational environment of special-needs students: (1) a full range of services; (2) suspensions, expulsions, and alternative interim educational placements; (3) incentives for the LRE; (4) IEP development, including access to the general education curriculum and participation in state- and districtwide assessments; (5) assessment, referral, evaluation, and placement guidelines; and (6) procedural safeguards.

Full Range of Services

Drafters of the EHA and IDEIA stipulated that a continuum of special education placement options must be available to meet the needs of special students in the LRE, the placement closest to the general classroom environment. However, teacher support is necessary for the LRE to have meaning. For instance, Rueda, Gallego, and Moll (2000) described the LRE using a sociocultural basis. To these authors, the LRE becomes a reality not because of a particular physical placement of students but because of social mediation and the careful structuring of the activities in the setting. These authors suggested that the linking of education, play, and peer interaction, structured around individual student needs, allows inclusion in the LRE to be accomplished successfully.

Even though inclusion is a popular choice because services are provided in the general education setting, inclusion is not a legal term. To ensure appropriate services, school personnel still must provide a continuum of alternative placements. Thus, students may need general education classes, special classes, special schools, home instruction, or education in residential facilities. (Chapter 1 illustrates the cascade of service delivery, one of the most common continua.) Federal law also makes preferable placement in the school the child would have attended if nondisabled unless participants in the educational process agree to some other arrangement. If a school district does not have a particular option, it may contract for the needed services.

Suspensions, Expulsions, and Alternative Interim Educational Placements

Due process protections must be extended to all students when imposing short-term and long-term suspensions and exclusions (including expulsions and alternative educational placements) (Yell et al., 2000). For instance, legally correct and educationally appropriate responses must be made when students with disabilities exhibit serious problem behaviors. Where a student with a disability violates school rules, the IDEIA permits a school district to remove the child from school for up to 10 days as long as there is not a pattern of removals. However, school personnel cannot impose a long-term suspension (i.e., one longer than 10 days) if the IEP team determines that the behaviors causing consideration of long-term suspension are a manifestation of the student's disability. Where the behaviors are not a manifestation of the student's disability and the school district follows its discipline policy by suspending a student with a disability for a period longer than 10 days, the school district must still provide special education services. The new IDEIA (04) also gives school personnel the authority, on a case by case basis, to consider unique circumstances when determining whether to order a change in placement for a child with a disability who violates a code of student conduct (CEC, 2004). Where a student with a disability is found

1. to have brought a gun or dangerous weapon to school,
2. to possess illegal drugs,
3. to have sold or solicited the sale of a controlled substance, or
4. inflicts serious bodily injury upon another person while at school, on school premises, or at a school function

the school district may unilaterally place the student in an interim alternative placement for up to 45 school days.

Incentives for the LRE

The current trend is to educate students demonstrating less severe mental, learning, or social disabilities in the general education class with normally functioning peers to the extent that these students can handle that setting. General educators and special educators are working together through inclusion models, consultation, and teaming formats. New directions in service delivery expand the legal role of teachers (Chapter 3 provides details of inclusion settings; Chapter 11 expands on consultation and teaming themes). As teachers are encouraged to collaborate and are supported in using known, effective practices in order to be more responsive to all students' learning characteristics, the focus for teaching and managing diverse students is shifting (1) from where interventions occur to which interventions are effective and (2) from viewing students as the problem to viewing teachers as the solution (Carpenter & McKee-Higgins, 1996). Thus, some educators view teachers' effective practices as the key to specially designed instruction in the LRE—no matter where students receive services.

In addition to being direct-service providers to students with disabilities, new special education teachers may be asked to consult and assist new general education teachers with instructional strategies, accommodations or modifications, behavior management, or classroom organization. Special education teachers may offer a combination of direct services and consulting assistance to make the general education classroom setting more appropriate to diverse students' needs. Special education teachers may help to develop, maintain, and evaluate prereferral strategies that general education teachers implement. Teachers in both general education and special education may use a variety of effective instructional formats to plan, implement, and evaluate appropriate learning materials or specially designed curricula for diverse students.

IEP Development and Access to the General Education Curriculum

A major component of the IDEIA is the emphasis on providing students with disabilities access to the general education curriculum (Hehir, 1999; CEC, 2004). School professionals and families address this component in each student's IEP. The IEP's present education level, annual goals, and participation in state- and districtwide assessments are relevant. In the present education level section, the IEP team must indicate how a student's disability affects involvement and progress through the general education curriculum. The new IDEIA (04) deletes benchmarks and short-term objectives, except for those children who take alternative assessments, therefore annual goals must reflect general education curriculum standards. Furthermore, the IEP must contain a statement of how progress toward annual goals will be measured and how parents will be regularly informed of student progress. IDEIA requires progress reports "to the extent to which that progress is sufficient to enable the child to achieve the goals by the end of the year" (CEC, 2004).

In order to coordinate a student's IEP with the general education curriculum, a general education teacher must participate in the IEP team whenever the student is expected to participate in the general education environment. Also, the IEP team must include statements about the student's inclusion in state- and districtwide assessments. Any accommodations or adaptations needed for the student to participate in these assessments must be delineated. If a student's participation in state- or districtwide assessments is inappropriate, then an explanation must be provided, and an alternative testing system must be used.

Further, transition issues must be addressed in the IEPs for all students who are 16 and older. For these students, the IEP must include "appropriate measurable post-secondary goals based upon age-appropriate transition assessments related to training, education, employment, and where appropriate, independent living skills." (CEC, 2004). In addition, the IEP must delineate interagency responsibilities and linkages and reflect programming that will affect postsecondary transitions. When the student is to reach the age of majority during the IEP cycle, the school district must notify the parents of the transfer of all parental rights to the student. (The age of majority varies from state to state.)

Assessment, Referral, Evaluation, and Placement

Federal regulations set up priorities for services given to those students who were unserved at the time of the EHA's passage and to the most severely involved students within each area of exceptionality receiving inadequate services. IDEIA (04) continues to maintain *Child Find*, a referral system for locating students with special needs. The overall purposes of Child Find, and the referral and screening services, are to determine whether or not a student has a disability and, if so, to identify the educational needs of that student. Teachers must follow the specific guidelines and time frames for the referral, screening, diagnosis, evaluation, placement, and reevaluation processes in order for their district to receive allocated funds. New teachers may be involved in every step—from referral to reevaluation procedures. Figure 2.2 presents a description of the various steps in the process. (Chapter 7 describes the paperwork involved in the referral, evaluation, and placement process.)

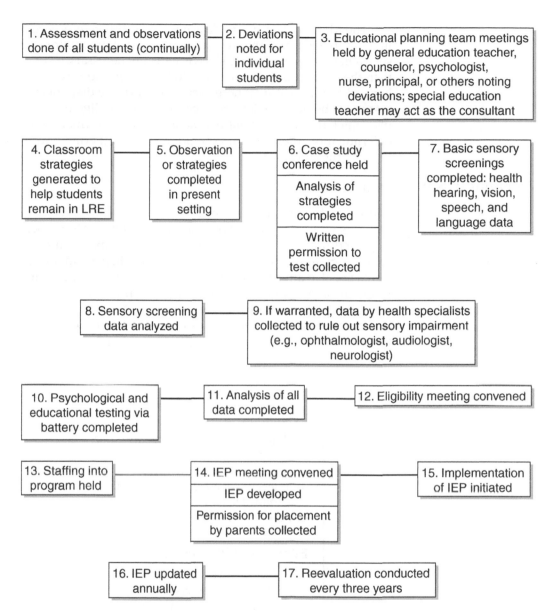

FIGURE 2.2   Steps in the Referral Process Used to Determine Eligibility for Special Education and to Plan Educational Programs

The IDEA established additional requirements for the evaluation and reevaluation of students with disabilities and those who are thought to have a disability. The multidisciplinary evaluation (MDE) team must address the individual student's ability to participate in and progress through the general education curriculum. Further, the MDE team needs to determine what, if any, modifications need to be made to the curriculum or instruction so that the student can be reasonably expected to achieve measurable annual goals. The team must assess cognitive and behavioral factors as well as physical and developmental factors. A student cannot qualify as having a disability if the determining factor is either a lack of instruction in reading or math or limited English proficiency.

The reevaluation process was changed significantly under IDEA (97) and is supported in the new IDEIA (04). Informed consent must be obtained for reevaluations as well as for initial evaluations. However, if the parents don't respond to reasonable attempts by the school district to obtain consent, the school district may pursue the reevaluation using due process procedures or mediation procedures.

The MDE team needs to determine first if there is a need to collect additional data in order to determine the student's continued eligibility for special education. If there is such a need, then the team proceeds with any necessary testing or data collection. If not, then the team must provide notice to the parents specifying why the team does not believe additional testing is necessary and informing them of their right to request that assessments be done to determine continued eligibility. If the parents and school district personnel are in agreement that no additional information is needed for an eligibility determination, then the team should focus on gathering information on how to instruct or assist the student.

Procedural Safeguards

Every developing and beginning teacher will be involved to some degree in legal proceedings with students, parents, and professionals. Due process rights, also referred to as procedural safeguards, are afforded to participants in the educational process. Parents are guaranteed active involvement in their child's educational program. These rights are also afforded to all professional personnel. Procedural safeguards, including rights in programming decisions and due process hearings and to confidentiality of record keeping, are illustrated in Figure 2.3. A new requirement under the IDEA (04) is that states must strengthen the provisions of their mediation system so that a written, binding, confidential agreement is enforceably in any state or district court of the US.

Evaluation

1. Written permission to evaluate (notice/consent)
2. Comprehensive battery
3. Nondiscriminatory practices
4. Independent educational evaluation
5. Informed results
6. Assessment by a multidisciplinary team

Educational Placement

1. Written permission to place (notice/consent)
2. Participation in educational decisions
3. Approval for proposed changes (notice/consent)
4. Input into creation, maintenance, and monitoring of IEP

Mediation and Hearings

1. Mediation
2. Prehearing conference
3. Due process hearing
4. Appeal process
5. "Stay put" policy until placement determined

Records

1. Review
2. Explanations and interpretations
3. Copies
4. Challenge
5. Assurance of confidentiality

FIGURE 2.3 Procedural Safeguards

The intent is to continue to reduce the number of due process hearings by providing a less adversarial process for resolving disputes.

Programming Decisions. IDEIA (04) requires all educators to follow specific notice, consent, evaluation, and placement procedures to ensure the nondiscriminatory evaluation and placement of students and appropriate development of the IEP.

Notice/Consent. Despite an emphasis on the general education setting, today's professionals still must gain consent or provide written notice to parents before school officials can initiate or change, or refuse to initiate or change, the identification, evaluation, or placement of students. Although implementation of these rights varies according to individual school practices, developing teachers will be involved in the process (e.g., sending written notices home to parents, holding informal conferences prior to the student's formal testing). All notices must be in the parents' native language or other principal mode of communication. New teachers should work actively to ensure that notices are written clearly and without teacher jargon. The notice must include a description of the proposed action, an explanation of the proposal, a summary of all options considered, and information as to why other options were rejected. Parents must be notified of each evaluation procedure, test, record, or report that teachers will use as a basis for any educational decision reached.

Parents must grant written permission prior to initial evaluation and placement into any special education program or related service. This includes specially designed instruction provided in the general education classroom. IDEA (97) extended the consent requirement to all reevaluations of students who are already receiving special education services; however, the frequency of reevaluations is not clarified in the new IDEIA (04) (CEC, 2004). Beginning teachers should be aware that parents can change their minds at any time and revoke their consent. School officials, however, have the right to initiate a due process hearing in the absence of parental consent for evaluation and reevaluation. A hearing officer, then, must determine whether the student should be evaluated or reevaluated. In turn, parents have the right to protest at a hearing any evaluation or programming action by school officials.

Evaluation. Evaluation safeguards include the right to an independent assessment by an evaluator of the parents' choosing. Parents have a right to be told where and how the evaluation will be conducted and to be given a list describing any available low-cost or free legal aid in the geographic area in which they reside. Parents have the right to request that the LEA or SEA pay for the independent evaluation if the agency evaluation was done incorrectly or inadequately. School districts must inform parents that a hearing officer may be asked to order an independent evaluation at public expense and that certain criteria must be met for the examiner to secure payment by the LEA or SEA.

The student must be given a full and individual evaluation using a battery of tests. The testing cannot discriminate on the basis of the student's language or culture. The evaluator must ensure that all testing devices and materials are sensitive to individual needs, including differences in sensory, manual, or speaking abilities. Professionals should assess all aspects of the student's strengths and abilities.

Placement. Teachers must use more than one criterion when specifying the appropriate educational program based on a student's specific instructional or behavioral needs. IDEA mandates that parents be given the opportunity for input into all aspects of the proposed placement. The program must be evaluated and implemented by a multidisciplinary team. Preservice teachers and beginning teachers should note that the student's individualized educational program (IEP) must be updated annually and that areas of functioning must be reevaluated by trained evaluators, including all team members, at least every three years, or more frequently if conditions warrant or if professionals or parents request it.

Individualized Education Program (IEP). The student's IEP is the most important document that teachers and parents will develop for the student. The IEP is formulated using multidisciplinary team input and parents' suggestions. Every student with special needs is provided with an IEP that specifies, in writing, measurable annual goals. For students qualifying for an alternative district or state-wide assessment, benchmarks or short-term objectives are required (IDEIA, 04). The plan must be current and in effect at the beginning of every school year. When a student is identified as having a disability during the year, teachers must hold an IEP meeting within 30 calendar days of the meeting at which eligibility for special education and related services is established. After parents give written consent for placement, the IEP goes into effect. (Chapter 7 describes the IEP in detail.)

Due Process Hearings. Due process hearings are among the methods of dispute resolution mandated by law. They are intended to allow dissenting or aggrieved parties opportunities to question educational decisions. To receive federal monies allocated by the IDEIA, representatives of the state education agency (SEA) and the local education agency (LEA) must guarantee to federal authorities that they have adopted appropriate due process procedures to address complaints relating to a student's identification, evaluation, or placement or to a student's right to a FAPE. In addition, parties participating in due process hearings have the right of review (e.g., they may appeal to a federal court any decision that they believe requires further interpretation).

For example, a new teacher may teach a student in the general education class. In the teacher's opinion, the student has been placed inappropriately and requires a change in placement to a full-time special class. The parents disagree with the need for change and request a due process hearing. Until a final decision is reached, the student remains or "stays put" in the present educational setting (i.e., general education class) unless all parties agree to an alternative placement. The review process may continue until the case is heard before the U.S. Supreme Court. Figure 2.4 presents levels of the review process.

Mediation. While due process hearings must be available, all professionals, and especially teachers in training and those new to the field, should strive for *mediation*, the process of resolving disagreements and deciding issues of FAPE before they escalate to the point where a due process hearing is requested. Mediation helps parents and professionals resolve differences without involving representatives of the legal system. Situations will arise in which the participants are unable to reach agreement. However, the new IDEIA requires that states strengthen their mediation provisions for developing a binding confidential agreement that is enforceable in any state or district court in the US (CEC, 2004).

When professionals have frequent opportunities to discuss evaluation results or placement issues with parents and advocates, the need for legal action may be lessened. However, legal authorities necessarily will participate in mediation, hearings, and reviews. During this stage, teachers may be asked to provide information they have collected on the student during the year. Mediation, the step prior to initiation of a hearing, often begins with a review of tangible data. Unfortunately, at times, litigation will be unavoidable.

Record Keeping and Confidentiality. The IDEIA stipulates that all teachers must ensure students' and parents' rights to fair record-keeping procedures and confidentiality of all records. Records may include informal and formal assessments, anecdotal records, behavior lists, and checklists. Federal law provides that parents have the right to inspect and review all data about their child. They have the right to copy all information and to receive a list of all types and locations of records being collected, maintained, or in any way used by LEA or SEA members. A teacher's data on the student are thus important pieces of information and may be used as evidence in legal proceedings.

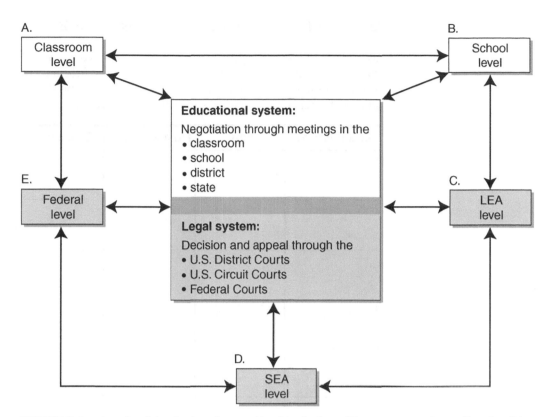

FIGURE 2.4 Levels of the Review Process Used to Redress Disagreements Regarding the Education of Individual Students

Parents may ask for an explanation of any information in the records and may ask for changes if they believe the records are incorrect, are misleading, or violate privacy rights. They also may initiate a hearing on the issue if school personnel refuse to change the data. Parents can restrict access to their student's records by withholding consent to disclose the data. School officials must inform parents about where and how information is to be used by others and before information in the student's file is destroyed.

RELATED LEGISLATION

Legislation beyond the IDEIA has had an impact on new teachers' roles as they serve students with disabilities. These are described briefly below.

Americans with Disabilities Act of 1990 (ADA)

Currently, state officials are required to provide facilities that allow students with disabilities the opportunity to participate with others to the extent possible. The Americans with Disabilities Act (ADA) of 1990 requires that all facilities afford students the access they need, including accessible public accommodations (e.g., school cafeterias, school lavatories) and telecommunications (e.g., relay services for students with hearing impairments and speech impairments) (National Loss Control Service Corporation, 1992).

In addition, all special education students have the right of access to supplementary services or aids. This means that the new teacher may provide prosthetic devices, assistive technology, adaptive equipment, flexible scheduling, or test modifications to make it possible for the student to remain in the LRE. Box 2.4 presents major components of ADA.

Pause and Reflect About the Profession 2.2

List with a partner five legal issues that have affected you or any of the professionals in your practicum or internship or at your student teaching or field placement site. Then, for each example, describe what might have been done to make the situation less stressful for you, your host teacher, the students, and/or the parents or guardians.

Legal Issues	You	Host Teacher	Students	Parents/Guardians
1.				
2.				
3.				
4.				
5.				

Section 504 of the Rehabilitation Act of 1973

Section 504 of the Rehabilitation Act of 1973 is important in today's classroom (Katsiyannis & Conderman, 1994; Zirkel, 2000). It prohibits discrimination against individuals with disabilities under any program receiving federal financial assistance. Section 504 provides rights for school-age students with disabilities in addition to those provided by the IDEIA because it protects students with disabilities who do not need special education.

Section 504 and the IDEIA have certain significant differences and many similarities (Zirkel, 1995, 2000). Section 504 applies to recipients of any federal assistance, including all programs or activities that receive or benefit from the assistance. The IDEIA, however, applies only to those states and political subdivisions receiving payment under the statute. Thus, to be protected from discrimination in a school setting, a student must be identified as disabled and must also be of an age for which a state is required to provide FAPE. An amendment to Section 504 excludes students with disabilities who use or are in possession of alcohol or illegal drugs. Such students may still be protected though, under IDEIA, if they otherwise qualify as disabled.

The full impact of Section 504 is only now being felt because of the interest of the Office for Civil Rights in the U.S. Department of Education in (1) implementing the LRE mandate and (2) meeting the educational needs of students with disabilities who qualify for services under Section 504 (Katsiyannis & Conderman, 1994).

However, some school districts have moved from underdoing to overdoing Section 504. Where the IDEIA typically leads to services for 10 to 15 percent of a school district's population, Section 504 should account for only another 1 to 2 percent. However, some school districts have trouble determining eligibility and rely on overidentification of students protected under Section 504 (Zirkel, 2000). In order to avoid overidentification, Zirkel suggested that the school district must have firm eligibility

Box 2.4   Accessibility Requirements of the Americans
with Disabilities Act (ADA)

Title 1: Employment

- Employers with 15 or more employees may not discriminate against qualified individuals with disabilities.

- Employers must reasonably accommodate the disabilities of qualified applicants or employees (e.g., by modifying workstations and equipment) unless undue hardship would result.

Title II: Public Services

- State and local governments may not discriminate against qualified individuals with disabilities.

- Buildings must be accessible.

- New buses and rail vehicles for fixed route systems must be accessible.

- One car per train must be accessible.

Title III: Public Accommodations

- Restaurants, hotels, theaters, shopping centers and malls, retail stores, museums, libraries, parks, private schools, day care centers, and other similar places of public accommodation may not discriminate on the basis of disability.

- Physical barriers in existing public accommodations must generally be removed. If removal is not readily achievable, alternative methods of providing services must be implemented.

- New construction in public accommodations and commercial facilities must be accessible.

Title IV: Telecommunications

- Telephone companies must provide telecommunications relay services for hearing-impaired and speech-impaired individuals 24 hours per day.

Source: From Americans with Disabilities Act of 1990 (ADA), Pub. L. no. 101–336, 104 Stat. 327–378 (July 26, 1990), 42 U.S.C. § 12101 *et seq.*

criteria. District personnel should determine that the student's impairment substantially limits a major life activity.

No Child Left Behind Act of 2002 (NCLB)

The No Child Left Behind Act is a landmark educational reform law designed to improve student achievement. With the passage of NCLB, Congress reauthorized the Elementary and Secondary Education Act, the principal federal law that affects education from kindergarten through high school. NCLB is constructed on four foundational pillars: (1) stronger accountability for results, (2) an emphasis on teaching methods that are based on scientific research, (3) expanded parental options, and (4) expanded local control and flexibility (Pennsylvania Department of Education, 2003).

In its short history, however, NCLB has already undergone several midcourse corrections in its implementation due to its complicated nature (U.S. Department of Education, 2004). Additional refinements are anticipated; therefore, any discussion on NCLB is subject to change, especially as the law relates to special education.

The special education community has been vocal in assuring policy makers and the public that students with disabilities should be expected to achieve and to perform; however, the field is rightfully confused and concerned about the differences in NCLB and the new IDEIA. Those contradictions include the following:

- NCLB requires that all students progress at a similar rate, while the new IDEIA recognizes that all students progress at different rates.
- NCLB uses standardized data sources to address progress, while, the new IDEIA uses multiple data sources aligned to a student's abilities.
- NCLB uses chronological age and grade as a basis for state assessment, while the IDEIA uses individualized instruction and assessment of a student's instructional level.
- NCLB requires student progress to be determined by a "proficient" score on state tests, while progress under the IDEIA is based on an IEP team decision, with test scores used as one contributing factor (Pennsylvania Department of Education, 2004).

In addition to these four issues, special educators are worried about the NCLB requirement for highly qualified teachers. Currently, NCLB requires that all teachers of core academic subjects be "highly qualified" by 2005–2006. This means they must have a college degree, have full certification or licensure, and demonstrate competency in the subject(s) they teach. Under IDEIA (04), this means that all practicing special educators must possess a full state certified special education certificate, or pass a state special education licensing exam and hold some sort of state license (CEC, 2004).

The language in IDEIA (04) attempts to directly tie special educators' "highly qualified" requirements to the subject matter requirements for general education in NCLB, without ignoring "the integrity of special educators, special education licensure, the multiple settings in which special educators deliver services, the diverse roles within which special educators function, and the very diversity of the individuals for whom they work" (CEC, 2004, p. 4). These criteria can be fulfilled by a college major in the subject, passing a state test, or demonstrating content knowledge through a state standard of evaluation (Pennsylvania Board of Education, 2004). This is a major problem for special education teachers and programs. Beyond the basic requirements, IDEIA contains additional requirements for special education educators who are teaching multiple subjects and those teaching students working on the "alternate achievement standards" (CEC, 2004). See Table 2.1. The content-area requirements are particularly burdensome to middle and high school special education teachers, who often work with students in several content areas. What it means is that to continue teaching, many special education teachers will need to acquire additional content-area credentials in

TABLE 2.1 NCLB and IDEIA (04) Requirements for "Highly Qualified"

If you are a practicing special educator teaching:	*Then* you must meet the requirements in NCLB:
1. Only students who area assessed with the NCLB alternative achievement standards	For elementary or secondary subject matter teachers
2. Multiple subjects	• For new elementary, middle, or secondary teachers OR
	• For elementary, middle, or secondary teachers not new to teaching through the HOUSSE process which is different in each state.

Source: CEC, 2004

more than one subject (Pennsylvania Department of Education, 2004). For example, if you are a learning support teacher assigned to a high school program where you are responsible for teaching math in a self-contained learning support program, you will need to be "highly qualified" as described above in the area of mathematics—basically in higher-level mathematics. This is problematic in the field of special education when there are already extreme shortages of special education teachers across the nation.

HOW TEACHERS CAN DEMONSTRATE IMPLEMENTATION OF THE SPECIAL EDUCATION LAWS

Preservice and beginning teachers can demonstrate a working knowledge of current trends and practices by adhering to federally mandated processes and procedures. All teachers can do the following:

1. View education as a process that continually changes in the face of evolving federal and state laws and regulations. To survive legal challenges, teachers must be flexible and adaptable within acceptable professional guidelines.

2. Be articulate consumers of public policy by talking with parents, teachers, community leaders, administrators, and legal representatives. Teachers should be familiar with local philosophies and goals of educational programs. Reading district procedures and other legal policies published by the state or local education office may help new professionals become familiar with current issues affecting their classrooms.

3. Be familiar with legal and professional guidelines to ensure the fairness and appropriateness of programs and to facilitate program accountability. This includes awareness of prereferral strategies, referral steps, testing procedures, program criteria, and exit criteria for all special education and related services provided.

4. Demonstrate knowledge of the major components of special education law, including the IDEIA, ADA, and Section 504 of the Rehabilitation Act.

5. Upgrade personal knowledge of legal changes that affect teachers or their students (e.g., legal issues related to teaching practices, research and services bearing directly on public policy) through in-service professional development opportunities, recertification, and so forth.

Major Challenges, Legal and Professional Responsibilities of Special Education Teachers

Positive educational changes have occurred in recent years for special-needs students of all ages from infants to 21-year-old adults. Efforts to meet the transitional needs of students in various life stages are examples of positive educational changes. These changes have evolved with the help of dedicated teachers fulfilling their legal and professional responsibilities to students, parents, themselves, and their profession. When dedicated professionals critically analyzed past practices, inadequacies were tackled head on, and the process of change helped initiate practices that better meet students' needs.

Federal mandates can make the job of new teachers especially difficult. Paperwork, data collection and conferences, often difficult students or parents, and the logistics of operating within a multidisciplinary team can be frustrating and stressful. New teachers, however, might adopt the approach that legal requirements will provide structure to their tasks. Federal and state mandates will help ensure consistency in the quantity and quality of the services provided. The more experience teachers have in implementing federal and state mandates, the easier their job can be.

Providing FAPE. Understanding important regulations and laws and abiding by legal mandates may help promote progress of all students. New teachers need to modify their programs to meet current federal and state laws and regulations, to modify the program according to current teaching practices, and to display professionalism.

Awareness of Legislation and Litigation. All teachers have a legal and professional responsibility to possess a working knowledge of legislation and litigation that affect students. Awareness of legislation and litigation can occur through a number of ways. Developing and beginning teachers can maintain their knowledge of current practices, laws, and court cases through active participation in conferences, workshops, in-services, continuing education classes, and professional development opportunities. Subscribing to relevant journals and newsletters may help teachers obtain information on research-based teaching practices, technology advances, and service activities. Working actively in local, state, or national advocacy groups may widen the contacts that teachers have and increase their political and legal awareness. Becoming an advocate may also provide new perspectives on the educational process occurring at the local level so that teachers can work effectively within the educational system.

Effective Teaching Practices. Changes within individual classrooms may affect the quality and quantity of services provided in the school, LEA, or SEA. Teachers can effect changes in their own classrooms in a number of ways. (Consult later chapters for specific research-based practices that have been found to provide positive changes.) However, all teachers should be skeptical of extraordinary claims about new methodologies in order to guard against charlatans (O'Shea, O'Shea, & Algozzine, 1998).

Implementing Problem-Solving Efforts Within the Educational System. To facilitate efforts to solve problems within the school, teachers should confer regularly with each other and parents about students or any aspect of the FAPE provided. Of course, effective communication skills should be used during all professional endeavors. Energies can be directed toward a team model, which encourages parental and professional involvement and which may enhance teachers' abilities to effect positive changes.

Communication. Communication is the foundation of all interpersonal relationships and the framework for every meeting with parents and professional contacts with peers. For teachers to be effective communicators, real effort is needed. Teachers new to the field can develop and enhance their communication skills by setting priorities, learning rapport-building techniques, and being flexible and adaptable.

In addition, new teachers should consider their roles in sending and receiving messages during the communication process. They should speak clearly and correctly, with consideration given to the meaning behind their words. Teachers should listen to what parents and other professionals say and be open to suggestions. They should consider their nonverbal messages, including body language, facial expressions, posture, and stance; demonstrate empathy and positive regard; and make only nonjudgmental statements to peers and parents. All of these suggestions may facilitate better communication, and the need for legal action may be lessened when the individuals closest to the student believe and demonstrate that they are working together.

Teaming. Involving others in the change process often helps if everyone perceives this involvement as a team effort. Individuals may assume ownership of the functions of the team and often may work harder to lessen legal difficulties for the benefit of the student. Teaming helps parents and professionals work together to ensure a FAPE to students and access to the general education curriculum. Some general strategies to promote teaming can be used within the context of any functional relationship with parents and other professionals:

1. From the first day, capitalize on the personal strengths of the student and always demonstrate that the major consideration is the student's best interests.

2. Provide constructive criticism by sharing information and by eliciting ideas from parents and other professionals about areas where the student needs to improve or ways to initiate this improvement. Provide encouragement through a balance of positive statements and corrective feedback statements.

3. Frame criticism with the goal of improved performance in mind. Although individual weaknesses that need discussion should never be glossed over, always mention some strength of the student at every meeting. It is wise to start and end each meeting with a positive statement. Even a single reference to the student's progress may aid in the teaming effort.

4. Strive for consistency at all team meetings by using verifiable data. Do not base information on personal opinion—provide facts. Communicate the data effectively, in speech and in writing, to parents, colleagues, administrators, and community members.

5. Get continual feedback from parents and other professionals to assess the reasonableness of the type and amount of programming requirements and others' roles in facilitating these requirements. Ask parents and professionals continually for their suggestions to improve the student's performance.

6. Involve parents and professionals in every step of the educational process. Elicit their suggestions for more appropriate programming for the student. Be flexible and open to their suggestions.

7. Always keep all members of the team informed of all records, evaluation results, and educational proposals. Keep a written, dated record of each communication attempt, and maintain the records where they can be located quickly.

Avoiding Unnecessary Litigation and Participating in Necessary Litigation.
   Mediation. Even with the best efforts during the communication process or teaming, problems over which the classroom teacher has little or no control may escalate. During this time, mediation efforts, with the help of other professionals, including administrators, peers, or even school attorneys, may be appropriate.

Classroom teachers can take a number of positive steps during in-school mediation to resolve disagreements over the student's evaluation, educational placement, or IEP:

1. Provide many informal conferences to attempt to remediate differences within the student's current placement. Invite all significant individuals to the mediation conference.

2. Designate a leader to chair all mediation attempts. It may be the classroom teacher, principal, supervisor, or legal counsel. Have a written agenda to share at all conferences.

3. Encourage all participants to sign, date, and identify their relationship to the student on a conference participation form.

4. Listen to all suggestions in order to ascertain the student's LRE. Strive for a group consensus on new strategies and procedures to try first in the student's immediate classroom environment.

5. Implement all suggested new strategies, procedures, and modifications within six weeks of the mediation conference.

6. Collect baseline data on the student's present levels prior to the introduction of treatments or changes in strategies. Keep data on all progress over time.

7. Document all modifications of the usual classroom techniques and procedures. Observe the student under different conditions within the classroom (e.g., individual assignments, group tasks, peer tutoring) and record all observations. Observe the student in different settings and while working or socializing with different individuals.

8. Ask various school professionals and parents to observe the modifications within the classroom and to document their observations on student progress. Compare professional and parental observations to determine interrater reliability.

9. Meet again in a structured conference to compare observation data and the student's progress to date. Strive again for group consensus on the next steps and "iron out" differences. Record the outcomes of all meetings.

10. Devise a written summary as soon as possible after each meeting concludes.

11. Send a copy of the written summary to each participant.

These suggestions will help the developing professional to document every attempt to ensure the LRE for the target student. Parties may still disagree, however, over best practices or specific treatment for individual students. Be assured that with dated, written data, new teachers need not fear legal actions. If litigation still results, preparation and professional attitudes may still provide relief.

Professional Attitude. If repeated mediation attempts fail, the only recourse may be a hearing in which the decision-making power passes from parents and school authorities to an impartial hearing officer, who determines the outcome of the case (Schrybman, 1982). It is vital that teachers in training and teachers new to the field not view litigation as an evil process. When seen as the catalyst for new and better laws for students, litigation may be considered a healthy and necessary process. When inappropriate management occurs, when procedures need to be redefined or refined, or when public policies require clarification that cannot be agreed on by local participants of the educational process, litigation can be a legitimate step in the process of providing FAPE for students with disabilities.

Advocating for New and Better Legislation.
Promotion of Progress. Professional attitudes can affect public policy, encouraging beneficial changes in the educational system. As demonstrated by past efforts, new legislation can result that will help guarantee gains in special education and related services. It is beneficial for all teachers to remember that much litigation was initiated during the past because individuals recognized and responded to inadequate services, poor practices, and unfair procedures occurring in schools; therefore new teachers should strive to provide students with FAPE. Past advocates were willing to work for change within the system but realized that the power of political forces and legal influences was necessary. These individuals acted when data verified that change was warranted. Today, new teachers should work within the established rules of the school, the district, and the state and strive for successful mediation when disagreements arise. They can respond when changes are necessary through simple modifications in school policies or classroom procedures.

Student Advocacy. Professionals who care about students and use established methods of intervention can be confident that members of the educational and legal systems will protect appropriate educational programming. To effectively protect the legal rights of their students, beginning teachers should recognize, implement, and monitor best teaching practices in their classrooms. This will provide the best assurance that all students are afforded legal justice in educational settings.

SUMMARY

In this chapter, we described how new teachers are involved in legal issues from the moment they enter teaching. They must be knowledgeable about the legal requirements providing the basis for special education practices. We emphasized that despite recurring changes in the legal interpretations and procedural aspects of federal law (i.e., the shifting sands of special education), new professionals must have a fundamental knowledge of the identification procedures for individuals with exceptional learning needs. They also require an understanding of assurances and due process rights related to assessment, eligibility, and placement for these students. We indicated that teachers will implement, through their effective practices, actions upholding the rights and responsibilities of parents, students, teachers, and schools as they relate to individuals with exceptional learning needs.

ACTIVITIES TO EXTEND YOUR KNOWLEDGE

1. Locate local school and community agencies, the library, advocacy centers, or legal aid offices, and prepare a list of the names, addresses, telephone numbers, web sites, and specific activities of contacts/resources related to Section 504, the ADA, and the IDEIA.
2. Ask for written school board policies on the local assurances and due process rights related to access to the general education curricula, assessments, eligibility, and placements for students with disabilities.
3. Obtain a copy of your district's attendance, discipline, and suspension and expulsion policies. Ask your special education director or supervisor to clarify assessment and placement practices for students with disabilities when questions arise about their infringement of such policies.
4. Interview local school board members; ask them to discuss their personal philosophies of special education, including its relationship to general education. Compare and contrast these statements with those of local advocacy groups and those of parents or guardians of students with disabilities.
5. Review the case study provided at the beginning of this chapter. What errors or problems discussed in this chapter will the district be confronting if staff continue to conduct evaluations and write IEPs in the fashion described?
6. Using the same case study, identify the problems that Natalie is facing as she prepares to write her first IEP. Brainstorm ideas on what she should do to improve the situation.
7. Review IEPs used in your district when possible. Sit down with a special education teacher to discuss procedure within the school district.
8. Walk through a local shopping mall and schools and visually inspect local restaurants and department stores. List any violations of accessibility for individuals with disabilities.

References

Abeson, A., & Zettel, J. (1977). The end of the quiet revolution: The Education for All Handicapped Children's Act of 1975. *Exceptional Student, 44,* 114–128.

Amendment to the Education for All Handicapped Students Act (PL 99–457). (1986). Washington, DC: Office of Special Education and Rehabilitative Services.

Americans with Disabilities Act of 1990 (ADA), Pub. L. No. 101–336, 104 Stat. 327–328 (July 26, 1990), 42 U.S.C. § 12101 *et seq.*

Ballard, J., Ramirez, B. A., & Weintraub, F. J. (1982). *Special education in America: Its legal and governmental foundations.* Reston, VA: Council for Exceptional Children.

Council for Exceptional Children. (2004). The NEW IDEA: CEC's Summary of Significant Issues. Arlington: Author.

Carpenter, S. L., & McKee-Higgins, E. (1996). Behavior management in inclusive classrooms. *Remedial and Special Education, 17*(4), 195–204.

Education of the Handicapped Law Report. (1977–1988). Alexandria, VA: CRR.

Hanley, T. V. (1995). The need for technological advances in assessment related to national educational reform. *Exceptional Student, 61*(3), 222–228.

Hehir, T. (1999). The changing roles of special education leadership in the next millennium: Thoughts and reflections. *Journal of Special Education Leadership, 12*(1), 3–8.

Hodapp, R. M. (1993, April). Comparison of families of students with mental retardation and families of students without mental retardation. *Mental Retardation,* 75–77.

Individuals with Disabilities Education Act of 1990, 20 U.S.C. § 1400 *et seq.*

Katsiyannis, A., & Conderman, G. (1994). Section 504 policies and procedures: An established necessity. *Remedial and Special Education, 15*(5), 311–318.

Maheady, L. (1988). An opportunity for developing instructional diversity. *Special Services Digest, 2,* 4–6.

McDonnell, J. (1993, March). Impact of community-based instruction on the development of adaptive behavior of secondary-level students with mental retardation. *American Journal on Mental Retardation,* 575–584.

McLaughlin, M. J. (1999). Access to the general education curriculum: Paperwork and procedures or redefining "special education." *Journal of Special Education Leadership, 12*(1), 9–14.

National Loss Control Service Corporation. (1992, Spring). *Americans with Disabilities Act: Whom does it cover?* Long Grove, IL: Author.

O'Shea, L. J., O'Shea, D. J., & Algozzine, B. (1998). *Learning disabilities: From theory toward practice.* New York: Prentice-Hall.

Pennsylvania Department of Education. (1995). *Pennsylvania 2000.* Harrisburg: Author.

Pennsylvania Department of Education. (2003). *Overview of No Child Left Behind.* Harrisburg: Author.

Pennsylvania Department of Education. (2004). *Pennsylvania's No Child Left Behind position paper.* Harrisburg: Author.

Rueda, R., Gallego, M. A., & Moll, L. C. (2000). The least restrictive environment. *Remedial and Special Education, 21*(2), 70–78.

Schrybman, J. (1982). *Due process in special education.* Rockville, MD: Aspen.

Tomlinson, C. A. (2000). Reconcilable differences? Standards-based teaching and differentiation. *Educational Leadership, 58*(1), 6–11.

Turnbull, H. R. (1993). *Free appropriate public education: The law and students with disabilities* (4th ed.). Denver: Love.

U.S. Department of Education. (2003). *No Child Left Behind: An overview.* Washington, DC: Author.

Weintraub, F. J., Abeson, A., Ballard, J., & LaVor, M. L. (1977). *Public policy and the education of exceptional students.* Reston, VA: Council for Exceptional Children.

Yell, M. L., Katsiyannis, A., Bradley, R., & Rozalski, M. E. (2000). Ensuring compliance with the discipline provisions of IDEA. *Journal of Special Education Leadership, 13*(1), 3–18.

Ysseldyke, J., & Olsen, K. (1999). Putting alternate assessments into practice: What to measure and possible sources of data. *Exceptional Student, 65*(2), 175–185.

Zirkel, P. A. (1995, May). *Special education law for regular educators.* Paper presented at Lehigh University Education Law Conference XXII, Bethlehem, PA.

Zirkel, P. A. (2000). Over-identification: Not all IDEA-ineligible students are Section 504. *Special Educator, 15*(12), 10.

Setting Up for Instruction

Chapter Outline

In this chapter, we will

- review the importance of being an organized manager of the instructional environment

- discuss alternatives for designing the physical classroom environment

- review the levels of instructional time and outline specific strategies for increasing the efficacy of time spent in school

- present approaches and strategies for scheduling activities and grouping students in both self-contained and inclusive classroom settings

- list methods that assist in the development, introduction, and maintenance of classroom rules and procedures

- outline strategies that assist in the coordination of resources

A PROFESSIONAL GLIMPSE

Clint Simon's first special education student-teaching placement was a self-contained upper-elementary program for students with severe emotional disturbance and behavior disorders. The classroom, taught by Ina Matrice, was composed of 14 boys, all between the ages of 9 and 11. Ms. Matrice had been teaching for 10 years and had developed a number of organizational routines that assisted in the promotion of an orderly learning environment. Indeed, it seemed that the students relied on the structures and prompts as they went through the day.

One of the first things that Clint noticed was that the classroom was arranged in a way that allowed for both distraction-free small-group instruction and common areas for discussion and socialization. Materials were organized, and there was a cheerful, pleasing décor to the room. On the large bulletin board in the back of the room was a master schedule that detailed the times that each student's activities were to begin and end as well as who was responsible for leading the activity (i.e., parent volunteer, related service provider, instructional assistant) and its location. Although the students were quite active, they seemed to know where they were supposed to be in the room and what was required of them during instruction.

As he was looking around the room, Ms. Matrice gave Clint a substitute teacher information packet. In that packet were the classroom rules and procedures; school policy information that detailed lunch, recess, and fire-drill duties; and specific student information such as seating charts, medication needs, and emergency contacts. Clint was most impressed that Ms. Matrice had folders for each student with weekly lesson plans formatted in a way that facilitated the monitoring of student progress toward IEP goals. Over lunch, Clint commented to Ms. Matrice that she was the most organized teacher he had ever seen. Ms. Matrice appreciated the compliment. However, she cautioned Clint that one could never be too organized when dealing with the immediate, variable, and unpredictable behaviors of students with special needs.

*A*s one can conclude from the case above, classrooms for students with mild to moderate disabilities tend to be busy places. Whether one is student teaching in a self-contained classroom, resource room, or "cotaught" inclusive setting, many and varied instructional and noninstructional events occur simultaneously. While a student teacher may be conducting a remedial lesson on long division for a small group of students in one corner of the room, several other students may be completing seatwork assignments with peer tutors from neighboring classrooms and still another group may be returning from music class. If these events are not enough of a management concern, most special education teachers are also often asked to assume a variety of responsibilities that go beyond the boundaries of traditional classroom instruction. In addition to being charged with the usual array of diagnostic and teaching responsibilities, teachers of students with disabilities are frequently called on to (1) complete full-scale educational evaluations, (2) field-test new and existing learning programs and instructional procedures, (3) monitor students' progress through the curriculum, (4) coordinate the logistics involved in implementing inclusive programming, (5) initiate and maintain collaborative working relationships with general educators and related service personnel, and (6) develop outreach programs with parents and significant others in the community.

Not surprisingly, special education teachers, as with most education professionals, meet these often overwhelming demands with differing levels of success. Variation in degree of success is not, however, a function of magic or luck; those able to deal effectively with the multitude of demands involved in teaching students with mild to moderate disabilities succeed because they work hard to produce conditions that promote

TABLE 3.1   Organizational Pressures of Classrooms

Organizational Pressure	Definition
Immediacy	Many events require immediate attention or action.
Publicness	Teacher is always on stage.
Multidimensionality	Classrooms are crowded and busy places in which limited resources are used to achieve a wide range of goals.
Unpredictability	Events in classrooms change daily, and many occurrences are difficult to predict.
History	Events that occur early in the school year set the tone for later happenings.
Simultaneity	Many things happen at the same time in classrooms.

Source: Adapted from *Classroom management*, by W. Doyle, 1980, West Lafayette, IN: Kappa Delta Pi.

success. The lesson is short and relatively simple: To successfully manage the daily demands of their busy classroom, special educators must be organized managers of their environments.

All classrooms, regardless of whether they contain special, "at-risk," or normally achieving students, contain organizational pressures that influence the teaching/learning process. Table 3.1 presents Doyle's (1980) conceptualization of the complex organizational pressures typical of most classrooms. It is interesting to note that these six factors portray the classroom as a public forum requiring frequent and immediate teacher actions in the face of almost overwhelming and, in many cases, unpredictable environmental variables. The range and intensity of the six pressures can vary according to a teacher's levels of experience, dedication, and competence and even the time of year. Whereas many veteran teachers are experienced in managing the busy classroom, preservice and beginning teachers face the challenge of managing the sensory overload of their first days in the classroom. This problem may be particularly evident in classrooms serving students with disabilities, where the unique learning and behavioral characteristics of such students often require explicit supports and additional external controls.

Fortunately, early recognition of the organizational pressures of the classroom can allow for the development of strategies to manage these ever-present demands. These strategies are best viewed as preventive—an approach in which the events of a busy classroom are anticipated and planned for by an organized and flexible professional who successfully manages multiple simultaneous events (Paine, Radicci, Rosellini, Deutchman, & Darch, 1983). In this chapter, we examine and provide guidelines for five interrelated preinstructional activities that will assist student and beginning teachers in preparing for successful teaching: (1) the design of the physical environment, (2) the management of instructional time, (3) the effective scheduling of classroom activities and grouping of students, (4) the formulation of meaningful and relevant classroom rules and procedures, and (5) the coordination of available resources.

DESIGNING THE PHYSICAL ENVIRONMENT

The first of the many organizational challenges facing beginning, experienced, and, to a certain extent, student teachers is to make effective use of the physical dimensions of the classroom. Whether one is working in a self-contained, resource, or inclusive setting, the chairs, desks, bookcases, tables, room dividers, and countless other pieces of furniture must be arranged for accessibility and safety. Instructional equipment such as computers, tape recorders, and filmstrip projectors must be arranged for controlled student access and efficient teacher use. Seating patterns for instruction, independent work, and appropriate socialization must be considered in relation to their effects on discipline and transitions among activities. Finally, those aesthetic features that promote pride in one's classroom, such as displays, plants, and bulletin boards, must be incorporated appropriately into the existing physical structure of the room.

This monumental task of orchestrating the physical learning environment is critical because classroom design is directly related to effective classroom management and student academic performance. These relationships among physical environmental variables and student performance variables are especially pronounced for students with mild to moderate disabilities, who typically require added structure in all facets of their educational experience. For all students, however, the appropriate arrangement of the physical environment can decrease the rate of student disruptions, improve the quantity and quality of desirable social interactions among students, and increase the amount of time that students attend to their assignments (Paine et al., 1983).

Figures 3.1 and 3.2 illustrate self-contained elementary and secondary resource classroom configurations. Each contains a common large-group area, an area for

FIGURE 3.1   Primary Self-Contained Classroom for Students with Mild Learning and Behavioral Problems

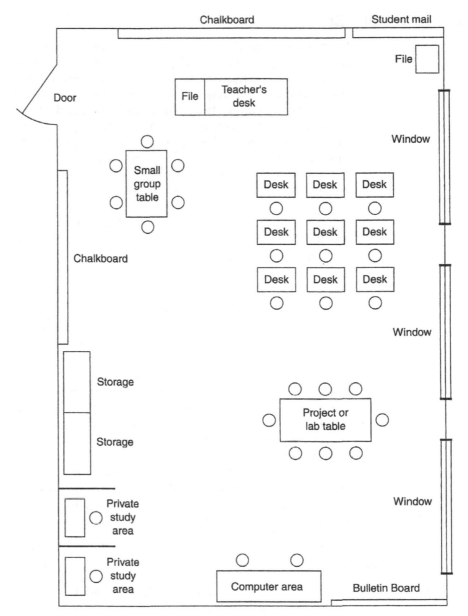

FIGURE 3.2 Secondary School Resource Room for Students with Mild Learning and Behavioral Problems

small-group instruction, and study carrels for private study. General education settings that are adapted for the inclusion of students with disabilities often integrate some of the features (e.g., study areas, group instruction areas, study carrels) found in self-contained and resource settings. However, the design of any physical classroom environment will vary according to a number of interacting variables, including (1) the actual physical layout and location of the classroom; (2) the number, age, and behavioral profiles of students in the class; and (3) the degrees of disability or levels of supports required by students. Still, several generic factors should be considered when arranging the physical layout of a special education classroom.

Public and Private Space

Regardless of the ages of or the types of problems exhibited by students with mild to moderate disabilities, the classroom environment should provide opportunities for work, study, and free time in both public and private areas. Public areas used for group instruction and the majority of independent practice activities should be arranged in such a way that all students can see the teacher's desk or the primary instructional area. Because students with mild to moderate disabilities have low rates of time-on-task under the best of conditions, exposure to potential distractors such as windows, free-time areas, and displays should be minimized.

Traditionally arranged student desks, class meeting tables, and large- or small-group instruction areas should be complemented with private quiet areas where students can work with limited distractions. Such areas can be easily designed through the creative arrangement of bookcases, filing cabinets, and study carrels. Partitions with greater portability and flexibility could be used as room dividers, providing privacy for small instructional groups, peer-tutoring activities, or counseling sessions.

Furniture

It is critical that teachers consider the patterns of movement typical of busy classrooms and plan furniture and seating arrangements to regulate such movement. Movement around the classroom can be facilitated by avoiding unnecessary congestion in high-traffic areas. Students should be able to move to high-traffic areas such as the teacher's desk, the pencil sharpener, and the front door without disturbing others. Moreover, these areas should be located in separate parts of the classroom so that students engaged in other activities are not overwhelmed or distracted by such activities. Open spaces that have no clear purpose should be avoided; such areas often become a breeding ground of problematic behaviors. Furniture should be used to regulate or channel movement in and around the room. Bookcases, room dividers, and filing cabinets can be used to limit movement in those areas that require regulation. For example, furniture can be arranged in such a way that movement around quiet or time-out areas can be easily monitored and regulated.

Easy Lines of Vision

In general, teachers should be able to monitor their students throughout the day. Because achievement of many of the instructional goals for students with learning and behavioral problems is determined by direct observation of behavior, it is critical that their teachers have an unobstructed view of the entire classroom. A teacher's attention is a powerful reinforcer of appropriate behavior—easily used to manage minor instances of disruptive behaviors. Teachers should also ensure that each student can easily see the key elements of daily lessons: the teacher, the teacher aide, the chalkboard, and so forth. Each key element should be in full view of students with minimal movement of their heads, desks, or chairs.

Storage of Instructional Materials

As observed by Evertson, Emmer, Clements, Sanford, and Worsham (1984), easy access to instructional materials and supplies increases the effectiveness of instructional procedures by minimizing the time needed for getting ready and cleaning up for individual lessons. Materials used frequently by teachers and students should be kept within easy reach at materials stations, activity centers, or other designated areas. Materials used on a more infrequent basis (e.g., overhead projector, craft supplies, seasonal decorations) should be stored in closets, storage bins, or bookcases.

Aesthetics

Classrooms that are pleasing to the senses can communicate a sense of pride to teachers and students. To contribute aesthetically pleasing elements to the classroom, teachers can use any of a number of items, including (1) displays of content or seasonally appropriate bulletin boards, (2) exhibits of students' work, and, when appropriate, (3) plants and animals. Students can and will respond with respect to an aesthetically pleasing learning environment.

In summary, the structuring of the physical environment is a critical variable in the design of a successful classroom. The levels of structure and intrusiveness required in different settings, however, will vary according to the developmental levels, severity of the disabling conditions, and instructional goals of the students being served. Teachers of young children or students with behavioral problems, for example, may find it necessary to assign seats to their students prior to the first day of school and to label desks, chairs, and lockers as belonging to specific students. In such situations, it may also be necessary to use discrete supports, such as markings on floors and tables, to prompt students where their chairs, desks, and materials are located during various parts of the day. In more inclusive settings, it may be useful to assign seating in a way that promotes social contacts among students with and without disabilities.

MANAGING INSTRUCTIONAL TIME

Effective teachers value instructional time and carefully control its allocation. Efficient use of instructional opportunities is critical if teachers are to maximize the effects of special education efforts. Fortunately, teachers of all experience levels—developing, beginning, and master—can become sensitive to and influence time-related factors that reduce instructional opportunities. Two interrelated activities can increase the appropriate use of instructional time: (1) an awareness of the different levels of instructional time and how they differentially influence classroom events and (2) the implementation of generic and lesson-specific strategies designed to increase the effectiveness and efficiency of the time that students are in school.

Levels of Instructional Time

As noted in Figure 3.3, instructional time is broadly viewed as a variable that consists of allocated time, actual instructional time, engaged time, and academic learning time. Allocated time is the amount of time that school systems or individual teachers set aside for the teaching of specific skills, concepts, units, or subject areas. Although school boards typically mandate how much instructional time students should receive in basic curricular areas, each individual teacher decides how much time is allocated to

FIGURE 3.3 Subsetting or Vanishing Nature of Instructional Time

the various skills within these areas. A readily available measure of how time is allocated to learning is a teacher's planbook.

Actual instructional time is a measure of the amount of time during which instruction is actually delivered to students. Unfortunately, numerous unforeseen events (e.g., fire drills, visiting related-service personnel) can reduce the time devoted to instruction. Moreover, noninstructional activities such as secretarial chores, the organization of materials, and the management of disruptive behavior can spill over into planned instructional time. Actual instructional time is the time during which a lesson is presented to a group of students, regardless of how much time is allocated. In most special education settings, instruction is actually delivered during 80 percent of the time allocated for instruction (Wilson & Wesson, 1986).

Engaged time refers to the actual time during which students pay attention to instruction. Because students can learn only the material to which they attend, engaged time is generally regarded as a sensitive measure of whether time is used effectively in classroom settings.

However, academic learning time is the most meaningful measure of instructional time. This final level of instructional time is the amount of time students are engaged in diagnostically and instructionally appropriate work. Thus, in evaluating whether academic learning time is occurring, variables such as task difficulty, teacher diagnostic ability, and student success rate must be considered.

Strategies for Time Management

Strategies that can be used readily by student and beginning teachers to increase the effectiveness and efficiency of instructional time fall into two major domains: generic classroom initiatives and lesson-specific procedures.

Generic Classroom Initiatives. Three generic strategies can increase the amount of productive time in classrooms for students with mild disabilities. First, teachers should conspicuously demonstrate that attendance and punctuality are expected and valued behaviors. Truancy, absenteeism, and tardiness are insidious thieves of instructional time. In addition to highlighting a policy that encourages school attendance, intermittent rewards for consistent participation and punctuality should be administered. These rewards can fit within the framework of the general classroom management plan and need not be elaborate or expensive. Moreover, systematic follow-up plans should be made for students who are absent or tardy repeatedly. Telephone calls, letters to students' homes, and other types of parental contacts can reduce instances of tardiness and unexcused absences.

Unfortunately, some children come from home environments where parents need help getting their children ready for school. In such cases, teachers may need to be active resources for parents and to recommend strategies that could promote attendance and punctuality. For example, problems with school attendance can be avoided if teachers remind or prompt parents to establish a morning routine. This routine would involve (1) setting out appropriate school clothes that children would wear the next day; (2) using alarm clocks; (3) eating a healthful, relaxed breakfast; and (4) keeping the television off in the morning (Bleichman, 1985).

Routines for home/school preparation can be put into a motivating and reinforcing format. Figures 3.5 and 3.6 illustrate how one school developed the "Take It Easy; Be Happy" strategy and checklist. Using a mnemonic and self-monitoring checklist format, teachers from Marley Middle School in Glen Burnie, Maryland, articulated the specific behaviors required of a well-prepared student.

Once students are attending school regularly, consideration should be given to a second concern: increasing the amount of the school day that is devoted to academic or task-relevant activities. Research on effective teaching has demonstrated that academic performance increases in special education settings where teachers maintain an academic

Pause and Reflect About the Profession 3.1

When real hours and minutes are plugged into the theoretical constructs of instructional time, it becomes readily apparent that, during the course of a typical school day, students receive a frighteningly small amount of instructional time. As illustrated in Figure 3.4, it is possible that a student could receive a mere *108 hours of academic learning time per year*. Clearly, instructional time is a valuable resource that can easily vanish.

	Hours per day	Hours per year
Academic learning time	0.6–1.5	108–270
Engaged time	1.5–3.5	270–430
Actual instructional time delivered	2–4	360–720
Time allocated to instruction	4.75	855
Typical attendance time	5.4	970
Total available time	6.0	1080

FIGURE 3.4 How Instructional Time Can Vanish

In response to these limited opportunities for learning, some policy makers have advocated that the length of the school day and year be extended. Is this the best alternative for addressing the issue of "vanishing" instructional time? What alternative are available for increasing the amounts of instructional time that are delivered to students? How can you ensure that you are maximizing the effectiveness of the time that students are in school? What sorts of activities can groups of educators plan and implement to ensure that instructional time is viewed as a valuable source?

focus. In such settings, effective teachers conduct more instructional activities and make more frequent use of directed questioning than do less effective teachers.

Clear danger signs of an environment at risk for a low academic or task-relevant focus include the following:

- Excessive amounts of time spent in open-ended, undirected discussions about personal opinions and beliefs
- Too much time allocated for noncontingent recess or free activity periods
- Large amounts of time spent on the management and discussion of discipline problems and disruptions
- Exceedingly long periods of time spent on attendance and other housekeeping or organizational chores
- Unscheduled but regular discussions of sporting events, movies, and television programs during academic work periods
- More than 25 percent of the day devoted to nonacademic activities
- Many seemingly harmless social interruptions from teachers' colleagues during academic periods

TAKE IT EASY; BE HAPPY

(Homeroom/Advisory Checklist)

Take all materials to class: notebooks, paper, pencils, special supplies.

Ask yourself if it's A or B Day: P.E., music, foreign language, etc.

Know your schedule.

Expect a lot from yourself. Excel!

it

(Morning Checklist)

Eat a good breakfast?

A or B Day?

Supplies all ready?

Your lunch money?

Be

(Morning Checklist)

Homework: Complete it, check it, and pack it.

Ask for help if you don't understand.

Pack your bookbag.

Parents or guardians: Tell them about your school day.

Yawning? Get a good night's rest. You need 8 hours of sleep.

This is our motto and checklist for success!

FIGURE 3.5   The "Take It Easy; Be Happy" Strategy

Planning and regularly scheduled monitoring of how time is used can ensure that appropriate amounts of time are delivered to academic or task-relevant activities. In terms of planning, it is important to be prepared for the teaching of lessons; instructional procedures should be mastered, and materials necessary for the entire lesson should be accessible. Teachers should regularly analyze how time is used in their own classroom settings. These continuous analyses can range from informal self-monitoring exercises to more systematic and precise observational regimens that require the help of peer observers. Regardless of the method chosen, it is critical that teachers determine how they use class time and, when necessary, consider alternative teaching methods that emphasize academic or task-relevant activities. A straightforward form for gathering data about instructional time during a typical school day is provided in Box 3.1.

TAKE IT EASY; BE HAPPY

Planning ahead and being organized will help you to succeed academically. We, at Marley Middle School, would like to assist you in developing those skills. Post this checklist at home in a convenient location. Every evening, check off the "HAPPY" sections as you complete them. In the mornings, check off the "EASY" sections. Soon your planning and organization will be routine. Have a great year!

		Mon.	Tues.	Wed.	Thurs.	Fri.	Mon.	Tues.	Wed.	Thurs.	Fri.
E	Eat a good breakfast.										
A	A or B Day?										
S	Supplies all ready?										
Y	Your lunch money?										
H	Homework, completed, checked and packed?										
A	Ask for help if you don't understand.										
P	Pack your bookbag.										
P	Parents or guardians: Tell them about your day.										
Y	Yawning? Get a good night's sleep!										

FIGURE 3.6   The "Take It Easy; Be Happy" Checklist

The final generic classroom initiative to maximize the effectiveness of instructional time is to facilitate fluid transitions among activities. The great majority of classrooms for students with mild disabilities have many activity shifts, which typically require movement from one area of the classroom to another or, in settings where there is resource room programming or extensive mainstreaming, from one part of the school building to another. Transitions are unavoidable by-products of comprehensive educational programs; the greater the variety provided to students, the more they will need to switch locations. Because students are not working during transitions, valuable instructional time is lost. Transitions also tend to be disruptive, requiring time for classroom management activities that should be spent teaching.

To facilitate efficient transitions, teachers need to arrange the physical environment appropriately, establish and enforce rules that encourage smooth transitions, and use

Box 3.1 **Monitoring Instructional Time**

Directions: For each classroom activity, record the amount of instructional time allocated and actually delivered. Also, indicate whether the major use of the delivered time involved teacher directed instruction (TDI), seatwork (SW), or nonacademic activity (NA). Use the formulas to calculate how instructional time is used. An illustration is provided on the first line of the form.

Activity	Allocated Time	Time Started	Time Ended	Actual Minutes	TDI/ SW/NA	Comments
Check H.W.	15	8:33	8:43	10	TDI	Discipline Problems

Total TDI minutes _____ Percentage of instruction delivered $= \left(\dfrac{\text{Actual minutes}}{\text{Allocated time}} \times 100 \right) =$ _____

Total SW minutes _____ Percentage of delivered instruction that is TDI $= \left(\dfrac{\text{TDI}}{\text{TDI} + \text{SW}} \times 100 \right) =$ _____

Total TDI/SW minutes _____

Total NA minutes _____

signals to indicate clearly that activity shifts are to occur. To teach effective transitioning skills, teachers should (1) analyze tasks and model appropriate methods of shifting between activities or locations, (2) provide directed practice in activity and location changes, (3) use a variety of group and individual cues to signal transitions, and (4) frequently evaluate the effectiveness of the types of transition signals used. Twenty-four transition cues are listed in Box 3.2.

Lesson-Specific Procedures. The most productive method for maximizing the use of time during lessons is to ensure that students attend to diagnostically and instructionally relevant instruction. Monitoring systems and corresponding instrumentation are available for the observation of on-task behavior. Each available alternative can be adapted to the unique features of any classroom. Box 3.3 contains a generic form for the

Box 3.2   **Transition Cues**

1. Teacher gives verbal cues to group.
2. An appointed child gives verbal cues to group.
3. Teacher gives verbal cues to individuals.
4. An appointed child gives verbal cues to individuals.
5. Teacher touches children to dismiss.
6. An appointed child touches children to dismiss.
7. Lights blink, a bell rings, a piano sounds, a buzzer buzzes, and so forth to signal dismissal.
8. Teacher begins a song that routinely tells children to move.
9. Teacher makes a routine gesture or stands in a routine place to signal dismissal.
10. Teacher or appointed child hands out individual necklaces or bracelets with a color, number, word, or symbol keyed to the children's intended destinations.
11. Teacher or appointed child distributes cards with symbols for the destinations printed on them.
12. Teacher calls for all children wearing a certain color, type, or pattern of clothing.
13. Teacher gives each child an object that will be needed in the next activity.
14. Teacher holds up something (e.g., coat, library book) for its owner to recognize and take to the destination.
15. Teacher tells children to go and find their names at the destination.
16. Teacher dismisses children by physical characteristics (e.g., brown eyes, red hair).
17. Teacher dismisses children by gender.
18. Teacher dismisses children by letters in name.
19. Teacher shows a letter, number, or word and asks for volunteers to identify it; correct answers earn dismissal.
20. Teacher dismisses children by tables at which they sit.
21. Teacher calls on all children who received stickers or "smiley faces" on this day to leave first.
22. Teacher calls first on those students who completed a valued task (e.g., remembered to clean out their cubbie yesterday, took a nap, said their telephone number).
23. Children look at a picture list on the chalkboard or cue card to learn where to go next after finishing an assigned activity.
24. Teacher dismisses using an if-then sentence (e.g., "If you have teeth in your mouth, then go . . . "; "If you could be a father when you grow up, then go . . . ")

From "Teaching mainstreamed children to manage daily transitions," by S. E. Rosenkoetter and S. A. Fowler, 1986, *Teaching Exceptional Children, 19*(1), 20–23. Copyright 1986 by The Council for Exceptional Children. Reprinted with permission.

measuring and recording of on-task behavior; it can be adapted for use under varying instructional conditions. Specific strategies for increasing on-task rates during both teacher-directed instruction and practice sessions are summarized in Box 3.4.

SCHEDULING ACTIVITIES AND GROUPING STUDENTS

The complicated, interrelated tasks of scheduling activities and grouping students are typically completed before preservice teachers enter a student-teaching situation. Consequently, those preparing to be teachers rarely have supervised experience in completing these frustrating activities. The following discussion is provided as an advance organizer for developing teachers who will be faced with scheduling and grouping responsibilities and as a set of guidelines for beginning teachers who are faced with the task of organizing their first classrooms.

Box 3.3

Recording Rates of On-Task Behavior

At 10-second intervals, record a plus sign (+) if the target student is on task and a minus sign (−) if off task. Operationally defined, **on task** means that the student is looking at the appropriate individual or instructional stimulus. Alternate among the targeted students at the prearranged 10-second intervals. Use tape recording of a low audible sound to signal an observation.

Name	1	2	3	4	5	6	7	8	9	10	11	12	13	14	15

Activity type _____   Time begin _____
_____   Time end _____

Note: To arrive at a percentage of the amount of time a student is on task, use the following formula:

$$\frac{\text{number of plus signs } (+ s)}{\text{number of plus signs } + \text{number of minus signs } (+s + -s)}$$

Scheduling Activities

Classrooms in which students with mild to moderate disabilities are effectively served are places where (1) schedules of daily tasks are relatively fixed and (2) routines consistently facilitate the completion of assigned tasks. When planning activities, two tools can facilitate the development and implementation of effective schedules: a master schedule and individual schedule cards.

Master Schedule. The most difficult and logistically complex step in developing consistency and predictability in the learning environment is the development of an overall class schedule. This overall or master schedule is directly related to the allocation of instructional time; teachers must determine how much of the school day is to be devoted to specific skill instruction and other relevant activities. Obviously, much of this information is gathered from students' records, recent IEP data, and current diagnostic test information. The master schedule is, however, a direct reflection of the relative emphases that will be given to content-area instruction for each student in the class. The schedule also reflects the level of each student's participation in general education or mainstreamed activities, as well as the amount of related service activities received each week.

Master schedules should contain (1) the precise times the scheduled periods are to begin and end, (2) a general label representing the subject area or general activity to be covered, (3) the adult (teacher, paraprofessional, parent volunteer) responsible for leading or supervising the period, and (4) the location where the assigned task should be completed. These components are illustrated in Figure 3.7 for several students with mild disabilities in a self-contained setting. This scheduling format can be adapted for resource placements as well. Any type of sturdy chart paper can be used for the construction of the master schedule, although large sheets of paper having preprinted rows and columns will result in a product that is neat and easy for students to read.

The master schedule should be posted in an area that is accessible in the classroom; smaller copies of the chart should be placed in the teacher's and instructional aide's planbooks. The master schedule should serve as a resource for (1) students who may

Box 3.4   Strategies for Increasing On-Task Behavior During Teacher-Directed Instruction and Independent Practice

Teacher-Directed Instruction

1. **Teach more and test less.** Rather than replicating diagnostic testing and repeatedly asking students to tell what they already know about the instructional subject matter, devote time to instructing students in what they need to know.
2. **Question students frequently.** Frequent questioning increases opportunities for students to respond. Pose randomly sequenced questions on a frequent basis. Whenever possible, have students respond both in unison and individually.
3. **Ensure that all students participate.** Structure instructional tasks so that all students can be actively involved in responding to learning opportunities.
4. **Use signals and prompts to indicate transitions and other attentional shifts within the lesson.** Signals can ensure smooth movement between the various components of lessons.
5. **Be enthusiastic.** Students participate more when teachers are excited about what they are teaching. Ways to show enthusiasm involve a touch of the "ham" in all of us and can include humor, animation, and gimmicks.

Practice Sessions

1. **Reward correct student responses frequently.** Because students with learning and behavioral problems tend to have high rates of off-task behavior when assigned independent practice, teachers need to provide frequent reinforcement of appropriate behavior. Methods that can be used include (a) directed content-related praise; (b) tangible reinforcers such as pencils, books, and food; (c) generalized reinforcers such as tokens, points, and checkmarks; and (d) activity reinforcers such as computer time, library time, and free time.
2. **Develop clear and concise rules, procedures, and instructions for practice activities.** What students should do both during and after completion of practice activities and how they should do it should be highlighted as a classroom rule. Procedures for the correct method of obtaining assistance should also be clearly defined.
3. **Use interesting and motivating practice activities.** In addition to using traditional "ditto" pencil-and-paper seatwork activities, intersperse assignments that require the use of microcomputers, learning centers, language masters, and filmstrip or filmloop projectors.
4. **Have private study spaces available**. Highly distractible students may find a "private office" helpful in maintaining the sustained attention necessary for the completion of practice assignments.
5. **Use peer-mediated or cooperative-learning strategies.** Tutoring systems and cooperative-learning strategies are effective in increasing the number of opportunities that students have to respond as well as in improving the academic achievement of students with mild disabilities.

Source: Adapted from "Instructional time and the teacher educator: Training preservice and beginning teachers to use time effectively," by M. S. Rosenberg and K. Baker, 1985, *Teacher Educator, 20,* 195–207; and "Making every minute count: Academic time in LD classrooms," by R. Wilson and C. Wesson, 1986, *Learning Disabilities Focus, 2,* 3–19.

have forgotten or misplaced their own personal schedules, (2) substitute teachers who need to ensure that quality programming continues when regular personnel are absent, (3) building administrators who may need to know where a student should be during a particular instructional period, and (4) parents and other interested visitors who need a guide to classroom activities.

Name	Opening exercises 8:45–9:00	Period 1 9:00 9:35	Period 2 9:40 10:15	Period 3 10:20 10:55	11:00–11:20	Period 4 11:25 12:00	Period 5 12:05 12:40	Period 6 12:45 1:15	Period 7 1:20 1:55	Period 8 2:00 2:30	
Jane A.		Reading decoding group A Bk. group table w/Mrs. Fisk	M Art w/class 3-303 MTWTh Music Rm. 202 F	Math group A Fr. group table w/Mr. Ross	Recess	Lunch	Spelling w/ peer tutor MWF / PE–TTh	Reading compreh. group A Fr. table group w/Mr. Ross	Written expression group A w/Mr. Ross	Social studies MW: Science; TTh: Free time; F: all	Dismissal at 2:35
Hector B.		Speech Rm. 302 MWF w/ Mr. Brooks / PE–TTh	R Reading group C Fr. group table w/Mr. Ross	Math group A Fr. group table w/Mr. Ross	Recess	Lunch	Spelling w/ peer tutor TTh / Art Rm. 202 MWF	Reading compreh. group B Bk. table group w/Mrs. Fisk	Written expression group A w/Mr. Ross	Social studies MW: Science; TTh: Free time; F: all	
Dale C.		Reading decoding group A Bk. group table w/Mrs. Fisk	Math group B Bk. group table w/Mrs. Fisk	Spelling w/ peer tutor MWF / Art Rm. 202 TTh	Recess	Lunch	M Art w/ class 3-301 MTWTh Music Rm. 202 F	Reading compreh. group A Fr. table group w/Mr. Ross	Written expression group A w/Mr. Ross	Social studies MW: Science; TTh: Free time; F: all	
Louise Z.		Reading decoding group B Fr. group table w/Mr. Ross	Math group B Bk. group table w/Mrs. Fisk	Spelling w/ peer tutor MWF / PE–TTh	Recess	Lunch	M Art w/ class 3-301 MTWTh Music Rm. 202 F	Reading compreh. group B Bk. table group w/Mrs. Fisk	Written expression group B w/Mrs. Fisk	Social studies MW: Science; TTh: Free time; F: all	

Key: M Indicates a "mainstream" activity
R Indicates a "related service" activity

Teacher: Mr. Ross
Aide: Mrs. Fisk

FIGURE 3.7　Master Schedule for a Self-Contained Setting

Individual Schedule Cards. To personalize the master schedule, each student should receive a personal schedule card. The card should be small enough to fit into the student's pocket, purse, or wallet or, when necessary, to be attached to the student's desk. Activities related to the construction of student schedule cards should be started on the first day of a new school year.

Scheduling Students in Inclusive Settings. When scheduling activities for students receiving instruction in inclusive general education environments, individualized scheduling matrices that explicitly operationalize how critical aspects of the students' educational program is to be delivered are useful. Any type of scheduling matrix format can be used as long as educational goals, general class activities, educational supports, and necessary personnel are highlighted. Figure 3.8 is an example of such a matrix from Giangreco, Cloniger, and Iverson's (1993) COACH (Choosing Options and Accommodations for Children) program.

FIGURE 3.8 Scheduling Matrix

Source: From *Choosing options and accommodations for children*, by M. F. Giangreco, C. J. Cloninger, and V. S. Iverson, 1993, Baltimore: Paul H. Brookes. Copyright 1993 by Michael F. Giangreco. Reprinted with permission.

Grouping Students

Grouping students for effective instruction is not an easy task; the process tests teachers' diagnostic, organizational, management, and decision-making skills. In special education, the process of grouping is tied directly to individualization of instruction. Individualization is based on the assumption that the adaptation of instruction to the individual characteristics or needs of students results in desired rates of learning. Individualization, however, must not be mistaken for one-to-one instruction; instruction appropriate to a learner's individual needs can be and often is presented in small and large groups.

Although compelling arguments can be made for most grouping alternatives (e.g., within-class ability grouping, learning-style approaches, specific-skill grouping), two preconditions must be met before any such alternative is considered. First, the alternative must result in success and achievement for all members of the group. Second, no stigma or negative feelings must be associated with group membership. To meet both of these preconditions, student and beginning teachers should do the following:

- Make grouping decisions based on the principle that each student possesses specific strengths and weaknesses. It is possible that a student will be placed in an advanced group for writing instruction while requiring a slower pace for math, story problems, and measurement.
- Do not consider group assignment to be permanent. As students progress through their programs, factors influencing group success may require changing a group's

composition. Reassessment of student characteristics and, when necessary, reorganization of groups highlight the fact that the ever-changing individual characteristics of students need to be regularly monitored and addressed.

- Consider the necessity of grouping. Content areas such as science and social studies, which do not have the "building block" character of math or reading, may be best presented in large-group settings (Slavin, 2003).
- Program for the size of groups on the basis of student ability levels. For average or high-performing students, groups of 6 to 10 students may be appropriate. Low-performing students may require a group size of three to five, and very low achieving students may need tutorial groups consisting of no more than three students (Paine, 1982).

When grouping for instruction, students should be assigned to groups on the basis of (1) criterion-referenced or curriculum-based placement tests, (2) standardized tests, (3) previous performance observations, (4) typical rates of acquisition, and (5) learning-style preferences. Attention should be paid to students' actual knowledge and skills rather than to inappropriate behavior. Once students are grouped, instruction should be tailored to meet the needs of each group. This tailoring typically involves adjustments to the content level, the pace of the lesson, and the dominant mode of presentation. For example, one group in an elementary class of students with and without identified disabilities may require three lessons to master the math content that another group of students can acquire in just one lesson. Moreover, the group requiring the additional instructional time may need substantially more visual cues or an explicit strategy for acquiring the necessary content.

In an inclusive secondary setting, it may be necessary to periodically group students who require explicit instruction in how to develop and use internally generated mediators when processing content area instruction. As noted by Bulgren and Lenz (1995), these mediators are learning strategies that a student uses to process information on an independent level. Appropriately implemented grouping within the general education setting can allow students to acquire these important adaptations as well as the necessary curricular material. (More specifics of strategy instruction and methods for developing effective instruction are provided in Chapter 6.)

Educators generally recognize that students with special needs, regardless of grade level and placement type, can benefit from a wide variety of grouping arrangements. Friend and Bursuck (1996) have organized the menu of grouping alternatives under two major categories: teacher centered and peer mediated. As noted in the brief descriptions of alternatives in Table 3.2, teacher-centered groups are groups in which the classroom teacher is primarily responsible for instruction; as noted in Table 3.3, in peer-mediated instructional alternatives, students are primarily responsible for instruction.

FORMULATING MEANINGFUL AND RELEVANT RULES AND PROCEDURES

Organization and management, two factors critical to the successful functioning of classrooms, produce much apprehension among beginning teachers. Their concerns are well founded, for a teacher's ability to organize and manage the classroom can affect students' academic performance and social-emotional behavior and both teachers' and students' attitudes toward school. Teachers present their organizational and management expectations through rules and procedures. Rules define and operationalize a teacher's specific principles of acceptable behavior. Routines and procedures specify a protocol of behaviors necessary for the appropriate completion of an activity, task, or classroom operation.

TABLE 3.2 Teacher-Centered Grouping Alternatives

Grouping Method	Description	Advantages	Disadvantages	Sources
Whole Class	Students spend class time being instructed by the teacher.	• Students less likely to go off task • Special-needs students not singled out • Less time spent transitioning/giving directions • More time for assessment and explanation	• Diverse needs of students may not be addressed	Friend & Bursuck (1996) Mason & Good (1993)
Small Group: Same Skill	Students are divided into groups on the basis of their ability to perform a skill. Teacher instructs each group separately.	• Overall academic achievement tends to increase • Diverse abilities can be addressed • Stimulation for high-ability students	• Low-performing students may be stigmatized • Increased time needed for transitioning/giving directions • Instruction may not be delivered equitably	Gamoran (1992) Hooper (1992) Kamps, Walker, Maher, & Rotholz (1992) Mason & Good (1993)
Small Group: Mixed Skill	Students are divided into groups randomly. Teacher instructs each group separately.	• Students observe positive peer role models • Opportunity for individualized instruction • Special-needs students not singled out	• Acceleration of high-ability students slowed	Friend & Bursuck (1996) Mason & Good (1993)
One-to-One	Students work one-to-one with teacher or computer. Students proceed at their own pace on their own ability level.	• Appropriate for students' ability level and pace • Students receive individualized attention • Early one-to-one interventions can prevent future academic failure	• Extensive one-to-one instruction allows less overall instructional time for everyone • Unattended students may go off task • Students encounter fewer peer models • Extensive one-to-one instruction is expensive	Kamps, Walker, Maher, & Rotholz (1992) Slavin (1993) Wasik & Slavin (1993)

The need for clear and concise rules and procedures for students with mild disabilities cannot be overstated. As a result of their unique learning and behavioral disabilities, these students tend to have difficulty in learning and/or complying with many of the more obvious standards of conduct typical of schools and classrooms.

In Chapter 8, you will see how rules and procedures fit into a comprehensive behavioral management system. Rules and procedures, however, also serve as discriminative stimuli, or antecedents, of appropriate situation-specific behavior. When used correctly, rules and procedures become the overt models and prompts for desired student (and teacher) behavior. They remind and motivate students to meet the standards of a specific learning environment. Finally, classroom rules and procedures, when used

TABLE 3.3 **Peer-Mediated Grouping Alternatives**

Grouping Method	Description	Advantages	Disadvantages	Sources
Peer Tutoring	Pairs of students, at the same grade level or at different grade levels, instruct one another.	• Students often increase in skill performance • Students often increase their social skills • General education students grow in their acceptance of special-needs students	• Considerable time commitment is required to ensure properly trained tutors • Considerable time commitment is required to monitor and evaluate tutoring	Ezell, Kohler, & Strain (1994) Garcia-Vazquez & Ehly (1992) Miller, Kohler, Ezell, Hoel, & Strain (1993)
Classwide Peer Tutoring	Students are divided into two teams and assigned to tutoring pairs, in which tutor and tutee roles rotate; the two teams compete against each other for points.	• Students increase skills in subject areas • At-risk students increase performance • Individual differences are addressed	• Unattended students may go off task • Considerable time commitment is required to monitor and evaluate pairs' progress	Maheady, Mallette, & Harper (1991) Simmons, Fuchs, Fuchs Mathes, & Hodge (1995)
Cooperative Learning	Students work in small mixed-ability groups, each group with a shared learning goal.	• Students learn social and work-related skills • Student self-esteem and motivation may increase as students learn their strengths in mixed-ability setting	• Teacher may expend much energy trying to force cooperation between students of widely varying abilities • Gifted students may be forced to act as task-masters to peers less gifted or else to accept a lower grade	Fenton (1992) Jules (1992) Manning & Lucking (1991) Mills & Tangherlini (1992) Tomlinson (1994)

in a positive context, can serve as specific behavioral targets to which teachers can direct reinforcers such as attention, praise, and tokens. The success of rules and procedures depends on (1) how they are introduced and presented to students and (2) how teachers plan for maintaining the integrity of their stated expectations.

Introducing Rules and Procedures

Classroom rules and procedures should not be designed in a quick or frivolous manner. Considerable forethought and troubleshooting are necessary to ensure that stated procedures match a particular school's and teacher's expectations for student behavior. The following guidelines, adapted from a number of sources (Evertson et al., 1984; Paine et al., 1983; Rosenberg, 1986; Rosenberg & Jackman, 2003; Strain & Sainato, 1987), can assist developing and beginning teachers in preparing and introducing rules and procedures.

- Be aware of school district policies. Have a working knowledge of the expectations for all students within the local education agency (LEA). Design classroom rules and procedures to be congruent with the prevailing expectations.
- Identify the specific behaviors expected of students. Reconstruct these expectations into overt, behavioral, and measurable pinpoints. Ensure that teachers and students will be able to agree on whether such expectations are met.

- The first order of business on the first day of school should be to discuss and teach classroom rules and procedures. Because rules and procedures govern daily classroom activities and events for the entire school year, it is important that they be in place and reinforced as soon as possible.
- Present a solid explanation of why classrooms need well-defined rules and procedures. Because a teacher's presentation of the need for structure can influence student compliance, discussions about rules and procedures should be conducted in a patient, businesslike, and sincere fashion.
- Involve students in the development of the rules and procedures. Solicit opinions as to what the consequences should be for both compliance and noncompliance. If students have a sense of ownership of the classroom system, they will feel a greater sense of allegiance to the rules and procedures identified.
- Keep the number of rules and procedures that students need to follow small, and for each rule generated, keep the wording simple and to the point. Students often view stated rules and procedures literally, and verbiage should be avoided. When specifying procedures, such as what a student should do after completing a seatwork assignment, an easy-to-follow, step-by-step sequence of behaviors is most effective.
- Phrase rules and procedures positively rather than negatively. Instead of accentuating what students should not do (e.g., "Do not call out during lessons"), highlight appropriate behaviors that students should engage in regularly (e.g., "Raise your hand if you wish to get the teacher's attention").

Maintaining the Integrity of Rules and Procedures

Unfortunately, the potency of classroom rules and procedures seems to diminish as the school year progresses. Factors as diverse as lapses in students' memories and lack of consistency in providing consequences for rule and procedure compliance and noncompliance account for this loss of effectiveness. The following guidelines, adapted from a number of sources (Evertson et al., 1984; Paine et al., 1983; Rosenberg & Jackman, 2003), will assist in promoting long-term compliance with the stated behavioral expectations.

- Keep rules posted where all students can see them. Prominently displayed rules and procedures can be powerful cues for appropriate student behavior and can prompt busy teachers to provide consequences for student compliance and noncompliance on a regular basis.
- Ensure different rules for various situations. One set of rules will not be appropriate for the range and variety of activities typical of most special education classrooms. For example, during highly structured instructional activities, such as directed reading and math lessons, rules and procedures should reflect the need for quiet, order, and a high degree of engagement in the task. In contrast, less-ordered activities, such as art and discussions or debates of citizenship issues, require a different, more relaxed set of rules.
- Teach and provide practice with all rules. Both overall classroom rules and activity-specific rules need to be taught and reviewed just like any other material that teachers want students to acquire. Lessons scheduled early in the school year can ensure rapid acquisition of the various rules and procedures of the classroom; brief reviews of rules prior to lessons can remind students of the expectations for that specific lesson. The potency of brief reviews of rules should not be underestimated. Rosenberg (1986) found that brief reviews (one to two minutes) of lesson-specific rules just prior to instruction increased time-on-task rates and the number of opportunities to respond.
- Model classroom procedures. Most classroom procedures, whether for the correct way to behave during a fire drill or to line up for lunch, involve a complex series of

behaviors. To ensure that students learn the correct way to comply with standard classroom procedures, teachers should (1) model or demonstrate how specific procedures are to be performed, (2) provide opportunities for guided practice in the initial performance of the procedures, (3) reinforce correct performance of the procedures, and (4) provide corrective feedback immediately if the procedures are not followed.

• Self-monitor performance with the documented rules and procedures. Two major reasons for the lack of maintenance in classroom organization and management systems is failure of the teacher to be consistent in following class procedures and the lack of regular enforcement of the rules. To promote high levels of consistency in the administration of classroom management systems built on a foundation of stated rules and procedures, teachers should (1) regularly sample, through peer observation or self-recording, their performance in providing consequences for rule and procedure compliance and noncompliance and (2) develop a personalized system to prompt regular and consistent enforcement of the class rules.

Developing Routines and Procedures

Student attention to task is often lost when procedures for successfully completing recurring classroom routines are not followed. The routines and procedures of specific schools and classrooms will vary according to the ages and developmental levels of the students. It is clear, however, that explicit and consistent routines and procedures are tools that help teachers orchestrate their classrooms with greater efficiency and effectiveness. Successful teachers know how to facilitate the completion of routine tasks such as morning arrival, dismissal from class, transitions to and from the cafeteria, and homework assignment checking. They do this by having clear and explicit procedures that (1) guide the successful completion of the task and (2) preclude the negative impact that can result from common, yet annoying, events that often interrupt the instructional flow of the classroom. These procedures are taught and practiced throughout the school year, and positive supports (e.g., self-monitoring procedures, buddy systems) are provided to assist those students who have trouble following the required steps. Figure 3.9 lists three typically troubling events, along with sample procedures designed to minimize disruptions.

COORDINATING RESOURCES

The final category of guidelines related to the successful organization of special education classrooms involves the coordination of the resources and personnel available to teachers. Developing and beginning teachers who create or coordinate several key instructional resources and who use the strengths of other school personnel will find that much of the time, they typically spend searching for or organizing materials and information can be filled with the more relevant activities of teaching or lesson planning.

Pause and Reflect About the Profession 3.2

List the explicit rules and procedures that are in effect in your classroom setting. In your opinion, do these rules and procedures promote a sense of organization and management in the classroom? Do these rules and procedures correspond to best practices for developing and implementing rules, routines, and procedures? What additions or suggestions can you offer to improve the quality and long-term effectiveness of these behavioral standards?

Procedures for Morning Arrival
- Check if it is an "A" or "B" schedule day
- Go directly to your locker
- Take all supplies needed for your morning classes
- Put hats and other personal items in your locker
- If you eat breakfast in school, report directly to the cafeteria
- Report directly to homeroom by the warning bell
- Upon arrival to homeroom, complete your morning log
- Listen quietly to morning announcements

Cafeteria Procedures
- Walk quietly when entering the cafeteria
- Remain seated until the teacher invites you to proceed to the lunch line
- Use quiet voices when speaking to your friends
- Remain seated at your table until the teacher signals for you to dispose of trash
- Remain in your seat until dismissed

Arrival to and Dismissal from Class
- Be seated when bell rings and begin working on warm-up
- After completing warm-up, wait quietly for teacher to begin
- The teacher directs preparation for dismissal
- When given the signal, clean up your workspace and pack your bookbag
- When bell rings, wait for teacher to dismiss the class
- Walk safely, quickly, and quietly to your next class

FIGURE 3.9   Procedures from a Typical Middle School Program

Five types of coordinating activities are considered: (1) using the Individualized Education Program (IEP) as a living and working document, (2) keeping files and materials organized and accessible, (3) using technology-based resources appropriately, (4) preparing a substitute teacher's packet, and (5) being aware of school- and community-based support services. Using the strengths of other personnel in the school environment is discussed in later chapters.

Using the IEP as a Living and Working Document

In most programs that prepare individuals to teach students with disabilities, considerable time is devoted to individualized education programs. As will be noted in Chapter 7, developing teachers require considerable practice in structuring the IEP document to ensure that it meets local, state, and federal standards. Sometimes overlooked in the activities related to technical and legal compliance is the notion that students' IEPs should be treated as working documents related directly to the ongoing instructional activities of the classroom.

Treating the IEP as a living and working document begins at the time of its preparation. When writing the document, the annual goals and short-term objectives should be treated as the foundation for the lessons that will be presented to students. When initially completed, IEPs should be placed in an accessible area close to the teacher's desk. An IEP should be monitored frequently regarding (1) the status of the goals and objectives listed and (2) the specific activities or instructional modifications necessary for successful attainment of the listed goals and objectives. When the teacher is communicating with parents or other professionals involved in the education of a student, the IEP should be used as the definitive record by which educational progress is measured and recorded.

Keeping Files and Materials Organized and Accessible

The time devoted to keeping files and resource material organized and accessible can pay rich dividends throughout a school year and, in many cases, a teacher's full career. A systematic filing system can save time and stress by providing quick and easy access to student records, instructional materials, and test protocols. Student records should be close to the teacher's desk; in case of emergencies, it is essential to have parents' or guardians' addresses, places of employment, and telephone numbers. Curricular materials can be filed according to subject areas, specific skills, or instructional objectives. McCoy and Prehm (1987) recommend that teachers file their material by sequenced instructional objectives within broad content categories. Material for each objective is coded according to a task-analytic hierarchy related to skill acquisition and the specific learning adaptations that each activity provides. Time devoted to ordering new instructional materials also can be saved if catalogs for instructional materials are filed according to this same system.

Using Technology-Based Resources Appropriately

In addition to the countless benefits associated with "information on demand" technologies, our rapid ascent into the use of computer and Internet-based materials presents all educators with a number of challenges. In the new millennium, our issues are no longer exclusively concerned with access; it is likely that most beginning teachers and their students know how to operate a computer and retrieve information from a range of commercially available search engines. Today, it is the ethical and appropriate use of the computer and the Internet that is critical.

Most school districts have practices and policies that govern how technologies are to be used by teachers, administrators, and students. For example, most school districts install software that restricts access to sexually explicit web sites, images of violence and drug use, and textual material that uses profanity and advocates racial/religious intolerance as well as to unmoderated and unpredictable chat rooms.

Still, student and beginning teachers should design a set of understandable policies and procedures involving the use of their classroom-based technologies and model ethical use of technology-based materials. Policies and procedures regarding the use of computers should state that

- modification of the system without permission and supervision is not permitted
- only programs authorized for student use are allowed
- confidentiality is essential and accessing another's data or work is not permitted
- downloading copyrighted material is not permitted
- e-mails must have user identifications (but not personal information) and objectionable content and language are forbidden

Moreover, teachers should model appropriate conduct regarding the downloading, transmission, and copying of electronic materials (Brownell, Youngs, & Metzger, 1999). This starts with knowing how to effectively search for and evaluate web-based materials as well as with employing ethical, fair-use practices when encountering copyrighted materials.

Preparing a Substitute Teacher's Packet

Under the best conditions, the job of substitute teacher is difficult. Even the best students behave as if the standards are relaxed when the regular teacher is absent. In special education settings, reports of disarray and confusion by substitute teachers are not uncommon. Consequently, many school districts have found it difficult to arrange for substitute teachers to fill in for ailing special education teachers.

TABLE 3.4   Components of a Substitute Teacher's Packet

Major Areas	Specific Information to be Included
Policy information	Floor plan or map of school Names of individuals to contact in case of emergencies, problems, or questions Entry, lunch, recess, and discussion policies and procedures Emergency and fire drill procedures
Schedules	Master schedule of student activities Teacher's duty schedule (e.g., lunch, recess) Schedules of parent volunteers, aides, peer tutors, and related service personnel
Specific student information	Seating chart and description of students Medication needs of students Names, addresses, and phone numbers of students' parents or guardians
Classroom procedural information	Attendance, charting, and record-keeping procedures Brief description of classroom management program Location of instructional materials and equipment Free-time activities
Daily plans	Location of students' IEPs Location of and guide to teacher planbook or daily lesson plans
Alternative activities	Bag of tricks containing fun and motivating student activities Structured recess plans

Source: Adapted from "Substitute teachers can do more than just keep the lid on," by J. M. Platt, 1987, *Teaching Exceptional Children, 19*(2), 28–31.

All student and beginning teachers should plan ahead for the occasional need of a substitute teacher. Because there is no way to know for certain when sickness or emergencies will strike, a generic substitute teacher packet should be prepared at the beginning of the school year. The packet should contain all the information needed to teach and manage the students left in the substitute teacher's charge. Platt (1987) has recommended that information be provided in six broad areas: policy information, schedules, specific student information, classroom procedural information, daily plans, and alternative activities. These six areas are further defined in Table 3.4.

Being Aware of School- and Community-Based Support Services

Students with mild to moderate disabilities require the coordinated efforts of a team of professionals. Fortunately, most schools have a cadre of support personnel who can and do assist as part of their typical responsibilities. For example, it is not uncommon for counseling and guidance personnel to assist with family outreach services or for the school psychologist to offer social skills instruction groups. Student and beginning teachers should find out about all the services available in their buildings and school districts and know the procedures to access needed services.

Unfortunately, school-based personnel are not nearly as knowledgeable about valuable community-based resources as they should be. Still, it has become increasingly clear that students with disabilities, particularly those with sustained and pervasive emotional or behavioral problems, require integrated and comprehensive services that involve education, mental health, social work, and family preservation personnel. It is critical that all of these human service professionals communicate and act in concert to meet the variety and multiplicity of needs presented by students and their families. The Child and Adolescent Service System Program (CASSP) (National Institute of Mental Health, 1990; Stroul & Friedman, 1986) provides a framework for understanding the interrelatedness of services within an integrated system of care. As implied by the

FIGURE 3.10 Components of an Integrated System of Care

overlapping circles in Figure 3.10, interagency communication and cooperation are necessary if professionals are to deliver integrated services for students and their families.

Preservice and beginning teachers should be aware of the range of services offered in their community and who in their school or district is responsible for agency access. Moreover, these teachers should be prepared to consult with and serve as liaisons among the many professionals involved in the lives of their students. Although specific liaison activities can vary from setting to setting, it is important for preservice and beginning teachers to (1) respect the belief systems and goals held by those in the other professions, (2) have a nonterritorial view of service provision, (3) share both the responsibilities and the rewards for providing services, and (4) recognize that interagency collaborations are developmental in nature and often require time and work to reach successful outcomes (Coleman, 1996; Johnson, Zorn, Tam, LaMontagne, & Johnson, 2003).

 ## SUMMARY

We conclude this chapter with the same message with which we started: To manage busy classrooms successfully, special educators must be organized. In this chapter, we provided practical suggestions for improving the organization of classrooms serving students with learning and behavioral problems. A theme that emerged throughout the chapter is that the organization required for successful teaching can be acquired, practiced, and mastered.

The first topic discussed was the challenging task of arranging the physical environment. Five interrelated preinstructional activities pertaining to classroom design were outlined, and specific illustrations of the physical layout of special education environments were provided. Second, the management of instructional time was considered. The different levels of instructional time were operationally defined, and both generic and lesson-specific strategies were presented for using instructional time effectively and efficiently. Third, the logistically complex tasks of scheduling classroom activities and grouping students were discussed. Strategies for organizing the school day into manageable segments were reviewed, and guidelines for the grouping of students were examined. Fourth, the formulation and maintenance of meaningful and relevant classroom rules and procedures were examined.

The chapter concluded with ideas related to the coordination of resources. Included were suggestions regarding IEP use, the organization of files and materials, the appropriate use of technology, the preparation of a substitute teacher's packet, and the development of a resource list of school- and community-based resources that can serve students and their families.

ACTIVITIES TO EXTEND YOUR KNOWLEDGE

1. Generate a series of strategies that you can use to organize your classroom environment. If you were to develop a checklist of things to consider in your "organizational strategy," which actions and items would you put toward the top of your priority list? What supports do you think you would need in order to maintain your level of organization?

2. What is the best way to group students? How children are grouped for instruction continues to be a most contentious issue. Is it best for high-achieving students to be grouped heterogeneously—that is, with low-achieving students or students with disabilities? Or should students be grouped homogeneously, so that they have similar abilities and instructional needs? What available instructional approaches (e.g., cooperative learning, differentiated instruction) can guide teachers in deciding how to best group students for instruction? What does the available research tell educators about these approaches? How do these general approaches address the special needs of students with mild to moderate disabilities?

3. Create your own resource manual of school- and community-based resources. In the first section of this manual, list the in-school and in-district personnel who can assist you in providing services to your students. Be sure to include each person's name, title, area of responsibility, telephone number, and e-mail address. In a separate section, list the available community services that may be of use to your students and their families. You may also wish to list organizations and support groups that may be helpful to your students and their families. Keep these resources handy, especially when you have parent conferences. In some instances, parents are searching for support mechanisms to cope with or address many of the same issues that teachers face in school.

4. With several of your colleagues, create a meaningful substitute teacher's packet. What information and items should be included in this packet? How can you ensure that the days you are absent will remain productive for your students?

POINT AND CLICK ABOUT THE PROFESSION

These web sites have information and links to additional information related to how one can best set up for effective instruction.

Mid-continent Research for Education and Learning
www.mcrel.org

Survival Guide for New Teachers
www.ed.gov/pubs/survivalguide

ERIC Digests
www.ed.gov/databases/ERIC_Digests/index

School Psychology Resources Online
www.schoolpsychology.net

Center for Effective Collaboration and Practice
www.air-dc.org/cecp

Teacher Expectations and Student Achievement
education.indiana.edu/cas/tt/v2i2/tesa.html

Teachers Discuss
oeri3.ed.gov:8000/Teachers

Ideas at Work
www.ed.gov/pubs/ideasatwork

REFERENCES

Bleichman, E. A. (1985). *Solving child behavior problems at home and at school.* Champaign, IL: Research Press.

Brownell, G., Youngs, C., & Metzger, J. (1999). *A PC for the teacher.* Belmont, CA: Wadsworth.

Bulgren, J., & Lenz, B. K. (1995). Strategic instruction in the content areas. In D. D. Deshler, E. S. Ellis, & B. K. Lenz (Eds.), *Teaching adolescents with learning disabilities* (pp. 409–473). Denver: Love.

Coleman, M. C. (1996). *Emotional and behavioral disorders: Theory and practice.* Needham Heights, MA: Allyn & Bacon.

Doyle, W. (1980). *Classroom management.* West Lafayette, IN: Kappa Delta Pi.

Evertson, C. M., Emmer, E. T., Clements, B. S., Sanford, J. P., & Worsham, M. E. (1984). *Classroom management for elementary teachers.* Upper Saddle River, NJ: Prentice Hall.

Ezell, H., Kohler, F., & Strain, P. (1994). A program description and evaluation of academic peer tutoring for reading skills of children with special needs. *Education and Treatment of Children, 17,* 52–67.

Fenton, C. A. (1992). Cooperative learning: A view from the inside. *Contemporary Education, 63,* 207–209.

Friend, M., & Bursuck, W. (1996). *Including students with special needs.* Needham Heights, MA: Allyn & Bacon.

Gamoran, A. (1992). Is ability grouping equitable? *Educational Leadership, 50,* 11–17.

Garcia-Vazquez, E., & Ehly, S. (1992). Peer tutoring effects on students who are not perceived as socially accepted. *Psychology in the Schools, 29,* 256–266.

Giangreco, M. F., Cloninger, G. J., & Iverson, V. S. (1993). *Choosing options and accommodations for children.* Baltimore: Paul H. Brookes.

Hooper, S. (1992). Effects of peer interaction during computer-based mathematics instruction. *Journal of Educational Research, 85,* 180–189.

Johnson, L. J., Zorn, D., Tam, B. K. Y., LaMontagne, M., & Johnson, S. A. (2003). Stakeholders' views of factors that impact successful interagency collaboration. *Exceptional Children, 69,* 195–209.

Jules, V. (1992). Cooperative learning: Student perceptions of the changing structure of learning. *Contemporary Education, 63,* 191–194.

Kamps, D., Walker, D., Maher, J., & Rotholz, D. (1992). Academic and environmental effects of small-group arrangements for students with autism and other developmental disabilities. *Journal of Autism and Developmental Disorders, 22,* 277–293.

Maheady, L., Mallette, B., & Harper, G. (1991). Accommodating cultural, linguistic, and academic diversity: Some peer-mediated instructional options. *Preventing School Failure, 36,* 28–31.

Manning, L., & Lucking, R. (1991). The what, why, and how of cooperative learning. *Social Studies, 82,* 120–124.

Mason, D., & Good, T. (1993). Effects of two-group and whole-class teaching on regrouped elementary students' mathematics achievement. *American Educational Research Journal, 30,* 328–360.

McCoy, K. M., & Prehm, H. J. (1987). *Teaching mainstreamed students: Methods and techniques.* Denver: Love.

Miller, L., Kohler, F., Ezell, H., Hoel, K., & Strain, P. (1993). Winning with peer tutoring: A teacher's guide. *Preventing School Failure, 37,* 14–18.

Mills, C., & Tangherlini, A. (1992). Finding an optimal match: Another look at ability grouping and cooperative learning. *Equity and Excellence, 25,* 205–208.

National Institute of Mental Health. (1990). *National plan for research on child and adolescent mental disorders.* Rockville, MD: Author.

Paine, S. C. (1982). Setting up for instruction. *Association for Direct Instruction News, 2,* 8–9.

Paine, S. C., Radicci, J., Rosellini, L. C., Deutchman, L., & Darch, C. R. (1983). *Structuring your classroom for academic success.* Champaign, IL: Research Press.

Platt, J. M. (1987). Substitute teachers can do more than just keep the lid on. *Teaching Exceptional Children, 19* (2), 28–31.

Rosenberg, M. S. (1986). Maximizing the effectiveness of structured management programs: Implementing rule-review procedures with disruptive and distractible students. *Behavioral Disorders, 11*, 239–248.

Rosenberg, M. S., & Baker, K. (1985). Instructional time and the teacher educator: Training preservice and beginning teachers to use time effectively. *Teacher Educator, 20*, 195–207.

Rosenberg, M. S., & Jackman, L. A. (2003). Development, implementation, and sustainability of comprehensive school-wide management systems. *Intervention in School and Clinic, 39*, 10–21.

Rosenkoetter, S. E., & Fowler, S. A. (1986). Teaching mainstreamed children to manage daily transitions. *Teaching Exceptional Children, 19* (1), 20–23.

Simmons, D., Fuchs, L., Fuchs, D., Mathes, P., & Hodge, J. (1995). Effects of explicit teaching and peer tutoring on the reading achievement of learning disabled and low-performing students in regular classrooms. *Elementary School Journal, 95*, 387–408.

Slavin, R. E. (1993). Preventing early school failure: What works? *Educational Leadership, 50*, 10–18.

Slavin, R. E. (2003). *Education psychology: Theory into practice.* Upper Saddle River, NJ: Prentice Hall.

Strain, P. S., & Sainato, D. M. (1987). Preventive discipline in early childhood. *Teaching Exceptional Children, 19* (4), 26–30.

Stroul, B. A., & Friedman, R. M. (1986). *A system of care for severely emotionally disturbed children and youth.* Washington, DC: Georgetown University, CASSP Technical Assistance Center.

Tomlinson, C. A. (1994). Gifted learners: The boomerang kids of middle school? *Roeper Review, 16*, 177–182.

Wasik, B., & Slavin, R. (1993). Preventing early school failure with one-to-one tutoring: A review of five programs. *Reuling Research Quarterly, 70*, 178–200.

Wilson, R., & Wesson, C. (1986). Making every minute count: Academic time in LD classrooms. *Learning Disabilities Focus, 2*, 3–19.

## CHAPTER 4

Classroom Assessment Practices for Instruction

Stephanie L. Carpenter and Margaret E. King-Sears

Chapter Outline

In this chapter, we will

- discuss the importance of classroom assessment

- identify the purposes of classroom assessment and suggest activities that address student performance and instructional design in relation to each purpose

- present guiding/overarching principles of assessment that should characterize all classroom assessments

- describe approaches to classroom assessment and examine ways that different approaches may be

used concurrently to provide different views of student performance

- outline a step-by-step framework (APPLY) for developing classroom assessments that both fulfill the purposes of classroom assessment and adhere to the guiding principles

- examine the relationship between assessments and grade assignment for student performance

CASE STUDY

Ms. Moore is a beginning special educator with responsibilities for teaching students with mild to moderate disabilities in a variety of content areas (e.g., science, mathematics, English) across two grades (sixth and seventh grades). Service delivery models include coteaching with general educators four periods per day, for which she travels around the school, and resource room instruction, for which the students with disabilities travel to her classroom for more intensive and specialized instruction.

It is the beginning of the school year. Ms. Moore is overwhelmed with the idea that she needs to assess who is where in which curriculum, in addition to determining how each student's Individualized Education Program (IEP) content will be taught both in content area classes (coteaching) and in the resource room setting. She realizes that she must use her organizational skills to develop and use assessments that will tell her who needs what instruction. She also realizes that she cannot do this alone; it is too much! She begins questioning other teachers about how they assess students.

One of the first teachers she talks with is Mr. Thomas, the sixth-grade social studies teacher, because he has about six IEP students in the class they will be coteaching. Mr. Thomas already has pretests developed for each grading period.

The next person she talks with is Ms. Bing, who has been teaching special education in middle schools for years. Ms. Bing shares her curriculum-based assessment (CBA) probes and graphs, scoring rubrics, and inventories specific to IEPs from previous students and related to middle school curriculum content.

Ms. Moore quickly begins working with Mr. Thomas to use his pretest results for the first grading period to determine what the students with IEPs already know and what areas she could focus on (such as vocabulary development) rather immediately with those students. Interestingly, Mr. Thomas finds that students without IEPs could also benefit from some of the social studies vocabulary instruction methods that Ms. Moore is designing.

Ms. Bing has CBAs for social studies vocabulary focusing on two skills. One CBA is a one-minute probe for pronouncing the vocabulary terms. This will help for word identification, which is a skill identified on students' IEPs anyway. Another CBA focuses on defining the vocabulary terms. Ms. Moore thinks this could be helpful for increasing students' comprehension skills as well because students need to understand what the terms mean in order to understand the social studies reading passages. Her concern, however, is that the text's reading level is so high and reading at grade level is something students had difficulty with. She discusses this with Mr. Thomas, who explains that he presents new content using varied methods, such as illustrations, graphic organizers, and small-group discussions, that he has found work well for many students in his classes.

Moreover, Mr. Thomas uses a variety of assessment techniques that provide students choices when showing what they know from the social studies content. For each unit, Mr. Thomas uses the same scoring rubric (he is firm—he always needs to include a scoring rubric no matter what type of project a student chooses to do), but students choose different ways to show mastery. These choices might include writing a research paper, designing a video with role-plays, audiotaping descriptions of cause-and-effect situations, developing a timeline with important events, and creating an individually designed project, enabling students to use their imaginations and strengths to show what they know.

Ms. Moore has a lot of work to do this school year just to develop and use classroom-based assessments for the students with disabilities she's teaching. But she is glad to know she has some colleagues like Mr. Thomas and Ms. Bing to work with. She can tell already that she will get some good ideas from them. More important, she really likes how their assessment techniques overlap so well with students' IEP content. There's more work to do, but at least she is not alone.

*A*ccountability for instructional programs and services for students with and without disabilities is a focus at all levels of education. Globally, students in the United States are being compared with students in other countries. Nationally, statewide assessment practices yield results that allow comparison with students in other states as well as comparison of students within different counties or districts in that state. No Child Left Behind (NCLB) contains many requirements for each state to improve accountability, ensure academic proficiency, and decrease achievement gaps for all students. Locally, administrators are concerned about how well students in their schools are doing compared with students in other schools. In the classroom, educators are focused on how each student is progressing within the local school curriculum.

For students with mild to moderate disabilities, progress is monitored on goals and objectives specified on their IEPs. Moreover, the Individuals with Disabilities Education Act (IDEA) requires students with disabilities to participate in their state- or districtwide assessment of student achievement with no modifications or with individualized modifications as noted on their IEPs. If the state/district assessment is not appropriate for a student with mild to moderate disabilities, then the IEP must note why that assessment is not appropriate and how the student will be assessed. Beginning teachers should consult their local and state guidelines to clarify how the state/district assessments are conducted and what assessment modifications are appropriate based on students' IEPs as well as what the criteria are for excluding a student from the state/district assessment and determining what alternative assessment will be used for that student.

Regardless of the level of accountability, the focus is on assessments that accurately portray how well students are progressing in critical curriculum areas. In the midst of pressures from different levels about accountability for students' progress, challenges facing developing teachers include using formal assessment reports and the IEP to plan instruction, deciding what to teach immediately, and linking assessment to both the IEP and the instruction (curriculum and methods). Beginning and developing teachers may find that their immediate concerns are as follows:

- What do I teach these particular students, starting tomorrow?
- How long should I spend on each area of instruction?
- How will I know whether students have mastered the required competencies?
- What should I do if students have not mastered the required competencies?
- What should I do if students seem to be making only minimal progress?
- What do I do when students seem to forget what they learned or don't continue to use new skills consistently in a variety of situations?
- How do I know what to teach next?

Although these questions will be addressed throughout this text, the answer to each begins with classroom assessments.

Beginning and developing teachers can demonstrate accountability by responding proactively and reactively to the assessment of students with mild to moderate disabilities in special and general education classrooms. Proactively, educators plan classroom assessments that effectively monitor both their students' response to instruction and their students' progress toward IEP goals and objectives. Reactively, educators make sound decisions about what to teach and how to teach on the basis of assessment results. In this chapter, we examine aspects of classroom assessment that will assist developing teachers in using classroom assessments proactively and reactively, including (1) purposes for assessment as related to the IEP and instruction, (2) overarching principles that characterize meaningful classroom assessments, (3) various approaches to assessing students' performance competencies, (4) a framework for developing classroom assessments, and (5) the relationship between classroom assessments and grading practices.

PURPOSES FOR CLASSROOM ASSESSMENT

Beginning teachers who understand the purposes of assessment are better prepared to develop and use assessments that provide functional, reliable, and valid information. The type of assessment administered is related to the purpose of assessment. Salvia and Ysseldyke (1991) note the differences between norm-referenced tests and criterion-referenced tests. Norm-referenced tests measure a student's performance in relation to the performance of his or her peers. Eligibility teams often use norm-referenced tests to determine the presence of a disability and whether a student qualifies for special education services. Criterion-referenced tests measure a student's performance in terms of absolute mastery of particular skills. Classroom teachers use criterion-referenced tests to help in planning instructional programs and monitoring students' mastery of skills. These "classroom" assessments serve four primary purposes related to planning instruction and documenting students' progress: (1) to identify students' entry-level competencies, (2) to monitor students' performance during instruction, (3) to determine students' mastery of competencies at the conclusion of instruction, and (4) to monitor students' maintenance and generalization of competencies. Developing and beginning teachers can engage in a series of activities to accomplish these purposes with their students with mild to moderate disabilities.

Identify Students' Entry-Level Competencies

The first step in classroom assessment is to identify students' entry-level competencies in order to plan for instruction. The domain of instruction must be known before students' current competencies can be assessed and before purposeful instructional planning can occur. Identification of students' entry-level skills is a step frequently overlooked in descriptions of classroom assessment and may cause confusion for beginning teachers. They may find that they are expected to teach, and that students are expected to learn, skills and content that are not specified on the IEP but that are encountered by students during the school day. The IDEA requires the IEP team to address how the student's disability impacts involvement and progress in the general education curriculum. As a result, beginning teachers must familiarize themselves with the general education curriculum and ensure that instructional content (whether the special educator delivers that content in a self-contained classroom or resource setting or via coteaching with the general educator) and, consequently, assessment include material general education curriculum. The challenge for developing educators is to integrate several sources of information, including the general education curriculum, in order to determine instructional domains or units and then to assess students' current performance so they have a basis for planning units of instruction (see Chapter 5 for detailed information on planning instruction).

The domain or content area that will be targeted for instruction is determined by considering a variety of information sources. Students with disabilities have IEPs with annual measurable goals that indicate domains for instruction and short-term objectives or benchmarks that indicate what students will do. Measurable IEP goals can be written in a variety of ways; beginning teachers should follow their school system's format, as the style and wording can vary within and across states.

Two goal formats are described here. The first format contains five components that summarize expectations for student performance within given domains of instruction (see Table 4.1 for examples of this format for goal statements):

1. Direction of the desired gain (e.g., increase, decrease, maintain)

2. Deficit area from which the student is operating (e.g., reading, written language, social skills)

TABLE 4.1 Examples of Exemplary Goal Statements from IEPs

Direction	Deficit Area	Starting Point	Ending Point	Resource
Increase	reading skills	from the third-grade level as measured by Woodcock Reading Mastery test	to the fourth-grade level as measured by Woodcock Reading Mastery test	using direct instruction teaching methods.
Decrease	inappropriate behaviors	from an average of five tantrums per day	to appropriately dealing with frustrating situations without a tantrum	using functional analysis and social skills training.
Increase tion	reading skills	from reading 7 words per minute from a fourth-grade reading list	to reading 90 words per minute from a fourth-grade reading list	using peer tutoring and direct instruc- techniques.
Increase	task completion	from turning in no homework or classroom assign- ments per week	to turning in all assignments	using self- management techniques.

3. Starting point for instruction (typically similar to the student's present level of performance)

4. Ending point for instruction (level of performance the student is expected to attain in a year)

5. Resources (instructional methods or techniques from which the student is most likely to benefit, given the student's individual learning characteristics)

The second format for writing measurable annual goals involves using verbs that are observable, a measurement guide, a timeline, and information that clearly references the general education curriculum when appropriate: "By the end of the school year, Jeremy will be able to complete 85% of multiplication and division problems correctly on the district math test . . ." (p. 135).

When IEP goals are vague (e.g., increase written language) or do not contain measurable information (e.g., the student's current performance level in written language, how written language increases will be measured, how written language can be linked to the general education curriculum), teachers should use the available IEP information to further develop more complete goal statements that contain all components for instructional information purposes. Teachers can conduct further assessments (typically, these are classroom-based assessments, such as those described in this chapter) to determine where to start in accomplishing the IEP goals. The available IEP information can help in both narrowing the possible curriculum areas and emphasizing the relevant curriculum content.

Short-term objectives on IEPs are directly related to the goal statements in that the objectives represent incremental and observable behaviors related to students' deficit areas that will denote and promote progress and growth. In this chapter, short-term objectives are conceptualized like benchmarks in that each represents a sequential endpoint for instruction. The IDEA requires that short-term objectives or benchmarks accompany each measurable goal on an IEP; consequently, the terms are used interchangeably. Again, beginning teachers will need to find out how their school system prefers or requires short-term objectives or benchmarks to be written, as formats may vary.

Short-term objectives or benchmarks may be written so that the time line they reference is a unit of instruction (*caution:* this is typically more detailed information than required for an IEP, but excellent for planning instruction), a grading period (which may be more realistic to find on an IEP and also prompts teachers to review the IEP content at the same time that they are reporting progress for students without IEPs—which is another IDEA requirement), or a semester/half-year. Typically, a minimum of two objectives are written per goal statement on the IEP. Objectives describe sequences, or benchmarks, from which progress toward accomplishing an IEP goal can be measured.

Exemplary IEP objectives contain information related to a student's observable behaviors, the conditions under which the behaviors should occur, and the degree or criteria that indicate a mastery performance. Each objective is assumed to refer to the student, or "audience," for whom the IEP is written. Many teachers use "ABCD" as a reminder when writing behavioral objectives:

- *Audience:* The student (other components of the objective explicitly address the student's learning characteristics and instructional needs)
- *Behavior:* The observable action performed by the student (the performance represents proficiency with the "content," ranging from low-order skills such as direct recall [e.g., spelling words correctly in a list] to high-order skills such as application of the skill in a unique format [e.g., spelling words correctly in a story])
- *Conditions:* The circumstances and/or materials used during assessment (the condition describes what is given to the student to perform the behavior [e.g., the content of the materials or the type of instructional cues])
- *Degree:* The criteria that indicate a mastery performance of the behavior (criteria include such descriptors as percentage, number of steps/items/trials, and duration that directly relate to the behavior and conditions portion of the objective)

Each of these parts (ABCD) is not merely required in exemplary behavioral objectives; these parts must match, or make sense when used together, for an objective to have internal congruence (see Table 4.2 for nonexamples of behavioral objectives and why they are nonexamples).

Behavioral objectives that result from careful thought and analytic preparation provide the foundation needed to prepare assessments for students with mild to moderate disabilities. See Table 4.3 for examples of behavioral objectives that contain each component (e.g., ABCD) and in which the components make sense when used together.

TABLE 4.2 Poor Behavioral Objectives

Poor Behavioral Objective	Why
Given 25 problems, the student will write the correct answer with 80% accuracy.	80% accuracy is not available with the number of problems in the condition, which is 25; 82% accuracy would be available. Clarify the content of the 25 problems.
The student will improve written language.	The objective does not contain observable behavior, conditions, or degree/criteria.
Given words to read in isolation, the student will answer comprehension questions appropriately.	The stated conditions do not relate to the behavior. Specify how the student will answer the questions: Writing is required in some classes, and verbal answers are required in others. The type of comprehension questions may also be important; recall, inferential, prediction?
The student will accurately define social studies terms.	The conditions are missing; the way in which degree/criteria is noted is ambiguous.

TABLE 4.3 Examples of Well-Written Short-Term IEP Objectives

Conditions	Observable Behavior	Criteria/Degree of Behavior
Given 25 math computations on basic addition and subtraction facts,	the student will write the correct answer	to 23/25 (92%) of the computations.
From memory when asked to define a biology science term,	the student will verbally identify a definition	that includes the term's function and relationship to the body system.
When given the opportunity to perform a seven-step task,	the student will perform* the task	accurately with 7/7 steps.
From memory,	the student will write the definition to terms	correctly.
When given choices of tasks to complete,	the student will identify sequences of task completion in priority order	so that the first task, second task, and so on are sequentially ordered.
Provided with a job to complete and a due date,	the student will perform each function	so that the assignment is completed by the due date.
When faced with situations in which criticism of performance may occur,	the student will perform*	in a socially acceptable manner.*

*Note: These behaviors need further description (refinement) to be accurately observed. In behavioral terms, this refinement is called an operational definition of behavior (ODB). An ODB allows teachers to provide a sequence of observable behaviors that either *exemplify* or *lead to* the objective; these ODBs provide educators with a terminology (e.g., the observable behavior) for succinctly identifying a behavior in the objective and further describing the constellation of behaviors (e.g., the sequence of behaviors that ultimately leads to the observable behavior) that the objective is intended to communicate to others (e.g., the student, parents, educators, and support personnel)

Even when IEP goals and objectives are well written, they may not give sufficient information for beginning teachers to plan instruction because of the influence of other variables on day-to-day teaching. To have a comprehensive idea of the areas that should be targeted for instruction, developing teachers should also keep in mind desired life outcomes for all students (What do students need to be successful when they transition from school to adult life?); expectations for students in school settings (What basic skills do students need to be successful academically, behaviorally, and socially in school settings?); and the curricula (materials, procedures, scope and sequence) used in the school (What resources are readily available? What content do the same-age students without disabilities experience in their classes?). Identifying areas to target for assessment prior to instruction requires teachers to look at the "big picture."

Once the domain or content area for instruction has been determined, teachers can identify students' current performance competencies in the targeted domain prior to beginning instruction. Informal inventories survey a sampling of key knowledge or skills within the domain. Commercially prepared inventories are available for many core achievement areas, including language arts, reading, and mathematics. These criterion-referenced devices usually contain a wide range of developmentally based skill sequences that provide educators "with lists of mastered and unmastered skills from which strengths and weaknesses as well as potential instructional objectives can be inferred" (Salvia & Ysseldyke, 1991, pp. 373–374). Teachers may develop their own inventories that correspond to the targeted domain and the local curriculum. The inventories should still address a broad spectrum of skills, beginner and advanced, from each domain (see Table 4.4).

Whereas inventories provide a broad overview of students' performance within the entire domain, pretests within specific areas will give the teacher more detailed information immediately prior to beginning a particular unit of instruction. These pretests can later be used as posttests. Similar to inventories, detailed pretests are available for some commercially prepared curriculum materials, or teachers may develop their own.

TABLE 4.4 Assessment Components Within Core Achievement Areas

Content Domain	Assessed Skills
Reading	*Decoding (accuracy, then fluency)* • letter recognition and letter sound correspondence • sight vocabulary, phonics, and morphology *Comprehension* • paraphrasing (retelling orally or in writing) the gist of the passage • recall and inference • rate of oral reading
Mathematics	*Skill topics* • readiness skills, vocabulary, and concepts • numeration and whole number operations • fractions and decimals • ratios and percents • measurement • geometry *Skill format* • problem sets requiring computation • word problems requiring selection and application of an algorithm *Skill difficulty variations* • number of steps in solution • amount of extraneous information • explicit versus implicit indicators of mathematical operation
Written Language	*Penmanship* • letter formation and rudimentary spelling *Content* • number of words written • quality, sequencing, or coherence of ideas • consideration of the audience *Style* • grammar (e.g., subject-verb agreement) • mechanics (e.g., punctuation or sentence structure) • word choice
Language Arts	*Skill topics* • alphabetization and spelling • reference skills (e.g., dictionary, phone book, newspaper) • correspondence skills and filling out forms

Compiled from information in *Assessment* (5th ed.), by J. Salvia and J. E. Ysseldyke, 1991, Boston: Houghton Mifflin.

The important feature of pretests is that they correspond to the material that will be taught. Once teachers have assessed students' entry-level competencies, they can plan instruction that addresses the levels at which students perform independently, require instruction, and are frustrated.

Monitor Students' Performance During Instruction

The second step in classroom assessment is to monitor students' performance during instruction in order to guide instructional content and methods; to accomplish this, teachers must decide how to measure performance and design the assessment device, administer the assessment, and respond to assessment results during future instruction. Before beginning instruction, teachers should develop their assessment devices and determine the assessment schedule they will use during instruction to assess students' performance on both short-term and long-term goals and objectives.

Pause and Reflect About the Profession 4.1

Hypothetically, the goals and objectives on students' IEPs should serve as guides to providing instruction for students with disabilities. Beginning teachers may find, however, that the IEP document does not give them enough information to begin daily instruction for a number of reasons. First, during the time lapse between the writing of the IEP and the start of instruction, students may either lose previously acquired prerequisite skills or make unexpected performance gains. Second, the goals and objectives may not address all areas in which students are required to participate in school. Third, goal statements and objectives may not be written in a way that clearly communicates expectations for students' performance in specific, observable, and measurable terms. Any of these inconsistencies between the IEP and expectations for students' performance in the educational setting will require teachers to gather additional information about their students' entry-level competencies in relation to units or domains of instruction.

Examine your students' actual performance levels, the daily expectations for them in school settings, and the IEP goals and objectives. Have your students' skills changed since the IEPs were written? Are any expectations for what they must do in school not addressed in the IEPs? Do the IEP goals and objectives clearly communicate what students should do? Your answers will influence your choice of the instructional domains or units that you will teach first and for which you will assess students' entry-level competencies.

Short-term assessments measure progress during a particular unit of instruction; they typically encompass all the individual competencies taught within the lessons that comprise the unit. Long-term assessments measure progress toward annual goals; they typically encompass the major competencies taught within the units that comprise the annual goals. The assessment device used for the pretest may be reused or adapted (by being shortened or presenting different stimuli for the same skill) for performance monitoring. Between the onset and conclusion of instruction for unit and annual goals, teachers should administer assessments several times. Teachers who assess their students' performance consistently and frequently receive timely indicators of whether students are making the desired achievement gains and whether changes in instruction are warranted. (Chapter 5 covers the diagnostic teaching model, which details possible explanations for students' lack of progress and strategies for adjusting instruction.)

Teachers can use a variety of methods to monitor students' progress during instruction. Beginning special educators should ensure they use the assessment techniques that provide the most information about students' responses to instruction. Some of these techniques may not be used as often as they should. For example, Arthaud, Vasa, and Steckelberg (2000) surveyed over 800 special educators about their reading assessment and instructional practices. They found that although teachers rated some reading assessment measures highly for their usefulness (e.g., oral reading fluency, miscue analysis, portfolios, and journal writing), they did not use these techniques regularly. Teachers reported that they most frequently reviewed the IEP (83 percent) and least frequently used oral reading fluency assessments (23 percent) and informal reading inventories (27 percent). Given that the latter two provide more specific diagnostic information that guides instruction, beginning special educators should ensure that they build more frequent use of such specific assessment techniques into their instructional plans.

Determine Students' Mastery of Competencies

The third step in classroom assessment is to measure students' mastery of competencies at the conclusion of instruction in order to confirm the effectiveness of instruction and students' readiness to proceed to the next unit of instruction (for details, see the discussion of the diagnostic teaching model in Chapter 5). Again, posttests may be available with curriculum materials, may be developed by teachers, and may be a readministration or adapted version of the pretest; however, the posttest should correspond to what was taught.

As is noted in this chapter's introductory case study, variety in how students can "show what they know" is desirable. For example, students can show what they know by writing a paper, designing a project, creating a video, or audiotaping responses. Providing students with choices for assessment methods can strengthen their self-determination skills as well as eliciting a more accurate gauge of what they do know and are able to do.

Monitor Students' Maintenance and Generalization of Competencies

The final step in classroom assessment is to monitor students' maintenance and generalization of competencies in order to determine whether additional teaching is needed. Maintenance refers to whether students remember what they have learned after instruction for that content has stopped. For example, do students who demonstrate mastery of addition and subtraction facts during the first month of school remember them in the second, third, or seventh month of school? Beginning teachers may find, to their dismay, that students who performed at a mastery level on the posttest seem to have forgotten how to add and subtract when they begin a unit on measurement.

Generalization refers to whether students use what they have learned in one setting or situation in other settings and situations that are different from the original instructional context. For example, do students who spell words correctly on a spelling test also spell those words correctly when they write paragraphs? Developing teachers are often disappointed to find that students who perform skills in one context will not transfer use of the skill or information to other appropriate situations. Thus, even after instruction has ended for a particular unit, teachers should conduct follow-up assessments of students' maintenance and generalization of previously mastered competencies.

PRINCIPLES OF ASSESSMENT

Educators can select from a variety of formats (paper-and-pencil tasks, spontaneous reactions, impromptu performances, writing samples) and systems (authentic, performance, portfolio, curriculum-based) in developing and using assessments. Assessments can cover a range of skills (word identification, concept formation, problem solving, self-help, vocational), and the skills can represent content from different curricula (reading, math, writing, social studies, science, social skills, work-related). Assessments can also occur in a number of settings (special education classroom, general education classroom, work site, community setting).

Regardless of what type of assessment format and system is used, what skills are assessed, what curriculum is being taught, or where assessment occurs, three principles guide assessment for students with mild to moderate disabilities:

1. Critical skills are selected for assessment.

2. Data are collected in a systematic manner.

3. Data on student performance are collected frequently.

Principle 1: Critical Skills Are Selected for Assessment

Given the wide variety of skills (or outcomes or standards) taught in educational settings, it is impossible to monitor each skill. Multiple student behaviors contribute to students' progress in reading, varied work behaviors are needed for employees to receive a satisfactory job performance rating, and several skills are executed when students solve math problems. Teachers feel responsible for teaching and assessing a wide range of skills, yet the logistics of conducting extensive assessments on each skill are prohibitive. Teachers make more efficient use of instructional time when they identify critical skills, or key final skills, to serve as guides or benchmarks. Consequently, the first principle of assessment is that the critical skills or skill areas (benchmarks) are selected for assessment and serve as indicators of progress for a student within an instructional unit.

Critical skills are the ending skills or concepts the teacher is teaching during the unit of instruction, not each skill or concept the teacher is teaching. In math, benchmarks might be proficiency and fluency in solving particular types of computations and solving multistep word problems. In reading, critical skills might be fluent identification of words with certain types of patterns and proficiency in answering recall and inferential questions about reading passages containing those words. A social studies curriculum unit might have such critical skills as identifying and defining the vocabulary, recalling important sequences of events, and discussing causes and effects of situations.

Principle 2: Data Are Collected in a Systematic Manner

Systematic data collection consists of using a predetermined plan for assessing students' progress that produces reliable and valid indicators of students' mastery of instructional objectives. Predetermination of instructional objectives is critical to systematic collection of data. When behavioral objectives are specified in advance, teachers are able to plan relevant instruction and assessment. Although a variety of activities may be used to accomplish any objective, the focal point during assessment remains systematic collection of information on the objective, and not extraneous or irrelevant information.

When teachers informally monitor students' involvement in educational activities during instruction and students successfully complete those activities, some educators claim that this observational information is sufficient to determine that the students are acquiring the targeted skills. Fuchs and Fuchs (1984), however, found that teachers' informal observations of students during activities do not necessarily provide reliable and valid information related to the lesson's goals and objectives; that is, some teachers noted that the student enjoyed the lesson or participated in the activity or was able to get the answer correct when cues were given. Although such information is interesting and can help the teacher make decisions about some aspects of instructional content and context, it may not be an accurate or reliable indicator of the student's mastery of the targeted skills. Reliable and valid assessments produce results that dependably measure the skills the teacher was intending to assess.

Reliability. Reliability refers to the extent to which assessment results are generalizable. In other words, reliable assessments provide similar information about students' performance competencies whether or not students are assessed with a different version of the assessment (alternate form or internal-consistency reliability), by a different person (interrater or interscorer reliability), or at a different time (stability or test-retest reliability). Although there are quantitative methods for determining the reliability of assessments, beginning teachers may find it helpful to ask themselves three questions related to the reliability of the classroom assessments they develop. Assuming no additional teaching or practice,

1. Will students perform similarly (with similar levels of mastery) on a different version of the test that contains items within the target domain?

2. Will another person (an instructional assistant, another teacher, a parent volunteer) who scores the students' performance on the assessment device obtain the same results in terms of levels of mastery?

3. Will students perform similarly (with similar levels of mastery) in the assessed area if they are assessed again at a different time?

Each version of the assessment should contain a similar sampling of the skills being taught but not necessarily identical items. For example, to assess students' mastery of addition operations that have two-digit addends requiring regrouping, teachers would provide different sets of math problems each time, but each set should require students to perform the targeted computation skill. In other words, the problem set, but not the computation skill, would vary from one test administration to the next. The extent to which the different versions of the assessment require students to use the same skills is an indicator of alternate form reliability.

The scoring guidelines for the assessment should be explicit enough that students' scores would be the same if two (or more) people were to evaluate students' performance. Interscorer reliability is easily obtained for factual items that have a clearly recognizable right or wrong response, as in spelling, decoding, mathematical computations, and direct recall of content. The more or less defined the range of acceptable responses is, the greater the variability among scorers may be and the less students may understand what signifies a mastery performance. Explicit scoring guidelines are important so that students understand the performance expectations and teachers know whether students have mastered the objectives. The extent to which two people using the same guidelines evaluate students' performance in the same way is an indicator of interrater reliability.

Assessment items or components should be presented in such a way that students must know the content or perform the skill in order to receive mastery scores. If students' performance is highly variable from one administration of the assessment to the next (in the absence of new teaching or practice), then variables other than the targeted skills may be responsible for the performance variations, and the teacher cannot be certain that students have attained mastery. The extent to which assessments require students to demonstrate a particular skill and reduce the opportunities for a "chance" performance is an indicator of test-retest reliability. Test-retest reliability—and hence overall reliability—will be enhanced when the content of assessments "is equivalent from test to test or probe to probe; [and] test directions, kinds of cues or hints, testing formats, criteria for correct responses, and type of score (for example, rates or percentage correct) [are] the same" (Salvia & Ysseldyke, 1991, p. 557).

Validity. To say an assessment is valid means that the skills it measures are indeed the skills it purports to measure. Salvia and Ysseldyke (1991) note that the validity of an assessment is inferred from a variety of information, and they identify three interrelated types of validity: content validity, criterion-related validity, and construct validity. Content validity will be the primary focus of beginning teachers for the assessments they develop.

Salvia and Ysseldyke (1991) recommend evaluating three factors to determine content validity: "the appropriateness of the types of items included, the completeness of the item sample, and the way in which items assess the content" (p. 146). When assessments require students to respond to content taken directly from the materials used during instruction and to perform tasks similar to those encountered during instruction, content validity is seldom a problem. If students are taught strategies for solving word problems and if the assessment requires students to solve similar word problems for which the strategies are appropriate, then content validity should be satisfied. However, if students are taught strategies for solving addition and subtraction word problems only and if the assessment requires application of multiplication and division strategies to solve word problems, then content validity is not satisfied. Furthermore, the types of word problems selected for the assessment must be the types of word problems originally selected for the instructional objective. If the teacher intended the student to be able to solve problems involving multiple steps and varied computational skills, then the word problems used to measure that objective need to include multiple steps and varied computations.

Gersten, Keating, and Irvin (1995) expand the technical features of validity to include social and instructional validity. To ensure that assessment is valid and can thus be used to inform instruction, they challenge researchers to "present evidence indicating that the assessment information is in fact used by teachers as intended and that it results in improved student learning" (p. 510). Teachers who develop sound assessment practices, yet do not use those results to make necessary changes in instruction, are not sufficiently fulfilling the purpose of the assessment process: to guide teaching.

Calhoon and Fuchs (2003) demonstrate how researchers are responding to social and instructional validity issues. They examined the impact of a peer-assisted learning technique and curriculum-based measurement (CBM) on the mathematics performance of secondary students with disabilities. In addition to analyzing research results based on the mathematics measures, the researchers sought feedback from the teachers and students. Students indicated positive attitudes toward the interventions, reported that they liked working with a partner, and believed that the interventions helped them improve and work harder in math. Teachers responded that they thought the interventions were beneficial for them and their students in promoting learning and enhancing decision making using CBM. Significantly, teachers also noted that the interventions enabled them to better prepare for statewide assessments and that they intended to continue using the interventions the following school year.

Principle 3: Data on Student Performance Are Collected Frequently

Frequent collection of data encompasses, at the very least, the use of pretests and posttests. Pretests confirm that students know prerequisite information and do not yet know the targeted content. Posttests confirm that students have learned the targeted content. Yet pretests and posttests do not inform the teacher how well students are learning while the instructional unit is in progress. Teachers who wait until the posttest to gather such critical information are missing timely opportunities to reteach content in different ways during the instructional unit. Thus, data should be collected on several occasions between the pretest and posttest dates, especially for students with special needs, who may benefit from alternative instructional strategies. Frequent data collection provides the teacher with information about how well students are acquiring the content while instruction is occurring.

It is important to note that teachers can use brief and informal ways to gather feedback from students about the content they are learning. Warm-ups at the beginning of class sessions and closures at the end of class sessions are excellent opportunities to gather information that guides instruction. For example, students' performance on brief warm-up problems can alert the teacher to how well students are remembering content that has been previuosly taught. Closure activities can include brief drills about content taught that day, which can guide the teacher for what to review the next day. We have worked with a middle school special educator to develop sets of questions that students can respond to at the end of class sessions. Students choose which question they want to respond to, and their responses guide the teacher for subsequent instructional sessions. Examples of questions include the following:

- What do you feel you need more work on?
- What content do you feel you know well?
- Which activities are particularly helpful for your learning, and why?

APPROACHES TO CLASSROOM ASSESSMENT

Traditionally, educational services for students with mild to moderate disabilities have been delivered by special educators in resource rooms, self-contained classrooms, or special schools. Consequently, assessment practices in the past largely focused on students' individual academic or social achievements within a relatively controlled environment, with small groups of students present for instruction, and with specific educational materials and practices as the cornerstone for their education.

In the 1990s, however, the emphasis on inclusion of students with all types and severities of disabilities resulted in more students, including those with mild to moderate disabilities, being educated in general education classrooms (Cullen & Pratt, 1992). More recently, the emphases have been differentiation for learners with and without disabilities (Hoover & Patton, 2004) and the achievement of all students on statewide assessments (No Child Left Behind Act of 2001). In addition, emphasis has been placed on the uses of community-based environments to promote students' opportunities to learn and practice skills in the authentic environment within which they are expected to perform. In short, educational classrooms for students with mild to moderate disabilities used to be primarily special education classrooms; now those classrooms may also be general education classrooms, work environments, community environments, and activities and locations around the school, such as recess, lunch, and homeroom.

Where the classroom is for these students may affect the assessment parameters teachers use to monitor instruction as well as the types of skills and strategies teachers are teaching. Authentic assessment is one of several terms used recently in general education. Other new terms are performance assessment and portfolio assessment. In the next section, we define and describe each of these terms and provide examples of how each system can be used for students with mild to moderate disabilities. Then we describe curriculum-based assessment. Curriculum-based assessment (CBA) is a system of assessment that has a solid research base for students with mild to moderate disabilities and can be directly linked to instructional decisions to ensure that students are achieving instructional objectives regardless of the setting where instruction occurs.

Authentic, Performance, and Portfolio Assessment

Authentic Assessment. Archbald (1991) notes that the term *authentic assessment* has been used more frequently and recently to represent varied interpretations of what meaningful, valuable, and realistic assessments can provide. Elliott (1992) describes authentic assessment as involving assessment activities like those commonly used in the world outside the classroom. Authentic assessments occur in the real environment and consequently require the student to perform behaviors that will successfully allow him or her to meet authentic setting demands.

The practice of authentic assessments is not new to education, although the application of the concept and terminology has increased in recent years. Poteet, Choate, and Stewart (1993) note that authentic assessments have traditionally been used in vocational education (consider on-the-job performance ratings), music education (e.g., participating in a recital), and sports programs (when students ultimately perform in competitions or games). Not only are students' behaviors assessed in these arenas by professionals who are typically evaluating individuals or teams according to exemplary standards, but also there are elements of student self-evaluation in the light of the familiar standards for which they are striving. Authentic assessment occurs when student performance is measured within the demands of realistic settings and real-life contexts.

In special education, generalization of a student's target behavior occurs when the student uses the skill or behavior in a real-life setting. In a classroom setting, a student may be learning to read words that have varied sound patterns (e.g., consonant blends, digraphs). The authentic assessment, or generalization, of the student's reading skill occurs when the student encounters a situation in which words with similar patterns need to be identified (e.g., in a book or magazine or on a bulletin board) and the student can identify the words correctly.

Another example of an authentic assessment, or generalization, is when a student is learning to complete a series of tasks for a "job" and he or she accurately completes those tasks in a way that satisfies the "employer." The job could be clearing and cleaning a work area (e.g., the student's desk, the student's bedroom, the office area at a work

Pause and Reflect About the Profession 4.2

Examples of authentic assessments for students with disabilities include the following: (1) when a student with an emotional or behavioral disorder responds appropriately to classmates who are making fun of her during recess, (2) when a student with a learning disability in reading correctly pronounces words when verbally reading paragraphs from a science text during a lesson, (3) when a student with moderate mental retardation correctly follows verbal directions while participating in a cooperative group activity, and (4) when a student with a learning disability in mathematics is able to use a calculator in a grocery store to determine when he has overspent his budget. What authentic assessments are already occurring for your students? What additional opportunities do you have to structure authentic assessments? Would identifying opportunities for authentic assessment assist you in teaching your students to generalize skills and behaviors to functionally relevant situations?

site), and the employer could be the student's teacher, parent, or supervisor. The student receives instruction in identifying the tasks that need to be completed, putting them in sequential order, and making decisions on how well the job must be performed. The employer constructs a checklist with this information and teaches the student how to use the checklist. Assessment of the student's use of the checklist may initially occur during instruction using simulated situations. The authentic assessment, however, occurs when the student is able to accurately and satisfactorily complete the tasks on the checklist when the appropriate situation arises.

Authentic assessment links very well with special education's emphasis on teaching and assessing skills within the actual environments in which students must perform. In fact, the concept of teaching for generalization is directly connected to the concept of authentic assessment. If students can use their learned academic and social skills only in artificial environments with controlled materials and cues (e.g., in the therapy room, in the special education classroom, with only small groups of students present, when given a cue from the teacher), then their specialized instruction is not yet completed.

It is appropriate that skills and behaviors measured in nonauthentic situations during instruction. However, the true assessment of instruction occurs when students use behaviors and skills in real settings and situations. Automatic and proficient student performance in authentic situations, with authentic setting demands and even with authentic consequences, is the ultimate aim of all instruction, whether the instruction is programmed and delivered by special educators, general educators, related service personnel, or employers. Educators should be teaching toward and measuring authentic results of instruction.

Performance Assessment. When student behaviors occur in simulated environments or in more controlled or "planned for" contexts, the assessment may be identified as performance assessment. Note that when students' performance occurs in authentic situations, the accurate term is *authentic assessment*. Sometimes, however, authentic demands can be presented within simulated situations, so that the same or similar student performance is required but the situation has not occurred within the "true" environment.

Meyer (1992) describes aspects of performance assessments that are authentic in nature. She delineates multiple features of tasks that can be considered authentic, including the stimuli presented, the complexity of the tasks, and the standards developed for performance (see Table 4.5).

The Office of Technology Assessment (U.S. Congress, 1992) defines performance assessment as students' creation or construction of knowledge, or what students do with

TABLE 4.5 Authentic Features of Performance Tasks

Task Feature	Question for Teachers	Example of Feature
Stimuli	Is the stimulus used identical to the stimulus encountered in real life?	Student can use a variety of vending machines to get a snack.
Task complexity	Does the task represent the difficulty level encountered in real situations?	Student completes a job application that has not been redeveloped for his or her reading level.
Spontaneity	Can the student perform the task when the situation requires it?	Student interacts appropriately with peers and adults throughout the day.
Conditions	Are the conditions present during assessment similar or identical to the conditions present in real life?	Student reads independently without someone there to tell him or her the words.
Criteria	Is the performance standard required in actual situations also required in the assessment situation?	Student must complete all steps in the task of making coffee, not 80% accuracy.
Locus of control	Is the student responsible for initiating or completing a response?	When the bus door opens, the student boards the bus before it departs.
Resources	Is the availability of materials similar to actual situations?	Student must locate art supplies and bring them to the work area.
Consequences	Are the consequences for performance similar to the consequences in real life?	Student gets to drink the soda after putting the correct change in the vending machine.

Source: Features derived from "What's the difference between authentic and performance assessment?" by C. A. Meyer, 1992, *Educational Leadership, 49*(8), p. 40.

what they know. The Office has identified six types—and related examples—of performance assessment: (1) constructed-response items, (2) essays and writing assessments, (3) interviews and direct observations, (4) exhibitions, (5) experiments, and (6) portfolios (see Table 4.6). Examples include assessment (1) during a role-play situation in which the student practices appropriate responses to criticism from peers, (2) during an oral reading of material that is similar to grade-level material, (3) while following a specific set of directions during a contrived group activity, and (4) while solving a math problem on a worksheet. Regardless of which method is selected, educators must predetermine criteria for successful performance in order to (1) explain the criteria to the student before and during instruction, (2) have a basis for discussing performance with the student during feedback sessions, and (3) develop valid and reliable assessment formats. Sarouphim (1999) notes that performance-based assessments must clearly and logically link to specific activities in order to be credible and effective. Teachers should be sure to incorporate those features that resemble real-life, or authentic, situations into their performance assessment sequence even when the authentic situations cannot be used.

Actually, many types of performances can serve to document a student's progress. For example, Woodward, Monroe, and Baxter (2001) analyzed how students with learning disabilities who received tutorial sessions fared in mathematics when compared to similar peers who did not receive tutoring. All students completed performance assessments developed to parallel outcomes for a statewide assessment, and they could solve problems and explain their thinking using pictures, tables, charts, and/or words. A rubric was used to score students' performance, and students with learning disabilities in the tutorial intervention scored significantly higher on performance assessments than their peers who had not received tutoring. The researchers indicated that the flexibility in performance was desired by the students and that the tutorials provided necessary discussion and practice opportunities for students.

TABLE 4.6 Descriptions and Examples of Performance Assessments

Type of Performance Assessment	Description	Examples
Constructed-response items	Students produce or construct their own answers.	• Mathematics calculation • Geometry proofs • Drawing graphs • Fill-in-the-blank • Matching • Definitions • Short written answers • Essays
Essays and writing assessment	Students' writing ability, and knowledge and understanding of content, is assessed.	• Direct writing sample in response to a writing prompt or question
Interviews and direct observations	Students verbally respond to or actively demonstrate knowledge.	• Give spoken response on or discuss a given topic • Perform tasks that have been taught in a simulated situation and/or spontaneously in a real situation • Observe dialogue of students spontaneously engaged in an academic activity • Collect work samples
Exhibitions	Students produce comprehensive products, presentations, or performances for the public.	• Recital • Activities, projects, or demonstrations are aggregated and displayed • Debate • Individual or group competitions • Dramatic presentation • Group project
Experiments	Students demonstrate the process of planning, conducting, and writing up experiments.	• Hands-on manipulative skills tasks • May include teamwork and interpersonal skills
Portfolios	Students contribute work samples to files, folders that portray their learning profile by documenting their experiences and accomplishments.	• Drafts and final products • Self-reflection

Source: Constructed from information in "Performance assessment: Methods and characteristics," in *Testing in American schools: Asking the right questions* (OTA SET-519, pp. 201–249), by U.S. Congress, Office of Technology Assessment, 1992, Washington, DC: Government Printing Office.

Portfolio Assessment. As students are learning and gaining proficiency in new skills and concepts, it is helpful for teachers to gather samples of their performances to review and indicate progress over time. Teachers can use a portfolio format to assist them in documenting such performances. Portfolio assessment can be conceptualized as an innovative notation of students' performances related to instructional objectives and can conceivably be an alternative "gradebook" for a teacher. The portfolio itself can be a folder, notebook, or some other "holder" of student work products. Paulson, Paulson, and Meyer (1991) describe a portfolio as a purposeful collection of student work that exhibits the student's efforts, progress, and achievements in one or more areas. Students must participate in selecting the contents, and the collection must include the criteria for selection, the criteria for judging merit, and evidence of student self-reflection (p. 60).

Paulson et al. (1991) emphasize the importance of deciding what type of information the portfolio is intended to communicate. A folder that merely holds a student's work does not represent portfolio assessment; decisions about what type of work can be placed in a portfolio and how that work relates to the curriculum (or IEP) goals and objectives must be clearly identified and discussed with the student. Paulson et al. suggest that teachers clearly identify the purpose of the portfolio, the type of content that can be included in it, the goals the student is working toward, and the standards for determining the quality of the content (see Table 4.7 for examples of these and other related questions on portfolio content).

Work products in a portfolio can represent either work in progress (e.g., writing outlines, drafts of a report being written) or the final work (e.g., the report that was turned in for a grade or for teacher evaluation). Work contained in a portfolio may be chosen by the teacher independently or by the student and teacher together. Teacher and student collaboration—in deciding what goes in the portfolio, and why, and how that work represents student growth and progress related to instruction—is required so that the portfolio represents assessment content decided with the student, not for the student. Duffy, Jones, and Thomas (1999) describe how portfolios can be used to promote independent thinking with students because they are encouraged to learn and use self-evaluation skills.

In addition to work products directly related to an academic area, the portfolio may contain the student's comments and reflections on how well he or she is learning and what he or she is learning from the academic content. More extensive content from a wide variety of sources can also be used in portfolios. For example, Viechnicki, Barbour, Shaklee, Rohrer, and Ambrose (1993) describe portfolio content that teachers developed for each student that included teacher anecdotal accounts of student learning, observations from lessons that were designed to elicit evidence of exceptional potential and

TABLE 4.7   Questions for Determining Portfolio Content

Question	Recommendation
1. Is the portfolio's purpose identified?	Clarify how the portfolio will be used in determining grades, guiding instruction, deciding content for instruction, and so on.
2. How closely will the portfolio content parallel the IEP/curriculum?	Link the content of the portfolio directly to the IEP and curriculum.
3. What type of content can be included in the portfolio?	Discuss with the student ways to make decisions about what goes into the portfolio. Content may also include alternative assessment formats such as projects and results from a role-play.
4. What are the standards for the content in the portfolio?	The teacher and student should be well aware of what an excellent product, or project, looks like. The criteria for selecting content may parallel the criteria statement of a behavioral objective.
5. How much student involvement will be elicited, and when?	Inform the student at the beginning of instruction what his or her choices are for including portfolio content. Guide the student initially in portfolio selection of content. Allow the student to make independent choices as he or she demonstrates more proficiency with making decisions.
6. How many purposes can the portfolio serve?	Use fewer purposes that coincide rather than more purposes that may fragment, isolate, or confuse the critical instructional objectives. The portfolio can inform the teacher about the student's progress, thinking processes, and preferences for demonstrating proficiency.
7. To what extent should growth and progress be evident in the portfolio content?	Growth and progress should be evident to a great extent. Furthermore, the teacher may want to include (for his or her future use) what methods were used to more consistently promote growth and progress.

performance, information from parents and/or peers, and examples of products produced by the student.

Nolet (1992) discusses portfolio assessment as a process that can be used for either instructional or assessment purposes, and his points can help guide teachers in clarifying their purposes for portfolio assessment. He distinguishes between uses of a portfolio that make it appropriate for assessment purposes and for instructional purposes. For example, if the purpose of the portfolio is assessment, then teachers need to ensure the reliability and validity of the portfolio contents in relation to instructional goals and objectives. In other words, teachers must ensure the content selected for inclusion in the portfolio is technically adequate for assessing students' performance competencies. For an instructional portfolio, in contrast, teachers may be less concerned with the technical features of the student work included in the portfolio; indeed, the student may select work to include that he or she believes reflects progress and performance but that the teacher knows does not represent reliable or valid measures (e.g., because the student had much assistance in completing the work instead of completing it independently).

By including the student's reasons for selecting a particular piece of work for the portfolio, the teacher can use the portfolio assessment process as an opportunity to gain insight into what the student is thinking about his or her learning experiences. Including the student's preferences for demonstrating knowledge (e.g., writing a report, constructing a model, developing a timeline, reflecting on his or her work) not only encourages student involvement and decision making but also is an excellent method of increasing student motivation and responsibility in the learning process.

Authentic, performance, and portfolio assessments represent relatively recent initiatives in general education. At this time, the research base on how well these assessments work for students with disabilities is relatively small, although some research is beginning to emerge (Nolet, 1992; Poteet et al., 1993; Sarouphim, 1999). Certainly, the basic premises of these assessment systems apply to the performance demands for students with mild to moderate disabilities, and flexibility for differentiated performance standards (e.g., the standard for a student with learning disabilities may be different from that of a student who is gifted) is available. Creative special educators can develop parallel and appropriate formats for students with mild to moderate disabilities that allow these students to participate in assessment formats similar to those used by general educators.

Curriculum-Based Assessment

An assessment system that does have a research base for teaching and assessing students with mild to moderate disabilities is curriculum-based assessment (CBA) (Deno, 1985; Deno & Fuchs, 1987; Fuchs & Fuchs, 1985; Salvia & Hughes, 1990). Elliott (1992) refers to CBA as techniques for observing a student's behavior that link assessment results to instructional interventions. CBA can be used as a formative assessment technique during instruction. Fuchs and Fuchs (1984) found that teachers who (1) conducted formative assessments during instruction, (2) used results from those assessments to change their teaching, and (3) graphically displayed those results to assist them in decision making were able to increase their students' academic achievement and to use instructional time more productively than teachers who did not conduct and use formative assessments. Although a variety of definitions and interpretations of CBA are used in the literature (e.g., Blankenship, 1985; Fuchs & Deno, 1991; Salvia & Hughes, 1990), the definition of CBA used for this chapter is based on the following principles of effective instruction:

- Observable behavior of critical student performances related to the curriculum being taught is used.
- Frequent and brief measurements of student behavior occur prior to, during, and after instructional units.
- Measurements are graphically displayed.
- Students and teachers use the graphic displays to make instructional decisions.

Systematically observing key student behaviors related to instructional content includes two of the principles of assessment presented earlier in this chapter: Critical skills are selected for assessment, and data are collected in a systematic manner. Methods for teachers' development and use of CBA have been described in as many as 11 and as few as 4 steps (e.g., Blankenship, 1985; Salvia & Hughes, 1990). In the next section, we describe the APPLY framework for developing and using CBA and provide case studies of students with mild to moderate disabilities in the elementary and secondary grades to illustrate varied examples of CBA in different content areas.

THE APPLY FRAMEWORK FOR DEVELOPING CLASSROOM ASSESSMENTS

Before using the APPLY framework to develop a CBA, teachers acquire critical information about the student from a variety of sources (e.g., IEPs, confidential files, parents, other teachers, standardized assessments, informal assessments, other CBAs, the student him- or herself). These sources provide indicators of the curriculum from which the student should be working and a general idea of the curriculum level at which the student can satisfactorily perform.

APPLY is a mnemonic (see Figure 4.1) that synthesizes the steps for teachers' development and use of CBA (Jorden & Haube, 1995; King-Sears, 1994; King-Sears, Burgess, & Lawson, 1999). It can be used as an initial diagnostic framework for determining a student's instructional curriculum and level. It can also be used as an ongoing diagnostic framework throughout the year when a student is progressing from unit to unit within a curriculum area.

Analyze the Curriculum

Target from the curriculum the critical objectives that will serve as benchmarks or indicators that the student is learning the content. For reading or social studies, for example, the new vocabulary throughout a unit of instruction and the types of comprehension questions used may represent benchmarking. The social studies curriculum might also include definitions of key terms or foundational concepts. The mathematics curriculum could include specific types of computations and word problems. The vocational curriculum could utilize a checklist of tasks to perform at a work site. A social-emotional curriculum might target specific verbal and nonverbal behaviors related to interpersonal skills.

Regardless of which curriculum is used, the teacher needs to predetermine the areas of that curriculum that can serve as critical markers across the instructional unit. Those markers can comprise low- and high-order thinking skills. A CBA cannot assess all information taught or anticipated for a student to learn, so key objectives need to be specified in advance. Consider that the key objectives are critical to a student's further understanding and use of the major information in the unit or domain.

FIGURE 4.1 APPLY as a Framework for Developing and Using CBA

Source: From *Curriculum-based assessment in special education* (p. 17), by M. E. King-Sears, 1994, San Diego: Singular. Reprinted by permission.

1. **A nalyze** the curriculum.
2. **P repare** items to meet the curriculum objectives.
3. **P robe** frequently.
4. **L oad** data using a graph format.
5. **Y ield** to results—revisions and decisions.

Nolet (1992) notes that the validity of portfolio assessments increases when teachers clarify the goals of instruction in a particular skill or knowledge area, design tasks that representatively sample those goals, administer the tasks reliably, and aggregate those data to arrive at conclusions about student performance. Teachers clarify the goals of instruction by analyzing the curriculum, determining the important goals, and specifying the behavioral objectives that will be used to monitor student progress related to the goals.

As has already been described, behavioral objectives specify observable student behaviors, the conditions under which the behaviors occur, and the criteria that indicate mastery of the objective (refer to Table 4.3 for examples of behavioral objectives that could guide the development of CBAs). After each component of the objective is determined, the method for assessing the objective can be developed more easily and clearly.

Prepare Items to Meet the Curriculum Objectives

Once the key objectives are targeted, the teacher develops short assessments, or probes, that can be used throughout instruction to elicit student responses. (*Note:* Probe is used as both a noun and a verb in CBA terminology. Probe is a noun when it represents the format used to elicit student responses; probe is a verb when it represents the act of eliciting student responses on a CBA.)

The item format is constructed so that it is brief in duration. It is useful to place a limit on the time a student will be given to respond. In developing—and, ultimately, administering—the CBA probe, teachers should address several time-related issues. First, the time limit can help teachers note both students' acquisition of and their performance fluency with content. For example, students may be able to compute math problems when given enough time to count the facts by using blocks, an indication that acquisition of the math concepts is occurring at a concrete level. Also important, however, is how quickly the student can compute math at the abstract level. A CBA that allows only a brief amount of time can provide that information. Second, a time limit is used to maximize the gathering of critical information in a minimal amount of time so that instructional decisions can be made more frequently. Allotting 20 minutes three days per week to gather CBA data may not be the best use of instructional time; 2 minutes on three occasions during the week is more realistic and manageable for teachers. Third, the time limit is not used to increase students' anxiety about an assessment. Prior to administering the CBA, teachers should discuss with students that the CBA will not result in a test grade; rather, they are using it to get indicators of student progress. See Table 4.8 for examples of brief CBAs.

Teachers should consider, when preparing items related to key curriculum objectives, how quickly relevant information can be acquired. Moreover, they need to consider the correlation between key learning that is representational of, or foundational to, more comprehensive learning. For example, students who are able to identify words quickly and correctly are better able to understand the reading passages they read. Consequently, CBA probes on the number of words identified correctly per minute are helpful. Students who can identify the correct steps to solve a problem are better prepared to use those steps in solving problems. A CBA might probe their ability to correctly identify the steps. Another CBA probe might elicit information on the correct application of the steps to a novel problem.

When preparing items to meet the targeted curriculum objectives, teachers can consider (1) providing a prompt for writing a response, (2) developing a checklist of behaviors required for completing a task, (3) listing words to identify, (4) designating words to define, and (5) describing a set of requisite behaviors. Regardless of the item format, teachers must consider the validity and reliability of the items in relation to the curriculum and instructional objectives. For example, listing steps in a problem-solving process can be used as a CBA when the objective is to have the student correctly list those steps. That CBA will not indicate, however, whether the student can apply the steps to novel

TABLE 4.8 Examples of CBA Brief Probes with Time Limit for Noting a Student's Acquisition and Fluency Rates

Content Area	Time	Description of CBA
Reading	1 minute	The probes are reading passages, which may be selected from any content area. The student reads aloud for 1 minute. Conduct CBA two times per week with each individual. Graph the number of words read correctly and incorrectly.
Math	2 minutes	The probe is a worksheet of math computations. The student solves as many problems as possible in 2 minutes. Conduct CBA three times per week by using group administration. Graph the number of digits computed correctly and incorrectly.
Spelling	2 minutes	The probe is an oral or audiotaped dictation of spelling words. Conduct CBA four times per week by using group administration. Graph the number of correct letter sequences or the number of words spelled correctly or incorrectly.
Written language	3 minutes	The probe is a story opener, which may be a topic or a brief story starter situation. The student elaborates on the story opener by writing for 3 minutes. Conduct CBA one time per week by using group administration. Graph the total number of words written, number of words spelled correctly, or other salient aspects.

Source: Curriculum-based assessment in special education (p. 21), by M. E. King-Sears, 1994, San Diego: Singular. Reprinted by permission.

situations. A CBA that provides a situation and requires the student to use the problem-solving process to arrive at a solution would be more appropriate. Although the ultimate goal of instruction may be to have the student independently apply problem-solving processes and use an appropriate solution when faced with varied situations (an excellent example of generalization or authentic assessment), the initial CBA may have a more limited focus, such as the student's recall of the problem-solving steps, or the student's ability to provide examples of how to use the problem-solving sequence when given a situation, or the student's identification of appropriate solutions for solving a problem.

Probe Frequently

Teachers should conduct brief CBAs two or three times a week. However, they cannot maintain this frequency if the CBAs require extensive instructional time to conduct. For that reason, brief CBAs are more desirable, manageable, and practical for teachers to use with consistency. Some teachers are able to use CBA probes daily; other teachers are able to conduct CBA probes weekly. Consider the time lapse between a pretest and a posttest: CBA occurs between the pretest and the posttest and lets the teacher and students know that progress is occurring.

Teachers who assess students' performance only at the end of instructional units are not able to make changes during instruction; by the time they know that the student or students are not "getting it," the end-of-unit test has already occurred—it's too late to make teaching changes. CBA functions as a frequent formative assessment that helps guide instruction for the teacher and learning for the student. Periodic assessments, or probes, during instruction ensure that teachers are gathering information that allows them to make teaching changes while instruction is occurring.

Load Data Using a Graph Format

After each probe is administered and evaluated, the score is plotted on a graph. The date of the assessment or the session number of the probe is identified on the horizontal axis. The assessed skill or competency, with its corresponding measure (e.g., percentage or number correct, number per minute), is identified on the vertical axis. It is important to plot the data point on the graph as soon as possible after the CBA is administered so that a timely and accurate performance line can be drawn. A delay in plotting students' data points reduces the usefulness of the CBA for making instructional decisions.

The graphic format of recording data accomplishes multiple purposes. First, the visual depiction provides teachers with a means to analyze students' performance and to make instructional decisions. Second, the visual depiction provides students with a concrete representation of their actual performance. Third, graphs provide parents with a visual representation of their child's progress. Fourth, the performance graphs provide other teachers with a quick comparison of individual students' current and previous progress and a guide for grouping students for instruction. When data are graphed, students can more efficiently note their progress (e.g., an ascending progress line), teachers can more readily know when to make changes in instruction (e.g., a stable or descending line indicates that teaching changes are needed), and others can more fully note ongoing performance (e.g., parents can see the results of their child's performance related to IEP objectives over time). Some teachers find computer-graphing applications to be an excellent time-saver for graphing.

Yield to Results—Revisions and Decisions

The visual depiction of a student's performance is used to make decisions about instruction. Wesson, Skiba, Sevcik, King, and Deno (1984) found that some teachers require extensive training or continuing support in order to use data to make ongoing changes in their instruction. Hasbrouck, Woldbeck, Ihnot, and Parker (1999) found that one teacher who was initially resistant to using curriculum-based measurement became convinced of its value after seeing the impact on student performance and receiving technical support and assistance. King-Sears, Burgess, and Lawson (1999) describe how the use of CBA in general education classrooms can more actively involve students in decision-making discussions and subsequent actions (e.g., students decide how they'd like to study information they still need to learn). In other words, for developing teachers, the issue may be how to make decisions based on the data, not how to collect and graph data. As Gersten et al. (1995) note, social and instructional validity of assessments does not occur unless the teacher uses assessment results to improve a student's future performance. Stecker and Fuchs (2000) found that it was essential for teachers to make decisions based on an individual student's CBA data. Students whose teachers made decisions based on their own data (versus a matched peer's data) performed significantly better on a global achievement test than students for whom CBA data were not gathered and used. Several techniques can be used to guide instructional decision making and evaluate data: the three-day rule, aimline performance, and quarter-intersect.

The three-day, or three-session, rule refers to any set of three consecutive connected data points on the graph. If the trend (direction) of the line connecting the three most recent consecutive data points is going in the desired direction (either increasing or decreasing), then the student is making progress, current instructional procedures seem to be effective, and instruction should continue in the present manner. However, if the trend of the line connecting the most recent three data points is not going in the desired direction or if it plateaus, then "it's time for a teaching change," and subsequent revisions of instruction should be planned.

Aimline performance is a modification of the three-day rule in which a line is drawn on the graph to connect the student's initial (sometimes considered the baseline) data point and the desired data point and session in which the teacher anticipates the student will have mastered the objective. Decisions are made using the aimline when data points fall below the aimline for three consecutive sessions; that is, progress may be occurring, but the progress is not at the anticipated rate. Instructional changes made when the aimline is not being met include revising teaching methods, talking with the student about how to improve performance, intensifying the amount of practice, and reteaching major concepts. In some cases, a decision may be made to set a more reasonable aimline for that student, although a decision to do this should be preceded by instructional alternatives to enhance performance toward the original aimline.

The quarter-intersect method can be used when seven or more data points are plotted and teachers use the following procedure to develop a line of progress:

1. Divide the number of data points in half by drawing a vertical line down the graph (midsession).

2. On the left half of the graph, find the midsession and draw a vertical line (middate).

3. On the left half of the graph, find the midperformance point and draw a horizontal line (midrate).

4. Repeat steps 2 and 3 on the right half of the graph.

5. Draw a line connecting the intersections (the intersection of the horizontal [midrate] and vertical [middate] lines from steps 2 and 3) of both halves of the graph. This is the quarter-intersect trend line.

6. Teachers may wish to further refine the line of progress by using the split-middle method, so that an equal number of data points fall above and below the line; start by counting the number of data points that fall above and below the line.

7. If the number of data points on and above the line is the same as the number on and below the line, then stop. The trend line is accurate.

8. If the number of data points on and above the line does not equal the number on and below the line, then move the line up or down until there is a balance of points above and below the line.

The resulting trend line may be ascending, descending, or stable. The trend line can be compared with the slope of the aimline to determine whether the aimline should be raised or lowered. The quarter-intersect trendline can be especially helpful when developing long-range goal data because the teacher can use the rate of performance on CBAs from the current year to develop realistic goals for the following year.

The case studies presented next describe how teachers have used CBA in a variety of settings and with students who have a range of mild to moderate disabilities. Throughout the case studies, note how teachers have used CBA to benefit themselves by making instructional decisions and revisions and how they have used CBA to benefit their students by (1) showing progress and performance in a more concrete manner, (2) encouraging goal setting, (3) sharing responsibility for learning, and (4) increasing motivation.

APPLY Case Study 1: Fractions and Decimals

Analyze the Curriculum. Ms. Joseph is teaching in a self-contained classroom of fourth- and fifth-grade students with emotional or behavioral disorders. She is responsible for delivering math instruction to each student (according to IEP goals and objectives), and during the math period, she is responding to varied levels of knowledge related to decimals and fractions. The school year has just begun, so she is determining what students know already about this area of mathematics. Her curriculum objective is

Given fractions to convert to decimals and decimals to convert to fractions, the student will correctly convert each problem.

Prepare Items to Meet the Curriculum Objectives. Because Ms. Joseph is surveying her class for a variety of learning levels in math, she develops a probe sheet featuring single items pertaining to benchmark math objectives from all curricula. The CBA probe shown in Figure 4.2 was used to determine each student's skill level related to a synthesis of decimal and fraction math objectives at varied grade levels. From that probe, she was able to graphically depict skill areas for students that led her to instructional groupings and starting points (see Figure 4.3 for the class profile).

1. $9/10 =$

2. $47.5/10 =$

3. $3.2/10 =$

4. $7.1 =$

5. $13.4 =$

6. $28.8 =$

7. Draw a picture to show 6/10:

8. Write a decimal to show 6/10:

BONUS: Develop your own question and answer that show your knowledge of this information.

FIGURE 4.2   CBA Probe for Fractions and Decimals

Note that Ms. Joseph's class profile not only allows her to determine who needs instruction in specific skills but also indicates which students already know the information for this math unit. She then develops three instructional groups according to the data from this CBA: Group 1 needs instruction on converting decimals to fractions and fractions to decimals, group 2 needs instruction on converting decimals to fractions, and group 3 already knows the information probed on this CBA. Group 3 needs to be probed on a different CBA that assesses the next set of math skills; students from group 3 would be involved in repetitive instruction for concepts they already know if Ms. Joseph were to erroneously include them in this particular math unit.

In essence, this CBA has also served as a pretest for students in determining who needs instruction in these math skill areas and who does not. Although one could argue

	MW	ME	BA	AS	DR	JI	JF	BK	DL	CE	BH	BI	ST
# 1.	X	X	X	X	X	X	X	X	X	X	X	X	X
# 2.				X		X	X	X	X	X	X	X	X
# 3.					X	X	X	X	X	X	X	X	X
# 4.										X	X	X	X
# 5.										X	X	X	X
# 6.										X	X	X	X
# 7.	X	X	X	X	X	X	X	X	X		X	X	X
# 8.	X	X	X	X	X	X	X	X	X	X	X	X	X
BONUS			X							X			

FIGURE 4.3   Class Profile of Decimal and Fraction Conversions

that avoiding repetitive instruction is important for any group of students, some might emphasize the added importance of focusing on pertinent instruction for students who have emotional or behavioral disorders because these students may be more likely to display inappropriate behaviors when they are bored with academic content. Conversely, when Ms. Joseph targets accurate academic skill levels, she is minimizing the likelihood of academic frustration or boredom, motivating students to focus on academic material they are capable of doing, and increasing the opportunities for time-on-task with relevant instructional concepts that can lead to enhanced academic achievement. The remaining portion of this APPLY case study focuses on students in groups 1 and 2, whose initial CBA results indicate they need further instruction in converting fractions and decimals.

Probe Frequently. Ms. Joseph can use varied forms of the CBA (that feature similar items) to conduct brief probes at the beginning of math instruction on several days during the week. Because Ms. Joseph is interested in what concepts students have remembered (e.g., from the previous day's instruction, from their homework assignments), she selects the beginning of the math sessions for CBA probes instead of the end. She has built into her math lesson plans for Mondays, Tuesdays, and Thursdays a two-minute period for students to complete a CBA probe. She wants to quickly gather the information at the beginning of the class session and briefly review the results to note what she may need to emphasize during the class session.

Ms. Joseph has several options for reviewing the CBA probe results: She can informally glance at the probes as she collects them at the end of two minutes, she can put them aside and review them at the end of the day; she can put them aside, have an instructional assistant or volunteer score them, and then review them at the end of the day; or she can have students correct their papers at the end of two minutes. She decides to have students correct their own papers at the end of two minutes; then she has the students themselves graph their correct responses on their progress graphs, which is the next step in the APPLY framework.

Load Data Using a Graph Format. Ms. Joseph has each student correct his or her own CBA probe, count the total number of correct responses, write that number at the top of the probe, and then graph the number correct on his or her progress graph. Initially, this procedure took about 15 minutes because Ms. Joseph wanted to ensure that students understood that the CBA probes were not the same as a test. Students were trying to make progress on answering the CBA probe items correctly, with their correct responses indicating progress over the instructional sessions, not to score 100 percent correct for each probe administration (note that group 3 students, who did score 100 percent correct, were not being instructed in these math concepts because they already knew the information). Figure 4.4 shows the progress for one student across 18 days of instruction.

Yield to Results—Revisions and Decisions. Ms. Joseph uses the "three-day/session rule" for deciding about student progress. She routinely reviews all student progress graphs on Fridays when she is writing lesson plans for the next week's instruction. When students have not made sufficient progress on their CBAs during the week, she knows she needs to work more on those concepts. Revisions may entail (1) reteaching using more concrete examples, (2) providing more guided practice activities using a variety of examples, (3) offering more demonstration examples using real-life situations that deal with fractions and decimals, (4) adding peer tutoring as an activity, and (5) including instructional games to provide more practice opportunities. The CBA data provide Ms. Joseph with instructionally relevant information that helps her in deciding about how well students are learning and when revisions in instruction may need to occur.

Student: Michael	Teacher: Ms. Joseph	Subject: Math
Objective: Given fractions and decimals (whole numbers and tenths), the student will correctly (1) convert the fraction to a decimal, (2) convert the decimal to a fraction, and (3) draw a picture to represent the fraction or decimal.		**Goal:** 8 out of 8 points earned. **Bonus:** The student includes something different than was asked for on the probe sheet.

Student Goal: I plan to get 8 out of 8 points by (write a date here): October 19

FIGURE 4.4   CBA Graph for Math (note bonus points awarded October 5, 12, and 17)

Extensions or Variations.

- Use newspaper advertisements of sale products to determine the amount of money saved on a sale item.
- Use a recipe for a favorite meal item to identify how the same denominator could be used in all ingredients. Provide a variety of measuring items so that equivalent measurements can be concretely seen.
- Use metric packages from products sold in stores (e.g., soda containers) to make connections to the decimal system.
- Identify everyday items or situations in which students may use the fraction/ decimal conversion skills. Students who are using portfolios to document their instructional progress may be responsible for adding items to their portfolio that illustrate how they see fraction/decimal conversion skills in their life. For example, one student may insert in his portfolio the following items to document his progress in this math area: (a) a copy of the probe sheet, (b) the progress graph that depicts his learning performance during instruction, and (c) a narrative that he has written that describes how he can use these fraction/decimal conversion skills when cooking and shopping for items.

APPLY Case Study 2: High School Essays

Analyze the Curriculum. Ms. Rodriguez is a general education teacher who teaches 10th-grade English. All the students in her fifth-period class, which includes three students with learning disabilities and one student with emotional or behavioral disorders, have an assignment to write an essay related to a contemporary topic. Ms. Rodriguez specifies the following objective for all the students: After selecting a contemporary topic and reading information related to that topic, the student will write an essay that (1) is well organized, (2) uses accurate and varied sentences,

(3) uses correct vocabulary, (4) uses correct mechanics of writing, and (5) is presented in an appropriate format.

Prepare Items to Meet the Curriculum Objectives. Ms. Rodriguez has done some research on the criteria other professionals use to assess students' writing proficiency. One article by Archbald (1991) displays a scoring rubric for essays that she has adapted for her use (see Figure 4.5). Ms. Rodriguez's probe is the rubric itself, which students received at the beginning of the instructional unit and can use as a self-assessment prior to turning in their essay drafts to Ms. Rodriguez.

Probe Frequently. Ms. Rodriguez reviews students' drafts an average of three times before the final essay is turned in for a grade. Students who have particular difficulty with written language, which includes all the students with learning disabilities and several other students in the class who have not been identified as needing special education services, will require more feedback sessions. Ms. Rodriguez meets with one student,

	1 2	3 4	5	Value	Total
O	Little or nothing is written. Essay is disorganized and poorly developed. Does not stay on topic.	Essay is incomplete. It lacks an introduction, well-developed body, or conclusion. Coherence and logic are attempted but inadequate.	The essay is well organized. It is coherent, ordered logically, and fully developed.	X 6	=
S	The student writes frequent run-ons or fragments.	Occasional errors in sentence structure. Little variety in sentence length and structure.	Sentences are complete and varied in length and structure.	X 5	=
U	Student makes frequent errors in word choice and agreement.	Occasional errors in word choice and agreement.	Usage is correct. Word choice is appropriate.	X 4	=
M	Student makes frequent errors in spelling, punctuation, and capitalization.	Occasional errors in mechanics.	Spelling, capitalization, and punctuation are correct.	X 4	=
F	Format is sloppy. There are no margins or indents. Handwriting is inconsistent.	Margins and indents have inconsistencies. No title or inappropriate title.	The format is correct. The title is appropriate. The margins and indents are consistent.	X 1	=
				TOTAL	=

The essays are scored using a 1–5 scale. The numbers in the boxes to the right indicate the relative importance of each factor in the overall grade. Thus, organization is valued the most and counts 30% of the grade; format counts 5% of the grade.

O = Organization
S = Sentence structure
U = Usage
M = Mechanics
F = Format

FIGURE 4.5 Scoring Rubric for Essays

Source: Adapted from "Authentic assessment: Principles, practices, and issues," by D. A. Archbald, 1991, *School Psychology Quarterly, 6,* p. 284. Adapted with permission of the publisher.

Maria, five times to provide her feedback using the rubric's scoring criteria. On each occasion, Ms. Rodriguez has had an opportunity to review Maria's essay in a formative manner and to emphasize/reteach those areas where Maria needs to improve. Maria's essay is formatted correctly from the very first draft; she receives the highest score (5), which is multiplied by the value for that criterion (format value is 1) for a total of 5 points for format. In organization, Maria initially earns a 3 for performance (multiplied by the value of 6 equals 18); sentence structure is a 3 (multiplied by the value of 5 equals 15); usage is a 3 (multiplied by the value of 4 equals 12); mechanics is 4 (multiplied by the value of 4 equals 16). For the first draft, Maria has earned 66 of a possible 100 points. In subsequent feedback sessions, Maria and Ms. Rodriguez review Maria's draft and determine a performance score. As Maria's writing improves, her score improves.

Load Data Using a Graph Format. Maria totals each rubric's score to find the cumulative number of points she has earned on each draft of her essay. Maria plots the total number on a graph and also sets a goal for herself about the areas she needs to concentrate on in her next draft to improve her score (see Figure 4.6).

Yield to Results—Revisions and Decisions. Ms. Rodriguez has drawn an aimline on Maria's graph to show how many points Maria should be accruing throughout the unit. By comparing Maria's performance to the aimline, Ms. Rodriguez and Maria are able to determine whether Maria is progressing toward satisfactory completion of the essay assignment.

Date	4 Feb	8 Feb	11 Feb	14 Feb	18 Feb
Goal Score	—	74	82	91	100
Actual Score	66	75	88	95	100

Date Assignment Given: February 1   Date Assignment Due: February 21
Student: Maria   **Teacher:** Ms. Rodriguez   **Class:** 10th grade English

FIGURE 4.6 Curriculum-Based Assessment for Essays

The rubric also provides Ms. Rodriguez with information about written language skills that she needs to reteach or reemphasize. Sometimes this instruction occurs with small groups, sometimes it occurs individually, sometimes peers can help edit each other's work, and sometimes there is content on which the whole class needs to work. Ms. Rodriguez is acquiring information about how well students in her fifth-period English class are progressing while they are completing the essay assignment. Using the scoring rubrics in both a formative and a summative manner makes it more likely that each student will successfully complete the assignment and that students will know what they will be scored on, what each score on the rubric means, and how the score will be assigned.

APPLY Case Study 3: Sight Word Recognition

Analyze the Curriculum. Mr. Jones is a special education teacher working with elementary students who have learning disabilities. Students are reading at different levels: Some are working on basic sight vocabulary, some are working on decoding skills, and all are working on comprehension skills. For his CBAs, Mr. Jones identifies the following objectives:

Given a listing of 45 words from the Dolch word list, the student will read the words at a rate of 25 correct words per minute. Given a 400-word reading passage, the student will read the passage, pronouncing each word correctly at a rate of 60 correct words per minute.

Given reading passages of factual information containing five to seven paragraphs each, the student will state the main idea and two details for each paragraph correctly.

Prepare Items to Meet the Curriculum Objectives. Mr. Jones prepares a series of probe sheets he can use with individual students when they reach certain levels of proficiency with each objective. Mr. Jones spends substantial time initially developing the probes for the reading curriculum area, but then he has a variety of probes readily available throughout the year (see Bui, Hlass, & Reda, 1995, for a compilation of probes and graphs that can be used for the Dolch words).

Mr. Jones can use two probe formats for the Dolch words. One format is flash cards, and he has a "deck" of flash cards for each set of words from the Dolch word list (e.g., preprimer level, primer level). The second format is a listing of the words on a worksheet, with the same words used repeatedly and each line precounted so that he can score the probe quickly after a student reads from it (Figure 4.7).

Probe Frequently. Three times a week, Mr. Jones conducts one-minute probes with each student working on this unit of instruction. He conducts the probe sessions at the beginning of the reading period, and he sets aside 10 minutes each day for the probes. Although it took more time when he first began using the probes, now he and his students are well acquainted with the CBA probe routine. Students begin seatwork at the start of the period, and Mr. Jones calls each student to a "CBA Center" in the classroom. Mr. Jones provides each student with a probe sheet, sets the timer for one minute, and marks on his laminated probe sheet any errors a student makes when orally reading the words. The student counts his or her number of correct and incorrect responses and gets ready to transfer those data to a graph.

Load Data Using a Graph Format. When Mr. Jones first began using the graph, he showed students how to figure out and write their correct and incorrect rates on the graph. Now each student is able to record his or her own data (see Figure 4.8) for correct and incorrect word identifications.

kind	fall	seven	about	laugh	far	shall		7
better	light	full	show	bring	long	got		14
six	carry	much	grow	shall	clean	myself		21
hold	start	cut	never	hot	ten	done	only	29
hurt	today	draw	own	if	together	drink	pick	37
keep	try	eight	warm	kind	fall	seven		44
about	laugh	far	shall	better	light	full		51
show	bring	long	got	six	carry	much		58
grow	shall	clean	myself	hold	start	cut		65
never	hot	ten	done	only	hurt	today		72
draw	own	if	together	drink	pick	keep		79
try	eight	warm	kind	fall	seven	about		86

DOLCH WORD LIST LEVEL 3 (Probe Form A)

FIGURE 4.7   CBA: Dolch Sight Word Probe

Yield to Results—Revisions and Decisions. Students are able to "see" their progress when they connect the sessions' data points across days of administration. Students can select individual goals for themselves by predicting the number of correct or incorrect words they want to get the next time they use a CBA probe. Some students are encouraged by the rising slope of their progress line, which documents that they are learning the words. Other students discuss with Mr. Jones ways to increase their progress line, such as reviewing the words more often by using the Language Master, using flash cards with a peer to study, finding the words in the school newspaper, or tracing the words on the bulletin board. Mr. Jones used to direct students in ways that they can increase their performance; now students formulate ideas to help themselves and each other.

Mr. Jones also uses the quarter-intersect and split-middle methods of assessing student performance. Once seven data points are gathered, Mr. Jones applies these methods to predict future performance rates.

Objective: Given words from level _3_ of the Dolch Word List, the student will verbally identify the words at a rate of _25_ correct words per minute.

FIGURE 4.8   CBA for Dolch Words: Equal Interval Graph

Extensions and Variations. Mr. Jones could use similar CBA formats for different IEP objectives:

Given words with different phonetic patterns, the student will verbally identify the word correctly.

After silently reading a brief passage that contains words the student already knows, the student will correctly answer five comprehension questions that are recall and inference level questions.

GRADING PRACTICES

The guiding principles for developing assessments described earlier in this chapter should also guide grading practices for students with mild to moderate disabilities. Whether grades are being determined for general education classes or for special education classes does not change the fact that the nature of the grading must be individualized for students—and for the latter group, completed according to the directions and directives in each student's IEP. Data still need to be collected in a frequent, systematic manner on critical instructional objectives. Much of the data collection described so far in this chapter may be used formatively to guide instruction; however, grades are usually derived from summative evaluations. Summative evaluations include homework scores, quiz grades, and test percentages that collectively comprise a student's final grade in a course. Effective teachers are able to present to students, at the onset of a course, those assessments and their relative value that will ultimately determine a student's grade in a course.

Ornstein (1994) notes several reasons that teachers use grades: (1) to ascertain mastery of specific content at a predetermined level, (2) to determine grouping of students, (3) to diagnose or plan instruction, and (4) to motivate students toward learning objectives. Wiggins (1988) notes that teachers are sometimes arbitrary when determining grades for students: "Students see that even teachers next door to each other, teaching different sections of the same course, employ different standards. . . . A grade is usable by students only if the criteria behind it are explicit and put in descriptive terms" (p. 23). To that end, several guidelines from Ornstein (p. 64) are applicable:

- Explain your grading system to students.
- Base grades on a predetermined set of standards.
- Base grades on the student's degree of progress.
- Base grades on a variety of sources.

 ## SUMMARY

In this chapter, we discussed how teachers who follow three principles of assessment are able to develop and use frequent and systematic assessments of critical curriculum objectives to make sound decisions about instruction. Furthermore, we described how involving students during their assessment process can promote responsible, motivationally oriented, and meaningful learning of instructional content and progress. We pointed out that teachers can gather information about student progress using a variety of assessment systems, including authentic, performance, portfolio, and curriculum-based systems. Effective teachers use the information gained from assessments to guide their teaching methods, materials, and techniques throughout the instructional process, not just on a pretest or posttest basis. Furthermore, encouraging student involvement by teaching students how to set goals for their learning and to self-evaluate their performance can increase students' achievement. We discussed how students with mild to moderate disabilities benefit educationally when their teachers involve them in their assessment practices. By collaborating with students during the assessment process, developing and beginning teachers can enhance achievement gains and improve learning opportunities for students with mild to moderate disabilities.

ACTIVITIES TO EXTEND YOUR KNOWLEDGE

1. Develop an inventory that samples a broad spectrum of students' skills or knowledge within an identified instructional domain or unit.
2. Identify a unit of instruction.
   a. Write a measurable goal and at least two corresponding objectives or benchmarks for student performance.
   b. Design a pretest to measure students' entry-level skills on the identified objectives.
   c. Compose an alternate form of the pretest you developed.
   d. Answer the following questions for the pretest and alternate form you developed:
      • Does each form of the assessment contain different items that require students to perform the same skills?
      • Are the scoring criteria for each form of the assessment explicit enough for different people to obtain the same scoring results?
3. An assortment of performance assessment methods are available to assess students' competencies in targeted areas. For your students, identify a domain or unit of instruction for which performance assessment could be used. Choose a method of performance assessment and predetermine the criteria for successful performance. What will you say to explain the criteria? When you talk with students during feedback sessions, what will the focus of your discussion be?

POINT AND CLICK ABOUT THE PROFESSION

IDEA. Several Internet sites provide paraphrases of IDEA content as well as access to the law itself. Because the IDEA contains important elements that guide instruction and assessment for students with IEPs, beginning teachers may find these sites useful not only for themselves but also for some of their general education colleagues. This important special education legislation may be reauthorized soon; visit these sites to keep up with the latest.

www.ideapractices.org/idea97a.htm
www.ldonline.org/ld_indepth/iep/idea97.html
www.ed.gov/offices/OSERS/Policy/IDEA/index.html
www.cec.sped.org/pp/

No Child Left Behind Act of 2001. There is considerable momentum nationally toward achievement and accountability for all students' performance, including the performance of students with disabilities. Statewide assessment formats and results, along with interpretations of adequate yearly progress, are receiving widespread attention. These Internet sites can provide information to help beginning special educators keep abreast of how assessments on a large scale are impacting assessments in the classroom.

www.wpllc.net/AYPConfSummary.asp
www.studentprogress.org/library/determining_Adequate_Yearly_Progress.pdf
www.ed.gov/nclb/landing.jhtml?src=pb

www.aasa.org/NCLB
www.cec.sped.org/pp

General Education Curriculum Standards from National Organizations. Beginning teachers may use local, state, or national curriculum standards to guide them when developing instructional and assessment content (check whether your state or school system posts its standards on the Internet). The following Internet sites identify different general education curriculum standards from national organizations. Special and general educators can use these or similar sites (e.g., their local school system) to assist in determining instructional and assessment items.

Curriculum Standards for Social Studies, National Council for Social Studies
www.ncss.org/standards/1.1.html

National Standards in Foreign Language Education
www.actfl.org/htdocs/standards/index.htm

National Council of Teachers of Mathematics
www/nctm.org

National Council for Music Education
www.namm.com/mktdv_ncme.shtml

National Geography Standards
www/cadgis.lsu.edu/lagea/natgeostand.html

National Standards for Arts Education
www.amc-music.com/srfact.htm

National Standards for Civics and Government: ERIC Digest
ericae.net/db/digs/ed380401/htm

National Standards for United States History
www.sscnet.ucla.edu/nchs/us-toc.htm

Standards for Science and Mathematics
ssdoo.gsfc.nasa.gov/education/standards.html

Assessment. The following Internet sites can be especially helpful for beginning special education teachers if the instructional and assessment content is a good match for their local school curriculum. If there is not a good match, some teachers may be able to adapt the content to achieve a good fit. Moreover, some sites contain generic information (e.g., literacy rubrics, math portfolios, CBA probes) that can easily be used for noting progress across many curricular and IEP areas regardless of what curriculum is used. These sites are particularly helpful for beginning teachers who are developing a number of different types of assessments (such as CBAs, performance assessments, and portfolio rubrics) because they include forms that can be individually tailored for students' IEPs and other general education content areas.

www.uvm.edu/~mhock/standards/rubric/altmath.html
www.aea1.k12.ia.us/transition/goalexamples/html
school.discovery.com/schrockguide/assess.html#rubrics
www.teach-nology.com/web_tools/rubrics
www.quadro.net/~ecoxon/Reporting/rubrics.htm
www.rubrics4teachers.com/
cresst96.cse.ucla.edu/CRESST/pages/samples.htm
www.rmcdenver.com/useguide/assessme/portfoli.htm?
brt.uoregon.edu/rctp/rctpcim/annweb/orfrationale/html
www.cse.ucla.edu/CRESST/pages/Rubrics/htm

www.emstac.org/registered/topics/cba/links.htm
www.lefthandlogic.com/htmdocs/tools/cbaprobe/cba.shtml
www.nasponline.org/certification/ss_module6.html
www.programevaluation.org/docs/cbamanall.pdf
www.cast.org/ncac/index.cfm?i2913

REFERENCES

Archbald, D. A. (1991). Authentic assessment: Principles, practices, and issues. *School Psychology Quarterly, 6,* 279–293.

Arthaud, T. J., Vasa, S. F., & Steckelberg, A. L. (2000). Reading assessment and instructional practices in special education. *Diagnostique, 25,* 205–228.

Bateman, B. D., & Linden, M. A. (1998). *Better IEPs: How to develop legally correct and educationally useful programs* (3rd ed.). Longmont, CO: Sopris West.

Blankenship, C. S. (1985). Using curriculum-based assessment data to make instructional decisions. *Exceptional Children, 52,* 233–238.

Bui, X., Hlass, J., & Reda, M. (1995). *Curriculum-based assessment and reading.* Unpublished manuscript, Johns Hopkins University at Rockville, MD.

Calhoon, M. B., & Fuchs, L. S. (2003). The effects of peer-assisted learning strategies and curriculum-based measurement on the mathematics performance of secondary students with disabilities. *Remedial and Special Education, 24,* 235–245.

Cullen, B., & Pratt, T. (1992). Measuring and reporting student progress. In S. Stainback & W. Stainback (Eds.), *Curriculum considerations in inclusive classrooms* (pp. 175–196). Baltimore: Paul H. Brookes.

Deno, S. L. (1985). Curriculum-based measurement: The emerging alternative. *Exceptional Children, 52,* 219–232.

Deno, S. L., & Fuchs, L. S. (1987). Developing curriculum-based measurement systems for data-based special education problem solving. *Focus on Exceptional Children, 19,* 1–16.

Duffy, M. L., Jones, J., & Thomas, S. W. (1999). Using portfolios to foster independent thinking. *Intervention in School and Clinic, 35* (1), 34–37.

Elliott, S. N. (1992). Authentic assessment: An introduction to a neobehavioral approach to classroom assessment. *School Psychology Quarterly, 5,* 273–278.

Fuchs, L. S., & Deno, S. L. (1991). Paradigmatic distinctions between instructionally relevant measurement models. *Exceptional Children, 58,* 488–500.

Fuchs, L. S., & Fuchs, D. (1984). Criterion-referenced assessment without measurement: How accurate for special education? *Remedial and Special Education, 5* (4), 29–32.

Fuchs, L. S., & Fuchs, D. (1985). Effectiveness of systematic formative evaluation: A meta-analysis. *Exceptional Children, 53,* 199–208.

Gersten, R., Keating, T., & Irvin, L. K. (1995). The burden of proof: Validity as improvement of instructional practice. *Exceptional Children, 61,* 510–519.

Hasbrouck, J. E., Woldbeck, T., Ihnot, C., & Parker, R. I. (1999). One teacher's use of curriculum-based measurement: A changed opinion. *Learning Disabilities Research & Practice, 14,* 118–126.

Hoover, J. J., & Patton, J. R. (2004). Differentiating standards-based education for students with diverse needs. *Remedial and Special Education, 25,* 74–78.

Jorden, J., & Haube, A. (1995). *A guide to using curriculum-based assessment: Do you know what your students know?* Unpublished manuscript (videotape & guide), Johns Hopkins University at Rockville, MD.

King-Sears, M. E. (1994). *Curriculum-based assessment in special education.* Belmont, CA: Wadsworth.

King-Sears, M. E., Burgess, M., & Lawson, T. L. (1999). APPLYing curriculum-based assessment in inclusive settings. *Teaching Exceptional Children, 32* (1), 30–38.

Meyer, C. A. (1992). What's the difference between authentic and performance assessment? *Educational Leadership, 48* (8), 39–40.

No Child Left Behind Act of 2001(NCLB), Pub. L. No. 107–110.

Nolet, V. (1992). Classroom-based measurement and portfolio assessment. *Diagnostique, 18* (1), 5–26.

Ornstein, A. C. (1994). Grading practices and policies: An overview and some suggestions. *NASSP Bulletin, 78* (561), 55–64.

Paulson, F. L., Paulson, P. R., & Meyer, C. A. (1991). What makes a portfolio a portfolio? *Educational Leadership, 48* (5), 60–63.

Poteet, J. A., Choate, J. S., & Stewart, S. C. (1993). Performance assessment and special education: Practices and prospects. *Focus on Exceptional Children, 26* (1), 1–20.

Salvia, J., & Hughes, C. (1990). *Curriculum-based assessment: Testing what is taught.* New York: Macmillan.

Salvia, J., & Ysseldyke, J. E. (1991). *Assessment* (5th ed.). Boston: Houghton Mifflin.

Sarouphim, K. M. (1999). Discovering multiple intelligences through a performance-based assessment: Consistency with independent ratings. *Exceptional Children, 65,* 151–161.

Stecker, P. M., & Fuchs, L. S. (2000). Effecting superior achievement using curriculum-based measurement: The importance of individual progress monitoring. *Learning Disabilities Research & Practice, 15,* 128–134.

U.S. Congress, Office of Technology Assessment. (1992). Performance assessment: Methods and characteristics. In *Testing in American schools: Asking the right questions* (OTA SET-519, pp. 201–249). Washington, DC: Government Printing Office.

Viechnicki, K. J., Barbour, N., Shaklee, B., Rohrer, J., & Ambrose, R. (1993). The impact of portfolio assessment on teacher classroom activities. *Journal of Teacher Education, 44,* 371–377.

Wesson, C., Skiba, R., Sevcik, B., King, R. P., & Deno, S. (1984). The effects of technically adequate instructional data on achievement. *Remedial and Special Education, 5* (5), 17–22.

Wiggins, G. (1988). Rational numbers: Toward grading and scoring that help rather than harm learning. *American Educator, 12,* 20–25, 45–58.

Woodward, J., Monroe, K., & Baxter, J. (2001). Enhancing student achievement on performance assessments in mathematics. *Learning Disability Quarterly, 24,* 33–46.

Planning for Instruction

Chapter Outline

In this chapter, we will

- provide reasons for lesson planning

- discuss the developmental aspect of lesson planning and its relationship to the diagnostic teaching model

- define strategic and tactical planning

- identify components of successfully planned lessons, including instructional activities and materials in planned lessons

- examine methods to evaluate lesson implementations, follow-up, and self-evaluation

- review unit and lesson plan formats, including those for inclusive programming

A PROFESSIONAL GLIMPSE

Colin O'Brien began his final student teaching internship confident that he could successfully complete the university's student-teaching requirements. Throughout his undergraduate program, Colin had worked at a shopping mall near the university. He saw no reason why he couldn't continue to work part-time at the clothing store while he completed his internship. After all, he had done it during his other practicum experiences. The first week of student teaching went along as expected. Dr. Mahoney, Colin's university-based internship supervisor, met with him and his master teacher, Mrs. Campanello, to review the internship requirements that she had discussed at the internship orientation meeting. To Colin, Dr. Mahoney seemed businesslike but supportive in her demeanor. He had no questions regarding Dr. Mahoney's expectations, although he wondered about how realistic both Mrs. Campanello and Dr. Mahoney were regarding the amount of time he would need to prepare his lessons. During the week, Colin spent his time observing Mrs. Campanello and working with students one to one or in small groups as they engaged in guided and independent practice activities. He also spent time reviewing the school's policies and procedures for its schoolwide behavior support program, crisis plan, and No Child Left Behind (NCLB) school improvement plan. He also met with the principal and guidance counselor as part of the school orientation activity that was assigned by Dr. Mahoney.

In week two, Mrs. Campanello had Colin prepare and implement a lesson on comparing and contrasting the use of various literary devices (e.g., personification, simile, metaphor, hyperbole, allusion). After the lesson, Mrs. Companello complemented Colin for treating simile and metaphor as concepts, defining them, giving examples and nonexamples, and testing the attributes. However, Mrs. Campanello expressed concern that while Colin followed the appropriate steps for treating concepts, he needed to provide multiple examples and nonexamples, engage students in guided practice activities, and have his materials ready and accessible during the lesson. Colin took the feedback well and promised to be better prepared for his next lesson. Sure enough Colin followed through two days later with a well-prepared and -executed lesson.

During the next three weeks, Mrs. Campanello relinquished more and more of her classes to Colin. Needless to say, the workload increased dramatically. But Colin continued his part-time job and his social schedule as usual. Upon Dr. Mahoney's third visit and second observation, Colin's preparation was poor, and his lesson was ineffective as a result. Dr. Mahoney met with Mrs. Campanello prior to meeting with Colin for his postobservation conference. Mrs. Campanello verified that Colin had been having more and more problems with his lesson preparation as she relinquished more responsibilities. She was contemplating taking back a couple of her class periods. In the postobservation conference, Dr. Mahoney presented Colin with the observation data and also discussed with him the comments from Mrs. Campanello. Colin became defensive and dismissed the criticism. He believed that his preparation was sufficient and that the lessons went well enough. He explained that he had seen teachers down the hall do half as much as he had.

Three-quarters of the way through his student teaching, Colin had not made sufficient adjustments to improve his preparation. His master teacher was frustrated with his recalcitrance, and Dr. Mahoney terminated Colin's internship.

*I*n any systematic approach to a task, planning is central. Consequently, effective teachers spend significant amounts of time planning for instruction in a variety of ways. The purpose of this chapter is to provide developing teachers with a rationale for planning, to show how planning relates to systematic teaching, to specify the components of well-designed lesson plans, and to provide suggestions for writing unit and daily lesson plans. Many teachers are skeptical about the need for written lesson plans.

Pause and Reflect About the Profession 5.1

Speculate on why written plans are valuable teaching tools. Provide at least five reasons why teachers write and use lesson plans.

1. _____

    _____

2. _____

    _____

3. _____

4. _____

    _____

5. _____

    _____

Some argue that the time spent writing plans could be better used developing or adapting materials, thinking through lessons, or consulting with other teachers.

All of these activities are important elements of instruction, and certainly teachers never seem to have enough hours in the day to complete all the planning and teaching functions expected of them. However, effective teaching includes written plans that specify the objectives of a lesson and detail the instructional activities that will be used to attain the objectives (Archer, 1991; Danielson & McGreal, 2000; Hofmeister & Lubke, 1990; Rosenshine, 1986). In the following paragraphs, we explain why written plans are valuable teaching tools.

REASONS FOR PLANNING

There are a number of reasons for planning. These include the increased probability of effective teaching; teacher's increased confidence, security, and direction; and the establishment of good habits.

Planning Increases the Probability of Effective Teaching

An old axiom that applies to travel—if you don't know where and how you are going, you won't be able to get there—applies to instructional planning as well. Specific goal statements provide a destination for teachers and students and the basis for evaluating the effectiveness of instructional activities and materials used to help students to arrive at some prescribed skill level. Describing in detail the means by which students are to attain these objectives is necessary as well. Researchers have found that teachers who set specific objectives and write more detailed lesson plans are more effective than teachers who write broadly stated goals and superficial lesson plans (Algozzine, Ysseldyke, & Elliott, 1997; Cooper, 1986; Hudson, 1996; Mager, 1996; Williams & Fox, 1996).

An important distinction needs to be made between written and mental planning. Many hours of mental planning precede the act of writing plans. Thoroughly thinking through instructional objectives and activities is often a necessary, but insufficient, means of planning. Mental planning alone still leaves a high probability that objectives and activities will be vague and loosely structured. Preparing a written document increases the chances that objectives will be clearly stated and activities thoroughly organized. Mager (1996) found that when teachers write out clear lessons, they make instruction work. Written plans help teachers derive appropriate learning outcomes and develop the instructional techniques to enhance their students' learning, anticipate and solve students' performance problems in advance of delivery, create instruction that matches student needs, and develop more effective instructional evaluations.

Planning Increases Confidence, Security, and Direction

Plans remind teachers what they are to do during a lesson. Considering the range of variables that teachers deal with during instruction, having a plan they can refer to tends to increase their confidence and sense of security. Effective teachers know that when uncertainty strikes, they can glance quickly at their notes, respond in an appropriate direction, and continue with their lesson (Clark & Yinger, 1979; McCutcheon, 1980).

Planning Helps Establish Good Habits

Developing teachers who consistently write lesson plans develop a systematic approach to instruction (Algozzine et al., 1997). Using a particular format to sketch out what and how to teach forces teachers to examine each element of a lesson, to sequence activities more carefully, and to organize materials more thoroughly. Once established, this routine should be followed when planning to teach any new content. And with changes in teacher roles to include more teaming models (discussed in Chapters 11), lesson plans can be approached creatively and collaboratively in traditional class settings or in cooperative settings, where teachers help each other adapt and deliver instruction (Rutherford & Warger, 1995; Thousand, Villa, & Nevin, 1994; Wood, 1991). Dieker (2000) reported that special education and general education teachers can coplan instruction for students with disabilities. Darch, Miller, and Shippen (1998) found that professionals who plan in advance of lesson presentation are proactive and can prevent learning and behavior problems before they occur instead of reacting to them. To accomplish this, teachers must consider how they think about lessons, how they talk to students, and how they anticipate and respond to problems in the classroom and the general school environment. These actions are essential for effective lesson planning.

DEVELOPMENTAL ASPECT OF LESSON PLANNING

Novice teachers will have more extensive written plans than more experienced teachers. This is a function of beginning teachers' unfamiliarity with students, materials, and content.

Written lesson plans are the first step for developing teachers as they learn to manage and carry out daily instructional activities. Although time-consuming and often tedious, writing out detailed plans helps developing teachers structure their thinking about teaching, which results in a more systematic course of action (Whitaker, 2000). Eventually, beginning teachers gain sufficient experience that the need to write down detailed daily lesson plans diminishes and they can spend more time attending to long-term planning needs. On the basis of interviews with experienced teachers, researchers have found that, ultimately, teachers think through, rather than writing down, their daily plans (Clark & Yinger, 1979; McCutcheon, 1980).

RELATIONSHIP OF PLANNING TO THE DIAGNOSTIC TEACHING MODEL

The diagnostic teaching model (DTM) (see Figure 5.1) is a framework for conceptualizing teaching as a hypothesis-testing process. Teachers systematically examine the variables (e.g., students' present skill levels, available teaching materials, strategies for presenting content, practice activities) associated with learning and how they apply to

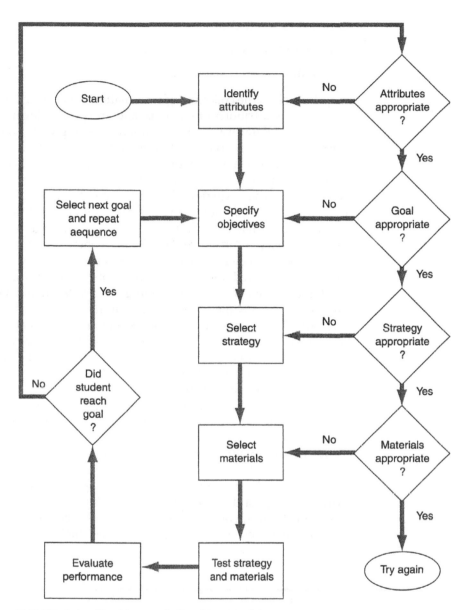

FIGURE 5.1 The Diagnostic Teaching Model

Source: Adapted from "Gilding the lily," by G. P. Cartwright & C. A. Cartwright, 1972, *Exceptional Children, 39,* pp. 231–234.

their students. They then construct a hypothesis in the form of an instructional plan. The plan is implemented, and student performance is monitored. If the plan to manipulate learning variables in certain ways changes the performance of students, then the hypothesis is supported. If the plan does not manifest the intended effects, then teachers analyze their plan to determine where changes are needed. Consequently, instruction is approached in a systematic way that acknowledges teaching as an inexact science and teachers' limited ability to determine the cause-and-effect relationship of the numerous variables in any learning environment (Cartwright, Cartwright, & Ward, 1981).

The DTM contains five core steps that teachers follow in planning for instruction:

1. Identifying attributes
2. Specifying objectives

3. Selecting strategies

4. Selecting materials

5. Testing strategies and materials

Step 1 involves the collection of information about the classroom setting, the behavioral and learning attributes of students, and any other relevant variables. Teachers first collect baseline data prior to intervention, allowing them to see what is occurring in the classroom under existing conditions. Next, they determine what skills or behaviors they want to decrease, maintain, or increase by specifying clear and behaviorally stated objectives that reflect how the target students are to respond (e.g., see-say, hear-write, see-write) and what criterion level they are to attain (e.g., 90 percent accuracy, 60 movements per minute) (step 2). Teachers then select alternative strategies (e.g., self-monitoring, semantic webbing, concept induction) and any accompanying materials (e.g., tangible reinforcers, reading books, concrete examples) needed to accomplish the stated objectives (steps 3 and 4). Once implemented by the teacher, the strategies and materials are tested through subsequent observations and data collection (step 5).

On the basis of the information gathered, teachers analyze students' performance on daily or weekly measures and determine whether the objectives have been reached. Accordingly, the sequence is repeated in one of two ways (see Figure 5.1). If the objectives have been reached, the teacher moves the student on to the next objective in the curriculum hierarchy (step 2) and continues through the other steps as described. If the objectives have not been reached, the teacher reexamines the accuracy and appropriateness of the baseline data, stated objectives, strategies, and materials. The teacher then makes any necessary modifications and the sequence is continued. When all steps seem to be accurate and appropriate, the teacher implements the strategies and materials again and retests (see Box 5.1).

One other point requires consideration. Often, teacher-training programs prepare their preservice teacher trainees to follow the steps in the sequence provided above. Researchers who have surveyed actual planning patterns followed by teachers in the field, however, suggest that teachers typically plan in a different sequence. Often, they focus first on activities, content, materials, or resources (Peterson, Marx, & Clark, 1978) instead of goals and objectives. In other cases, their planning is not a sequential process.

Box 5.1   **Case Study**

Christopher, a sixth-grade student, has just been referred to Ms. Theodore, a learning support teacher in an elementary school. Christopher has been having difficulties responding to comprehension questions. Ms. Theodore decides she wants to confirm his reported reading level by administering an informal reading inventory based on words, passages, and questions from the reading materials in the learning support class. In addition, she collects interview data from Christopher's classroom teacher and parents regarding the reading environment in the general education classroom and at home. She also asks Christopher what he does while he reads. From the information gathered, Ms. Theodore concludes that Christopher can recognize words by using phonic and semantic cues and can fluently read material written on a fourth-grade level but that he can answer comprehension questions with only 60 percent accuracy. He is provided with opportunities to read in the general education class, and his parents appear to provide a good reading environment at home (both parents read magazines and newspapers daily and encourage Christopher to read as well). When he was asked what he thinks about during reading and how he reads, Christopher reported that he reads the words and that sometimes he thinks about other things. He apparently does not correctly review what he has read, ask himself questions, or try to predict what will happen in the passages he reads.

Pause and Reflect About the Profession 5.2

See whether you can determine how Ms. Theodore used steps of the DTM in the example with Christopher.

1. What are relevant classroom attributes in Ms. Theodore's class?

2. What are important teaching considerations, given Christopher's reading comprehension skills?

3. What are appropriate reading objectives for Christopher, based on Ms. Theodore's use of the DTM?

4. How can Ms. Theodore use appropriate strategies to improve Christopher's written comprehension answers?

On the basis of the attributes derived from her assessments (step 1 of the DTM), Ms. Theodore specifies the following objectives (step 2 of the DTM):

- When given a passage at the fourth-grade reading level, Christopher will paraphrase the content after each paragraph read with 100 percent accuracy.

- When given a passage at the fourth-grade reading level, Christopher will see-write answers correctly for seven out of eight comprehension questions.

   To improve Christopher's written answers to comprehension questions, Ms. Theodore decides to train Christopher to paraphrase the content of each paragraph read during daily 15-minute sessions of small-group instruction (step 3 of the DTM). She selects a set of passages and accompanying comprehension questions written at the fourth-grade level to use for practice and as evaluation probes (step 4 of the DTM). Ms. Theodore then implements her teaching strategy and records Christopher's performance when using the paraphrasing strategy and writing answers to comprehension questions (step 5 of the DTM). If Christopher's performance increases at an acceptable rate (if he increasingly uses the paraphrasing strategy and answers more questions correctly), then Ms. Theodore will continue with her intervention program. If not, she will have to reevaluate each step of the DTM process and make necessary modifications.

Instead, teachers go back and forth among these steps, simultaneously working on each step. Regardless, the steps within the DTM are considered to be critical despite variations in the sequence with which they are carried out.

STRATEGIC AND TACTICAL PLANNING

Planning has two basic levels: strategic and tactical (Algozzine et al., 1997). Strategic planning refers to the broad, overall rationale for providing instruction to particular students. It includes justification for the content, activities, materials, and objectives that are included in the day-to-day operations of a classroom. Typically, at the strategic level, teachers reflect on their philosophy of instruction and the ultimate outcomes that should result from sound instructional programs. For example, teachers consider what the needs of students will be once they leave school and enter some vocation, how those needs can be most effectively met, and how the curriculum can be structured to provide the highest probability that those needs will be met. Thus, teachers plan functional skill activities that help students reach adult-life goals and objectives (Gable, Laycock, Maroney, & Smith, 1991). When teachers plan well, schools, community service agencies, private organizations, and family members can work together to help students make a smooth transition to adult life. Effective strategic planning supports students' transitioning and Individualized Education Program (IEP) processes (West, Corbey, Boyer-Stephens, Jones, Miller, & Sarkees-Wircenski, 1999).

On the basis of strategic considerations, teachers then plan how, on a day-to-day, week-to-week basis, they can provide instruction that builds on the bits and pieces of previous learning to attain the long-range goals of a program. These daily operational considerations, which take the form of daily lesson plans or unit plans, are the essence of tactical planning. Tactical planning includes determining prerequisite skills to be acquired by students, setting short-term objectives (e.g., what the teacher will teach the next day), describing specific teaching activities and related materials to be used to present particular concepts or skills, and designing daily evaluation procedures.

An example of strategic and tactical planning is the preparation of curricular interventions in learning strategies programs described by Carnine (1991). A group of content-area secondary teachers and the special education resource and consulting teachers discuss how they can better meet the needs of students with learning problems (strategic planning) in inclusion settings. After reviewing observational data, they conclude that these students appear to have few or no skills in monitoring and regulating their own learning. The teachers decide to set up a learning strategies course to be offered by the learning support teachers, cotaught with content instructors in the general education setting. In addition, the content-area teachers (e.g., science, mathematics, economics teachers) will modify their demands for content mastery, particularly during the first term of the school year, and provide opportunities for students to practice using the strategies they have learned. The expectation is that, with improved learning processes, students will be able to master more content.

With the overall plan sketched out, the teachers identify specific objectives to be mastered and learning strategies that they believe need to be taught. In addition, they identify the strategies intervention model (Deshler & Schumaker, 1986) as the set of procedures to be used. They then begin work on unit plans for the courses on learning strategies and on plans for content-area teachers to facilitate the use of strategies in their classrooms (tactical planning). Accordingly, as teachers approach lesson planning systematically, they can diagnose and use differentiated instruction to meet the needs of many students who have individual needs (Pettig, 2000).

In sum, planning occurs at a variety of levels, moving from more global to more specific considerations. It is important for new teachers to realize that the process of strategic and tactical planning is not necessarily sequential, whereby teachers make strategic plans and then move on to tactical planning. Teachers often move back and forth between global and specific considerations until both levels of planning are complete.

COMPONENTS OF SUCCESSFULLY PLANNED LESSONS

Effective planning is characterized by definable components that contain information on where and how students will reach some specified goal. These components include prerequisite skills, instructional objectives, instructional activities and materials to be used, methods to evaluate lessons, adaptations and modifications, anticipated problems, and self-evaluation of lesson plans (Garland, 1982).

Prerequisite Skills

To provide effective instruction, teachers must determine the present educational levels of their students; that is, they must determine what each student can and cannot do vis-à-vis the curriculum hierarchy. If one envisions a skill hierarchy for a given content area (e.g., reading, math, language) organized in some rational sequence, then teachers need to pinpoint which skills students have mastered and which skills they must learn or continue to practice. In some cases, published skill hierarchies may not be available, so teachers must determine the subskills for a given task.

Teachers can then collect baseline data on the skills identified. Depending on the target skills, baseline data may be derived from probe sheets, teacher observation, curriculum-based assessments, rubrics, formal assessment devices, task analyses, and so forth. In any case, these assessments enable teachers to determine the current educational levels of students and to specify the target skills that will form the basis for instructional objectives.

Instructional Objectives

Effective teachers know where they want to take their students. They have explicit goals and make students aware of them. Differences in how they guide students to reach those goals may not be as important as the need to specify where students are going. If they have set clear and specific goals, developing and new teachers can more easily determine what types of activities will help students achieve these goals. Without specific goals, teachers and students may flounder, completing one activity after another yet not making any progress toward the mastery of some predetermined skill or concept.

Written instructional objectives contribute to teacher effectiveness. For example, Mager (1996) found that when teachers identify, select, and write well-stated objectives, they create the foundation necessary to reach their instructional goals. Well-stated lesson plans include objectives that describe the performance that teachers expect to achieve. Lesson objectives can be benchmarks to help teachers identify the conditions under which they expect the performance to occur. Objectives can set criteria within lessons.

Hudson (1996) suggested that planned prelesson activities, also referred to as "lesson openings" (Archer, 1991) and "learning sets" (Hudson, Lignugaris-Kraft, & Miller, 1993), are necessary to link past and new sets of knowledge. Prelesson activities can be organized into two categories: review and introduction. The teacher first plans the review activities, including oral and written questions and lesson activities that permit students to practice content knowledge. Planning for reviews (Rosenshine, 1986) includes actively considering how to involve all students in response opportunities and how to tell students when they are correct and when they make errors. When introducing new information, teachers plan how they will set the stage for the upcoming content and tasks, how they will state the lesson and task objectives, and how they will tell students how the new skill or knowledge benefits them.

Characteristics. Behaviorally stated instructional objectives contain phrases identifying the target students, the behavior they will demonstrate, the conditions under which they will demonstrate the behavior, and the criterion for mastery. They are written in clear and concise language that makes it easy for others to understand the focus of instruction. The behavior is stated in observable, measurable terms indicative of the response mode the students will use (e.g., see-write, hear-say). Behavioral objectives are student-focused (reflecting what students will do or accomplish, not what the teacher will do). For example, the following statement contains all the attributes of a behavioral objective:

> When given a probe sheet with words beginning with bl, cl, and fl consonant blends, Calvin, Tony, John, and Tanya will see-say the words at a rate of 60 words per minute with two or fewer errors.

Often, teachers run into problems when they make unclear statements, such as "The teacher will work on decoding." It is unclear because "work on" connotes numerous possible activities. The same statement is flawed because it does not indicate a desired outcome; instead, it refers to the process of "working on." Also, the statement does

Pause and Reflect About the Profession 5.3

- During cleanup time, Perry begins to talk loudly. Ms. Martin looks at him sternly and tells him to "settle down and clean quietly."
- Both Jane and Freida complete work quickly and accurately.
- Five minutes before math class is over, Joan tells Aaron that if he completes his math assignment correctly, he may use her computer for the next 20 minutes.
- When asked to be Bill's partner for soccer practice, Andy responds with a statement that he doesn't want to be Bill's partner.
- Joe warns his friends: "Watch your language—there are small children here."
- Marsha fidgets, squirms, or seems restless whenever history class begins.
- Lorenzo often shifts from one uncompleted task to another and rarely finishes his assignments on time.
- Using a fifth-grade math book, Betsy will complete 10 fraction problems daily, with no more than two errors on each occasion.
- Sally often loses things necessary for class.
- Yasmine seems to have difficulty sustaining attention during school assemblies.
- Hillary often displays strong self-management skills.
- When Athena wanted to telephone her parents, she put in the quarter and dialed the number. She talked with her mother for two minutes.
- "I worked very persistently on my class readings and assignments. When the instructor gave an examination on Tuesday, I received a score of 95 percent."
- Given five minutes during class to complete her handwriting, Martha will form the letter c five times without errors.

1. What are student behaviors in each of the above examples?
2. Which of these examples contain all of the attributes of good behavioral or instructional objectives?
3. After identifying the student behaviors, specify the appropriate conditions and criterion level for each example.

not mention students. Finally, it lacks an observable, measurable behavior that indicates specifically how the students will respond to a stimulus, the most common error teachers make when writing objectives.

Behaviorally stated objectives focus on some desired outcome of instruction. However, this does not limit the utility of objectives to the end product of an academic task. Processes (e.g., metacognitive strategies, verbal rehearsal, self-instruction) used in attaining some end product (e.g., reading faster, comprehending more, writing better essays) can also be the targeted behavior(s). For instance, a student with writing difficulties may be asked to use a learning strategy such as TOWER (think, order, write, error monitor, and revise) in generating an essay (Mercer & Mercer, 1985). The objective could be stated in terms of the strategy, not the end product (the characteristics of the essay). For example:

> When asked to write an essay, the student will show evidence of using each step of the TOWER strategy with 100 percent accuracy for three consecutive days.

A second objective could reflect the intended effect of using the TOWER strategy (to be able to write a more coherent essay):

> When asked to write an essay, the student will think-write topics and supporting material that are coherently ordered as judged by the teacher in three consecutive essays.

Functions. Once teachers determine where students are functioning in a skill hierarchy, they determine how far up the hierarchy students should go over some period of time. Like a Sunday driver, a teacher without specific objectives may take a winding path in some unknown direction and never reach the appropriate destination (instructional objective).

Selection of Activities and Materials. With the objectives of instruction identified, teachers can begin to select activities and materials that will help students attain the objectives. Activities and materials act as vehicles for reaching some objective; they must help students understand a concept or remember the steps of an academic rule and provide sufficient practice to develop mastery. For instance, if, on the one hand, the objective of instruction is for students to discriminate between squares and rectangles, then the instructional activities and materials should help students identify the attributes that make one shape different from the other. The teacher could state or have students discover the attributes of each figure, listing them on the chalkboard, and have students methodically examine examples to see that all the attributes are present. If, on the other hand, students can already discriminate between a square and a rectangle, but the discrimination responses are slow, then the activities and materials should focus not on what the attributes are but rather on a quick and accurate response to examples and nonexamples of each. Students could quickly name shapes by using flash cards. Consequently, the activities and materials change as the objectives change.

Assistance in Tracking Student Progress. Clearly stated objectives indicate what students should be learning (Mager, 1996). All those with an interest in students' progress—teachers, administrators, parents, and students themselves—can draw conclusions about the effectiveness of instruction on the basis of whether or not students are meeting their objectives. Consequently, objectives form the basis for evaluation of instruction and accountability.

Task Analysis and En Route and Terminal Objectives. Objectives are generated by analyzing the components of a superordinate task or skill. Once a task or skill is selected for instruction, teachers or curriculum specialists often break down the task into steps. Instruction is then focused on mastering individual steps and sets of steps leading to mastery of the entire task or skill.

Depending on the complexity of the target task or skill and the existing skills of students, the number of steps (en route objectives) leading to mastery of the task (terminal objective) will vary. Another factor in determining the number of steps or en route objectives used to master a terminal objective is who makes the distinction between a task as the terminal objective and a task as an en route objective leading toward the mastery of some greater objective. One person may call mastery of consonant blends a terminal objective, whereas another may identify it as an en route objective leading to the mastery of phonics. Both persons may be right. The point is that teachers determine what they want to call en route or terminal.

In any case, the skill needs to be mastered. A rule of thumb for developing and new teachers is to break down tasks or skills to the largest units appropriate for the instructional situation. Some students can master multiple steps at once, whereas others will have to focus on each step individually. Again with the example of consonant blends, some students can master a set of blends containing the /l/ sound, whereas others may have to work on bl, fl, and cl separately.

Curriculum specialists and publishers of instructional materials have already done a task analysis of many basic academic tasks. The resulting skill hierarchies are lists of sequentially ordered subskills that lead to some terminal objective. Consequently, new teachers need not spend that much time analyzing the components of a task or skill. Hierarchies or curricula may not be available for a particular content area, however. In those cases, teachers must complete their own task analysis. And, even when skill

Pause and Reflect About the Profession 5.4

Practice the process of task analysis with the following academic skills. Sequence each of the following into component skills. Put each step in order, starting from the smallest step.

Reading
Names alphabet letters
Discriminates letter sounds
Uses dictionary skills
Sequences a story read
Finds a main idea in the written paragraph
Names the time, setting, characters, and story plot

Mathematics
Solves a division problem
Makes change for a dollar
Writes a check
Uses a calculator

Self-Help
Brushes teeth
Ties shoes
Dresses self
Feeds self
Takes care of personal needs
Makes a bed
Cooks a hamburger

Leisure
Gets a strike in bowling
Completes a word search puzzle
Bats a ball
Uses a jump rope
Plants a vegetable garden
Checks out a library book
Watches a home video

hierarchies or curricula are available, some task analysis may be needed to fit them to the learners' needs.

The benefit of following skill hierarchies is that planning is guided in a logical or sequential fashion. Teachers know where students are and where they need to go; they can see both the trees and the forest. This allows them to anticipate where instruction needs to go, to make adaptations, and to better assist students in reaching some terminal objective.

Instructional Activities and Materials to Be Used

Instructional activities should be designed to assist students in realizing targeted objectives. When designing instructional activities, teachers must consider the stage of learning to which the activity is directed. The simple four-stage model (acquisition, fluency building, maintenance, and generalization) illustrated in Figure 5.2 can be used to show how learning proceeds. The acquisition stage of learning is characterized by

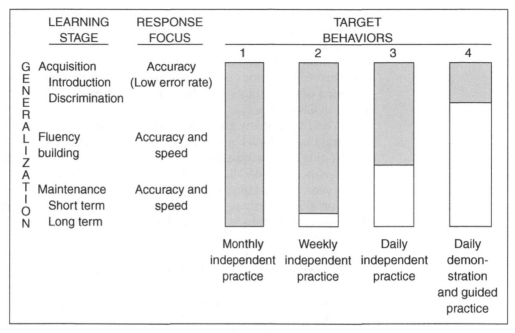

FIGURE 5.2 Illustration of the Interface of Stages of Learning, Response Focus, and Instructional Activities

a high rate of inaccurate responses. Students have little or no skill at this stage. With careful teacher-directed instruction, however, the rate of accurate responses rises and the rate of inaccurate responses declines.

When their responses reach 90 percent accuracy, students are moving into the fluency-building stage. They are now practicing their newly acquired skill in order to increase the speed with which they give accurate responses. For instance, instead of solving computational math problems at a rate of 40 digits per minute with five or fewer errors, students are increasing their speed and accuracy as they can solve 60 digits per minute with zero errors.

Once students respond fluently, instructional time for the target skill can be gradually reduced, but students must be provided with practice during the maintenance stage. At this point, students are largely engaged in periodic independent practice to ensure that they can still perform previously taught skills at an acceptable rate of speed and accuracy.

Generalization prepares students to use newly developed skills in settings and at times different from those used during acquisition and fluency building. Generalization is accomplished by reducing the level of teacher prompting and reinforcement so that students can demonstrate the behavior independently.

Instructional activities will be different at each of the four stages. Activities at the acquisition stage require intense teacher-student interaction in which the teacher models a response and students imitate. The teacher explains the steps to a skill or the definition and characteristics of a concept. Numerous cues are used to assist students in responding accurately, but fast responses are not the focus of instruction; the numbers of correct responses and errors are the important measures. During the fluency-building stage, teacher-student interactions continue but consist largely of providing corrective feedback as students work on daily independent practice activities. While these activities require less teacher supervision than at the acquisition level, teachers do periodically check student work and remind students of the need to respond quickly and accurately. Maintenance stage activities are largely the same type of independent practice activities used at the fluency-building stage, except that more review may be required beforehand and the practice is distributed over intervals of a week or month. Generalization stage activities are embedded into activities at all the previous stages and therefore do not occur necessarily as discrete independent activities. Further description of these stages and the types of strategies and learning activities used are provided in Chapter 6.

In addition, at any given point in time individual students will be developing multiple target behaviors. For the most recently introduced target behaviors students will be functioning at the acquisition or fluency building stage, while they are functioning at the maintenance or generalization stages for targeted behaviors that were introduced earlier in the year. For instance, students may be beginning to develop (i.e., **acquisition level**) addition skills involving regrouping with multi-digit numbers (e.g., 24 + 17 = 41). At the same time, the student is **maintaining** other addition skills such as addition of multi-digit numbers without regrouping (e.g., 21 + 13 = 34). The target behavior bars in Figure 5.2 illustrate this situation.

Regardless of the stage of learning, a lesson contains a beginning, a middle, and an end. This not-so-novel concept is surprisingly absent from the conceptualization of many developing teachers. Effective teachers usually begin a lesson by telling students what they will be doing during the lesson and linking previous lessons with the content of the current lesson. This often takes the form of a lesson-initiating review. Next, teachers demonstrate the concept or academic skill and provide appropriate practice activities for students. Finally, the lesson should end with some form of closure that indicates to students the transition from one session to another. A lesson-ending review often fills this need. The following sections detail the various sections of a lesson.

Lesson Initiation. It is necessary to prepare students for a lesson by telling them what activities they will do and how these fit in with previous and future lessons. Consequently, the first step in lesson description is to note the activities of the lesson. For example, an advance organizer may be used: "Today, we will discuss nouns and verbs. Then we will look at some magazine ads to find nouns and verbs. Finally, I have a worksheet for you to complete." To link this lesson with the previous lesson, a teacher may say, "Yesterday, we talked about nouns. We defined them and came up with some examples. Today, we will do the same, but we will discuss verbs, too." What may follow is a review of the definition and examples of nouns, either stated by the teacher or, preferably, elected from students by teacher questioning. The latter strategy provides students with an additional practice activity as well as a link to the previous lesson.

Demonstration. Once an initial review is conducted, instruction on new content begins (Hofmeister & Lubke, 1990; Hudson, 1996; Nolet & Tindal, 1993). Instruction initially involves a demonstration of target concepts, facts, skills, principles, or value judgments. The teacher either provides a model or induces the model from students. For instance, when teaching the concept of square, the teacher would begin the modeling strategy by presenting a diagram of a square and telling students what it is. Next, the teacher would write the definition of a square on the chalkboard: "A square is a quadrilateral with four congruent sides and four congruent angles." Using a diagram of a square, the teacher would then show how the example has four congruent sides and four congruent angles. In contrast, if using an induction strategy, the teacher would present a diagram of a square without naming its shape and proceed to ask students leading questions about the number of sides and angles and other attributes that distinguish a square. Using that information, the teacher could have students write a definition and give a name to the diagram. In either cases, the target content is explicitly provided to students in a systematic fashion.

Although lecturing is a primary way of presenting information in content classes, effective teachers use demonstration, guided practice, and independent practice

(Hudson, 1996). Nonetheless, Nolet and Tindal (1993) found that teachers actively lecture, demonstrate, and direct students through a task 70 percent of the time and that students are expected to listen 57 percent of the time. Effective teachers may realize that although students need to use listening comprehension and note-taking skills during demonstrated lectures, students with mild disabilities often lack such skills.

The manner in which the teacher conducts the demonstration phase of a lesson depends on the type of subject matter that students are learning. When teaching academic rules, the teacher needs to expose students to a stated rule (e.g., "bl makes the /bl/ sound"). Then students must apply the rule (e.g., sounding /bl/ in the word *blue*). When teaching concepts, the teacher needs to expose students to the definition or attributes (e.g., "a square is a quadrilateral with four congruent sides and four congruent angles") and give examples and nonexamples. In cases where the concept is too abstract to define for students, the teacher may simply use examples and nonexamples to teach the concept (e.g., when teaching the concept of square to children functioning at the preschool level). Special types of concepts called laws and lawlike principles refer to cause-and-effect relationships usually found in the sciences. They are taught by explicating the causal agent and the effect and by linking the two together. For example, the cause-and-effect relationship between temperature and moisture in the formation of rain is illustrated in Figure 5.3.

Teachers need to specify whether they will provide a teacher model or use an inductive strategy and to indicate what type of subject matter will be taught. Clear statements of the facts, academic rules, concepts, and principles, along with examples and nonexamples, should be written in the plan (see Figure 5.3).

Guided Practice. Once the target subject matter has been demonstrated, the teacher engages students in guided practice activities. Guided practice is characterized by teacher-student interactions in which the teacher provides many cues and prompts during a closely supervised activity. The following are examples of guided practice: asking students to state in unison the definition of a checking account, asking students about the attributes of a checking account, and asking students to evaluate examples and nonexamples of checking accounts. During guided practice, teachers model responses, lead students in practicing responses, and test students' skills in making responses with decreasing numbers of cues and prompts.

Often the shift from demonstration to guided practice is indistinguishable, especially when teachers use an inductive teaching approach. Being able to discern exactly when a lesson moves from demonstration to guided practice is not of primary concern. What is important is that the subject matter be clearly and explicitly presented and that students be given numerous opportunities to respond with high rates of accuracy (Greenwood, Delquadri, & Hall, 1984).

Independent Practice. When students respond accurately during guided practice, they are ready to work for fluency through independent practice activities such as seatwork (Hudson, 1996) or homework (Jayanthi, Sawyer, Nelson, Bursuck, & Epstein, 1995). Independent practice refers to activities in which students engage in repeated responding and require scant teacher supervision. Fluency refers to fast as well as accurate responding. Therefore, the focus of independent practice activities is on responding quickly and correctly. Students are ready to work independently on a target skill after they have attained 90 percent accuracy. If a teacher asks students who are unable to respond accurately to practice independently, they will either make numerous errors or constantly ask for assistance while the teacher attempts to work with others. In the case of homework, parents will begin to wonder about the effectiveness of instruction if their children cannot respond accurately and require parental assistance.

Demonstration and guided practice are used to prepare students for independent practice. It may take one or several lessons involving only demonstration and guided practice on a target skill before students are able to work independently. Consequently,

1. The teacher demonstrates the effect of rising moist air by reviewing a previously taught concept of *evaporation* (the sun's heating effect on bodies of water and atmosphere).

2. The teacher uses the diagram above to illustrate.

3. The teacher explains to students that the air high in the atmosphere is much colder, as illustrated in the diagram.

4. The teacher explains that as the heated, moist air rises up into the cold air, the little droplets of water begin to join and make bigger and bigger drops of water. When they are big and heavy enough, they begin to fall through the air down to the ground, in the form of rain.

5. The teacher shows students the following and explains:

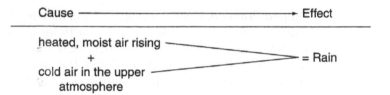

6. The teacher next demonstrates the cause-and-effect relationship by heating a pot of water on a hot plate and holding an aluminum tray filled with ice above the pot of water. Soon steam (hot, moist air) begins to rise, and as the steam reaches the tray, drops form on the bottom of the tray. As the drops get larger or condense, they begin to "rain" down.

Variation: Instead of the teacher "explaining" each step, the teacher may ask a series of probing questions to *induce* the steps in the cause-and-effect relationship.

FIGURE 5.3 Teaching steps for explicating the cause-and-effect relationship between rising moist air and cold air in the atmosphere in the formation of rain.

for a particular group of students, an instructional period may include demonstration and guided practice, demonstration and guided and independent practice, or demonstration and guided practice plus independent practice on another previously acquired skill.

Teachers of students with special needs need to consider two points when designing independent practice activities. First, teachers should mass practice sessions (providing daily practice) at the early stages of fluency building and then distribute them at weekly or monthly intervals to facilitate short- and long-term maintenance. Second, teachers should consider the number of opportunities to respond that each practice activity provides for the learner. Some gamelike activities are highly motivating, but students get only a few chances to respond after waiting for other students to take their turns. Other activities, such as worksheets, require students to make many responses in a relatively short period of time. Teachers working with special-needs students need to balance their practice activities so that the activities are exciting and motivational and provide the opportunity for students to make a sufficient number of responses.

Lesson Review. The final step of a lesson should be a summary review of the content being taught or practiced (Good, Grouws, & Ebermeier, 1983). A review allows the teacher to highlight the major points of the lesson, which helps students organize material. A review becomes practice when the teacher asks students to respond to questions about the major points of the lesson. A review also provides a sense of closure to the lesson, gives students a sense that the lesson has an explicit ending, and helps prepare them for the transition to the next lesson.

Methods to Evaluate Lessons

Effective teachers monitor and evaluate their instruction. Measuring instruction gives a teacher the power to (1) determine when instructional results have been achieved, (2) demonstrate that instructional results match the teacher's intended outcomes, (3) improve instruction, and (4) increase the value of the instruction the teacher creates (Mager, 1996). Teachers must identify a behavior or academic task, set goals, collect data to establish a baseline, introduce an intervention, and record the results over time until the goal has been reached or until no further progress has been demonstrated. A technique frequently used is the direct measurement and recording of student performance using data charts or graphs (Fuchs & Fuchs, 1986).

Graphing Performance. Graphs allow data organization and visual analysis of the effects of an intervention on behavior or academic achievement. In addition, the use of a pictorial rather than a narrative form saves time and space (Deno & Mirkin, 1977). Two basic types of graphs may be used by developing teachers to record data on a daily, weekly, or monthly basis: performance graphs and progress graphs.

Performance graph. A performance graph depicts a regular, frequent measure of a student's performance and behavioral changes on a specific task over time (Figure 5.4). An example is the number of times a student interrupts during a 30-minute interval. Plotted on the abscissa is the time interval during which the observations are recorded; plotted on the ordinate is the level of performance on that particular task. Vertical lines

FIGURE 5.4 A Decrease in the Frequency of Targeted Behavior

indicate periods of time or phases when specific instructional strategies are implemented.

The baseline phase is first and shows that no instruction occurred or that current instructional procedures remained the same. Data from this phase are used to identify the student's current level of functioning and to set instructional objectives. Next, a goal line (the horizontal dotted line) is plotted. Based on the median performance of a target student (represented by the number inside the teardrop shapes on the graph), the estimated time of intervention available, and the goal, a decision line (the diagonal line beginning at the end of the baseline phase and running until the estimated ending date for intervention) is then plotted.

After the baseline phase, intervention phases are implemented as needed. Each of these phases represents implementation of a different instructional strategy or a mix of multiple instructional strategies. Student performance is monitored and continuously compared with the pattern of performance displayed during the baseline phase. Data points are plotted until the goal is reached or until no further progress is made.

As the data points are plotted, the teacher decides whether to continue or to modify an intervention. Specific decision-making rules are used to make these determinations:

1. If for three consecutive sessions the data points fall above the decision line when attempting to decrease a behavior or fall below the decision line when attempting to increase a behavior, then that intervention phase is terminated, and a new or modified intervention is initiated.

2. After three weeks (15 sessions) of the same intervention, modify or change the intervention (to maintain interest and performance levels).

When necessary, additional intervention phases are introduced, with goal lines and decision lines reformulated. The teacher evaluates the effectiveness of instruction on the basis of changes in the level of student performance (how much higher or lower the student's current performance level is than the baseline performance) and the rate of change in student performance (how quickly the student's performance is improving).

In the example, the first intervention was the teacher talking with the target student about his behavior. Talking appeared to be effective, as the subsequent five data points fell below the decision line. This decrease in the frequency of the behavior changed, however, as indicated by three of the last four data points of this phase, which fell above the decision line. This result prompted the termination of the first intervention and the implementation of a second, planned ignoring. A new decision line was constructed by using the previous median performance level as the endpoint and drawing a line parallel to the first decision line. Ultimately, the target student did reach his goal during the second intervention phase. In fact, all three data points recorded during this phase fell below the adjusted goal line for the second intervention.

Progress graph. A progress graph (or chart) is intended to measure the time it takes a student to master a set of instructional objectives. The abscissa indicates the time, and the ordinate expresses the series of objectives. Data points are plotted sequentially and connected with a straight line, thereby illustrating graphically the student's progress in achieving the desired objectives. Unlike a performance graph, a progress graph is cumulative, meaning that the data points never descend: They either remain at the same level or ascend. Regardless, the same decision rules are used in both performance and progress graphs.

The progress graph example provided in Figure 5.5 is based on a districtwide primary-level mathematics curriculum goal of mastering three objectives per week. LaShonda, a first-grade student, mastered only one objective after six weeks of instruction (not shown on the graph). The teacher referred LaShonda to the resource teacher, and in consultation, it was decided that a goal of three objectives per week was appropriate even though LaShonda would be functioning slightly below grade level at the end of the school year. Initially, a trained fifth-grade student tutored LaShonda on her

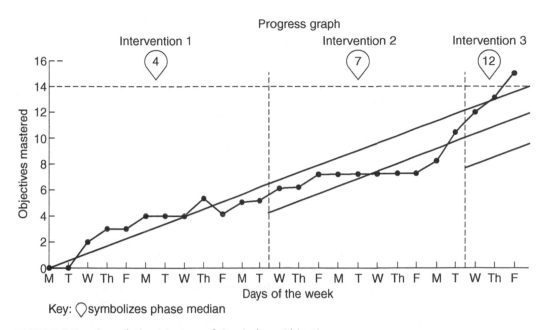

FIGURE 5.5 Cumulative Mastery of Curriculum Objectives

arithmetic skills for 15 minutes daily. This extra practice proved insufficient, and individual work with the resource teacher for 15 minutes daily was added to the intervention. In the third phase, LaShonda was given 25 minutes of daily practice with the resource teacher.

Graphs are an effective means of monitoring student performance on specific instructional tasks and progress through sets of curricular objectives. The choice of a performance graph or a progress graph depends on the type of data to be charted. If the rate of mastering a set of instructional tasks is of greater importance, use of a progress graph is recommended. If change in the level of performance on a specific task is to be highlighted, then the preferred medium is the performance graph. In both cases, the graphs provide a means for succinctly displaying the achievements of students and, consequently, the effectiveness of instruction. This conciseness can motivate students, teachers, parents, and other individuals interested in the students' attainment of educational goals. It should also be remembered that, in addition, graphs provide a vehicle for clear communication among teachers, administrators, and parents.

Adaptations and Modifications

An increasing concern as more and more diverse students spend time in the general education setting is the issue of adaptations and modifications (Lenz & Schumaker, 1999; Schumm, 1999; Simmons & Kameenui, 1999). When teachers adapt or modify the planned lesson, they help students acclimate to the task or activity through a change in the task, task presentation, or task evaluation. Teachers make changes by reworking the task, often making it easier for students to do. Teachers rely on adaptations and modifications when they use prosthetic devices, adaptive equipment, flexible scheduling, test modifications, and so forth to enable students to remain in the least restrictive environment (LRE).

Planning for adaptations and modifications allows teachers to identify adaptations that enhance student outcomes. Teachers can determine in advance such factors as other student outcomes for the activity, including outcomes from such content areas as social skills, communications, and problem solving. Teachers can determine whether those activity outcomes would benefit the students and what type of lesson format (e.g., large-group, small-group, teacher-directed, independent work) would be best suited to the students. Decisions can be made regarding current materials used, materials students need to use, and necessary changes in materials for individual students. Teachers also can pinpoint such factors as current response modes for the group (e.g., making choices, writing short answers, expressing thoughts and feelings), the students' modes for responding, and whether the response modes should be changed (Williams & Fox, 1996).

Teachers who plan adaptations and modifications for students with disabilities often include (1) social interactions between and among students and teachers, (2) the learning setting, (3) the teacher's lesson plans, (4) the instructional format and delivery, (5) equipment and materials, or (6) instructional evaluations. Box 5.2 illustrates adaptations and modifications that teachers have at their disposal for use with students with disabilities in the general education setting.

Anticipated Problems

An important step before implementing a lesson plan is to anticipate potential instructional and behavioral problems that might arise during the lesson. Regardless of how well teachers prepare materials and activities, they may still have to deal spontaneously with glitches in the subject presentation, different learning needs, or disruptive behavior by individual students. Such problems frequently can be addressed on the spur of the moment. Planning ahead, however, can help in either avoiding these problems before they occur or dealing with them with a minimal loss in instructional time. For example, developing teachers often have difficulties determining how long activities will take to complete and do not prepare backup activities when students complete the primary activity sooner than expected. By preparing a contingency plan, teachers can quickly move students into another activity and avoid the potential behavioral problems that arise when students are being engaged in constructive activities (see Box 5.3).

Self-Evaluation of Lesson Plans

To benefit fully from the experience of carrying out each instructional plan, teachers must spend time during and after the lesson analyzing and evaluating what occurred. Teachers who use responsive instruction evaluate their instruction (Englert, Tarrant, & Mariage, 1992). Thus, when they evaluate, teachers imbue instruction with new procedures or strategies at the point where students are likely to experience confusion. Teachers who evaluate adjust lessons on a moment-to-moment basis as they interact with and observe students during the lesson. Teachers accept and incorporate student ideas, examples, and experiences into the lesson content. They provide students with alternatives and opportunities to engage in decision making. They continually tie new data to those that students already know (before, during, and after the lesson).

When students make errors, reflective teachers use self-evaluation to link what students know and what they need to know (e.g., teachers bridge new knowledge to familiar knowledge). When teachers self-evaluate as a follow-up to lesson implementations, they respond to student mistakes as opportunities for students to gain new knowledge and meanings. Teachers who use self-evaluation can decrease their own behaviors that may be contributing to learning or behavior problems in the classroom (Allinder, Bolling, Oats, & Gagnon, 2000). Teachers who self-evaluate often are reflective—thus personifying master teachers.

The self-evaluation process affords teachers the opportunity to determine the strengths and weaknesses of the lesson. The focus of the postlesson evaluation is teacher and student performance. In evaluating their own performance, teachers may analyze their lesson organization and development, presentation of concepts or skills, or management of classroom behaviors. For example, they may determine whether sufficient examples were used to illustrate a target concept. In addition to their own effectiveness, teachers need to analyze the performance of students in terms of their participation in instructional activities and attainment of specified objectives. Consideration might be

B ox 5.2   **Adaptations and Modifications for Students with Mild to Moderate Disabilities**

1. Social Interactions.

Use a "communication booklet" to allow students to write about positive experiences or to express grievances and frustrations. Assign students in the classroom to be "peer buddies" or mentors for the at-risk students. Reduce the emphasis on social competition. Give students preferred responsibilities. Reduce distracting stimuli. Maintain consistency in daily routine. Limit students' independent movement in the classroom environment. Provide students with choices and behavioral options. Avoid physical contact with students. Avoid arguing with students. Have students avoid crowded areas. Provide students with predetermined signals (e.g., hand signals, verbal cues). Model appropriate social behaviors for students. Provide positive feedback. Use a positive behavioral support system in the class. Teach problem-solving skills and social skills.

2. Learning Setting.

Furnish students with their own personal spaces for belongings. Provide visual displays of progress (e.g., bulletin boards, charts). Post rules in various places throughout the classroom. Equip the classroom with a carrel for private study or time-out.

3. Lesson Plans.

Initially state the objectives, purpose, and relevance of the lesson. Review prerequisite information; define key terms for understanding the main points. Explain the relationship between the new material and previously covered material.

4. Instructional Format and Delivery.

Use ordinal numbers and temporal cues (first, second, finally) to organize data. Emphasize key concepts by varying voice quality and by using cue words—speaking them with emphasis, writing them on the chalkboard, and repeating them. Reduce extraneous information and stimuli. Discuss and summarize all main points. Ask factual and analytic questions throughout the presentation. Use cooperative learning techniques. Use collaborative discussion teams and sharing formats in place of lectures. Assign students shorter tasks; gradually increase the number of problems over time. Allow alternative assignments; gradually introduce more components of the regular assignments until these assignments are routinely performed (e.g., if the student feels uncomfortable giving an oral presentation, allow him or her to tape the assignment and play it for the class). Provide students with assignment choices. Use peer tutoring. Vary the schedule so that students are not passive for long periods of time. Select students randomly to respond. Vary response modes of instructional presentations. Integrate popular characters, items, and trends into classroom assignments. Offer students time at the end of class to review, summarize, and organize notes.

5. Equipment and Materials.

Use examples, illustrations, charts, diagrams, advance organizers, and maps to make material more concrete. Provide visual clues, including overhead transparencies, charts, graphs, and lists. Provide advance organizers that define lesson objectives and responsibilities. Make periodic appointments with students to discuss their academic progress. Underline correct responses. Highlight main points. Organize notebooks and work areas. Place students close to the speaker. Assign hands-on materials. Provide students with a list of necessary materials for each activity. Use structured study guides, information organizers, or skeletal outlines. Allow peer note takers and audiocassettes.

6. Instructional Evaluations.

Present oral tests for students with reading problems/learning disabilities. Use oral debates to check for student knowledge. Attempt to simplify responses to questions on tests to avoid frustration. Make certain that tests or quizzes measure knowledge of content and not related skills such as reading, spelling, or writing. Teach students to ask questions of their peers.

Box 5.2   **(continued)**

Expand on and use student responses to questions. Allow students to create study guides for tests and quizzes. Teach test-taking strategies. Give shorter tests or quizzes more frequently. Allow students to take tests in alternative settings. Remove the threat of public knowledge of results. Use test alternatives (e.g., computer usage, models, drawings). Modify question formats when necessary. Simplify the response level (e.g., develop a separate test form). Modify test procedures with regard to length, frequency, and content.

given to the degree to which students were motivated by an instructional activity or the materials used.

Teachers also need to consider students' mastery of the content. If students do not attain criterion performance levels, then teachers may need to recycle students through the DTM. If mastery has been reached, teachers can move on to the next objective in the skill hierarchy. In any case, self-evaluation of a teacher's ability to conduct an instructional activity and to facilitate students' behaviors is critical if effective teaching behaviors are to be maintained and ineffective ones are to be reduced or eliminated.

LESSON-PLAN FORMATS

Teachers plan at a variety of levels: They make yearlong plans, semester or term plans, unit plans, and daily plans. The focus of this chapter is unit and lesson plans. Selection of the unit or daily lesson-plan format must be based on classroom variables and individual needs at any given time.

Box 5.3   **Case Study**

Mr. Sarason, the teacher of an elementary learning support service, uses a thematic approach to teach units of concepts and skills. During one term, the theme was zoo animals. Students receiving learning support services for reading and language arts read about animals, listened to stories about zoos and jungles, and wrote compositions about the circus, the rain forest, and the desert. During math instruction, word problems and computation skill development were set in the context of animals' habitation needs, food supplies, and survival rates. With from 5 to 15 students working at different skill levels and on different types of activities at the same time, Mr. Sarason designed activities to fill in any "dead time" between activities. He used learning centers that involved activities that students could complete with scant or no assistance from him or his aide. (When activities required instruction, Mr. Sarason set aside a specific time to teach the necessary skills.) When students finished an instructional activity, they could spend time completing a papier-mâché zoo animal or sit at the listening post with a storybook and read along with a tape-recorded story.

The activities had five important characteristics:

1. "Dead time" was reduced.
2. Independence was promoted.
3. The learning of theme concepts and skills was enriched.
4. The teacher was able to work with other students.
5. The activities served as a reward for completing previous activities.

Pause and Reflect About the Profession 5.5

Five characteristics are evident in Mr. Sarason's teaching of the zoo animals unit. What are they?

1. _____

    _____

2. _____

    _____

3. _____

    _____

4. _____

    _____

5. _____

    _____

Daily Lesson Plans

The most commonly used lesson-plan format is the traditional group instructional plan. Such a plan lists objectives and provides a relatively detailed description of the materials, activities, and evaluation procedures for multiple small-group or single large-group instruction. Teachers using this format write down when and how they will provide instruction. An alternative format is the daily activity schedule, a succinct list designating when instruction will occur, with scant reference to how instruction will be carried out. Often this format is used in conjunction with a unit-plan format or in resource rooms where students work predominantly on their own, with their assignments for each day listed in a work folder.

Traditional Group Instructional Plan. Preservice teacher trainees have traditionally been taught to construct daily lesson plans with the assumption that, at any given time, they will be working with a single large group or with two to four small groups simultaneously. The generic lesson plan includes a statement of the lesson objective and a description of the materials, activities, and evaluation procedures to be used. This format continues to be used extensively because of its ease of use and applicability. In many classrooms for students with mild disabilities, large-group and simultaneous small-group instruction and practice are provided. In those classrooms where numerous students are individually placed at different points in the curriculum, however, the traditional lesson-plan format may not be feasible.

In fact, the chapter section entitled "Components of Successfully Planned Lessons" contains the categories used in the traditional daily lesson plan. Box 5.4 illustrates how the categories are laid out in the traditional lesson plan. Sections 1 through 6 are the contents of the actual plan; the remaining sections are used to self-evaluate after the plan has been implemented. The steps needed to complete the lesson plan are as follows:

1. Provide the teacher's name, the date, and the student's or group's name in the header.

2. Write behaviorally stated objectives that indicate how students will respond to demonstrate mastery.

Traditional Lesson-Plan Format

Lesson Preparation and Analysis Form

Name: Ms. Baldwell   Date: 5/12/05
Student(s) or Group: Cary, Carlos, Bill, Su-Lee, and Trone

1. Behavioral objectives of activity

When given a passage to read, students will be able to underline two important words or phrases for each paragraph with 90 percent accuracy.

When given a passage to read, students will be able to see-write answers to seven out of eight comprehension questions for three consecutive passages.

2. Description of activity

Demonstration

Explain the purpose of the underlining strategy (to help the student identify and recall important information). Tell students that the teacher will show them how to use the underlining strategy. Model the strategy by reading the first paragraph of the passage aloud. Verbalize the steps to the strategy:

"I need to underline two important words or phrases."

"Important words or phrases tell me about the main idea or details."

"Underline."

"Ask myself, why is this important?"

"Go on to the next paragraph."

Guided practice

Have students read the second paragraph.

Lead students through verbalizing the steps above.

Repeat the guided practice with paragraphs 3 and 5.

Lead students in summarizing the content of each paragraph by using the underlined key phrases.

After finishing the passage, lead students in using underlined phrases to read-write answers to comprehension questions.

Independent practice

None.

3. Measurement

Note each student's use of self-instruction statements.

Note each student's underlining of two words or phrases per paragraph.

Tally the number of comprehension questions answered correctly.

4. Materials

Story "Animals with Pouches"
Highlighter pens

5. Adaptations

Engage students in choral practice on self-verbalizations.

6. Problems that might be encountered

Students may not be able to discriminate important from unimportant words or phrases. If so, ask students to justify the importance of the words and phrases they underlined. Provide feedback on selections and justifications.

7. **Problems that actually arose**

   Students had difficulty identifying important words and phrases. Feedback was provided, and student selections were shaped into more appropriate responses.

8. **Behavioral techniques used during activity**

   Strategy modeling and specific academic praise for accurate self-verbalizations and under-lining were used.

9. **What you learned from this activity**

   Students respond well to modeling strategy steps. The model and lead steps provide sufficient support to students so that they can respond accurately and enjoy their success.

---

3. In the activities description section, write step-by-step procedures for each activity. Content information such as concept definitions and academic rules should be included as well.

4. List evaluation tools/measures and indicate whether the measures will be taken at daily, weekly, or monthly intervals. The evaluation tools selected should be designed to assess the mastery of the objectives, not the activity.

5. List all materials to be used in the lesson.

6. List any special adaptations and modifications needed for individual students.

7. List anticipated instructional or behavioral problems, along with strategies to deal with any problems if they arise.

8. After the lesson has been implemented, note any problems that occurred and the strategies used to resolve them. Include information that will be helpful in dealing with problems in the future as well as in preparing for the same lesson.

Daily Activity Schedule. The daily activity schedule replaces the traditional daily lesson plan with a daily time line depicting when instruction will occur. Teachers list the sequence of activities and document who will supervise each activity (teacher, aide, or students). The activities listed on the schedule are derived from either (1) a unit plan that contains a list of instructional objectives, a list of materials to be used, a description of the activities, and a list of evaluation procedures to be used to monitor progress toward attaining the objectives or (2) a set of materials from an individual student's work folder. The daily activity schedule provides planned activities without the details for each day of instruction.

A daily activity schedule is designed to provide

1. consistent, accurate, and meaningful planning for each student

2. a written record of previous activities to facilitate future planning, monitoring, and record keeping

3. a plan of action for the implementation of the unit plan

Alternative Forms: Option A. To complete a daily activity schedule using option A (see Figure 5.6)

ACTIVITY SCHEDULE

Teacher: Ms. Ley   **Date:** Wednesday, April 19

Groups:
G1: Willie, Brett, Jose, Errol & Juanita
G2: Barb, Sam, Myron, Amal & Robert
G3: Lindsay, Kelly & Chris
G4: Conor, Patrick, Kevin & Shannon

G5: Mike, Maria & Bo
G6: Greg, Jack, Carol & Paul

Time	Activity with teacher	Activity with aide	Independent practice
8:30–9:30	**G1** Flash card drill (sums to 10)	**G2** Language master: fluency building on phrases to 100 wpm	**Kevin & Conor** computer (Spell Blaster)
9:30–10:30	**G2** Reading comprehension, pp. 41–48: underlining strategy training with explicit text questions	**G1** Handwriting: copy and edit last week's language experience sentences	**G5 & 6** Peer tutoring, 2 digit × 2 digit multiplication w/regrouping
10:30–11:30	**G3** Oral repeated reading, pp. 31–36; fluency building to 120 wpm	**G4** Mastery test: fractions	**G1** Listening post; spelling quiz
12:15–1:15	**G4** Reading comprehension, pp. 98–107: paraphrase strategy training with explicit text questions	**G6** Probe: 2 × 2 multiplication	**G2 & 5** Sustained silent reading
1:15–2:00	**G3, 4, & 5** Written expression topic: fossils (based on field trip)	**G5** Handwriting: copy and edit last week's language experience stories	**Lindsay** implicit text questions from passage **Chris** listening post: main idea from "Over the Fence"

FIGURE 5.6 Completed Daily Activity Schedule for Option A

1. Enter your name and the date.

2. According to the time blocks that you determine, enter each student's name in the appropriate column:

   Activity with teacher: Teacher-directed activities are typically used to introduce, continue development, or review acquisition and/or provide guided practice.

   Activity with aide: These can be teacher-directed activities used by the teacher aide to introduce, continue development, or review acquisition of skills.

   Independent practice: These are practice activities to help the student develop fluency or maintain it for previously acquired skills. They are characterized by the student's ability to complete the activity with little or no teacher assistance once the directions for the activity have been reviewed.

3. Beside the student's name, list each activity. Be specific as to page number, cassette, filmstrip, disk, and so forth. Also indicate whether the activity entails demonstration, guided practice, or independent practice.

   Following are helpful hints for preparing daily activity schedules:

1. If your schedule remains the same on a daily/weekly basis, fill in students' names, time periods, and so forth. Then make a master copy of the activity schedule. As a result, you will have to complete only the activity columns from day to day or week to week.

2. A student can be a group, if consistent and clearly labeled initially.

FIGURE 5.7 Completed Daily Activity Schedule for Option B

3. A code may be developed to correspond to your unit plan. For example, in the unit plan, reading activities can be numbered as R–1, R–2, and so forth; math activities as M–1, M–2, and so forth. Then, when entering activities on the activity schedule, R–1 or M–2 could be used to refer to specific items on your unit plan.

Alternative Forms: Option B. An advantage to this format is that each student and teacher can readily see daily routines and expectations (see Figure 5.7). To complete a daily activity schedule using option B:

1. Use one sheet for each day of the week.

2. Fill in students' names across the top. Arrange by classes/grade levels to facilitate groupings. If pencil is used and space on the schedule is a priority, new students can replace those who leave your program.

3. Enter time (standard time) notations down the left side (e.g., 8:00, 8:30, 9:00, 9:30).

4. Enter each student's daily schedule (including lunch, recess, regular classroom activities, other specialists, and so forth). If desired, use consistent color coding for each different activity.

5. Block out periods in your classroom setting.

6. Record specific daily activities (e.g., reading, math, language, spelling) directly on the sheet. If a plastic or separate sheet is used, the master schedule can be reused each week/day.

Unit Plans

Individualized programming is not exclusive to special education settings, although it is a more common practice there than in general education. In addition, many special education settings are far more heterogeneous than are many general education classes. As a result, many special education teachers provide multilevel instruction to students who are functioning within a broad range of skills. Often this means that separate instructional activities must be prepared for each student. Because of these factors, preparing daily lesson plans can be an enormous task. To ask developing teachers to write traditional lesson plans for each student or each small set of students at each skill level each day is unrealistic. The unit-plan format is a viable option to accommodate the need to write effective lesson plans within the context of many resource rooms.

The unit plan is the vehicle whereby the specific objectives are translated into and correlated with specific activities, materials, and evaluation methods. A unit plan is designed to

1. provide a comprehensive plan for curriculum implementation

2. provide a foundation and rationale for all instruction

3. allow for creative planning from determination to implementation and evaluation of instructional objectives

---

Students: Groups 1 & 2   **Annual Goal:** Students will improve reading comprehension

Date of Initiation: September 18   **Date of Completion:**

Objectives	Materials	Activities	Evaluation
1. When given passage at their instructional level, SWBAT see-write correct answers to seven out of eight comprehension questions related to text explicit and implicit information for three consecutive sessions.	Stories from basal and supplemental reading series.	**Semantic Web (SW)** 1. Set purpose for reading (e.g., predicting events, main ideas, related facts). 2. Discuss theme of story and relate to students' background experiences. 3. Have students read first and second paragraphs. 4. Assign third paragraph. Have students predict what will happen next in the story. 5. Formulate a core question and write on the board. 6. Elicit possible answers to core question and write in list separate from web. 7. Ask students to accept, reject, or modify answers. 8. Draw web. 9. Build support for web strands. Ask students to examine them and accept, reject, or modify. (Students may reread prior to doing this.) 10. Guide students to relating strands (two or three relationships maximum).	Probe containing eight comprehension questions will be completed at the end of each passage. 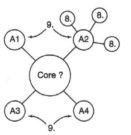

FIGURE 5.8 Unit-Plan Format for Option A

Alternative Forms: Option A. To complete a unit plan using option A (see Figure 5.8):

1. Enter the student's or group's name, subject, major goal, dates of initiation and completion, and charting method (progress or performance graphs).

2. Enter specific objectives that correspond to a major objective.

3. List all materials that might be used.

4. List activities that will help students reach the stated objectives. Under each activity, describe the specific step-by-step procedures. Content information such as definitions of concepts and academic rules should be included as well. The activity description is entered only at the initial entry point in the unit plan. If you wish to use the same activity to reach another objective, you need only list the activity title in the activity column next to subsequent objectives.

5. List evaluation tools/measures and indicate whether they are to be used daily, weekly, or monthly. The evaluation tools selected should be designed to assess the mastery of the objectives, not the activities.

Following are helpful hints for preparing unit plans:

1. Be as broad-based as possible. Build and adapt objectives, activities, and materials across groups and skill levels.

2. Be creative and flexible. Design a mixture of creative, high-interest activities, along with less-elaborate drill activities.

Alternative Forms: Option B. To complete a unit plan using option B (see Figure 5.9):

1. Develop a card file of successful activities. Code activities according to skill area.

2. Activity cards might include the name of the activity, identifying code, materials needed, objective, and appropriate instructional level.

3. Copy several cards onto one sheet of paper to be included with your unit plan.

This technique permits you to use the same activity with several skill levels without recopying the same information. In addition, the card file will be an invaluable resource.

FIGURE 5.9 Activity Card for Unit-Plan Format
Option B

STRATEGIC PLANNING FOR INCLUSIVE PROGRAMMING

With a growing number of students with mild to moderate disabilities being educated in inclusive environments, planning strategies have been developed to address the diverse needs of all students in general education environments. The Joint Committee on Teacher Planning for Students with Disabilities (1995) highlighted specific routines based on the premise that teachers in inclusive classrooms require plans that focus on (1) specific students' needs, (2) the skills and content to be acquired, and (3) the activities that students will engage in to learn the skills and content.

One such method is the lesson planning pyramid (see Figure 5.10), developed by Schumm, Vaughn, and Leavell (1994). Teachers use a mental template or graphic image of a pyramid to focus on the content of a lesson that will be learned by all students, most students, and some students and how the learning will be directed. The advantage to using the pyramid is that it focuses on the entire range of learners in the content-based class yet does not necessitate extensive paperwork. To use the pyramid, teachers first

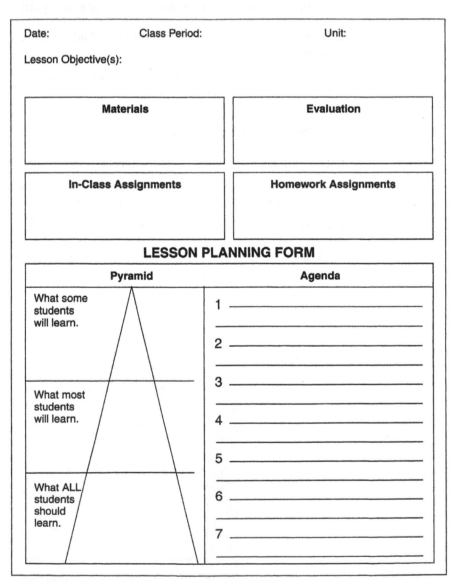

FIGURE 5.10 The Lesson Planning Pyramid Form

identify the concepts to be taught and then differentiate what all, most, and some students are to learn from the lesson. Second, teachers structure an agenda for the lesson. In developing the agenda of activities, teachers consider the unique aspects of their classroom, such as (1) class size, (2) how well their students work together in small groups, (3) resources available, (4) possible instructional adaptations, and (5) events that may distract students or alter instructional time. Finally, teachers list the materials to be used, specify in-class and homework assignments, and identify how student learning will be evaluated.

Another method, the lesson planning routine (Bulgren & Lenz, 1996), is an explicit planning process that requires teachers to reflect on the content and outcomes of a lesson and to create a graphic road map for the lesson (see Figure 5.11). When completing the graphic organizer, teachers use the acronym SMARTER to guide their reflective planning. The seven steps involved in the SMARTER prompt are described in Table 5.1. This type of lesson planning is most effective when used in conjunction with other strategic routines, such as reflective course planning and reflective unit planning. For additional information and specific implementation procedures regarding these techniques, we recommended that developing and beginning teachers consult Deshler, Ellis, and Lenz (1996).

FIGURE 5.11   Lesson Planning Routine Graphic

TABLE 5.1   SMARTER Reflective Planning

1. **Select** the critical content outcomes and develop a set of critical questions that all students should be able to answer by the end of instruction.
2. **Map** the organization of the critical content in a way that will show the structure of the content and that will be meaningful to all students.
3. **Analyze** why the critical content might be difficult to learn, based on amount, complexity, interest, student background, relevance, organization, abstractness, or external conditions (e.g., interruptions).
4. **Reach** decisions about how the content will be taught and how the content might be enhanced during instruction to reduce potential learning difficulties through specific teaching devices.
5. **Teach** students about the enhancements in ways that will inform them about how to use the devices, routines, strategies, or curriculum revision, and explicitly guide students to become actively involved in exploring and using the enhancements to improve learning.
6. **Evaluate** mastery of the critical content and related processes for high achievers, average achievers, low achievers, and others.
7. **Reevaluate** planning and teaching decisions for the next step in learning.

Source: Adapted from "Strategic Instruction in the Content Areas," by J. Bulgren, and K. Lenz, 1996, in D. D. Deshler, E. S. Ellis, & B. K. Lenz (Eds.), *Teaching Adolescents with Learning Disabilities*, Denver: Love. Copyright 1996 by Love Publishers. Reprinted with permission.

Lesson Plans and Computer Technology

School districts across the country are beginning to use computer technology to complement specially designed instruction. In addition to providing computers, districts are establishing local area networks that connect classroom computers to one another and wide area networks that connect schools. Increasingly, districts are enhancing their connectivity by providing access to the Internet through online and access service providers. Consequently, teachers are able to access resources and share methods and lesson plans locally or globally. For example, America Online (AOL) has an education area that allows users to download or upload lesson plans devised for a variety of subjects and student populations.

In addition, some school officials have reported that the laptop computer has improved the quality of other aspects of the instructional process, including special education referral-to-placement procedures, school-based conferences, and staff meetings (Johnston, Proctor, & Corey, 1995). Paperwork, including lesson plans and documents required for special education services, can be retrieved, modified, and stored more effectively. Staff can use their time and materials more efficiently. Data files can present an immediate visual display that helps teachers make informed decisions and track longitudinal progress. Teachers can easily generate data when reporting lesson results to parents in documenting progress for school records. Data can be easily compiled to help administrators and teachers make informed decisions about curriculum and instruction. Smith (2000) reported that technology is now integrated into teacher preparation programs.

Effective teachers can have an impact on students' educational placement decisions through the use of technology and lesson planning. For instance, some teachers now are planning for and including assistive technology resources in lessons in order to make it possible for students with disabilities to attend neighborhood schools and participate

Pause and Reflect About the Profession 5.6

How are your planning skills? Write a reflective summary indicating why writing out specific lesson plans will help you with your students. Include in your reflective summary five specific teacher behaviors you want to initiate/increase in order to provide effective lesson plans for your students. What can you do now to get started on these five behaviors?

successfully in general education classes (Webb, 2000). Milone (2000) also described a total inclusion program in which teachers planned lessons using technology in order to ensure that special needs students were fully integrated into general education classrooms. Computer technology will affect the quality of both the content and the presentation of lesson plans and other relevant classroom documentation in the 21st century.

SUMMARY

The bottom line for effective teaching is that teachers need to invest a substantial amount of time in preparing to teach. Although many developing and beginning teachers would like to think there must be a shortcut, there is none. To be effective, teachers have to work hard to develop their lessons and revise and polish them continuously.

This chapter provided beginning teachers with an overview of the rationale and principles of planning that lay the foundation for effective teaching. Plans help teachers identify clearly what they hope to accomplish and specify the means for accomplishing their goals. They help foster confidence and security. Plans provide the basis for an organized educational effort that ensures the success of students in developing academic, behavioral, and functional skills. To derive these benefits, plans must contain objectives, sound instructional and practice activities, and a method for evaluating attainment of the objectives (Garland, 1982).

Several suggested formats were presented that provide a starting point in developing a system of planning. Teachers need to examine the generic principles of effective planning and some possible formats for writing out their plans. Then they can devise a system that fits their own needs.

ACTIVITIES TO EXTEND YOUR KNOWLEDGE

1. Plan a science lesson on the weather involving a diverse group of five learners, two of whom require assistive technology. Use at least two web sites to locate creative lesson-plan themes.
2. Work in groups to task-analyze the following skills: tying shoes; using tense, pronouns, and possessives; using dictionary skills; naming numbers 0 to 20; counting objects 0 to 20; solving simple addition and subtraction problems; telling time; and using money skills. Be sure to sequence each component skill (put the task into small, ordered steps).
3. Using one of the task analyses above, determine a learning outcome or behavioral outcome for students at the grade or ability level you teach. Practice writing instructional objectives for the learning outcome. Practice writing behavioral objectives for the behavioral outcome.
4. Use the instructional objectives or behavioral objectives above to practice planning appropriate equipment and materials you will need to implement the objective.
5. Plan one modification to an instructional objective or behavioral objective. The modification may be to (a) social interactions between and among students and teachers, (b) the learning setting, (c) the teacher's lesson plans, (d) the instructional format and delivery, (e) equipment and materials, or (f) instructional evaluations.
6. Write out a teacher-student(s) script to implement the planned objective detailing teacher statements and desired student response. Include demonstration, guided practice, and independent practice scripts as appropriate for students in your class.
7. Write out the methods you will use to evaluate the objective while/after it is implemented. How will you link the objective to the next lesson? How will you review the lesson the next time it is taught? How will you evaluate student outcomes?

8. Share with your instructor and colleagues your results for each of the activities listed above. Discuss with your host teacher or university supervisor how you can implement your new ideas in your field site. How will you self-reflect on your own teacher behaviors?

REFERENCES

Algozzine, B., Ysseldyke, J. E., & Elliott, J. (1997). *Strategies and tactics for effective instruction.* Longmont, CO: Sopris West.

Allinder, R. M., Bolling, R. M., Oats, R. G., & Gagnon, W. A. (2000, July/August). Effects of teacher self-monitoring on implementation of curriculum-based measurement and mathematics computation achievement of students with disabilities. *Remedial and Special Education, 21*(4), 219–226.

Archer, A. (June, 1991). *Design of instruction: Lesson structure.* Paper presented at the Fourteenth Annual Intervention Procedures Conference, Logan, UT.

Bulgren, J., & Lenz, K. (1996). Strategic instruction in content areas. In D. D. Deshler, E. S. Ellis, & B. K. Lenz (Eds.), *Teaching adolescents with learning disabilities* (pp. 409–474). Denver: Love.

Carnine, D. (1991). Curricular interventions for teaching high-order thinking to all students: Introduction to the special series. *Journal of Learning Disabilities, 24,* 261–269.

Cartwright, G. P., & Cartwright, C. A. (1972). Gilding the lily. *Exceptional Children, 39,* 231–234.

Cartwright, G. P., Cartwright, C. A., & Ward, M. (1981). *Educating special learners.* Belmont, CA: Wadsworth.

Clark, C. M., & Yinger, R. J. (1979). *Three studies of teacher planning* (Research Series No. 55). East Lansing: Michigan State University, Institute for Research on Teaching.

Cooper, J. M. (1986). *Classroom teaching skills* (3rd ed.). Lexington, MA: Heath.

Danielson, C., & McGreal, T. (2000). *Teacher evaluation to enhance professional practice.* Alexandria, VA: Association for Supervision and Curriculum Development.

Darch, C., Miller, A., & Shippen, P. (1998). Instructional classroom management: A proactive model for managing student behavior. *Beyond Behavior, 9*(3), 18–27.

Deno, S., & Mirkin, P. (1977). *Data-based program modification: A manual.* Reston, VA: Council for Exceptional Children.

Deshler, D. D., Ellis, E. S., & Lenz, B. K. (1996). *Teaching adolescents with learning disabilities.* Denver: Love.

Deshler, D. D., & Schumaker, J. B. (1986). Learning strategies: An instructional alternative for low-achieving adolescents. *Exceptional Children, 52,* 583–590.

Dieker, L. A. (2000). *Co-teaching lesson plan book 2000.* Reston, VA: Council for Exceptional Children.

Englert, C. S., Tarrant, K. L., & Mariage, T. V. (1992). Defining and redefining instructional practice in special education: Perspectives on good teaching. *Teacher Education and Special Education, 15*(2), 62–87.

Fuchs, L. S., & Fuchs, D. (1986). Effects of systematic formative evaluation: A meta-analysis. *Exceptional Children, 53,* 199–208.

Gable, R. A., Laycock, V. K., Maroney, S. A., & Smith, C. R. (1991). *Preparing to integrate students with behavioral disorders.* Reston, VA: Council for Exceptional Children.

Garland, C. (1982). *Guiding clinical experiences in teacher education.* New York: Longman.

Good, T., Grouws, D., & Ebermeier, H. (1983). *Active mathematics teaching.* New York: Longman.

Greenwood, C. R., Delquadri, J. C., & Hall, R. V. (1984). Opportunity to respond and student academic performance. In W. L. Heward, T. E. Heron, D. S. Hill, & J. Trap-Porter (Eds.), *Focus on behavior analysis in education* (pp. 58–88). New York: Merrill/ Macmillan.

Hofmeister, A., & Lubke, R. (1990). *Research into practice: Implementing effective teaching strategies.* Needham Heights, MA: Allyn & Bacon.

Hudson, P. (1996). Using a learning set to increase the test performance of students with learning disabilities in social studies classes. *Learning Disabilities Research & Practice, 11*(2), 78–85.

Hudson, P., Lignugaris-Kraft, B., & Miller, T. (1993). Using content enhancements to improve the performance of adolescents with learning disabilities in content classes. *Learning Disabilities Research & Practice, 8,* 106–126.

Jayanthi, M., Sawyer, V., Nelson, J. S., Bursuck, W. D., & Epstein, M. H. (1995). Recommendations for homework-communication and problems: From parents, classroom teachers, and special education teachers. *Remedial and Special Education, 16*(4), 212–227.

Johnston, S. D., Proctor, W. A., & Corey, S. E. (1995). A new partner in the IEP process: The laptop computer. *Teaching Exceptional Children, 28*(1), 46–49.

Joint Committee on Teacher Planning for Students with Disabilities. (1995). *Planning for academic diversity in America's classrooms: Windows on reality research, change, and practice.* Lawrence: University of Kansas, Center on Research and Learning.

Lenz, K., & Schumaker, J. (1999). *Adapting language arts, social studies, and science materials for the inclusive classroom*. Reston, VA: Council for Exceptional Children.

Mager, R. F. (1996). *Preparing instructional objectives*. Atlanta: Center for Effective Performance.

McCutcheon, G. (1980). How do elementary school teachers plan their courses? *Elementary School Journal, 81*, 4–23.

Mercer, C. D., & Mercer, A. R. (1985). *Teaching students with learning problems*. Upper Saddle River, NJ: Prentice Hall.

Milone, M. (2000). Special teachers for special needs. *Technology & Learning, 20*(9), 40–44.

Nolet, V., & Tindal, G. (1993). Special education in content area classes: Development of a model and practical procedure. *Remedial and Special Education, 14*(1), 36–48.

Peterson, P. L., Marx, R. W., & Clark, C. M. (1978). Teacher planning, teacher behavior, and students' achievement. *American Educational Research Journal, 15*, 417–432.

Pettig, K. L. (2000). On the road to differentiated instruction. *Educational Leadership, 58*(1), 14–18.

Rosenshine, B. (1986). Synthesis of research on explicit teaching. *Educational Leadership, 43*(7), 60–69.

Rutherford, R., & Warger, C. (1995). *A collaborative approach to social skills instruction: An inclusionary approach*. Reston, VA: Foundation for Exceptional Innovations.

Schumm, J. S. (1999). *Adapting reading and math materials for the inclusive classroom*. Reston, VA: Council for Exceptional Children.

Schumm, J. S., Vaughn, S., & Leavell, A. (1994). Planning pyramid: A framework for planning for diverse student needs during content area instruction. *Reading Teacher, 47*, 608–615.

Simmons, D., & Kameenui, E. J. (1999). *Toward successful inclusion of students with disabilities: The architecture of instruction*. Reston, VA: Council for Exceptional Children.

Smith, S. J. (2000). Graduate student mentors for technology success. *Teacher Education and Special Education, 23*(2), 167–182.

Thousand, J. S., Villa, R., & Nevin, A. (Eds.). (1994). *Creativity and collaborative learning: A practical guide to empowering students and teachers*. Baltimore: Paul H. Brookes.

Webb, B. J. (2000, March/April). Planning and organizing assistive technology resources in your school. *Teaching Exceptional Children, 32*(4), 50–55.

West, L. L., Corbey, S., Boyer-Stephens, A., Jones, B., Miller, R. J., & Sarkees-Wircenski, M. (1999). *Integrating transition planning into the IEP process* (2nd ed.). Reston, VA: Council for Exceptional Children.

Whitaker, S. D. (2000). What do first year special education teachers need? Implications for induction programs. *Teaching Exceptional Children, 33*(1), 28–36.

Williams, W., & Fox, T. J. (1996). Planning for inclusion: A practical process. *Teaching Exceptional Children, 28*(3), 6–13.

Wood, J. W. (1991). *Adapting instruction for mainstreamed and at-risk students*. Upper Saddle River, NJ: Prentice Hall.

Delivering Instruction

Chapter Outline

In this chapter, we will

- identify elements of delivering instruction effectively

- describe generic procedures of direct instruction (DI) and guided discovery learning (GDL)

- provide applied examples of DI and GDL

- examine procedures for presenting concepts and academic rules in subject material

- analyze students' learning stages and teachers' behaviors during the learning process

- discuss the TEAL model—Teaching: Explicit Activation of Learning

- illustrate applications of various instructional strategies

A PROFESSIONAL GLIMPSE

Manor Elementary School was recently placed on the state's school improvement list. For the last two years, the number of students reaching proficiency in both reading and math was below the adequate yearly progress benchmarks. One of the research-based strategies the school improvement planning team decided to implement was the TEAL model. The team members had worked hard to align the school curriculum with state academic standards. They had identified assessment anchors—that is, items aligned with core standards—from the state assessments. With the curriculum aligned and an assessment plan, they wanted to shore up the faculty's instructional methods.

With state accountability funds, Washington and Jefferson School District contracted with Nemacolin Intermediate Unit to provide math and reading coaches. The coaches developed a "scorecard" that listed the effective TEAL strategies that teachers had to incorporate into each of their lessons. They presented a series of workshops for the teachers during common planning periods and after students had been dismissed for the day. They followed up with frequent visits to classrooms where they modeled the TEAL strategies and/or provided feedback to the teachers on their execution of the model using the scorecard. By using simple accuracy and fluency measures (e.g., words read correctly per minute, facts recalled by minute, digits correct per minute) two to three times a week, teachers and coaches monitored the impact of the strategies on students' academic performance.

With clear academic achievement goals identified, a scorecard to measure teacher and student performance, and a system for executing the school improvement plan and holding each other accountable, teachers were able to make dramatic improvements in the academic performance of their students.

Our purpose in this chapter is to describe for developing teachers a set of instructional elements related to effective instruction. These instructional elements derive from two instructional models prominent in classrooms today: direct instruction (DI) and guided discovery learning (GDL). These models form the conceptual and procedural basis for a variety of other instructional approaches. For example, DI steps underscore the strategies intervention model (Deshler & Schumaker, 1986) and classwide peer tutoring (Greenwood, Delquadri, & Hall, 1984). The GDL steps form the basis of proleptic teaching and scaffolding (Bruner, 1973; Rojewski & Schell, 1994; Vygotsky, 1978), cooperative learning (Johnson, Johnson, Holubec, & Roy, 1984; Slavin, 1990), language experience approaches, and process writing (Graves, 1994).

Then we provide specific procedures for presenting concepts and academic rules in subject material. All content areas in special education and general education reflect both concepts and academic rules to varying degrees.

Next, we describe learning stages that students pass through as they master the subject matter that teachers present. Our lesson development section presents teacher behaviors and instructional elements associated with initiating instruction, engaging students, and ending a lesson.

Finally, we synthesize the above material as represented in the TEAL model—Teaching: Explicit Activation of Learning (O'Shea & O'Shea, 1997). The TEAL model is used to present the chapter content in an integrated form. Also, we discuss teachers' use of particular instructional elements. We illustrate a variety of different content area examples to show how teachers apply the suggested strategies across different contexts.

*T*he central function of teachers is to deliver instruction to their students in the most efficient and effective manner possible. Developing teachers need to take into account the various instructional elements, weaving them into a form that will communicate clearly to students what target responses teachers expect.

Accordingly, in order to deliver instruction effectively, new teachers must be aware of and act on a number of complex factors that define how and whom they instruct in classrooms. For instance, teachers are confronted daily with an increasingly diverse student population, and they are expected to assist these students in meeting increasingly high standards. In order to instruct diverse students effectively, teachers must implement a growing range of instructional strategies that respond to the differentiation of students' needs (Holloway, 2000).

In addition, increasing numbers of students in American schools are affected by environmental, familial, educational, and interpersonal risk factors, all of which may interfere with students' needs being met and their ability to profit from instruction (Prater, Sileo, & Black, 2000). Teachers who implement effective instruction reach students at risk for and with identified problems because these teachers are aware of how students learn and how to organize, implement, and manage instruction geared toward student needs.

Effective teachers want to know specifically what to do with students and want to use a structured and organized way to get specific ideas across to students. There is research on linking the principles of learning and the principles of teaching to strategies and tactics for effective instruction (Algozzine, Ysseldyke, & Elliott, 1997). Accordingly, teachers involved in delivering instruction while implementing effective strategies and tactics rely on identified ways to instruct diverse students (Johns, 2000). A teacher planning to deliver instruction might focus on the following questions:

1. Is the amount of work appropriate for my students?

2. Is the work at the appropriate instructional level for my students?

3. Have I considered my students' specific learning needs when providing the instruction?

Algozzine et al. (1997) suggested that the most important aspects of effective teaching are tactics that bring broad components, general principles, and specific strategies of effective instruction to life. Appropriate instructional delivery relies on what works in instruction. Implementing appropriate planning, management, delivery, and evaluation processes contributes to instructional outcomes for students.

When teachers plan instruction, they are concerned with the degree to which teaching goals and teacher expectations of student performance and success are stated clearly and are understood by students. Teachers who manage instruction promote an effective and efficient learning setting. There is a sense of positiveness in the class. Such teachers deliver instruction by seeking an appropriate instructional match with their students, presenting lessons clearly, and following specific instructional procedures. They provide instructional support to individual students. They allocate sufficient time to academic and instructional time and ensure each student's opportunity to respond. When teachers evaluate their instruction, they actively monitor student progress and understanding, and they evaluate student performance appropriately and frequently. Thus, teachers who apply principles of effective instruction as they guide students toward the planned goals and objectives are able to reach their diverse students in significant ways.

DIRECT INSTRUCTION AND GUIDED DISCOVERY LEARNING: PRINCIPLES FOR EFFECTIVE INSTRUCTION

The two most broadly applicable models of instruction, which are often thought to be diametrically opposed, are direct instruction (DI) and guided discovery learning (GDL). DI proponents often focus on the need for students to master specific curriculum content; GDL proponents focus on the importance of teaching students how to solve problems and how to learn. In the former case, the instructional outcome is viewed as the demonstration of specific skills and knowledge about reading, math, social studies, science, and so forth (e.g., being able to sound out words, knowing facts about state capitals). In the latter case, the instructional outcome is viewed as the demonstration of skills and knowledge about the process of learning (e.g., how to solve problems, how to use study skills).

Although the philosophical underpinnings may be accurately thought of as being in opposition, the procedural applications deriving from these models can be seen as complementary. Each model has its strengths and weaknesses, and the weaknesses of one are compensated for by the strengths of the other. Therefore, to counter any shortcomings of DI, teachers can use GDL techniques in appropriate situations and vice versa.

In the sections below, we describe both models and their key components. We provide examples of how lessons are taught using each model. Remember that instructional procedures attributed to either DI or GDL are not so precise that variation in their implementation will significantly reduce their effectiveness. Developing teachers should instead consider the procedures outlined below as guidelines from which they can deviate based on the content being presented and their students' educational states.

Direct Instruction

In the areas of special and remedial education, the DI methodology has grown in popularity like no other instructional approach. Its roots date back to the mid-1970s, when Rosenshine (1976) coined the term *direct instruction* in reference to effective teaching behaviors. By extensive classroom observation, Rosenshine (1971) and others (Anderson, Evertson, & Brophy, 1979; Fisher et al., 1980) identified critical teacher behaviors that correlated positively with student academic gains. Englemann and associates (Becker, Englemann, & Thomas, 1971; Carnine & Silbert, 1979; Englemann & Carnine, 1982) expanded the term *direct instruction* to include the use of not only specific teaching procedures but also highly structured curriculum materials. Direct instruction also has been viewed as a positive behavioral support strategy, in that teachers focus on the integration of well-designed curriculum materials and effective instructional delivery to help in the management of student behaviors (Stein & Davis, 2000).

The purpose of direct instruction curriculum materials is to help a teacher systematically direct students in making accurate responses. The teacher uses scripted lesson plans to ensure that precise communication occurs between teacher and students. During instruction, the teacher models target responses, leads students in making these responses, and periodically tests students' ability to respond without teacher cues.

Direct Instruction Defined. DI refers to teacher-guided instruction directed toward the mastery of specific skills and includes activities in which students work in small groups with high rates of engagement. Teachers facilitate success through the use of fast-paced, structured lessons. They use structured curricula, corrective feedback procedures, and performance monitoring. The critical aspect of the DI model is that teachers control instruction. They determine what and how subject matter content is presented (they demonstrate target responses and lead students in making responses). They give extensive practice so that students have sufficient opportunities to respond and thus master the target skills. Practice activities are fast-paced to allow for a high density of responses during instructional periods. During initial learning, the teacher works with students in small groups to monitor the accuracy of their responses. When students err, the teacher provides corrective feedback that takes students through the model-lead-test sequence. As the teacher gradually fades cues, students increasingly are able to respond independently.

Principal Components of Direct Instruction. The three principal components of DI lessons are demonstration, guided practice, and independent practice. During each of these stages, teachers deliver instruction in a standard, systematic manner. If teachers use predictable steps in lesson development, students are able to participate in activities and perform responses in a more consistent manner.

Demonstration. During the demonstration stage of lesson development, the teacher models target responses for students. The responses relate to the performance of academic rules (sets of procedures for performing academic tasks such as solving computations with regrouping) or the formation of concepts (well-defined categories of information used for classification such as types of plants). For instance, if the target response for students is to see-say a set of words containing the medial short vowel sound /a/, then the teacher will point to each target word and sound out the letter sounds contained in the words (e.g., c-a-t, m-a-t, r-a-t). If the target response for students is to state a concept name and say the definition, the teacher will model the response by stating the target word and its definition (e.g., a square is a quadrilateral that contains four congruent sides and four right angles).

Guided Practice. The second stage of lesson development is supervised practice, with the teacher using cues and prompts to elicit target responses. The teacher leads groups of students in making the desired response (teacher and students perform the response simultaneously). As students demonstrate accurate responses, the teacher gradually fades the degree of leading. Instead of making the response with the students, the teacher presents the stimulus and has the group of students respond. Unison responding (groups of students making responses simultaneously) allows students more opportunities for responding during a period of time. The teacher must monitor the responses of individual students during unison responding to determine whether all students are responding accurately. In addition, the teacher tests students by calling on individual students to respond on their own.

As students become more accurate in their responding, the teacher shifts the performance criterion to fast and accurate responding. The teacher concentrates on asking for as many responses as possible during a guided-practice session. This focus increases the opportunities to respond and helps ensure skill mastery.

If the teacher is continuing the lesson on see-say words with medial short vowel sounds, after the sounding-out demonstration the teacher will have students sound out the words with him or her simultaneously. Similarly, in teaching the hear-say response for the concept of square, the teacher will demonstrate the response and then lead students in stating the definition with him or her.

During the interactive process of instruction, these two stages of lesson development often overlap, with little discernible differentiation between the end of one stage and the beginning of the next. Making such a differentiation when implementing these procedures is much less important than ensuring that responses are demonstrated and that students have numerous opportunities to practice the responses while the teacher leads.

Independent Practice. Once students have performed responses accurately without cues or prompts, the third stage of lesson development is initiated to provide students the opportunity to practice response accuracy and speed. Independent practice, therefore, is minimally supervised practice in which students respond with 90 percent or better accuracy.

Two important and closely related features of independent practice assist in skill development and efficient management of classroom activities. First, the teacher can work with other groups of students while one group practices independently. Second, students must be making accurate responses so that they can truly work independently of the teacher (without a constant parade of students moving over to the teacher to ask questions about their seatwork).

The most frequently used form of independent practice is seatwork. Seatwork typically involves independent reading and writing tasks that can be performed without direct and immediate teacher supervision. In general, students with and without mild disabilities spend up to 70 percent of their instructional day in assigned seatwork activities. Consequently, a major management concern for preservice and beginning teachers involves keeping "seatwork students" on task so that they can benefit from the independent work and not interrupt the other students who are receiving direct teacher instruction. For seatwork to serve as an effective independent practice activity, teachers should ensure the following:

1. The assigned exercises and activities are directly related to the objectives being taught.

2. Instructions are clear and concise.

3. Multiple stimulus and response formats are provided.

4. The assignments are age-appropriate, attractive, and organized.

5. Students can complete the activity with a high degree of success and can check the accuracy of their responses (Gaffney, 1987).

To manage students involved in seatwork practice activities effectively, teachers should (1) circulate and provide feedback and reinforcement for appropriate seatwork behavior, (2) arrange desks for easy monitoring of the instructional groups and those students assigned to independent seatwork, and (3) develop a seatwork routine so that all students understand the rules regarding seatwork and procedures for obtaining assistance.

In addition to independent seatwork, independent practice activities for students with disabilities can include instructional games and cooperative, peer-mediated activities (see later sections of this chapter). For students with persistent problems, particularly in the areas of basic skill acquisition and organizational skills, computer-assisted instruction may be especially potent. As noted by Schiffman, Tobin, and Buchanan (1984), the microcomputer is both user-friendly and nonjudgmental. It is especially suited to giving the student who needs additional opportunities to respond the undivided attention that most teachers (and peer groups) cannot physically deliver to individual students. Furthermore, the computer, with its powerful diagnostic and graphics capabilities, can be programmed rather easily by teachers to recognize, diagnose, and correct errors as soon as they are made. In more recent applications, Dawson, Venn, and Gunter (2000) evaluated the effects of reading previews, comparing models provided by a teacher to models provided by a computer. Their findings demonstrated that reading rates and accuracy increased when computers read information. In the absence of a teacher model, the computer model appeared to be a viable tool for increasing fluency. The computer model assisted in exposing students to repeated reading of a story and in scanning reading materials. Thus, technology can enhance students' independent practice activities.

Independent practice does not have to occur only during the school day; once students are proficient with the relevant task, independent activities can be given as homework assignments. If several basic "rules for homework" are followed, these additional practice activities can assist with the retention and integration of academic material. Friend and Bursuck (1996) have offered some general homework guidelines. First, preservice and beginning teachers should realize that the assignment of homework has different purposes at different grade levels. For younger students, a major goal of homework is to foster positive attitudes toward school and to instill good work habits; at higher grades, the main goal is to reinforce knowledge acquisition. Similarly, the frequency and intensity of the assignments should vary according to student age. Students in primary grades should receive no more than one to three assignments per week. On any given night, homework assignments should take a total of 15 to 45 minutes. In sharp contrast, students in the secondary grades should receive assignments four or five times per week. The total time for completing homework each night should be 60 to 120 minutes. Assignments for the intermediate and middle school grades should fall between the two extremes of this continuum. Second, in terms of composition, homework assignments should contain both mandatory and voluntary components, and the teacher should provide clear consequences for both homework completion and the failure to turn in the assignment. However, it is important to remember that homework is not to be used to punish or to teach complex skills directly; nor should teachers expect parents to play a formal instructional role in the completion of their child's assignment. Parents can, however, be asked to create a home environment that fosters the completion of independent work.

Even when following these general guidelines, it is possible that preservice and beginning teachers will find that students with disabilities are encountering difficulties in completing their homework assignments. Patton (1994) reviewed the available literature on the use of homework for students with learning disabilities and developed a comprehensive list of recommended homework practices (see Figure 6.1).

Other Components. Other components of DI have been developed for use during the three stages of lesson development. They are used by teachers to ensure that instruction is systematic and that students are engaged in academic tasks to the maximum extent possible and are evaluated continuously for their progress toward skill mastery (Carnine & Silbert, 1979).

Small-Group Instruction. In an ideal world, there would be one teacher for every student. Such an instructional arrangement is hardly practical, however. A ratio of one teacher for 100 students would provide economic efficiency but is not an effective instructional strategy. The practical compromise is to have 10 to 15 students in a special education classroom and 20 to 30 students in a general education classroom. Under these conditions, the most efficient and effective arrangement is to work with students in small groups during demonstration and guided practice. For those teaching exclusively in special education settings, three to five students is considered a small instructional group; for those teaching in a general education classroom, five to eight students is a small group.

Small-group instruction allows teachers to fulfill the criteria for effective instruction (discussed later in the chapter). A teacher can keep students engaged more easily, have students respond in unison, monitor group and individual performance, and provide corrective feedback. The close proximity of the teacher to students in small-group situations is a controlling force. Students are more likely to engage in desired tasks and to be responsive to teacher cues and prompts.

Engaged Time. Engaged time is the amount of time students spend actively performing the academic tasks presented to them. The concept of engaged time is simple: The greater the proportion of engaged time to allocated instructional time, the greater the academic performance of students. When students are off task, overtly or covertly performing nonacademic tasks, they are not working toward mastery of target responses. Teachers maximize engaged time by efficiently using instructional time, monitoring the rates of engagement in their classrooms, and avoiding dead time. Dead time occurs when teachers delay the start of instructional periods or do not have materials ready and close at hand, when students take unnecessary time to make transitions from one activity to another, and when discussions go off on tangents unrelated to the responses being taught. Developing teachers can minimize all these by being aware of the importance of engaged time and by monitoring the rates of engagement in their classrooms.

FIGURE 6.1 Recommended Homework Practices

Management Considerations

Assess student homework skills
Involve parents from the outset
Assign homework from the beginning of the year
Schedule time and establish a routine for assigning, collecting, and evaluating homework
Communicate the consequences for not completing assignments
Minimize the demands on teacher time
Coordinate with other teachers
Present homework instructions clearly
Verify the assignment given
Allow students to start homework in class
Use assignment books and/or folders
Implement classroom-based incentive programs
Have parents sign and date homework
Evaluate assignments

Assignment Considerations

Recognize the purpose of the homework assignment
Establish relevance
Use appropriate stage of learning demands
Select appropriate type of activity
Keep assignments from getting too complex or novel
Ensure a reasonable chance of completion and a high rate of success
Adapt assignment as needed
Avoid using homework as punishment
Consider nonacademic assignments

Student Competencies

Demonstrate minimum levels of competence
Possess academic support skills
Promote interdependent learning
Develop self-management skills
Foster responsibility

Parent Involvement

Serve in a supportive role
Go through training, if available
Create a home environment that is conducive to doing homework
Encourage and reinforce student effort
Maintain ongoing involvement
Communicate views regarding homework to school personnel

Source: From "Practical Recommendations for Using Homework with Students with Learning Disabilities," by J. R. Patton, 1994, *Journal of Learning Disabilities, 27*, p. 573. Copyright 1994 by PRO-ED, Inc. Reprinted by permission.

Unison Responding. During small-group instruction, teachers seek to maximize the number of opportunities students have to perform target responses. Unison responding, a technique used to maximize the efficiency of practice time, is the simultaneous performance of a response by a group of students. A synonymous term is *choral* *practice.* Each student is provided with more practice under unison responding than if individual students are asked to respond one after the other. The result is more efficient use of instructional time, which increases the likelihood of students mastering the response in the shortest amount of time (Greenwood et al., 1984).

Signaling. Signaling is used during unison responding. The teacher visually or auditorily prompts students to make the desired response to ensure that the responding is truly in unison. Without signaling, some students will lag behind and wait for another student to begin the response before they join in. For example, if a teacher has the word *mate* written on the chalkboard and does not train students to react to a signal, some students will wait for others to begin sounding out the /ma/ sound before starting their response. It is difficult for teachers to determine who is capable of making a response independently without cues.

When teachers begin to use unison responding, they must teach students to respond to their signal. Without explicit training in responding to signals, some students will persist in delaying responses.

Pacing. DI lessons are characterized by fast-paced practice sessions. Not only does a fast rate of stimulus presentation facilitate the efficient use of instructional time, but also it helps maintain interest and decrease off-task behavior.

Monitoring. To ensure appropriate instructional decisions, developing teachers need to know how well students are progressing toward skill mastery. Direct and continuous monitoring of students' rate and accuracy of responding allows developing teachers to determine the daily instructional needs of each student. Daily monitoring better ensures that students will not proceed through series of lessons with high error rates before instruction is modified to improve response accuracy. Monitoring can take the form of simply tallying the number of correct and error responses that students make during an oral practice session or on a paper-and-pencil seatwork assignment. These results can be recorded in a daily log or on a bulletin board chart or can be plotted on a graph. Chapter 4 contains a discussion on charting techniques used to monitor student performance and progress.

Corrective Feedback. The teaching precision under the DI model is designed to increase the probability that students will respond accurately. Accordingly, ideal instruction occurs when instructional procedures are so carefully designed that students make no errors; however, students invariably err, regardless of the teaching precision. In such cases, the following set of corrective feedback procedures is to be used when implementing the DI model in small groups: (1) Praise students making the correct response, (2) model the correct response, (3) lead students in the correct response, (4) test students by asking them to respond on their own, (5) alternate between the example where errors occurred and other examples, and (6) give a delayed test later in the lesson.

For high-level responses, restate or ask students to restate the rule or strategy used to arrive at the correct response. For instance, in teaching the spelling rule "i before e except after c," students can state this rule and then spell the word.

Box 6.1 contains excerpts from a DI lesson that includes the primary components—demonstration, guided practice, and independent practice.

Teaching Models Related to Teacher-Directed Instruction

There are a number of teaching models related to teacher-directed instruction. These include the strategies intervention model and classwide peer tutoring. Each is described below.

Box 6.1   **Example of DI Lesson**

The target skill being taught is two-digit plus two-digit addition with regrouping. This lesson has been preceded by instruction on prerequisite concepts (e.g., place value, regrouping) and skills (e.g., basic math facts, procedures for regrouping).

Demonstration

Ms. van Noord **models** the procedures for example problems by writing the computations and vocalizing the steps as she completes them:

"We begin with the ones column and add the two digits, 7 ones + 6 ones = 13 ones."

$$\begin{array}{r} 27 \\ +46 \\ \hline 13 \end{array}$$

"Thirteen ones can be regrouped into 1 ten and 3 ones."

"So we can place the 1 ten in the tens column and leave the 3 ones in the ones column."

$$\begin{array}{r} {}^{1}27 \\ +46 \\ \hline 3 \end{array}$$

"Next we add the digits in the tens column including the 1 ten we regrouped. 1 ten + 2 tens = 3 tens; 3 tens + 4 tens = 7 tens."

$$\begin{array}{r} {}^{1}27 \\ +46 \\ \hline 73 \end{array}$$

"Our complete sum is 7 tens and 3 ones or 73."

Ms. van Noord then introduces a second example problem, and, depending on the attentiveness of her small group of students, she may begin to include them in verbalizing parts of the computation or steps for completing the computations.

"Let's look at another example of two-digit plus two-digit addition with regrouping."

"We begin with the ones column and add the two digits. Let's say the addition together." **(Unison responding)**

$$\begin{array}{r} 53 \\ +29 \end{array}$$

Ms. van Noord **signals** the students to respond together by pointing to the 3 and says, "Begin." The teacher and group respond:

"3 ones + 9 ones = 12 ones."

$$\begin{array}{r} 53 \\ +29 \\ \hline 12 \end{array}$$

Ms. van Noord continues with the demonstration.

"Twelve ones can be regrouped into 1 ten and 2 ones."

$$\begin{array}{r} {}^{1}53 \\ +29 \\ \hline 2 \end{array}$$

"So we place the 1 ten in the tens column and leave the 2 ones in the ones column."

"Next we add the digits in the tens column, including the 1 ten we regrouped. Let's say the addition together."

Ms. van Noord signals by pointing to the regrouped 1 ten and says, "Begin." The teacher and group respond:

"1 ten + 5 tens = 6 tens; 6 tens + 2 tens = 8 tens."

$$\begin{array}{r} {}^{1}53 \\ +29 \\ \hline 82 \end{array}$$

Ms. van Noord continues:

"Our complete sum is 8 tens and 2 ones, or 82."

Guided Practice

During guided practice, Ms, van Noord **leads** students in completing the computations and vocalizing the steps as **they** complete them. Students write the computations on their worksheets, and together with the teacher they vocalize the steps.

As more examples are completed, the teacher fades her vocalizations until students "talk through" the computations and steps by themselves. Together the teacher and group of students complete the computations in the right column and vocalize the steps in the left column:

"Start with the ones column and add the two digits; 8 ones + 7 ones = 15 ones."

$$\begin{array}{r} 28 \\ +37 \\ \hline 15 \end{array}$$

"Fifteen ones can be regrouped into 1 ten and 5 ones."

$$\begin{array}{r} {}^{1}28 \\ +37 \\ \hline 5 \end{array}$$

"Place the 1 ten in the tens column and leave 5 ones."

"Add the digits in the tens column, 1 ten + 2 tens = 3 tens; 3 tens+ 3 tens = 6 tens."

"The sum is 6 tens and 5 ones or 65."

$$\begin{array}{r} {}^{1}28 \\ +37 \\ \hline 65 \end{array}$$

These procedures are continued with other examples in **unison.** Ms. van Noord intermittently has the members of the group complete an example individually **(tests).** When an individual student (Travis) errs, Ms. van Noord initiates the **corrective feedback procedure.**

"Everyone is adding the ones column correctly and stating the steps."	Step 1—Praise students making correct responses
"Let's make sure that we place the tens in the tens column."	Step 2—Model correct response.

Ms. van Noord **models** the steps, emphasizing the regrouping steps. She continues with the corrective feedback procedures:

"Let's complete the same example problem together. Add the ones column. . . ."	Step 3—Lead students in correct response.
"Travis, say the steps that you followed to complete this example."	Step 4—Test students individually.

Box 6.1   **(continued)**

"Do the next example problem by yourselves. As you write the additions, say the steps quietly to yourselves."

Step 5—Alternate between erred example and other examples.

Ms. van Noord **monitors** students as they complete the examples.

"Travis, write the additions and say the steps for the last problem we did. . . . "

Step 6—Give delayed test later in the lesson.

Independent Practice

Once students have demonstrated 90 percent accuracy in responding during guided practice, the teacher can have the group practice examples problems on their own in the form of seatwork. Independent practice on the target skill, two-digit plus two-digit addition with regrouping, may not occur during the first few lessons. Instead, independent practice on the target skill is delayed until students can follow the procedure. The first lessons usually involve only demonstration and guided practice.

Strategies Intervention Model. A widely applied example of the combination of DI methodology with metacognitive-based strategies is the strategies intervention model (SIM), conceptualized at the University of Kansas (Deshler, Schumaker, Lenz, & Ellis, 1984). Teachers can attempt to determine what setting demands their students need to meet and whether their students have the skills to meet these demands; then, if their students do not have the skills, they can teach students through SIM to use learning strategies they need to meet the demands (Rogan, 2000).

For instance, RAP, a three-step strategy, helps students in summarizing what they have read by following this mnemonic:

Early research by Alley and Deshler (1979) was based on the theory that educational delivery systems and curriculum at the secondary level were ineffective because they failed to address the underlying needs of students with learning disabilities. The researchers determined that these students could succeed in high school if the delivery system and curriculum focused on teaching them learning strategies—"techniques, principles, or rules that will facilitate the acquisition, manipulation, integration, storage, and retrieval of information across situations and settings" (Alley & Deshler, 1979, p. 13). Deshler and his colleagues have either revamped earlier strategies (e.g., the SQ3R method developed by Robinson, 1941) or developed new ones.

For instance, RAP, a three-step strategy, helps students in summarizing what they have read by following this mnemonic:

- Read paragraph.
- Ask self questions.
- Put it in own words. (Schumaker, Denton, & Deshler, 1984)

Other strategies are the word identification strategy (DISSECT), test-taking strategy (PIRATES), sentence-writing strategy (PENS), first-letter mnemonic strategy (FIRST), error-monitoring strategy (COPS), and visual imagery strategy (RIDER).

The SIM includes structures for what to teach and how to teach. Specifically, the "what to teach" component draws from the metacognitive needs of adolescents with learning disabilities; that is, teachers promote awareness and regulation of the information-processing demands of the secondary school setting. The SIM curriculum consists of learning strategies designed to enhance three processes: acquisition of information, storage of information, and expression and demonstration of competence (see Table 6.1).

TABLE 6.1   Strategies Intervention Model (SIM)

Acquisition of Information	Storage of Information	Expression and Demonstration of Competence
Word identification	First-letter mnemonic	Sentence writing
Paraphrasing	Paired associates	Paragraph writing
Self-questioning	Listening and note taking	Error monitoring
Visual imagery		Theme writing
Interpretation of visual aids tion		Assignment comple-
Multipass		Test taking
SOS		

The "how to teach" component is based on the behaviorally oriented DI model, in which teachers model, lead, and test students through the acquisition stage of learning. The strategy acquisition process consists of eight steps:

1. Teacher pretests and obtains student commitment to learn.

2. Teacher describes the new strategy.

3. Teacher models the new strategy.

4. Teacher and student verbally rehearse strategy steps.

5. Student practices on controlled materials.

6. Student practices on grade-appropriate classroom materials.

7. Teacher posttests and obtains student commitment to generalize.

8. Student generalizes.

During step 1, motivation to learn and use the strategy is developed by pointing out the inefficiencies or ineffectiveness of the student's present strategies. In addition, the pretest step is conducted to ensure that the student can perform all the preskills before the strategy is taught. In step 2, the teacher describes the procedures for executing the strategy. These procedures include the major behaviors in which the student will sequentially engage to complete the strategy correctly. In step 3, the teacher models the strategy through a "think aloud" process. In step 4, the student is led through a verbal rehearsal process designed to prompt the self-instruction process. Verbal rehearsal progresses from stating the steps aloud to stating the steps to oneself. So that the student can focus attention on learning the strategy without having to deal with new or difficult materials, initial practice, in step 5, is done with less-demanding materials. Once the students has demonstrated skill in executing the strategy with these materials, he or she then practices in grade-level materials (step 6) to further generalize strategy use to general education content. In step 7, the student is provided with a posttest to determine whether mastery has been achieved, and a behavioral contract is used to gain a commitment to use the strategy in general education classrooms (Deshler & Schumaker, 1986).

Generalization (step 8) is facilitated during and after the acquisition stage. Ellis, Lenz, and Sabornie (1987a, 1987b) describe the process of teaching generalization in terms of four stages:

1. **Antecedent:** Teacher changing negative student attitudes that might ultimately affect generalization behaviors

2. **Concurrent:** Student acquiring the skill well enough for it to become generalized

3. **Subsequent:** Student applying the skill to various contexts, situations, and settings

4. **Independent:** Student using self-instruction to mediate generalization

Antecedent steps are taken to encourage generalization by changing negative student attitudes that might ultimately affect students' efforts to generalize. In planning for instruction, teachers select, or are provided with in the SIM materials, extensive and diverse examples of the application of strategies. During strategy acquisition, concurrent steps are taken to facilitate generalization by having students learn strategies well enough to become generalized. By practicing strategies with controlled materials, students can attend to the steps for executing the strategy without having to focus their attention on reading material that requires attention to decoding or on comprehending complex semantic relationships. After students have demonstrated mastery of strategy use in controlled materials, they are taught to apply the strategy in various contexts, situations, and settings. Less emphasis is placed on completing the strategy steps in the regimented manner used in earlier stages. Instead, teachers vary formats, procedures, and examples as students gain mastery of a strategy in order to promote generalization. Ultimately, independence (executive functioning) is generated by teaching students to use self-monitoring procedures to mediate generalization and cue other teachers to provide reinforcement (Ellis et al., 1987a).

Other characteristics of SIM include explicit delineation of treatment outcomes, their importance, and techniques to be employed; use of self-verbalization; active participation by students in training; and an emphasis on generalization at all stages of learning (Deshler & Schumaker, 1986; Deshler, Schumaker, Alley, Warner, & Clark, 1982; Deshler et al., 1984).

Classwide Peer Tutoring. Classwide peer tutoring (CWPT) is a system of instruction in which students tutor peers in basic academic responses, using prescribed tutoring procedures that enhance the ecobehavioral interactions between classroom antecedents and overt student responses (Delquadri, Greenwood, Whorton, Carta, & Hall, 1986). The underlying principles include increasing students' opportunities to respond through practice activities. Often, when teachers are working with other groups, students outside the instructional group tend to engage in off-task behavior. For example, monitors who observed a fourth grader's oral reading performance noted that the student read for less than 10 seconds and was actively engaged in work for only 8 minutes out of 60 minutes of reading instruction. During reading instruction, the student typically sat alone at his desk while the teacher worked with reading groups. When his group was called for reading with the teacher, often the period was nearly over, and the group had to move to another activity. When peers work with each other, they are more apt to stay on task and to make responses related to academic learning.

In addition, the responses targeted for peer tutoring are functional and have high utility in the classroom; that is, they are skills the students can use often and in a variety

Pause and Reflect About the Profession 6.1

Try challenging your peers to use the strategies intervention model.

1. Without referring to notes or the text narrative, have peers list the eight SIM strategy acquisition steps presented here in the proper sequence.

2. Have peers try to sequence the SIM strategy storage steps.

3. Have peers try the SIM expression and demonstration of competence steps.

of situations. The strategy is to select those responses that are more likely to be practiced and maintained in the classroom environment, such as the following:

* textual oral reading
* responding to comprehension questions
* reading workbook practice
* math fact practice
* vocabulary practice involving meanings and definitions

Responses should reflect teacher outcome measures as much as possible. The focus is outcome variables, not process variables (e.g., rules for carrying out academic tasks or gaining meaning such as metacognitive strategies). Textual oral reading, for instance, focuses on such measures as sentences read, words written, and comprehension questions answered, not on phonetic rules, decoding skills, or comprehension rules.

The teacher reviews daily or weekly performance, giving the opportunity for the teacher to monitor and reinforce student gains. Daily and weekly team totals are posted on a classroom bulletin board (Delquadri et., 1986).

Student Training. Students are trained in three twenty-minute sessions. The teacher explains how the "game" works. Students are paired, and a variable number of pairs comprise a team. Each student functions as a tutor for part of the session, a tutee for part of the session, and the final segment of the session is used to add and total points for correct responses. The teacher then demonstrates the tutoring procedures by acting as the tutor with one student. Next, two students act as tutor and tutee while the rest of the class watches and the teacher gives feedback. A few more demonstrations are provided as needed, followed by a whole-class practice. The training is repeated twice more on other days. After students have demonstrated mastery of the procedures, the teacher assigns partners and teams.

After students have successfully completed the three training sessions, the regular daily CWPT sessions commence. The CWPT daily procedures are initiated with a remainder about tutoring partners, and then students are signaled to pair up. A timer is set for ten minutes. The first tutee in each pair responds to materials while the tutor observes, rewards, and gives feedback. At the end of ten minutes, the students switch roles and begin the second ten-minute tutoring segment. During the final 10 minute segment, the points are added and totaled. Each correct response earns two points, and each successful correction of an error earns one point. Bonus points are awarded for working immediately and cooperatively with the tutor. The winning team is applauded for their performance, and the losing team is applauded for their effort.

Guided Discovery Learning

From a philosophical perspective, the antithesis of DI is the pure form of discovery learning, of which guided discovery is a derivation. Barlow (1985) defines discovery learning as a process of presenting students with problem situations and encouraging them to identify solutions through group interactions or individually. Assumptions are made regarding the learners' psychological state (learners are viewed as processors of information and problem solvers who are curious and motivated to learn and who want to make sense of a situation).

Discovery learning methods emanate from a child-centered view of learning in which students decide what they learn and how learning proceeds. Teachers provide little structure for students. The tight control that teachers maintain under a DI model is largely absent in GDL. There are few specific teaching behaviors to be followed, and the content and materials are not prearranged or tightly structured.

Jerome Bruner is the leading proponent of the discovery model. In his conceptualization of "cognitive structure," Bruner (1966) emphasized the importance of students learning the structures and relationships of structures of a field of study. When they are taught generic problem-solving and information-processing techniques, students can learn how to learn independently. This "heuristic economy" is a means for accommodating the vast amounts of information that individuals must manipulate. School curricula should contain courses that transcend subject matter content and teach critical thinking skills.

Bruner's early work led to continued efforts by cognitive psychologists and special educators to develop cognitive routines, or strategies for developing internal processes for storing, manipulating, and retrieving information. These approaches are referred to as self-regulation, cognitive training, strategic learning, metacognitive learning, and a host of other related terms. The connection among these variations on a theme is that curricula are designed to help students learn about learning (Reid & Stone, 1991). Students learn when and how to use cognitive routines that enable them to process information better. Instruction revolves around students learning how to process declarative knowledge (factual information including concepts), conditional knowledge (knowledge about when to use strategies), and procedural knowledge (steps to follow to complete a cognitive task) (Paris & Winograd, 1990). Students learn to set goals, apply strategies, monitor their progress, and subsequently modify goals or strategies or both (Butler, 1995; Kirby, Booth, & Das, 1996). The learning strategies from the SIM and the skills for success program (Archer, 1991) are examples of strategic learning applications. The overall purpose is to provide students with the cognitive tools to be able to learn independently. These cognitive routines, or tools, are examples of what we refer to later in the chapter as academic rules.

The foundational principles of discovery learning are associated with the social constructivistic paradigm. Social constructivism is based on the assumption that students are self-directed, meaning-seeking, meaning-constructing individuals who act on their environments accordingly. Students' knowledge bases are shaped by contextual conditions and meaningfulness as well as by their individual interests and purposes. Self-directed learning is more motivating than teacher-directed learning, which imposes the problem and the solution. Academic programs designed without considering the context of purpose, use, and desired social relations fail to provide motivating and meaningful environments conducive to self-directed learning (Heshusius, 1986, 1989; Poplin, 1987, 1988; Smith & Heshusius, 1986).

With discovery learning, curricula and instructional techniques are developed so that learning is functional, genuine, and authentic. Curricula are integrated so that the focus of the content is real-life problem solving and skill development; that is, students study problems as they occur in nature or society, not as separate subject areas. Content area curricula are integrated to include problem solving that reflects knowledge structures across social studies, science, literature, art, music, and mathematics. For example, if students study the problem of balanced ecosystems, they may have to read narrative and expository prose, examine scientific principles, and use mathematical algorithms in order to show how an ecosystem works. The integrated curriculum approach is modeled after the British infant school tradition and the project approach of Kilpatrick (1918).

From a discovery learning perspective, the purpose of instruction is to teach students to be independent problem solvers, to teach them the generic steps to scientific inquiry and logical thinking. After learning the generic process of problem solving, it is believed that students can readily learn information from other content areas. Instruction is directed toward transferring the use of problem-solving strategies to new material and situations. Specific content information is learned incidentally, through the introduction of novel problems requiring similar problem-solving strategies and involving new but similar information. The bottom line is that the process of problem solving supersedes any learning of content material (Ausubel, Novak, & Hanesian, 1978; Biehler & Snowman, 1986).

Proponents of discovery techniques argue that DI techniques are too simplistic and authoritarian. They believe that DI methods are effective for low-level cognitive tasks but that discovery techniques using induction better facilitate the use of high-level cognitive skills. Also, they criticize the tight control that DI teachers exercise over content and instructional activities because students are taught to be passive and overly dependent on teachers and extrinsic rewards. With discovery techniques, students learn to be more independent learners, able to determine their own instructional needs.

Guided Discovery Learning Defined. Gagne (1980) has developed a variation of the pure form of discovery learning. Under Gagne's GDL model, curricular content and structure are integrated with a bottom-up, inductive approach to learning. Gagne asserts that learning is most effective when content is presented by starting with the specific and moving to the general. Concepts or rules are learned by assembling examples, making comparisons, identifying patterns, and then identifying the concept or rule that links the examples. A teacher's cues or hints and structured curricula are used to assist students in inducing the concept or rule identification. Curricula are to be analyzed and hierarchy developed from the top down, but instruction begins at the bottom and moves to the top (Belkin & Gray, 1977).

Guided discovery methodology focuses on gaining specific content as well as on teaching generic problem-solving skills. Instead of focusing solely on teaching students to be independent problem solvers, as is the case with the general format of discovery learning, GDL teachers guide students through a logical series of problem-solving steps to better facilitate learning specific content.

Principal Components of Guided Discovery Learning. Several components of GDL are the foundation of its effectiveness. Proponents of the guided discovery model, however, do not delineate these components as clearly as the proponents of DI delineate its components. From what can be discerned, the following components characterize GDL (Ausubel et al., 1978).

Contrasts. Contrasts are emphasized throughout this process as students identify and compare the distinctive features of like concepts. These distinctive features determine the relationships among concepts and help students in discriminating concepts, such as a square from a rectangle. For instance, teachers may guide students to identify the features of a square, such as the length of its sides, the comparative length of its different sides, the inside angles formed by each set of perpendicular sides, and its two-dimensionality. They also may examine nonrelevant features, such as its size and color. The distinctive features are then compared with those of other figures, with the characteristics of the square used as the comparison basis (Figure 6.2).

Example Selection. Example selection is critical for contrasts to be made. Examples are carefully selected and grouped by distinctive features so that when they are presented, void of a classification scheme, to students, the students will be able to identify the relationships themselves. By presenting numerous examples applicable to the target skill or concept, the teacher adds further cues as to the relationship shared by the concepts. For instance, in teaching the concept of chair, a kitchen chair would be a good first example. It contains the standard features of a chair, and it is a form of chair that students would see frequently and in different settings. Providing other examples of chairs with some variations from a kitchen chair, such as a living room chair (different shape and material) or a secretary's chair (different shape with wheel bases), helps students to form a concept set that accommodates varieties of form and enables them to identify distinctive features (e.g., the seat) and irrelevant features (e.g., wood, material). Gradually, less typical forms, such as a bean bag chair, can be introduced to elaborate the concept set further.

Informed Guessing. Students are encouraged to make informed guesses by using information they have identified as the basis for asking questions that lead to further information about the concepts. In reading a story, for instance, a student may use a self-questioning strategy that entails writing and answering questions about the content of

Early development of concept *square*

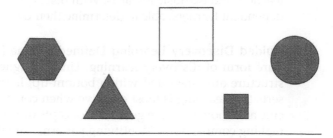

Advanced development of concept *square*

Square – a square is a closed figure with four equal
sides and four right angles

FIGURE 6.2 At early stages of concept development
during preschool and primary grades, students learn to
discriminate by using examples and nonexamples; later,
in a spiral curriculum, concepts are further developed
through formal definitions, examples, and nonexamples.

upcoming paragraphs to be read, based on the information gained from previous paragraphs. The questions are used to aid in "guessing" upcoming parts of the story plot and analyzing the concepts presented in the passage. Consequently, students are being taught to reflect on their state of understanding at any given time and to use questions to guide their acquisition of new information.

Awareness of the Underlying Problem-Solving Process. If students are asked to focus on the process steps they use to solve problems, they can form their own self-regulating strategies for problem solving. An obvious example is solving math word problems. Students are given problems to solve and are asked to state the steps used to determine the operation and to identify the variables and constants.

Active Participation. Participation is encouraged by having students work in various capacities as part of a group. In a group assignment, for example, students may be assigned or volunteer to research sources of information or to record answers to questions. The purpose of active participation is to ensure that students are involved in the process of solving problems, classifying information, or establishing rules.

The concept teaching model (Gregory, 1985) provides an example lesson format that incorporates the components of guided discovery:

1. Three to five well-chosen examples of the concept are presented one at a time. As they are presented, the teacher states, "This is an example of [concept name]."

2. Three to five well-chosen nonexamples are presented one at a time. The teacher states, "This is not an example of [concept name]."

3. Other stimuli representing the target concept or other concepts from the same form class are presented to students. Students answer yes or no when asked, "Is this an example of [concept name]?"

Pause and Reflect About the Profession 6.2

Which statement best illustrates the role of teacher effectiveness in a GDL framework?

1. Give me better students, and I'll give you better results.
2. Teach slowly, and students will absorb the information.
3. How well I teach = how well they learn.
4. Students will not learn until they are ready to learn.

Why did you choose the item you did?

4. The teacher, using leading questions, asks students to list the attributes of the examples and the nonexamples.

5. The teacher has the students construct a definition of the concept, based on a list of attributes.

The teacher provides practice by pointing to examples and nonexamples of the concept and having students answer the question "What is this an example of?"

Box 6.2 contains excerpts from a GDL lesson that includes the steps from the concept teaching model.

Teaching Models Related to Guided Discovery Learning

There are a number of teaching models related to guided discovery learning. These include proleptic teaching and scaffolding, cooperative learning, the language experience approach, and the process-writing model. Each is described below briefly.

Proleptic Teaching and Scaffolding. A model of instruction that includes many of the general features of guided discovery learning is proleptic teaching, the anticipation of competence (Vygotsky, 1978). The teacher provides a model of the strategy or skill being taught through a natural dialogue with students and gradually allows the students to take over the steps and procedures involved in applying the strategy or skill (Paris & Winograd, 1990; Rosenshine & Meister, 1992). As needed, the teacher provides the necessary support structures, or scaffolding (Bruner, 1973; Rojewski & Schell, 1994). The analogy is made to the tutelage of an apprentice by a master crafter; the master crafter provides the support that the apprentice needs to carry out some simple aspects of the task (Rogoff, 1990). In the instructional context, students are asked to perform a task before they really have the skills to do it. Teachers then guide them through the particular activity and gradually relinquish responsibility for completing the activity as students become more and more skilled in the task at hand.

This concept is closely related to Goodman's (1989) conceptualization of child-centered learning whereby teachers "lead from behind"; that is, as students demonstrate needs and seek out assistance, the teacher provides the guidance and support structures that allow them to learn what they need to know to complete the task at hand. The teacher does not establish and follow a preset curriculum sequence but rather follows the sequence dictated by each student's naturally developing needs.

In addition, a reciprocity occurs between teacher and student in what is termed a *community of learners*. Teacher and students learn from each other, and students learn from each other. Tasks often require a collaborative approach, as groups of learners study and solve problems. Students and teacher plan and develop curricular activities that are integrated across subject areas to facilitate growth and each student's emerging repertoire of skills. The teacher monitors student progress by *kid watching*, a term popularized by Yetta Goodman (1989). The social aspect of learning is heavily emphasized.

Box 6.2   Example GDL Lesson

The target concept being taught is story setting, a story grammar that describes the context in which a story takes place.

Example and Nonexample Presentation

Mr. Elkins presents three examples, listed on the chalkboard, excerpted from narrative prose that illustrate story settings. Students are asked to read each silently.

"This is an example of a story setting from the story 'Back of Burke.'"	The small Western town was at the base of a range of steep mountains. Most people in Burke owned cattle ranches that surrounded the town.
"This is an example of a story setting from the story 'Letter to the Editor.'"	Before he got dressed for school, Alan sat in his room with dirty clothes everywhere. Posters of his favorite sports players hung on all four walls. Alan typed quickly on his new computer.
"This is an example of a story setting from the story 'The Guilty Witness.'"	The sirens grew louder in the hot summer night's heat as the ambulance approached. Pat stood dazed by the sight of the bloody victim. Her mind raced back through the visions of what had just happened.

Mr. Elkins points to an adjacent chalkboard and has students silently read three nonexamples of story settings.

"This is *not* an example of a story setting."	It was all over. Adrian's cattle were back, and the town was a safe place to live.
"This is *not* an example of a story setting."	Alan wasn't going to let that stop him. He was determined to interview his hero.
"This is *not* an example of a story setting."	The jury returned their verdict to the judge. Pat knew, from the expressions on their faces, what they had found.

Mr. Elkins proceeds to have students open their textbooks to specific pages and read brief excerpts from several stories. After reading each, he asks, "Is this is an example of a story setting?" The students respond either yes or no (**informed guessing and active participation**).

Definition or Rule Induction

Next, Mr. Elkins asks a series of questions about the attributes of the examples and nonexamples in order to explicate **contrasts**, and the students respond.

"Let's look at our examples and non-examples of story settings. What did you learn about the story in the first example?"	"The story is in a little town." "The name of the town is Burkle." "People raise cows and stuff."

Mr. Elkins lists the students' responses on the chalkboard and continues to ask more leading questions.

"By learning these kinds of things, what does the story setting do for the reader?"	"Tell us things about the story."

"Yes, it does, but what kinds of things does the story setting tell us?"

"Where the people live."

"Yes, good thinking. The story setting tells us in formation about where and when the story takes place."

"If it's day or night."

To confirm this conclusion, Mr. Elkins directs the students to look at the nonexamples to confirm that the statement "The story setting tells us information about where and when the story takes place" adequately distinguishes examples from nonexamples (**contrast, informed guessing, and active participation**).

"Let's look at the nonexamples and see whether they tell us where and when the story takes place. Read the first nonexample. Does this statement allow us to answer the questions *where* or *when* the story takes place?"

"Sort of, it says the town."

"But that could mean any town."

"Well, I guess it really doesn't tell exactly where."

"What about telling us *when* the story takes place?"

"No."

After reviewing a few more nonexamples, Mr. Elkins includes students to **construct a definition** of story setting.

"How can we complete the following sentence beginning— 'Story settings tell us. . . .' "

"Where the story happens."
"When it takes place."

"Good, you've figured out the purpose of story settings. When in the story do we usually find the story setting?"

"In the first couple of pages."

"Yes, the story setting tells us where and when a story takes place and is usually found at the beginning of the story."

Mr. Elkins posts this definition of a story setting on a bulletin board and uses it in subsequent lessons when asking students to identify story settings in their reading passages.

Cooperative Learning. Cooperative learning involves sets of techniques that have students working together in groups to practice and master prescribed skills. While approaches may differ, they usually entail some form of student to student interaction, individual accountability, and positive student interdependence (Maheady, Mallette, Harper, Sacca, & Pomerantz, 1994). Students are sorted into teams, and their individual and team performances are evaluated. The two dominant approaches are student learning teams, developed by Slavin (1990), and the learning together approach, developed by Johnson and Johnson and their colleagues (Johnson et al., 1984). Following are specific applications of cooperative learning.

Jigsaw. Perhaps the most widely used and best example of cooperative learning is the jigsaw (Aronson, Stephan, Sikes, Bleney, & Snapp, 1978). Heterogeneous teams of three to five students are formed. All teams are given the same assignment, which is divided into the same number of parts as there are members on each team. Each team member is assigned a part (piece) of the assignment (puzzle). Students from the different teams who are assigned to the same part form "expert groups." The expert groups meet to review information regarding their part, determine the most important information, and return to their teams. The teams then review the important information from each part and synthesize the information (put the puzzle pieces together). Students are expected to master the information for all parts. Ultimately, students are individually quizzed on all parts of the topic.

Student Teams—Achievement Divisions (STAD). Students are arranged into heterogeneous teams of four to six. A pretest is provided on the lesson or unit content. Concepts, principles, and/or procedures are presented or elicited. The teams then work together on worksheets, study guides, or other practice activities. After students have mastered the content, they take individual tests on the material. Their scores are compared with their pretest scores to derive a gain score, and the individual gain scores are averaged for a team gain score. Points are awarded for individual and team gains.

Teams-Games-Tournaments (TGT). Students are arranged in groups, and lesson content is presented in the same way as with STAD. However, students participate in weekly games and tournaments rather than taking weekly quizzes. After practice sessions, students are arranged on the basis of ability levels into three-person tournament tables. The homogeneous grouping allows students with comparable skills to compete with each other and gives lower-functioning students the same probability of success as higher-functioning students.

Team-Assisted Individualization (TAI). TAI is designed to assist students in learning various math algorithms and problem-solving strategies. Students' skill levels are determined, placing them at a particular point in an individualized skill sequence. Students complete worksheets daily and progress through the curriculum at their own pace. Other team members help check responses on the worksheets. At the end of each unit of individualized instruction, students take a final unit test. Points are awarded for passing the unit tests, completing multiple units, and completing homework assignments.

Language Experience Approach. A narrower application of guided discovery is the language experience approach, in which students and teachers collaborate on story construction. Students unable to use all the technical conventions of written language (e.g., spelling, punctuation) dictate to the teacher their construction of a story, and the teacher writes down the oral statements. The stories are used as the stimulus for learning

Pause and Reflect About the Profession 6.3

Devise a cooperative learning activity for use with a set of students at the grade level in which you are instructing now.

List and describe the student grouping format for the content area (e.g., reading, science, mathematics) in which you are employing the cooperative learning activity.

Assign all students a group assignment for a 30-minute period.

Describe each student's role in the cooperative learning time frame.

Consider: What materials and equipment will students need to complete this activity?

language in written and oral forms and for learning about the content communicated within the story. Through constant exposure to their own writing and the writings of others (books), students begin to use vocabulary that they have written, heard, or read. They tell stories, create plots, and convey information (Holdaway, 1979). Readers construct their own interpretations of the text that authors have written. Meaningfulness and functionality are individualized, and there really is no teacher-directed interpretation. Individual students, with their own experiences and what they bring to a task, guide their own interpretation. This student-centered perspective on the construction of knowledge implies that a teacher's job is to understand what a student's interpretation is and how it came to be, not one of trying to correct and point the student to some single convergent response or interpretation.

Depending on students' needs, the teacher uses the student-constructed stories as the basis for leading students to recognize and understand principles of word recognition, spelling, grammar, and story structure and to utilize strategies for comprehending written and oral language. Guided discovery techniques such as contrasting and informed guessing are used to identify principles or procedures that students can apply to different stories.

Process-Writing Model. In process writing, a teacher guides students through a series of steps that include planning, drafting, conferencing/consulting, revising, and publishing. Although the degree of teacher directiveness can be high, the process-writing model is more often associated with student-directed approaches. The degree of teacher directedness is most controversial in the conferencing step. The fundamental concern is the difference between consulting and conferencing. The teacher's interaction with students is much more directive under the consulting mode than it is under the conferencing mode.

During planning, students collect information about the topic and begin to outline the content of what they are writing. Brainstorming is often used to map out information answering the basic questions of who, what, where, when, and how. The structure or sequence of the content is also listed. For a narrative story, the author maps out ideas about the setting, the problem encountered by the protagonist, the protagonist's goal, the order of actions taken by the characters to solve the problem, and how the problem is ultimately resolved (Zipprich, 1995). For expository prose, the author begins organizing the concepts and points to be presented. Next, the author begins drafting the initial version of the writing. During the conferencing step, the initial draft is shared with others, often by using an "author chair" (Graves & Hansen, 1983) or a "sharing conference" (Milem & Garcia, 1996). The author shares his or her writing with classmates, who in turn ask questions and give constructive suggestions that can be used for the revising.

Pause and Reflect About the Profession 6.4

Defend or refute each of the following statements.
The overriding issue associated with metacognition and strategies instruction is to help students become more knowledgeable of content.
Why did you choose the position?

The overriding issue associated with metacognition and strategies instruction is to help students become independent learners.
Why did you choose the position?

The overriding issue associated with metacognition and strategies instruction is to help students become responsive to cognitive demands.
Why did you choose the position?

The overriding issue associated with metacognition and strategies instruction is to help students become well-rounded students.
Why did you choose the position?

Next, the author revises the initial draft, taking into consideration the suggestions of others and his or her own reflections about the work. In addition to revising the content, the author edits the work for spelling, capitalization, and grammar. After the revision, the author may then conference a second time. This cycle may be repeated until the author is ready to publish the work. Publication involves reviewing the work to polish details and the visual presentation of the work (e.g., title page, accompanying pictures or graphics). It also provides students with opportunities to gain skills in proofreading and to learn to conform with the formal constructs of written discourse. With continued process-writing experiences, students become very comfortable sharing their work with others, discussing it with others, and receiving some assistance (Englert, Raphael, Anderson, Anthony, & Stevens, 1991; Graves, 1994; Richardson, 1991).

PROCEDURES FOR PRESENTING SUBJECT MATTER

In addition to concerns about how to teach, developing and beginning teachers often worry about what to teach. Although the scope of this chapter does not include specific curricular content, we present a description of the type of subject matter taught by most teachers. In most classrooms, two basic forms of subject matter—concepts and academic rules—are the focus of teaching and learning during any given day. These types of subject matter necessitate the use of specific steps that can be included within the more general procedures of either DI or GDL. For instance, when using a DI format, what the teacher models, leads, and tests on will be somewhat different when teaching concepts as opposed to teaching academic rules. Nonetheless, the same general DI procedures are used regardless of subject matter. This is equally true when using a GDL approach. Therefore, the relationship between the DI and GDL models and the presentation of concepts and academic rules is that the latter dictates more specific steps within the general framework of the former. Following is a description of how these two types of subject matter are presented effectively.

Presentation of Conceptual Knowledge

Concepts are the basis for categorizing and organizing one's understanding about the world. They provide a hierarchical structure for superordinate and related subordinate categories of ideas or information. Before students can master academic skills, such as in mathematics or reading, they need to have grasped the basic underlying skills (Stanger, Symington, Miller, & Johns, 2000). By categorizing information, students are better able to understand similarities and differences among various ideas or events and to use information in more efficient ways. To describe conceptual structure, the analogy of a file cabinet is often used: Superordinate categories are the file drawers, and within each drawer are file folders, the subordinate categories, and within the file folders are sets of papers, the second tier of subordinate categories.

Conceptual knowledge is the basis for all content areas. Language arts involves a seemingly infinite set of concepts about the human experience and the world. These concepts deal with the struggle among people, nature, and even supernatural powers. The foundation of mathematics comprises a set of fundamental concepts about numbers and their manipulation. The natural and social sciences also deal with a host of concepts used to categorize plants and animals and people and places. The sciences even have special cases of conceptual knowledge called laws and principles. Both involve cause-effect relationships that explain natural and social phenomena. In the physical sciences, for instance, Newton's third law of motion is an explanation of the equilibrium of forces acting on each other. In the social sciences, principles are used in explaining causal relationships such as the economics of supply and demand. Laws differ from principles in that there is greater certainty about their ability to account for what happens in nature. Natural laws are absolute, but principles are only guidelines that have exceptions. Although concepts differ from subject to subject and there are special categories of concepts such as laws and principles, teachers of conceptual knowledge can use a common set of principles to guide instruction.

How to Teach Concepts. The presentation of conceptual knowledge is centered on definitions of the concepts being taught. To teach students the category of information subsumed by the concept's name, developing teachers must set the limits for what fits and what does not. This can be thought of as a conceptual basket. A determination must be made as to what will fit in one basket and not another, just as clothes are sorted before washing.

Initially, the hierarchical structure of the categories must be determined (Figure 6.3). With reference to the selector dial on a washing machine, Mr. Gunn, who teaches daily living skills, might plan to start with three clothing categories: permanent press, heavy duty, and regular. Next, remembering his bachelor training, he separates whites from colors. So now Mr. Gunn has planned a two-tier system of sorting clothes requiring six baskets. To set limits, Mr. Gunn has to list the essential attributes of the clothes for each basket. For example, he might define white permanent press clothes as those clothes that are 90 percent or more white (when clean) and made of a permanent press material. He now has a definition of white permanent press clothes that can be used to classify the clothing piled up in the laundry room.

Mr. Gunn's definition has three components: concept name (white permanent press), class term (clothes), and essential attributes (90 percent or more white when clean and made of a permanent press material). The concept name simply serves as a label for the concept. The class term links the target concept to the broader, superordinate conceptual category to which it belongs. The essential attributes define the parameters of the target concept and help in distinguishing it from other related concepts (e.g., dark permanent press clothes, white heavy-duty clothes).

Definitions alone are insufficient for presenting conceptual knowledge. They are abstractions that need to be translated into more concrete examples. To do so, the class term and the essential attributes are used to identify those items that fit in the conceptual basket and those that do not. The students are taught to place each item of clothing into its appropriate basket by examining the item and first asking themselves whether it is a piece of clothing (the broad class of items) or some other item found in the dirty clothes pile. If it is a piece of clothing, then the students examine it more closely to determine the match between the essential attributes of the conceptual baskets and the

Dirty clothes

Permanent press   Heavy duty   Regular

colors   whites   colors   whites   colors   whites

FIGURE 6.3 Hierarchical Structure of the Categories of Clothing Used as Analogs for the Hierarchical Structure of Superordinate and Subordinate Concepts characteristics of the piece of clothing. If the piece of clothing is a white shirt (90 percent or more white when clean) and made of a permanent press material, then it is a good example of clothes that go into the white permanent press basket.

To complete the process of conceptualizing, Mr. Gunn needs to determine what does not fit in the baskets (nonexamples). The critical item for selecting nonexamples is the class term because it serves as a screening device for two types of nonexamples. Those items that are not members of the broader class are *between-class* nonexamples. They do not possess the essential attributes to even be a member of the broad class, let alone a member of a subclass. On the one hand, a wallet found in the middle of the clothes pile is a gross nonexample of clothing. On the other hand, a pair of blue jeans fits the class of clothing but does not share either of the essential attributes for the white permanent press basket. Consequently, it would be a *within-class* nonexample.

Within-class nonexamples have varying relations to the target concept (the more essential attributes an item of clothing shares with the target concept, the more alike it is and the finer the discrimination needed to sort it). For example, clothing must have only two essential attributes, in order to fit in the white permanent press category. So the degrees of fineness are limited to those pieces of clothing that have both of the essential attributes, those that have one essential attribute but not the other, and those that have neither of the essential attributes (see Figure 6.3).

These distinctions are important because the use of examples and varying degrees of nonexamples is critical in teaching students to discriminate among related concepts. If they are given clear examples that possess the essential attributes of the concept, students can more efficiently construct a stimulus set. After students have worked with a group of good examples and are clear on what fits in the conceptual basket, then they can effectively identify clear nonexamples as not fitting in the basket. This confirmation process is aided by moving from between-class to within-class nonexamples, which enables students to shape and fine-tune their understanding of the target concept.

Conceptual knowledge is presented in one of two ways. First, teachers may use a definition, examples, and nonexamples to teach a concept (Box 6.3). On the one hand, they may model the concept by defining it and then show students a set of examples and nonexamples to develop a more concrete understanding. This sequence is congruent with the DI teaching method. On the other hand, teachers may introduce a set of examples and nonexamples and induce students to formulate a concept definition based on common characteristics. This approach is more typical of a GDL approach commonly used at the upper elementary grades and above when complex related concepts are taught in science, math, and literature.

Second, teachers may choose to give DI examples and nonexamples or to induce students to give GDL examples and nonexamples without stating a formal definition. This strategy is applicable to situations in which a formal definition may be too complicated to be of value to the learner (e.g., teaching the concepts of redness and blueness to preschoolers) and to the early stage of a spiral curriculum where a concept is developed at progressively higher levels throughout students' educational careers (e.g., when teaching the concept of square to preschoolers as a visual discrimination of shape versus as opposed to teaching the concept to an elementary school student as a geometrical plane with essential characteristics involving sides, angles, and closedness, as shown Figure 6.2).

Box 6.3   **Procedural Options for Teaching Concepts**

Define (give concept name, class term, and essential attributes) and give examples and nonexamples.

   OR

Give examples and nonexamples.

Presentation of Academic Rules

A second type of subject matter that is taught on a large scale is the academic rule. Academic rules are procedures that are followed to complete an academic task. Such a rule contains two elements: (1) a situation or condition that denotes when or where a procedure is to be used (conditional knowledge) and (2) a command that pinpoints what is to be done (procedural knowledge) (Box 6.4). For example, students are taught to indent the first line when writing a paragraph. The situation or condition is "when writing a paragraph," and the command is "indent the first line." More complex academic rules contain a situation or condition and a series of commands that represent the steps needed to complete a task. For instance, students being taught to use multipass (Alley & Deshler, 1979), a study-skill strategy, are instructed that, when they set out to read a passage, they must first do a survey pass, then a size-up pass, and finally a sort-out pass. The learning strategies and self-regulation routines referenced earlier are forms of academic rules.

Academic rules also operationalize the application of conceptual knowledge. A prime example is mathematics. Numerous procedures for doing computations and solving problems entail the use of conceptual knowledge. Consider the concept of place value: the idea that, in a base 10 system, the placement of a number in a right-to-left progression determines the factor of the units it represents. For students to understand what it means to "carry" or "regroup" a number from one column to another, they must learn the concept of place value. Then the academic rule for "carrying" or "regrouping" will make sense to them (they will recognize that the digit they are regrouping represents sets of 10, 100, and so forth).

How to Teach Academic Rules. The principles for teaching academic rules are relatively simple. A teacher needs to state (DI) or induce students to formulate (GDL) the rule, including the condition or situation and the command(s). Next, the rule must be applied to examples, and ultimately students need to be able to distinguish when and where the rule is used appropriately. For instance, when the academic rule for decoding CVCe (consonant, vowel, consonant, e) words is being taught, the rule must be stated or discovered and applied to words that fit the pattern. Students then practice decoding the sounds of example words. Using a DI procedure, the teacher points to the chalkboard and states the academic rule as written:

> "When a consonant, vowel, consonant is followed by a final e (CVCe), the vowel is long and the final e is silent" (model).
> "All right, when I signal, say the rule with me. 'When a consonant. . . .'" (lead).
> "What is the rule, Sondra?" (test).

After several opportunities to practice, the teacher demonstrates the application of the rule and provides guided practice. When students are able to accurately state and apply the rule by using examples, then nonexamples are introduced (in this or a subsequent lesson) so that students learn when the rule is appropriate (examples) and not appropriate (nonexamples).

B ox 6.4   **Steps for Teaching Academic Rules**

1. State the academic rule:
   Condition or situation.
   Procedural step(s).

2. Apply the rule to examples.

Pause and Reflect About the Profession 6.5

Try to determine *academic rules* that teachers can teach, given the following examples:

(a)	(b)	(c)
book	stash	ax
look	cash	an
took	bash	at
hook	lash	as
Academic Rule:	Academic Rule:	Academic Rule:

(d)	(e)	(f)
replace	washing	ape
review	helping	cake
retake	fixing	place
rerun	spelling	brake
Academic Rule:	Academic Rule:	Academic Rule:

(g)	(h)	(i)
5, 10, 15, 20	2, 4, 6, 8	10, 20, 30, 40
Academic Rule:	Academic Rule:	Academic Rule:

(j)	(k)	(l)
0 × 150	6 × 156	(3 × 2) + 1
0 × 450	77 × 1577	(5 × 2) + 1
0 × 950	42 × 1542	(15 × 2) + 1
0 × 750	10 × 1510	(92 × 2) + 1
Academic Rule:	Academic Rule:	Academic Rule:

LEARNING STAGES

Another consideration in using either a DI or a GDL approach is the progression of students through the stages of skill development. As students' conceptual knowledge and academic skills improve, the DI and GDL procedures are modified to accommodate mastery. When initially learning a new concept or skill, students characteristically make numerous mistakes, require cues and prompts, and need corrective feedback. But with instruction and practice, students gradually become able to conceptualize information or execute the skill.

This progression is clearly evident when students are learning to decode and recognize words in print. At first, they read each individual word slowly, often saying the wrong sound or leaving out a sound. Teachers have to model letter-sound correspondence and sounding-out procedures. Gradually, young readers decode or recognize words with greater speed and accuracy as a result of instruction and practice. Ultimately, they are able to read fluently many varied types of reading material at school and home.

Learning to read exemplifies the stages of learning through which students pass when learning a new concept or skill. These stages are concept or skill acquisition, fluency building, maintenance, and generalization (Figure 6.4).

FIGURE 6.4 Teaching: Explicit Activation of Learning (TEAL)

1. **Acquisition Stage—Introduction**
   a. **Advance Organizer**—Outline the activities to be completed during the lesson.
   b. **Linkage**—Review related concepts, rules, or skills from previous lessons.
   c. **Demonstration**—Target concept, rule, or skill is demonstrated or induced. *Examples* are demonstrated or induced.
   d. **Guided Practice**—Target concept, rule, or skill is practiced with extensive prompting using *only examples*.
      1) Lead or induce student in stating definition, attributes, rule, or skill
      2) Lead or induce student in identifying concept examples or applying rules to examples
         a) use signaling to lead choral responses
         b) pose question, wait 3 to 5 seconds, call on reciter
         c) recognize student response
            1. give specific praise
            2. probe, amplify, restate student response
            3. ask peer for response
         d) follow corrective feedback steps as needed
      3) Test student's response
   e. **Independent Practice**—Target concept, rule, or skill is practiced daily without prompting using *only examples*.
      1) Give directions to complete activity tasks
      2) Lead students in completing example tasks
      3) Indicate deadline for completing activity
      4) Circulate and assist students
      5) Review student responses to activity tasks
   f. **Ending Review**—Review target concept, rule, or skill.
2. **Acquisition Stage**—Discrimination
   a. **Advance Organizer**—Outline the activities to be completed during the lesson.
   b. **Linkage**—Review related concepts, rules, or skills from previous lessons.
   c. **Demonstration**—Target concept, rule, or skill is demonstrated induced. *Examples and nonexamples* are demonstrated or induced.
   d. **Guided Practice**—Target concept, rule, or skill is practiced with extensive prompting using *examples and nonexamples.*
      1) Lead student in stating definition, attributes, rule, or skill.
      2) Lead student in identifying concept examples and nonexamples or applying rules to examples and nonexamples
         a) use signaling to lead choral responses
         b) pose question, wait 3 to 5 seconds, call on reciter
         c) recognize student response
            1. give specific praise
            2. probe, amplify, restate student response
            3. ask peer for response
         d) follow corrective feedback steps as needed
      3) Test student's responses
   e. **Independent Practice**—Target concept, rule, or skill is practiced *daily* without prompting using *examples and nonexamples.*
      1) Give directions to complete activity tasks
      2) Lead students in completing example tasks
      3) Indicate deadline for completing activity
      4) Circulate and assist students
      5) Review student responses to activity tasks
   f. **Ending Review**—Review target concept, rule, or skill.
3. **Fluency-Building Stage**—Target concept, rule, or skill is practiced *daily* with high rate of speed and accuracy.
      1) Review target concept, rule, or skill
      2) Give directions to complete activity tasks

FIGURE 6.4   (Continued)

> 3) Lead students in completing example tasks
> 4) Indicate deadline for completing activity
> 5) Circulate and assist students
> 6) Review student responses to activity tasks
>
> 4. **Maintenance Stage**—Target concept, rule, or skill is practiced *weekly or monthly* with high rate of speed and accuracy.
>   1) Review target concept, rule or skill
>   2) Give directions, to complete activity tasks
>   3) Lead students in completing example tasks
>   4) Indicate deadline for completing activity
>   5) Circulate and assist students
>   6) Review student responses to activity tasks

Acquisition (Introduction and Discrimination)

Students in the acquisition stage of learning typically make frequent errors when attempting to use a target concept or skill but gradually respond more and more accurately. Teachers provide effective instructional antecedents, which are characterized in this stage of learning by extensive direction or guidance, prompts, and cues that assist students in responding accurately. Through careful selection of examples and clear definitions of concepts or clear rule statements, teachers structure learning in ways that decrease the complexity of the learning environment and increase the probability that students will respond in a desired fashion.

The key principle associated with instructional antecedents at the acquisition stage is clear communication (Englemann & Carnine, 1982). This is accomplished when the teacher either provides directly or guides students in developing clear concept definitions or academic rules. A definition contains distinctive attributes that set the target concept apart from other similar concepts. An academic rule effectively describes the situation in which the rule is appropriate and provides clear steps to execute the task. In addition, clarity of communication is provided through the selection of effective examples. During the acquisition stage, examples should contain the prototypical dimensions of the concept or provide an easy stimulus for executing an academic rule. Our earlier reference to using a kitchen chair as a prototypical example is applicable here. Similarly, using the word *mat* would be a good example for introducing the CVCe sounding-out rule, whereas the multisyllabic word *material* would not.

The acquisition stage can be divided into two levels: introduction and discrimination. The differences between these two levels are minimal but significant. At the introduction level, only examples are used; at the discrimination level, both examples and nonexamples are used. The examples-only format at the introduction level helps to establish a pattern of accurate responding. When students respond accurately, those responses are reinforced by students' sense of success and by teacher praise. At the discrimination level, learning is solidified by having students distinguish between examples and nonexamples (they are able to determine whether the stimulus fits the concept category or the situation for using an academic rule).

The two levels occur sequentially in DI procedures but are presented in a more simultaneous fashion in GDL procedures. The time spent at the introduction level varies with the complexity of the response being taught. On the one hand, the presentation of three or four examples during five minutes of instruction may be sufficient. On the other hand, instruction at the introduction level may require presentation of numerous examples over three or four days before nonexamples are introduced. Similarly, several lessons may be needed at the discrimination level before mastery is attained.

Teaching the reading strategy of skimming can be used to exemplify instruction of an academic rule at the acquisition stage of learning. Using a DI approach, the teacher lists the steps for the procedure on poster board and uses it as the focus of a bulletin board in the front of the room (permanent model). Before reading a passage, the teacher first demonstrates the steps. Later the teacher leads students in reading the steps and applying them to their daily reading passage. The skimming procedure, to this point, is applied to passages for which skimming is appropriate (introduction level using examples only). As students respond by accurately following the steps, the teacher gives them very short passages for which skimming is not necessary (discrimination level using examples and nonexamples).

If a teacher uses a GDL approach to teach skimming, he or she demonstrates, using appropriate example passages, and says, "This is an example of skimming." Then the teacher fully reads short passages (nonexamples) and, after each, says, "This is not an example of skimming." The next step is to ask a series of guiding questions to induce students to identify the steps for skimming and to determine when it is appropriately used. Under the GDL approach, examples and nonexamples are presented in more of a simultaneous, rather than a sequential, manner.

Fluency Building

High rates of accuracy and increasing rates of response characterize the second stage of learning, fluency building. Once students have demonstrated consistently accurate responses, the focus of instruction changes to speed and accuracy. Instructional activities at the fluency-building stage involve the students in fast-paced drill. Using one-minute activities to measure a student's rate of performance, as done in precision teaching (see Precision Teaching Project in the References), is an example of a fluency-building strategy. Guided and independent practice sessions are scheduled on a daily basis to provide massed or concentrated practice. Once a prescribed level of fast and accurate responding is attained, the skill is considered to be mastered. A number of instructional strategies for building fluency through modeling, such as repeated reading, peer mediation, computer-guided practice, and previewing, have been evaluated empirically (Dawson et al., 2000).

During the fluency-building stage and continuing through the maintenance stage, the basic strategy is to wean students from their dependence on the teacher and the structures that have been built into the learning environment, such as demonstrations of the skill, instructions on performing the skill, and prompts to perform the skill (Wollery, Bailey, & Sugai, 1988). Fading out means that developing teachers monitor student progress and, as appropriate, decrease the intensity and frequency of instructional antecedents.

In the skimming example, for instance, the teacher moves students through the introduction and discrimination levels with elaborate and frequent demonstrations, prompts, and praise for accurate responding. As students are able to discriminate when and when not to use skimming, the teacher begins focusing on fast and accurate responding in the fluency-building stage. At this time, the teacher reminds students intermittently of the steps and instructs them to use the poster on the bulletin board as a reference.

The same fading procedure is necessary for those events that follow the use of a target skill (consequences). Teachers diminish the intensity and frequency of positive reinforcement by moving from a continuous schedule to an intermittent schedule. Initially, students are praised every time they successfully implement the skimming steps. As they become more accurate, the teacher praises them every two instances, then every six.

Maintenance

During maintenance, the third stage of learning, previously acquired concepts or skills are practiced for retention. Further fading of antecedent procedures and consequences continues the weaning process.

For example, once students demonstrate fluent skimming, the teacher begins implementing maintenance strategies. First, the poster board containing the skimming steps is moved from its prominent position in front of the room to the side of the room and replaced with a poster containing a simple prompt—"Skim before you read." Second, the teacher intermittently reminds students to skim when they appear not to be using the strategy.

These steps are taken to help students adapt to the use of skimming in a more natural environment. The teacher transforms the antecedents from contrived instructional techniques (demonstration and leading) to more naturally occurring events (the poster prompt and intermittent verbal reminders to skim). It is important to recognize that the beginning steps for maintaining skills are initiated from the first stages of instruction (Wollery et al., 1988).

As in the fluency-building stage, speed and accuracy are emphasized in maintenance activities. The practice sessions, however, are spaced at intervals ranging from one week to one month. They may take the form of an end-of-the-week or end-of-the-month review. As with the instructional antecedents and consequences for skimming, explicit practice and review of the procedures are gradually faded. Maintenance is based on the axiom "What you don't use, you lose."

Generalization

The ultimate educational outcome that underlies every instructional activity is to have the students function better in the world outside the school, either during or after their school years. This is achieved by fostering generalization of what is learned to other situations and times. Exhibiting learned responses in places other than where they were taught is referred to as *setting generalization*. For responses learned in a resource room, setting generalization occurs when the responses are performed in the general education classroom or at home. When learned responses are made after training conditions have been faded completely, then a second form of generalization, *time generalization*, has occurred. For example, a month after a unit of instruction on skimming, a student uses the strategy when reading a magazine during free reading time.

In the facilitation of both forms of generalization, three sets of variables need to be considered: antecedent, response, and consequence (Wollery et al., 1988). As mentioned above, teachers provide instructional antecedents when they demonstrate for, lead, and prompt students in making a conceptual or academic rule response. To facilitate maintenance, the intensity and frequency of antecedents are faded out gradually, with the aim of using naturally occurring antecedents to trigger a response. One objective is to maintain the response, but an additional objective is to facilitate setting generalization. Naturally occurring antecedents are operationally defined as those antecedents that occur in the setting to which the child needs to generalize the response. If resource room teachers want to prepare students to generalize a concept or rule to the general education classroom, they need to observe how the general education teacher triggers responses. Using the skimming example, if the general education teacher uses a verbal prompt (e.g., "Remember to skim your passage before reading"), then the resource room teacher should use the same prompt so that the student can make a setting generalization. Often, though, simply matching the antecedents will not suffice. The resource room teacher may need to tell students to use the procedure in the general education classroom and vice versa. Ultimately, both teachers should fade out their prompts completely.

Behavioral variables are attributes of the responses that students are taught. Generalization is more likely to occur if the behaviors selected for instruction have a high degree of utility in the target setting or over time. Students must be able to recognize that exhibiting the target academic behavior will be beneficial in some way. The benefit may be increased reinforcement or greater independence derived from learning new skills. These benefits should be conveyed explicitly to students so that they are aware of why they are learning a concept or academic rule.

Careful structuring of consequence variables can aid generalization significantly. The first strategy for manipulating the consequences of behavior to promote generalization is to develop the use of social reinforcers. Social reinforcers are important because they occur naturally and are the primary means of reinforcement in most classrooms. Social reinforcers come in a variety of forms, including smiles, verbal praise, pats on the shoulder, eye contact, and teacher attention. The second strategy is to prepare students for the usually thin schedule of reinforcement that occurs in most classrooms. In remedial and special education classrooms, students are often systematically or arbitrarily put on a very dense (i.e., frequency) schedule of reinforcement. Without thinning such reinforcement to levels equivalent to those in the general education classroom, the behavior may not generalize at all and may extinguish after a short period of time. The third strategy is to increase systematically the gap (i.e., latency) between the occurrence of the target response and the introduction of reinforcement. Such delays are designed to acclimate students to classrooms with larger numbers of students and fewer adults. In such environments, teachers and paraprofessionals or volunteers are unable to get to every student as often as in a remedial or special education classroom, where the adult-to-student ratio is lower. The fourth strategy also helps students to adjust to thin reinforcement schedules or delays in reinforcement by others. Students should be taught to self-reinforce for appropriate use of conceptual knowledge and academic rules. Self-verbalizations such as "You did it, big guy," a discreet little dance around the desk, and "low-fiving" themselves are effective ways in which students can self-reinforce.

LESSON DEVELOPMENT

The discussion to this point has focused on the principal elements of effective instruction for the sake of identification and analysis. Of course, practicing teachers soon realize that instruction is never a neat little prescriptive package with totally distinct and separate parts. Instruction is an integrated mass of interactive elements that vary in their form and sequence. In the section below, we present this integrated whole in the context of lesson delivery. We describe the three very general sequential elements of a lesson: initiating a lesson, engaging students during instruction, and closing a lesson. The section on lesson formats that follows later is more detailed, providing the specific sequence for lessons that incorporate DI or GDL techniques for teaching concepts and academic rules at different stages of learning.

Initiating a Lesson

The beginning of a lesson should accomplish three basic objectives: gain students' attention, orient students to the lesson content and format, and initiate lesson review (see Box 6.5).

Gaining Students' Attention. Learning is characterized by active participation in the manipulation of concepts and rules, either covertly through mental activity or overtly through responses like talking or writing. Regrettably, to those looking for an easy way to learn, unconscious, inattentive activities such as listening to foreign language audiotapes while sleeping do not result in learning. The first step in lesson development is to gain students' attention before engaging them in conscious efforts to manipulate concepts or rules.

| **B**ox 6.5 | **Example of Lesson Introduction** |

Mr. Ketcher is in the middle of a unit plan on home budgets. During the past few weeks, he has covered concepts and academic rules related to using a checking account. Mr. Ketcher has already introduced such concepts as *current balance, check charges, debits* and *credits*. Also, he has introduced the academic rules for filling out checks and maintaining a running record of transactions. Today, he will introduce the concept of *automated teller machine (ATM)* and the procedures for its use. Mr. Ketcher uses the following discourse to introduce the lesson, including gaining attention, orienting, and conducting a lesson-initiating review:

"OK, class, park it and eyes on the front of the class—that includes you, James." **(gaining attention)**

"Remember that we have been discussing home budgets for the past few weeks; in the last few days, we have focused on checking accounts. Today, we are going to discuss automated teller machines and the procedures for using them. We are going to practice using an ATM by using our computer, and next week we are going to apply for ATM cards." **(orienting)**

"Let's review first what we have covered so far relating to checking accounts. First, we discussed the concept of current balance and said that it is the amount of money that remains in your account to date." **(lesson-initiating review with teacher statements)**

"We also talked about the concept of a *running record*. How did we define the term *running record*?"

"It is the part of the checkbook where we write down how much checks were and any money we put in."

"Yes, Clyde, the running record is the section in the checkbook where we enter the amount or withdrawals, deposits, and current balance."

"Hey, I have used some of those fancy banking terms like *withdrawal* and *deposit*. What is the difference between withdrawals and deposits?" **(lesson-initiating review with teacher question)**

"We take out money, that's a withdrawal. When we put in money, that's a deposit."

"Good, Henry, withdrawals are the amounts of money we take out of the account, and deposits are the amounts we put into the account."

Mr. Ketcher continues the review of major points by asking students additional questions about how to keep the running record and so forth and then moves into the new material on ATMs. Students should now be aware of the important concepts and rules they have already covered and be ready to use that content in conjunction with the discussion of ATMs.

This can be done in some very simple and easy ways:

1. Start lessons on time so that students come to expect that a schedule is in place and will be followed.

2. Cue students—by sounding a bell or buzzer, by making a statement like "Let's get started," or by switching the lights off and on—that the lesson is to begin.

3. Become more creative in your lesson initiation by using more elaborate techniques that spur student interest and curiosity. For example, a pet rattlesnake placed in a conspicuous location in the classroom is sure to get students to focus their attention on the upcoming lesson on reptiles.

4. Solicit students to participate in an exciting lesson-initiating activity, such as playing word bingo.

5. Wear an article of clothing that is unusual and related to the lesson topic to stir interest.

Orienting Students to the Lesson. Providing a brief overview of the lesson sequence will make students aware of the content to be covered and the activities they will engage in during the lesson. Revealing the anticipatory set directly to students helps to orient them to the lesson. For instance, in orienting students to a reading lesson, a teacher may say, "Today, we are going to read a story about a pirate ship manned by a crew of ghosts. First, we are going to talk about pirates and ghosts, and then we are going to review the self-questioning procedures we have been using during silent reading. Then we will read and discuss the story." In addition to telling students about the lesson to follow, the teacher has established a bridge connecting what has been taught in previous lessons, the self-questioning strategy, and what is to take place during the present lesson. The teacher helps students recognize the links among successive lessons by cueing them to the fact that concepts and rules taught earlier will be used in subsequent lessons.

Initiating Lesson Review. To establish further the links among a set of lessons, teachers often engage students in a lesson-initiating review. The review is a connector between information introduced in previous lessons and information to be introduced in the new lesson. Teachers strategically integrate information across lessons to demonstrate the connections and to assist students in understanding the new information at a deeper level (Baker, Simmons, & Kameenui, 1994).

Teachers can use a block of time, usually between 2 and 10 minutes, to highlight pertinent information in one of two ways. First, they can simply state for students the relevant information for the upcoming lesson, emphasizing critical information. Second, teachers can ask a series of questions that cause students to rehearse information about concepts and academic rules. This form of review has the added benefit of providing an overlapping practice session: Not only is information reviewed, but also students practice verbalizing or applying the content.

Engaging Students During Instruction

Teaching at any stage of learning entails interaction between teacher and student. Two critical features of teacher-student interactions are the teacher's questioning skills and the teacher's treatment of students' responses.

Questioning Students. The teacher's questioning skills are important because the questions frame the responses received from students. They determine the complexity of students' responses in terms of the level of cognitive processing and the degree of elaboration required. For instance, teachers may ask students questions that require knowledge, comprehension, application, analysis, synthesis, or evaluation of information (see Box 6.6). It is important that teachers know the type of cognitive processing and response desired and are able to form questions that elicit the desired response (Martin, 1979).

In teaching a lesson on the concept of helping, for example, a teacher may want students to recall some basic facts from a story about a mouse, an elephant, and a lion and therefore asks, "Which two animals helped each other?" This query requires a relatively low level of cognitive processing and a brief response. In contrast, the teacher subsequently asks the class, "Why is it so odd that a mouse saved the elephant?" Here students are asked to analyze the relationship between the two animals, which requires a more complex level of cognitive processing and a more elaborate verbal response.

A related questioning strategy mixes the types of questions so that a variety of responses is required (Dunkin & Biddle, 1974; Rosenshine, 1971). Often, developing

Box 6.6

Hierarchy of Questions Ranging from Low-Level to High-Level Cognitive Processing Related to Social Studies

Low-Level Thinking ↕ High-Level Thinking	Knowledge:	Who is the president of the United States?
	Comprehension:	Why are there two Houses in the U.S. Congress?
	Application:	What is an example of a legislative "pork barrel"?
	Analysis:	What is the relationship between the spread of communism and the president's defense policies?
	Synthesis:	How do interest rates, inflation, and trade deficits affect monetary policy?
	Evaluation:	Has the president done an effective job in stimulating the economy?

teachers fixate on lower-level recognition and recall questions. These are certainly the easiest types of question to ask, but effective academic instruction requires students to do more than recognize and recall. Once basic factual information is presented or developed, teachers should require students to make responses that involve comprehension, application, analysis, synthesis, and evaluation. The above example involving the helping relationship between the elephant and the mouse illustrates how teachers can take basic factual information (who the animals were) and build on that base to analyze this relationship to determine why animals—and for that matter, people—help each other.

In addition to knowing what types of questions to ask, developing teachers need to know how to ask questions. Two strategies need to be applied. Using the first strategy, the teacher poses a question first and then calls on a student to respond, rather than calling a specific student's name and then asking the question. For instance, the more effective strategy would be to ask, "Why did the mouse help the elephant?" (pause) "Yes, Miguel,"—rather than "Miguel, why did the mouse help the elephant?" One benefit of stating the question first is that it enables teachers to get more "bang for their buck." All students must covertly process a response because they do not know who will be called on to make the overt response; consequently, a teacher can elicit an overt response and several covert responses with a single question. A second benefit is that students are less likely to engage in off-task behaviors because they are less able to predict who will be called on to respond.

The second strategy is called wait time (Rowe, 1974). One form of wait time, wait time I, refers to the gap in time between presenting a question and calling on a student to respond. By waiting three to five seconds after posing the question, the teacher provides students with time to formulate a response. Use of wait time I results in a greater frequency of accurate responses. Wait time I is used at the early stages of skill acquisition and when desired responses entail higher levels of cognitive processing. During fluency-building drills and practice activities, however, when speed and accuracy are being developed, wait time is not desirable.

A second form of wait time, wait time II, refers to the gap in time between the student's response and the teacher's subsequent response. Using the above story of the helpful mouse, wait time II would occur following Miguel's response to the teacher's question: "Why did the mouse help the elephant?" (wait time I) "Yes, Miguel." Miguel replies, "Because the elephant had helped the mouse." (wait time II) Miguel continues, "When the lion was going to eat the mouse, the elephant scared him away and the mouse was saved." Wait time II provides students with time to contemplate their responses and subsequently elaborate on or modify them, which results in increased accuracy and more elaborate responses. Wait time II is used more often when teachers ask questions that require responses generated from higher levels of cognitive processing.

Providing Feedback. Once questions have been asked and responses made, teachers evaluate students' responses and provide feedback. For accurate responses, teachers usually praise students, but often they do not inform students as to what was praiseworthy about their responses. Statements that praise students and provide information that indicates how they can receive praise in the future are referred to as specific academic praise. Such statements refer to the cognitive processes, strategies, or behaviors used to formulate the response. For example, the statement "Excellent answer, Caitlin. You made the connection between the two important events in the story" contains a praise component and indicates to the student that "making the connection" is what was praiseworthy. In contrast, by simply saying, "Excellent answer, Caitlin," the teacher focuses on the response, not on the process by which it was derived. The process is important because it provides generalizable guidelines for making similar excellent responses in the future.

Teachers can also respond to students' correct answers with feedback statements that paraphrase, elaborate, or clarify students' responses. Paraphrasing entails restating what the student said or did, which emphasizes the responses and ensures that other students observed the response. Returning to the reading lesson above, the teacher could state, "That nasty lion did try to eat the poor little mouse," following a student's response, "That bad lion was going to eat 'im." With elaboration, the teacher uses students' responses as a core and adds further information. For example, a student responds to the question "Why do lions have such big claws?" by stating, "They need them to climb trees." The teacher then states, "Yes, they often climb in trees to cool down and get away from flies." A clarifying response is used to either confirm what students have said or reformulate their responses in a more comprehensible way. For instance, when asked to state why people (or the mouse and elephant) become friends, a student responds, "Well, because they sort of think they're cool and they do stuff together, you know, like that." A teacher's clarifying response would be "So you are saying that people become friends because they are interested in doing the same kinds of things, like going to concerts or playing basketball, and enjoy doing those things with each other."

These forms of positive feedback are important because they provide information about students' responses without giving any explicit praise. Keep in mind that the gradual thinning of reinforcement is important for the maintenance and generalization of behaviors; the systematic use of combinations of specific academic praise and other feedback techniques is an important teacher strategy.

When students' responses are inaccurate, teachers can use the steps for corrective feedback associated with teaching low-level content using the DI model. Other options are to rephrase the question or request, provide additional cues to guide a student's responses, and indicate to students that a response is inaccurate and help them identify the nature of the inaccuracy. Rephrasing means presenting the stimulus question in a slightly different form, which may clarify the desired response or refocus students' attention. If a teacher asks, "How did the elephant use his trunk?" and the student responds, "He eats peanuts with it," the teacher may rephrase the question: "Let me ask that question a different way. In the story, when the lion was coming closer, how did the elephant use his trunk?" Providing additional cues is synonymous with giving "hints." For example, a teachers asks, "How did the lion sneak up on the mouse?" and when the student's response is inaccurate, the teacher adds, "Remember the tall grass."

The third option for teachers is to indicate that the response is inaccurate and help students determine what the correct response is. This may be done by telling students the response is inaccurate and then redirecting the question to another student or by telling students why the response does not fit the question. For instance, in the case where a teacher asks students to state the characteristics of someone who is helpful, and a student responds, "They leave other people alone," the teacher may redirect the same or a rephrased question to another student (e.g., "What do helpful people do to help other people?") or tell the student the response is incorrect and why (e.g., "Being helpful is judged by the things you do for others, not by the things you don't do").

Closing a Lesson: Ending Review

The closing review provides an end point and summary of what occurred during the lesson. The review cues students to the impending transition from one lesson to another. In addition, it is an opportunity for students to conceptualize the relationships among the discrete content elements of the lesson. For instance, as part of a written expression lesson, the teacher can guide students in restating the rule for writing a complete sentence and showing two or three examples and nonexamples of the rule application.

The review component proceeds in the same way as a lesson-initiating review, with the teacher either presenting verbal summary statements or physical demonstrations of the target responses or asking a series of guiding questions to elicit responses from students. The latter is the preferred format because it increases the opportunities for students to practice responses actively. With the sentence-writing lesson, the teacher might say, "When writing a complete sentence, a subject and predicate must be included. Examples are 'The dog barked' and 'The cow jumped over the moon.' 'The black angry dog' is not an example because it doesn't have a predicate." A guided review, however, would entail the teacher asking "What is the rule for writing complete sentences?" Subsequently, examples and nonexamples would be induced.

LESSON FORMAT FOR DIRECT INSTRUCTION AND GUIDED DISCOVERY LEARNING APPROACHES

To summarize the elements of this chapter, we designed the following section to show in outline form how the principles of DI and GDL can be overlaid with the procedures for presenting concepts and academic rules at each stage of learning. The integrated format is represented in Figure 6.4 as the TEAL model—Teaching: Explicit Activation of Learning (O'Shea & O'Shea, 1997). This integrated format can be used to structure lessons in a manner that incorporates the critical elements of effective instruction.

Acquisition Stage—Introduction

As described earlier, this initial stage of learning requires that significant teacher time and attention be directed toward planning and monitoring students' responses to target concepts and academic rules. The introduction phase of the acquisition stage is characterized by precise demonstrations and guided practice using only examples. The following sequence exemplifies this and other features of lesson development at this stage of learning:

1. Gain students' attention and orient students with an outline of the activities to be completed during the lesson.

2. Link the present lesson with previous lessons by reviewing related concepts or academic rules previously taught.

3. During the demonstration, model or induce through questioning the target concept or academic rule. Use only examples.

4. Provide extensive opportunities to respond through guided practice activities involving the target concept or academic rule. Use extensive prompts and cues to elicit responses involving only examples.

   a. Lead or induce students to state the definition, attributes, or rule.

   b. Lead or induce students to identify concept examples or apply rules to examples, using signaling to lead choral responses when appropriate.

      • Pose a question, wait three to five seconds, and then call on a student for a response.

      • Recognize a student's response by giving specific academic praise, paraphrasing, amplifying, clarifying, or redirecting to another student.

   c. Provide corrective feedback as needed.

5. For independent practice, provide daily activities involving examples of the target concept or academic rule that students can perform with minimal prompting or cues. Students should be able to perform tasks with 90 percent accuracy or better.

   a. Give directions to complete activity tasks.

   b. Lead students in completing example tasks.

   c. Indicate the deadline for completing activity.

   d. Circulate and assist students as needed.

   e. Review students' responses to activity tasks.

6. Engage students in an ending review to summarize the content covered in the lesson and to signal the transition to the next lesson.

Acquisition Stage—Discrimination

The acquisition stage continues with the introduction of nonexamples, which are used to teach students to discriminate between the target concept or academic rule and other similar concepts or academic rules. Accurate discrimination responses are indicators that students are improving their skills. The steps are identical to those under the acquisition—introduction stage except that examples and nonexamples are used during instruction.

Fluency-Building Stage

Lessons at the fluency-building stage entail independent practice activities. Teachers simply introduce the activity and monitor students' responses to a few example stimuli to ensure that they are responding with relative degrees of speed and accuracy. To ensure that students use their time productively and that fluency is built, the following steps are suggested:

1. Gain students' attention and orient students with an outline of the activities to be completed during the lesson.

2. Link the present lesson with previous lessons by reviewing related concepts or academic rules previously taught.

3. Provide daily independent practice activities that engage students in responding to examples and nonexamples of the target concept or academic rule. The focus of practice is on high rates of speed and accuracy. Students should be able to perform tasks with 90 percent accuracy or better.

   a. Give directions to complete activity tasks.

   b. Lead students in completing example tasks.

   c. Indicate the deadline for completing the activity.

   d. Circulate and assist students as needed.

   e. Review students' responses to activity tasks.

4. Engage students in an ending review to summarize the content covered in the lesson and to signal the transition to the next lesson.

Maintenance Stage

The primary characteristic of the maintenance stage is that practice activities are separated by longer intervals of time. These weekly or monthly practice activities are geared to assist students in retaining appropriate levels of fast and accurate responding. As the time interval between sessions increases, the need to conduct a brief review of the target concept or academic rule increases. In addition, instructional antecedents and reinforcement should be thinned. The following steps are guidelines for lesson development:

1. Gain students' attention and orient students with an outline of the activities to be completed during the lesson.

2. Link the present lesson with previous lessons by reviewing related concepts or academic rules previously taught.

3. Provide weekly or monthly independent practice activities that engage students in responding to examples and nonexamples of the target concept or academic rule. The focus of practice is on high rates of speed and accuracy. Students should be able to perform tasks with 90 percent accuracy or better.

   a. Give directions to complete activity tasks.

   b. Lead students in completing example tasks.

   c. Indicate the deadline for completing the activity.

   d. Circulate and assist students as needed.

   e. Review students' responses to activity tasks.

4. Fade out the frequency and intensity of response antecedents and consequences by using intermittent schedules.

5. Engage students in an ending review to summarize the content covered in the lesson and to signal the transition to the next lesson.

Generalization Stage

Unlike in the earlier stages of learning, the steps for generalization set out below are not taught in discrete lessons. Instead, these steps are incorporated, to varying extents, into lessons at all previous learning stages. The primary characteristic of generalization instruction is that students are encouraged to use their skills in other settings and at different times. The following suggestions are means to set the occasion for generalization:

(1) Use instructional antecedents and consequences that occur in other settings, (2) use materials found in other settings to practice target concepts or academic rules, (3) use delayed and intermittent reinforcement, (4) teach students to self-reinforce fast and accurate responding, (5) encourage other teachers to reinforce students' use of target concepts and academic rules, and (6) tell students to use concepts and academic rules in other classrooms.

WHEN TO USE SPECIFIC ELEMENTS OF EFFECTIVE INSTRUCTION

The lesson-format outline and overall discussion in this chapter deal primarily with what effective teachers do when they deliver instruction. The classroom examples provided throughout the chapter are aimed at illustrating how effective teachers operationalize the principles of effective instruction. Another important aspect of effective teaching is knowing when to use certain key elements. Following are some guidelines to assist developing teachers in deciding when they implement specific elements of effective instruction provided in the lesson-format section above.

Teaching Concepts and Academic Rules Using the DI and GDL Models

First, developing teachers must decide when to use either of the two general models of instruction presented in the chapter. The DI model can be used with either concepts or academic rules. It is more often used with content that entails rote learning of basic facts and skills. It can also be used, however, with content and learning tasks that involve high-order cognitive processes such as synthesis, analysis, and application. In the latter case, the teacher gives the concept definition and examples and nonexamples, but the students are asked to apply the concept to novel situations, thus requiring high-order cognitive processes. The GDL model, in contrast, can be used with both concepts and academic rules but is more frequently used with concept induction. GDL is more often used with high-order content and learning tasks than with rote learning tasks.

Second, developing teachers must decide when to treat content as concepts or academic rules. Concepts are ubiquitous; they are a part of all content area material, including reading, math, social studies, science, vocational, and daily living skills. When the developing teacher is teaching categories of information, the material should be treated as conceptual knowledge. Academic rules are not so pervasive; they are associated more with basic tool skills and, to some extent, other content areas, such as auto mechanics, in which a set of procedures must be followed to complete a learning task. When the subject matter requires students to learn how to complete a learning task, either covertly (e.g., using a learning strategy) or overtly (e.g., computing a math sum), the content should be treated as academic rule knowledge.

Third, developing teachers must decide the degree of precision with which to follow the prescribed steps. When first learning to implement either model, developing teachers should follow the model precisely until they can automatically carry out the steps. Then they can begin to focus more on students' responses to specific aspects of a lesson. At this point, developing teachers can make decisions about varying things, such as decreasing the number of examples presented or asking students to volunteer examples rather than the teacher giving them. Such decisions will be based on students' familiarity with the steps in instruction as well as on their interest in and prior knowledge of the content.

Stages of Learning

Decisions concerning when to move students through the different stages of learning should be based on the accuracy and rate of their independently made correct responses. In a very general sense, a criterion of 90 percent accuracy is a sound basis for moving students from the acquisition stage to the fluency-building stage. Movement into the other stages should be based on speed as well as accuracy.

The rate criterion can be derived from one of two sources. The first source, peer medians, is readily available, regardless of content area and grade level, but it may take a little advance work. To determine the rate for a particular response, developing teachers must sample the response rates of a peer group that has mastered the target response. The median rate of responding (responses per minute or some other unit of time) for the peer group is then used as the criterion for mastery. The second source, published proficiency rates, can be obtained for most tool skills in reading, math, and spelling but may not be available for other content areas. Table 6.2 is a sample of rate criteria from a variety of sources.

TABLE 6.2 Criterion Levels for Corrects and Errors per 1-Minute Sample for Reading, Math, and Spelling Skills

	PROFICIENCY RATES FOR READING SKILLS													
	Says Isolated Sounds				**Says Words in List**						**Says Words in Text**			
	K–Gr. 3		Gr. 2–4		Gr. 5–6		Adult		Gr. 1–3		Gr. 4–6		Adult	
	Cor.	Err.[a]	Cor.	Err.	Cor.	Err.	Cor.	Err.	Cor.	Err.	Cor.	Err.	Cor.	Err.
Koenig & Kunzelmann (1980)			140	0	120–130	0								
Starlin & Starlin (1973)									50–70	2	100–200	2	100–200	2

	PROFICIENCY RATES FOR MATH SKILLS						
	Addition Facts 0–9 Gr. 2–3	Sub. Facts (1–5) and Facts Top Numb. 2–9 Gr. 2–3	Add. Facts Sums and Sub. Facts Top Numb. 6–9 Gr. 3–4	Two-Column Addition with Re-grouping Gr. 4–5	Two-Column Subtraction with Re-grouping Gr. 4–6	Multiplies Facts Through ×9 Gr. 5–6	Divides Facts Through Divisor of 9 Gr. 6
	Cor. Err.	Cor. Err.	Cor. Err.	Cor. Err.	Cor. Err.	Cor. Err.	Cor. Err
Koening & Kunzelmann (1980)	60 —	60 —	90 —	60 —	60 —	90 —	60 —
Precision Teaching Project (Montana)	70–90 —	70–90 —	70–90 —	70–90 —	70–90 —	70–90 —	70–90 —

	PROFICIENCY RATES FOR SPELLING									
	Gr. 2		Gr. 3		Gr. 4		Gr. 5		Gr. 6	
	Cor.	Err.	Cor.	Err.	Cor.	Err.	Cor.	Err.	Cor.	Err.
Koening & Kunzelmann (1980)	60–90	—	90–100	—	100–120	—	110–130	—	120–140	—

	K–Gr. 2				**Gr. 3–Adult**			
	Instructional Level		Independent Level		Instructional Level		Independent Level	
	Cor.	Err.	Cor.	Err.	Cor.	Err.	Cor.	Err.
Starlin & Starlin (1973)	15–29	3–7	30–50	≥2	25–49	3–7	50–70	≥2

[a]Letters correct and errors

Source: Adapted from *Teaching Students with Learning Problems*, by C. D. Mercer and A. R. Mercer, 1985, New York: Merrill/Macmillan. Adapted with permission.

Lesson Development

The two decision areas in lesson development most often of concern to developing teachers are how frequently to review and how to mix low- and high-order questions. Some teachers are concerned that overdwelling on reviews may cause boredom and impede students' progress in mastering the full range of skills they need to complete in a school year. Both are legitimate concerns that can be the dysfunctional effect of reviewing too frequently or for too long a period of time. To help avoid these potential problems, developing teachers need to remember that the review need deal only with the major points of the lesson and not all the details. Also, developing teachers should use lesson-initiating reviews judiciously. When building an important conceptual bridge between two closely related concepts or academic rules, they should engage students in a thorough review at the beginning of the lesson. When the lesson is a continuation of work on a concept or rule that was introduced earlier, developing teachers can spend less time reviewing at the beginning of the lesson. Ending reviews appear to be more crucial. Developing teachers should be less willing to cut back on these reviews.

The second area of concern deals with the mix of low- and high-order questions. To begin with, developing teachers need to be aware of a trap into which many teachers fall: When working with academically lower-functioning students, many developing teachers fixate on asking low-order rote questions, believing that such students are not capable of handling high-order questions. The trap is that, without instruction and practice in answering high-order questions, these students will surely be limited in their ability to respond to questions involving comprehension, application, analysis, synthesis, or evaluation. Therefore, developing teachers should start units or segments of instruction with low-order questions but should plan in advance the introduction of high-order questions for students at all levels of ability once accuracy of rote responding reaches the criterion. Effectively using cues and prompts can help students in responding accurately to high-order questions. See Table 6.2.

 ## SUMMARY

This chapter presented a variety of elements that should be found in the effective delivery of instruction. These elements are very complex and are intricately interwoven into the fabric of teaching. They were artificially separated and described here for purposes of analysis, but when put into practice, they can be difficult to identify as discrete elements. Nonetheless, developing teachers who continuously analyze the instructional environment of their classrooms and their role in that environment can benefit from the application of these elements to their own instructional repertoire.

Educational researchers and philosophers continually strive to explain what makes effective instruction work. They have devised and revised a variety of instructional models. Two prominent models of instruction are direct instruction (DI) and guided discovery learning (GDL). Often, these models are viewed as diametrically opposed, but in another light, they can be viewed as complementary. DI offers developing teachers a set of procedures for presenting subject matter by modeling components of concepts or academic rules and then presenting examples and nonexamples. GDL generally entails presenting strong examples first and then having students induce the concept or academic rule through a series of guided questions. Many other features of these two models are similar, such as the importance of guided practice, of the development of content mastery through extensive practice, of the selection of strong examples, and of the need to identify essential attributes of concepts and steps for academic rules. Model selection can be guided by the applicability of subject matter to the instructional steps in each model and by the need to mix instructional techniques to enhance student interest. As Dixon and Carnine (1994) concluded, the proponents of different instructional models may not be as deeply divided when the respective practices are compared.

Another important element of instruction is the type of subject matter being presented. Two categories of content, concepts and academic rules, and the steps for presenting them were outlined. Concepts are central to all content areas. They provide a means by which students can categorize and classify information and understand the relationships among various superordinate and subordinate levels. Academic rules are procedures used to complete academic tasks that involve covert and overt responses by students. They, too, are found in a variety of content areas that require problem solving and the application of conceptual knowledge.

The third element of instruction discussed in the chapter is the stages of learning. Developing teachers can benefit by recognizing that students first acquire skills in responding to concepts and academic rules through careful presentation of examples and nonexamples. Once they have acquired a degree of accuracy in working with the target subject matter, fluency is built through daily practice sessions. For acquired skills to be maintained, practice sessions need to be provided, but distributed over longer periods of time. The final stage of instruction, generalization, is focused on having students use their acquired skills in different settings and at different times.

The final section of the chapter was an outline integrating the above elements. This lesson-development format is designed for developing teachers to use in guiding students to the ultimate goal of instruction: independently using subject matter in the appropriate setting at the appropriate time.

ACTIVITIES TO EXTEND YOUR KNOWLEDGE

1. Conduct a literature review on the use of metacognitive strategies by students with learning disabilities. Describe how teachers can assist students with attention problems during reading and mathematics instruction.

2. Take a position on each of the following issues: The purpose for having students practice learning strategies in controlled materials is to increase

   a. setting generalization
   b. readability of materials
   c. opportunities to use strategies
   d. skill maintenance

   Discuss your responses with peers.

3. List three advantages of peer tutoring, one of which should refer to work with culturally diverse populations.

4. Identify and describe in workshop presentations with peers strategies that facilitate learning in a specific academic situation. Discuss, in roundtable fashion, strategies that will take into account students' memory, attention, verbal mediation, visual imagery, rehearsal, relaxation, and/or subject-oriented instruction. Provide all class members and the instructor an up-to-date reference list and a two-page summary of important points on the chosen strategy presented.

5. Practice the classwide peer-tutoring model throughout your academic semester with peers in your university class. Use the topics of lesson planning and instruction delivery. Assign tutors and teams to distribute reinforcement. Tutors are to provide individual goals and reinforces. Work with your university instructor and other class teams to provide group goals and reinforces. Work with your instructor in posting the daily and weekly team totals. Compare and contrast the totals with those of your classmates.

6. Consider your field setting and briefly list five ways in which you have been an effective teacher who has integrated instructional strategies for your students. Give specific examples of what you have done in your field site.

7. After the announcement of your selection as Outstanding Rookie Teacher of the Year, your principal has asked you to describe for the rest of the faculty in your school the secret of your success—TEAL. Outline your presentation to the faculty. Give examples to illustrate your points; that is, select a concept, law or lawlike principle, academic rule, or value judgment and apply the TEAL model to it.

References

Algozzine, B., Ysseldyke, J., & Elliott, J. (1997). *Strategies and tactics for effective instruction.* Longmont, CO: Sopris West.

Alley, G. R., & Deshler, D. D. (1979). *Teaching the learning-disabled adolescent: Strategies and methods.* Denver: Love.

Anderson, L. M., Evertson, C. M., & Brophy, J. E. (1979). An experimental study of effective teaching in first-grade reading groups. *Elementary School Journal, 79,* 193–222.

Archer, A. (1991, June). *Design of instruction: Lesson structure.* Paper presented at the Fourteenth Annual Intervention Procedures Conference, Logan, UT.

Aronson, E., Stephen, C., Sikes, J., Blaney, N., & Snapp, M. (1978). *The jigsaw classroom.* Beverly Hills, CA: Sage.

Ausubel, D., Novak, J., & Hanesian, H. (1978). *Educational psychology: A cognitive view.* New York: Holt, Rinehart & Winston.

Baker, S. C., Simmons, D. C., & Kameenui, E. J. (1994). Making information more memorable for students with learning disabilities through the design of instructional tools. *LD Forum, 19*(3), 14–18.

Barlow, D. L. (1985). *Educational psychology: The teaching-learning process.* Chicago: Moody Press.

Becker, W. C., Englemann, S., & Thomas, D. R. (1971). *Teaching: A course in applied psychology.* Chicago: Science Research Associates.

Belkin, G. S., & Gray, J. L. (1977). *Educational psychology: An introduction.* Dubuque, IA: William C. Brown.

Biehler, R. F., & Snowman, J. (1986). *Psychology applied to teaching* (5th ed.). Boston: Houghton Mifflin.

Bruner, J. S. (1966). *Toward a theory of instruction.* New York: Norton.

Bruner, J. S. (1973). *The relevance of education.* New York: Norton.

Butler, D. L. (1995). Promoting strategic learning by postsecondary students with learning disabilities. *Journal of Learning Disabilities, 28,* 170–190.

Carnine, D., & Silbert, J. (1979). *Direct instruction: Reading.* Upper Saddle River, NJ: Prentice Hall.

Dawson, L., Venn, M. L., & Gunter, P. L. (2000). The effects of teacher versus computer reading models. *Behavioral Disorders, 25*(2), 105–113.

Delquadri, J. C., Greenwood, C. R., Whorton, D., Carta, J. J., & Hall, R. V. (1986). Classwide peer tutoring. *Exceptional Children, 52,* 535–542.

Deshler, D. D., & Schumaker, J. B. (1986). Learning strategies: An instructional alternative for low-achieving adolescents. *Exceptional Children, 52,* 583–590.

Deshler, D. D., Schumaker, J. B., Alley, G. R., Warner, M. M., & Clark, F. L. (1982). Learning disabilities in adolescent and young adult populations: Research implications (Part I). *Focus on Exceptional Children, 15*(1), 1–12.

Deshler, D. D., Schumaker, J. B., Lenz, B. K., & Ellis, E. S. (1984). Academic and cognitive interventions for LD adolescents (Part II). *Journal of Learning Disabilities, 17*(3), 170–187.

Dixon, R., & Carnine, D. (1994). Ideologies, practices, and their implications for special education. *Journal of Special Education, 28,* 356–367.

Dunkin, M., & Biddle, B. (1974). *The study of teaching.* New York: Holt, Rinehart & Winston.

Ellis, E. E., Lenz, B. K., & Sabornie, E. J. (1987a). Generalization and adaptation of learning strategies to natural environments: Part 1. Critical agents. *Remedial and Special Education, 8*(1), 6–20.

Ellis, E. E., Lenz, B. K., & Sabornie, E. J. (1987b). Generalization and adaptation of learning strategies to natural environments: Part 2. Research into practice. *Remedial and Special Education, 8*(2), 6–23.

Englemann, S., & Carnine, D. (1982). *Theory of instruction: Principles and applications.* New York: Irvington.

Englert, C. S., Raphael, T. E., Anderson, L. M., Antony, H. M., & Stevens, D. D. (1991). Making strategies and self-talk visible: Writing instruction in regular and special education classrooms. *American Educational Research Journal, 23,* 337–372.

Fisher, C. W., Berliner, D. C., Filby, N. N., Marliave, R., Cahen, L. S., & Dishaw, M. M. (1980). Teaching behaviors, academic learning time, and student achievement: An overview. In C. Denham & A. Lieberman (Eds.), *Time to learn*. Washington, DC: Government Printing Office.

Friend, M., & Bursuck, W. D. (1996). *Including students with special needs: A practical guide for classroom teachers*. Needham Heights, MA: Allyn & Bacon.

Gaffney, J. S. (1987). *Seatwork: Current practices and research implications*. Paper presented at the 64th Meeting of the Council for Exceptional Children, Chicago.

Gagne, R. M. (1980). *The conditions of learning* (2nd ed.). New York: Holt, Rinehart & Winston.

Goodman, Y. (1989). Roots of the whole-language movement. *Elementary School Journal, 90,* 113–127.

Graves, D. H. (1994). *A fresh look at writing*. Portsmouth, NH: Heinemann.

Graves, D. H., & Hansen, J. (1983). The author's chair. *Language Arts, 60,* 176–183.

Greenwood, C. R., Delquadri, J. C., & Hall, R. V. (1984). Opportunity to respond and student academic performance. In W. L. Heward, T. E. Heron, D. S. Hill, & J. Trap-Porter (Eds.), *Focus on behavior analysis in education* (pp. 58–88). Upper Saddle River, NJ: Prentice Hall.

Gregory, J. (1985). *The concept teaching model*. Unpublished manuscript.

Heshusius, L. (1986). Pedagogy, special education, and the lives of young children: A critical and futuristic perspective. *Journal of Education, 168*(3), 25–38.

Heshusius, L. (1989). The Newtonian mechanistic paradigm, special education, and contours of alternatives: An overview. *Journal of Learning Disabilities, 22,* 403–415.

Holdaway, D. (1979). *The foundations of literacy*. Sydney, Australia: Aston Scholastic.

Holloway, J. H. (2000). Preparing teachers for differentiated instruction. *Educational Leadership 58* (1), 82–83.

Johns, B. (2000). Reaching them through teaching them: Curriculum and instruction for students with E/BD. *Beyond Behavior, 10* (1), 3–6.

Johnson, D. W., Johnson, R. T., Holubec, E. J., & Roy, P. (1984). *Circles of learning*. Alexandria, VA: Association for Supervision and Curriculum Development.

Kilpatrick, W. H. (1918). The project method. *Teachers College Record, 19,* 319–335.

Kirby, J. R., Booth, C. A., & Das, J. P. (1996). Cognitive processes and IQ in reading disability. *Journal of Special Education, 29,* 442–456.

Maheady, L., Mallette, B., Harper, G. F., Sacca, K., & Pomerantz, D. (1994). Peer-mediated instruction of high-risk students. In K. D. Wood & B. Algozzine (Eds.), *Teaching reading to high-risk learners*. Needham Heights, MA: Allyn & Bacon.

Martin, J. (1979). Effects of teacher higher-order questions on student progress and product variables in a single classroom study. *Journal of Educational Research, 72,* 183–187.

Mercer, C. D., & Mercer, A. R. (1985). *Teaching students with learning problems*. Upper Saddle River, NJ: Prentice Hall.

Milem, M., & Garcia, M. (1996). Student critics, teacher models: Introducing process writing to high school students with learning disabilities. *Teaching Exceptional Children, 28*(3), 46–47.

O'Shea, L. J., & O'Shea, D. J. (1997). *Teaching: Explicit activation of learning*. Unpublished manuscript.

Paris, S. G., Cross, D. R., & Lipson, M. Y. (1984). Informed strategies for learning: A program to improve children's reading awareness and comprehension. *Journal of Education Psychology, 76,* 1239–1252.

Paris, S. G., & Winograd, P. (1990). Promoting metacognition and motivation of exceptional children. *Remedial and Special Education, 11*(6), 7–15.

Patton, J. R. (1994). Practical recommendations for using homework with students with learning disabilities. *Journal of Learning Disabilities, 27,* 570–578.

Poplin, M. (1987). Self-imposed blindness: The scientific method in education. *RASE, 8,* 31–37.

Poplin, M. (1988). The reductionistic fallacy in learning disabilities: Replicating the past by reducing the present. *Journal of Learning Disabilities, 21,* 389–400.

Prater, M. A., Sileo, T. W., & Black, R. S. (2000). Preparing educators and related school personnel to work with at-risk students. *Teacher Education and Special Education, 23*(1), 51–64.

Precision Teaching Project. Available from Skyline Center, 3300 Third Street Northeast, Great Falls, MT 59404.

Reid, D. K., & Stone, C. A. (1991). Why is cognitive instruction effective? Underlying learning mechanisms. *Remedial and Special Education, 2,* 8–19.

Richardson, P. (1991). Language as personal resource and as social construct: Competing views of literacy pedagogy in Australia. *Educational Review, 43*(2), 171–190.

Robinson, R. P. (1941). *Effective study*. New York: Harper & Row.

Rogan, J. (2000). Learning strategies: Recipes for success. *Beyond Behavior, 10*(1), 18–22.

Rogoff, B. (1990). *Apprenticeship in thinking: Cognitive development in social context*. New York: Oxford University Press.

Rojewski, J. W., & Schell, J. W. (1994). Cognitive apprenticeship for learners with special needs: An alternative framework for teaching and learning. *Remedial and Special Education, 15,* 234–243.

Rosenshine, B. (1971). *Teaching behaviors and student achievement*. London: National Foundation for Educational Research.

Rosenshine, B. (1976). Academic engaged time, content covered, and direct instruction. *Journal of Education, 160*(3), 38–66.

Rosenshine, B., & Meister, C. (1992). The use of scaffolds for teaching higher-level cognitive strategies. *Educational Leadership, 49*(7), 26–33.

Rowe, M. (1974). Wait-time and rewards as instructional variables, logic, and fate control: Part 1. Wait-time. *Journal of Research in Science Teaching, 11*, 81–94.

Schiffman, G., Tobin, D., & Buchanan, B. (1984). Microcomputer instruction for the learning disabled. *Annual Review of Learning Disabilities, 2*, 134–136.

Schumaker, J. B., Denton, P. H., & Deshler, D. D. (1984). *Learning strategies curriculum: The paraphrasing strategy*. Lawrence: University of Kansas.

Slavin, R. E. (1990). *Cooperative learning: Theory, research, and practice*. Upper Saddle River, NJ: Prentice Hall.

Smith, J. K., & Heshusius, L. (1986). Closing down the conversation: The end of the quantitative/qualitative debate among educational inquirers. *Educational Researcher, 15*, 4–12.

Stanger, C., Symington, L., Miller, H., & Johns, S. (2000). Teaching number concepts to all students. *Teaching Exceptional Children, 33*(1), 65–69.

Stein, M., & Davis, C. A. (2000). Direct instruction as a positive behavioral support. *Beyond Behavior, 10*(1), 7–12.

Vygotsky, L. S. (1978). *Mind in society: The development of higher psychological processes*. Cambridge, MA: Harvard University Press.

Wollery, M., Bailey, D. B., & Sugai, G. M. (1988). *Effective teaching: Principles and procedures of applied behavior analysis with exceptional children*. Needham Heights, MA: Allyn & Bacon.

Zipprich, M. A. (1995). Teaching web mapping as a guided planning tool to improve student narrative writing. *Remedial and Special Education, 16*, 3–15.

## CHAPTER 7

The Paperwork

with David Bateman, Ph.D.

Chapter Outline

In this chapter, we will

- discuss a rationale for developing useful paperwork when determining the need for special education services

- review paperwork required by prereferral and referral procedures

- review the use and interpretation of testing for determining eligibility for special education services

- delineate the required components of individualized education programs

- reiterate the importance of writing reports to parents and other professionals.

A PROFESSIONAL GLIMPSE

A fictitious student named Sarah Thompson, age nine, is followed throughout the chapter by using examples of required paperwork. Starting with pertinent data from her general education setting, examples of the kinds of data that professionals may collect are illustrated. Beginning and developing teachers will be able to note the types of data useful to families and professionals as Sarah moves through the screening-prereferral process. Background information (Box 7.1) is included to help beginning and developing teachers gain insights into Sarah's needs and strengths.

*A*lthough there may be some local differences in format and content, the documentation and paperwork required for special education are similar nationwide. We will summarize typical documentation in this chapter.

When asked to complete paperwork, developing and beginning teachers typically react with disdain and signs of stress. Most experienced members of the profession, however, can confirm that keeping careful, written records on students and on actions demonstrated by teachers is necessary for successful classroom management. Effective paperwork is one key to survival and success for many teachers. Accordingly, in this chapter, we identify the documentation necessary to ensure an appropriate team effort in all aspects of specialized services: from activities initiating the screening-prereferral

---

Box 7.1   Background Information on Sarah

Sarah is a well-mannered, attractive youngster currently attending a third-grade classroom in a large urban school. Sarah recently transferred from another school district in the state. As of this time, few prior school records are available. School officials from her previous school did send an incomplete cumulative record of her kindergarten experience, which indicate her progress was normal. However, no information was received describing her school progress during grades one and two.

During the current school year, Sarah is considered a potential candidate for special education because of problems in reading comprehension and study skills. On the Woodcock-Johnson Achievement Battery, given by her current teacher, Ms. Edward, Sarah performed at 5.7 in mathematics, 1.9 in reading, and 3.3 in spelling. Chapter tests from the Universal Reading Series, Level 3, were provided by her teacher. Sarah had not mastered the first group of objectives from chapter 1 of this reading series, suggesting to Ms. Edward some of Sarah's difficulties in reading comprehension.

Sarah's speech and language development appears to be adequate for a child of Sarah's age. Ms. Edward reported also that Sarah's motor development is adequate for a child in the third grade: She is able to run, jump, skip, and hop as most children her age; she competes satisfactorily in physical education with her classmates and performs exceptionally well in swimming. Sarah's medical history is not notable.

In the classroom, Sarah neither begins on time nor completes assignments in reading. Other subject area requirements do not appear to pose problems to her. She continues to perform well in mathematics and spelling, although assignments in social studies and science are beginning to contain more required reading than previously. Ms. Edward reported to her principal that she fears Sarah is falling farther and farther behind her classmates as the school year continues.

process for students who may have ability, learning, or behavioral problems to data-collection procedures necessary to exit students from special education.

As we discuss in other chapters, some special educators function as consultants or coteachers when students with mild to moderate disabilities receive their education in inclusive classrooms. Others are direct-service providers to students who meet the criteria for placement in specialized educational settings. All special education roles, however, necessitate professional skills in developing and maintaining paperwork.

Special education paperwork often reflects the types of assessment and instructional activities that school professionals conduct. Such activities, described by Mercer and Mercer (2004), include screening, determining eligibility for special education placement, and providing appropriate instructional services based on students' needs and strengths. Teachers are generally responsible for the following paperwork: (1) screening-prereferral documentation; (2) written records of individual student progress; (3) observation records; (4) assessment results; (5) eligibility placement information; (6) cumulative school files; (7) health and sensory notations; (8) annual individualized education programs (IEPs), including transition components; (9) written inquiries and responses to parents, guardians, general education teachers, or others; and (10) lesson plans or unit teaching summaries.

The completion of effective paperwork requires time, effort, and patience. There is a bright note: As they obtain experience teachers may find that paperwork demands are minimized considerably. Once teachers develop the habit of completing paperwork, this stressful task will be made easier. Gaining access to or investing in a laptop computer is worth the effort. Electronic management and storage of data can save hours of time.

DEVELOPING USEFUL PAPERWORK: A RATIONALE

Although tedious and time-consuming to prepare, written products are important for a compelling reason: Federal law requires written documentation by professionals on students suspected of having and identified with disabilities (Individuals with Disabilities Education Act [IDEA], 1997). The paperwork guides all parties through the special education process.

Critics view these procedures as burdensome and criticize the amount of time and effort that professionals must currently devote to paperwork (Bender, 2003). In addition, researchers report that hassles over legal procedures and paperwork contribute to the stress and burnout increasingly experienced by special education personnel (Hardman, Drew, & Egan, 2005). The legal requirements of paperwork continue to be stressful to teachers and are sometimes seen as detrimental to collaborative efforts with parents and other professionals. However, the importance of documenting systematic adherence to federal and state mandates cannot be overemphasized. Without such documentation, teachers and administrators are left unable to substantiate their actions, which can result in additional monetary and time costs to a district.

The time spent developing and using paperwork should not be considered wasted time. Accurate, written information helps in creating a conducive learning environment for students and a more organized workplace for adults. The development and maintenance of paperwork can also sharpen teachers' planning, instructional, management, evaluation, communication, and partnership skills. Maintaining paperwork helps professionals in making educational decisions about students and about classroom happenings.

Professionals working with students with diverse needs use paperwork when they

Pause and Reflect About the Profession 7.1

Describe what you believe are relevant reasons that paperwork helps in professional decision making. List at least three reasons why beginning teachers would want to participate in paperwork activities.

1. _____

_____

_____

_____

_____

2. _____

_____

_____

_____

_____

3. _____

_____

_____

_____

_____

- record professional observations, analyses, and judgments when making educational decisions for students
- provide varied explanations of variables, trends, and patterns appearing in students' past schooling, home, or community, offering clues to current behaviors
- determine the most effective and efficacious way to instruct and manage students in the least restrictive environment (LRE)
- modify curricula, strategies, or programs when students are served in inclusion classrooms
- explain the links between the general education placement and the special education placement based on students' strengths and needs
- continually verify whether students need to remain in or exit from special education and related services
- plan actions in the classroom (e.g., lesson planning and unit planning, as discussed in chapter 5)
- document transition planning, implementation, and monitoring as students progress toward mastery of learning outcomes, graduation, and pre-adult-life activities
- communicate efforts with other professionals and parents

Examples of potential problems confronting the teacher in completing paperwork and solutions to these problems are presented in Box 7.2. If implemented early in the novice teacher's career, these suggestions may reduce the time, effort, and stress associated with completion of paperwork.

B ox 7.2

Problems in Completing Paperwork and Potential Strategies to Prevent or Remediate Problems

1. Unawareness of required forms, data collection, paperwork, and so forth

Potential strategy: Take the time to become familiar with the content of forms prior to completion. Read directions in advance of completion. Be aware of and plan for required due dates, necessary signatures, and so forth.

2. No plan for handling paperwork

Potential strategy: Develop a plan to screen, consolidate, and prioritize the completion of forms. Use trial-and-error strategies in the implementation process. If problems arise, revise the plan with input from administrators, special education teachers, and general education teachers. Use self-evaluation techniques.

3. Unavailability of factual information

Potential strategy: Be prepared. Study past cumulative files, grade records, health histories, and attendance files of students. Talk with parents. Obtain information from the home, community, and former teachers. Store obtained facts in an accessible location for later use during school-based committee meetings, case conferences, and so forth.

4. Lack of time to complete paperwork

Potential strategy: Find the time. Complete a daily schedule, doing paperwork in a specified time slot. Work as a team. Elicit help from others (e.g., more experienced colleagues) to complete paperwork. Ask paraprofessionals to complete demographic information or any data not requiring confidentiality. Write down and make only written decisions that paraprofessionals can't.

5. Inadequate notice to/from others contributing to written product

Potential strategy: Ask for a written request for expected contributions and materials. Request written due dates if not given. Encourage others to specify notices in writing at all times. Provide an outline of required information when soliciting data from others.

6. Unrealistic priorities

Potential strategy: List what needs to be done first, second, and so forth. Put first things first. Resist unnecessary change.

7. Overplanning

Potential strategy: Monitor paperwork continually. Plan less (e.g., allow transition time for teachers and paraprofessionals). Write down only essential data. Use a tape recorder in lieu of writing whenever possible.

8. Lack of policies and procedures for completion of paperwork

Potential strategy: Clarify your role with administrators and other teachers in completing paperwork. Ask many questions. Persist. Be diligent.

9. Lack of skills for improving paperwork completion

Potential strategy: Set and meet deadlines. Use cues to remind yourself when paperwork is due (e.g., write out short daily to-do lists for yourself). Self-monitor progress. Solicit feedback from others. Attend workshops and professional conferences for updated information.

10. Lost data

Potential strategy: Keep in an accessible location a copy of all written data turned in to others. Initial and date all copies. Throw out all unnecessary, outdated copies.

Box 7.2   (continued)

11. **Lack of motivation to complete paperwork**

Potential strategy: Become aware of the impact of your own effectiveness on students, parents, peers, and so forth. Seek individual causes for lack of motivation and self-correct.

12. **Inadequate maintenance and storage of paperwork**

Potential strategy: Keep a copy of all written data in an accessible location. Set up a realistic filing system. File important documentation immediately. Computerize as much as possible. Use a tape recorder in lieu of written documentation whenever possible.

TYPICAL PROCEDURES USED FOR SCREENING—PREREFERRAL

Legal procedures for special education often determine the types and content of paperwork that teachers will produce and maintain.

Screening—Prereferral Process

During prereferral, students with academic and for behavior problems undergo screening and are provided with appropriate interventions by the multidisciplinary team (MDT) discussed below. These students and their teachers are provided assistance in the general education class, where the problems first arise. Prereferral actions are a logical first step in professional efforts to help students remain in the LRE. Today, with the emphasis on providing increased services in general education classes, professionals must collect extensive data and complete the necessary paperwork on the student's individual skills and abilities in the LRE, the setting closest to the general education class (IDEA, 1997).

Questions to ask during prereferral include the following:

- Under what conditions does the student seem to have the most trouble?
- What specifically are the student's problem areas?
- What specifically are the student's strengths?
- How does the student learn best (e.g., independently, in small groups)?
- Does the student display both academic weaknesses and problem behaviors?
- What have professionals tried thus far?
- Are current approaches successful? Why or why not? (Cartwright, Cartwright, and Ward 1981)

Professionals can collect written documentation to help them specify students' strengths and weaknesses. Effective beginning and developing special education teachers will consult with general education teachers and other professionals during prereferral. In the case example, prereferral questions were posed to Sarah's classroom teacher, Ms. Edward (Box 7.3). Ms. Edward provided important clues by specifying some of Sarah's strengths and weaknesses in the general education setting.

Present Educational Setting

Some general education students will experience problems with cognition, language, self-help, motor, behavior, and social-emotional skills as well as other areas. The teacher's task is to begin to discern whether students who display such differences require assistance through specially designed instruction and/or related services.

Box 7.3   **Prereferral Questions on Sarah**

Sarah's teachers were asked to answer prereferral questions about her classroom progress. This is what her teacher, Ms. Edward, wrote:

1. **Under what conditions does the student seem to have the most trouble?**

   Sarah demonstrates problems during independent study periods and unstructured class time. She also has difficulties with reading, especially when asked to complete read-and-answer sheets.

2. **What specifically are the student's problem areas?**

   Sarah's main problem appears to be self-management. She just doesn't seem to want to try in reading. However, I'm not sure whether she has the ability to comprehend the tasks required of her or she does not employ any cognitive strategy to aid comprehension. She lacks many reading comprehension skills for a child in the third grade.

3. **What specifically are the student's strengths?**

   Sarah demonstrates strong skills in basic mathematical operations. She has excellent abilities in spelling. However, none of these tasks has required much reading so far. Another strength I notice is how well she gets along with peers and adults. I think she really does try to please others.

4. **How does the student learn best (e.g., independently, in small groups)?**

   Sarah appears to learn best in small groups. I've noticed that she does well when she works with a classmate. She also works well in one-on-one situations with adults. I just can't always have someone there to work with her.

5. **Does the student display both academic weaknesses and problem behaviors?**

   Her main problem areas appear to be reading comprehension and completion of independent work.

6. **What have professionals tried thus far?**

   Sarah has worked with minimal success with our classroom paraprofessional. School volunteers have tried also to tutor her. It seems she would rather socialize with them than complete her tasks.

7. **Are current approaches successful? Why or why not?**

   Unknown at this time.

Classroom Diversity

Teachers face the daily challenges of implementing instruction and managing the behaviors of students. Most of them observe students and measure progress through curriculum-based assessments, teacher-made materials, chapter tests, portfolio assessments, student-made products, commercially prepared assessment devices, academic rating scales, or behavioral checklists.

Teachers observe and assess students daily, either by formal methods (e.g., checklists, rating scales, tests) or by informal methods (e.g., discussions with past teachers, unstructured comments based on task analysis). Effective teachers are able to discern their students' normal behavior patterns (Mercer & Mercer, 2004). After assessing and observing all students, teachers begin to note those displaying some variations from others in learning tasks, social behaviors, organizational skills, attention to tasks, study skills, developmental milestones, or cultural expectations. When teachers are familiar with students' backgrounds, they can use data that are continually being generated in the classroom, home, and community to identify students who may have low ability, learning difficulties, or problem behaviors.

Teachers should examine the data in a student's cumulative folder to determine grade levels repeated, school achievement, past test results, anecdotal information, and attendance patterns. Some teachers talk with parents and other school personnel involved with the student. Individuals whose behaviors differ greatly from the norm may require more formal observations and evaluations. When deviations are noted frequently over time and to such an intensity that the teacher believes that the student is in danger behaviorally or academically, other professional judgment is required. More data need to be generated on the targeted student so that appropriate educational decisions may be made. As an example, Figure 7.1 shows paperwork collected from Sarah's home, community, and school that is useful in educational screenings.

Data Collection by Multiple Professionals

The MDT is typically consulted when evidence indicates that a student stands out from his or her peers. The team may be called by a host of names, but the intent of these professionals is to gather more information on the target student, who differs in important ways from other students. The MDT may include principals, counselors, school psychologists, educational diagnosticians, content area teachers, nurses, therapists, special education teachers, and other school professionals. An MDT meeting has two purposes: (1) to generate classroom strategies (prereferral strategies) to help the student remain in the present setting and (2) to determine observation schedules needed to verify the student's progress toward the general education goals and prereferral objectives.

Home		**School**		**Community**	
Complies with parental demands?	yes	Displays academic needs?	yes	Frequents social organizations?	yes
Demonstrates good rapport with siblings?	yes	Has problem behaviors?	no	Demonstrates leisure-time activities?	no
Completes chores routinely?	no	Demonstrates adequate organizational skills?	no	Uses community resources?	yes
Displays self-help skills?	yes	Demonstrates adequate study skills?	no	Complies adequately with neighborhood peers?	yes
Are developmental milestones on time?	yes	Displays adequate socio-emotional development?	yes	Complies with community norms?	yes
Demonstrates adequate health/nutrition?	yes	Displays adequate speech/language skills?	yes	Has and uses a support system?	yes
		Has adequate motor abilities?	yes		

Comments: *Parents' report: Sarah does not always fulfill her family responsibilities at home. She sometimes completes household chores haphazardly. She will complete adequately if offered a reward. She needs to be reminded often. She doesn't always remember what her home chores are. School social worker's report: Sarah appears to function adequately in her community setting. She demonstrates no major problems with peers, neighborhood organizations, and community groups.*

Darby Olsen, Social Worker
1/7/04

Teacher's report: *Sarah's organizational and study skills are of concern. She doesn't complete required assignments and rarely brings in homework papers.*

Mr. Benjamin, Counselor
1/7/04

FIGURE 7.1 Home, School, and Community Data of Sarah

Prereferral Strategy Implementation

The general education teacher, with consulting help from the special education teacher, psychologist, administrator, clinician, counselor, or other professionals, often implements the prereferral strategies. A functioning MDT, however, shares rights and responsibilities in the efforts to help the student succeed with prereferral strategies. Rights pertinent to general education teachers and special education teachers (as based on Schulz & Turnbull, 1984) continue to be relevant in today's classrooms and include the following:

- The opportunity to attend all meetings in which educational decisions are made that affect the student and professionals involved with the student

Pause and Reflect About the Profession 7.2

Locate copies of the special education paperwork used in your local school district. Below, provide the specific name of the form and determine the form's purpose. Compare and contrast purposes with the paperwork listed in this chapter.

Paperwork Area	Form Name/Purpose	Local Form Name/Purpose
Present education setting		
	Data collection on deviations from the norm	
	Multiprofessional data	
	Prereferral strategies	
	Professional observations	
	Case study conference results	
Formalized testing		
	Sensory screenings	
	Consent for individualized testing	
	Individualized battery protocol	
	Testing requirements	
	Formal testing results	
	Eligibility meetings	
IEPs		
	Consent for placement by parents or guardians	
	Initial placement IEP forms	
	Results of IEP meeting	
	Notice of recommended assignment	
	Annual updated IEP	
Special education continuation or exit		
	Consent for reevaluation	
	Reevaluation results	
	Continuation or exit	
	Meeting notification	
	Consent for continuation or exit from services	
	Notice of recommended assignment	

- A chance to select the appropriate content, methodology, or objectives from a program to use in assessment or instructional activities implemented in prereferral attempts
- Access to all specialized materials, equipment, and curricula that would make instruction and management easier in the general education setting
- Participation in baseline data collection, strategies implementation, and teaching modification monitoring
- Input and feedback into all learning strategies and behavioral management steps devised as prereferral strategies
- Assistance in acquiring resources and extra classroom helpers, including parents, volunteers, aides, specialized itinerant help, and peer tutors

Responsibilities of professionals during implementation of prereferral strategies include the following:

- Demonstrating competency in given specialization areas
- Displaying effective organization of the learning environment
- Observing and collecting data on strategies and management steps
- Providing continual and objective assessment
- Individualizing instruction based on students' needs
- Making baseline data collections, prereferral strategies, observations, and other teaching modifications relevant so that students with diverse needs are a part of all general education activities
- Monitoring students' academic and social-emotional requirements over time
- Consulting with other professionals and with parents

Together with other team members, the special education teacher helps determine the success of attempts to remediate within the present setting. A team approach means that special educators, general educators, principals, counselors, school psychologists, librarians, therapists, paraprofessionals, students, parents, community volunteers, and professional/consumer organizations all can play a role in planning and implementing strategies to help students remain with their normally functioning peers. Emphasis is directed toward coordinating and monitoring all involvement carefully to maximize the ultimate benefit to students. Coordination, communication, and cooperation are keys to shared strategy implementation and successful programming.

The developing special education teacher and other team members may be called on to assist the general education teacher in devising and implementing strategies such as those listed in Box 7.4. Examples of applied activities of the teacher are listed under each strategy.

Examples of the paperwork used for prereferral strategies are illustrated in Figure 7.2. On these forms, modifications in prereferral strategies are planned, with implementers collecting data on Sarah's baseline level. There is a space to monitor modifications every day of the week for six weeks. Professionals at Sarah's school discovered the necessity of reviewing her educational program at the end of the six-week period. Prereferral modifications of teaching strategies were not enough to remediate her problems in independent study skills and reading comprehension. Teaming efforts must be intensified for her, and more formal data are required.

Professional Observations

As in Sarah's and other students' cases, observations of the strategies by professionals other than the general education teacher (e.g., special education teacher, psychologist, counselor, principal) provide evidence of modifications in teaching or changes in procedures. Observations may also indicate that students require more help by specialists than can be provided in the present setting.

Professionals who observe students with learning and behavioral problems highlight data on the appropriateness of the present setting. After many strategies have been tried, professionals familiar with the student in question can help determine the success

| **B**ox 7.4 | **Prereferral Implementation Strategies** |

1. Special modifications in teaching strategies

- Team teach with peers often, especially in individual areas of expertise.
- Write homework assignments on the chalkboard and have students copy them into their notebooks. Make sure the directions are clear.
- Team students (peer tutoring) who have complementary strengths and weaknesses. The entire class can begin independent study at the same time, using this buddy system.
- Let some students listen to taped reading assignments while others work on computerized assignments or read from texts. Change groups so that all students experience a variety of teaching modes.

2. Changes in classroom materials

- Break the work into short assignments. Place a marker over distracting pictures or other stimuli.
- Use audiovisual equipment with students as often as possible.
- Raise the stimulus value of elements to be learned: Any novel emphasis will help (e.g., color coding, emphatic use of voice, animation of materials).
- Block off sections of work the student has completed so that he or she is aware of where the assignment is on the page.
- Encourage the use of a typewriter or computer for students whose writing is slow and labored.
- Prerecord the classroom material to assist the slow reader.

3. Varying evaluation/schedules to be used

- Adjust grades so that the student is not constantly experiencing failing marks.
- Consider alternatives to grades, such as rewards for conduct and effort.
- Count intermittent scores on academic tests.
- Eliminate lowest and highest scores occasionally and go with average scores.

4. Modified curricula

- If students are required to take notes in class, provide an outline of general topics so that students can keep notes in order.
- Allow slow learners to complete work at their own pace.
- Integrate subject areas in which students succeed (e.g., let students draw the answer, rather than write it, if art is a strong subject for students).

5. Identification of effective assessment techniques for learning weaknesses and problem behaviors

- Consider that spelling and grammar need not be the basis for grading if mastery of the content is the objective.
- Draw lines on or fold worksheets and tests to divide them into various sections by types of questions or problems.
- Use a variety of formal and informal assessment techniques.
- Consider curriculum-based assessment rather than standardized assessment.

6. Behavioral management plans specific to the student's observed problems

- Set up contingency contracting: the completion of X before the student is able to do Y.
- Devise a token economy or point system: Students earn tokens that are exchanged for specific rewards.
- Use time-out: the removal of the student from an apparently reinforcing setting to a presumably nonreinforcing setting for a specified and limited period of time.

Student's Name Sarah Thompson				**Teacher** Ms. Edward			
School Howard Elementary				**Birthdate** May 14, 1993			
Date February 25, 2004				**Subject area** Reading			

Modification(s) in (circle):   (Teaching strategies)   Classroom materials
Evaluation schedules   Curriculum
Assessment   Behavior management
Other

Describe modification(s):   *Peer tutoring with another student to aid in Sarah's reading skills.

Reason for prereferral: *Sarah cannot complete classwork independently.

Target student's baseline level in problem area: *4/5 times Sarah does not turn in reading comprehension materials when asked to do so.

Student progress (describe):   Sarah's progress has been minimal. Tom W. (peer) has been assigned to help her complete reading comprehension papers.

Modifi-cation	Week 1	Week 2	Week 3	Week 4	Week 5	Week 6	Comments
M	R = 62% P	R = 59% P	—	—	—	R = 60% P	Papers turned in on Monday with teacher's cue. (Accuracy is low—60%.)
T	R = 40% P	absent	R = 60% P	R = 50% P	—	—	Accuracy is low, x = Papers turned in 3/6 times.
W	R = 10% P	—	R = 5% P	R = 62% P	—	—	Comprehension problems noted.
T	—	—	—	—	—	—	Low turn-in rate; 62% accuracy rate.
F	R = 50% P	—	—	—	absent	—	Sarah has not responded to peer tutoring strategy/less work requirements.

Professional's name/title   Ms. Edward—Teacher, Mr. Benjamin—Counselor, Ms. New—Special Education Teacher

P = Paper completed and turned in
R = Accuracy rate (percentage of correct comprehension questions) for independent work

FIGURE 7.2   Prereferral Strategies Implemented in Sarah's General Education Classroom

of the prereferral interventions. These individuals can provide an objective perspective on the student's opportunities to meet the classroom teacher's or parents' expectations. An appropriate observer may be an administrator, a school psychologist, a school counselor, or another teacher familiar with the target student.

For each observation, a valid data-collection procedure should be selected to match the student's needs. Data should be collected through systematic procedures ensuring replicability and use of discrete behaviors. This means that both strengths and problem behaviors of the student are specified (defined in observable terms for use by professionals). Efficient and consistent observation procedures ensure that the behaviors are actually observed. To increase the likelihood of interrater reliability, two or more observers must agree on the behaviors that occurred.

Pause and Reflect About the Profession 7.3

Briefly describe two observations that Sarah's teacher might conduct to help Sarah in the LRE. What should the school professionals observe? How should they observe? Who should do the observation?

1. What? _____

_____

How? _____

_____

Who? _____

_____

2. What? _____

_____

How? _____

_____

Who? _____

_____

Reflect on educational objectives that you believe teachers and other professionals should focus on to help Sarah remain in her present educational setting.

The use of a stopwatch or clock to time observations and a graph to document the results may help in producing evidence of strategy effectiveness. Tangible products can also be observed and measured systematically for clues to the target student's strengths or problem areas, including the student's organization or study skills, the appropriateness of the teacher-made product, and the student's approach to problem solving. Observations can result in (1) a record of the student's permanent products, (2) anecdotal records, (3) frequency counts, (4) duration recordings, and (5) time samplings (Hardman et al., 2005). Paperwork such as that shown in Box 7.5 helps teachers record observations in each of these categories.

Developing and beginning special education teachers may be asked to observe and/or help other members of the MDT observe a student's progress. Box 7.5 is used to highlight Sarah's data and includes Ms. Edward's descriptions of what she observed. Both Sarah's teachers and her counselor, Mr. Benjamin, collected data and examined written products to verify Sarah's strengths and weaknesses in the general education setting. Ms. Lytle, the school's special education teacher, participated actively in Sarah's observations.

MDT Meeting Results

After observations are completed, professionals meet with parents in an MDT meeting or similarly titled meeting to analyze the data and to discuss the student's current functioning. Parents should be involved in all meetings when educational decisions are made (IDEA, 1997). It is important that they be made aware of educational conferences where evidence is provided about their child's progress in the present educational setting. The purposes of this conference are to (1) analyze the results of the prereferral

Box 7.5   **Methods of Observations on Sarah**

A. Record of student's permanent products (e. g., worksheet, artwork, and so forth):

___✓___ 1. Collect and keep record of these products.
___✓___ 2. Systematically analyze the quality of the student's products.
___✓___ 3. Engage in error analysis (systematic analysis of the kinds of error students make).

Comments: During a 6-week period, work samples were collected 10 of 64 times (30% of total work required). Accuracy rate, reported by Ms. Edward, was in the low range (62%). Most errors were reported to be careless errors, although reading comprehension problems were noted. Ms. Edward suspected that the reading material may be too difficult for Sarah. Motivation may also be a problem.

B. Anecdotal records:

___✓___ 1. Write down recollections of the occurrence of specific behaviors.
___✓___ 2. Keep a log of teacher's comments.

Comments: Ms. Edward keeps a daily of Sarah's progress. Sarah appears to socialize during peer-tutoring sessions, rather than attend to assignments. She is reported to be off-task for more than 70% of the independent reading time. When given one-on-one instruction, she often completes the reading assignments accurately (if instruction provided by her teacher is a direct instruction format). This last instance of successful direct instruction was observed by Ms. New, special education teacher.

C. Frequency counts:

___✓___ 1. Record the frequency of observable behaviors.
___✓___ 2. Record the extent to which other students exhibit the same behaviors.
___✓___ 3. Compare target student's behaviors with those of others.

Comments: Relative to other students, Sarah's independent study skills are off-target (average observation was 8 of 12 times she did not complete and organize work). Independent reading assignments completed only 4/14 trials. Accuracy rates reported to be 85% when direct instruction was provided by Ms. Edward. (Observations were reported by Ms. New, special education teacher.)

D. Duration recordings:

___✓___ 1. Gather data on the occurrence of the behavior by recording the length of time it persists.
___✓___ 2. Indicate initiation time and ending time of the behavior.

Comments: Off-task behavior during peer-tutoring sessions averaged 28 minutes of 35 minutes during a 6-week period. Sarah was observed to be off-task for group reading instruction 73% of the time of 90% of independent seatwork. She was observed to be on-task 85% of time during one-on-one instruction with her teacher. Initiation and ending time for direct instruction reading was reported by Ms. New, special education teacher.

E. Time samplings:

___✓___ 1. Measure the number of times a behavior occurs during a preset observation period.
___✓___ 2. Measure the number of times a response occurs during a preset observation period.

Comments: Sarah appears to complete reading tasks 85% of the time during a direct-instruction format by Ms. Marshall. She cannot work independently on these same reading tasks. Apparently, she has begun to recognize some of the required vocabulary, but as observed by Ms. New, she cannot apply vocabulary words to independent reading tasks.

Source: Adapted from "An Analysis of the Incidence of Special Class Placement: The Masses Are Burgeoning" by B. Algozzine, J. Ysseldyke, & S. L. Christenson, 1983, *Journal of Special Education, 17*, 141–147.

strategies, (2) discuss the results of the observations, (3) review new data collected since the initial MDT meeting, (4) elicit the parents' perceptions of their child's functioning and needs, and (5) decide whether the student is to be provided with individualized testing and continue in the formal referral process. If the student is a candidate for formal testing, the team will (6) secure the parents' written permission and (7) complete the formal referral application for the student's testing, which is signed and dated by referring professionals and/or parents.

Examples of collected data relevant to the MDT meeting are illustrated in Figure 7.3. School academic documentation is highlighted, as are behavioral data from the school, home, and community.

An example of the paperwork used for a formal referral application is illustrated in Figure 7.4. This application should list the referring individuals and their titles, and the reason for referral and the results of prereferral strategies and observations should be summarized. In addition, recommendations for follow-up and testing must be targeted. In Sarah's case, information from prereferral strategies and results of professional observations verify the need for further testing by professionals, including the school psychologist and/or the educational diagnostician.

Summary of Present Educational Setting Documentation

Much paperwork is required before students with mild to moderate disabilities may leave the general education class. Comprehensive data collection, initial parental contact, and completion of the referral form must be accomplished (Gloeckler & Simpson, 1988). During the student's time in the general education setting, the special education teacher assumes the role of consultant, assisting in prereferral strategies and observations. Many students with mild to moderate disabilities are provided instruction with their normally functioning peers. When a student is determined to require the direct service model of special education, the comprehensive information collected supports professionals in initiating this change in educational placement. The student continues

SCHOOL DATA

Academic Documentation	Behavioral Progress Data
Prereferral data	Behavioral ratings
Classroom strategy results	Socioemotional progress reports
Observations by multiple professionals	Observation reports of attention-to-task
Previous formal/informal assessments	Data reports of rapport with others

FAMILY DATA

Parental observation notations	Family member observations
Interaction with other reports	Child behavior scale ratings by parents, siblings, other family members

COMMUNITY DATA

Interaction with neighbors' observations	Involvement in community reports
Access to community functions data	Habilitation plans
	Social worker's checklists

FIGURE 7.3 Data Relevant to the MDT Meeting

Name <u>Sarah Thompson</u>   Birthdate <u>May 14, 1995</u>

Class <u>3</u>   Parents <u>John & Mary Thompson</u>

Address/Phone <u>62 Sandalwood Dr./472-0765</u>

Teacher <u>Ms. Edward</u>

Referring individuals:

Name	Title	Date
Jane Edward	Classroom Teacher	February 25, 2004
Terry Benjamin	Counselor	February 25, 2004
Betsy New	Special Education Teacher	February 25, 2004

Reason for referral:

Sarah demonstrates problems in following directions, motivation, and independent study skills. She may have a reading problem—especially comprehension of third grade material.

Results of prereferral strategies:

Strategy

1. Peer tutoring was unsuccessful. During a 6-week period, she turned in only 10 assignments completed independently (highest accuracy rate = 62%).

Strategy

2. Amount of reading assignments required was reduced—she still did not turn in organized, completed work.

Results of observations:

Work may not be motivating for her, or assignments may be too difficult. Her reading level may be too low to complete requirements. She can comprehend, apparently, in a direct instruction, one-on-one format with her teacher.

Recommended follow-up and testing:

It is recommended that she be tested by Dr. Weiss, the psychologist, to determine whether Sarah has a learning problem (especially in reading).

FIGURE 7.4   Sarah's Formal Referral Application

in the formal referral process because evidence indicates that the general education setting may not be the LRE for that student.

REFERRAL AND FORMALIZED TESTING

Relying on their analysis of the general education class data discussed during a student's MDT meeting, professionals may determine the prereferral strategies were successful; that is, educators, psychologists, counselors, or others may find the data documents mastery of academic objectives or a decrease in inappropriate behaviors. Parents may confirm the success of prereferral attempts through home observation. In such cases, the student does not need to continue in the formal referral process.

Despite prereferral strategies, however, another student may continue to demonstrate low ability, problem behaviors, or academic difficulties. At this point, professionals should initiate the formal referral process by acquiring the parents' written permission to test the student. (If parents refuse to give their permission, school officials can resort to the mediation and hearing procedures detailed in Chapter 2.) An example of the paperwork

Student's name   Sarah Thompson
Parent/guardian's name   John & Mary Thompson
Parent/guardian's address   62 Sandalwood Dr.
Birthdate May 14, 1995   Parent's phone 472-0765
Class 3   Teacher Ms. Edward   Date February 25, 2004

Reason for testing

Level of class assignments may be too difficult for Sarah. Teacher suspects a learning problem in reading (reading comprehension may be too low to complete assignments). Classroom strategies reported to be unsuccessful. Observations verified low accuracy rates and incomplete assignments; off-task behavior observed to be high. On-task behavior and higher accuracy rate during direct instruction with teachers.

Check all test types to be given/name of tests

	Types	Name
Ability	✓	Wechsler Intelligence Scale for Children—4
Achievement	✓	Woodcock-Johnson Psychoeducational Battery
Socioemotional	✓	Achenbach Behavioral Scales
Process	✓	Developmental Test of Visual Perception
Adaptive behavior		
Others	✓	Brigance Diagnostic Inventories (Reading)
		Gates-McKillop Reading Diagnostic Test

Other comments   *Only the educational component of the Woodcock Battery
                       will be given.

Student's name Sarah Thompson

✓ I give permission to test my child Sarah. I understand I will be informed of all results. I have
been given procedural safeguards.
___ I do not give permission to test. I have been given procedural safeguards.
___ I wish to have another meeting prior to granting my permission to test my child.

Parent/guardian's signature John Thompson   Date February 25, 2004

FIGURE 7.5   Permission to Test Sarah

required for permission to test Sarah is included in Figure 7.5. As can be seen, Sarah's parents were involved in the decision to test her formally. The reasons for testing Sarah and the names of specific tests to be used with her are marked clearly on the form for her parents' perusal and consent.

Referral Process

During the referral process, documentation is collected from many sources, including data evaluating progress in the present educational setting, prior school records, sensory screening results, both formal and informal observations, assessments, and past health records. Among relevant data required to refer a student for a change in educational placement is evidence that the student was provided with the full opportunity to remain in the LRE (IDEA, 1997). To remove a student from instruction with general education students for even part of the day, professionals must collect written evidence establishing the need for a change in placement and in the type of instruction the student receives.

Documentating prereferral attempts to remediate problems is actually the first step in the formal special education referral process (Yell, 2001). The completed referral should include information related to (1) the present educational setting, (2) testing, and (3) the individualized education program. Box 7.6 delineates components of the completed referral. Each step of the referral process is explained below through typical actions of school professionals, and examples of required paperwork are provided in each section.

B ox 7.6   **Data of the Completed Referral Process**

Present Educational Setting Documentation

- Data of the student's deviations from the norm of classroom behaviors
- Data collected by professionals and parents from the home, school, or community
- School-based planning meeting results
- Prereferral strategy implementation results
- Professional observations
- Case study conference results

Testing Data

- Prereferral sensory screening results (vision and hearing assessments)
- Consent for individualized testing by parents
- Complete battery of tests
- Explanation and interpretation of formal testing in a written report
- Written results of eligibility meetings determining educational placement

Individualized Education Program

- Consent for placement by parents
- Initial placement IEP
- Annually updated IEP
- Results and implications of reevaluations

Beginning and developing teachers should note that the required paperwork may differ slightly in form and content from school district to school district. Names of meetings and professional teams (e.g., school-based committee meetings, educational planning teams) may differ from locale to locale. However, professional team members completing effective paperwork share a common goal: providing evidence that the student is served in the educational setting best suited to his or her needs.

Sensory Screenings

Prior to official testing by the school psychologist or other evaluator, sensory data on the student are collected, including health, hearing, vision, or speech and language screenings (IDEA, 1997). If the student fails any of the sensory or health screenings, more data must be obtained from health professionals (e.g., if the student fails the hearing screening, an audiometric report by a certified audiologist is pertinent; if the student fails the vision screening, a report from an ophthalmologist or optometrist is in order). These data are important for a number of reasons: (1) Evaluators must match the test to the student's needs; (2) a sensory impairment may be the major reason for the student's difficulties, suggesting a different interpretation and explanation of test results; (3) the discovery of a sensory impairment as the student's primary disability may yield different educational placement options; and (4) the discovery of a sensory impairment may suggest different goals/objectives on the IEP.

An example of the paperwork used to collect Sarah's sensory data is found in Figure 7.6. On close examination of this required paperwork, the teacher is able to confirm that Sarah has no sensory impairment. This information now is used to substantiate Ms. Edward's data from previous reports. Vision, hearing, speech and language, and overall health appear to be in the normal range.

Student's name Sarah Thompson   Class 3

Birthdate May 14, 1995   Teacher Ms. Edward

1.   **Vision screening**

Distance acuity results 20/20(l)   20/30(r)

Measure Snelling   Given by Ms. Parkens (nurse)   Date Oct. 2, 2003

Field vision results   Adequate

Measure n/a   Given by _____   Date _____

Follow-up required no   Reason Vision adequate.

Ophthalmologist/Optometrist: Name _____

                                     Address _____

(Enclose copy)   Phone _____

Recommendation Follow-up is not necessary at this time. Distance vision appears to be within the normal range in both eyes.

2.   **Hearing screening**

Auditory acuity results: Left ear Pass Right ear Pass

Measure Conversational speech   Given by Ms. Parkens (nurse)

Date Oct. 22, 2003   Follow-up required no

Reason Hearing (conversational speech) adequate.

Audiologist   Name _____

                                     Address _____

(Enclose copy)   Phone _____

Recommendation Follow-up is not necessary at this time. Both ears responded to stimuli (given conversational speech).

3.   **Speech/language screening**

Clinician Jan Jenkins   Date Oct. 14, 1999–Oct. 22, 2003

Test name	Results	Recommendation
Articulation Test of Language Development; VCS	Passed	No follow-up necessary at this time
Voice TLD	Passed	
Fluency Test of Language Development; VCS; PSLT	Passed	
Language PSLT	Passed	

Vocabulary Comprehension Scale; Test of Language Development; Picture Story Language Test

Follow-up required? No

Reason for speech/language placement option:

At this time, speech and language training not recommended.

Sarah's articulation, voice, fluency, and language skills appear to be within the normal range.

4.   **Overall health**

Physician's name Dr. Joseph Charles

Address 1608 Fairway Circle

Phone number 451-3928

Date of last physical December 18, 2003

Comments: Sarah appears to be in excellent health.

5.   Sensory/health screening comments: No notable sensory and/or health deviations to report at this time.

                                                Ms. Parkens (nurse)

                                                Jan Jenkins (Clinician)

FIGURE 7.6   Sarah's Health/Sensory Screening Results

Consent for Individualized Testing

Prior to their child's testing, parents must be assured of procedural safeguards (explained in detail in chapter 2). After all pertinent sensory data are collected and parents have signed the necessary paperwork giving their permission to test, the evaluator provides the student with the individually administered battery.

Individualized Battery

The purpose of the formalized testing situation is to link identification and intervention. Teachers need specific data to describe students' strengths and to help refine appropriate instructional strategies and techniques (Mercer & Mercer, 2004). Assessment must be multifactor, examining all areas of functioning. Through assessment, the guidelines for appropriate instruction begin.

Testing Requirements

Testing is to be completed in the student's native language, unless clearly not feasible to do so, with all testing materials sensitive to the student's abilities. Tests that may be included in an individualized battery are listed in Box 7.7. Teachers may be asked to complete part of these instruments (e.g., to complete a behavioral rating, to write down anecdotal information used by the psychologist in the test interpretation), or the instruments may be administered solely by the educational diagnostician or school psychologist. Many of the assessment devices used vary among different school systems. Box 7.7 is a partial listing of assessment devices used by psychologists and educational diagnosticians.

Explanation and Interpretation of Formal Testing

After testing is completed, all data are condensed into a written psychological report, which is shared with parents and professionals. Testing results must be interpreted and explained by the evaluator. Implications for instruction are generated from these results, and assessment should link the student's current abilities to teaching strategies and procedures used by general education or special education teachers. An example of Sarah's psychological report is included in Box 7.8. On this report, the psychologist provides evidence of Sarah's above-average intelligence and her lack of severe behavioral and sensory problems. Data support the claim that although she displays learning problems, her difficulties are not severe enough to remove her from the general classroom setting. Data from the present educational setting and the formal testing completed by Dr. Leigh, the school psychologist, have been summarized on the written psychological report. All information is explained and interpreted to parents and professionals by evaluators.

Eligibility Meeting

After completion of all formal testing, parents and professionals decide whether the student qualifies for specialized help. This decision occurs at an eligibility meeting.

Eligibility and placement decisions must be based on the results of all written data (IDEA, 1997). All data generated to date are compiled and synthesized during an eligibility meeting. For many students, the psychological report is explained and interpreted during this meeting.

Box 7.7　Examples of Tests in a Battery

Ability Measures

- Kaufman Assessment Battery for Children (K–ABC)
- Stanford-Binet Intelligence Scale
- Wechsler Adult Intelligence Scale (WAIS)
- Wechsler Intelligence Scale for Children (Fourth Edition) (WISC–4)

Achievement Measures

- Brigance Diagnostic Inventories
- Gates-McKillop Reading Diagnostic Test
- Gray Oral Reading Test
- Inventory of Elementary Reading Skills
- Key Math
- Metropolitan Achievement Test
- Peabody Individual Achievement Test
- Wide Range Achievement Test
- Woodcock-Johnson Psychoeducational Battery

Process Measures

- Auditory Discrimination Test
- Auditory Sequential Memory Test
- Bruininks-Oseretsky Test of Motor Proficiency
- Developmental Test of Visual Perception
- Frostig Test of Visual Motor Integration
- Purdue Perceptual-Motor Survey
- Wepman Auditory

Social-Emotional Measures

- Achenbach Behavioral Scales
- Burke's Behavior Rating

Adaptive Behavior Scales

- American Association on Mental Deficiency (AAMD) Adaptive

Behavior Scales

- Adaptive Behavior Inventory for Children
- System of Multi-Cultural Pluralistic Assessment
- Vineland Social Maturity Scale

Self-Report Techniques

- Bower-Lambert Screening Scales
- California Test of Personality
- Children's Apperception Test
- Piers-Harris Self-Concept Scale

Source: Based on *Assessment,* by J. Salvia and J. E. Ysseldyke, 1991, Boston: Houghton Mifflin.

Box 7.8   Psychological Report on Sarah Thompson

Name: Sarah Thompson

Birthdate: May 14, 1993

Parents: John and Mary Thompson

School: Howard Elementary School

Grade: 3

Teacher: Ms. Jane Edward

Evaluator: Betty Weiss, Certified School Psychologist

Date: 3/20/04

Background Information:

Sarah has been reported by her teacher, Ms. Edward, to be a well-mannered, attractive young-ster attending third grade at Howard Elementary School. Sarah recently transferred from Pelton School, Bowersville, another school district in the state. At the time of her entry into Howard, few prior school records on her were available. School officials from Pelton did send an incomplete cumulative record of her kindergarten experience, which indicates her progress was normal. However, no information was received describing her school progress during grades one and two.

During the current school year, Sarah has been experiencing problems in reading comprehension and study skills. On the Woodcock-Johnson Achievement Test, given by Ms. Edward on September 22, 2003, Sarah performed at 5.7 in mathematics, 1.9 in reading, and 3.3 in spelling. Chapter tests from the Universal Reading Series, Level 3, were provided by her teacher. Sarah had not mastered the first group of objectives from Chapter 1 of this reading series, suggesting to Ms. Edward some of Sarah's difficulties in reading comprehension. Mr. and Mrs. Thompson have reported also that Sarah has problems reading homework assignments and completing household chores and family responsibilities at home. The parents indicated, however, that she does not seem to have any difficulties in making and keeping friends in and around the neighborhood. She appears to get along well with her younger brother, Larry, age four.

Ms. Edward also reported Sarah's near-perfect handwriting and her love of drawing. Sarah's motor development is adequate for a child in the third grade. She is able to run, jump, skip, and hop as most children her age. She competes satisfactorily in physical education with her classmates and performs exceptionally well in swimming. Sarah's medical history is not notable.

Sarah's speech and language development appears to be adequate for a child of her age. She was screened by the school nurse, Mrs. Parkens, on October 2, 2003, for vision and hearing. Both vision and hearing screenings were unremarkable. Mrs. Jenkins, the speech and language clinician at Howard, screened Sarah on October 14, 2003, in areas of articulation, voice, fluency, and language by using the Test of Language Development, Vocabulary Comprehension Test, and Picture Story Language Test (refer to the completed screening report, dated October 22, 2003). On the basis of the results of these speech and language assessments, no speech/language training appears necessary at this time.

In the classroom, Ms. Edward reported Sarah's difficulty in beginning on time and completing assignments in reading. Other subject area requirements do not appear to pose problems to her. She continues to perform well in mathematics and spelling, although assignments in social studies and science are beginning to contain more required reading than previously. Ms. Edward reported her fears of Sarah falling farther and farther behind her classmates as the school year continues. For these reasons, prereferral strategies were proposed by an educational planning team on January 14, 2004. Teaching modifications applied in the general classroom were suggested and implemented by Ms. Edward. The school's counselor, Mr. Benjamin; special education teacher, Ms. New; and I participated in prereferral process. After six weeks, however, peer tutoring with a classmate during reading comprehension time was not successful. Lowering the amount of work required for her was also reported to be an unsuccessful strategy. For a majority of the time, Sarah continues to display problems in completing her work and in comprehending the assignments. Her papers continue to contain many errors (62 percent accuracy was the highest reported score). Observations by Ms. Edward, Mr. Benjamin, Ms. New, and me included an analysis of Sarah's work samples (during a six-week period, work samples were turned in 10 out of 64 times; problems in reading comprehension were noted); anecdotal records (Ms. Edward's daily log continued to verify problems specific to reading comprehension); and a frequency count of observable behavior during reading instruction (relative to peers, Sarah was on task during independent reading instruction only 4 out of 14 times; Sarah was off task for 73 percent of reading instruction and off task for 90 percent of seatwork during two independent observations by Mr. Benjamin and me). She appears to respond well to direct instruction strategies when working one-on-one with her teacher. When she was provided with direct instruction strategies geared to her level of learning (e.g., acquisition stage for reading comprehension), she improved in reading attention and level.

Testing:

Between March 4 and March 14, 2004, Sarah was given the following tests and obtained these scores:

- Wechsler Intelligence Scale for Children (Fourth Edition): Sarah obtained a full scale of 114 (verbal: 110, performance: 116) on the WISC-4, including raw scores on picture completion, picture arrangement, block design, object assembly, coding, and mazes. All are within the average or above average raw-score range.
- Woodcock-Johnson Psychoeducational Battery: Only the educational component was given to Sarah, and she scored 2.5 in reading, 5.7 in math, and 3.2 in language.
- Gates-McKillop Reading Diagnostic Test: On this measure, Sarah obtained a score of reading comprehension grade level 3.4.
- Brigance Diagnostic Inventories: This measure was given to determine more specific information about Sarah's reading abilities. An overall score of 2.3 was obtained with the breakdown of the subsets as follows:

Word recognition	3.1
Oral reading	2.7
Reading comprehension	2.3
Functional word recognition	2.4
Word analysis	2.4
Reference skills	2.0
Writing	2.1
Spelling	2.1
Forms	2.4

- Achenbach Behavioral Scales: The ABS was completed by both Sarah's parents and Ms. Edward, her classroom teacher, with no significant behaviors reported in any area of the behavior rating scale. Her social-emotional development appears to be adequate for a child of her age.
- Developmental Test of Visual Perception: To determine whether Sarah displays problems in visual processing, the DTVP was given. Sarah appears to have adequate functioning in all areas of the DTVP.

Box 7.8   (continued)

Summary of Data:

Sarah was given testing in the areas of ability, achievement, social-emotional development, processing, and reading-diagnostic skills. Classroom strategies were attempted and observations of her progress in Ms. Edward's class were conducted prior to testing. Peer tutoring and lowered rates of homework/seatwork requirements (teaching modifications) did not appear to aid Sarah in skills in which she needs to succeed in the general classroom.

On the current testing, Sarah performs at the above-average range of intelligence (ability results of the WISC-4 are one standard deviation above the norm). Reading scores range from a low of 2.1 to 3.1 on reading diagnostic testing. Overall reading comprehension is reported currently at the 2.3 level. There is no discrepancy between achievement and ability. Processing and social-emotional ratings are unnotable for a child of her age. Tentative strategies that may prove to be helpful to Sarah are suggested by Ms. New, Ms. Edward, Mr. Benjamin, and me:

1. Have Sarah repeat directions to assignments prior to the initiation of independent work problems.
2. Cue Sarah orally to read for facts before she starts reading comprehension assignments.
3. Work with Sarah to use underlining strategies (important details of assignments).
4. Teach Sarah self-questioning strategies so that she can ask herself whether she comprehends tasks.
5. Paraphrase important details to her in a variety of ways (e.g., orally say directions in two different ways).
6. Highlight assignments (color-code important information in each paragraph she is to read).
7. Set time limits on and monitor her completion of tasks.
8. Reward Sarah with tangibles, special class privileges, and so forth when she hands in assignments on time and follows classroom suggestions.
9. Post a record of her accomplishments for assignments and for successful completion of reading comprehension tasks (chart or graph).
10. Consider her stage of learning and plan instructional methods accordingly. If in the acquisition stage, consider direct instruction methods. Use independent and practice activities only when she demonstrates mastery or near mastery of the skills.
11. Continue to use, over time, peer tutors, student interns, and volunteers/paraprofessionals as warranted to assist her.
12. Plan for consultation time among her parents, the special education teacher, and the general education teacher to consider Sarah's individual progress.

The purpose of the meeting is to match the needs of the student to the appropriate setting. If an appropriate setting is unavailable, the school district may contract for the needed services. In all cases, a placement must be found for the student (placement options are described in Chapter 1). A representative of the assessment team, often the school psychologist or educational diagnostician who conducted the assessment, participates in the eligibility meeting. Other members include a school administrator, the referring teachers, the special education teacher, parents or guardians, and if warranted, the student. An example of the paperwork used in Sarah's eligibility meeting is included in Figure 7.7.

Participants in the eligibility meeting for Sarah determine that she does not have a disability and is not in need of a special education program. Sarah will remain in

Student's name Sarah Thompson   Teacher Ms. Edward   Class 3

Problem area defined Sarah appears to lack motivation. Her reading comprehension and study skills are reported as low.

Reason for referral She was referred for testing because prereferral strategies in the general education classroom were not successful. Multiple observations provided evidence of off-task behaviors and low accuracy rates in performance.

Prereferral strategies Peer tutoring and lower homework/seatwork requirements have not aided Sarah in completing tasks and reading comprehension.

Results Assignments over a 6-week period continue to be incomplete and to have low accuracy rates.

Observation 4 completed	Name(s)	Date(s)
	Benjamin	3/1/04
	Benjamin	3/5/04
	New	3/13/04
	Weiss	3/19/04

Result Off-task in group reading 73% of the time (4/14 times off-task). Does not keep up with others (28/35 minutes off-task 70% of time).

Test results Sarah's test results include: WISC-4 (verbal, 110; performance, 116; full scale, 114); Woodcock Johnson (reading, 2.5; math, 3.7; language, 3.2); Gates-McKillop (reading comprehension, 2.4); Achenbach (no significant problem behaviors); DTVP (adequate in all areas); Brigance reading (2.3). Although her reading comprehension appears to be low (2.3 level), results of testing indicate she is beginning to comprehend grade-appropriate material but is not ready for independent assignments at this time.
Motivation may be a problem.

Recommendation for placement Continue in general education class.

Reason Sarah does not meet the requirements for special education.
Teachers should continue to provide small-group and tutorial help on a one-to-one basis in the acquisition of reading comprehension skills. Tentative strategies as listed on the psychological report of 3/20/04 should be implemented. Team meeting should reconvene to update general strategies on 8/20/04 to provide direction for the coming school year. Continue to emphasize direct instruction.

	Participants' signatures	Date
LEA	Thomas Smart, Principal	4/5/04
Evaluator	Betty Weiss, School Psychologist	4/5/04
Teachers	Jane Edward, Teacher	4/5/04
Others	Betsy New, Special Education	4/5/04
	Terry Benjamin, Counselor	4/5/04
Patent/Guardian	Mary/John Thompson, Parents	4/5/04

FIGURE 7.7   Sarah's Eligibility Meeting

general education: She is not a candidate for special education because her formal test results, along with prereferral information and formal observation data, confirm the appropriateness of the general education program for her. Sarah does display learning problems, but she is not a student with severe enough problems to necessitate her removal from her present educational setting. She responds well to small groups, direct instruction techniques, and some modifications in the general education curriculum. Her achievement levels are low to moderate and not severe enough to require special education. Her eligibility team members do make an important recommendation: that the team reconvene at the start of the school year to update potential general class strategies. At this point, the special education teacher may continue to be a consultant to Sarah's general education teachers.

Pause and Reflect About the Profession 7.4

Briefly summarize the data that you believe Sarah's school professionals and family members will need during the eligibility meeting. Compare and contrast data collected during the prereferral strategy and observation processes with those accumulated in Sarah's formal testing. Can any relevant indicators of Sarah's needs and strengths help in determining her current strengths and needs for an IEP?

Eligibility Data Summary

_____

_____

_____

_____

Relevant Prereferral and Observational Summary

_____

_____

_____

_____

Formal Testing Summary

_____

_____

_____

_____

Strengths and Needs Summary

_____

_____

_____

_____

Pertinent Questions About Formal Testing Results

If the purpose of formal testing is to determine the need for a change in placement, important questions that developing and beginning teachers should ask during the eligibility meeting might include the following:

- What other information is relevant about the student's functioning that test results may not provide?
- Does the written report present a complete and accurate picture of the student's cognitive, language, social, motor, or other forms of development?
- Do test results conflict with previous data collected?
- What are the implications of the test results for instruction and management? That is, do the results provide a framework for instructing or managing the student in the special education situation?

B ox 7.9   **Pertinent Questions and Answers on Sarah Thompson**

These questions were answered by Ms. Edward, the general education teacher.

- What other information is relevant about the student's functioning that test results may not provide?
  Other information that may be helpful for us to consider includes readability level of the classroom material; distractions from peers, paraprofessionals, or volunteers; and expectations of parents and professionals. More emphasis on direct instruction techniques and less on independent assignments (for Sarah's learning stage) are important.

- Does the written report present a complete and accurate picture of the student's cognitive, language, social, motor, or other forms of development?
  The written report provides data about Sarah's functioning in the domains listed above, but the question still remains: How do we best instruct Sarah? No matter what the psychologist and educational diagnostician diagnose, we still must find strategies and techniques to teach and help Sarah succeed.

- Do test results conflict with previous data collected?
  Sarah's parents have reported her lack of initiation to study independently at home and to complete home chores, so there is some reliability across individuals and settings concerning the data. I really believed, however, that Sarah's reading scores would have been much lower than she actually obtained on the formal achievement test given by our school psychologist.

- What are the implications of the test results for instruction and management? That is, do the results provide a framework for instructing or managing the student in the classroom situation?
  How can we teach Sarah best if she remains in the general education classroom? Should we change her reading assignments? Should we provide another formal reading program? Should we allow her to attend reading class with second graders?

- If a change in placement is not warranted, do test results imply other strategies, materials, or evaluation systems that may help the student in the general education setting (Smith, Polloway, Patton, & Dowdy, 2004)?

Box 7.9 presents the responses of Sarah's classroom teacher to these questions. One key element not to be overlooked is Sarah's opportunity to remain in the general education curriculum and be provided with consultative services by a team, including her school's special education teacher. Even after formal testing is completed, many students may continue to display problems in the general education curriculum but not be candidates for specialized programming. When this happens, the role of the special education teacher continues to be that of consultant to the general education teacher. Not all students with individual differences in learning or behavioral needs are removed from instruction with normally functioning peers. As in Sarah's case, many students can remain in the inclusive classrooms when professionals work as a team to facilitate the LRE.

Summary of the Formalized Testing Situation

After securing parents' permission to test and obtain all sensory information about their child, a complete battery of testing is given. Each educational decision for the student should be based on comprehensive information. Because data have been collected by many professionals over time and in a variety of settings, much is now known about the student. An objective decision is more likely to be made on how best to offer instruction and management.

Some students, like Sarah, may have undergone formal testing but are ineligible for special education and related services. These students may be provided with remedial help in their general classrooms, with consultation by the special educator. An emphasis by professionals on teaching behaviors (e.g., use of modified materials, direct instruction techniques, management using tokens and rewards) will allow many students remain in inclusive classrooms. Other students, however, may have undergone formal testing and are eligible for special education and related services. For students requiring formal special education (removal from the general education placement for at least part of the school day), the special educator provides instruction using the direct service model.

INDIVIDUALIZED EDUCATION PROGRAMS

Prior to their initial placement in special education, an individualized education program (IEP) must be developed for every student (IDEA, 1997). All paperwork collected to date can be very useful in determining goals and objectives for the student in the new educational setting. All data are linked to the student's IEP.

Students' IEPs are the most important documents that teachers, school officials, and parents develop cooperatively. Developing and beginning teachers need to become familiar with (1) the necessity of obtaining parents' or guardians' consent for placement, (2) the requirements of initial placements, (3) the requirements of annually updated IEPs, and (4) the results and implications of reevaluations.

Consent for Placement by Parents

Each student placed into a special education program is provided with an IEP. The IEP must be current and in effect at the beginning of every school year or within 30 calendar days of the meeting at which the student is found eligible for special education and related services (IDEA, 1997). Prior to initial placement, parents or guardians must give their written permission for their child's program.

Also, consenting parents or guardians must be given the opportunity to attend the IEP meeting at a time and place convenient for them. Federal authorities have mandated school officials to give parents two types of notices of the upcoming IEP meeting. One notice must be written, with a copy saved for school records. The other notice may be by written request, personal correspondence, telephone call, or other means. Figure 7.8 illustrates the paperwork used in securing parents' permission to place their child. Sarah's example is a reminder that she will continue in her general education program. Although an IEP is not required for her, an IEP is required for all students who receive special education and related services.

Requirements of Initial Placement IEPs

Federal requirements are very specific for students receiving special education and related services for the first time. Documentation must be provided by school personnel in two major areas: (1) the required participants at IEP meetings and (2) the required components of the IEP document. Because developing and beginning teachers must demonstrate knowledge of the IEP from the first day of school, it is very important to become familiar with all requirements during preservice training.

IEP Participants

Federal regulations specify the presence of various individuals when an IEP meeting commences. Box 7.10 lists the titles and functions of the required participants. The IDEA extends participant requirements to include a general education teacher in cases where students will be receiving some or all of their educational services in a general

Student's name <u>Sarah Thompson</u>   Class <u>3</u>
Present setting <u>Howard Elementary</u>   Teacher <u>Ms. Edward</u>
Type of setting <u>General education classroom</u>   Date <u>June 20, 2004</u>

Results of tests <u>Results of ability, achievement, processing, and socioemotional testing were</u>
<u>discussed by the eligibility team. Motivation appears to be a major problem for Sarah. Learning,</u>
<u>ability, achievement, socioemotional, and processing appear to be in at least the average range.</u>

Recommended program name <u>General education classroom placement.</u>

Reason for recommendation <u>Sarah meets the criteria for general education classroom placement</u>
<u>continuation. Sarah does display learning problems (she appears to be at the three-level acquisition</u>
<u>stage of reading comprehension—rather than generalization as most of her peers).</u>
<u>She appears to need extrinsic, tangible motivation and small-group instruction to help her succeed.</u>
<u>Direct instruction in a small-group format should be highlighted.</u>

Delivery service provided <u>Sarah will continue to receive her educational placement in the general</u>
<u>education classroom, with consulting help provided by the instructional support.</u>

Recommended school name <u>Continue in Howard Elementary</u>

Address <u>230 Haystack Court Road, Maimlee, Florida</u>
<u>Continue in general education class, summer school, June 24, 2004–</u>
<u>July 23, 2004 J.C. M.C.</u>

Placement to begin on <u>August 8 2004</u> (**30 calendar days from eligibility determination**).
<u>✓</u> I have been given a copy of "Procedural Due Process".
<u>✓</u> I give permission to place my child <u>Sarah</u> in the recommended program.
_____ I do not give permission to place my child _____ in the recommended program.
_____ I request another meeting prior to making a decision.

Parent/guardian's name <u>John Thompson/Mary Thompson</u>
LEA representative <u>Thomas Smart, Principal</u>
Date: <u>4/5/04</u>   Evaluator <u>Betty Weiss, Psychologist</u>
Teacher: <u>Jane Edward (General Education Classroom)</u>
Others <u>Betsy New (Special Education Certified)</u>

FIGURE 7.8   Sarah's Parents' Permission to Place

education classroom. An IEP should never be written prior to the actual meeting but rather must be developed during the meeting, with all participants providing insights on how best to meet the student's needs. Each participant should be given the opportunity to (1) provide information on the student, (2) suggest IEP goals and objectives, (3) question interpretations and explanations, (4) examine educational alternatives, and (5) disagree with proposed actions.

Specific Components of the IEP. The IDEA mandates specific IEP sections. Seven areas must be specified in writing for every student:

1. A statement of the student's current level of educational performance, including to what extent the student's disability affects his or her involvement and progress in the general curriculum

2. A statement of measurable annual goals, including benchmarks or short-term objectives, related to meeting the student's needs that result from his or her disability

3. A statement of the particular special education services and related aids and services to be provided to the student, or on behalf of the student, and a statement of the program modifications or supports for school personnel that will be provided to enable the student (a) to advance appropriately toward attaining the annual goals, (b) to be involved and progress in the general curriculum, (c) to participate in extracurricular and other nonacademic activities, and (d) to be educated and participate with other children with disabilities and nondisabled children

---

Box 7.10   **Required IEP Participants and Their Functions**

1. **LEA representative:** The local education agency (LEA) representative provides meeting participants with pertinent data about available programs in the local area. The individual must be available to discuss service delivery options, transportation methods, and district procedures of program implementation. The LEA representative is usually a district administrator of special education or the principal of the local school attended by the student.
2. **Member of the evaluation team:** Someone knowledgeable about psychological and educational testing must be available to discuss, interpret, and explain all test results to those in attendance at the meeting. Usually, this person is the school psychologist or educational diagnostician who provided the testing to the student.
3. **Special education teacher:** A professional who is knowledgeable about the special education program to be provided to the student must be present. The person answers any questions posed by group participants and guides the writing of student-oriented goals and objectives on the written documents.
4. **Regular education teacher:** At least one regular education teacher of the child (if the child is, or may be, participating in the regular education environment) who is knowledgeable of the regular education curriculum.
5. **Other participants:** Other participants in the IEP meeting may include the parent, guardian, or surrogate parent and, when appropriate, the student. Also, any other person the student, parent, guardian, or surrogate parent wishes may attend. Lawyers, therapists, physicians, or other advocates may represent parents or school officials at meetings. Their functions are to provide input and feedback on goals and objectives proposed for the IEP.

---

4. An explanation of the extent, if any, to which the student will not participate with nondisabled children in the regular classroom and in other activities

5. A statement of any individual modifications in the administration of state or districtwide assessments of student achievement that are needed in order for the student to participate in the assessment, and if the IEP team determines that the student will not participate in a particular state or districtwide assessment of student achievement (or part of an assessment), a statement of why that assessment is not appropriate for the student and how he or she will be assessed

6. The projected date for the beginning of the services and the anticipated frequency, location, and duration of those services

7. A statement of how the student's progress toward the annual goals will be measured and how the student's parents will be regularly informed (through such means as periodic report cards), at least as often as parents are informed of their nondisabled children's progress, of (a) their child's progress toward the annual goals and (b) the extent to which that progress is sufficient to enable the child to achieve the goals by the end of the year.

Also, the transition services for students who are 14 years of age or older must be delineated. These services are provided as part of an outcome-oriented process that promotes movement from school to postschool activities, including postsecondary education, vocational training, integrated employment (including supported employment), continuing and adult education, adult services, independent living, and community participation. School professionals work with family members to identify pertinent transition activities.

For each student with a disability beginning at age 14 (or younger, if determined appropriate by the IEP team), the student's IEP must include a statement of the transition service needs of the student under the applicable component of the IEP that focuses on the student's course of study (such as participation in advanced-placement courses or a vocational education program). For each student with a disability beginning at age 16 (or younger, if determined appropriate by the IEP team), the student's IEP must include a statement of the transition services needs of the student, including, if appropriate, a statement of the interagency responsibilities or any needed linkages.

Also, in a state that transfers rights at the age of majority, beginning at least one year before a student reaches the age of majority under state law, the student's IEP must include a statement that the student has been informed of his or her rights under Part B of the IDEA, if any, that will transfer to the student upon reaching the age of majority (IDEA, 1997).

Box 7.11 details information that IEP meeting participants should analyze and discuss in the development of the written program. Figure 7.9 illustrates the component parts of IEPs. Beginning and developing teachers may be involved in every step shown in Figure 7.9, either as a consultant to some students (e.g., Sarah) in a general education placement or as a direct service provider to others requiring specialized programming.

The IEP as a Working Document

As described earlier, specific written statements provide (1) a destination for teachers, parents, and students to strive for and (2) the basis for evaluating the effectiveness of the instructional activities and materials in helping students arrive at some prescribed skill level. An IEP helps parents and teachers in describing annual plans for students with diverse needs. While some teachers may view the IEP process as a dreaded chore, the IEP provides a true opportunity to plan with parents and other professionals. The IEP is the focal point for planning a student's program and coordinating services to provide for the student's needs. Developing and beginning teachers are wise to recognize that IEPs will be only as useful as the individuals implementing them in schools. Only by actually devising, monitoring, and continually revising IEPs for students requiring special education and related services can the true intent of federal and state laws be implemented.

Effective IEP Meetings

Professionals and parents who can work together and agree on a common set of objectives can share in the decisions regarding a student's programs. The legal intent of the IDEA is for parents to be equal partners in decision making; unfortunately, several researchers have painted a rather bleak picture of parental participation (Goldstein, Strickland, Turnbull, & Curry, 1980; Lynch & Stein, 1982; Morgan, 1982). General education teachers, too, may have concerns over their involvement in the IEP process and the guarantee that they will receive the assistance they need to instruct students with diverse needs. The thinking is that if classroom teachers are required to provide specially designed instruction to students with learning or behavioral problems, they have both the right and the responsibility to share in decisions regarding the nature of students' programs ("CEC Leads IDEA Testimony," 2004; Cooley & Yovanoff, 1996; Smith, Polloway, Patton, and Dowdy, 2004).

Ms. Edward, Sarah's general education teacher, expressed legitimate concerns about instructing Sarah effectively after the formal testing situation (Box 7.8). Special education and general education teachers must continue to work on teaming ideas for all students requiring support from school personnel. School professionals in the 21st century must reaffirm that the input of parents, administrators, psychologists, counselors, and special and general education teachers is valued and that their concerns for students and their educational programming are legitimate. Effective special educators continue to offer consulting services when students exit from the referral process and/or exit from placement in special classes.

Rights and Responsibilities of All IEP Participants. IEP team members share rights and responsibilities. Every member must believe that he or she can contribute to the written product and should work to reach consensus on the best interests of each student. Participants should be able to provide input on responsibility for instruction,

B ox 7.11	Critical Information for the IEP Team to Review

1. **Present educational levels:** This is a statement of the strengths and weaknesses of present levels of functioning. The present educational levels may be derived from teachers' informal or formal observations, classroom assessments, prereferral strategy analysis, or case studies. Present educational levels are the bases for annual goals.
2. **Measurable annual goals:** These are broad statements of students' anticipated educational outcomes and behavioral outcomes for the year. Annual goals may include generic statements of subject or performance areas that students will encounter during the year. Annual goals should be linked to both the present educational levels and the short-term objectives.
3. **Benchmarks or short-term objectives:** These are very specific statements of the educational and behavioral areas that teachers and parents anticipate students will master within the year. Benchmarks and short-term objectives should be written concisely and clearly in concrete terminology. It is best to use behavioral terminology easily observed by objective observers. All benchmarks and short-term objectives specify conditions (circumstances under which objectives are presented to students) and behavior (specifically, what students must do or how students are to act or behave).
4. **Statement of special services needed:** This statement must reflect the specific special education program and related services provided for students. Usually, this is written in the form of the category assigned to students (e.g., specific learning disability or physical impairment to designate special education programs; specialized transportation, specific counseling, or social services to designate related services). The special services noted should be based on the results of assessment reports and data collected from case studies during prereferral or referral. All information can be reported to the multidisciplinary team at the eligibility meeting or continuation placement meeting.
5. **Programs to be followed:** Participants in the IEP meeting must agree to all educational programs provided to special students. This component specifies the degree to which students are integrated with general students. Writers of IEPs must specify the amount of general education, special education, and in some areas, vocational education. The need for adaptive physical education or general physical education should be determined for each student.
6. **Initiation date and expected duration:** These dates must specify when programs are to take place and how long they will last. Most programs run one year from the date of the initiation, when parents first give written consent. IEPs can be updated and rewritten, however, anytime during the school year.
7. **Criteria to assess objectives:** Every short-term objective written for students should be assessed continually to monitor progress made toward goals and objectives. Mastery levels for objectives should be specified. This is usually done in terms of duration (e.g., for two minutes), trials (e.g., four out of five trials), or percentages (e.g., 80 percent mastery level for acceptable performance). All materials, evaluation procedures, and schedules used to monitor should be specified. When students have met the criterion specified, the person responsible for implementing the program area should write the date of mastery by the objective. If objectives are not mastered by the ending date of the IEP, they may be eliminated or revised for continuation on the next IEP. During periodic monitoring of the IEP, teachers may write progress reports on students' completion of objectives (e.g., "On January 24, 2004, Mun-Hee mastered three out of five trials for decoding skills; on March 16, 2004, Mun-Hee mastered four out of five trials for decoding skills").

curriculum planning, scheduling, roles in implementing the IEP, and specification of reasonable goals and objectives.

The rights that developing and beginning teachers will share with all other IEP team members include (1) the opportunity to attend all IEP meetings; (2) a chance to determine appropriate goals and objectives for the students they serve; (3) access to all

ASSESSMENT RESULTS

A. Prereferral strategies
B. Observations
C. Data of classroom teachers
D. Psychological testing using battery of tests

PRESENT EDUCATIONAL LEVELS

A. Academic strengths and needs
B. Sociobehavioral strengths and needs

MEASURABLE ANNUAL GOALS

A. Yearly academic outcomes
B. Sociobehavioral expectations
C. Transition goals

BENCHMARKS, OR SHORT-TERM OBJECTIVES

A. Conditions
B. Behavior
C. Criteria

ANNUAL UPDATE

Reevaluation for program continuation

EXAMPLES OF ASSESSMENT RESULTS

A. Tim completed 3/5 chapters in the Global Reading Series at level 6. He was observed by his reading teacher to be struggling with oral reading skills. He could not answer any comprehension questions after reading a paragraph aloud.

B. Ruby was assessed by the school psychologist with the WISC-R and received 98 verbal, 109 performance, and 104 full scale. Her behavior ratings by the classroom teacher and parent yielded no significant problems. She received a 4.0 in reading, a 3.6 in mathematics, and a 4.1 in spelling, revealing average achievement for a student of her age.

FIGURE 7.9 Individualized Education Programs

specialized materials, equipment, and curricula; (4) input and feedback related to all learning and behavioral management strategies devised for the student; (5) the opportunity to call additional IEP meetings as indicated by the student's mastery of goals and objectives; and (6) assistance in implementing individualized instruction from other multidisciplinary team members.

The responsibilities of IEP team participants are also pertinent and include (1) demonstrated preparedness for all meetings; (2) display of professionalism during every meeting; (3) demonstrated organization and timeliness for every meeting; (4) display of empathy, positive regard, and nonjudgmental statements of other team members; (5) concerted effort to actually implement the written IEP; (6) continual attempts to evaluate the appropriateness of the IEP; and (7) ongoing collaborative efforts underscoring the importance of parents and other professionals.

Behaviors of Special Education Teachers. New special education teachers should focus on a few behaviors that will facilitate the involvement of others in the IEP process. These behaviors, listed below, occur prior to, during, and after the IEP meeting. Many of these behaviors are vital for students who continue to receive a majority of their educational services in the general education classroom after formal testing or who are exiting from specialized programs, as well as for students who require special education and related services.

Prior to the IEP Meeting

- Observe confidentiality, report objectively, and qualify subjective judgments whenever possible. Always demonstrate this attitude when working with others.
- Be sensitive to the attitudes of other professionals involved with the student. Try to display empathy for their situation while still seeking appropriate solutions for the student with diverse needs.
- Try to anticipate potential problems that could arise during the IEP meeting. Write down possible solutions prior to the meeting's initiation.

During the IEP Meeting

- Be sure a leader is present to organize the meeting.
- Complete introductions before starting the formal meeting. Participants should sign an attendance sheet and identify their relationship to the student.
- Determine in advance the length of the meeting. The leader should state the purpose of the meeting, provide a brief outline of the expectations of the meeting, and guide the meeting according to appropriate timelines.
- Encourage the administration to limit professional participants to the smallest number possible. Consider the professional/parent ratio and the special education/ general education curriculum ratio. Realize that some may feel awkward when outnumbered.
- In speech and all written statements, avoid the use of teacher jargon that may be confusing to or too technical for some participants. Speak and write in a clear, understandable manner, but never miscalculate any participant's ability to understand and use data.
- Ensure that the evaluator summarizes all testing done and that parents are provided with a copy of the summary.
- If disagreements arise over any components of the evaluation, try to ensure that the leader asks participants to specify their disagreements in writing. Secure a copy of the disagreements for administrators not in attendance.
- Ensure that the leader states the placement-delivery system most appropriate for the student's needs (e.g., resource room, special class). Be sure that parents understand placement options by asking questions and encouraging their questions.
- Develop and write the IEP during the meeting. Never have a completed form for participants merely to sign.
- Develop a complete IEP before requesting participants' signatures.
- Specify in writing any goals, objectives, and instructional procedures that are appropriate to the student on the basis of identified strengths and weaknesses.
- Link interventions to assessments. Ensure that the present educational level is tied to the psychological report and other pertinent classroom data. Link present educational level to annual goals, annual goals to short-term objectives, and so forth.
- Write verifiable objectives for the student in all areas of concern, specifying conditions, behaviors, and criteria.
- Solicit input from parents and all participants during the meeting. Actively encourage the input and feedback of others through visual cues, communication, and appropriate questioning and responses as warranted. Use empathy, positive regard, and nonjudgmental statements in all communication efforts.
- Encourage the leader to summarize the meeting and to plan for follow-up strategies during future meetings. The leader should write down all follow-up plans and promise all participants a copy of the plans.

- Discuss the tentative date for the next IEP meeting. Ensure participants that it is at least within one year's time.

After the IEP Meeting

- Implement all goals and objectives devised at the meeting.
- Strive to match actual programming for the student to the written plan.
- Monitor goals and objectives consistently. Date all monitoring efforts.
- If changes need to be made, hold another meeting to revise the IEP.
- Continue to solicit input and feedback from all participants, including parents and general education teachers. Demonstrate a team approach.
- Continue to keep written records and reports affecting students, parents, and other professionals and all educational decisions made about the student.

Specific behaviors of teachers before, during, and after the meeting are included to represent the continuing process of developing a useful IEP. Effective IEPs are implemented by concerned teachers who know their students well, who continually collect and maintain useful written data on the students, and act in accordance with the student's rights and responsibilities in the IEP process.

Requirements of Annually Updated IEPs

IEPs must be updated yearly for students who receive special education and related services (IDEA, 1997). This means that school professionals must ask parents to attend an annual IEP meeting to reconsider all goals and objectives. Again, parents must be notified twice, and one notice must be in writing with a copy saved for school records. Attempts should be made to establish a mutually agreeable time and place. If the parents then refuse to attend the annual IEP meeting, school officials may continue with the meeting as planned without the parents. It is the responsibility of MDT members to initiate additional meetings when a student's IEP no longer matches his or her needs as the school year progresses.

Results and Implications of Reevaluations

It is a professional responsibility to reevaluate students every three years (IDEA, 1997). However, some states may require more frequent reevaluations. Just as eligibility meetings are held to determine whether students meet program entrance criteria, they must be held to determine if exit criteria have been met. Figure 7.10 is an example of an observation-recording form that may be used to help verify a student's readiness to exit from specialized programming.

Reevaluations determine whether a student's program should change. Developing and beginning teachers should become familiar with local and state exit procedures when a change in educational placement is warranted for a student. Box 7.12 lists four phases of an exit process to remove a student from special education. These steps are important aspects of placing students back in a general education classroom. Many data are required to verify that the general education classroom is the LRE for the student. Again, the role of the special educator is as a consultant to the general education teacher when the student exits from special education. Professionals continue to team to implement the exit process steps of Box 7.12.

WRITING REPORTS TO PARENTS AND TO OTHER PROFESSIONALS

Providing reports to parents and to other professionals should be a continuous process that all teachers undertake. As discussed earlier, progress reporting to parents of students with disabilities must occur with at least the same frequency of reports to parents of nondisabled students. Developing and beginning teachers must realize the importance of

Student's name Jenny Wain   Grade 6   School Fiddler Middle

Date 4/14/04   Level –   Teacher   Mr. Metan

Subject area/class ESE (English/Math)

Dates of observation   April 1, 2004   to April 4, 2004 (3rd period)

Number of students present 12 Teaching format used Small group; independent self-management

Target student's behavior (description prior to observation) During functional English and math classes, Jenny continues to be on task for 95 percent of total allocated time.

Important antecedents Observation of 90 percent to 100 percent on task compliant behavior reported by Mr. Metan for six weeks during the last three months.

✓ = mastery   X = absent

Behavior	1	2	3	4	5	6	7	8	9	10	11	12	13	14	15	Comments
1. Describe: Functional English: Followed teacher's directions 90 percent of time after given oral instructions.	✓	✓	✓	✓	✓	✓	✓	✓	X	✓	✓	✓	✓	✓	✓	1. 100% compliance (except 1 day due to absence).
2. Functional math: Completed math assignment with 80 percent accuracy in self-instructional format.	✓	✓	✓	✓	✓	✓	✓	✓	X	✓	✓	✓	✓	✓	✓	2. Met criterion level for every day (except due to absence).
3. Functional English: Was able to read and complete homework during study time.	✓	X	✓	✓	✓	✓	✓	✓	X	✓	✓	✓	✓	✓	X	3. 12/15 days completed required assignment with 90 percent accuracy.
4. Functional math: On task at least 75 percent of small-group math instruction	✓	✓	✓	✓	✓	✓	✓	✓	X	✓	✓	✓	✓	✓	✓	4. Exceeded criteria (to 90 percent time on task).
5.																
Days	1	2	3	4	5	6	7	8	9	10	11	12	13	14	15	

Important consequences Demonstrated continued self-help, self-management, and self-evaluation skills in functional English and math class. Responded well in small-group format.

Comments

Reevaluation focus Jenny may be a good candidate for consideration of exit from specialized programming. She has been able to keep up with her required assignments in both the special class and her mainstreamed class for the past 3 months, as reported by Mr. Metan.

Observer's Name/Title   Mr. Chew, Counselor

FIGURE 7.10   Observation Recording form Useful for Exit criteria

communication. Special educators, general educators, other professionals, and parents need a continual communication process—more than can be provided through yearly IEP meetings or case conferences and school-based committee meetings. Reports may be formal statements of a student's progress, or they may be informal notes on the day's events or the student's reactions to them. Teachers may take simple steps to communicate with parents and other team members. Such things as writing down expectations, teacher's

Box 7.12   **Four Phases of an Exit Process**

PHASE I: Plan (prior to reevaluation/exit conference)

- Identify a systematic data-collection procedure for exit from special education programming.
- Identify pertinent strategies based on the student's needs.
- Determine how information is to be observed and collected.
- Identify data gatherers in the special education class and, as necessary, in the general education class.
- Develop a time frame and schedule for data collection.

PHASE II: Data collection (prior to reevaluation/exit conference)

- Identify student demographic attributes.
- Collect background data on mastery of general education goals/objectives.
- Provide observational data, including teacher-made tests and behavioral ratings in the general and special education classes.
- Compare and contrast past standardized test results with past and present criterion-referenced tests.
- Collect work samples from the general and special education classes.
- Analyze personal health and sensory data.
- Compare past prereferral strategies with current strategies.
- Collect individual interest surveys and goals.

PHASE III: Data analysis (prior to/during exit conference)

- Provide comparison with norms after individualized reevaluation.
- Analyze strengths and weaknesses within the individual.
- Note patterns of behaviors and changes across time.
- Determine goals and objectives for the mainstream class.
- Determine timelines for mainstream transition.
- Develop consultation teaming strategies and schedules of observation to implement during mainstream transition.

PHASE IV: Mainstream implementation (student returns to general programming)

- Continue to observe and modify practices as needed.
- Collaborate with other professionals.
- Consult with parents.
- Implement goals and objectives in the mainstream class.
- Monitor progress and continue to collect data.
- Evaluate continually appropriateness of the new LRE.

roles, and anticipated study units to share with parents and professionals are good to implement at the start of the school year. Special education teachers may also try to elicit from others how they perceive their role in the student's development. In an informal planning session, teachers may write down ways of working together. To establish and maintain a continual positive rapport with the student's family, initiate the first written contact with the parents or guardians at the beginning of the school year. Sharing responses intermittently will establish a positive rapport with others.

Also, a plan could be devised at the IEP meeting to maintain communication throughout the year. Such a plan could schedule updated review meetings for parents and teachers to discuss the student's progress or set up a notebook the student could take back and forth from the general education teacher to the special education teacher (Schulz & Turnbull, 1984). Getting together on a consistent basis with parents and other teachers may help the novice teacher in understanding the importance of continual communication with all individuals significant to the student.

Developing and beginning teachers should send written data home to parents on an informal basis. For example, the teacher may send home periodic newsletters or class happenings to keep parents informed of units of instruction, to target special activities, to announce special events, or to request inexpensive resources or household items from home. It's a good idea to send a copy of all newsletters and class happenings to the general education teachers to keep them updated as well. Some school systems provide server space so their teachers can maintain a home page on the Internet. This is an excellent medium for two-way communications with parents who have access to the Internet. Another example is sending home notes of progress and specific praise for tasks accomplished. (Try to accentuate the positive rather than contacting parents only when negative behaviors occur. Again, send the same positive correspondence to the general education teachers to alert them when students have had a particularly productive day.) Still another idea is to have a suggestion box available and actively solicit written feedback from parents and other professionals.

In all correspondence with parents and with other professionals, special educators should remember to translate all technical information. Write notes, e-mails, letters, and information sheets in clear, uncluttered language. In all contacts with parents, consider the language and tone used. Communicate respect for the family's values, ideas, cultural background, and needs in all written correspondence.

Finally, all teachers should strive to establish and maintain a positive rapport with parents and other professionals by meeting formally and informally throughout the year. Providing a written invitation to all get-togethers and following up with a letter of thanks for their attendance at functions coordinated by the teacher are effective ways to help maintain positive communication throughout the year.

Who Can Help the Novice Teacher Understand the Ins and Outs of Paperwork?

This chapter stresses the importance of paperwork in the special education process. After reading it, developing and beginning teachers should recognize the link between up-to-date, accurate paperwork and effectiveness in teaching.

Teachers must understand the crucial role that paperwork plays in ensuring effective communication and an appropriate education to students with diverse needs. Effective paperwork will pinpoint those students who need to be removed from general education programming and those who can function adequately in the general education classroom. Professionals should strive to implement effective teaming ideals. Developing and beginning teachers must not view either the vast amount of documentation needed for the IEP process or the less formal means of communication with parents and other professionals as busywork.

Just as it is important to recognize the value of paperwork and be aware of potential strategies to alleviate pitfalls of stress and conflict associated with paperwork, teachers new to the special education profession must realize that they are not alone in generating, collecting, and maintaining quality paperwork for the benefit of their students. When new teachers comply with local, state, and federal monitoring and evaluation requirements, and document their compliance through effective paperwork, they help ensure a free and appropriate public education (FAPE) to every student they serve. Colleagues can help. Peer teachers can answer many questions about the realities of paperwork. General educators and special educators can share documentation ideas as well as effective teaching strategies. Administrators may provide critical feedback about the proper paperwork procedures. Parents and students can provide valuable information necessary to complete forms or other documentation. The teacher's own experience during meetings can help in making sense of the necessity of and logic behind paperwork requirements. The novice teacher will function best by asking many questions. By using some of the strategies and teaming suggestions offered throughout this textbook, developing and beginning teachers may begin even to like using paperwork and to value the utility of well-written documentation.

In Sarah's case, a well-documented set of data was vital in determining her LRE—the general education classroom. The special education teacher can provide assistance to her general education teacher through continual teaming efforts and support. Teachers in the twenty-first century should continue to team to ensure all students the best educational opportunities in the public school setting.

SUMMARY

This chapter provided developing and beginning teachers with an overview of the data collection involved in special education. The theme of the chapter, paperwork, is central to the role of the special educator. Initially, a rationale for the importance of writing tasks was provided, as was a comprehensive description of the documentation required for referral and communication tasks.

In addition, IEPs and IEP meetings were discussed. Specific behaviors of classroom teachers before, during, and after the IEP meeting were suggested.

The chapter ended with ideas to help teachers write reports and inform parents and general education teachers of classroom activities and student progress. Maintaining effective paperwork facilitates the teaming efforts that ensure the most appropriate educational setting for each student.

ACTIVITIES TO EXTEND YOUR KNOWLEDGE

1. Set up a panel presentation on "the importance of conducting instruction and other professional activities consistent with the requirements of law, rules and regulations, and local district policies and procedures." How would you present the panel to your students' families?
2. Conduct a literature review to determine your role in preventing the behavioral management problems and/or academic difficulties of students who are culturally and/or linguistically diverse. What important data would help in the prevention process?
3. Given a variety of observation and data-recording systems during your term or semester, select appropriate observation and data-recording systems when presented with common classroom problems (e.g., calling out, teasing, name calling, swearing, not following directions, not completing class assignments). What important written data will you glean when you match the observation and data-recording systems to the problem behaviors? How can these data help your students in the LRE? How can these data be used in a prereferral process?
4. Apply a behavioral diagnostic protocol to a problem or cluster of problems presented by students at your field site to determine whether active intervention is appropriate. What are important written data that you will share with your host teacher and university supervisor when you use the intervention?

5. Describe in an essay the essential ethical and practical issues that must be considered if teachers are to respect the rights of families when applying confidentiality to record-keeping and data collection procedures for infants, children, and youth with mild to moderate disabilities.

 POINT AND CLICK ABOUT THE PROFESSION

The following web sites highlight the chapter's theme of special education paperwork. Each of these listings can assist new teachers in their compliance with local, state, and federal mandates on behalf of students with disabilities.

National Center for the Dissemination of Disability Research
http://www.ncddr.org
This web site offers to new teachers important information on special education research—publications and other information.

OSERS IDEA '97 Home Page
http://www.ed.gov/offices/OSERS/IDEA
New teachers can access relevant information from the U.S. Department of Education's Office of Special Education and Rehabilitative services.

U.S. Department of Education Publications and Products
http://www.ed.gov/pubs/index.html
New teachers can access the U.S. Department of Education's web site for a wealth of information.

U.S. Government Printing Office
http://www.gpo.gov
The U.S. Government Printing Office offers information on relevant governmental documents and service. It can be used as a general site to perform individual research on selected topics important to teachers.

InfoHandler.com Electronic IEPs
http://www.infohandler.com
InfoHandler.com produces electronic IEP, child accounting, medical assistance billing, and other data management software. The software is cross-platform and in some cases web-based. The use of electronic media can decrease paperwork time significantly.

REFERENCES

Algozzine, B., Ysseldyke, J., & Christenson, S. L. (1983). An analysis of the incidence of special class placement: The masses are burgeoning. *Journal of Special Education, 17,* 141–147.

Bender, W. N. (2003). *Learning disabilities: Characteristics, identification and teaching strategies.* Needham Heights, MA: Allyn & Bacon.

Cartwright, G. P., Cartwright, C. A., & Ward, M. (1981). *Educating special learners.* Belmont, CA: Wadsworth.

CEC leads IDEA testimony at congressional hearings. (2004, March/April). *CEC Today,* 1.

Cooley, E., & Yovanoff, P. (1996). Supporting professionals-at-risk: Evaluating interventions to reduce burnout and improve retention of special educators. *Exceptional Children, 62*(4), 336–355.

Gloeckler, T., & Simpson, C. (1988). *Exceptional students in regular classrooms: Challenges, services, and methods.* Mountain View, CA: Mayfield.

Goldstein, S., Strickland, B., Turnbull, A. P., & Curry, L. (1980). An observational analysis of the IEP conference. *Exceptional Children, 46,* 278–286.

Hardman, M. L., Drew, C. J., & Egan, M. W. (2005). *Human exceptionality.* Needham Heights, MA: Allyn & Bacon.

Individuals with Disabilities Education Act (Public Law 101–476). (1990, October). Washington, DC: U.S. Office of Special Education and Rehabilitative Services.

Lynch, E., & Stein, R. (1982). Perspectives on parent participation in special education. *Exceptional Education Quarterly, 3*(2), 73–84.

Mercer, C. L., & Mercer, A. (2004). *Teaching students with learning disabilities.* Needham Heights, MA: Allyn & Bacon.

Morgan, D. P. (1982). Parent participation in the IEP process: Does it enhance appropriate education? *Exceptional Education Quarterly, 3*(2), 33–40.

Salvia, J., & Ysseldyke, J. E. (1991). *Assessment* (4th ed.). Boston: Houghton Mifflin.

Schulz, J. B., & Turnbull, A. P. (1984). *Mainstreaming handicapped students; A guide for classroom teachers* (2nd ed.). Needham Heights, MA: Allyn & Bacon.

Smith, T. E. C., Polloway, E., Patton, J. R., & Dowdy, C. A. (2004). *Teaching students with special needs in inclusive settings.* Needham Heights, MA: Allyn & Bacon.

Yell, M. (2001). *Special education law.* Needham Heights, MA: Allyn & Bacon.

Ysseldyke, J., & Algozzine, B. (1984). *Introduction to special education.* Boston: Houghton Mifflin.

## CHAPTER 8

Positive Behavior Management and Support: Promoting Discipline and Self-Control

with Sunil Misra

Chapter Outline

In this chapter, we will

- review the importance of having comprehensive school and classroom management programs

- discuss alternatives for the prevention of problem behaviors

- specify how to develop rules, procedures, and behavioral supports that can facilitate the development of well-ordered instructional environments

- present alternatives for effectively responding to instances of student misbehavior

- present functional behavioral assessment and intervention alternatives for addressing student misbehavior

- discuss procedures that assist students in developing internal self-control and problem-solving protocols

- demonstrate a protocol for designing and implementing individual behavior-change interventions

A PROFESSIONAL GLIMPSE

Beginning his second practicum experience, Seth McCabe sensed that he was on the road to completing his teacher preparation program. Having changed his career from business administration (being a rental agent at the new luxury high-rise did little to fulfill his need for a job with impact) to teaching, Seth was anxious to finish the certification program and begin his new career. This second practicum was at Brookville Middle School, a placement that was generally regarded as a "good school." He was assigned to Ms. Morgan, an "inclusion teacher" who supported several general educators through consultation and delivered direct instruction in resource and cooperative teaching settings. Seth thought this was a great practicum because he was able to observe a variety of service delivery alternatives and see how several educators approached instruction and behavior management.

For the first two periods of the day, Ms. Morgan cotaught with two subject area teachers, Mr. Ropelt in English and Mr. Connelly in social studies. In each class, a group of six students met with her for a portion of the instructional period to reinforce aspects of the content area lesson; the remaining students worked with the general educator. From Seth's perspective, that is where the similarities between the two classes ended. Specifically, there were striking differences between the two classes in terms of student behavior. The English class was structured and positive, with Mr. Ropelt reviewing rules, procedures, and expectations routinely. He provided students with choices and supports for success, and prosocial behavior and solid academic performance were recognized in a developmentally appropriate, good-natured fashion. Inappropriate behavior was addressed immediately, and students were aware of the consequences of their actions. Both Mr. Ropelt and Ms. Morgan seemed to genuinely enjoy the academic and social interactions in their lessons.

In sharp contrast, the climate in the social studies class was dismal. The very same students from the previous period's class misbehaved at an extremely high rate. Mr. Connelly, the teacher, seemed ill at ease in front of the group and rarely engaged in positive interactions with the students. Few supports for success were provided, and it seemed like Mr. Connelly was more interested in what the students did not know rather than what they had completed. Unlike what was observed in Mr. Ropelt's class, there was no clear articulation of rules and procedures, and the students seemed to talk out and disrupt the lesson regularly. Mr. Connelly did little to stop the students until he became so frustrated that he would send a student to the office. Ms. Morgan tried to redirect the students by reminding them of how they were supposed to behave, but it was far too little to stop the spread of the group contagion.

Seth considered the differences between the two environments and how a series of preventative strategies and teacher interactions could alter how students respond to instruction. When asked by Ms. Morgan to comment on the differences between the two classes, Seth diplomatically mentioned how different the two teachers were in their approach to behavior management: specifically, Mr. Ropelt made greater use of explicit prompts and cues and recognized positive behaviors at a much higher rate than Mr. Connelly. Ms. Morgan smiled! The university had sent her a good one!

*W*hen asked what concerns them most about upcoming student-teaching assignments, developing teachers typically express apprehension and anxiousness about classroom behavioral management. Specifically, many preservice (and, unfortunately, many in-service) teachers worry about losing control of students in their charge and about possible encounters with students who do not comply with implicit and explicit behavioral standards. Most developing teachers find that they are able to apply management skills in their university-based training programs. Feelings of apprehension persist, however, when student teachers move on to their own first classrooms. In surveys of beginning teachers (e.g., Wilson, Ireton, & Wood, 1997), management and remediation of student misbehavior are among the most pressing problems reported. In a review of studies concerned with the perceived problems of beginning elementary and secondary teachers, Veenman (1984) found that classroom discipline and student motivation ranked 1 and 2 among a listing of 24 problems. These concerns are also shared by the general public: In almost all of the past two decades of Gallup Polls of Public Attitudes About Public Schools, lack of discipline in schools has ranked high among the major concerns facing the public schools.

Because many students with mild to moderate disabilities tend to engage in a wider range and higher rate of challenging behaviors than most other students in educational settings, it is essential that prospective special education teachers become effective classroom managers and be able to share successful approaches with general education colleagues. In most university-based training programs for special educators, issues and strategies related to discipline and the management of classroom behavioral problems receive considerable attention. Prospective special educators typically complete course work in and projects on (1) the characteristics of child and adolescent behavioral problems, (2) applied behavioral analysis, and (3) classroom management alternatives. The lesson that emerges is that there are no "magic" formulas or recipes to ensure appropriate student behavior.

On the positive side, however, a series of general and specific strategies, used correctly, can increase the probability of a successfully managed classroom. These general strategies provide the organizational structure for our discussion of effective classroom management. Because it is generally recognized that schoolwide comprehensive management programs form the foundation for successful management programs (e.g., Dwyer, Osher, & Hoffman, 2000), we first discuss the major components of successful schoolwide comprehensive management programs. Unfortunately, it is not always possible (or prudent) for developing and beginning teachers to advocate for, initiate, or organize important schoolwide reform efforts. Therefore, we provide specific techniques and basic teacher attitudes, consistent with the schoolwide approach, that can be used in the prevention, management, and resolution of problem behaviors in individual classrooms. We also provide guidelines for the completion of functional behavioral assessments and formal behavior-change efforts for individuals and groups of students.

COMPREHENSIVE SCHOOL AND CLASSROOM MANAGEMENT PROGRAMS

As it should be for all students, the development of effective management procedures for students with mild to moderate disabilities is a team effort. Although the ultimate responsibility for the maintenance of order in the special education setting rests with

Pause and Reflect About the Profession 8.1

Do students with disabilities present greater behavioral challenges in school than their nondisabled peers? According to reviews of the research (Alliance Project, 2000; Leone, Mayer, Malmgren, & Meisel, 2000), there is considerable evidence suggesting that a disproportionately high percentage (approximately 20 percent) of students who are suspended are students with disabilities, with those with learning disabilities and emotional disturbance being the most overrepresented. The suspension-related behaviors for those with disabilities tend to be similar in nature to those for students without disabilities and are for the most part nonviolent. How do these figures compare to your experiences at your practicum site? Can you articulate reasons why students with disabilities may be more prone to behaviors leading to suspension? Knowing that instructional time is a valuable commodity for these students, what can be done to reduce the numbers of suspensions among students with disabilities?

Pause and Reflect About the Profession 8.2

Discipline in the schools continues to be a major concern of the general public. Many claim that today's children and youth are more difficult to manage than those of the past and that schools are spending more time on discipline than on instruction. In your opinion, are these assertions true? If so, what factors are contributing to the breakdown in order in our schools? If these assertions are false, why is it that so many people believe that schools are failing to manage the troubling behaviors of students? Be prepared to back up your opinions!

the classroom teacher, active support and participation from building administrators, general education colleagues, and related service personnel are essential for the maintenance of successful management programs. Because most students with mild to moderate disabilities will have contact with members of the school staff, it is critical that management plans, classroom rules, and special interventions designed to foster inclusive programming be developed with input from all relevant personnel.

A prerequisite to successful collaborative and supportive working relationships within schools is clear and open communication. Unfortunately, open communication and cooperation in school settings do not automatically happen. As with most complex social systems, schools sometimes become places where individual and immediate concerns take precedence over activities that promote communication and teamwork. Successful cooperative efforts require hard work, persistence, diplomacy, flexibility, and a genuine belief that the efforts of a team can enhance the delivery of educational services to students. Box 8.1 provides some generic guidelines that beginning teachers can use to facilitate open communication and teamwork in their schools.

A number of models (e.g., Dwyer & Osher, 2000; Lewis & Sugai, 1999; Rosenberg & Jackman, 1997; White, Algozzine, Audette, Marr, & Ellis, 2001) for comprehensive school and classroom management have appeared in the literature. Rosenberg and Jackman (1997, 2003), for example, have presented an approach that promotes the development of positive, schoolwide comprehensive management plans. Adapted from the work of Curwin and Mendler (1988) and other researchers, this process-based, operational model has collaborative teams of teachers, school administrators, and related

---

Box 8.1

Three Strategies for Facilitating Open Communication and Teamwork in School

1. Meet with the school administrator responsible for student disciplinary actions prior to the start of the school year. The agenda for this meeting should include (a) the correspondence between schoolwide discipline policies and the behavioral management programs to be implemented as part of students' IEPs; (b) the proposed classroom rules, procedures, and consequences for noncompliance; and (c) suggested strategies to ensure consistency in instances when a student's behavior necessitates removal from the classroom.
2. Meet, both formally and informally, with other teachers in the building. The nature of the academic and classroom management program within the special education setting should be discussed, and issues related to the mainstreaming of eligible students should be highlighted. Arrange a mutually satisfying mode for communicating student progress throughout the academic year.
3. Alert the school support staff (e.g., psychologists, therapists, lunch aides, custodians) to the unique character and demands of your classroom. Discuss provisions that will enable easy access to support services.

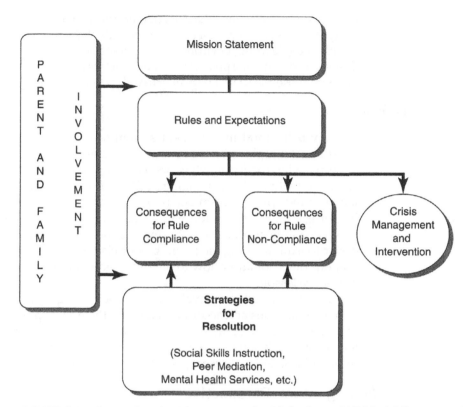

FIGURE 8.1 Comprehensive Management for All Students: PAR Model Components

service personnel work together within a prescriptive format to come to consensus on plans and strategies to (1) PREVENT the occurrence of troubling behavior, (2) ACT in response to instances of rule compliance and noncompliance in a consistent fashion, and (3) RESOLVE many of the issues that underlie or cause troubling behavior. In essence, the PAR model (signifying the emphases on prevention, action, and resolution) allows building-based teams to design their own unified plan of action using procedures that have been documented to work. Figure 8.1 illustrates the specific components of the PAR model that team members design.

As part of the collaborative process, each team completes a structured, jargon-free PAR management plan that is readily understood by all involved in the education and treatment of students (e.g., parents, students, related service personnel, bus drivers). Participants begin by agreeing on rules, expectations, and procedures that can preempt problem behaviors. This is followed by the development of specific procedures for the implementation of the positive consequences that promote rule compliance. An intervention hierarchy for negative consequences (for noncompliance) and specific crisis procedures are also developed. Finally, specific resolution interventions and logistical concerns regarding implementation are discussed.

The sections that follow suggest how developing and beginning teachers can apply these processes in their own schools and classrooms.

PREVENTING PROBLEM BEHAVIORS

The key to successfully managing the high-activity learning environments that serve students with mild to moderate disabilities is prevention. Developing and beginning teachers must be aware of the antecedent events related to student behavior that they as teachers can influence. Antecedent events include any expectations, attitudes, environmental conditions, and teacher behaviors that typically precede a student's response. As noted in Chapter 3, many antecedent events, especially those related to planning instruction and organizing the learning environment, are associated with increased academic achievement. Therefore, it is not surprising that many factors associated with effective instruction overlap with those associated with effective classroom management.

Effective Instruction

For any behavioral management system to succeed, effective, motivating instruction must be taking place. To that end, it is critical that developing and beginning teachers view their instructional behaviors as central to the management process. Effective instruction that is both challenging and structured for student success can be the biggest factor in reducing problem behaviors. In many settings, a major cause of troubling behavior is student frustration with academic content and how it is presented. Students who encounter repeated failure find it easier to "act out" than to "act dumb." It is far easier to explain being the tough guy or class clown to one's peers than it is to explain that one does not know how to organize and integrate the material from a social studies or science lesson.

The implication for developing and beginning teachers is clear: Planning instructional adaptations and accommodations is the first step in developing a comprehensive management plan. Students who are successful in meeting motivational academic challenges will be less likely to act up; they will be too busy garnering the internal and external reinforcers that accompany a job well done.

An Appropriate Management Perspective

The management of student behavior is not a cut-and-dried technical activity devoid of the human touches of empathy and emotion. Although systematic, scientifically validated techniques are applied for the purpose of maximizing student learning and social adjustment, management techniques are delivered through a series of interpersonal exchanges between teacher and students. Close examination of these exchanges reveals that several intangible (difficult to operationalize) behaviors, personal qualities, and attitudes are prerequisites for successfully managing students with mild to moderate disabilities.

Respect for Students. Successful classroom managers generally like their students and respect them as individuals (Good & Brophy, 1987). Demonstrations of this affection and respect, however, need not be superficial or overly dramatic. Genuine concern for the welfare of each student is demonstrated through (1) regular private interactions that exude warmth and a desire to know students individually, (2) facial gestures and body language that indicate acceptance and respect, (3) a vocal tone that shows patience and understanding, and (4) the use of enthusiasm and humor to ease tension in anxiety-filled situations. Even in the face of frequent misbehavior, effective classroom managers make it clear that students are differentiated from their behaviors. Students are shown that they are valued even when their inappropriate behaviors are not given approval.

Pause and Reflect About the Profession 8.3

It is relatively easy to say that we as teachers respect students or have high expectations for their continued growth and achievement. It is much more difficult to actually demonstrate that we hold these beliefs. How can teachers actually demonstrate to their students that they hold them in high regard and believe that they can have continued success in the school environment? Be sure that these are tangible things that students will be able to recognize.

Appropriate Expectations. Researchers investigating teachers' expectations of their students have found that students are aware of (Thorson, 1996) and tend to live up to the expectations their teachers have for them. The professional literature is replete with examples of how such negative self-fulfilling prophecies influence academic performance. Similarly, negative expectations can have a direct influence on rates of student misbehavior. Students considered to be behavioral problems are more likely to act out if expectations regarding the continuation of these types of behaviors are communicated with strength and consistency. In many instances, identified problem students have little incentive to change their behavioral patterns and typically conform to the negative expectations presented by significant others in their environment.

In several implicit and explicit ways, developing and beginning teachers can communicate positive expectations for behavior. First, similar to academic programming, reasonable goals related to how students should behave must be developed. This entails knowing what behaviors are expected of students during school and class activities. Second, expectations must be communicated to students in a no-nonsense, straightforward fashion. This communication can take several forms, including (1) the formulation of positively stated classroom rules, (2) the design of an overall classroom management system in which all students are treated equally, and (3) the delivery of consistent consequences for both compliance and noncompliance with the components of the management system. Furthermore, teachers need to convey that a student's acting-out history or "teachers' lounge hearsay" has nothing to do with how consequences will be applied under the current management system. Each student should be made aware that his or her current behavior is evaluated in relation to current standards rather than past years' rule infractions or subjective behind-the-scenes gossip.

Credibility, Dependability, and Assertiveness. Effective classroom managers are models of appropriate behaviors. They practice what they preach and can be counted on to be consistent and reliable in the enforcement of classroom rules and procedures. Teachers' credibility is established when (1) their verbal behavior coincides with their instrumental behavior and (2) they respect and adhere consistently to their daily responsibilities within the classroom. Once correspondence between words and actions is established, students will come to depend on teachers' verbal intentions and will test limits less frequently. Credibility and dependability will not develop, however, if a teacher chats sociably with other teachers during planned activities, makes empty threats, or enforces rules selectively rather than consistently (Good & Brophy, 1987).

Effective classroom management, like effective teaching, requires that a teacher convey strong leadership qualities. This does not mean that students with or without disabilities need to be taught by power-hungry, harsh, or "in your face" dictatorial men and women. Strong leaders convey authority with subtlety, tact, and diplomacy rather than through intimidation and intrusiveness. Developing and beginning teachers can convey a strong leadership presence by (1) using clear, calm, controlled, and defined statements when requesting student compliance; (2) being self-assured, confident, and consistent when delivering the consequences of a student's misbehavior; (3) not arguing with students; and, most important, (4) conveying to students that any problems and concerns that may arise will be addressed in an empathic and constructive manner (Weber & Roff, 1983; Westling & Koorland, 1988).

Withitness. Withitness refers to a teacher's ability to be aware of students' actions and to communicate that awareness to students (Kounin, 1970). Teachers possessing withitness position themselves so that they can readily monitor the multitude of events occurring in their classrooms. They seem to have a sixth sense or "eyes in the back of their head" and can deal successfully with more than one matter at a time. Their heightened sensitivity to the events in a classroom allows "with it" teachers to prevent disruptions before they grow into serious management problems.

Although withitness, per se, cannot be directly taught in methods courses, beginning and developing special education teachers can enhance their development of this important skill by (1) arranging their classrooms to allow for easy observations of all instructional activities, (2) regularly monitoring their classrooms, (3) responding to those small events and minor disruptions that often precede major behavioral problems, (4) attempting to handle multiple classroom situations simultaneously, and (5) communicating to students an awareness of what is going on in and around the classroom.

Preparation

One sure way to promote disruption among students is to be unprepared for lessons or activities. Most students, particularly those with mild disabilities, are likely to act out if they are not engaged in purposeful activities. Moreover, teachers who appear unprepared for the day's events are a poor model for their students. Lack of readiness on the part of a teacher signals to the students that planned classroom activities are not valued and that preparation for academic work is unimportant. Not surprisingly, teachers who are consistently unprepared for lessons have difficulties motivating and managing their students.

Thorough preparation is a difficult, time-consuming task, particularly for developing and beginning teachers. Nonetheless, time spent in preparation saves both time and anguish in the long run: Prepared teachers spend less time dealing with student behavior problems. Effective classroom managers prepare for their lessons and know how to keep their students on task with productive and educationally relevant work. Prepared teachers (1) have well-developed and -organized lesson plans, (2) start lessons promptly and keep to a consistent schedule, (3) have student assignments ready for distribution and board work prepared prior to the scheduled start of the lesson, (4) keep the materials necessary for a planned activity close at hand, and (5) take care of grading and record-keeping responsibilities promptly and efficiently. Teachers highlight the importance of class activities by preparing for them and by not wasting lesson time on clerical or organizational tasks.

Physical Environment

As discussed in Chapter 3, the physical design of the classroom environment can influence students' academic and social behavior. It is especially important to consider the relationships between physical environmental variables and behaviors of students with mild to moderate disabling conditions. Such students are easily influenced by events that are often regarded as merely neutral in most learning situations. Teachers of highly distractible students, for example, often find it essential to arrange tables for group instruction in such a way that students' lines of vision are narrowly focused in the direction of a chalkboard.

As a general rule, the proper arrangement of the classroom can assist teachers in managing their students by preventing student discomfort, decreasing opportunities for disruptive behavior, increasing levels of task-oriented behavior, and facilitating the quality and quantity of social interactions among students (Paine, Radicci, Rossellini, Deutchman, & Darch, 1983). What follows is a brief description of what teachers should consider when arranging the physical environment to prevent inappropriate behavior.

Ensure Student and Teacher Safety and Comfort. Students, particularly those with a low tolerance for frustration, may act out if they perceive a threat to their safety or experience physical discomfort. Teachers are also affected by the physical conditions of a school or classroom and may overreact to student behaviors if faced with persistent discomfort. The physical comfort of individuals in classrooms depends on such factors as lighting, temperature, ventilation, and noise level. Smith, Neisworth, and Greer (1978) recommend that, to ensure physical comfort in learning environments, (1) the lighting be warm and free from glare, (2) the room temperature be controlled to fall within a moderate range (68–74°F) with adequate humidity, (3) circulated fresh air be available at all times, and (4) the noise level be controlled so that the ongoing activities in one room do not disturb others.

Provide Security In and Around School. It is often said that events that occur in schools are a direct reflection of happenings in society at large. In the case of crime and the fear and anxiety associated with such violations, this is an unfortunate reality. Many students possess legitimate fears about attending certain schools. To many students, schools are not places of learning but rather places where they must contend with repeated threats to their safety, property, and psychological well-being. Obviously, the fear of injury or loss of property can deleteriously influence students' behaviors in the classroom. Safe learning environments are possible, however, if school administrators, teachers, parents, and students work together to promote a security-conscious philosophy.

Developing and beginning teachers can do their part by (1) following assignments related to monitoring student entry into, movement in, and exit from school; (2) ensuring that parents are made aware of safe avenues for students to travel to and from school; (3) closely monitoring students during recess activities and reporting any strangers who may be loitering either in or around the building; (4) securing the school's, teachers', and students' valuables and reporting instances of theft, vandalism, and property destruction; and (5) delivering immediate and effective consequences to those students who break the rules. Most important, however, teachers should educate students to be security conscious both inside and outside school. Furthermore, specific school and class policies regarding security should be developed and transmitted to students, parents, and the community.

Arrange Furniture to Minimize Disruptions. Classroom furnishings should be safe, comfortable, durable, and age- and size-appropriate for students in the class. Available classroom space should be organized to promote pro-social behavior and to facilitate academic achievement. In Chapter 3, several effective classroom configurations were presented, along with specific guidelines for the placement of furniture for students with mild to moderate disabilities. The classroom design should provide (1) both public and private student work spaces, (2) a convenient and unobstructed view of the entire classroom, and (3) easy access to instructional materials.

Teachers of students with greater tendencies toward overactivity, distractibility, and aggression should also attend to traffic patterns within their classrooms. First, students' desks should be spaced adequately, ensuring that each student can work independently without disturbing others. Second, access to high-action or -activity areas (e.g., the work "in-box," the pencil sharpener) should be designed to facilitate an easy flow of traffic. Paths to such areas should be away from major group and independent work centers, and teachers should try to limit the number of students moving to such areas at the same time. Movements within and between activities should be smooth, with little loss of positive momentum. Most important, the major high-traffic areas should be located in different quadrants of the room to avoid the oversaturation of one part of the room and allow for the maximum use of available space.

Keep Classrooms Neat and Trim. There are four good reasons for keeping learning environments neat and picked up. First, by taking care of and storing instructional materials in their assigned containers or areas, preparation time for lessons can be minimized. Students and teachers can begin their tasks with little need for frustrating "search" activities. Second, unsupervised high-interest materials can draw student attention away from an assigned task. By storing materials, teachers limit these potential distractions that often start instances of misbehavior. Third, the storage of personal belongings prevents minor and nagging disturbances involving lost and stolen possessions. By providing adequate and secure storage of personal belongings, conflicts involving personal property losses can be minimized. Finally, students with mild to moderate disabilities tend to be unusually hard on both the hardware and the consumable supplies in their classrooms. Highlighting and modeling procedures that promote respect for property can result in students demonstrating increased levels of care with instructional materials.

RULES, PROCEDURES, AND BEHAVIORAL SUPPORTS

Rules and procedures allow teachers to communicate the behavioral standards and expectations of the classroom environment to their students. Rules identify, define, and operationalize a teacher's specific conceptualization of acceptable behavior; procedures delineate the steps necessary for the successful and appropriate completion of an activity, task, or operation. Concise and unambiguous rules and procedures serve as discriminative stimuli for appropriate classroom behavior. When planned and implemented correctly, both rules and procedures can guide, motivate, and remind students to adhere to stated standards. The research literature is clear in its support of the use of rules and procedures: Teachers who establish reasonable, definable, and clearly understood rules and procedures are effective classroom managers (Smith & Rivera, 1995; Weber & Roff, 1983).

As was detailed in Chapter 3, rules and procedures need to be introduced correctly and maintained adequately throughout the school year. In regard to introducing rules and procedures, developing and beginning teachers should (1) identify the specific behaviors expected of students and the procedures they must follow, (2) discuss and teach rules and procedures beginning on the first day of school, (3) present students with a solid rationale for the rules and procedures, (4) involve students in the formulation and development of these classroom standards, (5) phrase rules and procedures positively rather than negatively, and (6) keep the number of rules and procedures to a minimum.

By following several guidelines, the strength and integrity of agreed-on rules and procedures will be maintained. First, rules and procedures should be posted in areas visible to students. Second, rules and procedures should be taught and practiced throughout the school year. Like any skill or concept, rules and procedures need to be taught in a complete and systematic fashion. Lessons should be designed that contain relevant exemplars, role-playing demonstrations, and opportunities for guided and independent practice. Brief reviews of lesson-specific rules can prompt students to adhere to the behavioral expectations specific to a particular activity. Third, teachers should model and demonstrate the correct way of adhering to school and classroom procedures at regular intervals throughout the school year. Finally, because the failure of many classroom management systems stems from less than consistent adherence to and compliance with the management system, teachers should monitor whether they themselves follow the stated rules and procedures and should provide consequences consistently. We further explore the development of effective consequences in the next section of this chapter.

It is also critical that positive behavioral supports be provided for students who have trouble complying with the rules. Rather than a change in the expectations for rule and procedural compliance, positive behavioral supports are proactive adjustments that assist a student in complying with a particular rule or procedural expectation. If a middle school student with an attention problem repeatedly has difficulty getting to a particular class on time, the teacher can choose to make a proactive accommodation (a buddy system, a self-monitoring plan) that will increase the probability that the student will have the expected level of success complying with the stated rule or procedure.

Figure 8.2 provides a format for the development of school and classroom rules as well as positive behavioral supports. The format provides a place for the general schoolwide rule, what the rule means in each teacher's individual classroom, how the

Rules Development Worksheet			
General Case Rule	Meaning of Rule in My Class	Teaching the Rule	Available Supports
The students will be prepared for class.	The students will be in their seat at the ringing of the bell with books, writing tools, drill, and homework.	• Role playing "The Prepared Student" • Display prepared materials	• Have pencils available for borrowing • Praise to those who are prepared. • Provide visual and verbal reminders. • Checklist of supplies needed to be prepared.

FIGURE 8.2   Rules Development Worksheet

teacher will teach the rule to students, and what supports are available for promoting rule compliance. Figure 8.3 provides a listing of support strategies adapted from the work of Topper, Williams, Leo, Hamilton, and Fox (1994) that can be used to prevent the occurrence of troubling behaviors.

TAKING ACTION: RESPONDING TO STUDENT MISBEHAVIOR

When we speak of taking action, we are referring to preplanned initial responses to student behavior. These responses include (1) surface management of minor annoyances, (2) functional behavioral assessments, (3) consequences for rule and procedure compliance and noncompliance, and (4) crisis management.

Surface Management Techniques

Surface management techniques are commonsense "stop-gap" methods for dealing with minor instances of troubling behaviors. As observed by Long and Newman (1965), the three techniques of planned ignoring, signal interference, and proximity control are positive alternatives for dealing with troubling behaviors because they do not embarrass or even identify the student who is misbehaving but still have the potency to get the student back into the flow of the lesson.

Most teachers use some surface techniques intuitively. For example, it is not unusual to see effective classroom managers using the technique of proximity control, moving close to a student who may be approaching a level of frustration to preempt a blowup. Because a teacher is typically regarded as a source of protection, strength,

Increase Students' Control and Choices

- Ask students what they need in order to have a better experience at school.
- Include students in planning and problem solving.
- Increase the number, variety, and importance of the decisions that students make.
- Support students having flexibility in their daily schedules.
- Grant students legitimate power—involve students in leadership roles.
- Support students in transitioning to the next class/activity at a different time.
- Add interesting activities and experiences matched to students' individual needs.
- Support students in self-evaluating their work.
- Support students in leaving class when needed.
- Support students in choosing testing methods.
- Develop assignments that emphasize students' strengths and talents.

Increase Students' Opportunities for Positive Attention

- Assign students to teacher advisors/mentors.
- Increase the number of friends or allies who know and spend time with students.
- Engage family, friends, faculty, and students in supporting the students.
- Identify an adult mentor within the community.
- Increase the number of community activities to which students have access.
- Support students in joining after-school groups/clubs/teams.
- Use teaching assistants to help all students in the class rather than pairing an assistant directly with one student.
- Speak and react to students in ways that model respect and friendship.
- Develop a peer buddy system for students.

Increase Students' Status, Self-Esteem, Image

- Support students in becoming peer mentors/tutors.
- Support student involvement in community service activities.
- Give students assignments that will "guarantee" success.
- Add pro-social skills to students' curricula.
- Give students high-status classroom/school jobs/roles.
- Increase the amount of time that students spend in roles that offer the best opportunities to express their natural abilities or strong interests (e.g., drawing, music, drama, pottery, sports, reading, math).

Match Expected Responses/Testing Methods to Student Strengths

- Support students in communicating ideas and demonstrating learning in a variety of ways (art, music, dance, poetry, oral presentations).
- Avoid requiring students to respond in ways that are likely to produce extreme stress or anxiety (e.g., reading aloud for a nonreader, essay exam for a poor writer).
- When anxiety-producing situations (e.g., oral presentations, final exams) cannot be avoided, provide additional support tailored to students' needs.
- Provide extra practice in nonthreatening, supportive situations.
- Read the test to students.
- Test students in private.
- Give students extra time.
- Break tests into short segments.

FIGURE 8.3 Support Strategies for Preventing Problem Behavior

Source: Adapted from *A Positive Approach to Understanding and Addressing Challenging Behavior*, by K. Topper, W. Williams, K. Leo, R. Hamilton and T. Fox, 1994, Burlington: University of Vermont.

Use the Physical Arrangement to Support Classroom Management

- Seat students in the classroom in a position that will best meet their needs (e.g., near the front of the classroom, near the teacher, near the door, near a window, near a supportive peer, away from unsupportive peers).
- Arrange the classroom to prevent problems from occurring and to facilitate cooperative interactions and the sharing of materials and ideas between students and adults.
- Support students in leaving the classroom (e.g., to go on a mission to the office, to run an errand, to go to the guidance counselor) when anxious, angry, or fearful.
- Limit student access to peers or adults who tend to set them off.
- Model appropriate ways of interacting with students and other adults.
- Make sure all materials are handy and set up in advance.

FIGURE 8.3   continued

authority, and identification, students will tend to stop their impulsive actions without the need for any type of verbal cue or prompt.

One of the most frequently used surface management techniques is planned ignoring. Similar to the behavioral technique of extinction, planned ignoring is the conscious attempt to not feed into the student's need for immediate gratification; this technique works best for minor behaviors that are likely to fade away if they are not reinforced.

Signal interference comprises the nonverbal gestures, eye contact, noises, and body postures that a teacher uses to communicate to students that their behaviors are inappropriate. These actions signal to students that their behavior needs to change.

Interest boosting is a direct intervention to reenergize a student's interest in the assigned activity. If a student's attention to an activity is diminishing, it is often helpful for an adult to demonstrate some genuine interest in the assignment. This interest can be expressed by asking how challenging the assignment is or by indicating a personal interest in the content areas being explored.

Tension decontamination through humor is the diplomatic use of humor to reduce a tense or anxiety-filled situation. In most situations, this tactic should take the form of teacher-based "self-deprecating" comments and should not be done at the expense of one or two vulnerable students. As with the use of humor in public-speaking situations, a good rule to follow here is "When in doubt, don't!"

Finally, antiseptic bouncing is a technique used to safely remove a student from a potentially serious behavioral event in a nonpunitive fashion. Some students just need some time away from the situation if they are to regain control over themselves. With antiseptic bouncing, the teacher can ask the particular student to deliver a message, wash up, or complete a task that requires movement to another part of the school. This intervention is characterized as "antiseptic" because the intent is to redirect the behavior rather than provide a negative consequence. Developing and beginning teachers should be cautioned that the overuse of this technique can be quite detrimental: With too much "bouncing," students will see that they can get out of their responsibilities by merely acting up.

These are just a sampling of the more common surface management techniques used by successful veteran teachers. For a more complete discussion, readers are urged to review the classic work by Long and Newman (1965). These techniques are by no means a substitute for a well-designed, comprehensive management program; they do, however, assist in getting students back in the flow of the classroom with minimal intrusiveness.

Functional Behavioral Assessments

What Is a Functional Behavioral Assessment? The IDEA calls for schools to implement specific disciplinary procedures when working with students who are identified as or suspected of having disabilities and who exhibit significant behavior problems.

Pause and Reflect About the Profession 8.4

Refer to the brief descriptions of the surface management techniques provided in the text, and reflect on how you have either observed or used these techniques. For each of the techniques listed below, specify the type of behavior to which it was applied. Also evaluate the effectiveness of each technique in managing the presenting behavior.

Technique	Type of Behavior	Efficacy
Planned ignoring		
Signal interference		
Proximity control		
Interest boosting		
Tension decontamination through humor		
Antiseptic bouncing		

A major component of these provisions is to conduct functional behavioral assessments (FBA) and to implement behavioral support plans. According to the Center for Effective Collaboration and Practice (1998), the logic behind the FBA is that most behavior occurs within a particular context and serves a specific purpose. As with most of us, students with behavior problems behave in ways that satisfy a need or result in a desired, purposeful outcome. In most cases, the desired outcomes are not inappropriate; it is the ways of getting to those goals and outcomes that are typically problematic. Changes in behavior will occur only when it is clear that a different pattern of behavior will result in the desired outcome. FBA is a problem-solving process that helps to identify the purposes of individual student behavior patterns and allows for the introduction of alternative and appropriate ways for students to attain their goals.

In general, students engage in problem behavior for one of two reasons: to get something (e.g., attention, a tangible object) or to avoid something (e.g., a difficult task or an embarrassing situation) (Lewis & Sugai, 1999). An FBA is a way of determining what influences behaviors in the classroom and then hypothesizing what purpose or purposes the behaviors serve (Maag, 1999). By identifying any environmental factors that may influence behaviors and by determining the purpose of those behaviors, one can design an effective set of interventions (Hawken & Horner, 2003). Such interventions are designed to teach the student to attain objectives in a way that increases his or her potential and respects the reasonable sensibilities of others.

Before FBAs, educators used methods to modify behavior without regard to the conditions that maintained it (Hanley, Iwata, & McCord, 2003; Sasso, Conroy, Stichter, & Fox, 2001). For those who are limited in their ability to express themselves, who are developmentally not able to offer explanations based on reflection, or who are nonverbal, the functional behavior assessment is a key way in which their behavior can offer testimony on why they do what they do, given the environment.

Educators have a legal, professional, and ethical obligation to participate in the development of FBAs. A team may recommend a functional assessment of behaviors, and that recommendation, particularly when made during an individualized education program (IEP) meeting, must be followed. Although it does not specify what constitutes a functional behavior assessment, the IDEA does require that a functional behavior assessment be performed for a child with a disability who has been suspended or whose placement has been changed because of behavioral issues (Asmus, Vollmer, &

Borrero, 2002). The FBA should be completed before or within 10 days after removal. Beyond the legal obligations are professional standards. Professional organizations such as the Council for Exceptional Children, the American Psychological Association, and the Association for Behavior Analysis have cited the importance of the functional behavior assessment as a preventative and not just a remedial practice.

Major Assumptions Underlying FBA. There are four major assumptions that underlie FBA. First, behaviors, both appropriate and inappropriate, are learned and can be reduced (Chandler & Dahlquist, 2002). The environment shapes the way in which people learn to satisfy or meet their needs. Appropriate behaviors can be taught, shaped, and encouraged by changing the environment to support the learning of acceptable behaviors and through the systematic reduction of inappropriate behaviors.

Second, all behaviors are purposeful. There is a reason that the individual is engaging in a behavior. Since behaviors arise from and are maintained by environmental factors, the FBA allows us to determine the factors that influence an individual's behaviors.

Third, multiple behaviors can serve one function, and, correspondingly, one behavior can serve multiple functions. For example, a student may sit for 5 or 10 minutes, begin to fidget, doodle, get up to sharpen a pencil, talk with others on the way back to the table, and openly defy attempts to redirect him to his assignment. These multiple behaviors may have one purpose, to escape difficult or confusing work. One behavior can also have multiple purposes: A student may loudly defy a teacher's attempts to have her complete an assignment, which may result in a referral to the office. The purpose of the student's behavior may be to escape difficult work and gain an opportunity to chat with other students and even staff about pleasant topics.

Finally, an FBA is most effective when members of a team collaborate in assessing the behavior, planning the intervention, and evaluating the treatment. The best way to do this is through transdisciplinary teaming, in which responsibility is shared and roles overlap. Certain team members may coordinate the functional assessment, but the team as a whole participates in developing it. Each task is performed collaboratively and, when needed, jointly. Organizing collaboration and communication can be a specific task of a member of the team, such as a case manager (Carpenter, King-Sears, & Keys, 1998).

Elements of FBAs: Behaviors, Setting Events, Antecedents, and Consequences. What exactly are we looking for when performing an FBA? We are looking for behaviors, setting events, antecedents, and consequences. A behavior is an observable, measurable verbal or nonverbal action that an individual takes (Maag, 1999). A behavior has a defined beginning and end. The reason to be concerned about a particular problem behavior is not only how severe and frequent it is, but also how it interferes with other factors such as academics and relationships and whether it is developmentally age appropriate (Chandler & Dahlquist, 2002).

Setting events are situations or contexts that influence antecedents, behaviors, and consequences (Mahon, Shores, & Buske, 1999). A setting event can precede a behavior or happen alongside it and may influence how an antecedent or a consequence affects a student (Davis & Fox, 1999). As there are no formal instruments to identify setting events, it is important to interview all those involved with the student in the instructional and, when possible, home settings, being careful to obtain as much detail as possible regarding specific behaviors (Fox & Conroy, 1995). There are four types of setting events: the physical environment, the quality and number of social interactions, the structure and nature of activities, and the biological disorders and discomforts. Examples of each of these types of setting events, gleaned from Davis and Fox (1999) and Fox and Conroy (1995), are found in Table 8.1.

An antecedent is an event that precedes or happens alongside a behavior of concern, that can increase the likelihood a behavior will occur, and that can increase the intensity and frequency of a behavior (Chandler & Dahlquist, 2002). Antecedents can also be referred to as discriminative stimuli or establishing operations. One of the most

TABLE 8.1 Examples of Setting Events

Type of Setting Event	Examples
Environmental	The physical setting (e.g., the noise or temperature level)
	The materials used (Are they developmentally appropriate? Do they pose challenges to fine or gross motor skills?)
	The people in the environment
Social interactions and skills	Individuals with disabilities tend to have difficulties in establishing meaningful or satisfying relationships with people
Deficits	Social isolation
	Deficits in social, play, conversational, study, and collaboration skills
Structure and nature of activities	Complexity of activity
	Whether an activity is developmentally appropriate
	Duration of an activity
	Order of tasks or activities
	Whether or not an activity is of interest to the person
	Whether or not an activity serves the function of a behavior
Biological disorders and discomforts	Type of medication (if any), dosage level, times of administration
	Sleep-related problems
	Food deprivation or satiation
	Pain
	Menses

Source: Adapted from Davis, C. A., & Fox, J. J. (1999). Evaluating environmental arrangements as setting events: Review and implications for measurement. *Journal of Behavioral Education*, 9, 77–96.

common mistakes made in functional behavior assessment is looking for an immediate or direct cause. When trying to identify antecedents, one should first simply identify the events preceding the behavior and not attempt to identify which particular event was a "cause." Conroy and Stichter (2003) identify three general types of antecedents: physiological states, social events, and environmental or instructional factors. Illustrations of each are provided in Table 8.2.

A consequence is any event that follows a behavior and may have an impact on that behavior by increasing, decreasing, or maintaining it (Maag, 1999). When observing for consequences, one should record all events that follow a behavior so they can be better classified at a later time (on-the-spot classification is often difficult). Keep in mind the following: Some consequences positively reinforce behaviors, some consequences negatively reinforce them (removing something unpleasant following a behavior of concern), some involve ignoring (i.e., extinction), some are punitive, and some are natural consequences. Table 8.3 summarizes the range of typical consequences.

A Stepwise Process for Conducting an FBA. Although the task seems involved and complicated, there is a time-efficient way to gather information necessary for an FBA. As illustrated in Figure 8.4, there is an order in which we should approach sources of information. We should review the records, interview those who know that child's behavior best, observe, and, finally, review findings with all those who must work with the child to ensure accuracy. At each step, one identifies more and more information about the behaviors of concern, setting events, antecedents, and consequences.

Reviewing Records. To save time, one should not ask in interviews what could have been gathered by a review of the records. As one goes through the records, list the behaviors of concern that need to be either decreased or increased in observable and measurable terms. Try also to note the frequency of behaviors of concern and circumstances surrounding those behaviors, with particular attention to the setting events, antecedents, and consequences. In effect, for each behavior or behaviors, one is collecting

TABLE 8.2 Examples of Antecedents

Type of Antecedent	Examples
Physiological	Being asked to perform a task that is physically difficult Being injured Loud alarms, other noises Being touched
Social	Negative interactions with others Being told "No" or "Stop" Being reprimanded Being greeted; being not greeted Ridicule Crowds Waiting periods Changes to schedule Arriving late Not earning a reinforcer
Instructional	Being given an instruction Being presented with difficult classwork Making a mistake Being corrected in an abrupt manner Running out of time Receiving a poor grade

Source: Adapted from Conroy, M. A., & Sticher, J. P. (2003). The application of antecedents in the functional assessment process. *Journal of Special Education, 37*(1), 15–25.

TABLE 8.3 Consequences: Definitions and Examples

Type of Consequence	Definition	Examples
Positive reinforcement	A consequence that increases the likelihood that the behavior of concern will happen more often and/or more intensely.	Greater assistance Closer monitoring Being told "No" and "Stop" Being warned of consequences Being counseled following behavior of concern Being promised reinforcers for doing better
Negative reinforcement	Stimuli that, when removed, increase the frequency or intensity of behaviors.	Reducing or removing difficult work Reducing demands
Extinction	The removal of any reinforcement that had been occurring after behaviors of concern, resulting in a reduction of those behaviors.	Ignoring minor misbehaviors
Punishment	A consequence that increases the likelihood that the behavior of concern will happen less often or less intensely.	Verbal reprimands Removal of work Removal of student from work area (e.g., time-out) Any corporal punishment

Source: Adapted from *Applied Behavior Analysis for Teachers* (6th ed.), by P. A. Alberto and A. C. Troutman, 2003, Upper Saddle River, NJ: Merrill/Prentice Hall; and *Behavior Management: From Theoretical to Practical Applications*, by J. W. Maag, 1999, San Diego, CA: Singular.

a cumulative setting event–antecedent–behavior–consequence report. A possible format for the gathering of this information may look like this:

Name of student	
Behavior of concern	
Frequency of behavior	
Setting events: What situations happened that might have influenced how the student responded to antecedents or consequences?	
Antecedents: What happened before the behavior or co-occurred with the behavior?	
Behaviors: Describe the behavior observed.	
Consequences: What happened following the behavior? What were the student's reactions to consequences?	
Functions: What are possible functions of the behavior?	
Date:	Information gathered by:

Review Records

Review psychological, psychiatric, behavioral, social and emotional, speech and language, augmentative and alternative communication, and medical assessments; IEPs; informal assessments; subject area assessments; data; report cards; portfolios; teacher notes; attendance records; referrals to the main office; parent-provided documents

⇓

Interview

Interview teachers, instructional assistants, related service providers, support staff, administrators, family, consultants, and the students

⇓

Conduct Direct Observations

Observe interactions between student and teachers, instructional assistants, related service providers, support staff, administrators, and, if possible and necessary, family and consultants.

⇓

Establish the Setting Event–Antecedent–Behavior–Consequence Chain for Each Behavior as a Team

⇓

Hypothesize Functions as a Team

⇓

Develop the Plan as a Team

⇓

Implement the Plan by the Team

⇓

Observe How Well the Plan Is Implemented by Designated Observer(s)
⇓
Continue Implementation of the Plan or Reassess

FIGURE 8.4   Stepwise Process for Conducting an FBA

Once this information is recorded, gaps in information will begin to emerge. For example, the records may show that loud disruptions to the class may have resulted in a referral to the office, but no information was collected on the setting events or antecedents to the incident. Since information in records is generally limited, it is likely that these gaps will be quite large.

Interviewing. As gaps in the records begin to emerge, interviews can be scheduled with key stakeholders. The purpose of interviews is to fill in the gaps in setting events, antecedents, behaviors, and consequences. Further, interviewing helps to determine in what situations the behavior is less likely to occur (Maag, 1999). Horner and Carr (1997) note that there are two major advantages to interviews: (1) the ability to review a large number of possible antecedents and consequences of behaviors and (2) the consequent ability to identify which of these factors are more likely than others to give rise to and maintain the behaviors of concern. A major disadvantage is that interviews are subjective.

Based on the review of files, one can develop a set of questions tailored to the individual. For example, if there are reports that more behaviors of concern have been exhibited during math class, one can ask the math teacher about the nature of the difficulties the student is having and how those difficulties have been so far addressed. A sample set of questions may include the following:

What behaviors of concern is the student exhibiting?

How often and for about how long are these behaviors displayed?

What behaviors are of greatest concern? Why?

Are there any physical reasons (e.g., missed medications, headaches, physical limitations) this student may be exhibiting the behaviors of concern?

Are there any environmental factors that precede the behaviors of concern?

Are there any social interactions with other students or teachers that precede the behaviors of concern?

Is there anything about the structure or nature of the activities that this student may find difficult?

Does the student seem to have any learning, organizational, time management, social, conversational, play, or other skills deficits?

What do you do when this behavior is exhibited?

Are there any existing strategies others have recommended?

How do fellow students react to these behaviors?

When is this student most cooperative?

What do you think the student is getting out of these behaviors of concern?

Because people are not used to conveying information in the sequential manner of a functional behavior assessment, be prepared to be an active questioner, listening carefully, plugging in information under the appropriate behavior, and classifying it as setting event, antecedent, or consequence. Obviously, one should point out that there is no "right" and "wrong" information.

Observing. Once interviews are completed, it may become evident that more information is needed before the FBA is adequate. To clarify ambiguities or fill in the gaps in the FBA following reviews of records and interviews, direct observations will likely need to be done. The person coordinating and conducting the functional assessment should schedule observations.

Remember that it is generally more difficult to observe low-frequency behaviors than high-frequency behaviors, more difficult to observe concealed behaviors than behaviors exhibited in public, and more difficult to observe problems with internal processes such as thinking than with observable behaviors. In these situations, interviews and data, such as an analysis of errors or amount of class work or tests completed, may provide more information useful to a functional assessment. In such situations, it may also be more worthwhile to observe the overall physical and social environment.

There are some basic rules for direct observation of students. While observing, one should try not to interact in any significant or obvious way with those in the setting. Stand or sit in a location that is close enough to hear interactions but not so close that it calls attention to one's self. Do not focus exclusively on the student being observed; this is in part to respect the student and in part to compare the student performance to the performance of peers. When observing, keep a running log of setting events, antecedents, behaviors, and consequences with times. As relevant antecedents and consequences become evident, the simplest way to track these is to use an "S," an "A," a "C," or an "R" to represent a setting event, antecedent, consequence, or reaction (see Table 8.4). When a function is suspected, an "F" can be placed next to the indicator. Once the observation is completed, the general information can be shared with the staff observed and corrections made and gaps filled in. For example, the observer may have misheard what was said, or what was said could have been said in a low volume and not heard. Once gaps are filled, functions should be hypothesized.

Writing the FBA Narrative. Once the review of files, interviews, and observations are completed, a narrative needs to be written. Each paragraph of the narrative should deal with one behavior or chain of behaviors. The paragraph should begin with a description of the behavior or behavior chain and the reported frequency of the behavior, followed by possible setting events, antecedents, and consequences. The paragraph

TABLE 8.4   A Running Log of Behavioral Events

Name of student:	
Class and teacher observed:	
Date:	
Time observation began & ended:	

Time	Running narrative

Place an "S" for Setting Event, "A" for Antecedent, "C" for Consequence, "R" for Reaction, and "F" for Function next to the relevant portion of the narrative.

should conclude with hypothesized functions of the behavior or chain of behaviors. The narrative should begin with the behaviors of greater concern and follow with the behaviors of lesser concern; descriptions of behaviors should be respectful to the student, teachers, other educators, and caregivers.

Reviewing Information to Check for Accuracy. Once the setting event, antecedent, and consequence chain is identified for each behavior of concern, the information should be put into narrative form and presented to the members of the team. The person or persons who wrote the narrative should review it with others, asking others to check if their report is accurate. Nothing should be eliminated that is accurate and has been reported by others or discovered otherwise during the assessment.

Hypothesizing Functions. Simply stated, hypothesizing functions is the making of informed best guesses (Maag, 1999). For every setting event, antecedent, and consequence of relevance, there can be a hypothesized function. Two typical functions of behavior are to gain something and to avoid something (Maag & Kemp, 2003), and social functions account for approximately 70 percent of challenging behaviors (Kennedy, 2002). Social functions include gaining attention, assistance, interaction, counseling, conversation, and power and control (Maag & Kemp, 2003). Other functions may include gaining foods and other reinforcements, gaining sensory stimulation, and escaping or modifying tasks or others' demands. Still, hypotheses as to why the problem is occurring are testable propositions and should include clear descriptions of antecedent and/or consequent events associated with the behavior. Finally, a behavior intervention plan is designed that can include one or all of the following strategies: (1) antecedent and setting event modifications (see Figure 8.3), (2) consequence interventions, and (3) the teaching of alternative or replacement behaviors, problem solving, and self-control procedures (Bambara & Knoster, 1998).

Consequences for Compliance and Noncompliance

The development of consequences is an essential component of successful management programs. Three important skills are needed for the development of effective consequences: creativity, the ability to provide recognition for rule compliance, and the ability to see the logical extension of rule violations (Curwin & Mendler, 1988; Rosenberg & Jackman, 2003). In short, good consequences (1) are clear and specific, (2) are not always punishments, (3) are natural and related directly to the rule, (4) preserve the student's dignity, (5) increase the student's motivation, and (6) promote an internal locus of control within students.

Thinking of effective consequences can be problematic, however, for developing and beginning teachers. Fortunately, four generic consequences can be effective for any rule. According to Curwin and Mendler (1988), these are (1) reminding the student of the rule, (2) warning, (3) developing an action plan for improving behavior, and (4) practicing appropriate behavior. Still, it takes considerable skill and practice to develop effective consequences that are not aversive. Strategies to assist developing and beginning teachers in creating good consequences are found in Table 8.5.

In providing recognition for rule compliance—consequences for appropriate behavior—many large-group or whole-class alternatives are available. Three such procedures—token economies, class contingencies, and level systems—are described below.

Token Economies. A system that employs tokens is referred to as a token economy. In such a system, tokens function in ways very similar to currency in the national economy. Tokens are used to purchase available backup reinforcers, which can include treats,

TABLE 8.5   Creating Effective Consequences: Five Strategies for Developing and Beginning Teachers

Strategy	Putting It to Practice
Reread and visualize the classroom rule	Close your eyes and imagine a student breaking a rule; consider the possible scenarios resulting from the various natural consequences.
Collect effective consequences	Observe master teachers. Ask them how they respond to specific instances of rule-breaking.
Ask the students	Early in the school year, have students provide input as to what they believe would be effective consequences. At the end of the year, ask students to comment on the effectiveness of each consequence.
Ask parents	At IEP meetings or parent conferences, ask parents what consequences have been effective at home.
Ask yourself	Remember your own days as a student and consider what consequences helped you (1) stop misbehaving, (2) learn from the experience, (3) cooperate, and (4) not feel embarrassed, angry, or resentful.

Source: Adapted from *Discipline with Dignity*, by R. L. Curwin and A. N. Mendler, 1988, Alexandria, VA: Association for Supervision and Curriculum Development.

trinkets, activities, and privileges. Token economies have been implemented in special education, remedial education, and general education classroom environments and have been successful in changing a variety of inappropriate classroom behaviors. Token systems have also been successful in improving academic performance and in raising standardized test scores.

Unfortunately, it is beyond the scope of this chapter to provide all the specifics necessary to design and implement a successful whole-class token economy (see Alberts & Troutman, 2003; Kazdin, 1975). It would be useful, however, to review several general guidelines prepared by Slavin (2003).

First, the specific behaviors that will be targeted for reinforcement need to be determined and articulated clearly. In general, these targeted behaviors should be similar in content to the stated rules, procedures, and behavioral standards of the classroom.

Second, a logistically appropriate point system must be developed. A range of alternative schedules for the systematic delivery of points is available. In some environments, teachers can wait until the end of an instructional period before awarding earned points; in other settings, the behavioral characteristics of students require that points be awarded more frequently. Similarly, there are alternatives for the recording of points. In some instances, students are able to keep track of their own points, whereas in others, record keeping must be the responsibility of the teacher.

Third, a selection of backup reinforcers must be developed. Each selection should be assigned a price, with many items being small enough that a student can earn a tangible backup in one day. A number of highly desirable big awards should require the saving of points over time.

Fourth, a response cost system that deducts points for specific instances of misbehavior should be considered. Although such a system is not necessary for routine and minor instances of misbehavior, it could be very effective in reducing instances of disruptive and aggressive behaviors.

Finally, plans must be made for the eventual fading of the extrinsic controls. The behavior modification program is considered successful only when appropriate behaviors occur without artificial points and non-normative backup reinforcers.

Class Contingencies. Although they are less systematic than token economies, class contingencies can be used to promote and maintain appropriate classroom behavior. In class contingency situations, the entire class receives consequences based on the behavior of its group members. Several types of informal, whole-class contingencies can be used. For example, the teacher can put marbles, chips, or paper clips into a canister whenever he or she catches students engaging in a targeted appropriate behavior or remove one of the objects if a rule is violated (Mastropieri & Scruggs, 1987). When the receptacle is filled, the whole class shares in a group reward, such as a party or field trip. In a second type of whole-class program, an individual disruptive student could be made responsible for earning reinforcers for the entire class of students on the basis of his or her performance alone (Kazdin, 1975). In such an instance, all members of the class share in the benefits when one troublesome student behaves appropriately.

The Good Behavior Game, originally formulated by Barrish, Saunders, and Wolf (1969) and applied successfully by a number of researchers (see Tankersley, 1995), is a formal group contingency program that has a long history of reducing disruptive behaviors. The game is implemented in four steps.

1. The classroom rules are stated, and the class is divided into two teams.

2. The teacher awards negative marks whenever any member of a team engages in a prespecified inappropriate behavior.

3. The team with the lowest number of marks is declared winner for the day and is given some form of reinforcement.

4. The losing team is required to do some extra work and/or forfeit a privilege.

It is generally believed that group contingencies work because group members encourage one another to do the things required to earn the reward. Overenthusiastic encouragement can, in some cases, get out of hand. Developing and beginning teachers who employ group contingencies should ensure that peers do not use coercive or threatening means to pressure others into behaving appropriately.

Levels Systems. A levels system is a group management alternative that accommodates the differing entry-level behavioral skills of students within a learning environment. The system is an organizational framework within which varying intensities of management alternatives are applied. Each level of a particular system has specific expectations, and corresponding privileges can be earned for meeting the expectations. Students' points of entry into a system and their progress through the levels depend on the intensity of their presenting problems (Bauer, Shea, & Keppler, 1986). The system shapes student behavior gradually by providing opportunities for movement through varying intensities of expectations and management alternatives. The ultimate goal of most level systems is self-management.

Levels systems are flexible and can be applied in resource, self-contained, day-school, and residential settings (e.g., see Braaten, 1979; Mastropieri, Jenne, & Scruggs, 1988). Developing and beginning teachers can employ these systems with both elementary and secondary students. Bauer et al. (1986) have provided guidelines for the planning and implementation of levels systems (see Box 8.2).

Crisis Management

Crisis is one of those terms that is often used, yet is difficult to define. We can all relate to how we have felt—physically, emotionally, and cognitively—when we have been in what we describe as crisis situations. Although signs and symptoms vary across individuals, typical descriptions of crisis responses from adults include (1) physical signs and symptoms such as headaches, rapid breathing, muscle tension, and nausea;

Box 8.2   Guidelines for the Planning and Implementation of Levels Systems

Step 1:   Determine the entry-level behaviors of the students with whom the system is to be applied.

Step 2:   Determine the terminal behavioral expectations for the students.

Step 3:   Formulate at least two but no more than four sets of behavioral expectations that seem to be appropriately graded steps between those expectations described in steps 1 and 2. Label each of the steps level 1 through level "x".

Step 4:   Consider the inclusion of a transition level. This would allow for part-time placement at a higher level for a portion of the school day.

Step 5:   Determine the privileges appropriate for students at level 1 and for students ready to terminate the program.

Step 6:   For each of the levels developed in step 3, list corresponding privileges that are appropriate. Ensure an equal distribution among the levels, and remember to reduce the amount of direct supervision as students progress through the levels.

Step 7:   Consider the following logistical concerns:

a. How, when, and at what frequency will a student's level status be reviewed?

b. Who will review a student's status?

c. How will self-monitoring procedures be implemented?

Step 8:   Determine how to facilitate communication among the many individuals (e.g., parents, administrators, related service personnel) involved in the student's education in the levels system.

Source: From "Levels Systems: A Framework for the Individualization of Behavior Management," by A. M. Bauer, T. M. Shea, and R. Keppler, 1986, *Behavioral Disorders, 12*, pp. 28–35. Reprinted with permission.

---

(2) emotional responses such as tension, depression, extreme anxiety, and panic; and (3) behavioral indicators such as a withdrawal from regular activities and an inability to pay attention or concentrate. Although most events that precipitate a crisis are beyond the control of school personnel, it is critical that educators be aware of what a child is experiencing when he or she is in crisis, what specific steps can minimize crisis responses, and how to manage such situations when they occur.

The physical and emotional by-products of a crisis situation are not pleasant. In many cases, the student in crisis has little or no control over his or her behavior. Therefore, the delivery of consequences for misbehavior or noncompliance with rules or procedures will have little or no effect. Steps must be taken to help the student though the crisis situation in a nonthreatening and nonpunitive fashion.

Formal crisis intervention is an involved process that requires considerable efforts from trained counselors, psychologists, and crisis personnel. Nonetheless, developing and beginning teachers should be prepared with a fixed set of steps or procedures in the event that a crisis situation emerges in their classroom. Figure 8.5 lists several steps adapted from Alpert (1989) for defusing crisis situations. However, all personnel should develop a mechanism to access psychological support personnel when necessary. For example, some schools have a code system that signals crisis personnel to report to areas of the school where a crisis is believed to be occurring.

Focus on Behavior, Not the Student.

- Describe, rather than evaluate, the presenting behavior.
- Deal in the present, not the past.
- Be firm, direct, and professional.

Take Charge of Emotions.

- Be in control of your own emotions and actions.
- Respond reasonably, rather than react impulsively, to student verbalizations and actions.
- Provide for a negative release or venting of student emotions.

Exercise Caution and Avoid Escalating the Situation.

- Be aware of your own body language.
- Avoid unsubstantiated accusations, hearsay, and generalizations.
- Do not back a student into a corner.
- Model appropriate "resolution" behaviors.

Make Plans to Discuss the Crisis Fully at a Later Time.

- Stress that people respond more rationally when they are calm.
- Stress the need to actually "hear" each other's points.

FIGURE 8.5   Steps for Avoiding and Defusing Crisis Situations

Source: Adapted from *A Teacher's Guide to Cooperative Discipline: How to Manage Your Classroom and Promote Self-Esteem*, by L. Alpert, 1989, Circle Pines, MN: American Guidance Service.

RESOLVING STUDENT MISBEHAVIOR

Although the keys to successful classroom management are prevention and action, many students, particularly those with mild to moderate disabilities, present problem behaviors that necessitate thoughtful and effective interventions for problem resolution. In this section, we review techniques that can be employed to intervene when students engage in problematic behaviors. First, we present a descriptive menu of generic behavioral techniques for influencing students' inappropriate behaviors. Then we discuss specific individual and group management alternatives. Keep in mind that the results of the FBA provide direction as to what interventions one should choose to apply.

Generic Behavioral Strategies

In most cases, interventions that are successful in managing and remediating student misbehavior involve both the strengthening and the reducing of different behaviors. Management programs designed to reduce or eliminate problem behaviors alone may be ineffectual because they do not directly teach or strengthen appropriate behaviors.

Pause and Reflect About the Profession 8.5

Develop a crisis plan for your setting. In your plan, be sure to identify how you can be reasonably confident that a student is in crisis and what steps you will take to secure assistance and to manage the crisis. How can you ensure that the crisis will be handled in a nonpunitive fashion?

Because a student may not be aware of, or proficient enough in, a correct mode of functioning in the classroom, the reduction or elimination of one series of problematic behaviors may lead to a situation in which other negative behaviors replace the initial problem behaviors. Clearly, dynamic management interventions are needed that simultaneously strengthen and weaken specific student target behaviors. Although techniques that increase and decrease student behavior are presented separately, it is critical that they be applied in a logical and dynamic fashion.

Increasing Behavior. When we speak of increasing behavior, we are referring to the process of reinforcement. Positive reinforcement occurs when the contingent presentation of a positive environmental consequence results in a corresponding increase in the frequency or intensity of a target behavior. Negative reinforcement, sometimes confused with punishment, occurs when the contingent removal of an unpleasant or aversive event results directly in the increased frequency of a targeted behavior. Whether positive or negative, reinforcement, by definition, always refers to an increase in a behavior's frequency or intensity. Therefore, praise, tokens, and free activity time will not always function as reinforcement. To be a reinforcer, an item, event, or activity must increase the strength or intensity of a behavior. For new and developing teachers, this functional definition of reinforcement highlights the need to identify potential items and events that have the greatest likelihood of increasing an individual student's appropriate behaviors.

According to Kazdin (1975), the effectiveness of reinforcement depends on several major factors: (1) the delay between the performance of a behavior and the delivery of the potential reinforcer, (2) the magnitude of the reinforcer, (3) the quality of the reinforcer, and (4) the schedule for reinforcer delivery. Developing and beginning teachers should ensure that positive reinforcers are delivered in close proximity to the target behavior. If the delivery of a reinforcer does not closely follow the target behavior, the risk is that behaviors other than the target behavior will be reinforced inadvertently. The magnitude, or amount, of reinforcement also influences the level of change in a target behavior. Quite simply, the greater the amount of a reinforcer delivered for the presentation of a behavior, the more frequent that response will be on future occasions. This relationship between amount of reinforcement and behavioral intensity is limited, however. Too much reinforcement can easily lead to satiation, a condition whereby reinforcers lose their potency. Teachers can combat satiation by using a variety of potential reinforcers in their classroom settings.

When we speak of reinforcement quality, we are referring to a student's reinforcer preference. In general, students will work with greater intensity if their efforts are recognized with items, behaviors, or events they value. Developing and beginning teachers can determine students' reinforcer preferences by directly observing the students or by administering a reinforcer preference survey. A comprehensive listing of items that may be included on a preference survey is found in Box 8.3.

Schedule of reinforcement refers to a specific arrangement by which reinforcers are delivered. Continuous reinforcement is an arrangement in which reinforcers are delivered after each instance of a target behavior. When reinforcement is delivered after only some instances of a target behavior, the schedule is considered to be intermittent reinforcement. The nature of classroom events necessitates the use of intermittent reinforcement schedules because they reduce the risk of reinforcer satiation and promote long-term behavioral maintenance.

The most common types of intermittent reinforcement schedules are fixed-interval (FI), variable-interval (VI), fixed-ratio (FR), and variable-ratio (VR) schedules. On FI schedules, reinforcers are delivered at prearranged, unvarying intervals of time. On VI schedules, reinforcers are delivered at prearranged, varying intervals that average a certain number of minutes. On a VI:15 schedule, for example, an average of 15 minutes would pass prior to the delivery of a reinforcer. For any given occasion, the interval would be more or less than the specific 15-minute interval. An FR schedule delineates

Box 8.3   **Possible Items for a Reinforcer Preference Survey**

Job Reinforcers

- Handing out paper, pencils, and so on
- Taking a note to the office
- Erasing the chalkboard
- Helping the teacher with a project
- Managing the class store
- Helping in the cafeteria
- Assisting the custodian
- Distributing and arranging reinforcers
- Watering the plants
- Running the copy machine
- Stapling papers together
- Feeding the fish or other animals
- Giving a message over the intercom
- Taking the class roll
- Serving as secretary for class meetings
- Raising or lowering the flag
- Carrying the wastebasket while other children clean out their desks
- Using the overhead projector
- Recording own behavior on a graph
- Teaching another child
- Helping the librarian
- Telling the teacher when it is time to go to lunch
- Sharpening the teacher's pencils
- Adjusting the window shades

Tangible Reinforcers Other Than Food

- Tickets to games or movies
- Personal grooming supplies
- Toys and games from the class store
- Colored chalk, pencils, or felt-tipped pens

Social Reinforcers

- Receiving verbal praise
- Having photograph displayed
- Getting personal time with the teacher, aide, counselor, or principal
- Having work and projects displayed
- Participating in show-and-tell
- Clapping and cheering by others when successful
- Being leader or organizer of an event
- Getting a hug, handshake, or pat on the back
- Sitting next to the teacher at lunch
- Playing with a classmate of choice
- Sitting and talking with a friend (adult or child)

Consumable Food Reinforcers

- Raisins
- Crackers
- Cookies

Box 8.3 **(continued)**

- Popcorn
- Peanuts
- Jelly beans
- Juice
- Ice cream
- Lollipops

Reinforcing Activities

- Reading books, magazines, and comic books
- Writing on the chalkboard with white or colored chalk
- Getting free time for self-selected projects
- Making things, such as kites, model cars, and airplanes
- Making bead jewelry
- Playing games (e.g., Monopoly)
- Doing puzzles
- Singing
- Finger painting
- Playing with puppets
- Drawing
- Reading with a friend
- Studying with a friend
- Tutoring younger children
- Eating lunch at a restaurant
- Decorating a designated area of the room in own style
- Taking field trips
- Going on outdoor walks
- Watching a movie
- Watching television
- Listening to music
- Doing a project of own interest
- Using the tape recorder or phonograph
- Getting extra recess
- Going home early
- Taking a class pet home for the weekend
- Going on a trip to a fair or museum
- Using a typewriter
- Doing "special," "the hardest," or "impossible" teacher-made arithmetic problems
- Reading the newspaper
- Reading or drawing a road map
- Listening to the radio with earphones
- Going to the library
- Doing a science experiment
- Weighing or measuring various objects in the classroom

the precise number of behaviors a person must perform to receive a reinforcer. In an FR:20 schedule, a student would earn a certain number of minutes on the computer for every 20 problems completed during a seatwork activity. With the VR schedule, the number of responses necessary to receive reinforcement would vary from occasion to occasion and reflect an average number of responses desired of the student.

Alternative procedures for increasing students' levels of appropriate behaviors are as diverse as the contingent delivery of edibles and the contingent awarding of tokens or free activity time. Because students with mild to moderate disabilities have individual and often unique needs, it is important that teachers apply the procedures with the knowledge that outcomes will typically vary from student to student. Table 8.6 presents a summary of the more common procedures for increasing appropriate student behavior.

Decreasing Behavior. Students with mild to moderate disabilities present a number of problematic behaviors that need to be reduced or eliminated. Three types of procedures exist for the systematic reduction of problematic behaviors: extinction, differential reinforcement, and punishment. Extinction is a process that decreases the strength and intensity of a behavior by withholding reinforcement previously given to the behavior. The most common and productive application of extinction is the planned ignoring of minor inappropriate behaviors (e.g., the tapping of a pencil on a desk) that had been reinforced previously through teacher attention. High-intensity problematic behaviors

TABLE 8.6 Procedures for Increasing Appropriate Behaviors

Type	Definition	Advantages	Disadvantages
Edible	A primary reinforcer. Potency varies as a function of deprivation and satiation.	Potency with students who possess severe handicaps. Useful in establishing reinforcing properties of other events (e.g., praise, smiles).	Delivery disrupts classroom functioning. Difficult to dispense in busy classroom settings. Need to be constantly aware of student allergies.
Praise and attention	Conditioned social reinforcers that can be delivered verbally and nonverbally (e.g., smiles, winks, physical contact).	Easily and quickly administered. Unobtrusive during classroom activities. Little preparation required.	Because the reinforcement value of praise and attention needs to be learned, some individuals may not respond. Limited potency with inappropriate behaviors that have high secondary reinforcing properties (e.g., theft, substance abuse).
High probability behaviors	The preferred activities of students can be used as reinforcers for low-probability behaviors.	Schools have many desirable activities available. Powerful and cost-free. Low probability of satiation.	Difficulty in delivering activity reinforcers immediately. Disruptions may occur during transitions between activities. Delivery mode tends to be all or none; little opportunity to portion out activities.
Performance feedback	Using the knowledge of progress or results to reinforce a target behavior.	Easily initiated in settings where performance criteria are explicitly stated. Low cost and motivating.	Effectiveness of feedback alone has been equivocal.
Tokens	Conditioned, generalized reinforcers whose strength is derived from items, activities, and desirable consequences they present.	Combat satiation in that a number of backups can be employed. Easily dispensed. Serve to bridge the period of time between the occurrence of a behavior and the delivery of a primary reinforcer. Allow for gradations of reinforcement.	Require effort in record keeping and other management activities, fading of tokens often neglected.

TABLE 8.7   Three Commonly Used Punishment Techniques

Type	Definition	Advantages	Disadvantages
Reprimand	A verbal statement or non-verbal gesture that expresses disapproval.	Easily applied with little or no preparation required. No physical discomfort to students.	Sometimes not effective. Can serve as positive reinforcement if this is a major source of attention.
Response cost	A formal system of penalties in which a reinforcer is removed, contingent upon the occurrence of an inappropriate behavior.	Easily applied with quick results. Does not disrupt class activities. No physical discomfort to students.	Not effective once student has "lost" all reinforcers. Can initially result in some students being more disruptive.
Time-out	Limited or complete loss of access to positive reinforcers for a set amount of time.	Fast acting and powerful. No physical discomfort to students.	Difficult to find secluded areas where students would not be reinforced inadvertently. May require physical assistance to the time-out area. Overuse can interfere with educational and pro-social efforts.

such as tantrumming, fighting, and noncompliance require the use of stronger behavior-reduction techniques.

Inappropriate classroom behaviors can be reduced indirectly by the creative use of reinforcement contingencies. With differential reinforcement of low rates of behaviors (DRL), teachers can reduce the frequency of a problem behavior by reinforcing a student for keeping the targeted problem at or below a particular level. Another technique, differential reinforcement of other behavior (DRO), involves the reinforcement of any behavior except the behavior to be reduced. To receive a reinforcer under a DRO schedule, the student must refrain completely from performing the behavior targeted for reduction. Thus, other behaviors are developed to replace the problematic behaviors being reduced or eliminated. The most stringent differential reinforcement technique is differential reinforcement of appropriate behaviors incompatible with a targeted behavior (DRI). The power of DRI is that students cannot engage in problematic behaviors if they are working under conditions that promote behaviors contradictory to the problem behavior. Because a behavior such as correctly completing seatwork cannot occur simultaneously with running around the classroom, the reinforcement of seatwork completion could result in the reduction of the room-running behavior.

Punishment, the manipulation and delivery of consequences designed to decrease the strength or intensity of a target behavior, typically takes one of two forms: (1) the presentation of an aversive consequence or (2) the removal of a previously earned reinforcer. Three common punishment techniques are reprimands, response cost, and time-out. These techniques are described in Table 8.7.

PROMOTING SELF-CONTROL AND PROBLEM SOLVING

Self-Control

The ultimate goal of any classroom management effort should be the development of student self-management. Students who are able to control their own behaviors independent of external agents in situations requiring delays in gratification, problem solving, and conflict resolution are better prepared to meet complex societal demands.

Self-control procedures allow students to assume a larger role in many aspects of their classroom behavioral management programs.

According to Hallahan, Lloyd, and Stoller (1982), most self-control programs include three major components: self-assessment, self-recording, and self-determination of reinforcement. First, in self-assessment, a student examines his or her own behavior and decides whether a target behavior (or series of target behaviors) was performed. This is followed by self-recording, a process in which a student records objectively the results of the self-assessment. Finally, in the process of self-determination of reinforcement, a student determines the nature and amount of reinforcement he or she should receive for the performance of the target behavior.

Self-monitoring, a combination of self-assessment and self-recording, should be employed regularly by developing and beginning teachers. Its use increases the probability that intervention efforts will be maintained. According to Hallahan et al. (1982), materials needed for a self-monitoring program include (1) a self-monitoring cuing tape or, if the student is advanced technologically, a handheld "Palm"-like personal computer (see Bauer & Ulrich, 2002), (2) a self-monitoring card (or computer application), and (3) an assigned task that a student can work on while self-monitoring.

The procedure is introduced by informing a student (or a small group of students) that it is important to keep track of the occurrence and nonoccurrence of a target behavior. The student is then introduced to the cuing tape, tape recorder, and self-monitoring card. Every time the student hears the tone of the cuing tape, he or she is to ask covertly, "Was I engaging in the target behavior?" and to mark the monitoring card appropriately. The procedures should be modeled and practiced initially to ensure that students can reliably differentiate between the occurrence and nonoccurrence of the target behavior. Once the procedure succeeds in teaching students to monitor and record their own behavior, procedures designed to teach the self-determination of reinforcement can begin.

On reaching an acceptable level of performance, it will become necessary to wean the student from the external aspects of the procedure. Hallahan et al. (1982) recommend that the process begin by removing either the tape or the self-monitoring card. If student performance begins to deteriorate, however, teachers should not hesitate to resume using the external prompts as part of a modified maintenance strategy.

Problem Solving

Many students possessing mild to moderate disabilities are deficient in their ability to solve interpersonal problems. The goals of problem-solving programs are to teach children (1) to be sensitive to interpersonal problems, (2) to develop the ability to generate alternative solutions to problems, and (3) to understand that one person's behavior affects the behavior of others.

Successful problem solving consists of several components, each of which can be taught directly to students who exhibit inappropriate patterns of behavior. The following list of these components has been gleaned from several sources, including D'Zurilla and Goldfried (1971) and Spivack and Shure (1982). Suggestions on how to apply these components are also provided.

1. **Develop a general sensitivity or orientation to the problem.** Students need to be instructed and given the opportunity to practice recognizing that interpersonal problems exist. This can take the form of role playing or examination of case studies in which problems appear.

2. **Articulate the specifics of a problem.** Students need to practice identifying the specific troublesome aspects of problem situations. For example, this could involve task analysis of hypothetical conflict situations.

3. **Develop step-by-step procedures for solving the problem.** Students require models and practice opportunities in the ordering of events that could lead to a problem's solution. For example, case studies and hypothetical problem situations that require several steps for possible resolution can be practiced through role playing and group discussion activities.

4. **Generate a set of alternative strategies to approach a problem.** Using the ordered steps necessary for problem resolution, students must be able to generate alternative solutions to the presenting problem. Through brainstorming sessions, students should be encouraged to think of all types of possible strategies that could result in problem resolution. This component of the process should not be neglected; considerable evidence suggests that the capacity to generate alternative solutions to problems is positively related to increased problem-solving ability and social adjustment throughout the life span.

5. **Consider the consequences of each generated alternative.** Once the set of possible alternatives has been listed, students should be encouraged to identify the possible consequences for each. This task can be structured by having students relate what the worst and best scenarios could be for each. This is a critical step. It requires students to project beyond the presenting problem and to determine what might happen if a particular alternative is chosen.

6. **Decide on a course of action.** On the basis of a thorough consideration of alternatives, students are to choose the best alternative for solving the presenting problem.

7. **Verify whether the selected alternative achieved the desired outcome.** Students should be made aware that the initial solution may not always resolve the problem as anticipated. It may be necessary to consider another alternative.

In terms of efficacy, self-monitoring and interpersonal problem-solving techniques show great promise for teaching appropriate behaviors to students with mild to moderate disabilities. These proactive activities can be used to intervene in problem classroom behaviors.

DESIGNING AND IMPLEMENTING INDIVIDUAL SUPPORTS AND BEHAVIOR-CHANGING INTERVENTIONS

When a student's inappropriate behavioral patterns cannot be prevented, many teachers use data gathered from FBAs and employ individual behavior-changing procedures. Although these often require considerable time for planning and monitoring, the initial effort is usually rewarded by increases in appropriate classroom functioning. A step-by-step sequence of activities for implementing individual behavior-changing procedures follows.

Pause and Reflect About the Profession 8.6

What are some specific problem-solving deficiencies that your students present? What specific curricular alternatives can you use to facilitate the development of problem-solving skills? How can such instructional alternatives be integrated into other aspects of your curriculum?

Rationale and Current Intervention Efforts

Two important concerns should be addressed before the implementation of formal behavior-changing procedures. First, the teacher should know why a formal change procedure is necessary. Second, the teacher should know the details of any previous (and presumably unsuccessful) behavior-changing efforts involving the student. Most of this information is gleaned from the FBA. In addressing concerns related to the rationale, developing and beginning teachers should be able to readily state why changing the observed problem behavior is necessary. If the change procedure is to be implemented, the benefits of the effort should be readily interpreted as being of social and educational relevance to the student. A listing of previously unsuccessful behavior-changing efforts is necessary to assist in planning for intervention; there is no need to repeat strategies found to be unsuccessful.

Pinpointing a Target Behavior

Educators frequently characterize the inappropriate behaviors of their students in general terms (e.g., hyperactive, lazy, aggressive) rather than in specific terms. These general descriptions are not especially useful for individual behavior-changing programs. Specific valid and reliable behavioral pinpoints are necessary. The pinpointing process involves moving from general to specific descriptors of behavior. For example, hyperactivity (a general descriptor that would vary from observer to observer) is not a good pinpoint; out-of-seat behavior would be a more useful and reliable descriptor of the problem behavior. A good rule of thumb when developing behavioral pinpoints is to ensure that targeted behaviors (1) are overt, (2) are easily observed, and (3) contain movement. Several individuals observing a student should be able to agree on whether a target behavior did or did not occur.

Selecting an Observation and Recording Procedure

Once an appropriate target behavior has been pinpointed, a convenient method for observing and recording the behavior should be selected. Alternatives range from labor-intensive, continuous-recording systems to more time-efficient systems such as behavior sampling (see Table 8.8).

Obtaining Baseline Measures of Targeted Behavior

Once decisions have been made on the pinpointing and recording of behavior, a baseline measure of the targeted behavior must be obtained. Baseline refers to the level or intensity of a behavior prior to the introduction of an intervention procedure. Data recorded during subsequent intervention phases are compared with the baseline data. There are no general rules on how long baseline data should be collected. The amount of time will vary according to the behavior pinpointed. Baseline data should be collected until a stable trend is noted. Stability is characterized as the lack of a significant slope in the data and only moderate variability in daily observations. It should be remembered, however, that many aggressive and destructive behaviors require rapid intervention. In such cases, short baseline periods are the only practical course of action even though they lack the predictive power of longer baseline periods.

Setting Goals

Once the presenting problem has been pinpointed and the baseline data have been recorded, a goal or set of goals for the intervention should be developed. Without goals, teachers would be unable to ascertain whether, when, or how well their interventions succeeded. Behavioral management goals are most often set by using normative data guidelines or consulting previous performance records.

TABLE 8.8 Alternatives for Observing and Recording Behavior

Format	Purpose	Advantages	Disadvantages and Cautions
Continuous recording	Narrative description of behavior allows specification of conditions in which behavior occurs. Can provide general information that will assist when seeking a more formal and objective recording alternative.	Provides a broad-based subjective account of a problem behavior's antecedent and consequent conditions. A useful diagnostic approach to determine the possible. Environmental interactions that elicit and maintain behavior.	Requires continuous attention and considerable time. Subjective nature can result in reduced accuracy.
Permanent product	A physical product of a behavior can be translated into numerical terms that provide a direct measure of an effect of a behavior. Examples include student worksheets, time-clock records, and videotapes.	Direct observation of student not necessary. Typical practice in most classroom settings. Tangible product allows for review at varying intervals.	Not practical for many behaviors in the socioemotional domain.
Event recording	A simple frequency count of discrete behaviors (e.g., number of swear words, number of times talking out) during a predefined period of time.	Useful with behaviors that have clear beginning and ending points. Easily recorded with a checklist, bead counter, or pencil-stroke procedure.	Not useful for behaviors of long or varying duration. Requires considerable attention during the predefined observation period. Lower accuracy with very-high-rate behaviors.
Duration recording	A record of how long a behavior occurs within a given time period. Can be used to record the total length of time for each occurrence of a behavior as well as response latency.	Most useful for low-frequency behaviors of moderate to long duration.	Usually used with only one student. Not useful for high-rate behaviors of short duration. Requires continuous attention during observation period and the use of a stopwatch.
Interval recording	A determination of whether or not a behavior occurred within specified time intervals (observation period is divided into smaller, equally sized intervals).	Applicable to a wide range of behaviors and can be used with multiple students. Provides estimates of both frequency and duration of behaviors. Provides information about student behavior across time intervals.	Difficult for teachers to use while instructing students. Length of interval must be appropriate for the behavior targeted.
Momentary time sampling	An on-the-spot determination of whether or not a behavior occurred immediately following specified time intervals.	Allows teaching and data collection to occur simultaneously. Applicable to a wide range of behaviors and can be used with multiple students.	Length of interval must be appropriate for the behavior targeted. Not useful for low-frequency and short-duration behaviors.

Normative Data Guidelines. Normative data guidelines attempt to bring students' problem behaviors into line with the expectations of the least restrictive or general environment. Therefore, social-emotional goals for students with mild to moderate disabilities should, in most cases, approximate or even match behavioral frequencies found in age-appropriate general classroom settings. Developing and beginning teachers can observe general classrooms and collect data on the behavioral frequencies of various pro-social and inappropriate target behaviors. These frequency counts can be used as terminal goals for students in special education settings. Such an approach to goal setting is consistent with the goal of normalization and can facilitate the process of returning students to less restrictive educational settings.

Previous Performance Guidelines. For certain behavioral problems, it is reasonable to expect student performance to match previous intervention outcomes. For example, if a student reduced the rate of hitting others by 80 percent under a particular contingency management program, it would be reasonable to expect that the same goal could be attained with another target behavior (e.g., out-of-seat behavior) under the same or a slightly modified management program.

Administering the Intervention

When selecting one or a set of intervention procedures, it is important to record all components of the program and to note all environmental changes that accompany the implementation of the procedures. Such precision will produce a resource bank of possible treatment alternatives and facilitate the replication of successful approaches.

To facilitate the precise recording of a program's components, many educators use written behavioral contracts, which are joint agreements between themselves and their students. These contingency contracts list the specific behaviors the contracting parties should exhibit and the consequences that will result. Contracts are advantageous in individual behavior-changing programs because they allow students to work at their own rates and involve them in the planning of interventions. According to Hall and Hall (1982), contracts should always (1) be stated in positive terms, (2) be designed to promote success (e.g., reward small gradations of change), (3) provide frequent and immediate reinforcement, and (4) be the result of mutual negotiation between teacher and student. The contract should contain the following:

- The dates on which the contract is to begin, end, and/or be renegotiated
- A clear specification of the behavior or behaviors targeted for intervention
- The consequences (rewards) for meeting the terms of the contract
- A listing of who is to provide the consequences
- The signature of each party involved in the contract

A sample contract is found in Figure 8.6. For more details on the construction of contracts, consult Hall and Hall (1982), Homme (1977), or Kazdin (1975).

Analyzing Results Continuously

Because data are collected throughout the intervention period, evaluation and interpretation of results are relatively straightforward. By merely "eyeballing" the continuously measured performance of the student in contrast to the goal of the intervention, an assessment of the treatment program's effects can be completed. If the treatment is on a successful course, then it should be continued; if it seems unsuccessful, then it should be modified, or alternative intervention procedures should be considered.

This is a contract between _____ and _____.

                                           Student's name   Teacher's name

The student _____ agrees to work on the following behaviors:

    1. _____

    2. _____

    3. _____

If I meet the above conditions, I will get from the teacher:

_____

_____

_____

_____

as a special reward. If the terms of the contract are not met by the student, all rewards will be withheld.

Signatures and date

_____	_____
Student	Date
_____	_____
Teacher	Date
_____	_____
Witness	Date

We will review this contract on _____ to reevaluate it.

                                        Date

FIGURE 8.6 Sample Behavioral Contract

Completing Follow-Up and Maintenance Procedures

Once a treatment goal has been achieved, two interrelated programming activities need to be completed to ensure that the positive outcomes maintain and generalize to nontreatment settings. First, all external and artificial treatment components should be gradually removed or faded. Rapid and unsystematic removal of external treatments will usually result in the return of inappropriate behaviors. Second, maintenance probes should be scheduled at regular intervals to assess the success of the fading procedure. If the probes indicate a significant loss of treatment gains, intervention procedures with modified maintenance plans will need to be reintroduced.

 SUMMARY

This chapter covered a range of issues related to the area of behavior management. Our goal was to provide a series of strategies that could be used to promote discipline and self-control. We began by noting that there are no magic formulas or recipes that guarantee appropriate student behaviors in classrooms for students with mild to moderate disabilities. The management of behavior in classrooms involves strategies and procedures designed to increase the probability that classrooms run effectively and efficiently.

The following strategies to prevent discipline problems were presented: (1) the development and maintenance of an appropriate management perspective, (2) teacher readiness, (3) the design of the physical environment, (4) the development of rules and procedures, and (5) the coordination of schoolwide cooperation. Procedures for intervening in student misbehavior were presented, with special emphases on methods for conducting a functional behavioral assessment as well as for increasing and decreasing behavior. Strategies for promoting self-control were also provided, as were step-by-step guidelines for the completion of individual behavior-changing efforts.

ACTIVITIES TO EXTEND YOUR KNOWLEDGE

1. How would you go about involving colleagues, both general and special educators, in the development of a comprehensive behavioral management system? What advantages of this approach would you like to highlight? What collaborative skills would you use to ensure that the others would stay involved?
2. Set up a system to monitor your own performance in behavior management. What specific behaviors would you monitor in the presentation and implementation of your management system? What behaviors would you look for in your students?
3. Some educators claim that providing students with positive consequences for appropriate behavior is nothing short of bribery and that such actions prevent the natural development of an intrinsic sense of right and wrong in many children. In your view, what, if any, are the differences between positive reinforcement and bribery? Is it possible for a teacher to develop a positively based management system that recognizes appropriate behavior without the use of tangible rewards?
4. Every once in a while, a teacher will require the services of a substitute teacher. How would you direct a substitute to implement your behavioral management procedures? What directions and materials would be necessary for the substitute to implement your well-developed plans?
5. Gather and organize the materials you will need to conduct an FBA on a student with troubling behavior. These materials can be readily downloaded from several web sites (see Point and Click About the Profession). Develop a plan for conducting the assessment. How much time will you need? Who will you need to interview? When and where should you conduct your direct observations? Once you have mapped out your plan, complete the FBA. After several weeks, evaluate the usefulness of the FBA.

POINT AND CLICK ABOUT THE PROFESSION

These web sites have information and links to additional information related to classroom management.

Addressing Student Problem Behavior: Functional Assessment Materials
http://www.air-dc.org/cecp/resources/problembehavior

Center on Positive Behavior Interventions and Supports
http://www.pbis.org/english/index.html

Behavior Home Page
http://www.state.ky.us/agencies/behave/ebs3.html

Johns Hopkins University PAR Project
www.parproject.org

Virginia Youth Violence Project
http://curry.edschool.virginia.edu/curry/centers/youthvio

School Psychology Resources Online
http://www.schoolpsychology.net

Center for Effective Collaboration and Practice
http://www.air-dc.org/cecp

REFERENCES

Alberto, P. A., & Troutman, A. C. (2003). *Applied behavior analysis for teachers* (6th ed.). Upper Saddle River, NJ: Merrill/Prentice Hall.

Alliance Project. (2000, May). *School discipline and students with disabilities.* Nashville, TN: Vanderbilt University.

Alpert, L. (1989). *A teacher's guide to cooperative discipline: How to manage your classroom and promote self-esteem.* Circle Pines, MN: American Guidance Service.

Asmus, J. M., Vollmer, T. R., & Borrero, J. C. (2002). Functional behavioral assessment: A school based model. *Education and Treatment of Children, 25*(1), 67–90.

Bambara, L. M., & Knoster, T. (1998). *Designing positive behavior support plans.* Washington, DC: American Association on Mental Retardation.

Barrish, H. H., Saunders, M., & Wolf, M. M. (1969). Good behavior game: Effects of individual contingencies on disruptive behavior in the classroom. *Journal of Applied Behavior Analysis, 2,* 119–124.

Bauer, A. M., Shea, T. M., & Keppler, R. (1986). Levels systems: A framework for the individualization of behavior management. *Behavioral Disorders, 12,* 28–35.

Bauer, A. M., & Ulrich, M. E. (2002). "I've got a Palm in my pocket": Using handheld computers in an inclusive classroom. *Teaching Exceptional Children, 35*(2), 18–22.

Braaten, S. (1979). The Madison School program: Programming for secondary-level severely emotionally disturbed youth. *Behavioral Disorders, 4,* 211–218.

Carpenter, S. L., King-Sears, M. E., & Keys, S. G. (1998). Counselors + educators + families as a transdisciplinary team = more effective inclusion for students with disabilities. *Professional School Counseling, 2*(1), 1–9.

Center for Effective Collaboration and Practice. (1998). *Addressing student problem behavior: An IEP team's introduction to functional behavioral assessment and behavior intervention plans.* Washington, DC: Author.

Chandler, L. K., & Dahlquist, C. M. (2002). *Functional assessment: Strategies to prevent and remediate challenging behavior in school settings.* Upper Saddle River, NJ: Merrill/Prentice-Hall.

Conroy, M. A., & Stichter, J. P. (2003). The application of antecedents in the functional assessment process: Existing research, issues, and recommendations. *Journal of Special Education, 37*(1), 15–25.

Curwin, R. L., & Mendler, A. N. (1988). *Discipline with dignity.* Alexandria, VA: Association for Supervision and Curriculum Development.

Davis, C. A., & Fox, J. J. (1999). Evaluating environmental arrangements as setting events: Review and implications for measurement. *Journal of Behavioral Education, 9*(2), 77–96.

Demchak, M., & Bossert, K. W. (1996). *Innovations: Assessing problem behaviors.* Washington, DC: American Association on Mental Retardation.

Dwyer, K., & Osher, D. (2000). *Safeguarding our children: An action guide.* Washington, DC: U.S. Department of Education.

Dwyer, K., Osher, D., & Hoffman, C. C. (2000). Creating responsive schools: Contextualizing early warning, timely response. *Exceptional Children, 66*(3), 347–365.

D'Zurilla, T., & Goldfried, M. (1971). Problem solving and behavior modification. *Journal of Abnormal Psychology, 78,* 101–126.

Fox, J., & Conroy, M. (1995). Setting events and behavioral disorders of children and youth: An interbehavioral field analysis for research and practice. *Journal of Emotional and Behavioral Disorders, 3*(3), 130–140.

Fox, J. J., Gunter, P., Davis, C. A., & Brall, S. (2000). Observational methods in functional behavioral assessment: Practical techniques for practitioners. *Preventing School Failure, 44*(4), 152–157.

Gartin, B. C., & Murdick, N. L. (2001). A new IDEA mandate: The use of functional assessment of behavior and positive behavior supports. *Remedial and Special Education, 22*(6), 344–349.

Good, T. L., & Brophy, J. E. (1987). *Looking into classrooms* (4th ed.). New York: Harper & Row.

Hall, R. V., & Hall, M. C. (1982). *How to negotiate a behavioral contract*. Lawrence, KS: H & H Enterprises.

Hallahan, D. P., Lloyd, J. W., & Stoller, L. (1982). *Improving attention with self-monitoring: A manual for teachers*. Charlottesville: University of Virginia, Learning Disabilities Research Institute.

Hanley, G. P., Iwata, B. A., & McCord, B. (2003). Functional analysis of problem behavior: A review. *Journal of Applied Behavior Analysis, 36*, 147–186.

Hawken, L. S., & Horner, R. H. (2003). Evaluation of a targeted intervention within a schoolwide system of behavior support. *Journal of Behavioral Education, 12*(3), 225–240.

Homme, L. (1977). *How to use contingency contracting in the classroom*. Champaign, IL: Research Press.

Horner, R. H., & Carr, E. G. (1997). Behavioral support for students with severe disabilities: Functional assessment and comprehensive intervention. *Journal of Special Education, 31*, 84–109.

Kazdin, A. E. (1975). *Behavior modification in applied settings*. Belmont, CA: Dorsey Press.

Kennedy, C. H. (2002). Toward a socially valid understanding of problem behavior. *Education and Treatment of Children, 25*(1), 142–153.

Kern, L., Choutka, C. M., & Sokol, N. G. (2002). Assessment-based antecedent interventions used in natural settings to reduce challenging behavior: An analysis of the literature. *Education and Treatment of Children, 25*(1), 113–130.

Kounin, J. S. (1970). *Discipline and group management in the classroom*. New York: Holt, Rinehart & Winston.

Leone, P. E., Mayer, M. J., Malmgren, K., & Meisel, S. M. (2000). School violence and disruption: Rhetoric, reality, and reasonable balance. *Focus on Exceptional Children, 33*, 1–20.

Lewis, T. J., & Sugai, G. (1999). Effective behavioral support: A systems approach to proactive schoolwide management. *Focus on Exceptional Children, 31*(6), 1–23.

Long, N., & Newman, R. G. (1965). Managing surface behavior of children in school. In N. Long, W. Morse, & R. Newman (Eds.), *Conflict in the classroom: The education of emotionally disturbed children* (pp. 233–240). Belmont, CA: Wadsworth.

Maag, J. W. (1999). *Behavior management: From theoretical to practical applications*. San Diego, CA: Singular.

Maag, J. W., & Kemp, S. E. (2003). Behavioral intent of power and affiliation: Implications for functional analysis. *Remedial and Special Education, 24*(1), 57–64.

Mahon, K. L., Shores, R. E., & Buske, C. J. (1999). Issues of conducting research on setting events: Measurement and control of dependent and independent variables. *Education and Treatment of Children, 22*(3), 317–332.

Mastropieri, M. A., Jenne, T., & Scruggs, T. E. (1988). A level system for managing problem behaviors in a high school resource program. *Behavioral Disorders, 13*, 202–208.

Mastropieri, M. A., & Scruggs, T. E. (1987). *Effective instruction for special education*. Boston: College-Hill.

McConnell, M. E., Hilvitz, P. B., & Cox, C. J. (1998). Functional assessment: A systematic process for assessment and intervention in general and special education classrooms. *Intervention in School and Clinic, 34*, 10–20.

McGill, P., Teer, K., Rye, L., & Hughes, D. (2003). Staff reports of setting events associated with challenging behavior. *Behavior Modification, 27*(2), 265–282.

O'Neill, R., Horner, R., Albin, R., Sprague, J., Storey, K., & Newton, J. S. (1997). *Functional assessment and program development for problem behavior: A practical handbook*. Pacific Grove, CA: Brooks/Cole.

Paine, S. C., Radicci, J., Rossellini, L. C., Deutchman, L., & Darch, C. R. (1983). *Structuring your classroom for academic success*. Champaign, IL: Research Press.

Peterson, S. M. P., Derby, K. M., Berg, W. K., & Horner, R. H. (2002). Collaboration with families in the functional behavior assessment of and intervention for severe behavior problems. *Education and Treatment of Children, 25*(1), 5–25.

Repp, A. C., & Horner, R. H. (Eds.). (1999). *Functional analysis of problem behavior: From effective assessment to effective support*. Pacific Grove, CA: Brooks/Cole.

Rosenberg, M. S., & Jackman, L. A. (1997). Addressing student and staff behavior: The PAR model. *The Fourth R, 79*, 1–12.

Rosenberg, M. S., & Jackman, L. A. (2003). Development, implementation, and sustainability of comprehensive school-wide behavior management systems. *Intervention in School and Clinic, 39*, 10–21.

Sasso, G. M., Conroy, M. A., Stichter, J. P., & Fox, J. J. (2001). Slowing down the bandwagon: The misapplication of functional assessment for students with emotional or behavioral disorders. *Behavioral Disorders, 26*(4), 282–296.

Scott, T. M., Nelson, C. M., & Zabala, J. (2003). Functional behavior assessment training in public schools: Facilitating systemic change. *Journal of Positive Behavior Interventions, 5*(4), 216–224.

Slavin, R. E. (2003). *Educational psychology: Theory into practice*. Upper Saddle River, NJ: Prentice Hall.

Smith, D. D., & Rivera, D. P. (1995). Discipline in special education and general education settings. *Focus on Exceptional Children, 27*(5), 1–16.

Smith, R. M., Neisworth, J. T., & Greer, J. G. (1978). *Evaluating educational environments*. New York: Merrill/Macmillan.

Spivack, G., & Shure, M. B. (1982). The cognition of social adjustment: Interpersonal cognitive problem solving. In B. B. Lahey & A. E. Kazdin (Eds.), *Advances in clinical child psychology* (Vol. 5). New York: Plenum.

Tankersley, M. (1995). A group-oriented contingency management program. *Preventing School Failure, 40,* 45–59.

Thorson, S. (1996). The missing link: Students discuss school discipline. *Focus on Exceptional Children, 29,* 1–12.

Topper, K., Williams, W., Leo, K., Hamilton, R., & Fox, T. (1994). *A positive approach to understanding and addressing challenging behavior.* Burlington: University of Vermont.

U.S. Department of Education, Office of Special Education and Rehabilitative Services. (2002). *A new era: Revitalizing special education for children and their families.* Washington, DC: Author.

Veenman, S. (1984). Perceived problems of beginning teachers. *Review of Educational Research, 54,* 143–178.

Weber, W. A., & Roff, L. A. (1983). A review of the teacher education literature on classroom management. In W. A. Weber, J. Crawford, L. A. Roff, & C. Robinson (Eds.), *Classroom management: Reviews of the teacher education and research literature* (pp. 7–43). Princeton, NJ: Educational Testing Service.

Westling, D. L., & Koorland, M. A. (1988). *The special educator's handbook.* Needham Heights, MA: Allyn & Bacon.

White, R., Algozzine, B., Audette, R., Marr, M. B., & Ellis, E. D. (2001). Unified discipline: A schoolwide approach for managing problem behavior. *Intervention in School and Clinic, 37,* 3–8.

Wilson, B., Ireton, E., & Wood, J. A. (1997). Beginning teacher's fears. *Education, 117,* 396–400.

## CHAPTER 9

Student and Family Transitions

with Janeen M. Taylor

Chapter Outline

Transition Faced by Students and Their Families

Transition Issues in Families of Young Children

Early Intervention and Early Childhood Special Education

Individualized Family Service Plans (IFSPs)

Teachers' Work with Families

Elementary- and Middle-School Students' Transitions

Linking School Opportunities

IEPs and Students' Transitions

High School Students' Transitions

Interagency Coordination Efforts

Teachers' Roles as Students Age

Facilitating the Transition Process for Older Students and Their Families

In this chapter, we will

- introduce transitions faced by students with disabilities and their families

- identify transition components of individualized family service plans (IFSPs) and individualized education programs (IEPs)

- discuss linkages in school opportunities, including interagency coordination

- review teachers' roles as students age

A PROFESSIONAL GLIMPSE

Elena Gorospe is a single mother with a three-year-old daughter, Anna, who has a genetic condition that causes overall developmental delays. Ms. Gorospe and Anna live with Anna's maternal grandparents and have received early intervention services as delineated in their individualized family service plan (IFSP) since shortly after Anna's birth. The health care providers in the neonatal intensive care unit (NICU) referred Anna and her family to the local early intervention program when Anna was only a few days old. NICU nurses and community-based early intervention practitioners worked closely to support Anna's transition from the NICU to home.

The early intervention team has made weekly home visits throughout the year. Visits are scheduled at times that are convenient for Ms. Gorospe, who works full-time, and her parents, who provide child care for Anna. Anna's service coordinator and the early intervention team have recently coordinated plans for Anna's enrollment in a local preschool program at the Sojourner Truth Child Development Center. She will receive special instruction and related services while she attends preschool with neighborhood children. Anna's mother is very anxious about Anna's impending participation in a preschool program. The early intervention team has become part of the family, and services have been delivered in a very sensitive, family-friendly manner.

Ms. Gorospe worries about the safety of transportation arrangements, attitudes of new teachers toward single parents, school-based routines, the level of playground supervision, and the behavior of children toward Anna, who is very petite and shy. Anna's early intervention practitioners know how stressful change can be and are working hard to provide Ms. Gorospe with information about Anna's new school, teachers, administrators, and routines. Early intervention personnel have scheduled tours of the new school, set up meetings with school personnel, and held meetings for parents whose children will be attending.

Ms. Gorospe is concerned about one of the many transitions Anna will encounter during her life. Families and practitioners face multiple challenges when planning and implementing smooth changeovers between programs and personnel. Ensuring seamless services for children and families is a critical component of a high-quality system of services for students with disabilities and their families. Developing strategies for supporting children and families during times of change can reduce family anxiety and stress.

*I*n this chapter, we provide an overview of transition issues related to very young children with disabilities and the effects on children's families. We review early intervention services and the transitions that students and their families face. We help new teachers examine the evaluation and assessment needs of young children and explore various medical or developmental issues related to implementation and monitoring of a child's IFSP (Epps & Jackson, 2000; McLean, Bailey, & Wolery, 2004; Sandall, McLean, & Smith, 2000). We explore these issues as they relate to teachers' roles in providing quality services to young children and families.

Next, we identify services offered to school-age children and youth with disabilities. Such services have undergone dramatic changes since the enactment of Individuals with Disabilities Education Act (IDEA) in 1990. We explore teachers' work with diverse families of school-age students involved in IDEA and other federal initiatives. The influx of diverse students is changing the shape and milieu of elementary, middle, and high school services.

A necessary prerequisite to school programs is interagency coordination. We identify helpful teacher roles as students age and as their families become increasingly involved with adult agencies. We examine strategies to facilitate transitions in high school years and beyond. Because new teachers will help in linking high school to postschool services, we offer ideas on how school curricula can provide a range of options in career planning (e.g., college-bound training, technical schools, vocational training, supported work, paid employment). Many high school teachers will focus on a curriculum model for high-functioning students that focuses on job training; postsecondary education requirements; self-advocacy, self-management, and awareness of learning strengths and weaknesses; and individual decision making related to leisure-time pursuits, marriage and living arrangements, and other adult considerations. Teachers providing a curriculum model for low-functioning students will stress community-referenced, integrated, longitudinal, and community-based experiences.

New teachers will be involved in making meaningful decisions regarding students' transitions (adjustments to change) and family concerns affected by students' transitions. Today, new teachers' roles and responsibilities are related to linking services within and between agencies. New service views, or what has been termed "life-long transition planning," require anticipation, planning, implementation, and analysis of systematic timeline procedures in order to prepare infants, children, and youth for adult roles and services (deFur, Getzel, & Kregel, 1994; deFur & Taymans, 1995; Karge, Patton, & de la Garza, 1992; Kolher, 1993; Martin, Marshall, & Maxson, 1993).

Preparing for transitions begins early in a child's life. Early and sequential planning increases the chances of successful adjustments for the child and the family. Developing and beginning teachers working with students of all ages and ability levels will be called on to assist students and their families as they make various transitions.

TRANSITIONS FACED BY STUDENTS AND THEIR FAMILIES

Students and their families face many transitions: exiting the cozy family-friendly environments of early intervention; beginning and coping with the daily demands of school or community programs as a very young child; advancing in school grades and interacting with different teachers; leaving parents' homes, marrying, and having children; getting jobs and being promoted; and moving to new homes or cities. When students and families make transitions, professionals can be a support. They can assist by offering coordinated and functional services that help students learn the concrete, everyday skills that allow them to achieve the kind of life they and their families want (Lambie & Daniels-Mohring, 1993). Functional skills learned in school are the foundation of students' adult success. When teachers link their functional skill instruction with services offered by other professionals, they are helping students and their families face and adjust to transitions.

Effective teachers who are focusing on functional skills need to consider real-life experiences that students will encounter as they age. Adult preparation increases in importance as students age. Changes are especially complex and difficult because, as students get older, they and their families must interact with various private and public agency personnel and systems. For instance, young children and their parents often spend an enormous amount of time in hospitals. Families may interact with countless numbers of doctors, nurses, therapists, and other health care personnel. Criteria for determining eligibility for services delivered to children in health care settings are usually medically based. Early intervention programs vary greatly from state to state and may be staffed by paraprofessionals, health care providers, educators, or other professionals. Families will interact with a myriad of practitioners while trying to obtain the best services for their infants and toddlers. By the time young children enroll in preschool or school, the professionals with whom families interact come from a different background; educational personnel usually deliver services in preschool and school settings. In addition, the eligibility requirements for receiving services, pertinent contact personnel available, and types and quantity of services provided differ from those in a health care facility. Such changes represent stressful adjustments for many young students and their families.

When students reach middle and high school, more changes occur in services, personnel, locations, and requirements. Families must interact with personnel from new agencies. In addition to medical and educational agencies, families may be involved with family support systems, legal services, counseling programs, social services, or welfare agencies. Often, agencies vary in the quality of services they provide. In addition, the focus of the interventions offered may vary from agency to agency. Some may continue to stress health or educational services, whereas others may be oriented toward social well-being and family interactions. Others may offer legal, community, or welfare supports. Nonetheless, students, families, and professionals must work together to address the changes in the activities, resources, and schedules. As time moves on and people adjust to the vast array of personnel, services, restrictions, and resources offered, working as a team is essential.

Teachers can help children, youth, and families make healthy adjustments to changes by providing support and information. Two life periods receiving particular attention are the transitions from preschool to public school and from school to work. Teachers providing services to students in or receiving students from both early and adult services assist students and their families when they target planned activities, anticipate time frames, and help coordinate integrated services and appropriate follow-through for student and family.

Pause and Reflect About the Profession 9.1

Are you well prepared to discuss with families, your host teacher, or your university supervisor the following transition and family issues regarding students in your field placement? Circle Yes or No for each of the following to indicate whether you are prepared to deal with the issue.

A. Early Life and Preschool Years

1.	Transition types	Yes	No
2.	Early services	Yes	No
3.	Evaluation and assessment	Yes	No
4.	Medical/physical issues	Yes	No
5.	Teaming issues	Yes	No
6.	Family-centered services	Yes	No
7.	Individual family service plans (IFSPs)	Yes	No

B. School-Age Years

1.	Family participation	Yes	No
2.	School-age transitions	Yes	No
3.	Diverse family strategies	Yes	No

C. Adult Preparation

1.	Linking schools and communities	Yes	No
2.	Individualized education programs (IEPs)	Yes	No
3.	Interagency coordination	Yes	No
4.	Adult issues	Yes	No
5.	Facilitating the transition process	Yes	No

Transition Issues in Families of Young Children

Ideally, transition planning is a careful process rather than a point in time. Transitions mean a variety of individual and family events as young children and their families enter into or change programs or service systems. Teachers need to recognize the importance of families as decision makers in the transition process and work toward the common goal of successful treatments and programs for young children and their families (McWilliam, 2000).

Transitions mean change and adjustment as infants and toddlers enter and exit various levels of service delivery systems (Kilgo, 1990). Transitions may entail a change from no services (e.g., students with mild disabilities typically are not identified until they reach school age) or multiple systems (e.g., health and social services are provided to students with more severe problems) to a unitary system (education).

Typical transition issues that teachers working with young children will confront are the adjustments and associated stresses that children and their families encounter when changing to and from various service delivery systems. These changes include the switch from physician to teacher as the family's primary information sources. New teachers may be called on to help families make the change from a program offered through a clinical or home setting to one that is provided in a preschool or school setting. Teachers may be the parents' or guardians' main resource for acquiring information on the scope of preschool offerings or additional legal requirements for services in a school setting.

Some teachers must assume different roles with family members, based on such factors as the severity of the child's disabling condition, parents' desires for and level of involvement in their child's programs, variations in local offerings of infant/family intervention programs that may or may not match families' expectations, coping strategies used by the child and his or her family, residential placement options, respite care needs, and independent functioning expectations. Nonetheless, adjustment and stress are evident in most children and families as they change faculty, staff, programming, adult-to-student ratios, service locations, schedules, communication methods, transportation methods, and service goals or objectives. Teachers can help families survive such adjustments.

Teachers can also help young children and their families make changes across service delivery systems by initiating the transition process. For example, teachers can provide a bridge across various program elements by collaborating with other service providers. Teachers can use effective communication techniques when children transition, for example, from a neonatal nursery to home and from home to school. Teachers can seek input from other relevant service providers when children change from child care centers to public school/preschool programs. Initial communication attempts by teachers are important because researchers have confirmed that a lack of communication among physicians, health care workers, social workers, speech and language therapists, physical therapists, and preschool staff can jeopardize the years of careful training and education provided to, or anticipated for, children in early childhood special education programs (Hanline & Knowlton, 1988). Important communication strategies include listening to family members' concerns, answering their questions honestly and promptly, and being a good resource to assist them with their child and family concerns.

Some researchers (Bailey, Simeonsson, Yoder, & Huntington, 1990; Craig & Leonard, 1990) suggest that teachers offering family-specific data on local contacts, program purposes, transportation information, times, and cost factors help families become more involved in and responsive to services. When teachers collaborate with other professionals, they help families address issues that define how families learn to live with and support their children. By working actively and assisting families, teachers pick up important home data on families' backgrounds, cultures, expectations, differences in coping styles, need for family support programs, parent training interests or accessibility, and teachers' influence on home environments. All of this information can be important when designing individualized treatments for children and their families (Gowen & Nebrig, 2002; Hooper & Umansky, 2004).

In addition, when teachers work well with such professionals as the medical and school services personnel also assessing families of young children, teachers help families enormously. They model for families how team building and group processes work. Teachers operating in effective professional teams support cross-disciplinary communication skills. They recognize how best to incorporate the basic terminology of other disciplines; they accumulate data about the roles, academic preparation, clinical experiences, and expertise of other professionals; they employ the principles and procedures underlying team building and the group process; they discuss family needs across settings; and they work together to facilitate students' school or community entrance or exit. During students' preschool years, teachers must be able to collect information on future skills and program requirements of the next school environment, while embedding training into current programming (O'Shea & Caldwell, 1990). Talking with other professionals and obtaining resources on new programs help the family while the child receives existing services. Transition coordination works when professionals cooperate and offer coordinated services.

Early Intervention and Early Childhood Special Education

Today, there are substantial differences between strategies for special instruction for very young children with disabilities (birth to age 6) and those for older children and youth with disabilities (ages 6 to 21) (Smith, 2004). The U.S. Congress recognized these differences by including Part C in the IDEA and by modifying Section 619, related to preschool special education. Part C and its accompanying regulations specify special instruction for infants and toddlers with disabilities as one of a long list of early intervention services. For children and youth ages 3 to 21, special education and related services are addressed in Part B of the IDEA. One section of Part B, Section 619, focuses on preschool children with disabilities and their special instruction and related services. Part C and Section 619 of the IDEA include unique features that hold importance for new teachers in terms of their knowledge and skills and their roles with family members.

Teachers' Roles in Early Transitions. There are three important transitions for children in early intervention or preschool special education programs. The first involves the transition from a hospital-based setting to the community in which a family lives. Hospitals usually have discharge coordinators who work with families to develop a plan for treatment after hospitalization. New teachers can help in the transition from the hospital setting by obtaining a list of the names and telephone numbers of area discharge coordinators. They can then work with each referring hospital's discharge coordinator to collect follow-through data, such as medical appointments, prescriptions, and/or therapies

Pause and Reflect About the Profession 9.2

Discuss at least four specific ways that teachers can help young children and their families when families are transitioning from physicians to teachers as primary informal sources.

1. _____

2. _____

3. _____

4. _____

Box 9.1　　　　**Community Programs for Three-Year-Olds**

_____ Before- or after-school care

_____ Child care

_____ Day camp

_____ Family child care (in-home)

_____ Head Start

_____ Library story times

_____ Play group

_____ Private lessons (e.g., gymnastics)

_____ Recreation center

_____ Residential camp

_____ Tutoring

begun in the hospital. Teachers can ensure a smooth adjustment from a health care setting to an early intervention setting by linking medical and educational services.

The second major transition for young children is from an early intervention program to a preschool or preschool special education program. Any transition can be stressful, especially for families who have grown accustomed to the staff and routines of their child's program (Nelson, Bennett, & Lingerfelt, 1992). Beginning personnel continue to play an important role in helping the family obtain accurate and timely information regarding their child's developmental strengths and needs. To do this properly, teachers can help in initially judging the likelihood of each child's eligibility for preschool special education or for a particular community-based program (Bowe, 2000; Lerner, Lowenthal, & Egan, 2003). It may be helpful to schedule regular information sessions for families of two- and three-year-olds. For example, Box 9.1 offers a list of possible program options for three-year-olds.

The third transition is from a preschool or preschool special education program to a primary education or primary special education program (i.e., grades one, two, and three). Families need a head start on the planning process, so having current written information about special education and community-based program availability is vital. As appropriate, handouts with registration cutoff dates, income eligibility requirements, geographic boundaries of programs, transportation availability, age restrictions, degree of parental participation required, and other program-specific criteria may help in the transition process (Governor's Office for Children, Youth, and Families/Maryland Infants and Toddlers Program, 1992).

Teachers work throughout the year to assist families in identifying the appropriate program(s) for their children. An important task is to orient families to the types of early services that are available locally. For example, teachers can provide accurate information on program eligibility criteria, resources, services, and contacts. Teachers' knowledge regarding unique family needs or priorities can make this a time of growth for families and children alike.

Evaluation and Assessment of Young Children with Disabilities. Determining the developmental strengths and needs of infants, toddlers, and preschoolers is critical to successful programming (Bagnato, Neisworth, & Munson, 1989; Guralnick, 2000; McLean, Bailey, & Wolery, 2004; Taylor & Fleming, 1997). Although some controversy surrounds specific terms used to describe developmental testing of young children, evaluation refers to instruments or procedures used to determine a child's (1) developmental diagnosis, (2) initial eligibility for a program, or (3) ongoing eligibility for a program (Campbell, 1991). Assessment refers to the process of monitoring or checking a child's developmental status for purposes of program adjustment (Fewell, 1991). For older students with disabilities, the terms *evaluation* and *assessment* are often used interchangeably (Henley, Ramsey, & Algozzine, 1993).

The birth to age three years can be a time of crisis for families (Fewell & Vadasy, 1986) when developmental test results confirm a serious problem that may carry long-term consequences (Turnbull & Turnbull, 1986). For families of premature infants, developmental testing can be especially difficult. Parents often spend days, weeks, or months visiting their child in the neonatal intensive care unit, watching their child struggle for survival. Many interact with a host of medical personnel, including doctors, nurses, technicians, and therapists. During this period, developmental testing can confirm or alleviate parental fears of permanent disability (Krajicek & Tompkins, 1993; VandenBerg & Hanson, 1993).

Given the inherent stress in the evaluation or assessment process, professionalism during the process of evaluating an infant or toddler is critical for families (Brown, Thurman, & Pearl, 1993; Katz, Pokorni, & Long, 1989). Teachers can take a number of steps to ensure evaluation and assessment preparation and professionalism. First, it is essential to determine the kinds of evaluation and assessment instruments or procedures operating in early childhood settings that will help families move from hospital or home-care support to educational support.

Teachers can begin to explore with parents the effects an exceptional condition may have on a person's life. They might provide written information to families on differential characteristics of children and youth with disabilities (including levels of severity, where applicable) and potential implications for parents, siblings, or other family members. They can assist families in understanding similarities and differences in children's development. They can become competent examiners of children's development (Bricker, 1989). Thus, new teachers can offer valuable information to parents on their child's developmental status and normal or exceptional milestones.

Box 9.2 presents suggested steps that teachers can take to become familiar with evaluation or assessment procedures. A beginning teacher's confidence in using a specific instrument or procedure will be transmitted to families whose infant or toddler may be under his or her care for months to come (Linder, 1993a).

In the preschool environment, however, the evaluation and assessment scenario is somewhat different. Curriculum-based assessment (King-Sears, 1994) is a common

---

Box 9.2

Steps for Selecting and Using the Appropriate Evaluation and Assessment Tools for Infants and Toddlers

_____ 1. Examine the scoring form.

_____ 2. Read the manual carefully.

_____ 3. Jot down questions you have.

_____ 4. Ask experienced examiners the questions you've formulated.

_____ 5. Observe an experienced examiner administer the instrument or procedure.

_____ 6. Obtain the test kit or assemble appropriate materials.

_____ 7. Practice using the instrument or procedure on children of friends or relatives.

_____ 8. Have someone videotape your efforts, and ask colleagues for suggestions on improving your test administration.

_____ 9. Reflect on the procedures and process.

_____10. Develop a plan to correct deficiencies.

_____11. Implement the plan.

approach to initial and ongoing assessment of a child's developmental status (McLean, Bailey, & Wolery, 2004). It is important to determine the specific curricular approach required by the child. If the school system or program does not have a standard curriculum, beginning teachers might choose a curriculum with an accompanying evaluation or assessment tool. At this time, teachers can begin to discuss curriculum options in relation to the child's educational strengths and needs. Teachers can discuss with parents or guardians similarities and differences among the cognitive, language, physical, social, and emotional needs of infants and toddlers who are developing in a typical fashion and those developing in an atypical fashion. Box 9.3 lists some commonly used curricula with accompanying evaluation or assessment materials. These early childhood special education curricula are in wide use throughout the United States and may be a helpful starting point for teachers' collaborations with family members. Box 9.4 lists criteria for choosing a curriculum.

Medical/Physical Issues Related to Working with Young Children with Disabilities. Advances in health care technology and practice ensure increased survival rates for many infants born prematurely and for newborns with formerly lethal congenital conditions (Bond et al., 1990). Many children born prematurely have special health care needs (Batshaw, 1997, 2001). Nonetheless, beginning teachers can take steps to make sure that the educational experience of children with special health care needs is positive and healthy:

1. It is helpful to complete a pediatric CPR course through the local Red Cross chapter (Urbano, 1992). Red Cross courses are relatively short and are especially important for pediatric health emergencies.

2. It is important to read the medical file on each student as soon as possible. Files often contain valuable information about a student's health status and relevant implications for educational intervention.

3. By asking the program director, principal, or supervisor for information concerning local policies related to children with special health care needs, new teachers may be able to gather a wide range of local support services and resources for families and children affected by medical conditions.

4. Reading relevant materials on special health care needs can help new teachers stay abreast of current medical practices affecting a child's educational needs. Two very good books about children with special health care needs are *Children with Disabilities* (Batshaw, 1997) and *Preschool Children with Special Health Care Needs* (Urbano, 1992).

Box 9.3   **Early Childhood Special Education Curricula with Accompanying Evaluation or Assessment Instruments or Procedures**

- Bricker, D., Capt, B., & Pretti-Frontczak, K., (Eds.). (2002). *Volume 2: AEPS Test for Birth to Three Years and Three to Six Years.* Baltimore, MD: Paul H. Brookes.
- Johnson-Martin, N. M., Attermeier, S. M., & Hacker, B. J. (2004). *The Carolina Curriculum for Infants & Toddlers with Special Needs* (CCITSN) (3rd ed.). Baltimore, MD: Paul H. Brookes.
- Johnson-Martin, N. M., Attender, S. M., & Hacker, B. J. (2004). *The Carolina Curriculum for Preschoolers with Special Needs* (CCPSN) (2nd ed.). Baltimore, MD: Paul H. Brookes.
- Furuno, S., O'Reilly, K. A., Hosaka, C. M., Inatsuka, T. T., Allman, T. L., & Zeisloft, B. (1997). *HELP Activity Guide (0–3).* Palo Alto, CA: VORT Corporation.
- VORT Corporation. (1999). *HELP for Preschoolers Assessment & Curriculum Guide.* Palo Alto, CA: Author.
- Linder, T. (1993). *Transdisciplinary Play-Based Assessment: Guidelines for Developing a Meaningful Curriculum for Young Children.* Baltimore, MD: Paul H. Brookes.

Box 9.4　　　　　**Criteria for Curriculum Selection**

In determining the appropriateness of a curriculum for use in an early intervention or early childhood special education program, consider the following:

1. Do you think children would like these curricular activities?
   Yes _____　　No _____

2. Are these activities family-friendly (easy to use, attractive, appealing)?
   Yes _____　　No _____

3. Is the curriculum teacher-friendly (logically formatted, understandable)?
   Yes _____　　No _____

4. Would this curriculum be consistent with community values?
   Yes _____　　No _____

5. Is the curriculum appropriate developmentally?
   Yes _____　　No _____

6. Are the criteria for success in the accompanying evaluation or assessment instrument or procedures clear and measurable?
   Yes _____　　No _____

7. Is there a range of opportunities for family members or caretakers to participate in (or lead) curricular activities?
   Yes _____　　No _____

8. Can these curricular activities be adapted for use with children who have a range of abilities and disabilities?
   Yes _____　　No _____

9. Does the curriculum require specialized or costly materials or equipment?
   Yes _____　　No _____

10. Does the curriculum have guidelines for staffing patterns (caretaker-child ratios)?
    Yes _____　　No _____

11. Are curricular activities suited for a child's natural environment?
    Yes _____　　No _____

12. Are all developmental domains addressed?
    Yes _____　　No _____

13. Are curricular activities sequenced appropriately?
    Yes _____　　No _____

14. Is the curriculum appropriate for individual children, as well as groups of children?
    Yes _____　　No _____

Another critical health issue is minimizing the transmission of communicable diseases in educational settings. Taylor and Taylor (1989) advise decreasing the incidence of infectious disease through specific guidelines for handwashing. Anderson, Bale, Blackman, and Murph (1994) advise: "Handwashing is the most important means of controlling infections. Staff and children should wash their hands upon arrival, . . . after using the toilet or changing diapers . . . or assisting with toilet use, after wiping a child's or their own runny nose . . . before serving or eating food, and any time hands may be contaminated with a body fluid" (p. 62). A 50 percent reduction in the incidence of diarrhea was noted in centers where careful handwashing procedures were instituted (Donowitz, 1993).

Washing classroom surfaces, instructional materials, and toys is a useful strategy for minimizing infection (Taylor, 1995). The school nurse or local health department official can suggest an effective cleaning solution. Teachers and classroom aides can wash boxes, shelves, counters, and other surfaces. Older children can help rinse them thoroughly with clean water. Work and play surfaces can be air dried. If the program does not have guidelines for handwashing and keeping materials cleaned, it is important that new teachers establish their own written directives. Guidelines should be placed in appropriate room locations where, on daily arrival, teachers, classroom aides, volunteers, parents, guardians, and/or classroom visitors can read the listings.

The Expanded Multidisciplinary Team. Early intervention and preschool special education continues a strong emphasis on serving children through a coordinated team effort (Smith, 2004). A multidisciplinary team typically includes representatives from three to five disciplines, including the physical therapist, occupational therapist, speech-language pathologist, and adaptive physical education teacher. Teachers work with other professionals daily and share data regarding young children's progress.

Further, teachers can offer families coordinated services with a variety of professionals. Communication and sharing with families and colleagues are vital if the expanded multidisciplinary team is to be successful. Early intervention entails a greater range of disciplines than special education for older students. The size of the team for younger children can be large, as illustrated in Table 9.1. The need for effective communication

TABLE 9.1   Possible Team Members for Part B and Part C of the IDEA

Part B	Part C
Parents	Parents
Audiologist	Audiologist
Counselor	Counselor
Medical service provider (for diagnostic purposes)	Medical service provider (for diagnostic purposes)
Physical therapist	Physical therapist
Occupational therapist	Occupational therapist
Orientation and mobility specialist	Orientation and mobility specialist
Special education teacher	Special education teacher
Speech-language pathologist	Speech-language pathologist
Recreation specialist	Health care provider (e.g., pediatrician, dysmorphologist, neurologist)
Psychologist	Psychologist
Social worker	Social worker
	Child care provider
	Service coordinator
	Nurse
	Nutritionist
	Vision specialist
	Assistive technology specialist

and collaboration increases in direct proportion to the number of individuals involved (Kroth, 1975).

Family-Centered Services. According to Sandall, McLean, and Smith (2000), early intervention and special education services for young children with disabilities must be family-centered. Family-centered services require teachers to be knowledgeable about individual and family needs and strengths. Teachers must provide functional instruction relevant to student diversity and family dynamics. They must respond to typical family concerns while individualizing appropriate student strategies. Further, implementing family-centered services means that teachers work with other team members to identify quality-of-life issues important to each family (e.g., leisure-time and recreation activities) and incorporate these issues into students' educational programs.

Part C of the IDEA is designed to be family-centered in recognition of the importance of the family to a child's developmental well-being (Brazelton & Cramer, 1990; Epps & Jackson, 2000; Fewell & Vadasy, 1986; Hanft, Rush, & Shelden, 2004; Johnson-Martin, Attermeier, & Hacker, 1990; Singer & Irvin, 1989). The ability to interact positively with a wide range of family members and to understand children and disabilities within a cultural context is a key factor in a successful career as an early interventionist or preschool special educator. Teachers are likely to be successful in providing family-centered services when they focus on implementing strategies that prepare students to live harmoniously and productively in a multicultural world.

Unfortunately, a lack of family knowledge can be problematic for teachers unfamiliar with students' ethnic backgrounds, cultural heritage, and/or family living arrangements. Teachers need accurate information on students' family diversity, lifestyles, cultures, and the many contributions that family diversity can offer in classrooms.

Lambie and Daniels-Mohring (1993) and Lynch and Hanson (2004) offer the following suggestions for facilitating team functioning in such a way that diverse family members are integral to the functioning of the multidisciplinary teams. First, the family must be involved in all aspects of decision making regarding their child and his or her services (Jeppson & Thomas, 1995). Parents or guardians need a say in their child's services. Family members have a lifelong relationship with their child and are central to their child's development and well-being. Family involvement in decisions regarding their child's program is extremely important to program success (McLean, Bailey, & Wolery, 2004; O'Shea, O'Shea, & Nowocien, 1993).

Second, teachers must develop an understanding of the cultural context necessary for communication and of the importance of culture and community to verbal and nonverbal communication. If all team members have the same cultural identity, this may not be an issue. It is common, however, for teams to comprise individuals from diverse backgrounds. Effective communication strategies for one cultural framework may not work in a different cultural context. Teachers need to be alert to communicating appropriate messages to families and students.

New teachers can use their observational skills to determine how best to communicate with diverse family members. Teachers can talk with parents or guardians about services that family members would like stressed in their child's program. Teachers can ask parents or guardians to provide input regarding priorities for their child's cognitive, language, physical, or social development. Teachers can help even the youngest child accept diversity by modeling appropriate acceptance behaviors when interacting with families or coworkers.

When new teachers take the time to acquire skills and competencies in cross-cultural communication, they maximize their group effectiveness. In the middle of fast-paced educational discussions, it might be easy to lose sight of important individual issues. Having written priorities based on each family's unique concerns before a meeting can facilitate team involvement in decisions. A written agenda may even help meetings run more smoothly.

B ox 9.5　　　　　　**Considerations for Multidisciplinary Team Meetings**

When preparing for a multidisciplinary team meeting, remember to
- Put ideas about each child in writing before the meeting.
- Bring paper and pencils (or pens) and take careful notes about concerns and suggestions.
- Consider the cultural context when communicating with team members.
- Know the rationale for each of your suggestions.
- Focus on each child and family.
- Maintain confidentiality with regard to the discussions.
- Follow up, when appropriate.

If a team has a difficult time with task completion, conflict resolution and group problem-solving strategies are available. For instance, Turnbull et al. (1993) and Turnbull and Turnbull (1986) offer useful ideas for successful team meetings and collaboration. Noonan and McCormick's (1993) recommendations for effective team functioning involve a multicultural context with wide applicability to many family or community needs. Box 9.5 lists strategies that will increase a beginning teacher's effectiveness as a contributing team member who is cognizant of unique family strengths and needs.

Parents often value practitioners who build rapport (Dinnebeil & Rule, 1994), take time to listen (Turnbull & Turnbull, 1985), are respectful (Harry, Allen, & McLaughlin, 1995), and demonstrate that they understand the incredible time and service demands necessary in effective early intervention and preschool services (Brotherson & Goldstein, 1992). To support families as they parent young children with disabilities, effective teachers need to take time to reflect on family encounters. Box 9.6 presents reflection questions that may help new teachers in developing and refining their abilities to support family efforts (DeGangi, Wietlisbach, Poisson, & Stein, 1994).

Individualized Family Service Plans (IFSPs)

Federal and state guidelines mandate active family participation in the transition process. As previously implied, even for the youngest child with disabilities, early intervention entails professionals working with families to document a family's resources, concerns, priorities, and interventions. The documentation results in a child's individualized family service plan (IFSP). A number of federal IFSP requirements are

B ox 9.6　　　　　　**Reflecting on Family Interactions**

_____ What went well during the session?

_____ What was awkward or uncomfortable for me or the family?

_____ Did I really understand the family's concerns for their child? If I'm not sure, a follow-up telephone call is in order.

_____ Did I avoid professional jargon and use lay terms?

_____ Did I go slowly when offering suggestions and allow time for new information to sink in?

_____ Was I nonjudgmental of the family and their parenting style?

_____ What do I need to know to support this family?

_____ How will I acquire the needed information (e.g., make telephone calls, consult a colleague, read texts or journal articles)?

Box 9.7

Federal Requirements for an Individualized Family Service Plan (IFSP)

Have I met all of the federal requirements for this IFSP? Have I provided information on the

____ Child's present level of development in
- Cognition
- Communication
- Social or emotional development
- Adaptive skills
- Physical status (including vision, hearing, health status)

____ Family's resources, concerns, and priorities

____ Projected completion date for major outcomes

____ Criteria, procedures, and timeliness for determination of progress toward or achievement of each outcome

____ Specific early intervention services

____ Frequency and intensity of services

____ Child's natural environment

____ Location of services

____ Payment for services

____ Linkages with services not required (under part C or Section 619 of Part B of IDEA)

____ Transition planning

Have all the participants signed the IFSP?

listed in Box 9.7. New teachers should query the program director to discover any additional state or local requirements. Figure 9.1 illustrates a sample IFSP.

Development of the IFSP continues to indicate the degree to which professionals and parents plan, implement, and evaluate appropriate programs. Input from families, professionals, and agency personnel is used to design and implement the IFSP. An IFSP focuses on child-related outcomes and supports the family-centered nature of early intervention services.

Given the number of agency providers involved in early intervention, service coordination is critical to success. Service coordination is the process of linking families with the services documented on the IFSP, monitoring child-related outcomes, and advocating on behalf of the child and family (Bennett, Nelson, Lingerfelt, & Davenport-Ersoff, 1992). Some services designed for children and families are easily available at the early intervention site. Other services may take time to identify or access. Creativity, perseverance, and the ability to communicate will increase the likelihood of children and their families meeting outcomes identified on the IFSP.

Box 9.8 offers a list of questions to help beginning teachers build resource files. To build resource files, new teachers can start with materials and information available at their own programs. It is also important to update notes about specific professionals who are especially helpful and to document the procedures for obtaining their services. A comprehensive resource file of local, state, and national services is one of the most important tools a service coordinator can offer to families and peers. Table 9.2 offers a list of national resources for young children with disabilities. Teachers can use it as a starting point for their resource file on national organizations. Relevant information should be kept in a central location and updated regularly.

Individualized Family Service Plan
Chesapeake County, MD
PART I: BIOGRAPHICAL INFORMATION AND SIGNATURES

Child: Date of Birth:
Address: Chronological Age:
Name of Parent/Guardian/Surrogate: Adjusted Age:
Address: Current Date:
Phone:
This is an: _____ Interim IFSP
           _____ Initial IFSP
           _____ Annual IFSP

Service Coordinator: Agency:
Address: Phone:

I (We) have had the opportunity to participate in development of this IFSP and have been provided with reasonable notice of the IFSP meeting. I (We) have been informed of my (our) rights under this program, understand the plan and parents' rights, and give permission to implement this plan.

_____   _____
Parent/Guardian/Surrogate's Signature   Date

Each agency or person who has a direct role in the provision of early intervention services is responsible for making a good-faith effort to assist each eligible child and family to achieve outcomes listed on the child's IFSP.

Service Coordinator	Date	Evaluator/Assessor	Date
Lead Agency Representative	Date	Other Participant	Date
Interpreter (if needed)	Date	Other Participant	Date

PART II: CHILD'S DEVELOPMENTAL STATUS

Child's Present Level of Development in:

LEVEL	CA	DA
Cognition		
Communication		
Socioemotional		
Adaptive		
Gross Motor		
Fine Motor		
Hearing		
Vision		
Health (including immunizations status)		

Primary Health Care Provider: Phone:

FIGURE 9.1 Sample Individualized Family Service Plan

School-Age Years and Adult Preparation. Important to meeting adult preparation needs are the necessary program elements and supports affecting older students. Teachers are instrumental in linking school opportunities across learning settings. This linkage occurs through students' IEPs. Thus, we examine changes in IEPs as students and their families prepare for school progressions and students move toward adult services.

PART III: CHILD/FAMILY INFORMATION

A. Please describe the child's developmental strengths and needs.

B. Please describe the family's resources, concerns, and priorities as they relate to their child.

C. Please describe the settings in which this child spends most of his/her time.

D. What strategies will enable the child and family to participate in early intervention in the desired settings?

PART IV: CHILD/FAMILY OUTCOMES

Directions: Complete one page per outcome.

OUTCOME:

TYPE OF EARLY INTERVENTION SERVICE TO MEET THE OUTCOME:

LOCATION/FREQUENCY/INTENSITY:

STRATEGIES/ACTIVITIES:

CRITERIA/TIMELINES:

PERSON[S] RESPONSIBLE:

AGENCY/ADDRESS/PHONE:

FINANCIAL RESPONSIBILITY:

INITIATION DATE:

ANTICIPATED DATE OF ACHIEVEMENT:

PART V: TRANSITION CHECKLIST

_____ By the child's second birthday, transition planning is initiated.

_____ Families have been given descriptive information about their child's options at age 3.

_____ The local child-find coordinator for special education has been contacted (for children who are likely to be eligible for preschool special education).

_____ Site visits for parents are scheduled.

_____ Evaluation/assessment results are reviewed and appropriate additional testing is scheduled.

_____ Parents are given copies of federal and state laws, regulations, and policies related to preschool special education.

_____ Parents are given information about advocacy groups in the state or region.

_____ Appropriate meetings are scheduled with school/community personnel.

_____ Other (please specify)

_____ Other (please specify)

_____ Other (please specify)

FIGURE 9.1   *Continued*

Program Elements and Supports Affecting School-Age Students. The U.S. Department of Education (1996) reported that approximately 4.8 million individuals with disabilities, ages 6 to 21, were served under the IDEA. Germane to all students with disabilities is federal legislation encouraging their early preparation for adult roles and responsibilities. Accordingly, the IDEA ensures collaboration among the agencies involved in service provisions to older students and their families. In essence, family-centered services are also becoming priorities for school-age children. Family practices

---

B ox 9.8   **Checklist for a Comprehensive Resource File**

- Where are resource directories kept in my center?
- Have I asked veteran colleagues (including parents) for suggestions regarding resources for families?
- Whom shall I call for help in obtaining immunizations for a family's child?
- Whom shall I call for an audiologic examination for a child?
- Who are the key contacts at relevant agencies or programs?
- Is there a file cabinet with relevant resource materials?
- Where are the resource files located?

---

now link funding provisions, inclusion, participatory school-based management, and school reform (O'Shea et al., 1993) to educational accountability. Teachers' family practices are made more meaningful when they encourage families to participate actively in their children's education.

Family Participation. Family participation proliferated during the 1980s (O'Shea et al., 1993; Turnbull & Turnbull, 1986). Parents participated not only in educational planning for their school-age children with disabilities but also in the development of home-to-school, within school, and school-to-community policies. Today, such family involvement includes parents' or guardians' participation on federal, state, and local interagency coordinating councils; their involvement in community-based decision making; and their formation of local and state parent advocacy groups affecting family policies and program decisions.

Family members of school-age children often participate in local educational services by attending open houses or "back to school nights." They attend parent-teacher conferences. Together with faculty and staff, they often plan and implement parent organization activities, such as fund-raising events or organized speaker presentations.

Pause and Reflect About the Profession 9.3

Anticipate at least four specific ways that teachers can help school-age children and their families when the children enter elementary school.

1. _____
2. _____
3. _____
4. _____

Anticipate at least four specific ways that teachers can help school-age children and their families when the children enter middle school.

1. _____
2. _____
3. _____
4. _____

TABLE 9.2 National Organizations for Families of Young Children with Disabilities

Resource	Address	Telephone
Association for the care of Children's Health www.acch.org	19 Mantua Rd. Mt. Royal, NJ 08061	(609) 224-1742
Beach Center on Families and Disability University of Kansas Haworth Hall www.beachcenter.org	1200 Sunnyside Ave., Room 3136 Lawrence, KS 66045-7534	(785) 864-7600 TTY: (785) 864-3434
Center for Developmental Disabilities University of South Carolina	Benson Building Columbia, SC 29208	
Frank Porter Graham Child Development Institute University of North Carolina at Chapel Hill www.fpg.unc.edu	CB#8180 Chapel Hill, NC 27599-8180	(919) 966-2622
The Genetic Alliance www.geneticalliance.org	4301 Connecticut Ave. NW Suite 404 Washington, DC 20008-2369	(202) 966-5557
Health Resources Services Administration U.S. Department of Health and Human Services www.ask.hrsa.gov	Parklawn Building 5600 Fishers Lane Rockville, MD 20857	(301) 443-3376
Institute for Family-Centered Care www.familycenteredcare.org	7900 Wisconsin Ave., Suite 405 Bethesda, MD 20814	(301) 652-0281
National Organization for Rare Disorders www.rarediseases.org	55 Kenosia Avenue P.O. Box 1968 Danbury, CT 06813-1968	(203) 744-0100 Tollfree: (800) 999-6673- (voicemail only) TDD: (203) 799-9590
NECTAC (National Early Childhood Technical Assistance Center) www.nectac.org	Campus Box 8040, UNC-CH Chapel Hill, NC 27599-8040	(919) 962-2001 TDD: (919) 843-3269
NICHCY (National Dissemination Center for Children with Disabilities) www.nichcy.org	P.O. Box 1492 Washington, DC 20013	Voice/TTY: (800) 695-0285
The Schiefelbusch Institute for Life Span Studies University of Kansas www.lsi.ku.edu/lsi/index.htm	1052 Robert Dole Human Development Center 1000 Sunnyside Ave. Lawrence, KS 66045	(785) 864-4295)
Zero to Three: National Center for Infants, Toddlers and Families www.zerotothree.org/ztt_aboutus.html	2000 M St., NW, Suite 200 Washington, DC 20036	(202) 638-1144

Many serve on school advisory panels or on strategic planning commissions. Often, they are active in school athletic events or in school volunteer projects.

Families of school-age students, in essence, are fast becoming more of a driving force in the provision of services to their children. Box 9.9 presents suggestions aimed at parents or guardians to help increase their active school participation-transition awareness.

| **B**ox 9.9 | **Suggestions for Parents or Guardians to Help Them Increase Their Active School Participation–Transition Awareness** |

1. Ask your child's teacher whether he or she uses a variety of resources in planning now for future needs of your child (e.g., does the teacher share information with you on a future school class or appropriate teaching materials?). Find out what is involved in the next educational setting by visiting your child's future class now or by asking now for concrete information from next year's teacher. In this way, you know what is in store for your child in the next program and can help prepare your child currently.
2. Ask your child's current teachers how the current educational program contains features that help with the transition to next year's class.
3. Ask yourself whether your school professionals are available to meet with you and your child often, but especially before your child's entry into new school programs.
4. Does your child's current teacher offer you information on community programs available now or ones in which your child can enroll next year?
5. Prior to your child's entrance into a new program or class, get the name of a school contact who can explain to you differences in programming requirements, legal issues, schedules, adult-to-child ratios, transportation, communication methods, and so forth. Ask for an appointment so that your questions can be answered concerning your child's specific needs.
6. Ask your child's present teacher how last year's goals and objectives on the IEP are related to this year's goals and objectives. Does your child's new teacher match instructional or management goals and objectives to new program features on the basis of your child's needs? Seek written assurance from school personnel that this is happening for your child.
7. Prior to your child's placement, visit the school and community programs and classrooms where he/she will be placed while they are in session.
8. Help your child's teacher write education and transition plans early enough so that your child has adequate opportunities to achieve goals. Realize that school professionals should be actively asking you for your input into your child's educational program.
9. Be willing to share information with others. Be open to help as much as possible before, during, and after your child's attendance in programs. Give teachers information on your child's behavior at home. If appropriate, share information from your child's doctor or recreational program personnel.
10. Ask professionals to provide you and other parents with workshops, meetings, reading materials, and so forth on expected stress and school adjustment difficulties. Ask them to talk with you and other parents about expected differences for children with various dis-abilities at home or in the community. Share with them your sources of stress with your child at home. Let them know when you can't find a baby-sitter to watch your child. Ask them to help you locate resources when your child's medical care is more than you can handle. Discuss how your other children at home include your child with disabilities in play and other activities. Discuss the impact of your child on grandparents, neighbors, and so forth. Also ask professionals to share with you and other parents information on expected similarities of your child to others. Ask to be provided with specific implications about re-sources, services, and programs beyond your child's immediate future so that you can help your child learn to adjust now.
11. Respect information on those involved in the transition process. Become familiar with the backgrounds, experiences, training, philosophical orientations, languages, communication styles, and expectations of your child's teachers. Share similar information about yourself as well in formal meetings, in informal get-togethers, or through written communications. Let the teachers know you and your child so that more appropriate programming can be offered.
12. Ask how your child's IEPs, Individual Transition Plans, or IFSPs and programs are changed on the basis of your child's needs for a particular service. Ask for, and keep a copy of, all records on your child. If you don't understand information in your child's records, know

Box 9.9 (continued)

that you have a right to have a professional explain all information. You may write down your concerns about any information with which you disagree, and your disagreements should be placed in your child's records.

13. Ask your child's school administrator or teacher to give you information in a variety of forms (e.g., books, materials) to help you, your child, siblings, and other members of your family anticipate changes in your child's needs.

14. Try to locate information on local services that will be available when your child is no longer of school age. Share, and ask others to share, resources and information.

15. Acknowledge stress and adjustment difficulties openly. Share your concerns with your child's teacher and with other parents and families. At all times, expect school and community professionals to treat you and your child with dignity. Demonstrate a willingness to listen to professionals and a common goal of solving problems together.

16. Realize your own coping levels and abilities without condemning yourself when you can't handle every situation with your child. Be willing to give help to others. Just as important is the willingness to receive help from others. Recognize your own strengths and weaknesses as a parent. Remember that your decisions about your child with disabilities will always be challenging despite the best intentions and planning. Also realize, however, that you are not alone and that you can receive some help for you and your child when you let others into your life.

17. Speak openly with school professionals often. Send notes to school about your child's progress at home. Let the teacher know when your child had a bad weekend, as well as about a toy or book your child especially likes. If teachers request it, let them share reports with you, have face-to-face contacts, or visit your home. Let them set up with you a scheduled time to talk about your child, the future, and your concerns.

18. Be open to working with your child's teachers and community helpers. Work from a team approach and expect that you should be treated as a contributing member of your child's team. When you disagree with professionals about your child, don't be afraid to speak up about your concerns. Remember that you will be with your child longer than any professional will, so your input about the future is vital. All your questions are appropriate, no matter how small. All your issues are of importance.

19. Include your child in future decision making as much as possible to enhance choices, emphasize independence, and consider your child's likes and dislikes, if appropriate. Changes in your child's life will be easier for all involved when your child believes that he or she is, and truly is, a part of the decision-making process.

20. Discuss with school personnel your ethnic and cultural customs, celebrations, and traditions. Help families and professionals work together in the change process through awareness, teaming, and action planning with others. Your child will benefit when you work together productively with professionals.

Teachers' Work with Families

Teachers of school-age students will be involved actively with diverse families. Recognizing and working with increasingly diverse American families are necessary competencies for new teachers. For example, information on families' backgrounds, home experiences, priorities, and expectations for their children contributes to students' school success and teachers' effectiveness. To work with families teachers must be skilled in effective listening, written expression, teaming, consensual decision making, problem solving, mediation, and compromise. By taking the first steps to establish and maintain a good rapport with students' families, teachers can build long-lasting foundations that help children at school and at home. Seeking family support for school projects and soliciting families' active participation in schools are ways of sending the message that teachers care and are responsive to family input.

Teachers can employ varied strategies to encourage families' active and productive participation in their children's school services. For example, new teachers can keep flexible hours to meet family needs (e.g., they can meet before or after the workday to increase parental participation or conduct home visits). They can communicate with families "in attitude more than in hours" by inquiring often about what parents do at home to help their children. Teachers can send home age-appropriate parent-child activities to supplement school objectives. They can directly ask families how to include parents or guardians as part of their children's team. They can use interest surveys, telephone calls, newsletters, or group forums.

Teachers demonstrate acceptance of family participation and a positive attitude toward diverse family input through interpersonal communication skills and behaviors. They might identify and employ the strengths of family members who are interested in participating actively in their child's education. For example, teachers can learn more about diverse family backgrounds, traditions, and priorities by inviting family members to demonstrate cultural traditions and family customs in open class discussions. They might invite family members to describe the family's holiday traditions (e.g., for

Pause and Reflect About the Profession 9.4

Put a check mark on your three top indicators of diverse family strategies in your field site. Discuss your indicators with a peer. Compare and contrast the reasons why you and your peer chose the indicators.

_____ 1. Endorse and support parents or guardians by making time for each other, sharing contributions, solving problems, and collaborating.

_____ 2. Offer written ideas to encourage family-friendly school programs, improve existing programs, and extend the opportunity for involvement of parents, siblings, or grandparents.

_____ 3. Participate in school advisory committees and programs charged with identifying family needs, developing plans, and assessing family-school outcomes.

_____ 4. Contact families regularly, using group meetings, written reports, letters, notes and notices, telephone contacts, and family-class newsletters. Consider families' primary language needs.

_____ 5. Work collaboratively with coalition groups, parent advocacy groups, and parent support systems to link home, school, and community practices. Empower each other through communication. Recognize that compromise is essential to communication.

_____ 6. Attend and actively participate in family programs and family in-service programs. Share experiences and collaborate with families in the identification of local home, school, and community improvement plans.

_____ 7. Strive to include diverse family suggestions and new ideas in the curriculum. Provide opportunities to share resources related to disabilities, family issues, school programming, community services, or family life.

_____ 8. Be willing to accommodate family diversity. Be open to family input that initially may not appeal. Use a variety of family involvement methods (e.g., parent questionnaires, family attendance at school functions, home visits and observations, family behavioral change, student performance systems).

Independence Day, Kwanzaa, Ramadan) and then ask students to compare and contrast their family customs with those of other class members.

New teachers can help students understand and accept individual differences and commonalities by directly supporting and sharing various ethnic celebrations, food, clothing, religious holidays, or special community celebrations. They can teach components of diverse family and community traditions in the curricula. By so doing, they let students, families, and peers know that they recognize family diversity as a strength. Again, communication strategies (e.g., teaming, displaying empathy, being open, sharing information, dealing with conflicts) have a huge impact on teachers' success with individual families.

Elementary- and Middle-School Students' Transitions

Teachers, students, and family members face various transition issues when children enter school-age services. These issues, however, often differ from those of younger children (George & Lewis, 1991; Stewart, 1989). Students exit single educational programs offering early intervention services and enter new situations in larger, elementary schools. The concept of least restrictive environment (LRE) implies learning opportunities across varied settings.

For example, students entering primary, elementary, and middle schools must adjust to teachers' alternative management systems within classrooms; opportunities with specialized teachers, such as media specialists, computer technologists, and reading specialists; teachers' and students' maintenance of academic momentum and flow between classroom events; and/or movement across special and integrated learning environments offered in the home, school, or community.

Teachers' transition involvement during the elementary and middle school years includes planning for students' involvement with peers, community personnel, and extended family members (e.g., parents, siblings, grandparents, neighbors) (George & Lewis, 1991; Stewart, 1989). Curricula often focus on maximizing the participation, independence, and productivity of students in varied learning domains.

New teachers will participate in planning activities that emphasize students' coping strategies within the home, school, or community setting. For example, the curricula and service delivery demands for many new teachers will relate to students' inclusion needs, available resources, and the "flow" implications when students change classrooms or teachers. Teachers may provide direct services to students and their families, or they may offer consultation and team-teaching options to other personnel. Curriculum offerings will target, for many students, their preparation for adult life. Teachers may offer training for work or discuss in class the students' home and family adjustments. "Functional academics" may center on such skills as independent living needs, students' leisure-time and recreational pursuits, and students' community involvement.

In addition to the basics of reading, writing, and arithmetic, self-management, independent study, social, and organizational skills may be the goals of learning activities developed by many elementary and middle school teachers. The effects of students' disabilities and levels of independence on their families' ability to function also pose challenges to teachers. Teachers will use their knowledge of students and families to plan and collect information on future skills and program requirements of the next learning environment (e.g., high school, job site) while embedding appropriate curricula into current programming.

Important to elementary and middle school students is teachers' preparation for transition events such as changes within and between schools and class programs; students' effects on family members; initiation of independence training; and implications of students' inclusive opportunities, including academic, behavioral, social, and learning adjustments in the home, school, or community setting.

Thus, as students grow, their learning environments expand from school boundaries to include opportunities in the community setting, vocational training sites, family units, and alternative educational instructional sites. Teachers' transition activities necessitate coordination throughout the school years. Most often, students' IEPs document the coordination. Successful transitions require goal specificity, concrete timeline planning, and cross-categorical focus on the varied needs of those served (Getzel, 1990).

LINKING SCHOOL OPPORTUNITIES

Implementing services for older students requires the coordinated efforts of many home, school, and community professionals involved with school-age children and their families. The IDEA is very specific concerning educational services and family involvement for school-age students with disabilities. For example, the law continues to mandate that an IEP be drawn up for every child or youth found eligible for special education or related services, pinpointing what kinds of services the student will receive. It reaffirms parents' right to participate in every decision related to the identification, evaluation, and placement of their child or youth with a disability. It calls for annual planning; assessment of students' strengths, needs, and interests; and programming by interagency personnel.

The law also promotes the linkage of school and community experiences, the development of postschool adult living objectives, and the development of daily living skills and functional vocational evaluations. Transition activities start occurring long before a student exits high school.

IEPs and Students' Transitions

The IDEA identifies "transition services" as a coordinated set of activities. Students' transitions must be designed within an outcome-oriented process that promotes movement from school to postschool activities, including postsecondary education, vocational training, integrated employment (including supported employment), continuing and adult education, adult services, independent living, and community participation.

The IDEA encourages students, teachers, and families to coordinate school programming with businesses and transition service agencies, beginning early in students' careers. As such, the law now mandates that the IEP contain a statement of transition services. This statement must be prepared for students who are age 16 or over, and when individually appropriate, for students who are age 14 or over.

The most substantive amendment to IDEA transition plans specifies that, if appropriate, a statement of the responsibilities or linkages or both of each participating agency must be completed before the student leaves the school setting. The agency, purpose, contact persons, and time by which the linkage is to occur are essential information for professionals and families. When teachers and other professionals work together with families in planning and establishing linkages, they help ensure students' long-term gains. Figure 9.2 provides an example of the transition component of school-age students' IEPs.

High School Students' Transitions

Although the IDEA's transition definition slants toward students' vocational needs, the federal definition also implies that many functional adult living skills should be taught long before high school students enter the adult world. Vocational training and employment opportunities, daily living skills, independent survival skills, and community participation skills, initiated earlier in elementary or middle school programs, now become necessary components of the high school curriculum requiring sequential placement in school programming (Tindall & Gugerty, 1989).

Professionals targeting high school transition help plan to-and-from programs through the individualized transition plan (ITP) portion of a student's IEP (Getzel, 1990). Teachers using a "top-down" curriculum can address longitudinal domains (Hawaii

INDIVIDUAL TRANSITION PLAN SECTION OF THE IEP

Transition services required for students with disabilities moving from school to adult life (beginning no later than age 16, and when determined appropriate, beginning at age 14 or younger). The IEP team addressed planning for transition services in the outcome areas checked below: (If an outcome area or instructional area is not needed, state and federal law requires a statement to that effect and the basis upon which the determination is made.)

I. EXPECTED POSTSCHOOL OUTCOMES:

[ ] Postsecondary Training/Education:

_____

_____

[ ] Employment:

_____

_____

[ ] Community Living:

_____

_____

[ ] Recreation/Leisure:

_____

_____

[ ] Residential:

_____

_____

I. INSTRUCTIONAL AREAS NEEDED TO SUPPORT EXPECTED POSTSCHOOL OUTCOMES:

[ ] FUNCTIONAL VOCATIONAL ASSESSMENT:

_____

_____

[ ] INSTRUCTIONAL AREAS: (may include, but not be limited to):
[ ] Academic Instruction
[ ] Career Education
[ ] Community-Based Experiences and Instruction
[ ] Community-Based Vocational Training
[ ] Functional Living Skills
[ ] Preparation for Postsecondary Education/Training
[ ] Vocational-Technical Education
[ ] Vocational-Technical Program Assistance
[ ] Work Experience
[ ] Other:

Instructional areas should support expected postschool outcomes. Instructional areas should appear in the IEP as annual goals, short-term objectives, and specially designed instruction.

FIGURE 9.2 Individual Transition Plan Section of the IEP

IIII. PERSON(s) RESPONSIBLE FOR IMPLEMENTING TRANSITION ACTIVITIES.

_____

_____

IV. INTERAGENCY RESPONSIBILITIES, OR LINKAGES, OR BOTH THAT WILL
BE PROVIDED BEFORE THE STUDENT LEAVES THE SCHOOL SETTING:

_____

_____

Agencies or individuals who may provide services support:

Agency: _____ Contact Person: _____

Address: _____ Phone: _____

Agency: _____ Contact Person: _____

Address: _____ Phone: _____

Agency: _____ Contact Person: _____

Address: _____ Phone: _____

FIGURE 9.2 *Continued*

Transition Project, 1987), including school survival skills; "functional management"; self-help skills; "follow-along" support programs in the school, home, or community setting; home and family training; family adjustment; self-fulfillment and self-advocacy training; integration realities after leaving school; recreation/leisure skills; financial support; emotional/physical well-being; health awareness; community awareness; and citizenship (guardianship/advocacy) rights and responsibilities. In addition, secondary school personnel may focus on students' and families' preparation for postsecondary adjustment, when teacher and school support is no longer available.

Accordingly, to teachers of older students with disabilities, transition implies a variety of changes: movement from a unitary system (education) to multiple service systems or sometimes to a nonsystem, from education to job setting, within the parental or natural home, from the parental or natural home to other living arrangements, and from relative dependence on professionals and parents to relative independence from them (O'Shea et al., 1993; Turnbull & Turnbull, 1985). New teachers can help prepare their students when they work to coordinate services for their students with family members and important interagency personnel. See Box 9.9 for suggestions for increasing parents' or guardians' active school participation and transition awareness.

Interagency Coordination Efforts

Today's schools require a high level of interagency coordination of frontline service providers, including teachers. Teachers increasingly work with other professionals and parents or guardians in a broader, community-oriented service delivery context. For example, the School-to-Work Opportunities Act of 1994 focuses on services linking students to adult life activities. It promotes collaboration and problem solving by the Departments of Education and Labor. The act also encourages partnerships between school-based and employment-based sites at the local level and encourages school and employment site personnel, along with family members, to plan, implement, and evaluate integrated school-based and work-based learning.

Among the components in the act are school-based learning components encouraging students' career awareness and exploration. However, the act also targets counseling to identify students' career interests and goals as well as to integrate their academic

---

Box 9.10

Examples of Linkage Component Activities to Promote the School-to-Work Opportunities Act of 1994

- Hold monthly meetings to address local collaboration and problem-solving initiatives espoused by the Departments of Education and Labor.
- Initiate partnership models between school-based and employment-based sites at the local level.
- Hold quarterly sessions for school and employment site personnel to plan, implement, and evaluate integrated school-based and work-based learning. Invite families, students, and educational and business leaders.
- Have bimonthly meetings with teachers and employers to match students with employers.
- Plan student and family orientations or conferences on career education, career development programs, and work-based linkages. Invite guidance counselors, local college or university personnel, and educational and business leaders.
- Plan transition-coordinating councils to develop and implement interagency agreements, technical assistance, and services to employers, educators, case managers, and others.
- Prior to IEP meetings, send home surveys to parents or guardians and students to ascertain, in advance, postschool options and assistance anticipated for training, vocations, residence, recreation, and so forth.
- Share written resources with family and community services on youth development activities, academic and vocation learning, and employer strategies for upgrading worker skills.

---

and vocational learning. Work-based learning components include workplace mentoring and instruction in general workplace competencies. Connecting activity components include provision of technical assistance to schools and employers to integrate school-based and work-based learning. Linkage of youth development activities with employer strategies for upgrading worker skills is also relevant in program initiatives. Box 9.10 presents examples of linkage components that new teachers may find beneficial when they combine home input with school and employment opportunities inherent in the School-to-Work Opportunities Act.

?

Pause and Reflect About the Profession 9.5

Review at least two major considerations for each of the following areas that teachers need to consider regarding students' transitions into adult services.

Linking Schools and Communities

1. _____

2. _____

IEPs

1. _____

2. _____

Interagency Coordination

1. _____

2. _____

TEACHERS' ROLES AS STUDENTS AGE

As students transition across school-age programs and enter into adult services, professionals and families must continue to work together to plan, implement, and evaluate program services. New teachers will continue to help coordinate services through students' IEPs, and team members will again consider students' varied needs and strengths as the students grow toward adult roles. For example, beginning teachers may work with others to determine location and accessibility of local community-based service delivery systems. They may work with parents and business leaders to secure appropriate jobs with the degree of integrated opportunities that families want for their children. They may work with other professionals and families to match students' needs to available housing resources when students are ready to leave their parents' home, marry, or move to a new city. They may help to evaluate curricula as students leave school, enter the armed forces, and/or accept jobs or take advantage of training opportunities.

As students age, teachers can work cooperatively with job coaches, employment trainers, supported employment personnel, and other vocational personnel at local vocational training sites or jobs. Teachers might be sharing data related to students' opportunities in community-based vocational training, in vocational-technical education, or in work experiences offered through the armed services. Many teachers may be reorienting their school curricula from academic outcomes to adult outcomes and experiences.

Facilitating the Transition Process for Older Students and Their Families

As was the case with early intervention services, teachers can help older students and their families make adjustments in new settings. They can help families secure advance written information about training requirements and community-based programs available in the local area. They can help arrange for students and families to visit new programs before the students exit high school programs. Teachers can help organize orientations. They can also obtain necessary resources (e.g., handouts with registration cutoff dates, income eligibility requirements, geographic boundaries of programs, transportation availability, age restrictions, degree of parent participation required).

Teachers' involvement with their students' families and communities, thus, is vitally important to the continuing success of older students. Unfortunately, educational, social, and medical professionals with whom teachers work often have various family conceptualizations (e.g., administrators, counselors, family legal advocates, family therapists, health care workers, psychologists, teachers, and social workers may clash in IEP meetings). Nonetheless, understanding the views of others is vital.

As new teachers integrate knowledge of their students' families with what they can do to help students' successful transitions, they will be in a better position to value, respect, and accept the perspectives of others. Teachers can select, with families and other professionals, student assessment and instructional strategies that are age and ability appropriate. They can offer functionally based curricula geared to meeting daily and long-term needs. Family expertise can be targeted as a valued and recognized variable in school services. Families, as allies, can help increase resources important to students, schools, and communities.

As teachers gain information on the unique experiences of families, they are in better positions to offer realistic programming. Successful adjustments occur when individuals guide program and service options based on the needs and strengths of their individual students and families. Box 9.11 provides a checklist to help teachers facilitate the transition process for school-age children.

| **B**ox 9.11 | **Checklist to Help Teachers Facilitate the Transition Process for School-Age Children** |

_____ Encourage families, students, and significant professionals in the students' lives (e.g., therapists, social workers, health workers, coaches, employers) to visit programs and classrooms while in session prior to students' placement in the program.

_____ Use a variety of formal and informal assessment devices to gather and determine goals and services for the existing program and to plan for the future program.

_____ Plan, teach, and evaluate relevant skills required of students in the next setting (an appropriate number of weeks before leaving the existing program). Consider the impact on the home, school, and community settings for the students and their families. Write education and transition plans early enough that students have adequate opportunities to achieve goals.

_____ Devise educational plans with families and significant professionals in the children's lives (e.g., therapists, social workers, health workers), describing specific skills students will need to be successful in the home, school, or community.

_____ Include a clear description of what students will gain from the current programming with respect to future functioning in the home, school, or community setting. Specify in writing the potential gains and expectations across settings for the future.

_____ Be specific in sharing information with others. For example, teachers in sending and receiving programs need to be aware of the necessity of initiating and maintaining contacts as long as necessary for individual students and families. Be open to help as much as possible before, during, and after students' attendance in programs.

_____ Provide families and significant professionals with workshops, meetings, and reading materials about expected stress and adjustments in developmental ages.

_____ Talk about expected differences for students with disabilities. Include specific information about resources, services, and programs beyond the immediate future.

_____ Be available to meet with families, students, and significant professionals prior to students' entry into new programs.

_____ When students are ready to exit from the current program, visit the new program with students and families to act as a familiar link and support system for them.

_____ Provide families and significant professionals with specific details about the current program's components (e.g., curriculum, transportation, meals, therapies, job training, job placements) before students enter the programs.

_____ Provide students, families, and significant professionals with information on placement and service options available in the home, school, and community settings. Collect pertinent information about the local programming options. Share information continually and ask others to share.

_____ Initiate and maintain ongoing contact with families and significant professionals throughout students' involvement in the current program. Actively encourage program input from families and significant professionals at all times.

_____ Invite others to express their questions, comments, and concerns through open communication methods such as letters home, progress reports, face-to-face contacts, and home visits.

_____ Demonstrate empathy, congruence, and availability to students, families, and significant professionals before, during, and after students' attendance in programs.

_____ Facilitate parent-to-parent contacts and information sharing throughout students' involvement in the program. Encourage the same with other service providers.

_____ Observe and obtain information on the new learning environment, prior to students' exit from the existing program, so that current programming anticipates the next setting.

_____ Provide information in a variety of forms (e.g., books, materials) to help families and other professionals anticipate changes in students' needs.

_____ Provide students with the skills and training required in the next environment to reduce adjustment difficulties and associated stress of the "unknown."

_____ Match instructional goals and objectives to new program features as soon as possible for students' needs in the current setting.

_____ Modify IEPs, ITPs, and programs on the basis of student and family needs for a particular service. Continually collect data on program effectiveness. Document all attempts. Make adjustments when changes are required.

SUMMARY

This chapter emphasized that collaboration with families must start in the early years of a child's life, not just in the months before students enter the adult world. Teachers must be aware of relevant transitional periods and accompanying activities for children, youth, and families. In addition, the individual developmental and educational needs of students and families should be foremost in teachers' professional planning and conduct.

Next, the chapter offered an overview of the need for new teachers to have a realistic base to match planning, programming, and evaluating. Present and future environmental conditions must be considered in relation to school programming. By assuming transition responsibilities related to both students and families in a wholehearted manner, teachers help ensure an effective education to all students.

ACTIVITIES TO EXTEND YOUR KNOWLEDGE

1. Interview several families of young children with disabilities. You can get names of families from the local chapter of the Association for Retarded Citizens (ARC) or another agency with a focus on children with disabilities. Ask families to share their impressions of important issues surrounding their child's transitions from the hospital to home, home to early intervention services, early intervention services to preschool special education, and preschool special education to elementary-level special education. Be sure to ask the families to indicate which people and transition strategies were helpful and which were not. Ask whether families have suggestions for improving the transition process.

2. Read books or articles written by parents of children with disabilities to better understand families' perspectives. Visit your local library or bookstore and ask for guidance at the reference desk. Ask staff members of professional organizations (e.g., ARC) to suggest reading material.

3. Explore computer programs and/or library resources to locate more information related to the influence of students' diverse learning, behavioral, linguistic, and cultural characteristics on home, school, and community opportunities. How does this information help students in your field site?

4. Interview a social worker or family community worker on age-appropriate rules and reinforcers necessary for students' transitions from preschool to adult services. What are additional curriculum implications for students in your field site? What can you begin teaching your students now?

5. Visit various potential job sites for your students. Ask employers and employees about specific ideas for improving student motivation and cooperation on job sites. Share your findings now with your students and school personnel.

6. Discuss group problem-solving techniques within the context of students in your current site. Find out more on conflict resolution techniques and related social skills that can help your students transition into a relevant new setting. What can you begin teaching your students now?
7. Complete a log on successful assessment instruments and transition techniques appropriate in identifying and meeting the needs of your students. Target specific ways that you can communicate assessment and transition results to parents.
8. Develop a transition management plan that will address specific academic, behavioral, social, vocational, and other functional needs of students at your site. Ask parents or guardians for their input.
9. Offer to provide a few hours of respite care for parents of more severely involved children. Respite care is often difficult for families to find. As you provide respite care, you'll not only give families a break from caregiving routines, but also learn about the strengths and needs of the children in your care. The old saying about walking a mile in someone else's shoes is especially relevant when a child has a disability.

POINT AND CLICK ABOUT THE PROFESSION

www.eparent.com/default.htm
This is the web site for *Exceptional Parent* magazine. In addition to information for parents of children with disabilities, there are links to other relevant sites such as the Disability Network, an Internet directory, financial planning, mobility, and appropriate toys.

www.cec.sped.org
This web site is the home page for the Council for Exceptional Children (CEC), the leading professional organization in the area of the education of individuals with disabilities. There are also divisions (e.g., the Division for Early Childhood), each with a specialized focus. CEC's web site has numerous links to other web sites related to disability issues.

www.nectac.org
This site offers a wealth of resources related to young children with disabilities and their families. The National Early Childhood Technical Assistance Center (NECTAC) is housed at the University of North Carolina in Chapel Hill. Of particular interest are the links to information about service coordination, an important component of many transitions for young children and their families.

www2.edc.org/NCIP/Default.htm
The web site of the National Center to Improve Practice in Special Education Through Technology, Media, and Materials (NCIP) offers a wide variety of resources related to the education of children and youth with disabilities. The site's links are especially helpful in finding information on specific kinds of disabilities.

REFERENCES

Anderson, R. D., Bale, J. F., Blackman, J. A., & Murph, J. R. (1994). *Infections in children: A sourcebook for educators and child care providers.* Rockville, MD: Aspen.

Bagnato, S. J., Neisworth, S. J., & Munson, S. M. (1989). *Linking developmental assessment and early intervention: Curriculum-based prescriptions.* Rockville, MD: Aspen.

Bailey, D. B., Simeonsson, R. J., Yoder, D. E., & Huntington, G. S. (1990). Preparing professionals to serve infants and toddlers with disabilities and their families: An integrative analysis across eight disciplines. *Exceptional Children, 57*(1), 26–35.

Batshaw, M. L. (1997). *Children with disabilities* (4th ed.). Baltimore, MD: Paul H. Brookes.

Batshaw, M. L. (2001). *When your child has a disability: The complete sourcebook of daily and medical care* (rev. ed.). Baltimore, MD: Paul H. Brookes.

Bennett, T., Nelson, D. E., Lingerfelt, B. V., & Davenport-Ersoff, C. (1992). Family-centered service coordination. In T. Bennett, D. E. Nelson, & B. V. Lingerfelt (Eds.), *Facilitating family-centered training in early intervention.* Tucson, AZ: Therapy Skill Builders.

Bond, N., Farquahar, B., Hentz, P., Luckenbill, D., Prumo, M., Ralabate, P., Santelli, J., Taylor, J., Trice, C., & Weintraub, F. (1990). *Guidelines for the delineation of roles and responsibilities for the safe delivery of specialized health care in the educational setting.* Reston, VA: Council for Exceptional Children.

Bowe, F. (2000). *Birth to five: Early childhood special education.* Albany, NY: Delmar.

Brazelton, T. B., & Cramer, B. G. (1990). *The earliest relationship: Parents, infant, and the drama of early attachment.* Reading, MA: Addison-Wesley.

Bricker, D. D. (1989). *Early intervention for at-risk and handicapped infants, toddlers, and preschool children* (2nd ed.). Palo Alto, CA: VORT.

Brotherson, M. J., & Goldstein, B. L. (1992). Time as a resource and constraint for parents of young children with disabilities: Implications for early intervention services. *Topics in Early Childhood Special Education, 12*(4), 508–527.

Brown, W., Thurman, S. K., & Pearl, L. F. (Eds.). (1993). *Family-centered early intervention with infants and toddlers: Innovative cross-disciplinary approaches.* Baltimore: Paul H. Brookes.

Campbell, P. H. (1991). Evaluation and assessment in early intervention for infants and toddlers. *Journal of Early Intervention, 15*(1), 36–45.

Craig, E. R., & Leonard, C. R. (1990, April). P.L. 99–457: Are speech-language pathologists trained and ready? *ASHA, 32*, 57–61.

Cripe, J., Slentz, K., & Bricker, D. (1993). *Assessment, evaluation, and programming system for infants and children: Vol. 2. AEPS curriculum from birth to three years.* Baltimore: Paul H. Brookes.

deFur, S., Getzel, E. E., & Kregel, J. (1994). Individual transition plans: A work in progress. *Journal of Vocational Rehabilitation, 4*, 139–145.

deFur, S., & Taymans, J. M. (1995). Competencies needed for transition specialists in vocational rehabilitation, vocational education, and special education. *Exceptional Children, 62*(1), 38–51.

DeGangi, G. A., Wietlisbach, S., Poisson, S., & Stein, E. (1994). The impact of culture and socioeconomic status on family-professional collaboration: Challenges and solutions. *Topics in Early Childhood Special Education, 14*(4), 503–520.

Dinnebeil, L. A., & Rule, S. (1994). Variables that influence collaboration between parents and service coordinators. *Journal of Early Intervention, 18*(4), 349–361.

Donowitz, L. G. (Ed.). (1993). *Infection control in the child care center and preschool* (2nd ed.). Baltimore: Williams & Wilkins.

Epps, S., & Jackson, B. J. (2000). *Early intervention programs that work.* Washington, DC: American Psychological Association.

Fewell, R. R. (1991). Trends in the assessment of infants and toddlers with disabilities. *Exceptional Children, 58*(2), 166–173.

Fewell, R. R., & Vadasy, P. F. (Eds.). (1986). *Families of handicapped children: Needs and supports across the life span.* Austin, TX: PRO-ED.

George, N. L., & Lewis, T. J. (1991). Exit assistance for special educators: Helping students make the transition. *Teaching Exceptional Children, 23*, 35–38.

Getzel, E. E. (1990). Entering postsecondary programs: Early individualized planning. *Teaching Exceptional Children, 23*(1), 51–53.

Governor's Office for Children, Youth, and Families/ Maryland Infants and Toddlers Program. (1992). *Transition at age three: Guidelines for implementing policies and procedures.* Baltimore: Author.

Gowen, J. W., & Nebrig, J. B. (2002). *Enhancing early emotional development: Guiding parents of young children.* Baltimore, MD: Paul H. Brookes.

Guralnick, M. J. (Ed.). (2000). *Interdisciplinary clinical assessment of young children with developmental disabilities.* Baltimore, MD: Paul H. Brookes.

Hanft, B. E., Rush, D. D., & Shelden, M. L. (2004). *Coaching families and colleagues in early childhood.* Baltimore, MD: Paul H. Brookes.

Hanline, M. F., & Knowlton, A. (1988). A collaborative model for providing support to parents during their child's transition from infant intervention to preschool special education public school programs. *Journal of the Division for Early Childhood, 12*(2), 116–125.

Harry, B., Allen, N., & McLaughlin, M. (1995). Communication vs. compliance: African American parents' involvement in special education. *Exceptional Children, 61*(4), 364–376.

Hawaii Transition Project. (1987). [Transition resources]. Honolulu: University of Hawaii, Department of Special Education.

Henley, M., Ramsey, R. S., & Algozzine, R. (1993). *Characteristics of and strategies for teaching students with mild disabilities.* Needham Heights, MA: Allyn & Bacon.

Hooper, S. R., & Umansky, W. (2004). *Young children with special needs.* Upper Saddle River, NJ: Merrill/Prentice Hall.

Individuals with Disabilities Education Act (Public Law 101–476). (1990, October). Washington, DC: U.S. Office of Special Education and Rehabilitation.

Jeppson, E. S., & Thomas, J. (1995). *Essential allies: Families as advisors.* Bethesda, MD: Institute for Family-Centered Care.

Johnson-Martin, N. M., Attermeier, S. M., & Hacker, B. (1990). *The Carolina curriculum for preschoolers with special needs.* Baltimore: Paul H. Brookes.

Karge, P. D., Patton, P. L., & de la Garza, B. (1992). Transition services for youth with mild disabilities: Do they exist, are they needed? *Career Development for Exceptional Individuals, 15*, 47–68.

Katz, K. S., Pokorni, J. L., & Long, T. M. (1989). *The chronically ill and at-risk infant: Family-centered intervention from hospital to home.* Palo Alto, CA: VORT.

Kilgo, J. (1990). Early intervention. *Research Forum: DEC–CEC, 17*(1), 4.

King-Sears, M. E. (1994). *Curriculum-based assessment in special education*. San Diego, CA: Singular.

Kohler, P. D. (1993). Best practices in transition: Substantiated or implied? *Career Development for Exceptional Individuals, 16*, 107–121.

Krajicek, M., & Tompkins, R. (Eds.). (1993). *The medically fragile infant*. Austin, TX: PRO-ED.

Kroth, R. (1975). *Communicating with parents of exceptional children*. Denver: Love.

Lambie, R., & Daniels-Mohring, D. (1993). *Family systems within educational contexts: Understanding students with special needs*. Denver: Love.

Lerner, J. W., Lowenthal, B., & Egan, R. W. (2003). *Preschool children with special needs: Children at risk and children with disabilities*. Boston, MA: Allyn and Bacon.

Linder, T. W. (1993a). *Transdisciplinary play-based assessment: A functional approach to working with young children* (rev. ed.). Baltimore: Paul H. Brookes.

Linder, T. W. (1993b). *Transdisciplinary play-based assessment: Guidelines for developing a meaningful curriculum for young children*. Baltimore: Paul H. Brookes.

Lynch, E. W., & Hanson, M. J. (2004). *Developing cross-cultural competence: A guide for working with young children and their families* (3rd ed.). Baltimore: Paul H. Brookes.

Martin, J. E., Marshall, L. H., & Maxson, L. L. (1993). Transition policy: Infusing self-determination and self-advocacy into transition programs. *Career Development for Exceptional Individuals, 16*, 53–61.

McLean, M., Bailey, D. B., & Wolery, M. (2004). *Assessing infants and preschoolers with special needs* (3rd ed.). Upper Saddle River, NJ: Merrill/Prentice Hall.

McWilliam, P. J. (2000). *Lives in progress: Case stories in early intervention*. Baltimore, MD: Paul H. Brookes.

Nelson, D. E., Bennett, T., & Lingerfelt, B. V. (1992). Facilitating transitions between settings. In T. Bennett, D. E. Nelson, & B. V. Lingerfelt (Eds.), *Facilitating family-centered training in early intervention*. Tucson, AZ: Therapy Skill Builders.

Noonan, M. J., & McCormick, L. (1993). *Early intervention in natural environments: Methods and procedures*. Pacific Grove, CA: Brooks/Cole.

O'Shea, D. J., & Caldwell, L. (1990, Fall). *Transition services for students with mental handicaps* (University Internal Research Grant). Boca Raton: Florida Atlantic University.

O'Shea, D. J., O'Shea, L. J., & Nowocien, D. (1993). Parent-teacher relationships in school renewal and educational reform. *Learning Disability Forum, 18*(3), 43–46.

Sandall, S., McLean, M., & Smith, B. J. (2000). *DEC recommended practices in early intervention/early childhood special education*. Longmont, CO: Sopris West.

Santa Cruz County Office of Education. (1987). *HELP for special preschoolers ages 3 to 6: Activities binder*. Palo Alto, CA: VORT.

School-to-Work Opportunities Act of 1994, Pub. L. No. 103–239, 108 Stat. 568–608 May 4, 1994 20 U.S.C. § 6101 et seq.

Singer, G. H. S., & Irvin, L. K. (Eds.). (1989). *Support for caregiving families: Enabling positive adaptation to disability*. Baltimore: Paul H. Brookes.

Smith, D. D. (2004). *Introduction to special education: Teaching in an age of opportunity* (5th ed.). Boston, MA: Pearson, Allyn, and Bacon.

Stewart, D. (1989). *A curriculum framework for secondary-aged handicapped students designed for use in the state of Georgia under Technical Assistance Activity-03-GA-88-06 (Transition)*. Washington, DC: OSERS.

Taylor, J. M. (1995). Staying healthy. In V. Y. Rab & K. I. Wood (Eds.), *Child care and the ADA: A handbook for inclusive practices*. Baltimore: Paul H. Brookes.

Taylor, J. M., & Fleming, J. A. (1997). *Guidelines for the evaluation or assessment of three-year-old children transitioning from early intervention services to pre-school special education*. Baltimore: Maryland State Department of Education.

Taylor, J. M., & Taylor, W. S. (1989). *Communicable diseases and young children in group settings*. Boston: Singular.

Tindall, L. W., & Gugerty, J. J. (1989). Collaboration among clients, families, and service providers. In D. E. Beckell & J. M. Brown (Eds.), *Transition from school to work for persons with disabilities* (pp. 127– 160). New York: Longman.

Turnbull, A. P., Patterson, J. M., Behr, S. K., Murphy, D. L., Marquis, J. G., & Blue-Banning, M. J. (Eds.). (1993). *Cognitive coping, families, and disability*. Baltimore: Paul H. Brookes.

Turnbull, A. P., & Turnbull, H. R. (1986). *Families, professionals, and exceptionality: A special partnership*. Upper Saddle River, NJ: Merrill/Prentice Hall.

Turnbull, H. R., & Turnbull, A. P. (1985). *Parents speak out: Then and now*. Upper Saddle River, NJ: Merrill/Prentice Hall.

U.S. Department of Education, Office of Special Education Programs. (1996, February 7). *Seventeenth annual report to Congress*. Washington, DC: Author.

Urbano, M. T. (1992). *Preschool children with special health care needs*. San Diego, CA: Singular.

VandenBerg, K. A., & Hanson, M. J. (1993). *Homecoming for babies after the neonatal intensive care nursery: A guide for professionals in supporting families and their infants' early development*. Austin, TX: PRO-ED.

## CHAPTER 10

Collaborative Programming and Consultation

Chapter Outline

In this chapter, we will

- discuss the beginning teacher as the recipient and provider of consulting services

- provide a collaborative model for consultative processes

- examine important interpersonal communication skills and general procedures for collaborative consultation

- analyze basic procedures in the conference model and the means by which to operationalize them

A PROFESSIONAL GLIMPSE

Dr. Lopez, the assistant principal of West Peco High School, had been working with her second- and third-year teachers to meet the Corpus Christi School District teacher performance standards. This is an important function not only to ensure that students are the benefactors of effective instruction, but also to ensure that her developing teachers are granted tenure with the school district.

One of her teachers, Nelda Hernandez, was having difficulty with her interpersonal communication skills. When she interacted with other teachers in the high school math department, she came across as condescending, judgmental, and sometimes aloof. Likewise, she was unable to establish a positive rapport with her students because they, too, sensed arrogance. Dr. Lopez frankly had difficulties with Nelda whenever she had presented constructive criticism on Nelda's interactions with her students.

The speculation around the school was that Nelda was hired because of her uncle's prominence in the community as a successful businessman. She had also completed her bachelor's degree at an Ivy League school and went straight into a master's degree program. Other faculty members in the school resented her Ivy League education and the presumption that her uncle pulled a few strings to get her hired.

Using a teacher evaluation instrument based on the National Council for the Accreditation of Teacher Education (NCATE) standards and *Enhancing Professional Practice: A Framework for Teaching* (Danielson, 1996), Dr. Lopez arranged for a conference with Nelda. She laid out the information from prior observations, both formal and incidental, including comments from the faculty and parents. When she met with Nelda, Dr. Lopez presented the data to Nelda in a nonthreatening manner. She demonstrated a genuine, positive regard for Nelda by presenting feedback to her in a straightforward manner. Although Dr. Lopez was businesslike in her presentation of the facts, she was at the same time demonstrating empathy by acknowledging Nelda's emotional response to the information. Nelda explained that the experienced faculty intimidate her and she is scared of being duped by her students. Nelda admitted that her behaviors could be interpreted as arrogant and aloof. She was aware of the rumors about her uncle and had heard comments about her Ivy League education. Dr. Lopez and Nelda both agreed that there is little or nothing they could do about the rumors and resentment, but they decided to examine the other issues and focus on dealing with those that Nelda could control. Dr. Lopez used open-ended questions to help Nelda develop strategies to improve her relationships with other faculty and students. They decided to ask one of the more seasoned faculty members, Mr. Clapsaddle, to act as her peer coach. He is highly regarded by the other faculty, and the students think he is an effective an approachable teacher. Nelda committed to using this strategy to help her with her relationships with other faculty and students.

One area often overlooked or given only superficial attention in teacher-training programs is professional interaction. In this chapter, we discuss how communicating with other professionals requires a set of critical skills that will enable developing teachers to use the resources available in a school more effectively. Developing teachers new to a school are given greater than usual attention. Other professionals, paraprofessionals, parents, and students observe and begin to make decisions about the kinds of persons new teachers are and whether or not they will be effective teachers, helpful associates, or even personal friends. Consequently, there is a need to be cognizant of how individuals come across to others.

By verbal and nonverbal actions, developing teachers can manipulate the perceptions of others. On the one hand, if they want to be viewed as aggressive, they can make demands about what they will and will not do and what resources they expect to have available. On the other hand, they may act passively by being very acquiescent and giving in to the demands of everyone else. And, of course, there are myriad degrees of aggressive/passive behavior between these extremes. The point is that developing teachers have a degree of control over how they are perceived by others within this continuum. Consequently, the perceptions of others determine how cooperative they will be and what human and other resources will be made available.

We discuss roles that developing teachers will assume. In the first section, we offer commonsense ideas about interacting with consultants (consulting teachers, supervisors, or principals). Then we include more technical information regarding interpersonal communication skills and procedures for conferring with others. Developing and beginning teachers should know how to play the roles of both recipient and provider of consultative or supervisory services. Therefore, they must look at the discussion from both points of view and envision how they would apply principles of interpersonal communication and collaborative problem solving in any one of the roles they may play at any given time. Their ability to function effectively in these roles will help shape the perceptions of others toward them.

INTRODUCTION

Developing and beginning teachers take on a variety of roles in the professional relationships they develop with other school staff (see Figure 10.1). Obviously, they will take on the role of a beginning teacher and therefore be the consultee (recipient of consultative services) with respect to supervisory personnel (e.g., principal, program supervisor, consulting teacher). It is also likely that they will have paraprofessionals in their classrooms whom they will manage (e.g., assign instructional tasks, train in different teaching techniques). Thus, in this capacity, their role will be that of a consultant (provider of supervisory services).

In addition, with the emphasis on providing special education services in general education classrooms with normally functioning peers and giving diverse students access to the general education curricula, many special education teachers will be asked to consult with other teaching staff in their school as well as with parents. These expanding roles and responsibilities require teachers to have the teamwork and communication skills needed to meet the challenge of diverse educational opportunities (Glatthorn, 1990; Villa, Thousand, Nevin, & Malgeri, 1996).When teachers consult with others, they often use coaching models to support the communication process. In fact,

FIGURE 10.1   Relationship of the Developing Teacher to Other Education Professionals in the Consultant and Consultee Roles

the Council for Exceptional Children (CEC) defined the CEC standards for the preparation and licensure of new special educators (CEC, 2000a). Special educators who collaborate with families and other professionals recognize and acknowledge the competencies and expertise of others. They strive to develop positive attitudes among others. They cooperate with families and other agencies involved in serving persons with exceptionalities. They provide consultation and assistance, where appropriate, to both general and special educators as well as other school or nonschool personnel. They maintain effective interpersonal relations.

New teachers often rely on coaching models to support their collaboration and consultation with others. New teachers profit from mentorships (Council for Exceptional Children, 2000b). CEC (2000a) found that each new special educator should have a mentor throughout at least the first year of professional special education practice. The mentor should be an experienced professional in the same or a similar role as the mentee who can provide expertise and support on a continuing basis.

New teachers can develop greater practical competence and maintain enthusiasm for teaching when they engage in consultative mentoring experiences with novice and veteran teachers (Boyer & Gillespie, 2000; Caccia, 1996; McCaffey, 2000; Whitaker, 2000). For instance, in peer coaching seminars, teachers learn content practices and implementations from each other. Peers can help each other analyze their teaching skills, especially students' responses (Showers & Joyce, 1996). New teachers may consult with fellow teachers when creating and evaluating prereferral strategies intended to support students' learning. They may ask more experienced teachers for implementation tips in the general education classroom. Teachers in both general education and special education may join in implementing a variety of management strategies through peer coaching and assistance consultations. In some schools, teachers use consultative formats to modify and adapt learning materials, evaluations, or specially designed curricula.

When new teachers work with consulting teachers, they are involved in collaborative planning and data collection, which increase the time needed for and the cost of staff development activities. However, to the extent that such activities result in greater clarity about means and ends, more thorough implementation of planned changes, and more immediate information about effects on students, the additional effort is well worth the investment. Teacher induction programs are beginning to use consultation formats to help new personnel learn the ropes of the system. The formation of supervisory assistance and peer coaching teams produces greater faculty cohesion and focus and, in turn, facilitates more shared decision making.

Some new personnel may be fortunate enough to work in a system where initial orientations, administrative consultations, and ongoing mentoring opportunities are the rule rather than the exception. Other new teachers may experience informal staff development meetings, such as those that occur in faculty lounges. Whether informal or formal means are used to help new members learn how the system operates, a skillful staff development program results in a self-perpetuating process for change as well as new knowledge and skills for teachers and increased learning for students (Showers & Joyce, 1996).

CEC (2000b) suggested that school administrators and school directors provide opportunities for teachers to pursue actively professional growth activities that include collaboration. Because planning and preparation time is essential, administrators and directors can organize the school day and week so that school professionals have time to work collaboratively.

Through peer coaching from new and experienced peers, new teachers receive help in increasing their teaching effectiveness. New teachers also receive administrative and peer assistance in refining their communication, management, and teaching behaviors. Consulting in supportive contexts is one key to successful professional growth and role development and to subsequent teacher change (Bos, 1995; Caccia, 1996; Showers & Joyce, 1996). In fact, opportunities for administrative support and peer collaboration, along with stress management, show promise as interventions for reducing burnout in special education and related services personnel (Cooley & Yovanoff, 1996; Westling & Whitten, 1996). Effective consultation and collaboration often rely on developing teachers' skills in recognizing how they are affected by and affect others through the use of consulting services.

DEVELOPING AND BEGINNING TEACHERS AS RECIPIENTS OF CONSULTING SERVICES

Preservice teacher trainees and developing teachers are invariably the recipients of consulting services. Consulting services are activities or interactions provided by other professionals to help novice teachers improve their teaching performance. They may be provided by a consulting teacher or supervisor who formally assists setting up a classroom program on an ongoing basis, another teacher who informally takes on the role of mentor and assists as needed, or a principal who evaluates teaching performance and offers corrective feedback. Team support from others, including university and district collaborators, often helps beginning teachers make strides in instructional practices,

Pause and Reflect About the Profession 10.1

What are potential roadblocks to "getting around the system" when you enter a school for the first time? Identify at least two areas of concern for college or university students initially entering a field site. Then, determine two different areas that may be potential roadblocks for student teachers. Next, list two avenues of concern for first-year teachers. Last, discuss with a peer one way to overcome each identified roadblock in your examples.

Students	Student Teachers	First-Year Teachers
Potential roadblock 1	Potential roadblock 1	Potential roadblock 1
A way to overcome potential roadblock 1	A way to overcome potential roadblock 1	A way to overcome potential roadblock 1
Potential roadblock 2	Potential roadblock 2	Potential roadblock 2
A way to overcome potential roadblock 2	A way to overcome potential roadblock 2	A way to overcome potential roadblock 2

classroom management, and curriculum modifications (Karge, Lasky, McCabe, & Robb, 1995).

More-experienced teaching personnel can help new teachers avoid mistakes. They have gone through the process and have, more than likely, learned a lot that can be passed on to new personnel. For instance, teaching materials that would be of interest may be tucked away in some remote closet, or the school system may have an extensive library of videotapes, but they must be reserved far in advance. Often, asking the right person may better ensure receipt of needed materials. More experienced teachers know how the school system really works and how to get around potential roadblocks.

Interactions with consulting teachers, supervisors, or principals can give developing teachers insights as to what is important in the eyes of key school personnel. Accordingly, new teachers can learn where to focus their time and attention. Administrators, for instance, may place more emphasis on classroom management and presentation of content than on having attractive bulletin boards. They may implicitly indicate hidden agendas, such as the expectation that teachers handle discipline problems in their rooms and not send students to the principal for reprimanding.

Appreciating the Competence of Other Professionals

A large part of learning from experienced teachers and administrators is accepting that others are skillful and willing to be helpful when asked. Other teachers have refined their teaching skills so well that they make teaching and classroom management look simple. They have developed styles that may or may not be congruent with the style of teaching that developing and beginning teachers wish to emulate. Nonetheless, developing and beginning teachers can learn a great deal about why specific teachers use certain styles and may find that what experienced teachers do can be modified to fit their conception of teaching and management. For example, a new teacher may observe that a teacher has excellent control of her students but seems to be verbally rough with them. This style may not be appealing, but beyond the surface, the new teacher may notice that this teacher is very consistent in reinforcing appropriate behavior and in punishing inappropriate behavior. For the new teacher's own development, the rough tone may be dispensed with and the consistency incorporated into his or her approach to student behavior management.

Another point to consider is developing and beginning teachers' evaluation of and interaction with individuals in authority. Supervisory and administrative personnel are granted a degree of authority simply by the positions they hold. On the one hand, new teachers are expected, if nothing else, to respect the positions of such individuals in the organizational hierarchy. On the other hand, new teachers will make judgments about the competence of supervisory and administrative personnel and accordingly afford them varying degrees of respect for their professional competence. In either case, developing and beginning teachers will have to subordinate their views in order to survive in a hierarchical organizational system. If they find that a person with whom they work warrants respect for his or her competence, they can acquiesce to the dominant view with little or no resentment. If they respect a person only for the position he or she holds, it may at times be exceedingly difficult to subordinate their own views.

The safest strategy for developing teachers is to concede to authority in the early stages of induction into the school system unless such a concession entails committing an immoral, unethical, or illegal act. As developing and beginning teachers become more familiar with the system and demonstrate their own professional competence, they may become more assertive and challenge the system. Also, it should be remembered that new teachers are not necessarily alone; professional organizations and teachers' unions may be of great help, especially when an issue at hand is a serious one.

Often, developing and beginning teachers find that the consulting teachers, supervisors, and principals with whom they work have a different training background or teach different types of students or subject matter. Ideally, those professionals who are assisting with a developing teacher's growth have direct experience teaching the same content area, material, and category of students. But that may be a luxury that new teachers will not experience. Accordingly, they may be inclined to underestimate the quality and relevance of the assistance that teaching professionals in other areas can lend.

The fact remains, however, that the principles of effective instruction and behavioral management used by skilled teachers are, by definition, generalizable rules that guide teacher behavior (Box 1.1). They are appropriate for most populations and content (although those principles might need to be modified for application to different populations and content). Teachers unfamiliar with the specific content of instruction may not be able to assist with issues of content accuracy and structure. But teachers in other content areas and with different types of students and age groups can demonstrate techniques or help developing and beginning teachers recognize effective or ineffective techniques they are using in their instruction.

Box 10.1   Effective Instructional and Behavioral Management Principles

Instructional Organization and Development

- Uses instructional time effectively
- Provides reviews of subject matter frequently
- Signals the initiation of lessons and lesson transitions
- Varies levels of questioning
- Provides numerous opportunities to respond
- Uses wait time to mediate question presentation and signal to respond
- Acknowledges and elaborates on student responses
- Provides specific academic feedback
- Provides and monitors guided and independent practice

Presentation of Subject Matter

- Defines and gives examples and nonexamples of concepts
- States cause and effect for laws and lawlike principles
- States and applies academic rules
- Establishes criteria and assembles facts to make value judgments

Management of Student Conduct

- Sets, monitors, and enforces classroom rules
- Is aware of student behavior
- Manages multiple activities simultaneously
- Uses positive reinforcement
- Uses contingent punishment

Communication: Verbal and Nonverbal

- Presents discourse clearly and logically
- Emphasizes important information
- Makes academic tasks attractive and challenging

Source: Adapted from *Domains: Concepts and Indicators of Effective Teaching—Florida Performance Measurement System*, by Florida Coalition for the Development of a Performance Measurement System, n.d., Tallahassee: Florida Department of Education.

Making the Most of Consultative Services

If developing and beginning teachers view the supervision process as a service being provided by their employer, then they can view their role in the process as that of a consumer receiving a service. Consequently, they should take advantage of supervision by making full use of the process. The consultative service should entail a systematic approach to the supervision process whereby regularly scheduled conferences and observations target specific performance objectives. Critiques of developing teachers' instructional or management behaviors should be presented in conjunction with constructive suggestions for alternative teaching behaviors. Novice teachers should also be given increasing responsibility for identifying their own strengths and weaknesses and for devising prescriptions for their improvement.

If developing and beginning teachers tactfully indicate to supervisory personnel that these are their expectations for the consultation process, then they communicate to others that they are knowledgeable about the process, are serious about developing their skills as teachers, and want some control over their own professional development.

Accepting Constructive Criticism

The most difficult aspect of consultation is being critiqued. When participating in a collaborative consultation conference, the first priority for developing and beginning teachers is to maintain objectivity to the greatest extent possible. They need to suppress their desires to defend their performance, listen to what is being conveyed, and objectively present their rationale for their actions. If developing teachers are experiencing such a strong emotional response that they are on the verge of losing self-control, they should say as little as possible, allow the supervisor to finish, and then indicate the need to think over the points that were made and schedule another conference. During this cooling-down period, developing teachers can vent any anger and then spend time carefully analyzing the supervisor's or consulting teacher's comments. In most cases, the new teachers will find that the feedback is not as terrible as first thought and that it is valid.

Before reconvening with the consulting teacher or supervisor, developing teachers should reflect on how they could have approached instruction in a different, more effective way. Making some notes about what they think went wrong and how they can avoid the same mistakes in the future is a helpful strategy. In contrast, if developing teachers believe that the feedback is invalid, then they need to reflect on what occurred during instruction and build a case to defend their performance. Again, they should make notes that can be taken to the next conference. (The conference planning guide, Figure 10.2, may be helpful to record notes.)

Regardless, keep in mind that effective teachers are made, not born. No one should expect developing and beginning teachers, and that includes themselves, to walk into a classroom and do a flawless job of managing classroom behavior and providing instruction. Developing effective teaching skills takes years of practice and conscious effort. Developing and beginning teachers should be patient and work toward the goal of becoming effective teachers.

DEVELOPING AND BEGINNING TEACHERS AS PROVIDERS OF CONSULTING SERVICES

Now that these great expectations have been built up for exemplary consultative services to be provided to developing and beginning teachers, consideration must be given to how these teachers can do the same for other teachers and paraprofessionals.

Developing teacher _____ Clinical professor _____

Clinical teacher _____

A. Behaviors to continue/maintain   Specific examples

    1. _____   _____

    2. _____   _____

    3. _____   _____

B. Behaviors to increase   Specific examples   Specific prescriptions

    1. _____   _____   _____

    2. _____   _____   _____

    3. _____   _____   _____

C. Behaviors to reduce/eliminate   Specific examples   Specific prescriptions

    1. _____   _____   _____

    2. _____   _____   _____

    3. _____   _____   _____

D. Responsibilities   Owner

    1. _____   _____   _____

    2. _____   _____   _____

    3. _____   _____   _____

Date of next conference _____   Date of next observation _____

FIGURE 10.2   The conference planning guide can be used in planning and documenting strategies and responsibilities for solving problems.

When they have to be the consultants, developing and beginning teachers quickly realize the amount of work, frustration, and skill involved. The kinds of skills needed are outlined in the next section and are categorized as interpersonal communication skills. A description of these skills is provided in some detail, but before reading about that, developing and beginning teachers should consider a few simple concepts when acting as consultant.

Novice teachers have the potential to become effective teachers and consultants, but they have to accumulate a great deal of experience in both roles before becoming effective in either. In working with others during the early stages of their careers, developing and beginning teachers need to accept that they know some things but that they have a great deal more to learn. They need to consider the sensitivity of others to constructive criticism. Again, they need to use the skills outlined below, always being aware that the feedback they provide may not be the information that others want to hear. They need to tune into the verbal and nonverbal reactions to what is being said.

COLLABORATIVE MODEL FOR CONSULTATIVE PROCESSES

As recipients of consultative services (consultees) or as providers of consultative services (consultants), new teachers are active participants in a collaborative consultation process. As consultees, developing and beginning teachers need to assist in scheduling

Pause and Reflect About the Profession 10.2

How Well Do You Take Constructive Criticism?

1 = Would listen quietly and comply with the feedback
2 = Would sense a degree of panic but would comply with the feedback
3 = Would not be affected by the feedback and would do nothing
4 = Would sense a degree of panic but would not comply with the feedback
5 = Would react emotionally (e.g., cry, scream, argue) and reject the feedback

Directions: Use the above scale to rate your behaviors in the following:

_____ 1. Your university supervisor asks you to redo your paper on classroom management strategies for lack of recent citations.

_____ 2. Your consulting teacher asks you to redo your science lesson plans for lack of specific instructional objectives.

_____ 3. Your university supervisor and your consulting teacher tell you to use a softer voice.

_____ 4. Students tend to avoid you in mathematics class, as indicated to you by your peer mentor.

_____ 5. Parents have noted that you spell many words incorrectly. They inform your consulting teacher, who in turn tells you to check your spelling before sending notes home.

_____ 6. Your university supervisor informs you that although your lesson plan was written neatly, you should spend more time on analyzing why your students did not meet the history objectives.

_____ 7. Your principal asks you to change your attire so that you are dressed more professionally for the job.

_____ 8. You overhear your consulting teacher tell another teacher that although you have been a help this semester, she can't wait to get her class back. It seems that the students pay you more attention.

_____ 9. Your university supervisor and consulting teacher indicate that they would like you to spend more time on assessing your students' writing skills before giving increased written expression assignments.

_____ 10. Your principal tells your consulting teacher that your students tend to act up (e.g., getting out of their seats, becoming noisier) when you take over lunchroom duty.

Is there a way to turn constructive feedback around in these examples? What would you do if this feedback were given to you? Discuss a possible course of action that could turn these constructive critiques into positive actions.

conferences and observations. They have to prepare lesson plans and present them to their supervisor in advance. They are expected to reflect on their own teaching performance and to analyze their strengths and weaknesses. During conferences, they are asked to communicate their perceptions of their own teaching in an honest and uninhibited way and to assist in devising strategies for improving their teaching. Follow-up responsibilities are devised, and tasks must be completed before the next conference (e.g., practicing new techniques, observing other teachers demonstrating alternative teaching behaviors, reading reference texts).

As a consultant to other teachers, paraprofessionals, or parents, a developing or beginning teacher has to schedule conferences, direct the conferences toward achieving some set of goals, analyze information related to the situation at hand, determine a strategy for resolving target problems, and determine the procedures and responsibilities for consultant and consultee (Warger & Aldinger, 1984).

Consensual Decision Making

The overall goal of collaboration is agreement on what is to be accomplished and how it is to be accomplished (Bos, 1995; Glatthorn, 1990; Karge et al., 1995; Villa et al., 1996). Individuals working on a problem need to feel a part of the problem-solving process. To accomplish this, the consultant and consultee in a working relationship need to participate actively in the process. This concept of active participation to achieve group consensus is referred to as consensual decision making. Consensual decision making requires a commitment of individuals within a working group to three principles (Chandler, 1982):

1. A belief that others understand their point of view

2. A belief that they understand others' points of view

3. Committed support for decisions made, whether or not they prefer the decisions, because they were arrived at in an open and fair manner.

Consensual decision making relies on individuals working as a cohesive group, perceiving the process as fair and worthwhile, and committing to the outcome of the efforts made. As consultees, developing and beginning teachers want to know that they have contributed to the problem-solving process, instead of being criticized on how they should improve their teaching skills. As consultants, they want to help others (e.g., teachers, paraprofessionals, parents) develop ownership and commitment to the decisions.

Balance of Control

In successful collaborative consultation, the balance of control typically moves away from the consultant and toward the consultee. Early in the consulting relationship, consultees tend to be more reliant on others to provide them with information and directions on how to complete job-related activities. They do a lot of asking and a lot of listening. Consultants, in contrast, usually have a great deal of information about the school and views as to how the system should work. In the early stages of the process, consultants typically do a lot of telling and a lot of directing. Researchers like Blumberg (1980) refer to this as a directive style of behavior. Conversely, as the consultees become more knowledgeable and confident in what they are doing, they ask fewer questions and seek less direction. They begin to do more talking in conferences and to ask consultants to confirm their suspicions about a situation. Consultants do more listening and ask leading questions to guide consultees in analyzing their own teaching performance. This consultative behavior is referred to as an indirective style of behavior (Figure 10.3).

The directness or indirectness of a consultant's style is related to the degree of emphasis given to the task at hand (improving the consultee's performance) or to the interpersonal relationship between the consultant and the consultee. A directive consultant tells developing consultees what their strengths and weaknesses are and how to improve their performance. Telling is usually a more efficient means of identifying problem areas and strategies in order to remediate them. With direct consultation, however, little attention is given to a consultee's self-esteem or the development of his or her self-evaluation skills. An indirective consultant, in contrast, asks developing consultees questions that lead them to recognize problem areas and deduce possible

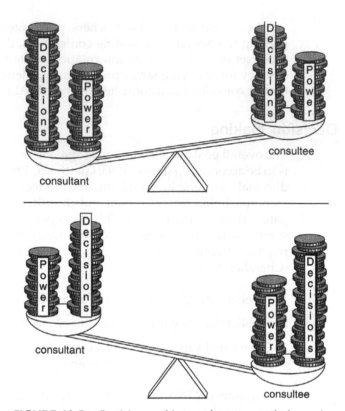

FIGURE 10.3 Decision making and power are balanced between consultee and consultant although, at different points in the process, the consultant or consultee may have more or less of each.

solutions. Under this indirect style, consultees tend to feel more in control of their performance, accept ownership for the diagnosis and intervention strategies, and develop self-evaluation skills.

Productive interpersonal work seems to be achieved best by maintaining an overall balance between energy directed toward improving the consultee's teaching and energy directed toward establishing good interpersonal relationships among team members. Effective consultation is a combination of both direct and indirect approaches. The results of at least one study (Copeland, 1982) indicate that teachers (consultees) positively evaluate their supervisory interpersonal relations when they perceive their supervisor's (consultant's) behavior as being high direct, high indirect (Style A) or low direct, high indirect (Style C) (Table 10.1.).

In sum, in the collaborative model for consultative processes, the consultant and consultee actively participate in decision making and problem solving. The two people understand that the purpose of the process is to improve instruction and that they must agree about the goals of consultation and the means for attaining them. Consensual decision making helps facilitate a commitment to the consultation process and ownership of the responsibilities associated with the goals and strategies agreed on by the team. For a true consensus to occur, the process requires a balance of control. That is not to say that, at each conference, there will be an equal distribution of control between consultant and consultee, but over the course of a series of conferences, each will contribute equally to the decision-making process. Early in the process, the consultant will usually dominate, but this will shift to the consultee as the relationship develops.

TABLE 10.1   Styles of Behavior Applicable to Consulting

Style A	High direct, high indirect	The consultee (teacher) sees the consultant (supervisor) emphasizing both direct and indirect behavior—he or she tells and criticizes but also asks and listens.
Style B	High direct, low indirect	The consultee perceives the consultant as doing a great deal of telling and criticizing but very little asking or listening.
Style C	Low direct, high indirect	The consultant's behavior is rarely direct (e.g., telling, criticizing); instead, he or she puts a lot of emphasis on asking questions, listening, and reflecting back the consultee's ideas and feelings.
Style D	Low direct, low indirect	The consultee sees the consultant as passive, not doing much of anything. Some consultants may appear passive as they try to engage in a rather misguided democratic role.

Source: From *Supervisors and Teachers: A Private Cold War*, by A. Blumberg, 1980, Berkeley, CA: McCutchen.

INTERPERSONAL COMMUNICATION SKILLS

Some constructs taken from the work of Carl Rogers (1965) may be helpful to developing and beginning teachers in building a cooperative rapport with those with whom they work. Developing and beginning teachers must keep in mind that they will apply these constructs primarily in their role as consultants but that these constructs are also applicable to their role as consultees. There will, however, be differences in how the constructs are operationalized, depending on whether the new teachers are acting as consultants or consultees.

Pause and Reflect About the Profession 10.3

Below are examples of activities that new teachers will engage in as active participants in a collaborative consultation process. For each of the following examples, analyze how you and others will operate as consultees or consultants. Provide a brief script for what you, your consultant teacher, the principal, your university supervisor, or parents might say or do.

1. Identifying discrepancies in a student's academic progress within general education content areas
2. Planning and using a variety of assessment strategies for a serious problem behavior
3. Observing students in the special education learning-support program
4. Collecting and reporting social skills data on students' peer-tutoring sessions
5. Adapting specialized equipment to help a small group of students in the physical education class
6. Modifying one part of the general education language arts curriculum to make it easier for a student to remain in the grade-level curriculum
7. Creating an individualized behavioral support plan for one student displaying signs of attention deficit disorder
8. Locating for parents some resources on normal developmental milestones in language and social domains

The first construct is positive regard for others. This is the ability to maintain a degree of respect for others simply because they are fellow human beings. Although developing and beginning teachers may respect others as individuals, this does not mean they necessarily agree with them or condone their actions. In essence, the person is separated from his or her actions. For instance, a fellow teacher may photocopy copyrighted material in a way that violates the law and a new teacher's own moral values. The new teacher does not condone the behavior but can still maintain a degree of respect for the individual as a skilled teacher. The benefit of developing a positive regard for others is that greater objectivity is gained in dealings with others.

Positive regard for others can be shown by providing honest feedback and by offering encouragement. Honest feedback describes frankly what the target behavior is, the perceptions that the speaker has of the listener's attitudes and behaviors, and the response that the speaker has to the listener's behavior. For example, rather than saying to the classroom paraprofessional who was obviously not prepared, "Well, I thought the tutoring went fairly well . . . considering," the developing teacher might provide honest feedback by saying, "This lesson did not go well because you were not fully prepared. You didn't have any visuals ready, and you weren't organized. Can we talk about why you weren't prepared?"

Encouragement is the acknowledgment that another person has the skills and behavioral repertoire to overcome problems and to extend existing skills to higher performance levels. Behaviors that express encouragement help in building and maintaining self-esteem and should increase the probability that similar positive behaviors will be demonstrated in the future. Statements of encouragement need to include specific, descriptive praises. Such statements describe the observed behavior and the observer's response to it. When a consultant observes that a consultee has displayed an effective behavior and comments on the behavior and her impressions of its effect, then descriptive praise is being used. For instance, the consultant might say, "I thought it was very effective when you stopped the talking by walking over to the student, yet continued to discuss regrouping of numbers without a moment's interruption."

A second construct is empathy. Empathic responses indicate an understanding about what another person is going through. In everyday life, individuals often make empathic statements regarding both the positive and the negative experience of others. For instance, in acknowledging a colleague's successful instruction of a student, a new teacher might say, "Oh, you must have been thrilled to see that Darius finally was able to conquer regrouping." When unpleasant experiences occur, teachers often console friends or colleagues with empathic statements such as "Getting a parking ticket first thing in the morning is aggravating." Being empathic toward the experiences of others often helps convey the fact that individuals are concerned and can appreciate the emotional responses of others to situations or events.

Burke (1984) describes responding behaviors as skilled expressions reflecting an empathic attitude for another person. Empathy for another person as described by Rogers (1965) is not an overt behavior. The attitude of empathy, however, can be expressed through outward behavior in the form of active listening. Active listening entails the following:

1. Using open-ended responses that focus on the other person, are nonjudgmental, seek further information, and are uncomplicated utterances.

   Example: "How do you think the lesson went today?"

2. Using paraphrasing/clarifying responses to help the speaker hear his or her own words, help the listener understand what the speaker's concerns are, and relate back to the speaker that the listener has carefully considered the statements.

   Example: "You said they didn't understand the concept very well. Do you mean they had difficulty with the follow-up activity?"

3. Focusing on emotions so that this component of a person's message is objectively and openly acknowledged as existing and not ignored.

Example: "I can see that you're upset with this situation. Let's talk it over."

The third construct, congruence, refers to the degree to which individuals' perceptions of their behaviors or experiences correspond to the actual pattern of behaviors and experiences. Developing and beginning teachers in a state of congruence are psychologically well adjusted (comfortable about what they do and about their experiences). Consultants and consultees in a state of congruence are genuine and sincere when interacting with each other. They project the fact that they are being honest and expressing their true impressions of a targeted problem area. Burke (1984) refers to statements with these characteristics as attending skills, which involve the use of self-disclosure statements. Such statements are characterized by three criteria (O'Shea & Hoover, 1986):

1. Taking responsibility for thoughts, behaviors, and emotions

Example: "If I had planned that transition a little better, we wouldn't have lost so much time."

2. Making concrete rather than vague or abstract statements

Example: "I find that my school day goes so much better if I get a good night's sleep, eat a full breakfast, and arrive half an hour before the students."

3. Referring to conditions in the immediate environment

Example: "I plan the math lesson for late morning, before the music teacher comes in. After she leaves, the students are so excited that spelling is more easily accomplished."

Statements with these characteristics objectively convey the position of the consultant or consultee, specify the exact subject of the statement, and put the subject into the immediate context. One subset of self-disclosure statements is that of "I" statements (Gordon, 1974). These statements involve three components (O'Shea & Hoover, 1986):

1. The consultee's target behavior is described in nonjudgmental terms.

Example: "I heard you ask 12 literal-level recall questions and 2 evaluation questions."

2. The effect of the target behavior on the speaker is described in concrete terms.

Example: "I can't keep my roll book up to date when you fail to give me the weekly test results for your students on time."

3. The emotional response of the speaker to the other person's behavior is specified.

Example: "I am delighted to have a developing teacher who is as interested and as willing to put forth effort as you are."

These kinds of statements convey that the speaker is a clear, honest, and sincere communicator.

Again, these interpersonal communication skills are applicable to both consultant and consultee. When individuals in both roles use positive regard, empathy, and congruence, communication is clear and effective. Without clear communication, collaborative consultation will be muddled by ineffective attempts to communicate ideas instead of resulting in effective attempts to resolve targeted instructional problems (Figure 10.4).

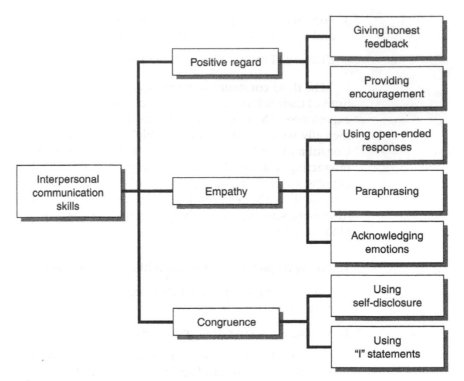

FIGURE 10.4 Rogers's (1965) Constructs of Interpersonal Communication and the Overt Behavior Used to Exhibit Them

GENERAL PROCEDURES FOR COLLABORATIVE CONSULTATION

The focal point of interpersonal relations in collaborative consultation is the series of conferences among members of the consultation team (consultee, consulting teacher, supervisor, or principal) that occur throughout the consultation process. In addition to the energy and attention spent on the interpersonal relationship between consultant and consultee, an equal amount of energy needs to be directed at identifying and resolving instructional problems. An important facet of collaborative consultation, therefore, is the systematic implementation of procedures for conducting conferences. Whereas interpersonal communication skills aid in establishing positive relationships among members of the collaborative consultation team, the procedures for conducting conferences focus on the activities that need to be accomplished. Initially, the conferences are devoted to discussing team members' roles, scheduling conferences and observations, and identifying important classroom variables (e.g., types of students, classroom rules and schedules). After the first few weeks, however, conferences focus on diagnosing problems and testing strategies to resolve them (Garland, 1982; Goldhammer, Anderson, & Krajewski, 1980).

Three Basic Procedures

Many of the procedures incorporated into the collaborative consultation process are derived from behavioral principles and decision-making systems. These procedures are designed to help developing teachers define the roles, functions, and goals of the collaborative consultation team (Bos, 1995; Caccia, 1996; Cooley & Yovanoff, 1996; Karge et al., 1995; Westling & Whitten, 1996). The three general procedures described below underlie the entire conference process and are designed for use by both consultant and consultee in collaboratively solving instructional problems.

Pause and Reflect About the Profession 10.4

Review the three major interpersonal communication skills applicable to both consultant and consultee. For each, name a person you observed who demonstrated the skill this past week in your class or school. Describe a specific example that indicated to you that clear and effective communication was occurring.

Interpersonal Communication Skill 1:

_____

Person demonstrating the skill:

_____

Specific example that indicated clear and effective communication was occurring:

_____

_____

Interpersonal Communication Skill 2:

_____

Person demonstrating the skill:

_____

Specific example that indicated clear and effective communication was occurring:

_____

_____

Interpersonal Communication Skill 3:

_____

Person demonstrating the skill:

_____

Specific example that indicated clear and effective communication was occurring:

_____

_____

The first general procedure is to formulate behaviorally descriptive statements related to the targeted instructional problem. Behaviorally descriptive statements are those that operationally identify a behavior in specific, accurate, and concise terms. They refer to quantities or frequencies of behavior occurrences. Behavioral statements do not contain subjective descriptions that imply a judgment of the behavior. A statement like "The developing teacher is not enthusiastic" is imprecise and may lead to poor communication. Vague statements should be avoided or backed up with a more objective statement of observable behaviors to indicate clearly the basis for the statement.

In addition, the conditions of behaviors need to be stated. These elements provide a clear reflection of the context in which behaviors occur. For instance, the consultation team may have agreed that the consultee should praise students each time they provide an accurate response to a question (condition) and not when they simply respond with any answer (noncondition). When a change in a specific teaching behavior is targeted, the desired level (greater or lesser) or direction (increase or decrease) of the change should be clarified. Behaviors must be referenced in clear, quantifiable, and observable terms. In this way, documentation and monitoring of changes in behavior are made easier and more objective (Piper & Elgert, 1979).

The second general procedure is to develop and maintain schedules for consistency and to routinize collaborative consultation procedures. In addition to their roles as consultants, developing and beginning teachers often have their own classroom responsibilities. Direct instructional services to students take priority over consultations with other teachers. As a result, new teachers may fail to make time available for conferences with consultees, be they other teachers, paraprofessionals, or parents. Unless consultants and consultees make the time by setting goals and scheduling observations and conferences, they are likely to defer these activities in favor of others. Following through with schedules establishes, over time, distributed practice of the procedures for various collaborative activities, which in turn better ensures that consultation activities occur.

To ensure that schedules are maintained, it is important not only to write down the series of activities to be completed but also to set a time and date to engage in each of the activities. Each subsequent conference should end with the confirmation of the next interaction as well as of projected meetings that are to follow in the near future. Following this strategy ensures that the schedule is constantly used, reviewed, and modified throughout the consultation program.

Another general procedure involves the collaborative problem-solving process. During collaborative consultations, the principal activity is that of identifying relevant classroom variables, identifying instructional program strengths and weaknesses, and formulating alternative strategies to improve student performance. These steps are delineated by the diagnostic teaching model (Cartwright & Cartwright, 1972) discussed in Chapter 5. The steps in the model are (1) identify attributes, (2) specify objectives, (3) select strategies and materials, and (4) test strategies and materials.

The first step, as applied to consultation, involves the collection of information about the classroom setting, the behavioral and learning attributes of the students, the teaching style and behaviors of the teacher, and any other relevant variables. Consultants and/or consultees collect baseline data prior to any systematic intervention, allowing team members to form a picture of what is occurring in the classroom. Next, the team members determine what they want to maintain or modify by specifying clear and behaviorally stated objectives that reflect the desired outcomes of the instructional program (step 2). Team members then select alternative strategies for accomplishing the stated objectives (step 3). Once implemented by the consultee, the strategies and materials are tested through subsequent observations and data collection (step 4).

On the basis of the information gathered, team members analyze the feedback and determine whether the objectives have been reached. Accordingly, the sequence is repeated in one of two ways. If objectives have been reached, the team forms new ones (step 2) and continues through the other steps as described. If objectives have not been reached, the team reexamines the accuracy and appropriateness of the baseline data, stated objectives, strategies, and materials. If modifications in any of these areas are necessary, the team makes the changes and the sequence is continued. When all steps seem to be accurate and appropriate, the team implements the strategies and materials again and retests.

Behaviorally descriptive statements, schedules, and problem-solving procedures are used in conferences to identify and remediate instructional problems (Figure 10.5).

OPERATIONALIZING CONFERENCE PROCEDURES

During the preobservation conference that occurs at the beginning of the consultation experience, the consultant and the consultee focus on obtaining a baseline measure of salient situational variables involving the students, teacher aides, or a new teacher. At

Use behaviorally descriptive statements

Write down schedules and keep appointments

Solve problems collaboratively

FIGURE 10.5 Three Basic Principles That Underlie the Collaborative Consultation Process

this point, the team members will discuss anecdotal observations of the members, the most important being those of the consultee. Areas of possible concern to the consultee may set the agenda for the initial observation by the consultant. Any additional areas dealing with planning, student conduct, management of classroom procedures, presentation of instructional material, building rapport, and so forth that the observer will attend to should be discussed with the consultee.

Next, the means for collecting data on these areas need to be devised or selected. In systematic observation models, some form of data recording is used to monitor behavior and to provide feedback. Recordings of teacher behavior can take a variety of forms: (1) continuous event recording, (2) time sampling, and (3) interval recording. Judgments about the situation and type of information sought from an observation dictate the type of recording system used. In any case, the recorded data provide the basis for discussion between the observer and the new teacher.

Used in conjunction with specific operational definitions of behaviors, observation records effectively communicate by providing a clear, quantifiable picture of the consultees' and/or students' behaviors. Observation records also serve as a prompt in follow-up conferences. For instance, after having observed and conducted a postobservation conference using a systematic observation record, consulting teachers can use the record in the subsequent preobservation conference to remind consultees of behavioral patterns and to guide the consultees in varying the patterns during the upcoming observation.

If a predesigned recording instrument is to be used (e.g., COKER, Flanders Interaction Analysis), then the team members should simply review the target behaviors on the instrument and the recording method to be used (e.g., continuous event recording, time sampling). If an informal instrument is to be designed and used, the team should design the form and recording method together, incorporating the principles of interpersonal communication and participative decision making outlined in previous sections.

During the postobservation conference, feedback on earlier observations is provided. This critical step involves providing consultees with objective data reflecting environmental variables, including student and teacher behavior in the classroom. Observers should present the data and explain how they were collected but should avoid making any value judgments about the performances of the students, the teacher aide, or the developing teacher. Both the consultant and the consultee should then discuss the data and analyze it to discern any recognizable patterns where specific behaviors occur in the context of antecedent or consequent events. For instance, every time a new teacher sits at her desk during seatwork assignments, the class noise level may begin to rise. This may become evident to the consultant and consultee when a recurring pattern is noted on the observation records.

As consultees become more skilled at analyzing data, more responsibility should be shifted to them for identifying patterns, with increasingly less direction from the consultant. This gradual fading process will help consultees in developing self-evaluation skills. In addition, by analyzing the data with consultees and by helping them identify salient patterns, consultants create an atmosphere that is less defensive and more productive in locating and solving problems.

Once patterns of behaviors have been identified, team members need to specify those student, teacher aide, or new teacher behaviors to maintain or increase and those behaviors to reduce or eliminate. Here, again, the emphasis is on behaviorally stated target behaviors that the consultant and the consultee will focus on in the future. In addition, the team members should determine alternative strategies for modifying the behavior of the students, teacher, or aide. These strategies may also involve modifications to the classroom setting (e.g., rearranging the physical space) or the curriculum (e.g., moving students to more appropriate points in the curriculum, changing the curriculum).

Finally, the responsibilities of each member for the next observation and conference should be documented. For instance, if the strategies for changing the consultee's behavior include the consultant modeling a specific teaching technique, then arrangements for the consultee to observe the consultant should be made. If the consultee is to review some reference books, then arrangements for getting those books need to be made. This documentation helps to ensure that the activities identified by the team are

Pause and Reflect About the Profession 10.5

Hold mock collaborative consultation conferences (include preconference and postconference sessions) for the following. Role-play what you, your consultant teacher, the principal, and/or your university supervisor might say or do.

1. Planning assessment strategies for a student's memory and retention problems in reading

2. Observing a student in a learning strategies classroom; devising generalization tips for the student's mathematics and science teachers

3. Modifying a penmanship lesson plan to accommodate a student with physical support needs

4. Devising a group management game for whole-class participation during art class

5. Designing, with fellow teachers, plans to prevent calling-out disruptions during a schoolwide assembly

6. Using positive behavioral management strategies in biology instruction

7. Encouraging students' self-evaluations during computer science instruction

carried out. Included within this step is the scheduling of the next observation and conference. The conference planning guide (Figure 10.2) can be used to document the decisions made in postobservation conferences and provide a permanent record of the process.

SUMMARY

This chapter described how developing and beginning teachers are involved in the consultation process in two ways: as recipients and as providers of consultative services. In the first case, as consultees, their role is to assist in the process of developing their own teaching and classroom management skills. They need to accept the consultant's assistance and, to some extent, acquiesce to the consultant's control and authority. In the latter case, as consultants, developing and beginning teachers will be required to direct others carefully in their development. This will entail being sensitive to the perceptions of those with whom they work. For both of these roles, the following principles and procedures of a collaborative consultation model have been suggested.

The chapter described the critical facet of collaborative consultation as the establishment and maintenance of productive interpersonal relationships between consultants and consultees. This can be accomplished through the application of the constructs of positive regard, empathy, and congruence. These constructs are displayed through verbal and nonverbal communication techniques during systematically implemented conference procedures. Consultants and consultees can operationalize these constructs through facilitating, responding, and attending. By facilitating, team members provide honest feedback regarding instructional variables but encourage continued professional development as well. A consultant responds to consultees' concerns by recognizing the affective elements of the learning process and by exploring and clarifying consultees' perceptions of their situation. Team members attend to the situation at hand by making concrete, nonjudgmental statements about the behaviors and emotions of the people within the instructional environment (e.g., teachers, paraprofessionals, students).

Facilitating, responding, and attending are the elements of the indirect style whereby consultants ask questions of consultees and attentively listen to their responses. Although, under a direct consultation style, active listening is replaced by telling and criticizing, facilitating and attending still can be employed. There are times and places for both indirect and direct approaches as long as team members strive to maintain a complementary mix.

Important elements that appears to influence consultees' responses to varying consulting styles are their levels of skill and confidence. During the early stages of consultation, more directive approaches by consultants may be necessary. As skills and confidence grow, consultees are better prepared to participate in the decision-making processes during conferences. Under these circumstances, consultees are able to self-evaluate more objectively and to commit themselves to decisions made by the consultation team.

ACTIVITIES TO EXTEND YOUR KNOWLEDGE

1. Plan a presentation in your student teaching or field placement seminar on consulting with general education teachers, administrators, and other school personnel. Use the theme of characteristics of students with specific exceptional learning or management needs. List 10 specific teaching or management strategies on which professionals in your area can consult to assist your students.

2. Revisit issues in the development of teachers' feedback and consultation skills by reviewing recent articles on these themes. Summarize at least five new understandings that you gained regarding your own feedback and consultation skills.
3. Describe ways in which technology can assist with planning and managing the consultative environment. Plan and present one workshop activity with peer mentors on the use of technology as a consultation strategy.
4. Demonstrate proficiency in oral and written communication by researching a topic relevant to consultative services. Prepare overhead transparencies for a guided discussion on local and state consultative services available to parents and fellow professionals at your school site. Include a handout with five anticipated questions that parents and professionals may have. Include the answers that you will provide regarding consultative services in your area.

REFERENCES

Blumberg, A. (1980). *Supervisors and teachers: A private cold war*. Berkeley, CA: McCutchen.

Bos, C. S. (1995). Professional development and teacher change: Encouraging news from the trenches. *Remedial and Special Education, 16*(6), 379–382.

Boyer, L., & Gillespie, P. (2000). Keeping the committed: The importance of induction and support programs for new special educators. *Teaching Exceptional Children, 33*(1), 10–15.

Burke, J. B. (1984). Interpersonal communication. In J. M. Cooper (Ed.), *Developing skills for instructional supervision*. New York: Longman.

Caccia, P. F. (1996). Linguistic coaching: Helping beginning teachers defeat discouragement. *Educational Leadership, 53*(6), 17–22.

Cartwright, G. P., & Cartwright, C. A. (1972). Gilding the lily: Comments on the training-based model for special education. *Exceptional Children, 39*, 231–234.

Chandler, T. A. (1982). Can Theory Z be applied to the public schools? *Education, 104*, 343–345.

Cooley, E., & Yovanoff, P. (1996). Supporting professionals-at-risk: Evaluating interventions to reduce burnout and improve retention of special educators. *Exceptional Children, 62*(4), 336–355.

Copeland, W. D. (1982). Student teachers' preference for supervisory approach. *Journal of Teacher Education, 33*, 32–36.

Council for Exceptional Children. (2000b). *Bright futures for exceptional learners: An action plan for quality conditions, teaching, and results for every exceptional learner*. Reston, VA: Author.

Council for Exceptional Children. (2000a). *What every special educator must know: The standards for the preparation and licensure of special educators* (4th ed.). Reston, VA: Author.

Danielson, C. (1996). *Enhancing professional practice: A framework for teaching*. Alexandria, VA: Association for Supervison and Curriculum Development.

Florida Coalition for the Development of a Performance Measurement System. (n.d.). *Domains: Concepts and indicators of effective teaching—Florida Performance Measurement System*. Tallahassee: Florida Department of Education.

Garland, G. (1982). *Guiding experiences in teacher education*. New York: Longman.

Glatthorn, A. A. (1990). Cooperative professional development: Facilitating the growth of the special education teacher and the classroom teacher. *Remedial and Special Education, 11*(3), 29–50.

Goldhammer, R., Anderson, R. H., & Krajewski, R. J. (1980). *Clinical supervision: Special methods for the supervision of teachers* (2nd ed.). New York: Holt, Rinehart & Winston.

Gordon, T. (1974). *T.E.T.: Teacher effectiveness training*. New York: Peter H. Wyden.

Karge, B. D., Lasky, B., McCabe, M., & Robb, S. M. (1995). University and district collaborative support for beginning special education intern teachers. *Teacher Education and Special Education, 18*(2), 103–114.

McCaffrey, M. E. (2000). My first year of learning: Advice from a new educator. *Teaching Exceptional Children, 33*(1), 4–9.

O'Shea, L. J., & Hoover, N. L. (1986). *Conferring with teachers about teacher performance*. Tallahassee: Florida Department of Education.

Piper, T. J., & Elgert, D. B. (1979). *Teacher supervision through behavioral objectives: An operationally described system*. Baltimore: Paul H. Brookes.

Rogers, C. (1965). *Client-centered therapy*. Boston: Houghton Mifflin.

Showers, B., & Joyce, B. (1996). The evaluation of peer coaching. *Educational Leadership, 53*(6), 12–16.

Villa, R. A., Thousand, J. S., Nevin, A. I., & Malgeri, C. (1996). Instilling collaboration for inclusive schooling as a way of doing business in public schools. *Remedial and Special Education, 17*(3), 169–181.

Warger, C. L., & Aldinger, L. E. (1984). Improving student teacher supervision: The preservice consultation model. *TEASE, 7*, 155–163.

Westling, D. L., & Whitten, T. M. (1996). Rural special education teachers' plans to continue or leave their teaching positions. *Exceptional Children, 62* (4), 319–335.

Whitaker, S. D. (2000). What do first year special education teachers need? Implications for induction programs. *Teaching Exceptional Children, 33*(1), 28–37.

## CHAPTER 11

The Master Teacher

with Vickie McGinley

Chapter Outline

In this chapter, we will

- discuss professional teaching standards, particularly the National Board for Professional Teaching Standards and the CEC and INTASC standards

- discuss PRAXIS testing for preservice teachers

- provide tips for conducting job searches and writing résumés

- examine typical job interview procedures

explore the professional portfolio process

discuss how master teachers work effectively in partnerships with other professionals, parents and guardians, and paraprofessionals

elaborate on the signs and symptoms of, and strategies to reduce, teacher stress and burnout

articulate how continual professional growth and active involvement are components in a "teacher career cycle"

challenge developing teachers to analyze their personal philosophy of special education as they develop into master teachers

A PROFESSIONAL GLIMPSE: A CASE STUDY

Sarah had graduated in May with a bachelor's degree and dual certification in elementary and special education. However, her life experiences, growing up with a sibling with Down Syndrome, had also prepared her, she thought, for the type of classroom she wanted and the interview she faced with the Dorinth School District. Sarah's brother Michael had been in an inclusive setting throughout his schooling—he was now 11 years old. At times Sarah's parents had to push for inclusive classrooms, at one point even threatening due process but working it out through in mediation instead.

Sarah felt that the elementary school position in the Dorinth School District would be ideal for her as it was located geographically next to the school district where she had attended school her whole life. This job would enable her to live at home for a while and pay back some of the loans she had accumulated while attending college. In addition, Sarah felt so strongly about inclusion that even though the advertised position was in "special education," Sarah just knew that once employed in the school, she would teach both typically developing children and children with disabilities in an inclusive setting, the situation in which she clearly wanted to be. After all, directly stated on her résumé was

Goal: To teach in an inclusive classroom at the primary level.

Sarah felt great on the way to the interview. She was prepared, having sent an electronic professional portfolio ahead of time; she carried her disk, just in case, as well as some copies of her work samples and a copy of her résumé. Sarah had also done her homework on this district, having spent three hours on the Internet last night reading the district's web page. Sarah knew that the elementary school where she was interviewing was the largest in the district and housed the full continuum of placements for children with disabilities. Sarah felt she had a lot to offer this school.

Sarah was both a bit nervous and confident at the same time as she walked into the board room where five people were waiting to interview her. The interview seemed to be going well as they asked Sarah questions about her portfolio and her student teaching experience. Finally, the principal of the elementary school described the position for which they were interviewing. It was a special education position in a self-contained life skills classroom working with 12 children and 2 aides. The principal described how all of the children with low-incidence disabilities were served in her school since services could be centralized and thus children could receive more hours of needed related services.

As the principal continued to describe this position, Sarah began to get extremely tense. When given an opportunity to ask questions, Sarah's demeanor became judgmental—clearly they hadn't read her résumé's goal. In addition, her brother had done just fine in an inclusive setting his whole life, even though other children with more severe disabilities like her brother had been in more restrictive settings. Sarah became argumentative about the class situation, suggesting ways she could change the model of services when she arrived. As the interviewers became increasingly quiet, Sarah felt the need to continue to speak to justify the things she was saying. When she paused, the principal thanked her for coming in and stated that they would be interviewing all this week and would get back to her either way. Sarah was shown to the door.

---

*I*n this chapter, we provide direction to beginning or developing teachers who are determined to make teaching a long-term career. Our goal is to increase awareness of the necessity of continual professional growth and active involvement. Professional growth and active involvement are vital steps in becoming and remaining master teachers.

We open the chapter with a discussion of teaching standards and testing in professional preparation programs. More and more pressure is being applied to novices to enter the field with the appropriate knowledge, skills, and dispositions to reach an increasingly diverse student population. However, while a consensus is emerging that beginning or developing teachers need to meet standards for practice that will attest to their grasp of essential skills (National Commission on Teaching & America's Future, 2004), specific fields such as special education rank in the top 10 in terms of teacher shortages nationally (American Association for Employment in Education, 2004).

Teachers seeking initial employment must be prepared to face the reality of school-to-job transitions. Accordingly, we offer tips for conducting job searches and writing résumés. Teachers seeking employment must present themselves well on paper initially. They must articulate their past work experiences, professional qualifications, and career goals during face-to-face interviews. We also discuss the professional portfolio development process. All teachers must begin early to create professional portfolios that provide evidence of their professional expertise.

Further, strategies to move from a student teaching viewpoint to that of a master teacher frame the next portion of the chapter. We discuss cooperation and the necessity of teaming. We also delineate practical strategies for observing peers and other professionals when mentor-protégé opportunities are provided and strategies appropriate for working with parents or guardians. Master teachers daily face typical parent or guardian concerns and must apply their professional expertise to help parents or guardians deal with these concerns.

The next portion of the chapter we devote to approaches for managing paraprofessionals (or paraeducators, instructional assistants, and/or volunteers). Teachers no longer work in isolated settings. Today, classrooms often must operate with paraprofessionals in order to run successfully. Many students served in new service delivery systems require the attention of dedicated paraprofessionals. The ability to manage paraprofessionals is evolving into a key requirement for the successful classroom performance of master teachers.

All teachers must be able to recognize and deal with stress and burnout, factors that impede the master teaching process. We provide a discussion of the sources, signs, and signals of stress and burnout in teachers as well as strategies to lessen their negative effects.

Finally, we review steps that facilitate the master teacher process. Professionals making teaching a career need to articulate a personal philosophy of special education and field advancements. They must remain committed to their profession. They also must help promote appropriate education for all students by being involved in professional organizations, participating in professional development activities, obtaining advanced degrees, and renewing teacher certifications and credentials.

TEACHERS' TESTS

Praxis

Prior to entering the teaching profession, you will learn the skills and knowledge expected of you, and of course you will be assessed along the way to see if you exhibit those skills necessary to be a successful teacher. Almost upon entering a teacher education program, you will hear the word "Praxis" and will quickly learn that The Praxis Series refers to tests that nearly 80 percent of states rely on (www.ets.org/praxis).

As you complete your certification, you will take a number of Praxis tests, and, in addition, you may have to be tested during the first year in your classroom. The Praxis Series is produced by the Educational Testing Service (ETS), which provides tests for states to use as part of their teacher certification process (*Praxis Registration Bulletin*, 2004, p. 3). You will need to take tests at a number of levels before entering your classroom. One of the first is the Pre-Professional Skills Test (PPST) in Reading, Writing, and Mathematics. Some colleges and universities require this test before admitting you to teacher education. The second assessment is the Subject Assessment, and the final assessment is the Classroom Performance Assessment.

It is natural to be nervous when facing testing: most people experience some amount of stress—which can be good. However, there are ways to prepare for these tests, and good preparation is the best way to ease stress. One way to prepare is to review the Praxis Registration Bulletin, which ETS puts out every year. This bulletin include a section called "Tests at a Glance," which provides detailed test descriptions, sample questions, and answers with explanations. Trying out the sample questions in this section will enable you to refresh previously learned knowledge and skills to focus on areas that you may need to review in more detail. In addition, the bulletin provides test-taking strategies. For more detailed help, you can order Praxis study guides directly from ETS. Also check with your college or university to see if any study tools are available. Finally, the best preparation for the Subject Area test is to develop good study and classroom skills in all of your education courses.

Information on such things as what to take to the test center, test-taking locations, and test center regulations can also be found in the Praxis bulletin. In terms of scoring, each state will set the criteria for pass/fail. Scores are sent to you and to any institution you designate on your application. Passing these tests is a requirement for becoming a teacher, and, with preparation, you will be successful.

PROFESSIONAL PREPARATION STANDARDS

Beginning in the latter part of the twentieth century, the movement to develop educational standards caught on nationally. The resulting initiatives establishing national standards for teacher performance, such as those of the National Board for Professional Teaching Standards (NBPTS) and Interstate Teacher Assessment Standards Consortium (INTASC), gained support in professional circles. While most of the NBPTS and INTASC activity was devoted to developing national standards for program development and teacher assessment for general education, program planners also explored the potential of standards for preparing all new teachers. For example, national standards for performance and assessment practices special education were circulated within INTASC (INTASC, 1994).

The standards-setting efforts of the Council for Exceptional Children (CEC) provided a structure for special educators that helps new teachers understand the master teacher process. New teachers preparing to instruct exceptional students need a solid grounding in the professional, ethical, legal, historical, and philosophical aspects of the field; in human development, the characteristics of exceptional students, and the way these characteristics may interact with a student's culture and environment; in assessment procedures that contribute the sound information needed for individualized educational decision making and program improvement; in effective instructional practices that support successful access to challenging curricula and that enhance self-advocacy and independence; and in effective programs that help exceptional students use social skills to enhance learning and independence. They also need to have developed collaborative partnership skills that are characterized by mutual and reciprocal respect and responsibility and communication skills that enable the professional to be sensitive, culturally competent, and effective (CEC, 2000a).

In addition to articulating its standards for knowledge and skills that all new special educators should possess, CEC collaborated with other national programs, projects, and agencies in its work to develop national teacher standards for experienced educators working with diverse students. For example, CEC worked with NBPTS, which has approved standards for exemplary teachers of students with "exceptional needs" (NBPTS, 1999). Its standards for accomplished practice for an "exceptional needs specialist" were designed so that accomplished teachers demonstrate what they know and are able to do to provide exemplary support for students in a broad range of settings and roles (O'Shea, Hammitte, Mainzer, & Crutchfield, 2000).

INTASC identified a knowledge base and performance measures for beginning educators that are aligned with CEC's recognized standards for beginning special educators. CEC's recent work highlighted its collaboration with INTASC in developing standards and performance assessments covering the knowledge, skills, and disposition beginning educators need in order to teach students with exceptionalities in general classrooms (O'Shea et al., 2000).

As these national standards initiatives emphasize, all beginning and developing teachers are expected to be able to teach their students so as to meet high standards. But doing so requires preservice and in-service programs based on clear standards that define high-quality teaching. Such standards also establish a blueprint that all new teachers and their mentors can use to gauge new teachers' development (National Association of State Boards of Education [NASBE], 2000).

All teachers can profit from important guideposts for their professional preparation as they face more and more diverse students in their classrooms. In order to meet the teaching standards and support special needs students wherever these students receive their education, all general and special educators must understand the knowledge demands of the standards and the curriculum. Master teachers accept or believe in the purposes and the value of having high standards. However, teachers' knowledge and ability to integrate high standards into pedagogy are affected by the quality of professional development and the strength of teachers' collaborative efforts to support each other (McLaughlin, 2000).

Unfortunately, even among teachers who survive their early years, many never receive the targeted professional development they need to acquire teaching skills that foster high-quality student learning (NASBE, 2000). New teachers benefit from the kind of sustained support that takes time and effort, particularly from each other and from those helping them to become master teachers. Such activities as attending professional development events, participating in peer evaluations, and investing considerable time in discussions and observations can make the difference in teachers' attrition (that is, exit from the field) or retention (that is, commitment to remain in the field). These activities also contribute to new teachers' job satisfaction as they work to achieve master teacher status.

The attrition rate is highest among the newest teachers (Billingsley, 2002). A brand new teacher will learn that it takes a long time to become a great teacher, with the need for professional development and mentoring, which is crucial, along the way (Ingersoll, 2003).

Chronic Shortages

Unfortunately, at a time when education is focusing on the quality of the professional, chronic shortages of well-prepared and -qualified special educators loom large (American Association for Employment in Education [AAEE], 2004). Specific fields such as special education rank in the top 10 in terms of teacher shortages nationally (AAEE, 2004), and an end to this shortage over the next decade is not probable due to growing student enrollment. In special education, the population of children with disabilities in the last five years increased at a rate three times faster than the general population (U.S. Department of Education, 2002).

Stemming these chronic shortages, while simultaneously ensuring that teacher education programs prepare the next generation of educators for the responsibilities they will assume, was and will continue to be daunting. Nevertheless, even in the face of these critical shortages, the focus on quality, rather than any lowering of standards, remains necessary.

THE JOB SEARCH

Knowing what potential employers seek in job candidates can increase your employment prospects. Doing your homework during the job search process will pay off. First, you must research the state in which you are planning to teach. Each state has a state education agency, which oversees licensing. However, individual school districts handle their own screening and hiring. As a general rule, school districts will need a cover letter, a résumé and/or job application (submitted online and/or in hard copy; be prepared with both), official transcripts, and letters of reference. Some school districts may provide you with the forms they want you to use to obtain references (AAEE, 2004). Being familiar with districts' screening procedures, interviewing processes, and faculty selection criteria will make your job search and your transition to employment smoother. Be aware that school districts are relying more on Internet web sites to recruit teacher applicants, even offering virtual job fairs in some instances.

Equal Opportunity Employment Procedures

Districts nationwide are committed to selecting and employing the most qualified persons for available teaching positions. To prevent the use of discriminatory hiring, promotion, or retention practices, district policies include equal opportunity employment procedures for all candidates. This means that school districts cannot discriminate on the basis of age, cultural or ethnic background, gender, religious orientation, disabling condition, and so forth. Policies for filling teaching positions must be written before teaching opportunities are posted.

Posting Teaching Opportunities

Vacancy and new position notices are prepared and posted in accordance with contract agreements existing in school districts. During the initial screening steps, school district personnel scan applications, review cover letters, and identify key elements in résumés for faculty positions. Many districts have interview teams composed of school board members, administrators, teachers, and parents. Interview teams most likely are obligated through contractual or union agreements to review substitute lists and appraisal forms prior to selecting interview candidates. This means that, before new district personnel are interviewed and hired, interview teams will consider (1) substitute teachers, (2) permanent substitute teachers, (3) long-term substitute teachers, and/or (4) half-day teachers.

Pause and Reflect About the Profession 11.1

Describe what you believe school district personnel want candidates to do after the personnel office posts available teaching opportunities. List at least three things a new teacher can do to participate in the employee search.

1. _____

_____

_____

_____

_____

2. _____

_____

_____

_____

_____

3. _____

_____

_____

_____

_____

It is very helpful to get on substitute lists even if no immediate positions are available. Not only does substituting provide the new teacher with experience, but also it can be a way to "get a foot in the door." Many school district personnel recognize their obligation to screen and employ as well as to provide a thorough introduction to the school district. Substituting is a fast way to get the initial orientation and name recognition. In this way, new teachers can begin their positions on the best possible grounds. They also have an edge in observing teacher induction criteria for that district.

Employee Searches

School districts are looking for good people: candidates who are bright, professional, motivated, and collaborative. Since school districts nationwide want to select high-quality professional employees, they often begin their employee searches by posting available positions in key locations. State education agency, educational organization, and school district web sites, as well as career counseling centers in colleges or universities, have up-to-date job postings from local, state, and national employment searches. Job postings for vacancies and new positions include information on the position(s) available, qualifications, major responsibilities, salary, and application deadlines. They also list the names, addresses, and telephone numbers of contacts.

New teachers wanting a teaching position for the beginning of the school year ideally will initiate job searches in late February. Most positions begin with the start of a new school year; however, some positions are available in January. Teachers who submit the necessary information to district personnel offices by mid-October can be considered for January positions.

> 127 Lincoln Drive
> Smithtown, Pennsylvania 15249
> 412-987-6543

February 14, 2005

John Doe, Personnel Director
Main Street School District
One Main Street Drive
Main Street, USA 12345

Dear Mr. Doe,

I am interested in applying for the special education teaching position in Main Street School District that was advertised recently. I will be graduating from Smithtown University in May 2005 and am available to begin teaching in the fall of 2005. Upon completion of my undergraduate studies, I will be certified to teach in special education and elementary education. I am especially interested in consulting with parents and general educators concerning students with mild to moderate disabilities in your school district.

Please send me more information on the posted elementary-level teaching position, including the grade level, subject(s) taught, the school in which the class is located, and its geographic relationship to Main Street River. Please send me a copy of your district's professional application form and any other forms I need to complete in order to be considered for an interview.

Thank you for your time and consideration of my request.

Sincerely,

Martha Barton

FIGURE 11.1   An Introduction Letter to Main Street School District

When the new teacher locates a desirable teaching position in a geographic area in which he or she would like to work, the next logical step is to write an introduction letter to the district's personnel director. The teacher should identify him- or herself in the introduction letter and express an interest in working for the district. It is a good idea to request more written information on the job listing, including the grade level, subject(s) taught, school name, and geographic region. The introduction letter should also request the district's professional application form. All introduction letters should be neatly typed, signed, and dated. Figure 11.1 illustrates an introduction letter to the fictitious Main Street School District.

Professional Application, Résumé, and Cover Letter

Completing the Professional Application. The new teacher completes the professional application form by listing personal information (e.g., name, address, emergency telephone number), professional preparation (e.g., undergraduate institution, degree, graduation date), professional experience (e.g., prior teaching experience, student teaching experience), and references (e.g., people who have supervised the candidate or observed the candidate's teaching experiences).

Further, many personnel directors require documentation relating to background checks and clearances (including fingerprints), FBI clearance for nonresidents, drug use checks, child abuse checks, and communicable disease clearances. Districts require the additional data to eliminate the possibility of hiring people who have criminal backgrounds and/or have been exposed to diseases that potentially may be dangerous to others. (Most recent graduates will have undergone these background checks prior to

---

Main Street School District
One Main Street Drive
Main Street, USA 12345

PROFESSIONAL APPLICATION FORM

1. Fill out information as completely as possible. Forward the following application and the materials listed below to **Personnel Office, Main Street School District, One Main Street Drive, Main Street, USA 12345.** Completed applications include: (**A**) cover letter, (**B**) application form, (**C**) three (3) professional reference forms, (**D**) college/university transcripts, (**E**) copy of teaching certificate, (**F**) criminal and child abuse clearances, and (**G**) NTE scores.

2. This application will remain active for a period of 1 year. If you desire to have your application remain active after the termination date, please contact the Personnel Office at the Main Street School District.

3. Appointments for interviews will be arranged by this office for those individuals who meet screening criteria.

PERSONAL INFORMATION

Last Name _____ First Name _____ Middle _____

Business Address _____ Telephone _____

Town _____ Zip Code _____

Home Address _____ Telephone _____

Town _____ Zip Code _____

Number to Call in Case of Emergency _____ Social Security Number _____

Area of Certification _____ Date Issued _____

(Copy of Certificate or Letter of Verification from your college must accompany application.)

Present Position _____ Present Annual Salary _____

Type of Position Desired _____ Date of Availability _____

Salary Expected _____ Total Time Taught _____ Time Taught in State _____

PROFESSIONAL PREPARATION

INSTITUTION & LOCATION	MAJOR/MINOR	DEGREE	GRAD. DATE
High School			
Undergraduate			
Graduate			

Main Street School District Is an Equal Rights and Opportunities Educational Agency

---

FIGURE 11.2 Professional Application Form

their student teaching assignments.) The new teacher should type the professional application form or print it neatly. Figure 11.2 illustrates a professional application form used by the Main Street School District.

After the new teacher has completed the professional application form, he or she should send it to the district personnel office. A current résumé and a cover letter should accompany the completed professional application form. (It is wise to make a copy of all information prior to mailing the completed package.) Upon receipts, the personnel office will initiate an individual credentials file for the candidate.

PROFESSIONAL EXPERIENCE

INSTITUTION & LOCATION	POSITION	FROM/TO	YEARS	SIZE/UNIT

OTHER VOCATIONAL OR GENERAL EXPERIENCES THAT YOU BELIEVE ARE PERTINENT

_____

_____

_____

_____

_____

REFERENCES

Please list the names of at least three persons who have supervised your work or teaching and will be providing a completed Main Street School District Reference Form.

Name _____ Position _____

Present Address _____

Town, State, Zip Code _____ Telephone _____

Name _____ Position _____

Present Address _____

Town, State, Zip Code _____ Telephone _____

Name _____ Position _____

Present Address _____

Town, State, Zip Code _____ Telephone _____

SIGNED _____ DATE _____

Main Street School District Is an Equal Rights and Opportunities Educational Agency

FIGURE 11.2 *continued*

Writing the Résumé. With a résumé, the new teacher markets him- or herself to a prospective employer. A résumé is a one- to two-page written summary supporting the candidate's personal information, professional preparation, and professional experiences. The goal of any résumé is to stimulate interest in the candidate. Since it has been reported that recruiters will spend, on average, 25 seconds scanning a résumé (AAEE, 2004), it makes sense that the résumé should state that the candidate is worth pursuing. There are standard ways to write a résumé, which generally should include the following: (1) teaching objective, (2) educational background, (3) certification, (4) awards/

endorsements, (5) teaching experiences (whether paid or volunteer), (6) field work and student teaching, (7) any coaching and tutoring experiences, (8) employment, and (9) related activities. If it might help land a particular job, the candidate may want to include language competencies, technology skills, interests, conferences and workshops attended, and any special interest.

Writing the Cover Letter. Writing the cover letter is an important task. The cover letter briefly highlights pertinent information from the application form and résumé. Often, district personnel offices post more than one position. Therefore, it is helpful to indicate the specific position one is interested in obtaining within the cover letter's initial paragraph. (Figure 11.3 illustrates a typed cover letter with an introduction, a body, and a closing—the standard format for a cover letter; Figure 11.4 illustrates a résumé.) School districts will look at the resume first to screen applicants. However, cover letters do matter, and the recruiter will look at this to see if the candidate can write. According to the American Association for Employment in Education (2004), there are 10 rules of cover letter writing:

1. Don't draft generic letters; make each letter unique to a specific school district.

2. Address your letter to a specific person at the school district, with the correct spelling of that person's name and title.

3. Communicate something unique to that person.

4. Show how you can meet the needs of the school, rather than what you hope they will do for you.

5. Use the body of the letter to highlight your education and experiences that are relevant to the job.

6. Qualify and quantify your experiences and achievements using examples.

7. Ask for a meeting to discuss your qualifications in more detail.

8. Keep to minimum sentences that begin with "I."

9. Write a one-page letter; check your spelling, proofread, and print a clean copy.

10. Sign the letter, make a copy for your files, and attach it on top of your resume. Send your letter and resume in a 9" × 12" manila envelope.

Many job opportunities are posted electronically. In turn, more and more districts are accepting candidates' application forms and résumés electronically. This system offers both the candidate and the personnel office a chance to screen potential employee-employer matches more efficiently and effectively. Innovations in electronic applications and résumé inquiry include job banks that are interactive and résumé-friendly; online application-interview processes; and local district web sites that boast of incentives and opportunities available. If the cover letter and résumé are sent electronically as an attachment, it is recommended that the candidate also include this information in the body of an e-mail, with an indication that a hard copy is on its way.

Professional References

Professional references are important to the job selection process. Most personnel offices will ask the new teacher to name at least three contacts that have supervised the teacher's work or student teaching; thus, the selection of references is vital. (The candidate should not rely on relatives, neighbors, or other significant individuals unfamiliar with teaching responsibilities or professional job qualifications.) If the candidate is completing the application process prior to graduation, the teacher supervising the candidate during the student teaching or internship assignment is an important reference choice. Further, when the candidate is familiar with a school administrator, such as a

April 10, 2005
127 Lincoln Drive
Smithtown, Pennsylvania 15249
412-987-6543

John Doe, Personnel Director
Main Street School District
One Main Street Drive
Main Street, USA 12345

Dear Mr. Doe,

Enclosed is my completed professional application form for the fourth-grade special education consulting position in Main Street School District. Your district personnel office advertised this position and recently sent me the forms to complete. I am very interested in moving to the Main Street area. I include my résumé and a brief summary of my professional endeavors for your perusal.

I completed my student teacher experience at George Roberts Elementary School in April 2005. I worked under the direction of Mr. Tom Mallory. My major instructional responsibilities under Mr. Mallory included planning, implementation, and evaluation of the reading, language arts, mathematics, and science curricula. I worked with third-, fourth-, and fifth-grade students receiving special education services. All of my students had Individualized Education Programs delivered in the general education setting. My main responsibilities were conducting assessments, programming, and evaluating both learning strategies and positive management practices aimed at supporting the students' success in their general education classes. I received specialized training in computer technology and specially designed instruction while working at George Roberts Elementary. Consequently, I am very familiar with adapting the general education curricula from third to fifth grade, as well as with adapting and modifying computer technology for the curriculum areas. Further, my teaching experiences included work in curriculum-based assessments, portfolio assessments, and classroom management techniques for special education services.

Finally, while completing my undergraduate degree, I worked nights for the past three years at the Smithtown University Student Center. My responsibilities included maintaining product inventories at the University Book Store.

I am very interested in a third- or fourth-grade teaching position at Main Street School District. Following are my professional contacts, who will be able to provide you more information concerning my professional training:

1. Mr. Tom Mallory
   Teacher, Elementary Education Department
   George Roberts Elementary School
   Smithtown, Pennsylvania 15249
   412-987-3456
2. Dr. Bob Lennon
   Supervisor, Special Education Services
   Smithtown School District
   Smithtown, Pennsylvania 15249
   412-987-1298
3. Dr. Mary Reynolds
   Professor, Special Education Department
   Smithtown University
   Smithtown, Pennsylvania 15249
   412-456-7890

Please let me know whether you require any other information from me at this time. Thank you for your time and consideration. I look forward to hearing from you at your earliest convenience.

Sincerely,

Martha Barton

FIGURE 11.3   A Typed Cover Letter to Main Street School District

Martha Barton
127 Lincoln Drive
Smithtown, Pennsylvania 15249
412-987-6543

Educational Background

High School:	**Dates:**
High School Diploma	June 2001
Smithtown High School	
Smithtown, Pennsylvania 15249	
University:	**Dates:**
Bachelor of Science	August 2001–May 2005
College of Education	
Smithtown University	
Smithtown, Pennsylvania 15249	

Professional Certifications: **Effective Dates:**
Special Education, Instructional I   May 2005
Elementary Education, Instructional I   May 2005

Professional Experience: **Dates:**
Student Teaching, Grades 3–5   January 2005–May 2005
Special Education Services
George Roberts Elementary School
Smithtown, Pennsylvania 15249
412-987-3456

Student Teaching, Grades 7–8   August 2002–December 2004
General Education
Sammel Middle School
Smithtown, Pennsylvania 15249
412-987-4000

Practicum, Ellis Preschool Center   January 2003–May 2005
George Roberts Elementary School
Smithtown, Pennsylvania 15249
412-987-1007

Specialized Training Experience: **Dates:**
Computer Technology   January–May 2005
Specially Designed Instruction
Curriculum-Based Assessment
Portfolio Assessment
Classroom Management
(George Roberts Elementary School)

Professional Organizations:
Association for Retarded Citizens, Member (2002–present)
Council for Exceptional Children, Member (2002–present)
Division on Mental Retardation, Member (2002–present)
Division for Learning Disabilities, Member (2002–present)
Division for Behavioral Disorders, Member (2002–present)

FIGURE 11.4   Résumé

Career Goal Expectations: **Anticipated Dates:**
Special Education Consulting Teacher   August 2005
Master's Degree, Special Education   May 2010

Previous Employment: **Dates:**
University Bar and Grill   August 2001–April 2002
Maintenance Supervisor
Smithtown University Student Center

Awards/Recognition: **Dates:**
Dean's List   August 2003–May 2005
College of Education
Smithtown University
Smithtown, Pennsylvania 15249

Professional References
Mr. Tom Mallory
Elementary Education Department
George Roberts Elementary School
Smithtown, Pennsylvania 15249
412-987-3456

Dr. Bob Lennon
Supervisor, Special Education Services
Smithtown School District
Smithtown, Pennsylvania 15249
412-987-1298

Dr. Mary Reynolds
Professor of Special Education
Smithtown University
Smithtown, Pennsylvania 15249
412-456-7890

FIGURE 11.4 *continued*

program supervisor or principal, that administrator can be another good reference choice. Finally, college or university instructors, supervisors, or professors from whom the candidate took classes can be important contacts.

Each contact most likely will complete a professional reference form, such as that illustrated in Figure 11.5. On this form, the individual will rate the candidate in areas such as teacher performance (e.g., knowledge of subject matter, maintenance of classroom control); professionalism (e.g., participation in professional organizations, demonstration of initiative and leadership); and personal qualities (e.g., display of emotional stability, positive relationships with students, collaboration with administration and staff). In addition, the contact will rank the candidate, comparing him or her with others in the same position whom the contact has supervised or managed. Finally, most personnel offices ask the contact to provide written comments about the candidate's attendance and overall teaching performance. The contact also provides his or her name, school address, and telephone number for future reference, if necessary.

College Transcripts, Verification of Previous Employment, and Teaching Credentials

In addition to a professional application form, cover letter, résumé, and references, the candidate will often have to provide the district personnel office with copies of his or her college or university transcripts (verified on official college or university letterhead).

Main Street School District
One Main Street Drive
Main Street, USA
12345

Mail to: John Doe, Director of Personnel
Room 1234
Main Street School District
412-123-4567

PROFESSIONAL REFERENCE FORM

Candidate's Name _____ Position Desired _____

Please assist me in my application for a position with Main Street School District by completing the form below and returning it in the enclosed self-addressed envelope. You have my permission to complete this evaluation based on your knowledge of my background.

I further understand that the information provided will be kept confidential by and become the property of Main Street School District.

Applicant's Position _____ Full Time _____ Part Time _____

Exact Dates of Service: From (mo./yr.) _____ Total (mo./yr.) _____

Total Years Served _____

Reason for Leaving Employ/Reemploy? _____

Would You Employ/Reemploy? _____

1. TEACHER PERFORMANCE	Out-standing	Above Average	Average	Unsatisfactory	No Opportunity to Observe
A Has knowledge of subject matter					
B Is consistently thorough in lesson planning; manages learning environment, including student materials, activities, and time					
C Uses a variety of teaching techniques, resources, and materials that relate effectively to the individual needs and maturity of children					
D Exhibits enthusiasm for teaching and has the ability to arouse interest; stimulates intellectual growth					
E Maintains classroom control; is respectful, positive, fair, firm, and consistent with children					

Main Street School District Is an Equal Rights and Opportunities Educational Agency

FIGURE 11.5 Professional Reference Form

2. **PROFESSIONALISM**	Out-standing	Above Average	Average	Unsatisfactory	No Opportunity to Observe
A Follows ethical and professional practices in working with others					
B Keeps accurate and up-to-date records (e.g., IEPs, portfolios)					
C Participates in general school activities					
D Participates in a variety of professional organizations					
E Demonstrates loyalty and dependability					
F Shows initiative and leadership skills					
3. **PERSONAL QUALITIES**					
A Displays emotional stability					
B Has positive relationships with students					
C Collaborates with administration and staff					
D Communicates and works with parents effectively					
E Maintains professional appearance					
F Demonstrates professional oral and written communication skills					
G Responds positively to constructive criticism					

4. **COMPARATIVE RANKING**

   How would you rank this person as compared with others in the same position whom you have had under your supervision?

   TOP 5%   NEXT 20%   MIDDLE 50%   LOW 25%

   Main Street School District Is an Equal Rights and Opportunities Educational Agency

FIGURE 11.5 *continued*

In addition, the personnel office may request verification of previous employment and copies of teaching certifications. (Because these are requested by, but not mailed in by, the candidate, these additional materials can be received in the personnel office at a later date than the application form, cover letter, and résumé.)

Personnel offices will ask candidates to send written documentation of summary grade point averages from college or university course work. When determining which candidates to interview, many personnel directors assign points on the basis of

---

5. **PLEASE COMMENT ON THE FOLLOWING:**

    A. OVERALL PERSONALITY AND CHARACTER _____

    _____

    B. ATTENDANCE _____

    C. OVERALL PERFORMANCE AS A TEACHER _____

        _____

        _____

    D. ADDITIONAL COMMENTS _____

        _____

        _____

EVALUATOR'S NAME (Print/Type) _____

TITLE _____

SCHOOL ADDRESS _____

_____

DAYTIME PHONE NUMBER _____ DATE _____

SIGNATURE _____

Main Street School District Is an Equal Rights and Opportunities Educational Agency

---

FIGURE 11.5 *continued*

summary grade point averages. For example, candidates might receive points as indicated below:

A. Cumulative College Grade Point Average (with a grade point average of 3.0, based on a 4.0 scale, as the cutoff for interviews):

Grade Point Average	Points
4.0–3.6	2
3.59–3.0	1
Below 3.0	No interview

B. Cumulative Master's Grade Point Average (if applicable) (with a grade point average of 3.5, based on a 4.0 scale, as the cutoff for interviews):

Grade Point Average	Points
4.0–3.5	1
Below 3.5	No interview

Pause and Reflect About the Profession 11.2

How would you rate if the district personnel office were to assign points on the basis of your summary grade point averages? Determine your points and your interview potential on the basis of your grade point averages as indicated below. Would you be eligible for an interview?

A. Cumulative college Grade Point Average (with a grade point average of 3.0, based on a 4.0 scale, as the cutoff for interviews):

Grade Point Average	Points
4.0–3.6	2
3.59–3.0	1
Below 3.0	No interview

Your cumulative college grade point average: _____

B. Cumulative Master's Grade Point Average (if applicable) (with a grade point average of 3.5, based on a 4.0 scale, as the cutoff for interviews):

Grade Point Average	Points
4.0–3.5 or higher	1
Below 3.5	No interview

Your cumulative master's grade point average: _____

C. Grade Point Average in Certified Area(s) (with a grade point average of 3.0, based on a 4.0 scale, as the cutoff for interviews):

Grade Point Average	Points
4.0–3.6	3
3.59–3.2	2
3.19–3.0	1
Below 3.0	No interview

Your college grade point average for certified areas: _____

Are you eligible for an interview on the basis of this rating system?_____

C. Grade Point Average in Certified Area(s) (with a grade point average of 3.0, based on a 4.0 scale, as the cutoff for interviews):

Grade Point Average	Points
4.0–3.6	3
3.59–3.2	2
3.19–3.0	1
Below 3.0	No interview

In addition, district personnel offices often request the candidate's score(s) on a national teaching test, such as the National Teachers' Examination. A passing score in core areas, such as written expression and mathematics, as well as in the candidate's content area specialization (e.g., special education, reading, science) can be determinative in initial candidate screenings.

Completed Credentials Files

Completed credentials files for teaching positions contain much information. Most personnel offices consider a candidate's application to be incomplete until they receive the following:

- A professional application form
- A cover letter
- A current résumé
- Recent background checks and clearances
- Letters of recommendation (usually three)
- Official undergraduate and (if applicable) graduate transcripts
- Verification of previous employment (if applicable)
- A copy of applicable teaching certification(s)

Some school districts that have insufficient candidates will readvertise the positions. If the number of candidates is still insufficient, many districts select the highest-scoring applicants to interview. Most districts hold candidates' files for only six months to a year. Candidates will need to reactivate their files for additional consideration when positions are reposted.

Interview teams often use an initial screening form, such as that illustrated in Figure 11.6, when choosing candidates for interviews. Interview teams discriminate among candidates by rating them in terms of (1) college grades, (2) national teaching scores, (3) professional experience, (4) specialized training or experience, and (5) references. Many interview teams indicate that candidates who have evidence of completing multiple tasks simultaneously (e.g., holding a job, raising a family, having university or community leadership experiences, in addition to completing college course work) are often selected for job interviews. Such candidates demonstrate on paper that they have what it takes to be a teacher—a professional who is required to complete competing, multiple tasks in classroom settings.

Main Street School District
One Main Street Drive
Main Street, USA
12345

INITIAL SCREENING

Rate based on "0" to "5", 5 being the highest score

Candidate's Name _____   Date _____

Area(s) of Certification:

1. COLLEGE GRADES ASSESSMENT _____
2. NTE SCORE _____
3. PROFESSIONAL EXPERIENCE _____
4. SPECIALIZED TRAINING OR EXPERIENCE _____
5. REFERENCES _____

CANDIDATE QUALIFIES FOR AN INTERVIEW: YES / NO

Main Street School District Is an Equal Rights and Opportunities Educational Agency

---

FIGURE 11.6 Initial Screening Form

Face-To-Face Interviews

The top-rated candidates are chosen for face-to-face interviews with the interview teams. The face-to-face interview may require the candidate to travel to the district or to a job fair that partners local university, district, and community resources. Before the interview, the candidate should prepare (i.e., learn about the school district), should practice for the interview, should be prompt and polite, and should dress professionally (a conservative suit and shoes in neutral colors are the best choices). During the interview, the new teacher sits before the interview team members, answering probing questions. Questions are either in a group format or provided by individual interview team members. The questions often relate to the candidate's (1) background, (2) strengths and weaknesses, (3) instructional techniques, (4) content matter, (5) behavioral support or classroom management, (6) planning ability, and (7) knowledge of teaching. See Table 11.1.

Interview teams look for candidates to demonstrate initiative during face-to-face contacts. To do so, the new teacher should be prepared to ask pertinent questions about local practices. This part of the interview is intended to allow the interview team to determine if there is a match between the candidate's interests and qualifications and what the district can offer the candidate. It further gives the candidate an opportunity to decide whether the district is the right employment choice.

Pertinent questions that the new teacher might raise in face-to-face interviews include those related to the district's average class sizes, number of students in the building, number of students receiving special education services, and number of students provided special education services through inclusion models in the general

TABLE 11.1 Questions Applicable to the Interview Team and Candidates During Face-to-Face Interviews

Interview Team Questions to Candidates	Candidates' Questions to Interview Teams
What is relevant in your background that qualifies you for this teaching position?	What grade levels does the position entail?
	How many students are in the school?
What are some methods that you would use in teaching a reading lesson . . . mathematics lesson . . . science lesson, and so forth?	What is the student-teacher ratio?
	How many students receive special education services?
How do you determine that students have learned what you have taught? What are assessment methods you use?	Where do the students receive the special education services?
What do you do when your students forget homework assignments?	Who attends the IEP meetings with the special education faculty?
How would your supervisor determine whether you were well organized in your classroom?	What peer-mentoring and/or professional development services does the district offer?
What steps would you take if your principal provided constructive criticism on some aspect of your lesson plans?	How often are family members invited to participate in school functions?
How do you promote positive communication with parents?	How are teaching faculty evaluated or observed? What is the process, and who conducts the process?
What are several ways you maintain classroom control? How would you begin teaching [subject area] if you were not provided teaching materials?	What are the beginning and ending times for teachers' school attendance?
What are specific consulting strategies you will use with general education teachers if you are to use a learning strategies approach?	How are resources provided for individual students, classes, and teachers?
	What extracurricular duties are expected of teachers?
How will you manage and evaluate your paraprofessionals and classroom volunteers?	

Pause and Reflect About the Profession 11.3

What pertinent topics might you raise in a face-to-face interview with an interview team? Determine what you would want to ask to help you in deciding whether the position is the right employment choice for you. Write down at least five questions you would want to ask if you were involved in a face-to-face interview.

1. _____
_____
_____
_____

2. _____
_____
_____
_____

3. _____
_____
_____
_____

4. _____
_____
_____
_____

5. _____
_____
_____
_____

education classroom. Other questions include number of teachers, starting and ending times for teachers, extracurricular activities, classroom resources, and professional responsibilities. Still other pertinent questions relate to the specifics of job demands and incentives for employment. Table 11.1 presents questions that might be asked by interview team members and candidates during face-to-face interviews.

Candidate Recommendations

Many districts require top-rated candidates to conduct a classroom demonstration lesson or a computer technology demonstration in front of the interview team and other teachers, administrators, or parents. These requests most likely will take place during a second or third round of face-to-face interviews. Interview teams consider these results prior to recommending the final two or three candidates to the district personnel director. Many district personnel directors will submit top-rated candidate recommendations to the superintendent and board of education. School board members, however, often make the final selection for the faculty positions. The board of education approves final faculty selections, with all credentials and processing papers completed in full before final appointment.

PROFESSIONAL PORTFOLIOS

Portfolios have been a part of job searches in other disciplines for many years. However, they are relatively new in education. A professional portfolio is a purposeful collection of pedagogical work that tells the story of the teacher's efforts, progress, or achievements. It is different from a student portfolio, which you may have had to compile while still a student at your college or university.

Some teacher preparation programs currently use the professional portfolio, with most moving to electronic professional portfolios, to document new teachers' accomplishments and how well beginning or developing teachers meet professional standards. The process of compiling a professional portfolio often functions to account for assessment decisions, improved teaching, and student performances in teacher preparation. For example, Kenney, Hammitte, Rakestraw, and LeMontagne (2000) summarized their professional portfolios process, coupled with the statewide move to teacher preparation course work delivery. As programmatic changes focused on raising university standards in teacher preparation, these authors detailed how new teachers prepared professional portfolios and received instructional modeling of effective teaching practices across grade levels, educational settings, and teacher placements in primary through grade 12 classrooms. These authors provided data on their college's use of professional portfolios to document performance-based assessments and dynamic assessment strategies, programmatic change effectiveness, and special education course work.

Professional Portfolio Purposes

There is a variety of professional portfolio purposes. If you're about to graduate, you may have been developing a professional portfolio along the way as part of your graduation requirements. However, now you will select the evidence (documents) to keep in your portfolio for a different audience and for a very specific goal—to obtain employment. Therefore, at this time, the professional portfolio serves very specific purposes directed toward that goal.

First, through the professional portfolio, beginning or developing teachers can specify the knowledge, skills, and dispositions essential for them as professionals. Second, they can use the professional portfolio to display teaching progress, efforts, and achievements. By creating a professional portfolio during preservice experiences, new teachers show evidence that they have what it takes to assume professional responsibilities. Next, they can use the professional portfolio to present the contents, products, and processes that will help convince employers that they can solve, create, design, debate, perform research, collaborate, interact, and explain—all essential behaviors for the master teacher. Professional portfolios reveal new teachers' work in real-world situations, where they learn actively rather than passively as they explore the art and science of teaching. Finally, new teachers who compile a reflective professional portfolio can make judgments about their own work as they reflect on their instructional assessments and the management, teaching, and collaborative activities they initiated during their teacher preparation experiences.

Portfolio Evidence

Relevant portfolio evidence is similar across teacher preparation programs. For example, evidence (i.e., artifacts) includes academic achievements and tangible rewards, such as accolades earned in college or university programs. Also relevant is community or service recognition that demonstrates teachers' efforts. Actual assessment, instructional, or behavioral materials, including specially designed items, learning strategy materials, curriculum-based assessments, and functional behavioral assessments, are valuable products. Pertinent data also include positive behavioral strategies used during instruction; student work samples; cooperative learning tasks; record-keeping systems used to manage student groups; and web sites, photographs, video recordings, films, or tape recordings of teacher-student interactions (written parent/guardian permission is necessary for the last). Finally, evidence of written reflections, responses, or notations made during university courses or student-teaching seminars and journal entries summarizing professional dispositions, behaviors, or feelings during teaching experiences can be important.

Professional Portfolio Process

The new teacher takes the first step in the professional portfolio process by participating in the teaching-learning process and building reflections. The teacher collects artifacts that represent his or her initial experiences in university course work, tutoring sessions, field experiences, and/or student teaching opportunities and that provide multiple concrete examples of the teacher's growth and development in terms of the content and processes of teaching. For example, the teacher saves and collates examples of his or her first attempts at writing lesson plans, creating teaching games, or analyzing behavioral charts that he or she created. Initial examples often are trial and error. Examples of planning or assessments, behavioral support systems or discipline procedures, and collaborative or consultation experiences are also among the items that should be included in the professional portfolio. Thus, artifacts provide evidence of the teacher's professional contacts with students, families, school-based professionals, and community professionals with whom the teacher interacts that demonstrate the new teacher is acquiring basic pedagogy. Artifacts also include examples of the content and processes of teaching that are meaningful to the teacher's self-esteem as a professional educator.

As the new teacher implements and refines his or her teaching skills in classroom settings, a second step is to choose those artifacts that the teacher deems important to represent him- or herself as a professional. The teacher must eliminate unnecessary documentation and key in on meaningful data, selecting and highlighting what is essential to describe him- or herself as a professional. This second step emphasizes a sorting process. After examining and analyzing artifacts, the teacher keeps those that hold self-importance. The teacher must be willing to discard lesson plans prepared, teaching games devised, behavioral systems implemented, and other items that hold little or no relevance to the teacher's evolving picture of him- or herself as a professional.

The third step in the process, self-evaluation, requires the new teacher to explain the inclusion of artifacts in the professional portfolio. The teacher must be willing to state in writing why the included evidence is meaningful and contributes to an awareness of his or her individual knowledge, skills, or dispositions in the teaching process. The self-evaluation step includes the preparation of a dated, individualized self-assessment statement. Insights gained and mistakes made that contributed to professional growth and development are important inclusions. The teacher articulates the hows and whys of artifact contribution as he or she acquires, becomes fluent in, maintains, refines, and generalizes important teaching behaviors.

Many new teachers are aligning their professional portfolio reflections with data from the Council for Exceptional Children's *What Every Special Educator Must Know: The Standards for the Preparation and Licensure of Special Educators* (2000a) and other standards-based teaching references. For example, some personnel preparation programs are encouraging their teacher candidates to reflect on artifacts aligned with standard-setting efforts related to teaching responsibilities (e.g., the framework components from *Enhancing Professional Practice: A Framework for Teaching* [Danielson, 1996].

Accordingly, new teachers reflect on why and how their chosen artifacts provide evidence of the integration of standards and teaching responsibilities into research-based practices (Danielson, 1996).

Keep the following in mind when compiling the professional portfolio:

- Be creative and make it attractive.
- Present material in an organized manner.
- Be selective.
- Include credentials (résumé, transcripts, child abuse clearance, criminal background clearance, teaching certificate); awards/honors; philosophies; teaching samples (unit plan, lesson plan, homework, assessments, photos of bulletin boards); samples of student work; student-teaching evaluations/recommendations; continuing professional development; community service; and letters of recommendation.

MOVING FROM STUDENT TEACHER TO MASTER TEACHER

Once selected by a school district to fill a faculty vacancy or new position, the developing teacher begins the transition to master teacher. Cooperative approaches and specific teacher induction efforts structure the master teaching process.

Cooperative Approaches

Cooperative approaches are being used increasingly in American schools. Competence in interaction often differentiates master teachers from less skilled teachers. Classrooms are no longer the exclusive domain of teachers. Peer teachers, related services providers, student teachers, paraeducators, instructional assistants, and volunteers are becoming members of the instructional and management team (Dettmer, Thurston, & Dyck, 2002). Many schools now provide core teams to lead and support the entire school community, to model effective problem-solving approaches, and to enhance the child-focused atmosphere. Such schools facilitate school and community collaboration. All of these instructional arrangements require ongoing cooperation and support.

Important changes that occurred during the 1990s are now being felt in educational circles during the twenty-first century. Among the factors that shaped these changes are elements of cooperation:

- Reports suggest that cooperative learning experiences designed to increase teachers' and peers' acceptance of diverse students are a necessary component of effective classroom programming (U.S. Department of Education, 1994).
- Students, and especially students with disabilities, demonstrate improved interactions and improved learning outcomes when community members, school faculty, and staff team with, problem-solve with, and support each other and family members (Dettmer et al., 2002).
- Partnerships (e.g., across general education and special education settings) are necessary if learning outcomes for students are to improve (CEC, 2000a, 2000b).
- Those involved in the education of students with disabilities face major philosophical and logistical changes. That is, The Individuals with Disabilities Education Improvement Act, as passed in 2004, contains a number of provisions designed to improve outcomes for students with disabilities. (Chapter 2 describes the IDEIA in detail.)

Many contend that school personnel who work together to provide a supportive schoolwide climate and respond early to at-risk students' academic and behavioral problems can prevent such issues as school violence and its preceding behaviors

(Dwyer, Osher, & Hoffman, 2000). In fact, schools that are academically responsive and prosocial contribute to prevention. When reflective practices and teacher decision making become part of a school culture, new teachers are naturally expected to collaborate with more experienced university and school-based colleagues (Weiss & Weiss, 1999). Accordingly, when professionals model sharing and teaming, they provide a supportive school wide foundation. Such professionals are more likely to address students' academic and behavioral problems early.

A comprehensive picture of integration trends based on national special education statistics emerged (Sawyer, McLaughlin, & Winglee, 1995). Sawyer and peers found that full-time placement in the general education classroom increased relatively consistently, over time, for most disability categories. Currently, special needs students are served more and more in inclusive general education settings (Hehir, 1999). As Chapter 2 reiterates, the IDEIA mandates that the general education curriculum be the basis for students' individualized education programs (IEPs).

Accordingly, the newly hired teacher will find that many school districts nationwide are changing their special education services to accommodate the needs of diverse students. Many changes in services are controversial. Some proponents report that curriculum changes and the emphasis on the general education classroom were long overdue and that such opportunities to be integrated with nondisabled peers benefit students with and without disabilities academically and socially (Westling & Fox, 2004). Other researchers question these changes and the ability to meet the many unique learning needs of these students in the general education setting (Kauffman & Hallahan, 2003).

Newly hired personnel must embrace cooperation and a teaming spirit—during school activities as well as extracurricular functions. The fact that teachers work in close proximity has much influence on what happens to teachers, students, and the classroom environment. New teachers will be able to expand their service delivery roles when they involve themselves in shared decision making and mentoring experiences. They also need to be aware of the additional stress and conflicts that teaming will create.

Pause and Reflect About the Profession 11.4

What makes your role as a new teacher different from that of teachers working in special education services 20 years ago? List at least 10 factors that make teachers' roles in the twenty-first century different from teachers' roles in the 1980s:

1. _____
2. _____
3. _____
4. _____
5. _____
6. _____
7. _____
8. _____
9. _____
10. _____

Compare and contrast your ideas with those of your peers.

Team Approach

Even some veteran teachers have had little experience in meeting some of the new service demands (e.g., accommodating or adapting the general education curriculum). In some cases, meeting these demands may be viewed as an overwhelming or intimidating task—especially so to newly hired personnel. This problem can be overcome by a team of professionals who meet together when needed to brainstorm and provide suggestions regarding objectives for students and to discuss how the objectives can be met in classrooms (Stainback, Stainback, & Stefanich, 1996).

A team is composed of adults and students who work together and share common activities and experiences. Drury (1986) defines a team as highly involved people who are committed to achieving common objectives, who work well together and enjoy doing so, and who produce high-quality results. Box 11.1 is based on Drury's identification of attributes that differentiate a team from a collection of individuals.

Teacher Induction Programs

Teams can help new teachers enormously, especially through teacher induction programs that include mentoring experiences. Mentoring experiences help the new professional by offering support in (1) planning flexible learning objectives, (2) adapting activities to individual students, (3) using multiple adaptations simultaneously to accommodate diverse student needs, and (4) implementing successful curriculum strategies (Stainback et al., 1996).

Box 11.1   **New Teachers Who Operate as a Team Versus Those Who Operate as a Collection of Individuals**

A Team

New teachers who

- listen and try to understand
- share common visions
- share in decision making by consensus
- use clear communication within and outside the team
- display ability to talk through conflicts and problems in a constructive way
- display openness, honesty, mutual respect, and trust
- focus on the task
- make use of all team resources, including parents and professionals from other disciplines

A Collection of Individuals

New teachers who

- fight for their own views without consideration of others
- do not use effective listening skills
- operate on right-or-wrong premises
- have no clear group vision
- operate on negative assumptions and hidden agendas
- display suspicion, distrust, and competition
- often are sidetracked

Source: Adapted from *Team Effectiveness*, by S. S. Drury, 1986, Newark: University of Delaware.

Teacher induction programs that include opportunities for mentor-protégé relationships are found to not only reduce attrition rates among new teachers but also improve their teaching capabilities. The availability and structure of formal induction programs vary among states and local school districts. However, effective programs help new teachers move into their teaching positions and help retain them (Weiss & Weiss, 1999).

Although there may be some local differences in format and content, the processes involved in hiring and retaining teachers are similar. Most districts follow typical hiring processes, and many rely on teacher induction to smooth the transition from preservice to in-service activities. Local school districts' links between preservice and in-service activities may be based on research. For example, Ralph, Kesten, Lang, and Smith (1998) found that the collaborative efforts of those having an interest in the hiring process (e.g., university preparation personnel, public school administrators, and teacher union representatives) contribute jointly to the successful preparation, hiring, and induction of new teachers.

Critical faculty shortages in special education have resulted in renewed attention to the specifics of recruiting and retaining qualified educators to instruct diverse students with special needs. Cooley and Yovanoff (1996) indicated that the shrinking supply and demand nationally for special educators both contribute to and are affected by the high rate of attrition among these professionals. New teachers' early job experiences have a huge impact not only on whether they remain in teaching for the long term, but also on the kind of teacher they become. Dissatisfying experiences during the first five years are related to attrition rates among teachers, rates that now range from 30 percent to 50 percent nationwide (NASBE, 2000). In order to survive and succeed, all new teachers need exposure to high-quality induction programs that will help them remain committed to their profession.

High-Quality Induction Programs. High-quality induction programs share at least four characteristics: (1) mentoring relationships between new and experienced teachers, such that beginning or developing teachers have a sustained relationship with at least one accomplished, experienced teacher; (2) targeted professional development for participating teachers, so that new teachers have activities specifically designed to address their needs and concerns as new teachers; (3) a support focus during at least the first year of actual teaching experiences; and (4) a system to evaluate and improve the performance of beginning or developing teachers, including remediation and counseling efforts (NASBE, 2000). When preservice and in-service personnel work together to support new teachers' transition, these new teachers have increased survival and success rates.

In addition, school districts have existing team models that may be helpful to the new teacher. For example, many classroom teams that serve students with disabilities rely on cooperative models, including collaborative consultation (Idol, 1988), coteaching (Walther-Thomas, 1996), child study/resource teams (Hayek, 1987), and cooperative teaching (Bauwens & Hourcade, 1995). All these models emphasize active participation and stress the importance of trust, mutual respect, and the valuing of each person's roles and contributions to group effectiveness.

Walther-Thomas (1996) described coteaching, a popular cooperative model that will be helpful to newly hired personnel initiating collaboration attempts. In coteaching, teacher teams provide all students with instruction, discipline, and support. This helps coteachers avoid unintentionally stigmatizing students based on identified needs and helps eliminate mental walls that some teachers possess. Coteaching reminds teachers to think about all class members as "our students."

Researchers report that coteaching offers new teachers many benefits (e.g., opportunities to work on teams, solve problems, make joint decisions, and share responsibilities and accountability). Coteaching can provide new teachers with assistance in the development, delivery, and evaluation of effective instructional programs. It can provide them with much critical data about classroom setting demands, teacher expectations, and current student performance levels. This knowledge enables new teachers to make more appropriate recommendations regarding the instructional procedures that are most likely to benefit their students with disabilities and many of their students who are low achievers. Coteaching provides professionals with ongoing support, opportunities for problem solving, and professional development—all elements necessary to the transition from new teacher to master teacher.

Accordingly, teacher preparation programs around the country are recognizing that it is time to integrate cooperation-building competencies into professional development and teacher preparation practices. Many of the groups developing professional preparation standards reiterate the fact that collaboration and team-building skills are essential (CEC, 2000a; NASBE, 2000; National Board for Professional Teaching Standards, 1999). O'Shea, Williams, and Sattler (1999) reported on new teachers' perceptions of collaboration training and the types of collaboration patterns that evolve in university preparation across special education and elementary education course work. They found that most new teachers support collaboration opportunities and welcome activities designed to encourage partnerships across curriculum areas. In their study, O'Shea and peers reported that many new teachers indicated that collaboration preparation helped to support their efforts to increase the benefits and avoid the pitfalls of inclusion. New teachers offered important insights into why collaboration preparation focusing on curriculum areas contributes to their readiness for future instructional roles.

Mentoring Activities

To ease their transition to full-time teaching, many school districts have mentoring programs to support beginning teachers. Teacher educators are responding to research reports that peer-mentoring opportunities are significant in the preparation and professional growth of teachers (NASBE, 2000; Weiss & Weiss, 1999). During mentoring activities, new teachers are paired with peers and experience sharing, problem-solving, and conflict resolution situations. Many districts offer teacher induction programs to support new teachers as they address these situations. In addition to problem solving with other new teachers, mentorship experiences include opportunities for experienced and inexperienced personnel to work together. Mentorship activities imbue the process with an ethic of caring that teachers ideally will bring to their own classrooms. New teachers have opportunities for modeling, observations, dialogue, and practice; continuity in caring; teaming; reflection; and confirmation of actions—ingredients essential to the facilitation of cooperation expected in classroom endeavors.

Working with Students' Parents, Families, or Guardians

Many of the skills gleaned from teaming, coteaching, and mentorship programs can be used in working collaboratively with students' parents or guardians (Karp, 1993). New teachers profit from those opportunities to practice and model sharing, problem solving, teaming, and reciprocity—while gaining the pedagogical knowledge and skills they will need in their work with students' families. (Chapter 9 details family transition approaches.)

Master teachers recognize that beliefs, traditions, and values vary across cultures within society and affect the relationships among child, family, and school. Despite the differences that students bring to school, teachers work actively to create family-friendly schools that encourage family advocacy. Master teachers accept and support the diversity and dynamics of students' families, backgrounds, and communities. In essence, master teachers establish and maintain rapport with students' families, valuing, respecting, and/or accepting the families, backgrounds, cultures, languages, and approaches to child care even when these differ from their own.

When teachers work to maintain family-friendly interactions between parents of special needs students and the local school system, they are demonstrating master teacher behaviors. They help to ensure that parents engage in positive, successful interactions facilitated by their peers and school personnel. Master teachers help parents and

Pause and Reflect About the Profession 11.5

How Do Mentorship Experiences Help You in Your Current Field Placement?

List at least five advantages to you personally of working with other new teachers during your classroom experience. Are there advantages to working with experienced teachers? List at least five advantages to you personally of working with experienced teachers that are different from the advantages of working with new teachers.

Mentorship Advantages with New Teachers	Mentorship Advantages with Experienced Teachers
1.	1.
2.	2.
3.	3.
4.	4.
5.	5.

guardians new to the system gain knowledge and skills concerning legal rights to family involvement guaranteed by state and federal mandates. In short, master teachers empower and support family members. Box 11.2 presents a summary of important strategies that master teachers use with families.

Working with students' families entails knowledge and skills concerning students' home backgrounds. Table 11.2 lists such knowledge and skills. New teachers can acquire the knowledge, skills, and dispositions they need to work with diverse families by imitating master teachers as they work with students' families. By observing how effective teachers problem-solve and work toward mutually agreed-on goals with students' families and by imitating experienced peers, new teachers move toward master teacher status.

Developing teachers who work with students with disabilities will participate in family support programs. Effective teaming requires the new teacher to demonstrate listening skills and empathy. Communication skills and constructive problem-solving abilities are also important. Effective interpersonal skills are vital, as are the abilities to

| **B**ox 11.2 | **Important Strategies That Master Teachers Use with Families** |

1. **Implementing effective communication skills** (e.g., demonstrating active listening, positive regard, and empathy) **and interaction skills** (e.g., encouraging families to express, share, disagree, problem-solve, form partnerships, decide, and/or reach group goals; considering how individuals share with others)

2. **Overcoming barriers** (e.g., relying on limited knowledge and skills; ignoring family priorities, family values, customs, and traditions) **that potentially block effective rapport with students' parents or guardians**

3. **Providing family members with opportunities for shared planning and decision making with district officials** (e.g., offering direct support for parents and guardians new to special needs services; setting up opportunities to talk with district officials and teachers about school conferences, grades, consulting reports, IEPs, management strategies, learning supports, adaptations, and modifications)

4. **Creating matched goals and objectives between home and school, such as family members' desire for school participation** (e.g., talking about such topics as amount of homework, number of acceptable conferences, resources, persons responsible for task completion, potential outcomes, and individual expectations over the course of the school year; offering choices in meeting times and places conducive to families' involvement)

5. **Encouraging parent or guardian mentoring and leadership opportunities at the local level** (e.g., setting up after-school opportunities for family members to meet with and share information with other families)

6. **Recognizing that families who lack knowledge or are inactive do not necessarily lack interest in their children's education and achievement but rather need alternatives and choices in school involvement** (e.g., valuing, respecting, and/or accepting others whose training, culture, concepts, skills, and values differ)

7. **Planning and conducting collaborative conferences** (e.g., assisting families in making informed decisions regarding educational opportunities available for their child; helping empower families by sharing, questioning, clarifying, or problem solving during meetings or activities set up to explain students' learning; clarifying students' work samples and assessment records)

8. **Sharing learning resources for home use when feasible** (e.g., lending media, learning aids, and educational materials appropriate to students' learning skills and abilities; having and sharing reading materials, computer technology, and videos highlighting management and learning strategies; offering a lending library for families' use)

9. **Ensuring that families understand the scope of educational resources available to them and their child** (e.g., when asked, interpreting professional journals and summarizing major findings in language appropriate to parents or guardians; securing local and state resources on programs and services)

10. **Collaborating with general classroom teachers and other school and community personnel** (e.g., when appropriate, integrating students into various learning environments; seeking to improve communications with teachers, administrators, and other school personnel about characteristics and needs of students with diverse strengths and deficits)

11. **Being accessible and responsive to family needs; recognizing the strengths and positive attributes of students, families, and other team members**

TABLE 11.2 Examples of Knowledge and Skills That Teachers Require Concerning Students' Home and Community Backgrounds

Knowledge	Skills
Awareness of the number of individuals in the family, sibling makeup, birth order of child with a disability, and type of family structure (e.g., nuclear, single parent, stepfamily)	Discussing with families the expected similarities and differences for the child, including discussions of the impact on siblings, grandparents, neighbors, and so on
Understanding of the cultural, ethnic, and environmental milieu of the family	Encouraging questions and comments; specifying resources, services and programs that will help
Recognition of the effects that problems in ability, behavior, learning, social skills, and so forth may have on one's home life	Contributing and providing personal insights to help facilitate family expectations
Awareness of the child's self-directedness encouraged or expected by parents or guardians	Demonstrating respect for the family's contributions in decisions; working toward a common goal of successful programming
Awareness of the family's school and life expectations for their child	Providing information in a variety of forms (e.g., books, materials) to help the child, siblings, and other family members
Recognition of specific family-school involvement priorities	Using open communication methods often, such as letters home, shared reports, face-to-face contacts, and home visits
Understanding of the unique family differences in coping with the demands and challenges of a child with a disability	Scheduling time to discuss program issues, student progress, parent options, community input, or other issues
	Modifying IEPs or family progress on the basis of the family's needs for a particular service

be task-oriented and resource-oriented. Students with disabilities thrive when there are respectful and beneficial relationships between families and professionals. Family support involves appropriate management and efforts by all teachers.

Many school districts are electing to serve diverse students through cooperative services. As in most situations, however, teaming is not easy, and conflicts can arise. Many problems with team approaches will not be readily apparent but can be stumbling blocks in new teachers' efforts to work cooperatively with those around them. Problems that surface are often related to teachers' lack of planning time, student scheduling, caseload concerns, limited administrative support, and needed, but often lacking, staff development opportunities (Walther-Thomas, 1996; O'Shea et al., 1999). School districts are only beginning to address realistically the legitimate concerns of planning, scheduling, and so forth. Nonetheless, master teachers have been able to face these persistent problems, operate in a cooperative mode, and continue to serve their diverse students effectively. New teachers who are mindful of both the benefits and the pitfalls of teaming are in a good position to identify ways to overcome problems and make teaming work.

Making Teaming Work

Special education teachers must work effectively with general education teachers to make IEPs work well for students. At some point, every teacher must cooperate with family members, paraprofessionals, peers, and administrators as they adapt the general education curricula to accommodate individual students' needs.

The effectiveness of teaming is influenced heavily by the teacher's disposition toward working with others. In fact, the teacher's disposition and style will encourage or sabotage the abilities of other adults to interact effectively with students and to succeed in schoolwide projects. For example, when another adult is present in the classroom,

---

Box 11.3

Important Teacher Attributes Influencing Teaming Effectiveness

- Skills in organizing and planning for students, adults, and activities
- Leadership ability
- Observational skills
- Ability to communicate needs and wants to all present in the group
- Experience in training, managing, and monitoring students and adults
- Skills in taking and following directions from others
- Educational background and experiences
- Awareness of others' educational background and experiences
- Philosophy of education

Source: Adapted from *Paraprofessionals in Special Education*, by V. Lombardo, 1980, Springfield, IL: Charles C. Thomas.

---

students' attention will shift to that adult to some degree, a factor to which the teacher may react. On schoolwide projects, the teacher may have to share recognition for success rather than being singled out for individual accomplishment. Individual teachers' dispositions are especially important to the interplay of individuals and team effectiveness. The skills and abilities needed to enhance team effectiveness are listed in Box 11.3.

Walther-Thomas (1996) reported that, for teaming to be effective, classroom teachers must have the motivation and ability to make changes in their assessment, instructional, or management procedures. They must be open to having another person come into their classes and observe them. They must know how to collaborate. Teachers are more effective when they believe in the benefits of and use teaming, open communication, and joint decision making.

Peer Observations

New teachers can benefit from teaming when they interact with more experienced colleagues through peer observations. After observing experienced peers, new teachers can ask questions to clear up role conflicts and ambiguities. They can ask for tips on proven practices, and they can view how teachers survive in the system and problem-solve. New teachers can also develop their own effective teaching styles and function more proficiently in teaming models when they observe experienced peers.

While new teachers who observe experienced colleagues will have more opportunities to imitate and strive for best practices, it is important to keep expectations realistic. Initial mistakes are bound to occur until teachers accumulate experience. Nevertheless, many benefits will result from observation:

1. Observing experienced peers conduct similar activities can confirm in the new teacher's mind the appropriateness of the strategies, materials, procedures, and techniques used in his or her classroom.

2. Observing experienced peers model research-based practices will generate new approaches and techniques.

3. The new teacher can record and analyze patterns of students' behaviors in and across various class settings.

4. Teachers can share observations during team meetings and conferences with families, peers, and supervisors.

5. The new teacher can analyze factors influencing the success of peer teachers' behaviors.

Box 11.4   **Classroom Observation Factors That Are Important to New Teachers' Success**

- Detailed physical description of the classroom, including information on visual, auditory, and/or other environmental factors (e.g., seating arrangements, location of materials, equipment, and other relevant classroom features)
- Descriptions of age levels, cognitive/ability levels, academic grade levels, pertinent behaviors of individual students, learning styles, and other relevant descriptive data
- Behavioral management plan for the entire class, including all classroom rules, strategies for increasing positive student behaviors, and strategies for decreasing negative student behaviors
- Uses of informal assessments and data collection procedures, including teacher-made checklists, rating scales, inventories, and curriculum-based assessment devices
- Uses of formal assessments, including title, publisher, publication date, and brief description of the purpose of each assessment device
- Descriptions of the teaching format used for various subjects (e.g., "used individual instruction for reading skills; used large-group instruction for social skills")
- Descriptions of instructional strategies and teaching methods, including use of learning strategies, peer tutoring, direct instruction, and guided discovery learning
- Uses of volunteers, paraeducators, teacher aides, or other adults in the classroom
- Methods of communicating with parents or guardians
- Methods of working cooperatively with other professionals in the school (e.g., administrators, guidance counselors, speech-language pathologist, general education teachers, other special education teachers)
- Names and locations of relevant personnel (e.g., principal, assistant principal, office secretaries, guidance counselor, special education coordinator, special education teachers, general education teachers, school district superintendent, area superintendent)
- Names and locations of relevant rooms (e.g., teachers' lounge, cafeteria, office, health suite)

---

6. Peer teachers can aid in the communication process and provide corrective feedback. Developing and new teachers can discuss behaviors of concern during peer reviews as a means for change. Box 11.4 lists classroom observation factors that are important to new teachers' success.

Peer observation can encourage a teacher's professional and skill development. By reviewing what they observe with others and sharing information through either formal or informal methods, teachers are implementing a collaborative approach (O'Shea & Hoover, 1986). Teachers can share the benefits of teaching that make the field rewarding and challenging.

Managing Paraprofessionals

In addition to interacting with families and peers, new teachers will use teaming models in their own classrooms. For example, the vast majority of teachers serving children with problems will be responsible for supervising paraeducators and/or adult volunteers in the classroom. These individuals, whether they are paid or volunteer their time, are referred to as paraprofessionals. Paraprofessionals (aides, teacher aides, paraprofessionals, and auxiliaries are used interchangeably here) are all nonprofessionals who relieve teachers of some nonteaching duties (Beach, 1973). In terms of teaming responsibilities, the new teacher is a consultant to the paraprofessionals, but he or she also functions as their leader, supervising, managing, and evaluating their ability to interact in the classroom.

Paraprofessional are especially important to new special education teachers because students with special needs often require the assistance of more than one adult for a majority of the day. Paraprofessionals have a noticeable, positive impact in the classroom if used effectively in a team format. Paraprofessionals (1) improve the adult-to-student ratio in the classroom; (2) facilitate the implementation of the curriculum; (3) enable the teacher to develop more effective programs based on the individual or small-group needs of students; (4) make it possible for teachers to use more variety in structured classroom activities; (5) enable the teacher to use more instructional media and materials; (6) allow the teacher increased time for evaluating learning situations, using behavioral management techniques, and counseling or guiding students; and (7) relieve the teacher of the numerous semi- and nonprofessional tasks that consume a disproportionate amount of his or her time and energy.

However, the new teacher may be asked to manage a paraprofessional who has been in the class for many years prior to the new teacher's arrival. The new teacher may be assigned to work with an aide who displays an inappropriate disposition or whose personal goals and aspirations conflict with those of the teacher. Without proper management and insight into these sources of difficulty, the new teacher may develop a negative working relationship with the paraprofessional, which may affect classroom interactions. Stress and conflict may arise from the difficult situation, and effective teaming may come to a halt. The new teacher who is aware of management techniques that facilitate teaming with paraprofessionals may make a smoother transition to class supervision and operation.

Strategies Useful with Paraprofessionals. Drury (1986) discussed teaming techniques pertinent to teachers who manage aides and volunteers. As a team consultant and leader in the classroom, the new teacher should consider the following:

1. **The team makes major decisions with a team consultant or leader facilitating the decision-making process.** New teachers need to consider the differences in their roles as group consultees for some teams (e.g., observing peers, consulting with supervisors) and as group consultants or leaders for other teams (e.g., supervising students and paraprofessionals). New teachers must take the lead in making classroom decisions—no matter how long the aide has been working.

2. **Goal setting and action plans are based on team analyses of problems.** New teachers must set goals and objectives for classroom activities and follow up with action plans designed to implement team decisions. Problem solving can often be accomplished more quickly when many individuals share strategies. Teacher aides are a good source of information, particularly pertaining to their classroom, and new teachers can use their suggestions when developing goals and objectives. Teachers have the major say, however, on goal setting and action plans.

3. **Team members have input into team decisions.** All members of the educational team can make special contributions to the team. New teachers will benefit from appropriate suggestions of other adults, especially paraprofessionals, who often know students and classrooms well.

4. **Team members need access to all data relevant to decisions.** Sharing information in written form promotes team cohesiveness and effective team functioning. Sharing data with paraprofessionals who are working with particular children is one aspect of effective communication. (Teachers must remember to safeguard confidentiality of pertinent data.)

5. **Communication is encouraged for all team members.** Being part of a team entails listening to and receiving messages from all other members of the team. By being open with the paraprofessional, the new teacher is encouraging a healthy working rapport.

Working with Paraprofessionals. Because they provide day-to-day support in the classroom, paraprofessionals are very important. However, most paraprofessionals are not trained in general and/or special education. Therefore, the new teacher will be required to lead the classroom team. The keys to success with paraprofessionals are maintaining effective communication and modeling how things should be done in the classroom. The teacher may need to train the paraprofessionals in ways that various tasks should be done; the paraprofessionals should not have to figure out how the teachers wants things done.

Paraprofessionals may not be given independent responsibility for classroom teaching, management, or organization. The teacher functions as the team consultant and must facilitate major classroom decision making. However, under the teacher's direction and support, the paraprofessionals can assist in classroom management, supplemental teaching, housekeeping chores, and extracurricular activities. If a paraprofessional is to be used to the best advantage, there must be a correspondence between the tasks the teacher expects to have performed and the paraprofessional's ability and opportunities to carry them out.

Box 11.5 provides tips to help paraprofessionals get oriented to the special education situation. An in-service orientation conducted by the new teacher builds rapport with the paraprofessionals and helps to establish a team model. Paraprofessionals are vital part of the classroom team, and it may be helpful to collaborate with and get input from them, but the teacher is always the person responsible for making decisions (Doyle, 2002).

Box 11.5 | **Tips to Orient the Paraprofessional When Working with Special Needs Students**

Introduce the paraprofessional to other adults and the students with whom he or she will be working. The intent is to plan for early interactions with the paraprofessional. Help the paraprofessional acquire as much information about each student as quickly as possible.

Expose the paraprofessional to written guidelines and review those materials (e.g., classroom or board of education policies, teacher's handbook, aide's handbook) with which the paraprofessional should become familiar.

Tour the school with the paraprofessional if the principal has not already done so. Provide a tour of the classroom and areas where the following necessities are kept: supplies, books, games, charts, desks, curriculum guides, district course of study, picture files, and audiovisual collection.

Have the paraprofessional become familiar with the following during his or her first days of work:

- **Personnel names and locations within the school:** principal, assistant principal, dean, other supervisors, psychologist, social worker, speech clinician, therapist, librarian, other ancillary personnel, custodian, nurse, cafeteria director, cooks and lunchroom personnel, teachers, other paraeducators, other paraprofessional (e.g., playground, lunch, bus, special education)
- **Location of important school areas:** special education classrooms, library, supply room, storage areas, workroom, bookstore, cafeteria, auditorium, gymnasium, faculty lounge
- **Location of things within the school:** audiovisual equipment, storage cabinets, copying machine, art supplies, other machines

Provide the paraprofessional with a job description that outlines the functions of the position. Spell out specifically all clerical, housekeeping, technical, and supervised instructional tasks assigned. Also point out tentative activities that might occur irregularly (e.g., field trips, school projects). Help the paraprofessional devise his or her own weekly schedule to be filled out each week.

Source: Adapted from *Tips for Using Teacher Aides Effectively* (Monograph No. 16.), by D. J. O'Shea and J. M. Hendrickson, 1987, Gainesville: University of Florida Diagnostic and Teaching Clinic.

O'Shea and Hendrickson (1987) offered these suggestions to classroom teachers to encourage teaming with paraprofessionals. These suggestions are pertinent for today's classroom interactions as well.

1. Treat the paraprofessional with respect in all dealings.

2. From day one, capitalize on the personal strengths of the paraprofessional. Point out these strengths whenever possible in a written fashion and share them with the paraprofessional, administration, and other teachers or paraprofessionals.

3. Give the paraprofessional plenty of compliments on work that is well done.

4. Maintain high performance standards and encourage the paraprofessional to do the same.

5. Make the communication process as optimal as possible. Be willing to listen and respond with empathy as necessary to the paraprofessional's concerns.

6. Strive for consistency in the working relationship with the paraprofessional. Don't tell the paraprofessional one thing one day and something different the next day.

7. Organize the classroom in a manner that promotes good order and a sense of forward movement. Tell the paraprofessional specifically how the class is to operate. Discuss directly with the paraprofessional what, where, why, when, and how duties are to be done. Demonstrate the correct procedures as well. Elicit feedback and input from the paraprofessional on the success of classroom procedures.

8. Distribute duties in a fair and equitable manner. Get continual feedback from the paraprofessional to assess reasonableness of the type and amount of assigned work. Ask questions and encourage the paraprofessional to do the same.

9. Within a structured conference, explain to the paraprofessional the importance of increasing the quality and quantity of the duties as his or her expertise grows.

10. Help the paraprofessional to observe and follow the disciplinary measures used by the teacher; make adjustments only after a conference together.

11. Encourage the paraprofessional to handle his or her own disciplinary problems, but offer advice and help if serious problems occur.

12. Do not correct the paraprofessional in front of others, especially in front of students. (If you must provide corrective feedback, do it privately at a scheduled conference.)

13. Provide constructive criticism by telling the paraprofessional what needs to be improved and how it is to be improved. Offer criticism with the goal of improved performance.

14. Encourage the paraprofessional to keep a sense of humor whenever possible.

Paraprofessionals have lives outside school. Effective teachers get to know and respect the personal side of the people with whom they work so closely. It is important to show interest, when appropriate, in the paraprofessional's personal stories.

Finally, Box 11.6 presents descriptions of tasks that paraprofessionals can do to provide the teacher with more quality time with students. Some of these tasks are supplemental instructional activities; others are classroom housekeeping chores. All these tasks can be accomplished by paraprofessionals with direction and guidance from the classroom teacher. As new teachers will discover, managing, organizing, and supervising paraprofessionals and volunteers effectively are necessary steps toward becoming master teachers.

| **B** ox 11.6 | **Teaming Tasks That Paraprofessionals Can Do to Assist Special Education Teachers** |

- Assist students in academic subject areas in which the teacher believes that tutoring is necessary
- Circulate around the room to check students' progress
- Provide individualized assistance, such as conducting flash card drill or listening to oral reading
- Prepare charts, graphs, or teaching bulletin boards
- Correct written assignments from the teacher's key or model
- Work with those students who were absent to review or summarize lessons or activities
- Collect assignments from the general classroom teacher for completion in the resource classroom
- Assist students with written compositions, especially with spelling, punctuation, and grammar
- Correct homework and workbooks; note and report weak areas
- Call the class to order
- Collect money for lunch, class pictures, field trips, or special items
- Care for bulletin board appearance and overall appearance of the room
- Help students move from one activity to another
- Assist students in the lavatory
- File correspondence and other reports in students' records
- Keep inventories of classroom stock: equipment, books, and instructional supplies

Source: Adapted from *A Handbook of Effective Techniques for Teacher Aides*, by D. B. Clough and B. M. Clough, 1978, Springfield, IL: Charles C. Thomas.

STRESS AND BURNOUT

Any career can be stressful; however, being a professional educator today can be very difficult. Stress occurs in all aspects of one's life, but when it is not controlled, it can lead to burnout. Teacher burnout will affect not just the teacher but also the children, other professionals, and family members with whom the teacher must interact and team on a daily basis.

The stress response is a series of physiological and psychological changes that occur when one perceives that one's coping resources are inadequate (Wood & McCarthy, 2004). Teachers, on a daily basis, are dealing with the demands of the school setting and weighing the resources they have for coping with stress (Troman & Woods, 2001). Symptoms of stress include exhaustion, absenteeism, boredom, depression, cynicism, moodiness, impatience, headaches, excess eating, frustration, anxiety, impaired performance, and problems with relationships at home and work (Kyriacou, 2001). When stress occurs over a long period of time, teachers may experience burnout, described as a loss of idealism and enthusiasm for one's work (Matheny, Gfoerer, and Harris, 2000). It is generally accepted practice in the mental health field that it is better to deal with stress before teachers become burned out.

Ballinger (2000) described the stress many teachers reported when leaving their jobs for good. Among the causes were low pay; lack of support; increased problems with student discipline; lack of job knowledge, especially in classroom management; and the top-down management style of administrators. Weiss and Weiss (1999) reported that first-year teachers experience stress when they are left in a "sink or swim" position with little support from colleagues and few opportunities for professional development. Informal, haphazard teacher induction experiences have been associated with higher levels of attrition as well as lower levels of teacher effectiveness (National Commission on Teaching and America's Future, 1996).

As more and more general education teachers continue to instruct students with special needs, stress and burnout will influence many teachers' desire to stay with education as a chosen career. Stress is part of everyday life and, in manageable doses, can motivate individuals to improve and grow. Too much stress, however, will cause serious repercussions for an otherwise healthy person. Certain working conditions are very stressful and often lead to burnout and eventual attrition. In other words, teachers often leave their jobs when stress takes over their lives (Billingsley, 2002; Weiss & Weiss, 1999).

Many educators have observed changes over the past few decades that make teaching, especially special education, a more stressful profession (Cooley & Yovanoff, 1996; Crane & Iwanicki, 1986; Greer & Greer, 1992). In fact, when CEC (2000b) recently identified those barriers that obstruct high-quality special education, three compelling realities emerged:

1. Many individuals with diverse needs do not receive the quality education they need to reach successful adult outcomes;

2. Many special educators teach under conditions that prevent them from delivering quality instruction; and

3. Many special educators are asked to fulfill roles that are fragmented, ambiguously defined, and obscured by conflicting responsibilities.

Today's schools represent the composition of society. As society becomes more complicated and stressful, it follows that so, too, do schools. Schools are, in essence, minisocieties and can reflect, among other things, (1) the growing and diverse population of students and their needs; (2) the changing social, ethical, and moral values of society; and (3) the increased external pressures on teachers (e.g., the intent of parents and administrators to hold educators accountable in instruction and management).

Stress is a very real problem for educators and cannot be overlooked by new teachers. As reported in Chapter 3, Doyle's (1980) conceptualization of complex organizational pressures portrays the classroom as a public forum requiring frequent and immediate actions by the teacher in the face of almost overwhelming and often unpredictable environmental variables. New teachers who deal with intense pressures on a daily basis because of the often unpredictable nature of students with special needs and the added responsibilities of working from team models, working with difficult parents, and managing and supervising paraprofessionals are most vulnerable to school and classroom stress. Teachers face their own and others' expectations about what they can accomplish. In addition, public demands and increased public expectations reflect the changing roles of educators and make the job of master teacher very difficult.

Stress and Special Educators

O'Shea, Stoddard, and O'Shea (2000) reported on stress related to the reauthorized mandates of the IDEA. They found teachers' stress associated with special education paperwork, functional behavioral assessments, accommodations and adaptations, and overall perceptions of peers needing to support each other in such areas as procedures, assessment, curriculum, and instruction. The effects of social change on schools and the ways teachers perceive these changes as affecting themselves personally impede their development as master teachers. Public perceptions and demands of teachers, as well

FIGURE 11.7 Potential Sources of Stress to Special Educators

STRESS FACTORS

Effects of social changes
Increased legal responsibilities
Lack of administrative support
Career stagnation
Lack of training
Teaching competencies
Vast paperwork
Poor salaries/benefits
Public perceptions
Unrealistic expectations
Lack of time-management skills
High teaching loads
Low self-perceptions
Daily confrontations with students
Uncooperative/uninvolved parents
Feelings of loneliness
Feelings of lack of control
Lack of recognition
Little planning time
Lack of input into school policies/procedures

as the teachers' own perceptions of what they believe is expected, are related to the successful completion of their roles.

The increased legal responsibilities of educators are a source of conflict (O'Shea et al., 2000). Many teachers consider too much red tape in their jobs to be a major source of their discontent. An additional problem for developing teachers is their lack of time-management skills (Brownell & Smith, 1992). Time-management skills may influence the effectiveness of teaming models and opportunities to work with peers, paraprofessionals, families, and students. Teachers perceive themselves as failing to do their job well when they are overwhelmed by changing legal, behavioral, and social responsibilities; by daily confrontations with the problems of students, parents, peers, paraprofessionals, and administrators; by complex and extensive paperwork connected with IEPs; and by feelings of loneliness and helplessness, especially in the first year of teaching (Fimian & Blanton, 1986). When added together, all these factors help make teaching, especially teaching special education students, a demanding profession.

Figure 11.7 illustrates potential sources of teacher stress, factors that new teachers should examine closely. Awareness of stress factors is a first step in lessening the negative effects of stress.

Signs and Signals

Many professionals do not agree on common definitions or strategies for remediation of stress, although most agree on the variable ways that stress and conflict affect teachers: loss of productivity, work refusal, physiological disorders that are psychologically based, and loss of quality teachers (who leave the field due to burnout, the emotional overload associated with teaching, schools, students, or the entire educational process) (Crane & Iwanicki, 1986; Morsink, 1982). Many quality teachers are lost to the profession because they do not heed warning signals.

Signs and signals of stress are provided in Box 11.7. If a teacher recognizes many of these signs frequently, over time, and to such intensity that coming to school becomes a

---

B ox 11.7   **Signs and Signals of Stress**

- Avoidance of school through many absences, continual tardiness, or an intense desire to leave the building before the school day is over
- Apathy toward students, parents, and teachers
- Lower productivity, especially in teachers who at one time were highly productive
- Continual negative self-statements concerning teacher effectiveness
- Physical signs, including prolonged headaches, stomach pains, and voice problems
- Real or imagined mental fatigue over time
- Blatant refusal to comply with school policies and rules
- Prolonged crying and depression
- Deep feelings of loss of control over career, personal life, or business matters
- Continual complaints to loved ones

---

daily chore, it is time to reevaluate and redefine personal priorities and coping strategies. Even teachers new to the field will experience some of these after a few weeks in school. It is vital to target strategies to alleviate these sources of conflict as soon as they are recognized.

Reducing Stress and Burnout

Cooley and Yovanoff (1996) identified potential interventions that reduce or alleviate burnout and improve retention among special educators. Short-term interventions include the individual responses of professionals to the stressors they encounter, the quantity/quality of collegial interactions available to them, and access to appropriate alternatives to administrative support when such support is lacking. There are factors over which teachers themselves have some control or that fall within administrators' purview to address. Other strategies are to equip teachers with coping skills and to reduce the collegial isolation that special educators commonly experience. Opportunities for teaming and work-related problem solving are useful. Support and constructive collaboration among professional peers can help reduce stress and burnout.

Strategies to reduce stress and burnout are listed in Box 11.8. Some of these strategies are implemented by others (e.g., administrative support to reduce class size) and some by the teachers themselves (e.g., commitment to exercise, adequate sleep). It is important to note that administrators can recognize the need for strategies to help teachers cope better with their jobs, but they do not necessarily have the authority to change policies (e.g., they may recognize the need to increase teacher pay but lack the power to change school financial policies). Administrators also can have a direct influence on their own schools by enforcing personnel policies that lessen teacher stress and burnout (e.g., principals can schedule weekly sessions in the faculty lounge so that teachers can discuss concerns or exchange ideas to reduce tensions). Thus, as listed in Box 11.8, external controls can take the form of administrative support (the administrator recognizes the need for the strategy and does or does not have personal control to implement the strategy) or administrative intervention (the administrator has personal control within his or her own school to implement the strategy). Self-control strategies for teachers include physical controls (related to bodily functions) and interpersonal controls (related to commitment to family or community involvement). Self-control strategies can be continually implemented directly by new teachers.

Time-management strategies will also be useful stress reducers for developing teachers (Youngs, 1986). They include the following:

1. **Be proactive, not reactive.**   Learn to anticipate and plan for stress. By being prepared, new teachers can learn to avoid sources of difficulty.

Box 11.8   Strategies to Reduce Stress and Burnout

Externally Controlled Strategies

Administrative support (recognized/supported by administrators)

- Access to counseling
- Reduced class size
- Reduced teacher loads
- Adequate resources/materials
- Adequate paraprofessional and volunteer help
- Tangible incentives for successful teaching
- Increased pay
- Increased job benefits
- Environmental variables (e.g., lighting, acoustics)
- Opportunities for teacher advancement

Administrative interventions (controlled by administrators)

- Increased planning time
- Increased responsibility for job performance
- Teacher's lounge discussion sessions
- Organized personnel social functions
- Functioning feedback mechanisms in school (e.g., school suggestion box)
- Teacher input into curriculum and scheduling
- Increased involvement of teachers in faculty decision making
- Analysis of school-classroom expectations

Self-Control Strategies

Physical controls

- Relaxation training
- Adequate diet
- Adequate sleep
- Regular exercise
- Self-verbalization of positive dispositions

Interpersonal controls

- Hobbies
- Clubs/organizations
- Family
- Sports/leisure
- Community support systems
- Increased networking
- Increased professional skills and training

2. **Plan time.** Try not to be controlled by events and persons around you beyond your own personal limits. Assert yourself so that others do not push you beyond these limits. Communicate to others and yourself what your limits are.

3. **Identify and plan for quality time.** This is a time during the day when you can focus your awareness on a specific task without interruption. Avoid doing more than one thing at a time.

4. **Don't place demands on yourself that you can't meet.** Be honest with yourself and with others. Demanding too much of yourself causes stress and will create failure. Effective teachers know when to say no as well as yes.

5. **Know where your time goes.** If necessary, make a list of what you did during a day and evaluate whether you spent your time wisely. New teachers need to self-evaluate continually.

6. **Build your strengths and not your weaknesses.** Concentrate on what you can do rather than on what you cannot do. As with special needs students, new teachers must be kind to themselves.

7. **Be aware that, in general, poor time management includes the following:**

   a. excess time spent in crisis situations

   b. more time spent on trivia than is necessary

   c. frequent interruptions that destroy planning incentive and momentum

   d. less time spent on high-priority items than low-priority ones

   e. little quality time spent on items requiring creativity and productivity

8. **Set long-term as well as short-term career goals.**

9. **Reward yourself for what you do well.** Put what you don't do well in proper perspective. Time-management strategies can help reduce stress and facilitate the master teacher process. New teachers can help reduce their feelings of lack of control over their teaching careers and advance within their profession.

Tips for New Teachers' Survival

Policy makers have devoted attention to new teachers' survival (CEC, 2000). As new teachers make their way into the world as a professional special educators, they must seek actively to reduce stress. The following tips may help:

- Get to school early in order to establish important relationships.
- Get to know students in order to become familiar with their demographics and needs.
- Organize files in order to locate previous lesson plans and projects.
- Learn time management, as described above, including how to set priorities.
- Look professional, choosing proper and comfortable attire.
- Reach out for help, as by locating a mentor.
- Socialize with peers in order to initiate collaboration with peer teachers.
- Sponsor a club or team in order to know varied students and colleagues.
- Join professional organizations, where questions about concerns or problems can be answered quickly and confidentially.

FACILITATING THE MASTER TEACHER PROCESS

Continued professional growth and active involvement are characteristics of master teachers. By continually upgrading their commitment to the field, teachers move closer to becoming master teachers. Seeking advancements within teaching, becoming involved in professional organizations, and obtaining higher degrees and renewed certifications in areas of specialization all inform, reinforce, and challenge teachers. These steps will help encourage professionalism and continued active involvement (Dudzinski, Roszmann-Millican, & Shank, 2000). As teachers begin to feel confident of their abilities and develop a prolonged commitment to the field, master teachers evolve.

Advancement Within the Field

There are ways other than direct contact with students to effect changes in the field of education and to advance personally within the field. Many teachers change with their jobs and still provide services to their field. Other services that make a noticeable difference include involvement in research, administration, teacher training, service organizations and advocacy groups, curriculum planning and development, parent training, and support services and counseling. Work in each of these areas helps increase benefits to teachers and to all students with special needs as well as to their parents and peers. Teachers who are committed to these other areas will also become master teachers by making a difference in the field. By expanding services and professional memberships, committed teachers remain in the field but specialize in areas outside direct contact with students.

Involvement in Professional Organizations

New teachers can maintain knowledge of current strategies and best teaching practices through active participation in professional organizations. Many professional organizations provide and promote conferences, workshops, in-services, and continuing education classes. Working actively in local, state, or national professional groups will widen the contacts that teachers have and will increase their professional awareness. By actively participating in professional organizations, new teachers are exercising some control over their teaching careers. Increasing professional awareness helps maintain master teachers and invigorate and challenge new teachers.

Involvement in Professional Development Activities

More and more experienced teachers participate in professional development activities that support their continued expertise. Many take advantage of intense and ongoing professional growth opportunities in order to keep pace with current knowledge and skills. Many districts are offering local educational incentives to experienced teachers. For instance, some are providing tuition for teachers who pursue recertification or add-on certifications. Some are offering stipends and books to those in degree programs in critical teaching areas. Some are partnering with colleges and universities to offer distance education or online course work. Others are using recruitment incentives to encourage mid-career changes through fast-track alternative certification programs.

Continued professional development activities provide teachers with opportunities to collaborate and influence major decisions and policies that guide their work. Such activities enhance teachers while fostering collegial support. Teachers can work in both discipline-specific and cross-disciplinary professional communities to exchange and generate new knowledge. When they participate in ongoing professional development, they engage in practice-based inquiry and have opportunities to team with colleagues. They model the reciprocity of roles and collaboration among disciplines that effective special and general educators promote.

Higher Degrees

Many universities offer advanced degrees in education. Often, local school districts provide in-service training modules that can be exchanged for college credit or advanced standing, leading to additional degrees for teachers. By obtaining higher degrees, teachers increase their competency levels and mastery of teaching objectives—all relevant to their feelings of success and confidence. When teachers feel successful and confident in their teaching, their teaching abilities increase.

Certifications

Many current general educators and special educators are renewing certifications to teach. With increased numbers of diverse students in general education, more and more general education and content area teachers are also adding on special education certification in order to be able to instruct and manage students with special needs. Certification provides a mechanism for establishing regulations to carry out the intent of the IDEIA. It is often the foundation for the establishment of minimum training and experience levels for teachers. In a sense, certification assures teachers and administrators that employees are trained, competent, and able to carry out the responsibilities they have been assigned. Teachers with varied and/or updated certifications have obtained more than the minimum necessary to survive in teaching and to maintain their status as master teachers.

WHAT CAN TEACHERS DO TO REMAIN INVIGORATED AND COMMITTED TO THEIR CAREERS?

Teachers with advanced degrees and additional certifications are in an excellent position to effect changes in their individual classrooms and the total school system. Armed with updated information on current research and teaching practices, these teachers help ensure students with disabilities a free and appropriate public education. They remain invigorated and committed over time. Teachers who respect the teaming model and who actively target strategies to minimize stress are enhancing their own professionalism. As these teachers develop and change in conjunction with the needs of the students they teach, they are on the road to becoming master teachers.

These teachers continually observe students and discuss ways of meeting these students' needs with their peer teachers. They implement learning strategies and behavioral support strategies consistently. They work well in teams with parents, professionals, and paraprofessionals. They recognize stress factors and seek ways of reducing stress when they begin to feel burnout. They are committed to special education success through active professional involvement, participation in additional training, and development of specialized areas of expertise. These teachers have made the transition from student teacher to master teacher. They have found that teaching students with diverse needs is rewarding and stays a challenging career over the years.

SUMMARY

The chapter opened with a discussion of professional teaching standards, now common nationwide. Next, we examined how to conduct job searches and write résumés. Typical job selection procedures emphasize skills in oral and written communication. We discussed ways and means to create a professional portfolio.

Then, we discussed the transition to employment, working with families, participating in peer teaming and reviews, and observing fellow educators in other settings. Observation and continual professional discussion lead to positive changes as teachers collaborate and share successful teaching techniques and strategies. Tips on successful teacher induction programs and mentor-protégé relationships received attention.

A portion of the chapter was devoted to strategies for dealing with paraprofessionals. In addition to working with peers, many teachers work in close proximity to other adults, either paraeducators or volunteers. A team approach was advocated for a successful teacher-paraprofessional relationship.

All teachers must be able to recognize and deal with stress and burnout, factors that impede the transition to master teacher. We discussed potential sources, signs, and signals of stress and burnout in teachers and the strategies to lessen their negative effects.

We reviewed techniques to facilitate the master teacher process: seeking advancement within the field of special education, becoming involved in professional organizations, obtaining higher degrees, and renewing and adding on teacher certifications. Master teachers are committed to the field and change in accordance with the needs of their students.

ACTIVITIES TO EXTEND YOUR KNOWLEDGE

1. Choose one local, state, or national professional organization dealing with individuals with disabilities, and request information on how to join, fees, and resource materials available. Analyze your letter to the organization and the information you received; write a one-page summary of the organization's purpose and target audience.
2. Compile a list of at least 15 community service agencies (including postal or electronic address, telephone number, contact person, and purpose of the agency) that are available in your area to assist individuals with mild to moderate disabilities and their families and/or teachers.
3. In a collaborative effort with peers, develop a list of 15 educational programming ideas that will help you become or remain a master teacher. Include the rationale for each idea based on current reference citations.
4. Participate in an in-class presentation dealing with the prevention and/or amelioration of teacher stress and burnout among those providing special education services. Include handouts and current reference citations for your peers. If you feel comfortable doing so, discuss the possible etiology of a stress and burnout problem that affected you in your field placement.
5. Explore computer and/or library resources to locate more information on specific locations where you can obtain an advanced degree and/or renew a teacher certification.
6. Discuss with students' families what they believe new professionals can do to demonstrate commitment to a lifelong teaching career. Compare and contrast your findings with those of your peers.
7. List 10 ways you believe you demonstrate positive regard for the cultures, religions, gender, and sexuality of students in your field setting. Do not name students, but rather discuss your specific strategies with your peers.
8. Write a paper (without using references) that articulates your personal philosophy of special education. Include what you believe your relationship will be with general education professionals, fellow special educators, administrators, families, and paraprofessionals. Describe how you will maintain active involvement with these other individuals. Discuss how you can become and remain a master teacher.
9. Reflect on your current knowledge, skills, and dispositions related to working with special education students in the general education curricula. Analyze your professional strengths and needs.

REFERENCES

American Association for Employment in Education, Inc. (2004). *Job search handbook for educators*. Columbus, OH: Author.

Ballinger, J. (2000). Programs aim to stop teacher washout. *Journal of Staff Development, 21*, 92, 2833.

Barner, A. (1982). Do teachers like to teach? *Pointer, 27*(1), 5–7.

Beach, R. G. (1973). *Help in the school: Establishment of a paraprofessional program.* Philadelphia: Dorrance.

Billingsley, B. (2002). *Research summary: Teacher retention and attrition.* Gainesville: University of Florida, Center on Personnel Studies in Special Education.

Council for Exceptional Children. (2000a). *What every special educator must know: The standards for the preparation and licensure of special educators* (4th ed.). Reston, VA: Author.

Council for Exceptional Children. (2000b). *Bright futures for exceptional learners: An action plan for quality conditions, teaching, and results for every exceptional learner.* Reston, VA: Author.

Crane, S. J., & Iwanicki, E. F. (1986). Perceived role conflict, role ambiguity, and burnout among special education teachers. *Remedial and Special Education, 7*(2), 24–31.

Danielson, C. (1996). *Enhancing professional practice: A framework for teaching.* Alexandria, VA: Association for Supervision and Curriculum Development.

Dettmer, P. A., Thurston, L. P., & Dyck, N. T. (2002). *Consultation, collaboration, and teamwork for students with special needs.* Needham Heights, MA: Allyn & Bacon.

Doyle, M. B. (2002). *The paraprofessional's guide to the inclusive classroom* (2nd ed.). Baltimore, MD: Paul H. Brookes.

Doyle, W. (1980). *Classroom management.* West Lafayette, IN: Kappa Delta Pi.

Drecktrab, M. E. (2000). Preservice teachers' preparation to work with paraeducators. *Teacher Education and Special Education, 23*(2), 157–164.

Drury, S. S. (1986). *Team effectiveness.* Newark: University of Delaware.

Dudzinski, M., Roszmann-Millican, M., & Shank, K. (2000). Continuing professional development for special educators: Reforms and implications for university programs. *Teacher Education and Special Education, 23*(2), 109–124.

Dwyer, K. P., Osher, D., & Hoffman, K. C. (2000). Creating responsive schools: Contextualizing early warning, timely response. *Exceptional Children, 66*(3), 347–365.

Fimian, M. J., & Blanton, L. P. (1986). Variables related to stress and burnout in special education teacher trainees and first-year teachers. *Teacher Education and Special Education, 9*, 9–21.

Frank, A. R., & McKenzie, R. (1993). The development of burnout among special educators. *Teacher Education and Special Education, 16*(2), 161–170.

Greer, J. G., & Greer, B. B. (1992). Stopping burnout before it starts: Prevention measures at the preservice level. *Teacher Education and Special Education, 15*(3), 168–174.

Hayek, R. A. (1987). The teacher assistance team: A prereferral support system. *Focus on Exceptional Children, 20*(1), 1–7.

Hehir, T. (1999). The changing roles of special education leadership in the next millennium: Thoughts and reflections. *Journal of Special Education Leadership, 12*(1), 3–8.

Idol, L. (1988). A rationale and guidelines for establishing special education consultation programs. *Remedial and Special Education, 9*(6), 48–58.

Ingersoll, R. M. (2003). *Who controls teachers' work? Power and accountability in America's schools.* Cambridge, MA: Harvard University Press.

Interstate New Teacher Assessment and Support Consortium. (1994). *Model standards for beginning teacher licensing and development: A resource for state dialogue.* Washington, DC: Author.

Karp, N. (1993). Collaborating with families. In B. S. Billingsley (Ed.), *Program leadership for serving students with disabilities* (USDOE #H029H10034–93). Richmond: Virginia Department of Education.

Kauffman, J. M., & Hallahan, D. P. (2003). *Exceptional learners: Introduction to special education.* Boston: Allyn & Bacon.

Kenney, S. L., Hammitte, D. J., Rakestraw, J., & LeMontagne, M. J. (2000). Special education and the P-16 Initiative: Addressing CEC standards through portfolio development and assessment. *Teacher Education and Special Education, 23*(2), 89–97.

Kyriacou, C. (2001). Teacher stress: Directions for future research. *Educational Review, 53*(1), 28–35.

McLaughlin, M. J. (1999). Access to the general education curriculum: Paperwork and procedures for redefining "special education." *Journal of Special Education Leadership, 12*(1), 9–14.

McLaughlin, M. J. (2000). *Reform for every learner: Teachers' views on standards and students with disabilities.* Alexandria, VA: Center for Policy on the Impact of General and Special Education Reform.

Morsink, C. V. (1982). Changes in the role of special educators: Public perceptions and demands. *Exceptional Education Quarterly (The Special Educator as a Professional Person), 2*(4), 15–25.

National Association of State Boards of Education. (2000, April). *Teacher induction programs.* Alexandria, VA: Author.

National Board for Professional Teaching Standards. (1999). *Exceptional needs standards.* Washington, DC: Author.

National Commission on Teaching and America's Future. (1996). *Summary report—What matters most: Teaching for America's future.* New York: Author.

Office of Special Education Programs. (1999). *To assure the free appropriate public education of all children with disabilities: Twentieth annual report to Congress on the implementation of the Individuals with Disabilities Education Act.* Washington, DC: Author.

O'Shea, D. J., Hammitte, D. J., Mainzer, R., & Crutchfield, M. (2000). From teacher preparation to continuing professional development. *Teacher Education and Special Education, 23*(2), 71–77.

O'Shea, D. J., & Hendrickson, J. M. (1987). *Tips for using teacher aides effectively* (Monograph No. 16). Gainesville: University of Florida Diagnostic and Teaching Clinic.

O'Shea, D. J., Williams, A. L., & Sattler, R. O. (1999, March–April). Collaboration across special education and general education: Preservice level teachers' views. *Journal of Teacher Education, 50*(2), 147–158.

O'Shea, L. J., & Hoover, N. L. (1986). *Conferring with teachers about teacher performance.* Tallahassee: Florida Department of Education.

O'Shea, L. J., Stoddard, K., & O'Shea, D. J. (2000). IDEA '97 and educator standards: Special educators' perceptions of their skills and those of general educators. *Teacher Education and Special Education, 23*(2), 125–141.

Otis-Wilborn, A., & Winn, J. A. (2000). It's the standards and the process. *Teacher Education and Special Education, 23*(2), 78–87.

Praxis: For test requirements by state and the Praxis, visit the Educational Testing Service (ETS) at www.ets.org/praxis/index.html.

Ralph, E. G., Kesten, C., Lang, H., & Smith, D. (1998). Hiring new teachers: What do school districts look for? *Journal of Teacher Education, 49*(1), 47–56.

Sawyer, R. J., McLaughlin, M. J., & Winglee, M. (1995). Is integration of students with disabilities happening? An analysis of national data trends over time. *Remedial and Special Education, 15*(4), 204–215.

Snell, M. E., & Janney, R. (1994). Including and supporting students with disabilities within general education. In B. S. Billingsley (Ed.), *Program leadership for serving students with disabilities* (pp. 219–262) (USDOE #H029H10034-93). Richmond: Virginia Department of Education.

Stainback, W., Stainback, S., & Stefanich, G. (1996). Learning together in inclusive classrooms. What about the curriculum? *Exceptional Children, 28*(3), 14–19.

Taylor, L., & Salend, S. J. (1983). Reducing stress-related burnout through a network support system. *Pointer, 27*(4), 5–9.

Top tips for new teachers. (2000, June/July). *CEC Today, 6*(8), 6–7.

Troman, G., & Woods, P. (2001). *Primary teachers' stress.* New York: Routledge/Falmer.

U.S. Department of Education. (1990). *Twelfth annual report to Congress on the implementation of the Individuals with Disabilities Education Act.* Washington, DC: Author.

U.S. Department of Education. (1994). *Sixteenth annual report to Congress on the implementation of the Individuals with Disabilities Education Act.* Washington, DC: Author.

U.S. Department of Education. (1997). *Nineteenth annual report to Congress on the implementation of the Individuals with Disabilities Education Act.* Washington, DC: Author.

U.S. Department of Education. (2002). Annual report tables: IDEA Part B Personnel (1998–99), Tables AC1 and AC2. Retrieved January 5, 2003, from http://www.idea-data.org/arc_toc2.html# partbPEN.

Walther-Thomas, C. S. (1996). Inclusion and teaming: Including all students in the mainstream. In T. Dickinson & T. Erb (Eds.), *Teaming in middle schools.* Columbus, OH: National Middle Schools Association.

Weiss, E. M., & Weiss, S. G. (1999, Spring). *New teacher induction.* Washington, DC: American Association of Colleges for Teacher Education.

Westling, D. L., & Fox, L. (2004). *Teaching students with severe disabilities* (3rd ed.). New Jersey: Merrill/Prentice Hall.

Wood, T., & McCarthy, C. (2004). *Understanding and preventing teacher burnout.* (ERIC Document Reproduction Service No. ED477726)

Youngs, B. B. (1986). *Stress in children: How to recognize, avoid, and overcome it.* Melbourne, Victoria: Nelson.

Ysseldyke, J., & Olsen, K. (1999). Putting alternate assessments into practice: What to measure and possible sources of data. *Exceptional Children, 65*(2), 175–185.

Appendix A
CEC Code of Ethics and Standards
for Professional Practice
for Special Educators

CEC CODE OF ETHICS FOR EDUCATORS OF PERSONS WITH EXCEPTIONALITIES

We declare the following principles to be the Code of Ethics for educators of persons with exceptionalities. Members of the special education profession are responsible for upholding and advancing these principles. Members of the Council for Exceptional Children agree to judge and be judged by them in accordance with the spirit and provisions of this Code.

A. Special education professionals are committed to developing the highest educational and quality of life potential of individuals with exceptionalities.

B. Special education professionals promote and maintain a high level of competence and maintain a high level of competence and integrity in practicing their profession.

C. Special education professionals engage in professional activities which benefit individuals with exceptionalities, their families, other colleagues, students, or research subjects.

D. Special education professionals exercise objective professional judgment in the practice of their profession.

E. Special education professionals strive to advance their knowledge and skills regarding the education of individuals with exceptionalities.

F. Special education professionals work within the standards and policies of their profession.

G. Special education professionals seek to uphold and improve where necessary the laws, regulations, and policies governing the delivery of special education and related services and the practice of their profession.

H. Special education professionals do not condone or participate in unethical or illegal acts, nor violate professional standards adopted by the Delegate Assembly of CEC.

CEC STANDARDS FOR PROFESSIONAL PRACTICE

Professionals in Relation to Persons With Exceptionalities and Their Families

Instructional Responsibilities

Special education personnel are committed to the application of professional expertise to ensure the provision of quality education for all individuals with exceptionalities. Professionals strive to

(1) Identify and use instructional methods and curricula that are appropriate to their area of professional practice and effective in meeting the individual needs of persons with exceptionalities.

(2) Participate in the selection and use of appropriate instructional materials, equipment, supplies, and other resources needed in the effective practice of their profession.

(3) Create safe and effective learning environments, which contribute to fulfillment of needs, stimulation of learning, and self concept.

(4) Maintain class size and caseloads that are conducive to meeting the individual instructional needs of individuals with exceptionalities.

(5) Use assessment instruments and procedures that do not discriminate against persons with exceptionalities on the basis of race, color, creed, sex, national origin, age, political practices, family or social background, sexual orientation, or exceptionality.

(6) Base grading, promotion, graduation, and/or movement out of the program on the individual goals and objectives for individuals with exceptionalities.

(7) Provide accurate program data to administrators, colleagues, and parents, based on efficient and objective record keeping practices, for the purpose of decision making.

(8) Maintain confidentiality of information except when information is released under specific conditions of written consent and statutory confidentiality requirements.

Management of Behavior

Special education professionals participate with other professionals and with parents in an interdisciplinary effort in the management of behavior. Professionals

(1) Apply only those disciplinary methods and behavioral procedures, which they have been instructed to use, and which do not undermine the dignity of the individual or the basic human rights of persons with exceptionalities, such as corporal punishment.

(2) Clearly specify the goals and objectives for behavior management practices in the persons with exceptionalities individualized education program.

(3) Conform to policies, statutes, and rules established by state/provincial and local agencies relating to judicious application of disciplinary methods and behavioral procedures.

(4) Take adequate measures to discourage, prevent, and intervene when a colleague's behavior is perceived as being detrimental to exceptional students.

(5) Refrain from aversive techniques unless repeated trials of other methods have failed and only after consultation with parents and appropriate agency officials.

Support Procedures

Professionals

(1) Seek adequate instruction and supervision before they are required to perform support services for which they have not been prepared previously.

(2) May administer medication, where state/provincial policies do not preclude such action, if qualified to do so or if written instructions are on file which state the purpose of the medication, the conditions under which it may be administered, possible side effects, the physician's name and phone number, and the professional liability if a mistake is made. The professional will not be required to administer medication.

(3) Note and report to those concerned whenever changes in behavior occur in conjunction with the administration of medication or at any other time.

Parent Relationships

Professionals seek to develop relationships with parents based on mutual respect for their roles in achieving benefits for the exceptional persons. Special education professionals

(1) Develop effective communication with parents, avoiding technical terminology, using the primary language of the home, and other modes of communication when appropriate.

(2) Seek and use parents' knowledge and expertise in planning, conducting, and evaluating special education and related services for persons with exceptionalities.

(3) Maintain communications between parents and professionals with appropriate respect for privacy and confidentiality.

(4) Extend opportunities for parent education utilizing accurate information and professional methods.

(5) Inform parents of the educational rights of their children and of any proposed or actual practices, which violate those rights.

(6) Recognize and respect cultural diversities which exist in some families with persons with exceptionalities.

(7) Recognize that the relationship of home and community environmental conditions affects the behavior and outlook of the exceptional person.

Advocacy

Special education professionals serve as advocates for exceptional students by speaking, writing, and acting in a variety of situations on their behalf. They

(1) Continually seek to improve government provisions for the education of persons with exceptionalities while ensuring that public statements by professionals as individuals are not construed to represent official policy statements of the agency that employs them.

(2) Work cooperatively with and encourage other professionals to improve the provision of special education and related services to persons with exceptionalities.

(3) Document and objectively report to one's supervisors or administrators inadequacies in resources and promote appropriate corrective action.

(4) Monitor for inappropriate placements in special education and intervene at appropriate levels to correct the condition when such inappropriate placements exist.

(5) Follow local, state/provincial, and federal laws and regulations which mandate a free appropriate public education to exceptional students and the protection of the rights of persons with exceptionalities to equal opportunities in our society.

Professionals in Relation to Employment

Certification and Qualification

Professionals ensure that only persons deemed qualified by having met state/provincial minimum standards are employed as teachers, administrators, and related service providers for individuals with exceptionalities.

Employment

(1) Professionals do not discriminate in hiring on the basis of race, color, creed, sex, national origin, age, political practices, family or social background, sexual orientation, or exceptionality.

(2) Professionals represent themselves in an ethical and legal manner in regard to their training and experience when seeking new employment.

(3) Professionals give notice consistent with local education agency policies when intending to leave employment.

(4) Professionals adhere to the conditions of a contract or terms of an appointment in the setting where they practice.

(5) Professionals released from employment are entitled to a written explanation of the reasons for termination and to fair and impartial due process procedures.

(6) Special education professionals share equitably the opportunities and benefits (salary, working conditions, facilities, and other resources) of other professionals in the school system.

(7) Professionals seek assistance, including the services of other professionals, in instances where personal problems threaten to interfere with their job performance.

(8) Professionals respond objectively when requested to evaluate applicants seeking employment.

(9) Professionals have the right and responsibility to resolve professional problems by utilizing established procedures, including grievance procedures, when appropriate.

Assignment and Role

(1) Professionals should receive clear written communication of all duties and responsibilities, including those which are prescribed as conditions of their employment.

(2) Professionals promote educational quality and intra- and interprofessional cooperation through active participation in the planning, policy development, management, and evaluation of the special education program and the education program at large so that programs remain responsive to the changing needs of persons with exceptionalities.

(3) Professionals practice only in areas of exceptionality, at age levels, and in program models for which they are prepared by their training and/or experience.

(4) Adequate supervision of and support for special education professionals is provided by other professionals qualified by their training and experience in the area of concern.

(5) The administration and supervision of special education professionals provides for clear lines of accountability.

(6) The unavailability of substitute teachers or support personnel, including aides, does not result in the denial of special education services to a greater degree than to that of other educational programs.

Professional Development

(1) Special education professionals systematically advance their knowledge and skills in order to maintain a high level of competence and response to the changing needs of persons with exceptionalities by pursuing a program of continuing education including but not limited to participation in such activities as inservice training, professional conferences/workshops, professional meetings, continuing education courses, and the reading of professional literature.

(2) Professionals participate in the objective and systematic evaluation of themselves, colleagues, services, and programs for the purpose of continuous improvement of professional performance.

(3) Professionals in administrative positions support and facilitate professional development.

Professionals in Relation to the Profession and to Other Professionals

The Profession

(1) Special education professionals assume responsibility for participating in professional organizations and adherence to the standards and codes of ethics of those organizations.

(2) Special education professionals have a responsibility to provide varied and exemplary supervised field experiences for persons in undergraduate and graduate preparation programs.

(3) Special education professionals refrain from using professional relationships with students and parents for personal advantage.

(4) Special education professionals take an active position in the regulation of the profession through use of appropriate procedures for bringing about changes.

(5)   Special education professionals initiate, support, and/or participate in research related to the education of persons with exceptionalities with the aim of improving the quality of educational services, increasing the accountability of programs, and generally benefiting persons with exceptionalities. They

- Adopt procedures that protect the rights and welfare of subjects participating in the research.
- Interpret and publish research results with accuracy and a high quality of scholarship.
- Support a cessation of the use of any research procedure that may result in undesirable consequences for the participant.
- Exercise all possible precautions to prevent misapplication or misutilization of a research effort, by self or others.

Other Professionals

Special education professionals function as members of interdisciplinary teams, and the reputation of the profession resides with them. They

(1)   Recognize and acknowledge the competencies and expertise of members representing other disciplines as well as those of members in their own disciplines.

(2)   Strive to develop positive attitudes among other professionals toward persons with exceptionalities, representing them with an objective regard for their possibilities and their limitations as persons in a democratic society.

(3)   Cooperate with other agencies involved in serving persons with exceptionalities through such activities as the planning and coordination of information exchanges, service delivery, evaluation, and training, so that duplication or loss in quality of services may not occur.

(4)   Provide consultation and assistance, where appropriate, to both general and special educators as well as other school personnel serving persons with exceptionalities.

(5)   Provide consultation and assistance, where appropriate, to professionals in nonschool settings serving persons with exceptionalities.

(6)   Maintain effective interpersonal relations with colleagues and other professionals, helping them to develop and maintain positive and accurate perceptions about the special education profession.

Appendix B
CEC Knowledge and Skill Standards Common Core

Standard I: Foundations

CC1K1: Models, theories, and philosophies that form the basis for special education practice.

CC1K2: Laws, policies, and ethical principles regarding behavior management, planning, and implementation.

CC1K3: Relationship of special education to the organization and function of educational agencies.

CC1K4: Rights and responsibilities of students, parents, teachers, and other professionals, and schools related to exceptional learning needs.

CC1K5: Issues in definition and identification of individuals with exceptional learning needs, including those from culturally and linguistically diverse backgrounds.

CC1K6: Issues, assurances, and due process rights related to assessment, eligibility, and placement within a continuum of services.

CC1K7: Family systems and the role of families in the educational process.

CC1K8: Historical points of view and contributions of culturally diverse groups.

CC1K9: Impact of the dominant culture on shaping schools and the individuals who study and work in them.

CC1K10: Potential impact of differences in values, languages, and customs that can exist between the home and school.

CC1S1: Articulate personal philosophy of special education.

Standard II: Development and Characteristics of Learners

CC2K1: Typical and atypical human growth and development.

CC2K2: Educational implications of characteristics of various exceptionalities.

CC2K3: Characteristics and effects of the cultural and environmental milieu of the individual with exceptional learning needs and the family.

CC2K4: Family systems and the role of families in supporting development.

CC2K5: Similarities and differences of individuals with and without exceptional learning needs.

CC2K6: Similarities and differences among individuals with exceptional learning needs.

CC2K7: Effects of various medications on individuals with exceptional learning needs.

Standard III: Individual Learning Differences

CC3K1: Effects an exceptional condition(s) can have on an individual's life.

CC3K2: Impact of learner's academic and social abilities, attitudes, interests, and values on instruction and career development.

CC3K3: Variations in beliefs, traditions, and values across and within cultures and their effects on relationships among individuals with exceptional learning needs, family, and schooling.

CC3K4: Cultural perspectives influencing the relationships among families, schools, and communities as related to instruction.

CC3K5: Differing ways of learning of individuals with exceptional learning needs including those from culturally diverse backgrounds and strategies for addressing these differences.

Standard IV: Instructional Strategies

CC4S1: Use strategies to facilitate integration into various settings.

CC4S2: Teach individuals to use self-assessment, problem-solving, and other cognitive strategies to meet their needs.

CC4S3: Select, adapt, and use instructional strategies and materials according to characteristics of the individual with exceptional learning needs.

CC4S4: Use strategies to facilitate maintenance and generalization of skills across environments.

CC4S5: Use procedures to increase the individual's self-awareness, self-management, self-control, self-reliance, and self-esteem.

CC4S6: Use strategies that promote successful transitions for individuals with exceptional learning needs.

Standard V: Learning Environments and Social Interactions

CC5K1: Demands of learning environments.

CC5K2: Basic classroom management theories and strategies for individuals with exceptional learning needs.

CC5K3: Effective management of teaching and learning.

CC5K4: Teacher attitudes and behaviors that influence behavior of individuals with exceptional learning needs.

CC5K5: Social skills needed for educational and other environments.

CC5K6: Strategies for crisis prevention and intervention.

CC5K7: Strategies for preparing individuals to live harmoniously and productively in a culturally diverse world.

CC5K8: Ways to create learning environments that allow individuals to retain and appreciate their own and each other's respective language and cultural heritage.

CC5K9: Ways specific cultures are negatively stereotyped.

CC5K10: Strategies used by diverse populations to cope with a legacy of former and continuing racism.

CC5S1: Create a safe, equitable, positive, and supporting learning environment in which diversities are valued.

CC5S2: Identify realistic expectations for personal and social behavior in various settings.

CC5S3: Identify supports needed for integration into various program placements.

CC5S4: Design learning environments that encourage active participation in individual and group settings.

CC5S5: Modify the learning environment to manage behaviors.

CC5S6: Use performance data and information from all stakeholders to make or suggest modifications in learning environments.

CC5S7: Establish and maintain rapport with individuals with and without exceptional learning needs.

CC5S8: Teach self-advocacy.

CC5S9: Create an environment that encourages self-advocacy and increased independence.

CC5S10: Use effective and varied behavior management strategies.

CC5S11: Use the least intensive behavior management strategy consistent with the needs of the individual with exceptional learning needs.

CC5S12: Design and manage daily routines.

CC5S13: Organize, develop, and sustain learning environments that support positive intracultural and intercultural experiences.

CC5S14: Mediate controversial intercultural issues among students within the learning environment in ways that enhance any culture, group, or person.

CC5S15: Structure, direct, and support the activities of paraeducators, volunteers, and tutors.

CC5S16: Use universal precautions.

Standard VI: Language

CC6K1: Effects of cultural and linguistic differences on growth and development.

CC6K2: Characteristics of one's own culture and use of language and the ways in which these can differ from other cultures and uses of languages.

CC6K3: Ways of behaving and communicating among cultures that can lead to misinterpretation and misunderstanding.

CC6K4: Augmentative and assistive communication strategies.

CC6S1: Use strategies to support and enhance communication skills of individuals with exceptional learning needs.

CC6S2: Use communication strategies and resources to facilitate understanding of subject matter for students whose primary language is not the dominant language.

Standard VII: Instructional Planning

CC7K1: Theories and research that form the basis of curriculum development and instructional practice.

CC7K2: Scope and sequences of general and special curricula.

CC7K3: National, state or provincial, and local curricula standards.

CC7K4: Technology for planning and managing the teaching and learning environment.

CC7K5: Roles and responsibilities of the paraeducator related to instruction, intervention, and direct service.

CC7S1: Identify and prioritize areas of the general curriculum and accommodations for individuals with exceptional learning needs.

CC7S2: Develop and implement comprehensive, longitudinal individualized programs in collaboration with team members.

CC7S3: Involve the individual and family in setting instructional goals and monitoring progress.

CC7S4: Use functional assessments to develop intervention plans.

CC7S5: Use task analysis.

CC7S6: Sequence, implement, and evaluate individualized learning objectives.

CC7S7: Integrate affective, social, and life skills with academic curricula.

CC7S8: Develop and select instructional content, resources, and strategies that respond to cultural, linguistic, and gender differences.

CC7S9: Incorporate and implement instructional and assistive technology into the educational program.

CC7S10: Prepare lesson plans.

CC7S11: Prepare and organize materials to implement daily lesson plans.

CC7S12: Use instructional time effectively.

CC7S13: Make responsive adjustments to instruction based on continued observations.

CC7S14: Prepare individuals to exhibit self-enhancing behavior in response to societal attitudes and actions.

Standard VIII: Assessment

CC8K1: Basic terminology used in assessment.

CC8K2: Legal provisions and ethical principles regarding assessment of individuals.

CC8K3: Screening, prereferral, referral, and classification procedures.

CC8K4: Use and limitations of assessment instruments.

CC8K5: National, state or provincial, and local accommodations and modifications.

CC8S1: Gather relevant background information.

CC8S2: Administer nonbiased formal and informal assessments.

CC8S3: Use technology to conduct assessments.

CC8S4: Develop or modify individualized assessment strategies.

CC8S5: Interpret information from formal and informal assessments.

CC8S6: Use assessment information in making eligibility, program, and placement decisions for individuals with exceptional learning needs, including those from culturally and/or linguistically diverse backgrounds.

CC8S7: Report assessment results to all stakeholders using effective communication skills.

CC8S8: Evaluate instruction and monitor progress of individuals with exceptional learning needs.

CC8S9: Create and maintain records.

Standard IX: Professional and Ethical Practice

CC9K1: Personal cultural biases and differences that affect one's teaching.

CC9K2: Importance of the teacher serving as a model for individuals with exceptional learning needs.

CC9K3: Continuum of lifelong professional development.

CC9K4: Methods to remain current regarding research-validated practice.

CC9S1: Practice within the CEC Code of Ethics and other standards of the profession.

CC9S2: Uphold high standards of competence and integrity and exercise sound judgment in the practice of the professional.

CC9S3: Act ethically in advocating for appropriate services.

CC9S4: Conduct professional activities in compliance with applicable laws and policies.

CC9S5: Demonstrate commitment to developing the highest education and quality-of-life potential of individuals with exceptional learning needs.

CC9S6: Demonstrate sensitivity for the culture, language, religion, gender, disability, socio-economic status, and sexual orientation of individuals.

CC9S7: Practice within one's skill limit and obtain assistance as needed.

CC9S8: Use verbal, nonverbal, and written language effectively.

CC9S9: Conduct self-evaluation of instruction.

CC9S10: Access information on exceptionalities.

CC9S11: Reflect on one's practice to improve instruction and guide professional growth.

CC9S12: Engage in professional activities that benefit individuals with exceptional learning needs, their families, and one's colleagues.

Standard X: Collaboration

CC10K1: Models and strategies of consultation and collaboration.

CC10K2: Roles of individuals with exceptional learning needs, families, and school and community personnel in planning of an individualized program.

CC10K3: Concerns of families of individuals with exceptional learning needs and strategies to help address these concerns.

CC10K4: Culturally responsive factors that promote effective communication and collaboration with individuals with exceptional learning needs, families, school personnel, and community members.

CC10S1: Maintain confidential communication about individuals with exceptional learning needs.

CC10S2: Collaborate with families and others in assessment of individuals with exceptional learning needs.

CC10S3: Foster respectful and beneficial relationships between families and professionals.

CC10S4: Assist individuals with exceptional learning needs and their families in becoming active participants in the educational team.

CC10S5: Plan and conduct collaborative conferences with individuals with exceptional learning needs and their families.

CC10S6: Collaborate with school personnel and community members in integrating individuals with exceptional learning needs into various settings.

CC10S7: Use group problem-solving skills to develop, implement, and evaluate collaborative activities.

CC10S8: Model techniques and coach others in the use of instructional methods and accommodations.

CC10S9: Communicate with school personnel about the characteristics and needs of individuals with exceptional learning needs.

CC10S10: Communicate effectively with families of individuals with exceptional learning needs from diverse backgrounds.

CC10S11: Observe, evaluate, and provide feedback to paraeducators.

Appendix C
Table of Contents Linked to CEC Common Core Standards

1   Field Experiences with Students with Mild to Moderate Disabilities

Section	CEC Common Core Standards
Students with Mild to Moderate Disabilities: Definitions and Characteristics	CC1K1, CC1K5, CC2K2, CC2K5, CC2K6
How Special Education Services Are Delivered	CC1K3, CC5S3, CC5S11, CC10K1, CC10S6, CC10S7
Roles and Responsibilities	CC1S1, CC9K3, CC9S1, CC9S2, CC9S3, CC9S4, CC10S4
Preparing for a Successful Practicum Experience	CC5K4, CC9S8, CC9S11

2   Legal Aspects of Special Education

Section	CEC Common Core Standards
Legal Basis of Educational Rights for Students with Disabilities	CC1K1, CC1K2, CC1K4, CC1K6, CC8K2, CC9S4
Major Components of the Federal Law	CC1K2, CC1K4, CC1K6, CC8K2, CC9S4, CC10S1, CC10S2
Major Challenges of the IDEA for Developing Teachers	CC1K2, CC1K6, CC8K2

3   Setting Up for Instruction

Section	CEC Common Core Standards
Designing the Physical Environment	CC5K1, CC5S4, CC5S5
Managing Instructional Time	CC7S12
Scheduling Activities and Grouping Students	CC4S3, CC4S6, CC5K1, CC5K2, CC5K3
Formulating Meaningful and Relevant Rules and Procedures	CC5K3, CC5S12
Coordinating Resources	CC5S15, CC8S10, CC10K2, CC10S6

4   Classroom Assessment Practices for Instruction

Section	CEC Common Core Standards
Purposes for Classroom Assessment	CC2K5, CC2K6, CC7S2, CC7S6, CC7S13, CC8K3, CC8K4, CC8S1, CC8S2, CC8S4, CC8S5, CC8S8, CC8S9, CC9S9
Principles of Assessment	CC7S6, CC8K1, CC8S1, CC8S2, CC8S8, CC8S10, CC9S9
Approaches to Classroom Assessment	CC4S2, CC8K1, CC8S1, CC8S2, CC8S4, CC8S5, CC8S8, CC8S10
The APPLY Framework for Developing Classroom Assessments	CC8K1, CC8S1, CC8S4, CC8S5, CC8S8, CC8S9, CC8S10
Grading Practices	CC8S5

5   Planning for Instruction

Section	CEC Common Core Standards
Reasons for Planning	CC5K3, CC5S12, CC7S6, CC7S10, CC7S11
Developmental Aspect of Lesson Planning	CC7S10
Relationship of Planning to the Diagnostic Teaching Model	CC1K1, CC5K3, CC7S6, CC7S13, CC8S8
Strategic and Tactical Planning	CC1K1, CC4S3, CC5S6, CC7K1, CC7S1, CC7S2, CC7S13, CC8S8, CC10S9
Components of Successfully Planned Lessons	CC7S1, CC7S2, CC7S5, CC7S6, CC7S10, CC7S11, CC7S12, CC7S13, CC8S1, CC8S4, CC8S5, CC8S8, CC8S9, CC8S10, CC9S9
Lesson-Plan Formats	CC5K3, CC5S12, CC7S1, CC7S5, CC7S6, CC7S10, CC7S11, CC7S12, CC8S10
Strategic Planning for Inclusive Programming	C5K3, CC7K4, CC7S10, CC7S11, CC7S12, CC8S10, CC9S9

6   Delivering Instruction

Section	CEC Common Core Standards
Direct Instruction and Guided Discovery Learning: Principles for Effective Instruction	CC4S3, CC5K3, CC5S4, CC7K1, CC7S5, CC7S10, CC7S11, CC7S12
Procedures for Presenting Subject Matter	CC4S4, CC5K3, CC7S10
Learning Stages	CC4S4, CC5K3, CC5S10, CC7S6, CC7S10
Lesson Development	CC5K3, CC7K1, CC7S10
Lesson Format for Direct Instruction and Guided Discovery Learning Approaches	CC4S4, CC5K2, CC5K3, CC5S10, CC7S6, CC7S10
When to Use Specific Elements of Effective Instruction	CC5K2, CC5K3, CC7S10

10 Collaborative Planning and Consultation

Section	CEC Common Core Standards
Introduction	CC1K1
Developing and Beginning Teachers as Recipients of Consulting Services	CC9S2, CC9S7, CC9S11
Developing and Beginning Teachers as Providers of Consulting Services	
Collaborative Model for Consultative Processes	CC10K1
Interpersonal Communication Skills	CC9S2, CC9S8, CC10K1, CC10S9
General Procedures for Collaborative Consultation	CC10K1
Operationalizing Conference Procedures	CC10S7

11 The Master Teacher

Section	CEC Common Core Standards
Teachers' Tests	
Professional Preparation Standards	CC9K3, CC9K4, CC9S1, CC9S2
The Job Search	CC9S1
Professional Portfolios	CC9S9
Moving from Student Teacher to Master Teacher	CC1K7, CC5S15, CC7K5, CC9K3, CC9K4, CC9S12, CC10S3, CC10S4, CC10S5, CC10S6, CC10S8, CC10S9, CC10S11
Stress and Burnout	CC9S7
Facilitating the Master Teacher Process	CC9K3, CC9K4, CC9S2
What Can Teachers Do to Remain Invigorated and Committed to Their Careers?	CC1S1

Index